Love and Music

The Glorious History of the Dublin Grand Opera Society (1941 - 1998)

Gus Smith

Atlantic Publishers
1998

DEDICATION

This book is dedicated to the members and artists who
through their tireless work and ideals, helped to make
the Dublin Grand Opera Society an organisation with a
proud and honoured tradition.

Published by Atlantic Publishers, Baggot St., Dublin,
and Henrietta St., London,
and printed by the Smurfit Print, Dublin.
Design by The Design Room, Dublin, Tel: 01 66 170 80

CONTENTS

JUBILEE TRIBUTES

Warmest congratulations to the Dublin Grand Opera Society on their Silver Jublilee. What they have done for Grand Opera in Dublin in the last twenty-five years is worthy of the highest praise. All lovers of good music are in their debt. Go mba seacht mó a réim sna blianta atá rompu.

President Eamon de Valera
(his special tribute penned in Spring
Season programme book of 1966)

During this year, the Dublin Grand Opera Society will not only give its fiftieth season but will also celebrate its twenty-fifth birthday. Looking back through these years and considering what has been achieved, one feels a sense of gratitude as well as satisfaction.

Professor John F Larchet, DGOS
president, also in the 1966 programme

AUTHOR'S ACKNOWLEDGEMENTS

In the preparation of this operatic text I wish to express my grateful thanks to numerous people, from chorus member to diva, backstage manager to designer, who willingly gave of their time to help me build up a picture of a truly great musical society. I am, however, especially indebted to Paddy Brennan who took on the painstaking task of compiling a detailed record of DGOS performances since the society's foundation in 1941. In addition, he included the principal artists in the operas concerned, something every opera-lover with a feeling for operatic history will surely appreciate.

I was fortunate also to be able to discuss the society's early years with such as Aileen Walsh, Maura Mooney, Moira Griffith and Nick Lewis and to meet the families of the pioneering triumvirate, Professor John Larchet, Lt.-Col. Bill O'Kelly and Lt.-Col. J M Doyle and draw on their memories. The following are others I'm indebted to for their generous recall:

PRINCIPALS: Paulo Silveri and his wife Delia, Virginia Zeani, Ugo and Angela Benelli, Aurio Tomicich, Veronica Dunne, Adele Leigh, Barbara Howitt, Dermot Browner, Rita Lynch, Suzanne Murphy, Ruth Maher, Mary Sheridan, Renée Flynn, Nick Lewis, Paddy Ring, William Young, Frank Dunne, Moira Griffith, Brendan Cavanagh, Pádraig O'Rourke, Patricia Bardon, Mary Hegarty, John O'Flynn, Virginia Kerr, Peter McBrien, Frank O'Brien, Cara O'Sullivan, Deirdre Grier Delaney, Kate McCarney, Angela Feeney.

CONDUCTORS: Giuseppe Morelli, Vilem Tausky, Lt.-Col. J M Doyle, Sir Charles Mackerras, Albert Rosen.

CHORUS MASTERS: Jeannie Reddin, Giuseppe Giardina, John Brady, Patrick Somerville.

PRODUCERS:Dario Micheli, Tom Hawkes, Michael McCaffery, Patrick Mason, Paddy Ryan.

DESIGNERS: Patrick Murray, Dario Micheli.

RTÉ: Geraldine O'Grady, Sheila Larchet and Brian O'Rourke (Symphony Orchestra); Fachtna O Hannracháin and Norris Davidson (Music Staff).

CHORUS MEMBERS: Monica Condron, Aileen Walsh, Maura Mooney, Dympna Carney, Brigid Finucane, Joan Rooney, Mary Troy, Florrie Draper, Anne Deegan, Caroline Phelan, Mona Brase, Charlie Dunphy, Paddy Brennan, Dick Hanrahan, Seán Kelly, Jimmy Brittain, Barry Hodkinson, John Allen, John and Tom Carney, Jack Doyle.

BACKSTAGE STAFF: George McFall, Josephine Scanlon.

REMAINDER OF CAST: Donnie Potter, Dr Dermot O'Kelly, Frank O'Rourke, Dermot Kinlen, Kitty Browner, Barry and Margaret Healy-Doyle, Paula Donlon, Paddy and Ann Fagan, Martin and Mary McCullough, Elizabeth Lovatt-Dolan, Mrs Máire Hogan, Maureen Lemass, David Collopy, Frank Byrne, Harold Johnson, Tony O Dalaigh, Marie Maxwell, Michael and Frances McCarthy, Gerry Larchet, Carmel McHale, Margaret McDonnell.

AGENCIES; Angela McCrone, DGOS, Opera Ireland, RTÉ Tapes Dept., Irish Times Library, Irish National Library, Trinity College Library, Frances McCarthy, Dublin, for lending historic photos from her Dundalk Concerts Album, and the editors of the following newspapers for their permission to quote from opera reviews and special features:
Irish Independent, Evening Herald and Sunday Independent; Sunday Tribune, The Examiner and the Irish Times.

Publishers' note

We wish to thank the following without whose support this historical book would not have been possible: Bank of Ireland. Independent Newspapers, British Council, Opera Ireland, IMRO, Guinness Ireland Group Ltd., Italian Cultural Institute of Ireland, Margaret McDonnell (Opera Ireland Patron), Nico's Italian Restaurant, Dame St., Opera House Cork, Matt Farrelly, managing director Aisling Technology Ltd., and an Opera Ireland Patron.

FOREWORD

A living record of the achievements, past and present, of any outstanding music organisation is essential, it seems to me, and in the case of the Dublin Grand Opera Society this has been waiting to be written since the society celebrated its golden jubilee in 1991. Therefore, it is with particular pleasure as chairwoman of the Opera Ireland Board that I welcome the publication of Gus Smith's aptly named book, Love and Music.

It is timely, it fills a music gap, and its statistics compiled by Paddy Brennan, are an important adjunct to the text. And at a glance, it is undoubtedly a fascinating pictorial record dating back as it does to the very first performance.

For my own part, growing up in Limerick I was constantly reminded of my grandfather's operatic life and achievements - the Joseph O'Mara memorabilia was everywhere in our house, the most important item being the framed scroll recording the occasion he was given the Freedom of the City of Limerick. There were, too, Gaiety Theatre programmes of seasons there - in the same theatre where much later I would enjoy exciting performances by the Dublin Grand Opera Society. It was an enriching experience musically and one soon became aware of the tradition from which that success sprung. It must have been no easy matter to maintain an operatic society amid the austerity of wartime Dublin, yet it appears that the legendary DGOS chairman Bill O'Kelly had the loyalty of his officers and troops. From all accounts, he was an inspiring figure and opera in Ireland is indebted to him.

Gus Smith's book will no doubt revive interest in those early decades of the society's history, as when it presented renowned German companies at the Gaiety as well as festivals of Italian Opera. There were times of financial crises in the sixties and seventies which the society bravely survived and anyone with any love of opera will be grateful for that. But the struggle to present opera in the Gaiety did not become in any way easier and even today Opera Ireland has to work tremendously hard to secure opera's place in the musical sphere in Ireland. With the continued support of the Arts Council of Ireland, our friends and patrons as well as our sponsors, we can approach the future with confidence.

As this new book amply shows, the society has a very proud past and is guaranteed a prominent place in any musical gallery; indeed since it involved so many idealistic people from the beginning it would be invidious to try to single them out. I congratulate Gus Smith on this publication and for taking the trouble to record for history the achievements of a society that is as synonymous with Dublin as Anna Livia herself.

Eileen O'Mara Walsh
Chairwoman Opera Ireland
November 1998.

Birth of the Society

It began, like other similar ventures, with an advertisement in the newspapers inviting people to a public meeting. About the same time, and in a more personal approach, a letter was circulated to music lovers and friends, simply stating: 'A meeting of those interested in the presentation of a Spring Season of Grand Opera in Dublin at the Gaiety Theatre will be held in the Central Hotel, Exchequer Street, at 8 p.m. on Thursday next, February 20, 1941. You are cordially invited to attend.'

The letter was signed by William O'Kelly (Capt.) and Miss Ann Clarke. It was the first indication of an unusual development in the capital's operatic scene and was puzzling insofar as the Dublin Operatic Society was already mounting successful seasons at the Gaiety Theatre in South King Street. Furthermore, William O'Kelly was not only an Irish Army officer but a prominent member of the Dublin Operatic Society chorus since the mid 1930s. He was reckoned to be one of the prime movers behind the efforts to form a new society. 'The DOS was falling apart at this time', O'Kelly would say later in a Radio Eireann interview.

Nonetheless, the DOS had a proud history since it was founded in 1928 by Maestro Adelio Viani, senior professor of singing at the Royal Irish Academy of Music and had made a notable debut with Rossini's comic opera, *The Barber of Seville*. When Viani resigned in 1936 his work was carried on by the chairman George Sleator, a man with a passion for opera. A well-known jeweller, he was dapper and an elegant dresser but could be prickly. He was not slow, however, in propping up the society with his own money. Apart from staging popular Verdi and Puccini works, the DOS also presented Thomas's tuneful *Mignon* and Donizetti's much loved *L'Elisir d'Amore*, operas infrequently seen in Dublin. And he and his committee managed to engage first-class guest artists including English tenor Heddle Nash and soprano Elena Danieli who sang together in *La Traviata* in the society's spring season of 1937. And for *Mignon* the principals were baritone Leslie Jones and leading Welsh tenor Ben Williams and soprano May Devitt.

Sleator also provided opportunities for talented Irish artists such as Geraldine Costigan, May Devitt and baritone John Lynskey to take on leading roles. Lynskey was discovered in the west of Ireland where he was a blacksmith and invited to Dublin for vocal training. It was a smooth voice of fine range and natural colour. Among the society's conductors were Captain J M Doyle, Dr Vincent O'Brien and Arthur Hammond from London. The society's 1940 season was noteworthy for the arrival of the young soprano Joan Hammond to sing Pamina in DOS's new production of *The Magic Flute*. She had been engaged to sing Mimi and Violetta at La Scala, Milan, in that year, when she was advised to leave Italy. Although she had been born in New Zealand, she liked to call herself 'Aussie'; her parents had settled in Australia when she was a child. To Arthur Hammond (no relation), Miss Hammond possessed one of the most meltingly beautiful voices he had ever heard.

Ironically, it was Capt. O'Kelly who had discovered the Belfast tenor James Johnston for the Dublin Operatic Society when he heard him in Derry in *Merrie England*, the Edward German musical. So impressed was O'Kelly by the purity and tonal quality of the voice, that he invited him to Dublin where he was cast by George Sleator as the Duke of Mantua in *Rigoletto*. It was the first indication that the army officer and opera lover had a genuine flair for recognising real potential in voices.

For Sleator it was the beginning of a worrying period. At the best of times he found it almost impossible to break even with his operatic seasons, having to rely almost entirely on box-office takings to see the society through. Any new competition could be serious. Soprano Moira Griffith was one of the first to learn what was taking place behind the operatic scene. Her brother Andrew, a priest and founder member of the Our Lady's Choral Society, had kept her informed. He was a friend of Louis Elliman, the proprietor of the Gaiety Theatre.

'Andrew told me he was in Louis Elliman's office in the Gaiety at the first meeting between Bill O'Kelly and Elliman when the matter of the new operatic society was being discussed. He said that Elliman was very enthusiastic about the plans and encouraged O'Kelly. It seems that the DOS owed money to the Gaiety Theatre and although Elliman was a friend of George Sleator he was not prepared to go on any further. The bills were mounting up and the DOS hadn't the money to clear them.' O'Kelly's version of his meeting with Louis Elliman was summed up later in his own words: 'I went along and met Louis Elliman. I hadn't a shilling, just what I stood on and he said to me, "You go ahead and put on the operas and I'll do the rest for you." '

With a world war raging, resulting in the cessation of both operatic and theatrical tours from overseas to Dublin, Elliman, whose family also ran the 4,000-seater Theatre Royal in the city, was concerned about filling his theatres and welcomed any new musical societies, professional or amateur, capable of doing so. Obviously he saw in the sturdy O'Kelly someone with the vision and push to make a success of any new operatic society. To O'Kelly, complacency had set in in the Dublin Operatic Society and he felt it was going nowhere. He was already assured of the support of his friends and he was not slow to convey this point to Elliman, a businessman to his fingertips. Yet Sleator's contribution to opera had been substantial and his mixture of charm and persuasiveness and knowledge of the subject had made him numerous friends. Moira Griffith regarded him as a gentleman, ever since she began singing minor roles for him like Flora in *Traviata*. The more she talked to her brother Andrew about him, the more her sympathy grew for him. 'We knew that he had poured lots of his money into the DOS and got no return. George just wasn't a businessman; he couldn't delegate authority.'

Richard Hanrahan got to know Sleator when he joined the DOS chorus. 'I found him a nice man with a genuine love of opera. I mean, it was his whole life, apart from his jeweller's shop. He was a great man for taking chances, a risk-taker, you might say. He never knew where his next penny was coming from. I remember he worked very hard for the cause of opera and in order to keep the society afloat he put money he couldn't afford into it. And he was the kind of man who inspired loyalty in one and there were singers who would sing for nobody else except George..'

Nick Lewis, a Dun Laoghaire builder and a chorister in the DOS, had heard the rumours about efforts to start a new company and he wondered if Dublin would be able to support the two. He had joined the DOS as a baritone and sang beside Capt. O'Kelly. He came to the view that both O'Kelly and Sleator, who he happened to like, were ambitious go-getters and there could be a clash of personalities. 'I was enjoying my singing and didn't take much notice of what was going on behind the scenes.'

Meanwhile the response to the meeting at the Central Hotel was enthusiastic and the attendance filled one large room. It was jointly chaired by Capt. O'Kelly and Michael Dinnigan. O'Kelly explained that they were there to discuss the holding of a grand opera season at the Gaiety Theatre in May of that year 1941 and that they would endeavour to build up a society worthy of the art of opera. It was their duty to the opera-loving public of Dublin to do so. He told the gathering that their principal singers would include Eily Murnaghan, John Lynskey and Patricia Black. Rehearsals would start on the following Monday and the big rehearsal room in the Theatre Royal had been placed at their disposal.

Capt. O'Kelly was elected chairman and Michael Dinnigan as the vice chairman. Bertie Timlin, a civil servant and a former DOS chorister, was elected honorary secretary, while Capt. J M Doyle would be the group's musical director. It was expected that John F Larchet, professor of music at University College Dublin, would be the first president. Surprisingly, the society was named the Dublin Grand Opera Society, a name that appeared provocatively close to Sleator's Dublin Operatic Society. It was said at the time that Capt. O'Kelly was anxious to have the word 'Grand' but its inclusion caused bitterness and resentment in the Sleator camp. And despite the breakaway of chorus members from his society, about one-third in all, he was determined to carry on and already had finalised plans for his 1941 spring season at the Olympia Theatre.

Falling out with Elliman over money did, if anything, act as a spur to Sleator who could still draw on the support of guest artists like Heddle Nash and Elena Daniele and others. He wasn't prepared to sit back and let the new society monopolise the operatic scene. To Moira Griffith, however, he had spent nearly all his money propping up the Dublin Operatic Society. She felt sorry for him. In her view the DGOS was little more than the DOS without George Sleator and this was the reason she decided to join O'Kelly's society..

'I didn't mind which society I was attached to as long as I was enjoying my singing,' recalled Nick Lewis. He held the view that Sleator and his committee had done a good job and no-one could deny that. However, he too like others in the DOS chorus saw his future with the DGOS.

Capt. O'Kelly also saw the more amusing side of things. Asked later about his new society, he quipped, 'Imagine it - an army officer forming an opera society during the war years.' But he said he was reassured by the fact that they could draw on some excellent principals such as tenors James Johnston and John Torney as well as soprano May Devitt and mezzo soprano Patricia Black. Having his army colleague Capt. Jim Doyle as musical director pleased him perhaps most of all.

Despite the war raging on various fronts, Dublin remained a busy entertainment city with crowds flocking to cinemas, theatres and musical shows. Travel restrictions, including the absence of electric trams in the evening, proved no real deterrent as Dubliners used the bicycle in many cases as the chief mode of transport. With food and coal often scarce, especially for the poor, entertainment acted as a tonic, the cinema perhaps most of all. Capt. O'Kelly and his colleagues had no doubt that Dublin was ready for a more progressive operatic company. The cigar-smoking and dapper Louis Elliman - 'Mr Louis' to his friends in the business - was of the same mind. He was no opera buff but said he had been enormously impressed from the beginning by Capt. O'Kelly's sheer determination to get the new company off the ground.

For a new society the programme for the first season certainly looked an ambitious one. Four operas would be staged - *La Traviata, Il Trovatore, Faust and La Bohème*. Moira Griffith was approached by Capt. O'Kelly to sing Leonora in Verdi's *Trovatore,* and although George Sleator also wanted her to sing the part for the DOS, she now saw herself as a DGOS guest artist. The same thing applied to others like May Devitt and James Johnston. Everyone seemed encouraged by the newfound enthusiasm that was to be the *modus operandi* of the new society.

Nowhere was it more evident than at the rehearsals under chorus mistress Julia Gray. An excellent pianist, she was outstanding at her job and an inspiration to chorus members. Among them were Maura Mooney and her husband Gerard who had a good baritone voice. 'We worked very hard for Julia and we all wanted the season to be a big success,' recalled Maura. 'It was important that everyone did their best. Bill O'Kelly and Bertie Timlin were also in the chorus and no different from the rest of us. I remember we had men and women from all kinds of occupations, from banks, the Corporation and shops. It was such fun to be singing together.'

However, it wasn't going to be easy for the society to launch itself successfully. It lacked permanent rehearsal rooms, costumes and funds. And with most of the chorus members working a six-day week the rehearsals could only take place at night. Furthermore, the Radio Éireann Orchestra was not available for opera, being committed to live studio broadcasts and evening concerts, so the DGOS orchestra was usually made up of freelance musicians and members of the Irish Army Band. It wasn't a satisfactory arrangement as some of these musicians were attached to theatres and were unavailable for week-night rehearsals..

'During these early months it was hard work and it was confidence in the future of the society that kept us going,' Capt. O'Kelly was to say. The society quickly ran into problems. Raynes of London provided the costumes, but the first set for *La Traviata* went down in a cargo steamer sunk in the Irish Sea five weeks before the opening of the season, and a second set of costumes arrived in Dublin just in time for the first performance.

Maybe the fact that its name was not unlike that of the Dublin Operatic Society or because the chorus and guest artists were, it seemed, no different from those who sang with the DOS, the announcement of the DGOS's first season that May in the Gaiety Theatre did not arouse immediate excitement or grip the public's imagination. Was it, after all, a mistake to call it the Dublin Grand Opera Society? Only time would tell. Nonetheless, the theatre was filled to capacity on Monday, May 19 for the opening performance of *La Traviata*. True, this opera was a great favourite with Dubliners but it also seemed by now that opera buffs suspected that something new and exciting was happening that might have positive long-term results.

On the following evening the *Evening Mail* stated: 'Although the Dublin Grand Opera Society is new, the leading players are all well known to Dublin audiences, and the production as a whole was well up to the standard of any reading of the opera given here in recent years. The staging throughout was bright, full of colour, and a particularly commendable feature was the clear diction of both principals and chorus. That splendid artist May Devitt was Violetta. Her interpretation of the part was intensely dramatic, especially in the final scene which was played with a degree of realism rarely aimed at. James Johnston sang with power and spirit and his acting has considerably improved. The scenes with the elder Germont (Robert Irwin) were genuinely touching in their simple pathos.'

The majority of the other reviews were equally favourable. 'The newly-formed Dublin Grand Opera Society made a most auspicious and encouraging start, when it presented *La Traviata* to a large audience at the Gaiety Theatre,' commented the *Irish Times*. The critic attributed most of the success to May Devitt's performance as Violetta for she not alone sang the role in brilliant fashion but acted with an understanding and wealth of passion that brought the character to real life. 'The Dublin soprano has rarely been in better form, her voice control especially being outstanding. Her only fault was that in the excess of emotions she was inclined, notably in the final act, to hold up the rhythm.'

James Johnston sang Alfredo but it was a performance that he afterwards liked to forget. Originally he had been engaged to sing the title role in *Faust* but when he arrived at the railway station he was told by Capt. O'Kelly that he would be singing Alfredo as well. The tenor protested and argued that he could not possibly learn the role of Alfredo in a few weeks. 'You will, Jimmy,' was O'Kelly's blunt reply. Subsequently the tenor spent a week in a Greystones hotel being taught the part by Julia Gray. That first night in the Gaiety was an ordeal for him nonetheless and he was to say later, 'In the first act I had to stand on a chair for the big duet with Violetta and as I wore tights, I could see my knees shake and I hoped that nobody else noticed me. I was really frightened, but I got through the performance despite the fact that by the last act I was nearly hoarse.'

Johnston was blessed with a witty turn of phrase and had already endeared himself to the society members. A butcher in his native Belfast, he had come to opera somewhat late but he was a decided asset to the Dublin Grand Opera Society. His singing of Faust that season won great praise from the critics and roused the audience. Unfortunately the Marguerite, young Waterford soprano Helen Paxton, was too inexperienced for the part and upset the balance of the production, though John Lynskey was an impressive Mephistopheles.

La Bohème, a perennial favourite with audiences, packed the theatre. Directed by John Lynskey, it was notable for the outstanding portrayal of Mimi by May Devitt. 'The soprano scored yet another triumph, both vocally and dramatically,' stated one morning newspaper critic. 'Those simple little mannerisms introduced with perfect precision: that glorious voice that could at times soar over the most forte orchestral passages and yet return again to pianissimo phrases with delightful clarity: the physical appearance of the woman racked by mental pain were all features of a very fine characterisation.'

If James Johnston had been nervous singing Alfredo, the same could be said of Moira Griffith as she prepared to sing the taxing role of Leonora in *Il Trovatore.* Although she sang Eily O'Connor in November of 1940 opposite John Lynskey's Danny Mann in *The Lily of Killarney* for the Dublin Operatic Society, she still felt short of stage experience. And it was no help to her that John Torney, from Belfast, was also new to the part of Manrico in *Trovatore.* 'John probably believed that I had sung Leonora before and I thought the same about his Manrico. How we both got through the performance I'll never know.'

No-one seemed to notice their inexperience or unconvincing acting. As was the custom with critics at the time, the musical and vocal content took precedence over everything else, though Harold White, the doyen of Irish newspaper critics in the thirties and forties, sometimes was critical of design and staging. Dublin-born, his parents hailed from Devon and as a boy he had a beautiful voice. He went on to study singing with Arthur Barraclough and joined the Leinster School of Music as vocal professor, doing also advanced harmony and orchestration. An able songwriter, he wrote a hundred songs in all - the best known of which was "Macushla", a concert favourite with John McCormack. Of his three operas, Shaun the Post enjoyed some popularity and Shaun was Limerick-born tenor Joseph O'Mara's last operatic creation for the stage. In White's own opinion, it was 'an electrifying performance, with the tenor bringing to the role more romance and dramatic significance than he himself had thought possible.'

It was important to Capt. O'Kelly and his fellow officers in the society that Harold White pass favourable judgment on that first season. They respected him as a critic and musician and were relieved that he had found the week's operas more than 'creditable and of a reasonable standard.' Everyone read Harold White in the *Irish Independent,*' recalled Moira Griffith. 'He could be hard on singers but for the most part he was very fair. I think, though, his pen was feared. I was lucky in this respect as he seemed to like my singing voice.'

The production of *Il Trovatore* had impressed him and, like his colleagues, he felt that Patricia Black's performance as the vengeful gypsy woman Azucena was outstanding and emotionally powerful. The conductor was Capt. Doyle and the orchestra was led by Miss Terry O'Connor.

Despite their off-stage commitments, people such as Capt. O'Kelly, Bertie Timlin and Michael Dinnigan found time to sing in the chorus. To Maura Mooney, who remembers that first historic season vividly, it was 'a smashing week of opera.'

'I knew after the splendid reception we got on the first night for *Traviata* we had got off on the right foot. There was this buzz in the Gaiety, you could feel it, and we all gave of our best in the chorus. Bill O'Kelly came up to my husband Gerard and me afterwards and said, "Keep it up and we'll get there." I can say I never enjoyed myself more, not that it was easy work and we staging four big operas in seven days.'

The fact that two operatic companies were now operating in the capital had not gone unnoticed either by the public or the press; indeed it provoked the *Irish Times* to comment in an editorial: 'Although we may go short of tea and petrol in the city, we shall not, it seems, go short of song. The people of Dublin who in time of peace patronise all the touring companies who come to our shores, in the absence of these companies have formed their own musical societies. Up to a short time ago Dublin was without a grand opera company and amateur performances of light opera were few and far between. In Ireland unfortunately whenever anybody forms one society, either somebody else forms another of precisely the same type, or else the original society had divided itself into several opposing camps before it has time to accomplish anything.

'This failing it appears is as common among singers as it is among politicians, and the result is that Dublin at the present moment is suffering from a glut of opera and musical comedy. For example, the musical season in the city began when the Dublin Operatic Society presented a grand opera season at the Capitol Cinema Theatre. The choice of theatre itself showed a surprising change in the order of things, and a certain proof that the people of Dublin are beginning to forsake the cinema for the theatre once more. Next, the Rathmines & Rathgar Society presented a week's season of Gilbert & Sullivan operettas at the Gaiety Theatre. In both cases the theatres were well filled every night. This week the Old Belvedere Society is performing Franz Lehar's *Count of Luxembourg*, a musical comedy of the type which has not been seen in the capital for some time; while next week, hot upon its heels, as it were, comes *The Belle of New York*, another musical comedy of more or less the same kind. After that, to round off the whole proceedings, the Dublin Grand Opera Society is presenting a season of opera, including at least two of the works performed recently by the DOS and "starring" several of the same guest artists.'

While the leader writer believed it was most reassuring to find Dublin become so music-conscious as to form separate societies, he deemed it at the same time a great pity that at least some of them should not be amalgamated so as to obtain the best possible combination of musicians and singers. Under the present circumstances it seemed that talent would be shared among the same companies.

Undeniably, this was the paper's criticism of the 'split' that led to the formation of the DGOS as well as the expressed hope that the two would join forces. This of course was impossible as George Sleator was understandably angry at the action of the breakaway group and felt he could go it alone with the support of some loyal guest artists and new chorus members. Louis Elliman's action in banishing him to the Olympia Theatre did not go down well with George's friends.

Surprisingly, there was no response to the paper's pungent comments which clearly suggested that there was scarcely room for two grand opera societies drawing more or less on the same pool of guest artists. It was in another way questioning the logic of the establishment of the DGOS and if it was needed in view of the Dublin Operatic Society's artistic policy that provided much the same operas for the public. It was an opportunity for George Sleator to reply but he evidently didn't want to be drawn into a public debate.

Capt. O'Kelly, for his part, was at this time more concerned about his forthcoming opera season at the Savoy Theatre in Limerick. Following the success of the Gaiety Theatre season, the society was invited south and O'Kelly was quick to accept the offer. 'I was happy to carry the flag of grand opera to the provinces.' His vision proved correct. The Savoy week of opera was a great success, with packed attendances and admirable performances. It was also clear that he saw the society as national in dimension and he made no secret of his willingness to tour when possible.

Back in Dublin, meanwhile, Louis Elliman was chuffed by the box-office takings for the DGOS opening week at the Gaiety as they amounted to nearly £900 in cash. He was already looking forward to the winter season for which the programme was already announced. Elliman's faith in O'Kelly had been fully vindicated and the future for the society looked bright. Capt. O'Kelly, for his part, would say he had found a genuine friend in Elliman who wanted the society to succeed. As he put it, 'While we worked on a business basis, he became interested also in every aspect of the society and that pleased me.'

And he himself would write later, 'It speaks volumes for the courage of its founders that, while the greatest war history has known has already raged for nearly two years, the society was launched without financial aid, save the personal guarantee of a small group of enthusiastic opera lovers.'

The society's joy was in another way shortlived, however, for scarcely had that spring season begun when the horror of war came tragically home to Dublin's citizens, quickly erasing memories of operatic successes and variety laughter at the Gaiety and Theatre Royal. Early on the morning of May 19, a German aircraft unloaded its bomb cargo on the streets of the North Strand scoring direct hits on houses and causing devastation. The attack left 34 dead and 90 seriously injured with 25 houses completely destroyed and 300 damaged to such a degree that many hundreds became homeless.

It was stated that the attack was a German reprisal for the Irish government's earlier response to bombings in Belfast, when they sent fire engines to fight the blazes. Later the Ulster Union Club in Belfast proposed raising funds for the Dublin disaster and conveyed their deepest sympathy to the homeless and the relatives of the people who had lost their homes.

Irish newspapers were slim during the war years because of the shortage of newsprint and their editorial content was mainly news from the war fronts, so coverage of the arts scene inevitably suffered; indeed opera drama reviews were often no more than four or five paragraphs in length. Now the North Strand bombings filled the columns for days and days, leaving practically no space for the arts. The DGOS was fortunate therefore with the timing of its spring season; more fortunate still that none of its amateur choristers was killed or injured in the bombing. It was a grim reminder, nevertheless, that danger was ever present despite the country's neutrality.

The Triumvirate

As a triumvirate they shared an essential belief in the society's future and an ambition to raise artistic standards. Dr John F Larchet and Captain J M Doyle were full-time musicians while Capt. Bill O'Kelly devoted almost all his spare time to ensuring that the society not only survived but went forward. He was greatly assisted in this respect by his friends, vice-chairman Michael Dinnigan and the meticulous honorary secretary Bertie Timlin. Behind their idealism was a practicality that recognised problems and how they might be resolved. Running an opera company, however, was new to all of them and their dedication would be tested.

'Rome wasn't built in a day,' was Bertie Timlin's good-humoured riposte when O'Kelly in typical Army style wanted to rush fences. As a team, though, there was no evident clash of temperament and O'Kelly, as chairman, prided himself in being able to gather around him the right people for the job. He was energetic, the chief motivator, and enthusiastic leader of his band of musical musketeers. The choice of Dr Larchet as president could hardly be bettered. By now he was a household name in Irish music: composer, arranger, advisor and teacher. In his mid fifties, he was slight of build, sharp featured and his urbane, gentle manner made him genial company. And as a front-of-house man in the Gaiety foyer on gala operatic occasions he would present the right image for the society. His knowledge was extensive and embraced not only all aspects of music but Irish history, French literature and art. As a composer he liked to describe himself as 'a miniaturist' and hoped his compositions would epitomise the Irish spirit. His name would be always associated in later years with "Padraic the Fiddler" and "By the Waters of Moyle". That he hadn't as yet attempted an opera was a source of disappointment as his songs and song arrangements reflected his appreciation of vocal technique and expressiveness. His interest in opera was summed up in his own words: 'Among all branches of great music, opera makes the widest appeal.'

In conversation, as well as in print, he sometimes recalled the Italian operatic tradition in Dublin and dated its development from the late 1770s onwards when the annual Italian season became an important cultural feature in the life of the city. Every renowned singer of the 19th century was heard, including Jenny Lind, Adelina Patti, Giulia Grisi and Catherine Hayes, the Limerick-born coloratura. And he went on to describe the kind of excitement their appearances generated. 'After the performance the diva in her carriage would be escorted from the stage-door to her hotel by a large procession, the horses having been removed, some male members of the crowd drawing the carriage. The diva would then appear on the balcony or at an open window of the hotel and sing a song to a crowded street.'

Since becoming DGOS's first president he had privately expressed the hope that opera-going in Dublin would again become a memorable social occasion marked by colourful gala nights, post-opera parties and suppers. He was realist enough to accept that divas could no longer be expected to serenade their admirers from the windows of the Gresham or Shelbourne hotels. In his own home, 8 St Mary's Road, Ballsbridge, he and his wife Madeleine loved to entertain singers and musicians and relive concert or operatic performances. They regarded it as all part of the city's musical scenario, nothing at all elitist.

'Music was the life and soul of our house,' recalls Gerard Larchet. 'Musicians were invited in all the time, Irish and foreign. I remember nights when we had people like Paul Tortelier, Arnold Bax, Constance Lambert and there was lively chat over a glass of wine or whiskey. My father was a good mixer and a great raconteur and a charming host, as was my mother who enjoyed herself as much as the others.'

The gangling playwright Lennox Robinson was a frequent visitor to No 8, for his and Dr Larchet's friendship dated back to the latter's days when he conducted the small Abbey Theatre orchestra that entertained playgoers at the intervals. To Gerard Larchet, this was an important period in his father's career and in later years, he talked about his meetings with Yeats, Lady Gregory, the Fay brothers Frank and Willie, and actors FJ McCormick, Michael Dolan and Sara Allgood. 'He used to take pride in the fact that he saw history being made, I mean the trouble over O'Casey's *Plough and the Stars* and even earlier, the riots over *The Playboy of the Western World*. I'm sure that my father and Lennox Robinson sometimes discussed them.'

Looking back, he says his father was incredibly industrious, as he divided his time between UCD, writing songs, arranging others, radio commitments and directing music examinations in secondary schools. He managed even an *Obbligato* for Fritz Kreisler which the violinist acknowledged. He later was to wonder how on earth his father would find the time to preside over DGOS management meetings and involving himself in the spring and winter seasons. Fortunately he enjoyed good health and had boundless energy.

Maybe the fact that Dr Larchet had French ancestry was a contributing factor. His grandfather had come from France to manage a gaming club in Dublin and was so successful that he went on to open his own hotel in Dame Street, Larchet's Hotel, which he ran with his Dublin-born wife. Young John Larchet grew up in this unusual atmosphere and would say later, 'Although my parents didn't appreciate my burning desire to be a musician, they never tried to stop me. I had no interest in hotel business and I remember from the age of seven I was captivated by music.'

He was educated by the Marist Fathers at Catholic University School, Leeson Street, and later became a pupil of the distinguished Italian musician Michele Esposito at RIAM, studying piano and composition. A gifted pupil, he gathered degrees with exemplary ease. And he was subsequently acknowledged as a brilliant teacher. He met his wife-to-be, Madeleine Moore, when she also was a student of Esposito and they were married in 1913. 'It was a wonderful partnership, artistically and otherwise,' recalls Sheila Larchet. 'My mother became a staff teacher in the academy and taught violin. She also was an outstanding accompanist.'

'It was my mother who organised everything for my father,' said Gerard Larchet. 'She had this extraordinary combination of artistic and business acumen. She told him who he was every day as he could get completely lost in the music.'

Predictably, the Larchet children began to study music and followed their father's advice as to the instruments they should choose. Sheila became an orchestral harpist, Maire followed suit as a violinist, and their brother Gerard qualified as a French horn player but later decided to become an engineer.

Later on both he and Sheila were surprised by how their father and Bill O'Kelly struck up such an easy rapport, particularly as they were characteristically different. 'My father regarded O'Kelly as a great organiser and motivator of people,' said Miss Larchet, 'and together with conductor Jim Doyle they chose the operas for the society. Sometimes they came to our house for talks.'

James Doyle had been considered one of Dr Larchet's most talented students at UCD in the early thirties and in the record time of three years instead of five, he took his degree of B.Mus. with first class honours. Young Doyle had begun his musical studies at eight years of age, when he entered the Royal Irish Academy of Music and became a pupil of Signor Esposito. While there he won the Coulson and Vandaleur Academy Scholarships for piano and harmony. A brilliant musical career was predicted for him by the critic Harold White. 'This boy' he wrote, 'will go far.'

He was then aged thirteen and although he hailed from a musical family, it was moderate in circumstances, money being scarce and he was soon sent out to work. But he displayed unusual ambition and was determined to make music his career. He left school after his primary education and found a job behind a shop counter - his sister was employed in a candle factory. His parents did not, however, stand in their son's way and took pride in his early music achievements. They were well known in musical circles, his mother, singing under her maiden name Lucy Brady, being much in demand as a concert artist. J C Doyle, his uncle, had a fine baritone voice and sang duets with Count John McCormack. James Doyle was eighteen when he joined the Irish Army School of Music as a bandmaster cadet, and after eighteen months' tuition under Col. Fritz Brasè (famous as one time leader of the Band of the Prussian Guards) young Doyle was given complete command of a band. Realising his shortcomings in education, he studied for the matriculation while in the army and passed it before deciding to go to UCD to complete his music studies.

'My father was self-taught,' recalls his daughter Margaret Healy-Doyle. 'He had, it seems, lots of self-educator books and was very dedicated and eager for knowledge. He had also a most enquiring mind. And, in order to make some money, he used to play the piano at silent movies in cinemas for which he got a few shilling. He would also accompany my mother as well as his sisters at concerts and earned a guinea a time for this. It was a busy time for the young musician. He was still under twenty when, to the tune of "A Nation Once Again", and an emotional response from the crowd, he led the No 1 Army Band into the RDS arena for the first Aga Khan showjumping competition.

The soft-spoken army officer who cut a striking figure in uniform, liked to recall other proud moments in his career such as the day he conducted the No 1 Band at the Tailteann Games, where they were awarded the McCormack Cup which he was to receive from the singer himself; marching at the head of the band along the city quays from the Phoenix Park to O'Connell Bridge at the Eucharistic Congress in 1932; and most of all, the pride he felt when he was commissioned and later appointed bandmaster to the band. And in 1936 when he was to become part of Radio Eireann history as he was seconded to the broadcasting services as musical director and conductor of the newly-formed orchestra. Early challenges awaited him in that first year, particularly when he was called on at very short notice to conduct Beethoven's difficult Choral Symphony (the Ninth) and passed the test.

As in the case of his mentor Dr Larchet, James Doyle was to choose a young musician as his bride. She was Nance McLoughlin, a cellist, and RIAM scholarship winner and Feis Ceol gold medallist. They had met shortly after he had graduated from UCD in 1934. Doyle could on occasions display a mischievous sense of humour and Nance McLoughlin, who was more correct, did not always appreciate it. Margaret Healy-Doyle tells the story of how her father once led a pipe band past her mother's door as she was practising the cello. 'Apparently he was trying to tease her but disliking pipe bands anyway, my mother didn't think it funny at all.'

After their wedding, the Doyles settled in a two-storey house in Rathgar Avenue which they named "Halcyon". Like the Larchets' home, it too was to often echo to the soft strains of music. Nance Doyle continued with her musical interests, sometimes playing at concerts and at Robert's Café in Grafton Street, and later she joined the Radio Eireann Symphony Orchestra as a permanent casual. Temperamentally, the Doyles were suited to each other and it was a happy home. James liked to accompany himself on the piano as he sang ballads and Victorian songs while Nance on other occasions quietly practised on the cello.

Captain Doyle was recalled to the army on the death of Col. Fitz Brasè in 1940 and was appointed Assistant-Director of the Army School of Music. Before long, he would be made its director, making him the first Irish-born director to fill the post. The energetic Doyle had also found the time to conduct operas for George Sleator's Dublin Operatic Society and showed himself a skilled as well as an adaptable practitioner. And he was quick to respond to an operatic crisis. Once, in the Gaiety Theatre, he conducted a successful performance of Gilbert & Sullivan's *Iolanthe* for the Old Belvedere Musical Society at very short notice and without a rehearsal of any kind. Ironically, Harold White's *Shaun the Post* was the first opera he conducted. White was of course among the first to spot his early talent.

In subsequent years Capt. Doyle's wife Nance played in the Radio Eireann Symphony Orchestra for some of the DGOS's biggest nights of opera, often conducted by her husband. Their eldest daughter Ann, a French horn player, would in time join the same orchestra. Discussing James Doyle with his other daughter Paula (Donlon) she remembered being brought to the Gaiety Theatre for rehearsals. 'I was very small and as my father stood on the rostrum I thought he had great authority. He seemed also to be very patient with the chorus. I think he realised they were amateurs and were giving up their Sundays to come into the theatre. I remember how he would go over again and again, say, the Humming Chorus in *Madama Butterfly* until it was what he wanted.' And at home in the evenings he would sit with a musical score on his knees and proceed to mark passages. Later, he and my mother would have supper together and maybe chat about happenings in the musical scene.'

Her father, she recalled, was friendly with John McCormack and he sometimes invited him to the house. As a child she was in her cot once when the great singer was brought up to see her. 'I was told I must wait in my cot until the musical evening was over. I remember as I waited a long time, I could hear the singing voices below and wondered if they had forgotten me. My parents weren't party people but sometimes liked to have singers and musicians for a meal or a drink. My father used to find James Johnston and Veronica Dunne jovial company and enjoyed their humour.'

There were only a few occasions on which his daughter Margaret saw him annoyed. One was when Bill O'Kelly sold the boxes on either side of the proscenium arch in the Gaiety Theatre without telling him. 'It was a big opera he was conducting, probably *Aida,* and he wanted to increase the size of the orchestra so he arranged at rehearsals to put a few of the double basses in the boxes and it had worked out well for him. Can you imagine his dilemma when Bill told him they had been sold to first night patrons. All my father said, it seems, was, "Those front-of-house people have no idea about musical demands." Generally, I'd say, Bill O'Kelly and himself got on well, though my father was not slow to show he was the boss musically.'

Fred O'Callaghan, Doyle's army colleague and himself a musician, was of opinion that James Doyle was a musician's conductor. As he put it, 'His direction was always informed and secure, his baton work elegant, purposeful and supremely legible. And he had that mysterious ability of some conductors to make his musicians feel at times that they were achieving what in other circumstances would have seemed impossible.'

To Capt. Bill O'Kelly the conductor's greatest asset was his reliability. As he liked to say, 'I can ask Jim Doyle to do any opera and he'll make a good job of it. When I first thought about forming the Dublin Grand Opera Society, Jim's name was the first I pencilled in in my notebook.'

He was just turned forty years when he was elected chairman of the DGOS. Low-sized like a front row rugby forward, he tended to keep his dark hair closely cropped and so presented a somewhat rugged image, though in his well-fitting army uniform he looked smart. Since he didn't smoke or drink he kept himself fit and was blessed with ample stamina. His loves in life were his wife Margaret and large family, sport - swimming in particular - and opera. In his home at Hannaville Park, Terenure, he had an impressive collection of records, among them the voices of Gigli, Caruso and McCormack. Verdi was his favourite operatic composer though he also enjoyed *Carmen, Faust, Cavalleria Rusticana* (the latter for the sheer emotional intensity of the music), Puccini's *Madama Butterfly and Tosca.* Singing in the chorus of the Dublin Operatic Society had afforded him great enjoyment earlier on and he made some firm friends, even if he and George

Sleator weren't always the best of friends.

Some of the women choristers regarded the stocky army officer as a fussy individual, even bossy, and his short fuse sometimes affected his relationships with people. He could on the other hand be amiable, cheerful and inspire those around him and not a few of them believed him a born optimist. Few could deny his leadership qualities. Born in Dublin in November 1900, he was educated at O'Connell Schools and displayed a keen intelligence in the classroom and later on an ambition to improve himself. He had a happy childhood, a fact he emphasised when as DGOS chairman he was interviewed by newspapers and radio.

In 1918, he joined the Irish Volunteers as a member of E Company, 2nd Battalion of the Dublin Brigade, In Christmas week, 1920, he was arrested, brought to Dublin Castle, from there to Belfast Jail and shortly afterwards interned in Ballykinlar Camp until the Anglo-Irish truce was signed. With the setting up of the Irish Free State, he joined the Irish Army and became A.D.C. to the Chief of Staff, General Sean McKeown.

He had earlier experienced personal anguish when his brother Jack, also a young army officer, was killed during the Civil War in an ambush in south Tipperary. As he tended to become emotional about the killing, William O'Kelly rarely if ever talked about it. Subsequently he came to know leading politicians on a personal basis when he became a member of the security force guarding their homes, among them William Cosgrave and Richard (Dick) Mulcahy. He was reckoned a first-class soldier, loyal and patriotic and able to keep confidences. Off-duty, he pursued his interest in sport and it was while playing tennis in Terenure Club that he met his wife-to-be, Margaret. She was outgoing, spirited and good-humoured. Most of all she loved people and was a popular member of the club and a promising player.

As Capt. O'Kelly's commitments grew between the army duties and the Dublin Grand Opera Society, it was Margaret O'Kelly who kept their home in Terenure running smoothly. Talking to their daughter Máire (Hogan), she says her mother was a good housekeeper. 'Like most mothers of big families in those days she worked hard but as we grew up we were expected to play our part. I think we got used to the fact that our Dad was busy either coming or going to the Curragh Camp or planning opera productions. I do remember him bringing singers and conductors to the house for supper and playing records for them. He was a good father and the home was happy.'

She says they got their appreciation of music from him and at an early stage were sent along to the Gaiety for opera matinees. Opera became almost her father's whole life and as the years progressed his interest deepened. 'I can recall him coming home after a performance and entering in his notebook the amount of money taken at the box-office. As administrator he was always conscious of the society's financial standing. He might say to me, "We had a record crowd in last night, and Louis Elliman opened a bottle of champagne to celebrate the occasion. Dad was close to Bertie Timlin and confided in him about the society's finances but I don't think he worried that much about them; he was more anxious if a guest artist cancelled at short notice and he had to find a replacement, He was very proud of his chorus, as he liked to call it, but he demanded loyalty and was loyal to those who were loyal to him. People either liked him or they didn't. It wasn't an easy job trying to keep the society going and he fought tooth and nail to ensure it survived. He was remarkable in that way.'

Growing up, Sean Kelly remembered his father talking about opera matters and listening to Björling on record sing Puccini and Verdi arias. 'My father raved about the Swedish tenor and also had a lot of time for Gigli. He was a good judge of a singer and this would be proven later when he auditioned singers for the DGOS. He had a good sense of humour although this wasn't always visible. Some of his one-liners could be funny. I think that he and Dr Larchet enjoyed a very good rapport and he telephoned my father regularly at our home to tease out something or other about a production or an individual problem. Although Dr Larchet was busy at UCD and other places he always found time for the DGOS and my father considered him a first-rate president. There were others, too like Bertie Timlin and Michael Dinnigan whose contribution couldn't be measured in words, and my father used to say they helped to lift the society off the ground.'

Not surprisingly, Capt. O'Kelly got his own children involved in the opera. Sean was eleven when he played in *Hansel & Gretel* for the DGOS and was also in performances of *La Boheme and Tosca*. 'My father encouraged our interest and he was always on the lookout for volunteers for the position of "Super". Later, I was one in *Aida*.

It's well to explain that "Supers", or to give them their full name, supernumeraries, are the "extras", male and female, who do not sing or open their mouths at all for the duration of their time on stage. They appear in the programme under the guise of soldiers, village people or street urchins. The contribution they make is an invaluable one. It would be impossible to stage many operas effectively without the aid of "Supers". For example, the manhandling of Cavaradossi to and from Scarpia's prison is the handiwork of Roberti and his henchmen, all roles for "Supers", as is the firing squad in act three of *Tosca*. Furthermore, in many scenes where a chorus is of necessity static, creating a balance of voices, "Supers" create movement. It was not always easy to recruit them for the society as the "Super's" job can be after all a rather thankless one. But Capt. O'Kelly and his colleagues regarded it as one of the utmost importance.

Later on Sean Kelly and his brother Liam would be staunch members of the DGOS chorus. 'I enjoyed chorus work,' Sean recalled, 'as it was a break from everything else. Although we rehearsed very hard I found the whole thing relaxing and you made friends. My father treated Liam and myself like any other chorus member and that's what we liked. But he appreciated what we were doing and the sacrifices we were making to sing for the society. He was not a man to say that out loud. He saw the amateur chorus as something special, the bulwark of the society.'

Meanwhile, the 1941 winter season in November looked an overcrowded programme, with seven operas scheduled to run on consecutive nights, directed by a newcomer from London, Kingsley Lark, and the augmented orchestra conducted in turn by Capt. J M Doyle and Charles Lynch. Young baritone Nick Lewis, a builder by day, had been chosen by Capt. O'Kelly to sing the elder Germont in *La Traviata*. 'It was my first major role and I worked very hard on it with Julia Gray. I loved Verdi's music and the part lay within my range.'

Soprano Moira Griffith was cast as Gilda, Rigoletto's artless daughter, with John Lynskey in the title role; John Torney was the Duke. The opera, one of Verdi's greatest, had a problematic background mainly over censorship. Its theme is based on Victor Hugo's play *Le Roi s'amuse* depicting Tribolet a hunchback court jester. Because the Venetian censorship deemed that the opera's libretto undermined a sovereign ruler, and the religious authorities condemned Monterone's curse on the jester and the Duke, Verdi had to rework the script. Eventually a compromise was reached and the names were changed with Tribolet becoming Rigoletto.

The opera was an enormous success at its performance in Venice in March 1851, and in its first Paris season was performed over one hundred times. And in Dublin it has remained one of the most popular of the composer's works. On this occasion Moira Griffith recalled happy memories of the production. 'I thought that John Lynskey was outstanding as the jester, in both his acting and singing, and was very convincing, especially at that agonising moment when he discovers I've been abducted. I can still see the look of anger and despair in his face. One funny thing about John, though, and it is this. He always kept time with his big toe. On this occasion he was wearing the jester's shoes with his toe protruding and close to the artificial bell, with the result that every time he beat out time it caused a swishing sound. The audience realising what was happening, began to giggle aloud but John didn't know what they were giggling at. When he did, he quickly ceased beating out time. It was funny at the time'

Off-stage, she found the baritone somewhat shy and detached and it wasn't always easy to make conversation with him. But she was fond of him as he was considerate to his fellow artists. By now he was married to Eily Murnaghan who was beginning to direct operas for the society. Harold White for the *Irish Independent* lavished praise on Lynskey's performance and added that it was a personal triumph for him. 'He does not,' the critic wrote, 'try to make sense out of the rather ridiculous situations, but he seizes on the human qualities of the jester's character and makes the most of them. His duets with Gilda, too, were very satisfying, for in Moira Griffith we had a Gilda whose sense of musicianship is a decided asset in the rendering of the music. Her phrasing of "Caro Nome" was artistic and her acting, even in this melodramatic opera, was comparatively restrained. She needs, however, to attack her notes in the centre if she is to make her intonation unmistakable.'

White thought that 'Charles Lynch conducted cautiously', but the chorus was excellent. And he was impressed by John Torney's singing as the Duke and Sam Mooney's Monterone. Likewise in *Traviata*, Nick Lewis came in for favourable mention, even if as expected Renée Flynn stole the show as Violetta. One of the highlights of the season was James Johnston's performance as Turiddu in *Cavalleria Rusticana*, opposite Patricia Black's Santuzza, while Dublin soprano Renée Flynn got good notices for her portrayal of Nedda, the heroine in *I Pagliacci*.

It was considered a successful season by most of the critics, particularly by the influential Harold White. The audience favourite at this time was questionably soprano May Devitt who was impressive as Floria Tosca, though Puccini's melodic opera failed to pack the Gaiety. Tenor James Johnston again sang a glorious Faust, his "All Hail thou Dwelling" winning spontaneous applause from the crowded house.

Capt. O'Kelly had a habit of marking in his notebook the takings at the box-office and after this, only the society's second season, he was able to mark down over 85 per cent business. Louis Elliman would be pleased.

The Girl from Macroom

She arrived in Dublin at the outbreak of war hoping to make a career as a singer. It was a new adventure for the girl from Macroom, Co. Cork, and all she had to show for her efforts so far were medals and trophies won at Feis Matiu, Cork. 'I felt I would get nowhere in Macroom,' she recalled, 'and decided I must get away to improve my voice.'

Rita Lynch was fortunate to have two brothers in Dublin, both civil servants. 'I persuaded them to take a flat and that I would look after them, but they soon complained that I didn't look after them enough, that I was always out. It wasn't quite true. I did do a certain amount for them and stayed on.'

After a few months she gave a recital in the Royal Irish Academy of Music. The programme had been prepared for her by her former teacher in Cork, Mary Sheridan. It comprised Mozart arias and Lieder. Her sweet soprano made an immediate impression and as she was unknown, people in the hall asked about her. At that moment she was approached by a woman who introduced herself as Jean Nolan, a voice teacher. Ms Lynch told her she had just come to Dublin to live. 'I would like to train you,' said Ms Nolan, 'and I will do it for nothing.'

Looking back, Rita Lynch says she was overwhelmed by the generous offer, especially in view of the fact that she was earning no money. 'I thanked her and in the following months I trained hard with her. She was an excellent voice coach.'

She went on to win major awards at the Dublin Feis Ceoil, prompting the adjudicator Topliss Green to remark, 'Ms Lynch is a singer whose breath control is perfect and her vowel sounds are better than any other singer I have heard at the festival.' It was a very musical performance by a singer who ought to do well and she was a delight to listen to. She sang "The Last Rose of Summer" with the ease and simplicity of an outstanding artist.'

The young soprano was soon in demand for concert and oratorio engagements and began to earn fees that though small helped to improve her wardrobe. Jean Nolan was anxious to introduce her to opera and approached George Sleator early in 1940 and he gave Ms Lynch a part in

DOS's new production of Donizetti's *L'Elisir d'Amore*. But she would have to wait another two years for her "break". This came when she was chosen to sing a principal role in the DGOS's bi-centenary performance of Handel's *Messiah* in the Gaiety Theatre in April 1942. It was one of Dublin's biggest musical occasions of the year, with a 230-strong chorus comprising the choirs of the Culwick Choral Society, Trinity College Choral Society, the UCD Musical Society and the DGOS chorus. The other soloists were James Johnston and Patricia Black; Capt. J M Doyle conducted. The occasion made a deep impression on Rita Lynch and the *Irish Times* critic commented that she sang with exquisite purity of tone and a delicate artistry.

It was no surprise therefore when Capt. O'Kelly chose her to sing Susanna in the society's spring season's Marriage of Figaro. Again her performance received impressive press notices. Her own abiding memories, however, were singing the lovely Letter Duet with Renée Flynn and working with a cast that included Josephine O'Hagan, Moira Griffith and the bass-baritone Michael O'Higgins. He had heard her sing at the Feis Ceoil and gave her a volume of Hugo Wolf's songs. 'He couldn't have been more helpful to me,' she recalls, 'and young singers remember gestures like that.'

When the society brought the opera to Cork, it was for the soprano, like going back home, except that it took hours and hours to get there by train. Sometimes the train would stop for some reason or other and it was eventually nearly five hours before it pulled into the station. Since there were eight brothers in her family, she could expect a few of them to attend the performance of *Figaro* at the Opera House. She stayed at the Victoria Hotel and was looking forward tremendously to singing before her own people. A shock, however, awaited her. Getting ready to go to the theatre for the matinee performance of *Figaro* at the Opera House, the hotel lift suddenly stalled and she was left 'calling out madly' for someone to get her out. Eventually, she was rescued and reached her dressing-room with about forty minutes to go to curtain up. 'I got an awful fright and to this day I'm terrified of lifts. I was in the circumstances happy enough with my performance. Mozart's music fitted perfectly into my voice. It was special to me.

Capt. O'Kelly considered the short season highly successful and in his curtain speech on the final night promised a return visit, if possible to Cork. Among the packed audience was Frank Byrne, an avid opera fan whose firm Hickey & Byrne printed programmes for visiting companies for many years, including the programmes and posters for the Joseph O'Mara Company's last visit to the city. In Byrne's view, touring opera had always been popular in the city and the visit of the newly-formed Dublin Grand Opera Society was no exception. Artists such as James Johnston, JC Browner, John

Lynskey and Patricia Black had visited Cork in the previous year with the Dublin Operatic Society and created a big impression, with Browner's being acclaimed for his vivid portrayal of Mephistopheles and Johnston for his beautifully sung *Faust*. 'I remember that Rita Lynch was little known at the time but for a young soprano making her way she displayed a natural talent. After that she was offered recitals and concerts in Cork.'

Back in Dublin, the soprano experienced some tough times due to wartime shortages. While she admits she never went hungry, she was often short of fuel at her flat in Sandymount Avenue which she still shared with her brothers Gerry and Con Lynch. With winters tending to be severe she sometimes felt the chill and missed warm fires. She got over the transport restrictions - electric trains did not run in the evenings - by purchasing a bicycle which she used to get her to rehearsals and singing lessons with Jean Nolan.

'Despite the hard times I was enjoying myself,' she recalls. 'Best of all I was meeting important people in the music world like John McCormack, Margaret Burke Sheridan, Dr Vincent O'Brien and the producer Sydney Russell. When I was cast in the small role of Ines in Donizetti's *La Favorita*, I experienced at first hand the outstanding talents of Patricia Black. Fascinated, I used to watch her at rehearsals as she combined dramatic singing with real acting ability. We became friends in no time.'

The society was presenting the work for the first time, mainly because Miss Black was available to sing the role of Leonora di Guzman, the Mistress of Alfonso, King of Spain. In the opera *Fernando,* a novice in a monastery is attracted to her and such is his passion that he decides to renounce his novitiate. Premiered in Paris in December 1840, it has enjoyed universal success. By 1904 the opera had been performed no fewer than 650 times at the Paris Opéra alone. The tenor aria "Spirto gentil" and the mezzo-soprano's "O mio Fernando" have become popular concert pieces.

The DGOS production, from all accounts, was successful and featured what was described as 'a good team of principals'. A Continental tenor, Herman Simberg, was appearing for the first time with the society and apparently acquitted himself well, his 'light pleasant tenor voice making the most of Donizetti's tuneful music.' He was singing Fernando in Italian while the rest of the principals and chorus sang in English. There was praise for Michael O'Higgins's King Alfonso and John Nolan as the Prior Baldassare. 'He acted the part with becoming dignity and his singing was rich in its sonority and expression,' commented the *Evening Mail*. But once again it was Patricia Black who stole the honours. 'I can still remember her singing "O mio Fernando", recalls Rita Lynch. 'It made me so happy to be one of the cast.'

Moira Griffith had sung with Miss Lynch in *The Marriage of Figaro* and their careers ran along similar lines except that Miss Griffith's priority was the piano at the outset and she picked up various trophies and scholarships before she ever thought of opera. It was when she attended the convent at Eccles Street for a year that she met Sister Clements, Margaret Burke Sheridan's first singing teacher, and asked her if she could sing. 'I'm a pianist, not a singer,' she told the nun politely. But Sr. Clemens persisted, 'Margaret Sheridan comes to visit me here occasionally and I'll get her to listen to you sing.'

The appointment was made for the Gresham Hotel some months later. Moira Griffith was still unconvinced. 'I packed some music into my bag and went along to see her in her suite. She was very charming but direct and, taking my bag, picked out the music for "One Fine Day", the Puccini aria. I had never sung it before and it belonged to someone else. I accompanied myself on the piano. When I'd finished, Miss Sheridan looked at me and remarked, 'You're a marvellous pianist!'

Miss Griffith went on to be a brilliant piano and organ student at the Royal Irish Academy of Music, winning gold medals and scholarships for both instruments. She had to forego a scholarship to the Guildhall, London, because of the war and instead got a grand piano. Later, she was introduced to Lady Hamilton, wife of the composer Sir Hamilton Harty, who told her that her soprano voice was very good. She took her "Matric" at the Loreto Convent, St. Stephen's Green, and enrolled in UCD for her bachelor of music degree and studied harmony with Dr John F Larchet.

In the late 1930s she began to enter for vocal competitions at the Dublin Feis Ceoil and after winning the Dramatic Cup, received a letter from Louis Elliman offering her an engagement at the Theatre Royal, where she would be partnered by Michael O'Higgins and tenor Alfred O'Shea in excerpts from the ballad opera, The *Lily of Killarney*. When her father saw her name on bill posters in city streets he became very annoyed and tried to stop her appearing. 'My father loved music and had often brought me to operas at the Gaiety Theatre,' she recalled, 'but he thought I was too young and the show would be a distraction. Eventually I got round him to let me sing.'

Popular variety artist Noel Purcell, a gangling, bearded figure, acted as Moira Griffith's guardian for the week and on the Friday said to her, 'The ghost walks tonight, girl.' She stared at him puzzled, believing that the place was haunted. He laughed as he said, 'No, not that. I mean you'll get paid tonight.' She felt foolish. Later, Louis Elliman handed her the envelope with her fee and she opened it in her dressing room and reckoned it was a lot of money. She went upstairs and said to him, 'Isn't there something wrong, Mr Elliman? I think you've made a mistake.' He took the envelope and assured her he hadn't made a mistake. 'Don't you see, I'm giving you a pound for each performance.' She had mistakenly believed she would get one pound for the week's work. Again, she felt a little foolish.

She had, meanwhile, kept up her friendship with Margaret Burke Sheridan and they sometimes met for coffee and a chat about music. The diva liked to walk with her down Grafton Street and seemed in need of company. It was by now the summer of 1942 and Moira Griffith had been offered the role of Rosina in the DGOS's winter season production of *The Barber of Seville*. 'I will teach it to you,' said Miss Sheridan. 'I know it will suit your voice.'

Moira Griffith had regarded Sr. Clements as a brilliant voice teacher and had accompanied her pupils on the piano; but Burke Sheridan was also painstaking and she remembered her going over the lovely first act aria "Una voce" on numerous occasions until she was satisfied. She would hum it and sing the music and then say to the soprano, 'I think we have it now.'

While she would be grateful for the diva's help she was not prepared for her behaviour at the Saturday matinee. Miss Sheridan, ensconced in her usual box near the stage, inevitably attracted the attention of people around her. After Miss Griffith had sung the aria "Una Voce", the diva rose from her seat and shouted, 'Brava! Brava!' and in the second act words like 'You're great, Moira!' and 'Isn't she great!'

'I was mortified,' recalls the soprano. 'I was lucky it was a matinee and not an evening performance as I would never have got through it. I knew she meant well but she got entirely carried away. I went to Bill O'Kelly afterwards and told him she mustn't be in that box for the rest of my performances. He understood; he had seen her act like this before.'

Rossini's *Barber*, premiered in Rome in 1816, has remained exceedingly popular because its score bubbles with freshness, charm and high humour, and the characterisation is well drawn. The role of the Count Almaviva has attracted outstanding lyric tenors, Tito Schipa among them, and Figaro, the town barber, was one of Tito Gobbi's favourite parts.

Love and deception, French-style, characterises the opera's inventive comedy, though it is set in Seville. The sparkling overture is often performed at concerts. The DGOS was staging this comic masterpiece for the first time and judging by the critics' reaction, underestimated its production demands - it has never been an easy work to direct because of the copious comic business.

Most of the reviewers agreed that the first act was weak and the tempo too slow with the cast failing to come to grips with the quick-changing stage business. Others held that John Torney did not possess the lyric voice for Almaviva's mellifluous music, though his acting was convincing. Even John

Lynskey's singing of Figaro's scintillating first act aria "Largo al Factotum" failed, it was stated, to rouse the audience. The orchestra under Charles Lynch fared somewhat better, his reading of the overture winning praise. Moira Griffith recalls that the audience for the most part responded enthusiastically and enjoyed themselves. She was unhappy, however, about one particular aspect.

There is a scene in the opera where Rosina can accompany herself on the piano as she sings and she saw this as an opportunity to show that she was a pianist as well as a singer, so she asked Charles Lynch if he would allow her to do this. His reply was instant. 'Oh, no, I won't have that. You can have a piano off-stage and someone else can play for you.' But she persisted with her plea and was allowed a piano on stage but it was turned in such a way that the audience didn't know she was actually accompanying herself. The next morning one newspaper critic stated it was a pity that Miss Griffith did not make some attempt to play the piano herself. It was the kind of comment that tended to annoy her intensely.

The director of *The Barber* was the experienced Sydney Russell who had made such a marked impression in his direction of the society's *Marriage of Figaro*. By now he was a household name in Dublin operatic circles. Since 1936, when he was engaged by George Sleator to direct for the Dublin Operatic Society, he had missed only two seasons - those given by the DGOS in 1941 at the Gaiety Theatre. Russell was liked and respected by artists. Both Rita Lynch and Moira Griffith said they learned a good deal of stage craft from him and that he went about his direction quietly and effectively.

It was a surprise when he decided to work with the DGOS as for years he had been George Sleator's right hand man. But he needed the money and to supplement his income he also taught singing. In fact, he had started his career as a singer and in 1922 sang with Nelly Melba at Covent Garden. He was stage director at the Old Vic and Sadler's Wells companies. His philosophy about directing opera was summed up in his own words, 'With regard to changes from the traditional, I very soon decided that unless one was sure that the change was a good one and a definite improvement on the old, it was much wiser to leave very well alone. While changes can effect improvement and be necessary, I am in favour of sticking to tradition whenever it is reasonable or practical.'

If he welcomed the opportunity to be part of the DGOS - and he undoubtedly did - he was also aware of the shortcomings that militated against achieving higher artistic standards. The lack of time for dress rehearsals was in his view a serious drawback and he said he would give a great deal for a week with three Sundays at least, so as to give the time necessary to do justice to the great operatic masterpieces that the society put before the public. How far they succeeded or not was not for him to say. At any rate it was not for lack of trying. And more than once he declared, 'I do hope a real national opera house is founded and endowed by the State, for no more promising field could be found for its nucleus than the Dublin Grand Opera Society.'

He was struck by the dedication of the chorus members who worked well and cheerfully, but as they had had already done a hard day's work at desk, counter or bench, they were often tired before they commenced rehearsing. Nevertheless, no stage director could wish for a more willing and hard-working chorus. 'Many a time I have called attention to the clock because of the transport restrictions, only to be told, "Never mind that, Mr Russell, we can walk or cycle home all right." '

One of those who cycled home was Aileen Walsh, a teacher, who had joined the chorus early in 1942 and was enjoying every moment of the experience. 'We had no fears in those days of cycling home at night,' she said, 'and most of the choristers had bicycles which we used to come to both rehearsals and performances. Since there was no public transport after 7.30pm, it was the only way we could get home at night. Usually we left our bicycles into an empty depot near the Gaiety Theatre and paid three pence for the privilege. At other times a few of us would walk home at night, especially during the summer, and there was no danger whatsoever, not like nowadays.'

There was, she said, great camaraderie in the chorus and it was made up of both married and single men and women. It was a lively set of about 80 people who simply loved to sing. Sometimes in the summer if they had a free weekend, a group of them would cycle together to Greystones or Glendalough for a picnic. To Aileen Walsh it was a way of making new friends and at the same time ensuring that a good spirit ran through the chorus. At the outset she found Capt. Bill O'Kelly could be gruff in manner, acting like a commander, so everyone did as they were told. She suspected, though, that he cherished the chorus as a group and would do anything for them. Although she had sung in a choir she found the atmosphere around opera more exciting. As she said, 'It was a funny thing, but once you donned a costume you tended to be a different person, losing your identity and inhibitions. It was a new experience for me. I devoted most of my spare time to the chorus but I didn't mind that, nor did others.

Maura Mooney continued to be a stalwart member of the chorus, as did her husband Gerard. She left it for some seasons when her children were born but admitted she couldn't wait to return. 'Eventually when I did go back, I remember saying to everyone how much I had missed singing and the fun that goes with being a chorister. I loved being part of that, meeting the principals, hearing the applause on first nights, and feeling the excitement around you. The Gaiety audience were great to us and let us know if we were good.'

Opera, like pantomime, drama and variety, was regarded as a useful form of escapism in the midst of the prevailing economic austerity and gloom, and an antidote to the grim war news that people listened to on Radio Eireann daily and read in newspapers. Food continued to be scarce, as well as fuel, and there were large pockets of poverty in the inner city, indeed within a stone's throw of Nelson's Pillar which attracted many visitors from the provinces eager to climb its steep steps to catch a panoramic view of the surrounding city.

James Johnston, meanwhile, remained the jewel in the operatic crown as far as Capt. O'Kelly was concerned, for tenors of his class were desperately scarce. When he wasn't singing either opera, oratorio or in concert he went back to his butcher's shop in Belfast and earned more money in a month than he could hope to earn in six months' music engagements. He liked to joke Bill O'Kelly about this, in particular when he was seeking higher fees, but the chairman assured him he would pay him more if the society could afford to do so.

Coming as he did from a staunch Methodist background, Johnston displayed an untypical liberalism and no trace of an anti-Catholic bias. Bigotry, like violent extremism, was anathema to him. He enjoyed travelling to Dublin and Cork and made numerous friends. He was popular with women and at least one pretty DGOS chorister would later fall for his charms and puckish humour.

Strangely, he began his singing as a bass and then baritone and won various competitions. He became alarmed when one adjudicator told him he could not award him any more prizes in that section as he was, in his view, a tenor. Young Johnston believed the adjudicator was talking nonsense and he had no intention of changing to tenor. 'I associated tenors with pansies,' he later explained, 'but after a few of them sang in competitions I revised my opinion and said to myself, "Maybe not all tenors are pansies", so I decided to go up an octave.'

He found singing an enjoyable diversion and his English-born vocal tutor John Vine greatly encouraged him, though he was amused when Johnston enquired about the fees to be paid. 'I don't want a fee from you, Jimmy,' Vine said, 'but instead when the electricity bill comes to me I want you to pay it.'

Around this time a wealthy businessman, who had heard the tenor sing in concerts, offered to send him to Italy to study the Italian language and learn operatic technique. Excited by the prospect, Johnston confided in his father whose reaction shattered him. 'No son of mine,' he declared, 'is going on stage for it's a sure way to hell.'

For the tenor it was an opportunity lost. Shortly afterwards, however, he was advised by Vine to accept Capt. O'Kelly's offer of parts with the Dublin Grand Opera Society.

It was the society's policy to build a new production around a leading singer or singers, so the choice of Patricia Black for Saint-Saens' biblical opera *Samson and Dalila* made good sense. Dalila dominates the story as the unscrupulous enchantress determined to trap the mighty Samson and learn the secret of his strength. The singer must be capable of projecting allurement and passion, especially in the big act two love duet. Miss Black had already shown as Carmen and Azucena that she could cope in this respect. Finding a tenor to match her seductive powers posed a problem, for while John Torney's voice was equal to the role he did not conjure up the heroic figure of Samson and he lacked sex appeal.

The work was first performed in December 1877 and is now in the repertory of nearly all of the leading opera houses. On the choral side one is reminded of oratorio and its air of nobility. Capt. O'Kelly at the time was confident the big DGOS chorus could cope with the composer's demands. Despite the beauty of the music, the opera was slow to catch on in the Dublin of the forties. For one thing, newspaper reviews were mixed and Harold White's introduction must have raised eyebrows and did no good at all for box-office takings. He was after all the leading critic of the day.

As he stated, 'It is not an opera I find attractive - its lack of action and dramatic progress makes it laboured. Indeed, until Dalila's entrance the music is more appropriate to oratorio. Certainly John Torney did his best to infuse some energy into it by his singing, but his efforts were spasmodic and scarcely convincing. However, both his singing and acting were generally effective.

'In this opera, of course, everything depends on the Dalila. Saint-Saens took a great risk in confining the female cast to one woman - and that a contralto. I have to say that Patricia Black acted well and sang her three arias with much expressiveness and deep romantic feeling. She looked handsome and dignified, if not alluring, and effective in the dramatic scenes. Capt. Doyle conducted the work with surprising skill.'

To Florrie Drapier, Patricia Black was ideal casting at this time; she was slim and sultry-looking in the part and certainly raised the temperature of the audience. 'Her love scene I remember with Samson was terribly convincing in the sensual sense, but she needed a more macho Samson, as we say, for the sparks to fly.'

Aileen Walsh thought Patricia Black coped as well with Saint-Saens' music as she had with Verdi (*Azucena*) or Bizet *(Carmen)*. 'To me she looked every bit the enchantress.'

In the winter season of that same year, 1942, Capt. O'Kelly had wanted to build the society's first production of Verdi's Aida around Joan Hammond but was stymied in his plans by George Sleator, who held the soprano to the expiry date of her short-term contract with him. It was a disappointment for the chairman and instead he was obliged at short notice to ask May Devitt to sing the part, with Patricia Black as Amneris. Some members of the DGOS chorus were not surprised by Sleator's action as he had earlier threatened to hold May Devitt to her contract with the Dublin Operatic Society. In retrospect it was perhaps understandable, for the DOS had engaged both Miss Hammond and Miss Devitt before the DGOS was established.

Leonora's Fee

It was not unusual in the Dublin of the 1940s for sopranos like May Devitt, Renée Flynn and Moira Griffith to do vocal spots in shows at the Theatre Royal, and these went on prior to the showing of the big movie. In November of 1943, Miss Griffith was appearing in a new show "Flying High" and by her own admission enjoying herself, though she was well aware that artistically it was some way behind a Mozart opera. Usually Louis Elliman asked her to do about eight weeks in the year and it wasn't taxing on her voice.

It was now around the time of the opening of the DGOS winter season and since she was not engaged in the season, she had decided to take up the 'Royal' offer and other concert dates. She was therefore unprepared when Comdt. O'Kelly asked to see her urgently. The society's vice-chairman Michael Dennigan was with him when they met and the men quickly came to the point. Joan Hammond was unwell and would not be able to sing Leonora in Trovatore on the opening night of the season. Would she get them out of the crisis?

'As you know, I'm singing in the Theatre Royal show,' she reminded them.

'Louis Elliman has agreed to let you off for the night,' said Comdt. O'Kelly. 'If you don't agree to sing, we'll have to cancel, which means closing the theatre for the night.'

After a pause, Miss Griffith told them she would sing for the same fee as they intended paying Joan Hammond. 'Don't you think this is only fair as it's the same part and, anyway, I have to refresh it in my mind?' Normally she received a fee of around eight pounds for singing a leading role, and although money was never a priority with her, she would actually be losing money transferring for one night to the Gaiety. Eventually both O'Kelly and Dennigan agreed to give her the same fee as Joan Hammond was getting, though the figure was not specified. It was later that Dennigan told Miss Griffith that Hammond's fee per performance was one hundred pounds plus expenses.

Since she had got only twelve hours' notice, Moira Griffith spent most of the next day sitting at the piano in her home going over Verdi's music and working on the big arias. 'I told Jim Doyle I'd prefer to revise the score alone and he left me to get on with it. It's a big part and I hadn't sung it for nearly twelve months.'

At this time Joan Hammond was singing regularly with the Carl Rosa Opera Company througout Britain as Butterfly, Mimi, Marguerite and Violetta and she would soon be recording the captivating Puccini aria "O My Beloved Father" that would go on to sell a million copies. She made no secret of her liking for Dublin and had promised Comdt. O'Kelly that whenever she could she would sing for the society. 'I think she loved eating our big steaks,' the chairman used to say later.

Moira Griffith, meanwhile, got through the performance in admirable fashion. *The Irish Times* noted, 'Owing to the illness of Joan Hammond, the Dublin soprano Moira Griffith had taken the role of Leonora at short notice and received a well-deserved ovation.' Likewise, the *Irish Press* critic stated it was the most satisfactory operatic performance he had seen the soprano give. And Joseph O'Neill *(Independent)* congratulated her on her performance and also praised James Johnston for his artistic approach to the role of Manrico. Once again, however, Patricia Black as Azucena won the greatest acclaim for her impassioned singing.

When Miss Griffith went along next day to Louis Elliman's office in the Gaiety Theatre to collect her fee from Comdt. O'Kelly and Michael Dennigan, she was thanked for getting the society 'out of a corner' and handed a closed envelope. Normally she would not have bothered to open it until later but she decided on impulse to do so at that moment. To her dismay it contained eight pound notes instead of the bigger fee agreed. Without uttering a word, she tore up the envelope with the money and let the paper pieces drop on the floor, closing the door after her. There was no doubt in her mind about their agreement. Surely she had made herself clear enough?

Three years before she had sung Eily O'Connor in The *Lily of Killarney* for the Dublin Operatic Society and afterwards George Sleator had sent her a letter, stating, 'Dear Miss Griffith - For your performance of Eily O'Connor kindly accept my gratitude and heartfelt congratulations. I feel very happy in the thought that you kindly accepted the part. It will be my dearest wish to have you in our April season. Thank you, and may the coming Easter season bring you many joys.'

Although she had received no fee from the DOS, her contribution had been gracefully acknowledged. She regarded her fee for Leonora as a matter of principle, yet she was determined not to let it stand in the way of future engagements with the   DGOS. She was the first to admire the way Bill

O'Kelly had got the newly-formed society on the road, but she expected him to be more grateful. She had after all been taken out of the Theatre Royal show against her own wishes.

Joan Hammond recovered in time to sing the November 25 performance of *Trovatore* but she was to make her biggest impact as a memorable Elizabeth in Wagner's *Tannhauser*. The production was worth every penny for it gave an over-flow audience the opportunity in that spring of `43 to hear Miss Hammond in a role and in music that suited her. Her voice had a glorious ring with exquisite tonal colour, her artistry was inspiring.

To Joseph O'Neill *(Independent)*, the soprano's range of expression was remarkable and she was always in full vocal control, her singing of the Prayer being very moving. There were other fine performances, according to the critics, notably John Lynskey's Wolfram - his singing of the aria "O Star of Eve" being considered a *tour de force* - and JC Browner's commanding Landgrave. Soprano Renée Flynn, as Venus, sang her opening scene with 'beautifully sustained tone', suggesting to at least one experienced critic that she was 'born to sing Wagner's music'. In the 1930's she had appeared in Die Walküre at Covent Garden and afterwards was handed a contract which she has to this day, but her husband Tom (Attwood) was against her spending weeks on end in London and discouraged her putting her signature on it. All she will say today is, 'In those days you were inclined to carry out your husband's wishes.' On that occasion the Siegmund was sung by Lauritz Melchior and Sieglinde by the illustrious Lotte Lehmann.

Although there was a shortage of strings in the DGOS orchestra, led by Terry O'Connor, they were said to have played well under Comdt. Jim Doyle, and the chorus after a tentative start, gave a very fine account of themselves. Sydney Russell's staging of the work was described as 'notable' and his finest of the week. However, it seemed once again that the society had taken on more than it could manage for in December 1943 it prompted the heading in the *Sunday Independent*, TOO MUCH ATTEMPTED?, and the paper went on to warn the society about over-crowding the programme. 'It does not seem possible to give adequate rehearsal to seven operas, even if a number of them are in the repertory,' it stated. 'For neither the chorus nor many of the principals are full-time operatic artists, so rehearsals have to be fitted in when other claims are being made on their time. Not that anything went wrong with the performances last week that could at once be attributed to insufficient rehearsal, but in some of the productions there was communicated and atmosphere of "feeling our way".

There were, the critic added, slight lapses of memory in parts that were quite well-known by the principals, hesitant singing by the chorus, and a constraint in the acting took the brilliance out of some of the performances. The 'happy family' feeling where each one could rely completely on the other was missing. He could be quite wrong in that, but he got that uneasy feeling at times, though there were many fine performances, notably Miss Griffith's singing of Leonora at short notice and of course Joan Hammond's brilliance as Aida and Elizabeth. The society seemed to have, however, the same problem as other musical societies in finding talent to fill minor roles. The importance of casting these to provide a reasonable balance with the principal roles should not be overlooked.

The winter season of that year, 1943, looked particularly interesting. The society planned a centenary performance of William Balfe's *The Bohemian Girl* for November 27, exactly one hundred years since the opera was first staged at the Drury Lane Theatre, London. The work held a special place in the hearts of Irish music lovers. Born in the city on May 15, 1808, the son of a dancing master, young Balfe was a child prodigy, composing a polacca for a band at the age of seven and giving a violin recital at the age of nine. He went to London in 1823 to learn the violin and later obtained a post as violinist in the orchestra at Drury Lane Theatre. After a short spell in Italy, he settled in Paris where he met Rossini who offered him an engagement with the Italian Opera, as a baritone. He made an acclaimed debut there as Figaro in The *Barber of Seville* in 1827. Following an engagement in Palermo, he composed his first opera *I Rivalli di se Stessi*, and also met and married a Hungarian singer, Lina Roser. His first English opera was *The Siege of Rochelle* but few of his remaining operas ever achieved the same popularity as *The Bohemian Girl*. He made the journey to London for its premiere which turned out to be a huge success. Subsequently the libretto was translated into Italian *(La Zingara)*, German, French, Swedish and Russian. Later it was given in Paris as *La Bohemienne* in a French version. The opera's storyline is dramatic, if sentimental, and is woven around a young girl Arline, daughter of Count Arnheim, who is kidnapped as a child and taken to a gypsies' encampment and brought up by them. But twelve years later, through an odd twist of fate, she is reunited with her father and he agrees to give her in marriage to the Polish nobleman Thaddeus, despite the fact that he is a political exile.

"The Bo Girl", as it came to be affectionately called, is Balfe's best known opera and was undoubtedly the most popular English opera of the nineteenth century and the only one to win universal acclaim abroad. Its melodic arias such as "I dreamt I dwelt in marble halls" - recorded by Margaret Burke Sheridan - "When other lips", a great favourite of Count John McCormack and "The heart bowed down" contributed to the work's popularity, and it was not unknown for characters in the Gaiety 'gods' up to 1955 to belt out one of the arias during an interval of a performance.

The DGOS assembled an all-Irish cast for the centenary celebrations, with James Johnston singing Thaddeus, Patricia Black the gypsy queen and JC Browner as Devilshoof. Sean Mooney was given the role of Count Arnheim. Rita Lynch appeared the natural choice to sing Arline and it came as no surprise when Comdt. O'Kelly offered her the plum part. The soprano's purity of voice and look of vulnerability fitted the character and at the time it was not unusual for her to sing "I dreamt I dwelt" at concerts. She deemed it an honour to be asked to sing on this auspicious occasion for the society.

'I worked hard with Julia Gray and producer Sydney Russell', she recalls, 'and I had no fears about singing the part. I knew that every soprano in Ireland would have given the world to sing in the opera, and here I was, the girl from Macroom, being cast in the leading role. I remember how thrilled I was and could not wait to tell my family and friends.'

Prior to the opening performance, Dublin's Lord Mayor Ald. Martin O'Sullivan unveiled a marble plaque in the Green Room as a tribute to Balfe in the presence of a gathering that included Dr Vincent O'Brien, Louis Elliman, the Gaiety Theatre's managing director, and the officers of the Dublin Grand Opera Society, Dr Larchet (president), Comdt. O'Kelly (chairman) and AE (Bertie) Timlin (hon. Secretary). Indeed, the theatre was celebrating a double event as on that day seventy-two years before it had first opened its doors to the public.

There was also a buzz in the rest of the theatre on that November evening. Chorus members Aileen Walsh and Florrie Draper recalled the 'definite air of expectancy' that prevailed, mainly because it was an all-Irish cast. According to Miss Walsh, this fact 'had gone down well' in the society served by Irish singers. To Florrie Draper it was about the best cast that could be got. 'I remember we were all looking forward to Jimmy Johnston singing Thaddeus. The rehearsals had gone very well and I'd say that producer Sydney Russell was happy, as was Comdt. Doyle.'

For the occasion, Comdt. O'Kelly and Bertie Timlin joined the chorus ranks. The theatre was packed when Comdt. Doyle took his place on the podium. For many oldtimers in the audience it was an evening of nostalgia as they remembered perhaps pre-war performances by cross-Channel touring companies, and this would be evident in their subsequent enthusiastic applause for the big arias.

Rita Lynch became upset though in the second scene of act two, which takes place in a street in Presburg, when some of the scenery above her began to creak and were it not for the quick intervention of the backstage hands she feared the worst. 'I remember Jimmy Johnston whispering to me,

"You'll be alright, you're singing like a trooper, girl." I felt nervous at the time and was afraid my voice would be affected. Thankfully, I got through it and in the final scenes I can still hear the lovely applause.'

James Brittain, an aspiring young tenor, played the small part of a peasant and was particularly impressed by Johnston's voice and musicianship. 'I used to love the way he sang and how he made it look so easy. You could hear every word he sang and never forced the voice. You knew he had got a good vocal training and as a tenor myself, hoping to go places, I studied his technique. His Thaddeus was a first-class interpretation, and for that matter, so was Sean Mooney's Count Arnheim. Sean had a natural baritone voice and a good stage presence. With proper coaching he would have gone further in his career.

Rita Lynch was pleased with her progress. Apart from Arline and Susanna, she had sung Micaela (*Carmen*) and Zerlina (*Don Giovanni*) for the society, as well as innumerable concerts throughout the country. She always welcomed the opportunity to work with Sydney Russell as he knew everything, it seemed, about the opera he was directing. She made friends with Charles Lynch, though as a conductor he lacked the decisiveness of Jim Doyle; she would come to admire him more as a concert pianist and it suited his temperament better.

Her next part for the society was that of Gretel in Humperdinck's fairytale opera *Hansel & Gretel*. Since it had not been staged in Dublin for a long time the critics welcomed its revival. The rehearsals were sometimes an unhappy experience for Rita Lynch as May Devitt, who was singing Hansel, was unfriendly and inclined to adopt a superior air. 'I felt a little slighted in fact and could see no need for her attitude. I was, you could say, a beginner in opera so she hadn't anything to fear from me. I was disappointed because I regarded her as a very good actress-singer. It was the first time I had come up against someone acting the prima donna.'

In the subsequent reviews, however, she shared the honours with Miss Devitt, a fact that pleased her. A 'very successful partnership' was how one critic described their performances; while the *Evening Mail* reviewer commented, 'The society is fortunate to have two such outstanding sopranos.'

Around this time Comdt. O'Kelly was hearing rumours that the Carl Rosa Company was anxious to sign up James Johnston, Patricia Black and Moira Griffith, and in the case of Johnston, especially, he was worried because it was virtually impossible to get suitable tenors. When he heard about a young Derry-born tenor singing in *Show-Boat* at the Theatre Royal he went along to hear him. Joseph McLaughlin was single and over six feet in height, good-looking, a matinee idol with a voice made in heaven. To Comdt. O'Kelly, it possessed a warm, appealing tone and the young singer appeared to derive personal delight in hitting top notes. The chairman believed that with painstaking coaching McLaughlin would be able to tackle roles like Pinkerton, Rodolfo and may be Romeo in Gounod's *Romeo & Juliette*. The women in the audience seemed to love him. He decided to speak to May Devitt about the young singer. By now she and McLaughlin were lovers which in some more 'proper quarters' was a source of scandal as May was married. If anything, though, the affair enhanced their stage appeal. The singers' private lives did not worry Comdt. O'Kelly; he was more anxious about discovering a Pinkerton for the society's new production of *Madama Butterfly*.

McLaughlin, who could be outspoken, expressed astonishment when May Devitt told him what O'Kelly had in mind. 'May knew I'd never seen an opera,' he recalls, 'and Pinkerton meant nothing to me. But she was terribly persistent and I gave in to her when she finally said, "Joe, I'll teach the part to you." And, God bless her, she did with the help of Julia Gray. I felt I could manage the part, I mean it isn't all that big - he doesn't appear in Act two.

'Together, they hammered the words and music into McLaughlin,' said Comdt. Doyle, the conductor, when I talked to him in his Rathgar home in the early 1990s. 'It wasn't easy work, he was an untrained singer, but he did work very hard to get it right. I had to admire the women's patience.'

James Brittain, whose brother Harry had been in the chorus since the foundation of the society, was immediately struck at rehearsals by the beauty of McLaughlin's voice. 'It was a natural tenor voice, fresh-toned and flexible and when he sang softly it was like listening to Richard Tauber. He was a pure-voiced operatic tenor and people don't know that when they hear him today as Josef Locke adopting a different kind of voice. I was intrigued by the manner in which May Devitt taught him how to walk onto the stage, every movement, you might say. They were fantastic together in the big love duet at the end of act one and I remember on the first night you could almost hear the women in the audience swoon as he carried his Butterfly in his arms into the geisha's house. It was a magical moment.'

It was a strong cast. Michael O'Higgins was the American consul Sharpless, with Richard Mason as Bonze, a Japanese priest, and Patricia *Black as Suzuki*.

The production received favourable reaction, the *Irish Press* critic commenting, 'The society would have to go a long way to find a better combination than May Devitt and Joseph McLaughlin as Butterfly and Pinkerton.' Dublin audiences simply adored Miss Devitt's portrayal of the tragic heroine in Puccini's opera, as she built up the hope and expectancy reflected in her big aria, "One Fine Day". There were those in the audience who found it difficult to watch her final agonising moments before she stabs herself in despair.

McLaughlin, for his part, was pleased by the audience's warm response and his own ability to sing the role. 'I thought our voices blended very well in the love duet,' he told me once. 'May was beautiful to sing with, an artist to her fingertips.'

In Comdt. O'Kelly's view the tenor had done even better than he had expected and later on he cast him as the poet Rodolfo to May Devitt's Mimi in *La Boheme*. O'Kelly believed this would be his best part, that he had the range to sing Puccini's music. Again, it was Devitt, Julia Gray and Comdt. Jim Doyle who ensured that the tenor would be ready by opening night. Devitt, in particular, worked like a trojan on him, humming the music as they strolled hand in hand in Grafton Street, or even as they sat together in the corner of a café.

Sometimes Comdt. Doyle was amused when McLaughlin fluffed his lines at rehearsal. 'I had to pull him up when he got the words mixed up. It was just as well there was no audience around to hear some of the weird lines spoken by Rodolfo. But we were glad to have him and he more or less mastered the part.'

The critics were divided about his Rodolfo, with the *Irish Press* reviewer saying that it was not the tenor's best work and wondered if he was suffering from a cold. The *Irish Times*, though, stated it was a good all round production, not perfect, but thoroughly enjoyable. While May Devitt was intensely dramatic and at times almost too passionate her Mimi nevertheless was very convincing. As for Joseph McLaughlin, he was making his debut in the role and came through the ordeal creditably, projecting a fine ringing tone, although in the ensemble singing he appeared uncertain. To his credit, added the critic, the young tenor bravely managed to pull through.

According to Joseph O'Neill in the *Irish Independent,* the society set the tenor a difficult task by casting him as the poet. Vocally, the part was well within his scope but much more than ability to sing the notes was required. His big duet with Marcel, for instance, was spoilt by his failure to observe a pause note entering the second verse. Unlike his colleagues, O'Neill did not make allowance for the fact that McLaughlin was new to the role and as an actor was a novice. The critics didn't worry the ebullient Derryman; he was satisfied that he had got through the evening. He was receiving £10 a performance and sometimes reckoned he was mad to be singing for that kind of money. He was on friendly terms with James Johnston and knew that he admired his voice and had said so to colleagues. 'I used to joke Jimmy about his butcher shops in Belfast, telling him that he could afford to sing opera and I couldn't. He had a grand sense of humour and to him Protestants and Catholics were all alike. He was a prankster like myself.'

Thursday, October 26, 1944. It is the evening of the society's first patron's dinner and 250 men and women, elegantly attired, are gathered in the Metropole Ballroom. Among the guests are the Lord Mayor of Dublin, Ald. Martin O'Sullivan, Count John McCormack and his wife Lily, Louis Elliman, civic and diplomatic representatives, and Alfie Byrne, the quintessential Dublinman, and other VIPs including Eamonn O'Neill, president of the Cork Operatic Society. Presiding over the unique event is the advertising tycoon Charles McConnell, DGOS vice-president and patron. It is the society's first big social get-together, an aspect that chairman Comdt. Bill O'Kelly and his fellow officers are anxious to develop in the future. The main purpose is to focus everybody's attention on the patron membership in the hope of raising it to at least 500. For three guineas per person a year, a member is entitled to two seats in the Gaiety Theatre dress circle or boxes on Patrons' Members Night, or on some alternative night during each season, as well as being guaranteed priority booking.

It is a convivial occasion with speeches kept suitably short. Glasses are raised for numerous toasts and there is little doubt that the function is being hugely enjoyed. Dr Larchet says that although the society is less than four years old, it has presented nineteen different operas. 'It's our aim and ambition to try to recapture the great sense of discernment and critical faculty of grand opera which was a feature of Dublin's past history.' Comdt. O'Kelly proposes the toast of the patrons, and tells those present that the position of the society is satisfactory, but the object is artistic perfection and, with the fullest co-operation of all members, they cannot fail to reach that standard.

In proposing the toast of the visitors, Bertie Timlin likens the society to an infant which has not grown up and when its future has to be sponsored by patrons; these now, he says, are the assembly before us in the ballroom. The cheerful Charles McConnell is happy to say that patrons members have subscribed £500 and this will be used to stage operas that are less known to the public. There is applause as Count John McCormack, looking portly and prosperous, gets to his feet and proceeds to speak in his unmistakable Irish brogue, 'We should get the best possible talent available and bring it to this country as an encouragement and as an example. Let them show what they have to give grand opera and let them see what we have to give, and no doubt in this way we will learn a lot and they likewise, but in the end grand opera will certainly benefit.'

To mark the occasion, a special souvenir brochure is distributed to all the tables. It is both revealing and informative with contributions by Comdt. J M Doyle, the society's musical director, Sydney Russell and Dr Larchet, who sums up, 'Our first efforts have been modest, as were those of the now recognised great schools of European opera during the formative years, but in the course of time, with experience and encouragement - financial and otherwise - the DGOS hopes to achieve much.'

There are songs and arias to conclude what has been a most entertaining evening. These are performed by DGOS principals, Michael O'Higgins, Patricia Black, John Lynskey, Renée Flynn and Rita Lynch. Soprano Moira Griffith is in fine voice and has evidently patched up her differences with the chairman, in fact she has recently sung Leonora in *Trovatore* with the society.

The choice of Ponchielli's *La Gioconda* ("The Joyful Girl") for the 1944 winter season was another reassuring example of the society's determination to stage more spectacular operas. The action is set in Venice in the seventeenth century, with act one depicting the Ducal Palace; other scenes like the celebration in act three, demands visual grandeur. At this time the work was virtually unknown to Irish operagoers, though not a few of them would have been familiar with the orchestral version of the ballet music, "The Dance of the Hours" from act three. It has remained the composer's most successful and popular opera, dramatically powerful and musically noteworthy. And it is strong in characterisation.

Casting the work was by no means an easy task. With James Johnston, engaged to sing the Duke of Mantua, Don José and Ottavio, Comdt. O'Kelly had no hesitation in casting Joseph McLaughlin with May Devitt singing La Gioconda. 'I was prepared to tackle any new role as long as May was by my side,' he told me later. 'Anyway, sure I hadn't let the side down with either Pinkerton or Rodolfo.'

Jimmy Brittain has always held the view that Comdt. O'Kelly demonstrated unusual courage in casting McLaughlin in big operatic parts, ignoring at the same time the obvious risks involved. 'I think he knew like all of us that "Big Joe" had the voice and that it was only a matter of coaching him properly and getting him to act.'

Like all of the society's productions, it would be sung in English. The work had been premiered at La Scala in 1876 and was a resounding success, being described as 'a typical example of popular grand opera'. The story revolves round La Gioconda, a ballad singer, who rejects the advances of Barnaba, a spy in the Venetian Council of Ten. In revenge he accuses her blind mother of witchcraft but the old woman is saved from the crowd by Enzo Grimaldo, a Genoese prince whom La Gioconda secretly loves.

There was no reason why Irish operagoers would not fall under the opera's spell; indeed, the booking was unusually brisk and the Gaiety was well filled for the first night. The critics were for the most part impressed by the production. 'It's an enormous success for the society,' stated the *Irish Times*, and added that it was truly lavish and spectacular. 'Typically Italian, the opera is full of flowing melodies with wonderful choral effects, while the ballet music is brilliant.'

May Devitt's acting was described as 'forceful' and her singing as 'luminous'. Patricia Black, as Laura, rose to splendid heights, shining in the big dramatic moments. As for Joseph McLaughlin, the *Irish Press* critic thought he had greatly improved on his Rodolfo and Pinkerton, though his acting was still wooden. His singing of the great aria, "Heaven and Ocean", was 'highly artistic.' Joseph O'Neill in the Irish Independent was less impressed. 'The tenor role in *La Gioconda* abounds in graceful music,' he observed, 'but Joseph McLaughlin did not make the most of his opportunities as often his tone was muffled by varying methods of vocal production.'

Count John McCormack and his wife Lily were guests of honour on the occasion and occupied a box close to the stage. Afterwards, the tenor was accompanied on stage by Comdt. O'Kelly and proceeded to meet the chorus and principals. Joseph McLaughlin said later that he was rebuked by the tenor who had said to him, 'As for you McLaughlin, grand opera is not your forte.' When I talked to Comdt. J M Doyle later at his home, he said he had not heard the remark despite being close to the stage. 'I remember seeing McCormack shake May Devitt's hand as he congratulated her and I suppose he did make a fuss of her, as he was to do also in the case of Patricia Black. Although McCormack could be blunt, I don't believe he would deliberately snub a fellow artist. He might have said to Joe McLaughlin in a whisper to confine himself in future to operetta, songs and ballads. I would perhaps have said the same thing myself.'

McCormack, in spite of failing health, tried to attend the opera as often as possible as the society's guest. Occupying another box on such occasions could be Margaret Burke Sheridan but the celebrities rarely, if ever, met - she did not particularly care for the tenor. In music circles it was felt that the diva envied the wealth he had accumulated from his record royalties in the United States and elsewhere; in contrast, she had made few records and was by now living in moderate circumstances. Nonetheless, she had retained her deep love of opera and adored meeting singers, the more famous the better. Nor had she forgotten Irish artists such as Moira Griffith and Rita Lynch; strangely, Miss Sheridan and May Devitt for some inexplicable reason avoided one another.

'I continued to meet her for coffee,' recalled Moira Griffith, 'and walk her up or down Grafton Street. While she could be lively company she was living in the clouds.'

Earlier that year, after a performance of *Faust* at the Gaiety, the diva was called on to make a speech from her usual box and told the enthusiastic audience she was overwhelmed as it was more than ten years since she had last addressed a gathering in public. In typical fashion, she refused to single out any of the principals and, instead, had encouraging words for the chorus and the wider accomplishments by the society, especially its musical director Comdt. J M Doyle and his colleague Charles Lynch. She went on to wish the society more success in the future. Clearly, Maggie from Mayo was still a force and as popular as ever with her fans.

The year closed on a note with the unexpected death of JC Browner, one of the most devoted servants of opera in the country; first with the Dublin Operatic Society and later with the DGOS. His final appearance was in the Opera House in Cork during the society's spring season, when he again sang his renowned interpretation of Mephistopheles. On that occasion the chairman, Comdt. O'Kelly, in his curtain speech on the final night, singled out Browner for his magnificent performance.

New Era Dawns

The dark war clouds lifted and gradually rolled away, heralding a new era for the society in the spring of 1945. Comdt. O'Kelly was particularly relieved and declared frankly, 'Without the help of our great friend Louis Elliman we would not have survived the forties. He gave us the benefit of his great experience, the help of his stage staff, and during all the period we dealt with him we never signed a contract for our seasons. He is a man of his word, and we owe him a great deal.'

O'Kelly's own contribution was also considerable. From the outset he was an inspirational figure whose vision and drive had made dream into reality; he exuded enthusiasm in what he did and it was infectious as his fellow officers Bertie Timlin, Michael Dinnigan and perhaps most of all, Dr Larchet, wholeheartedly agreed. The chairman was forgiven if sometimes this enthusiasm got the better of him and he wanted to do the impossible on the society's very limited resources. The DGOS was not the only company to survive the difficult war years. George Sleator's Dublin Operatic Society was still presenting operas at the Olympia and by early `45 the new National Opera Society of Ireland was doing the same thing. The capital, it seemed, had an insatiable appetite for opera.

Comdt. O'Kelly and his colleagues now realised that Irish opera buffs wanted to see new faces and hear new voices and be able to enjoy more imaginative productions, provided of course that the society could afford to mount them. Quickly he arranged meetings in London with agents and forged new contacts in an atmosphere of considerable goodwill. Sometimes Bertie Timlin or vice-chairman Michael Dinnigan accompanied O'Kelly on these trips and were agreeably surprised by the number of artists available, many of them demobbed servicemen who wanted to resume their singing careers.

They had to work in haste as the scene in Ireland was about to change. James Johnston and Patricia Black had signed contracts with the Sadler's Wells Company so that their appearances with the society would in future only be on an irregular basis. Moira Griffith was soon to concentrate on accompaniment, in between her secondary school commitments. In truth she said she wanted to carve a career outside of opera. Meanwhile, Rita Lynch had met her husband-to-be, Patrick Shaw, at a concert in the Opera House, Cork, and settled in the southern capital, though she continued to take on numerous concert engagements. Charles Lynch, her firm friend, and the country's leading piano soloist, could no longer spare the time for operatic conducting as he pursued a solo career. It was at the same time rumoured that Joseph McLaughlin and May Devitt were together contemplating a move to Britain, as was Belfast tenor John Torney.

Before the year was far advanced the society had engaged a bevy of new names to opera in Ireland; they included Owen Brannigan, Gwen Catley, Eva Turner, Parry Jones, Ruth Packer and Ivan Dixon. Usually Comdt. O'Kelly greeted them on their arrival and was photographed by press photographers; it was useful publicity and the chairman never let such an opportunity escape him. Once, when he introduced a famous soprano to reporters, he quipped, 'She's come here for our big steaks." There was more than a modicum of truth in this for in the immediate post-war years, food in Britain remained rationed and it was no secret that singers welcomed engagements in Ireland where it was in good supply.

Although the general public eagerly looked forward to hearing the new artists, some Irish singers soon resigned themselves to the fact that in future they would be playing secondary roles. Moira Griffith was prepared for that eventuality. 'I had sung principal roles only with the society and suspected that before long I would be asked to take on lesser parts and maybe end up in the chorus. I was by then church organist in Bray, a busy accompanist and occasionally a chorus mistress. I felt a bit sorry, though, for some of my colleagues.'

Nonetheless, the Irish were still needed and Comdt. O'Kelly reminded his critics that one of the chief aims of the society was to foster home talent and this remained a priority. He was aware of the criticism from some quarters but he was not a man to ever let criticism stand in the way of progress. Like his colleague Dr Larchet, he knew the time had arrived to expand their repertory. His timing was right and his choice of cross-channel artists would in time also prove him a good judge of voices. For example, the soprano Eva Turner made an immediate impact as Aida. She was by now in her early fifties and already a renowned Turandot. She was partnered in Aida by Welsh tenor Parry Jones whose singing of "Celeste Aida" in act one was greeted by warm applause, though it was the soprano who enraptured the audience by her opulent voice that swept over the orchestra into every corner of the Gaiety. The *Evening Mail* summed up: 'Together these two singers overshadowed all others on stage, both vocally and dramatically; they were magnificent.'

Ruth Packer, an unusually tall soprano, was soon also to attract the admiration of audiences by her dramatic singing in the winter season of '45 as Leonora in *Trovatore,* displaying a true Verdian line and real acting ability. 'Miss Packer is a discovery,' wrote the *Evening Herald* critic. 'The society must have her back again.' Likewise, another English newcomer, Victoria Sladen, was a touching Butterfly, even if Dublin oldtimers were understandably reluctant to place her above 'their own' May Devitt in the same role. Ivan Dixon, as Pinkerton, partnered Miss Sladen impressively in the love duet in act one.

It was the new production of *Rigoletto* that however drew the most enthusiastic response of the season. Roderick Jones was very popular with Dublin audiences and his portrayal of the tormented jester was eagerly awaited. This was borne out by *Irish Independent* critic Joseph O'Neill: 'I had looked forward to Jones's appearance in the role and I can say he gave me all the pleasure I had expected. His flexible baritone voice is eminently suitable for the portrayal of this complex part and he conveyed the character's mixed emotions in a thoughtful and intelligent manner.'

James Johnston had returned from Sadler's Wells to sing the Duke while Gwen Catley, the young English coloratura soprano, won a lot of friends in the audience by 'her delicate artistry and vocal agility' as Gilda. Owen Brannigan, one of the leading British basses of the day, combining a large and rich voice with assured acting ability, sang the assassin Sparafucile, and was described by one critic as 'a magnificently honest villain.'

By now the society had introduced gala nights and they injected a welcome touch of colour and glamour that helped to make opera-going a social occasion. Newspapers dispatched photographers to the Gaiety Theatre and subsequent photographs helped to boost attendances. A gala night was certainly different, recalled Aileen Walsh. There was an added buzz in the auditorium and the boxes were always filled. In her view empty boxes did not look well and could convey the wrong impression. To Florrie Draper, a chorister like Miss Walsh, a gala occasion prompted the ladies to dress in their most elegant finery. She saw nothing elitist about this. 'I think everyone agreed that on big occasions there was no harm in a bit of colour - and that went for the gentlemen too.'

The casting of Joseph McLaughlin and May Devitt in Gounod's romantic opera, *Romeo & Juliette* was a talking point in the spring of 1945. No one could deny they looked the part and as well as that their off-stage love affair had some of the elements of the opera itself. Sometimes they attracted the attention of people in the streets as they passed by in a horse-drawn carriage - the handsome tenor liked to do things in style. DGOS chorus members wondered if he was in fact serious about making a career in opera for he seemed more showman than opera singer. A veteran photographer of the social scene once told me that McLaughlin and Devitt attracted people to the Gaiety who wouldn't normally go to opera. 'I think he had a big effect on women and it was one of the reasons at the time why everyone was looking forward to his Romeo.'

Behind the scenes the 'big fellow' from Derry was finding difficulty learning Gounod's music and both May Devitt and Julia Gray had to spend painstaking hours on the score with him.. McLaughlin made no secret of his dilemma and conductor J M Doyle was only too aware of it when rehearsals began, for he was obliged to give him more musical cues than usual. The fact that the tenor wasn't a musician and lacked training as a singer did not help matters. There were times when Miss Devitt expressed real worry and hoped that by opening night her 'lover Joe' would be a convincing Romeo on stage. The opera, which when premiered in Paris in April 1867 was a resounding success, would on this occasion be sung in English.

The critics' reaction was favourable though not over-enthusiastic. 'May Devitt and Joseph McLaughlin in the leading roles were convincing,' stated the Irish Times, 'their singing in the Garden Scene of act two and the Vault Scene of the last act being among the best things they have sung together.' After commenting on Miss Devitt's convincing acting as Juliette and the beauty of her singing voice, the Irish Independent described Joseph McLaughlin's approach as romantic, but criticised his reading of the part because of his over-restraint as compared with Miss Devitt's intense show of passion. He did however 'rise to dramatic heights in the Duel Scene and his farewell to Juliette.'

Because McLaughlin was considered 'a bit of a character' he was not always easy to handle, though he rarely got the better of Comdt. O'Kelly. He sometimes played tricks on Jim Doyle but the conductor was inclined to laugh them off. He saw the tenor as 'somewhat incorrigible' and did his best to keep him to the music. Pianist Jeannie Reddin believed that with more discipline and dedication to the music he would have made it in opera. 'I suspect though he found opera restricting and was more at home in show business.'

Comdt. O'Kelly offered Joseph McLaughlin the role of Cavaradossi in the following season's *Tosca* but he turned it down, explaining to the chairman that he and May Devitt were shortly off to England. O'Kelly expressed his deep gratitude and wished him well. He knew that McLaughlin was fond of the good life and that the money he could pay him would never satisfy him. In subsequent years, the tenor, singing under the name of Josef Locke, would attain millionaire status and buy a half share in the Grand Theatre, Blackpool. But he has no regrets about his stint in opera in Dublin. As he told me in more recent years, 'I showed them I could sing it, the audiences loved me, and Bill O'Kelly was pleased. But I couldn't go on singing for buttons, even for Bill and, God knows, he put a lot into the DGOS, so he did.'

The spring season of 1946 promised to be one of the most innovative - and ambitious - since the society was founded. It was decided to stage Verdi's *Otello* and Wagner's *The Flying Dutchman* for the first time, along with the popular 'warhorses' *Trovatore, Traviata* and *Tosca*. Comdt. O'Kelly and his colleagues were taking a risk but believed it was again time to expand the repertory. They were also determined to keep ahead of rival companies in the capital in their choice of operas. To Dr Larchet, *Otello* was a masterpiece and undoubtedly a challenge for the society but he accepted his chairman's word that they had the resources to stage it.

The opera's history is particularly interesting as it was written seventeen years after Verdi wrote *Aida* and at a time when it was feared he would not write again - he was now 73 years of age. Eventually, however, he gave in to his friends and agreed to collaborate with the poet and librettist Arrigo Boito, an avid admirer of his genius. Boito almost ended the collaboration when he was quoted in the newspapers as saying that he would himself have loved to set Shakespeare's play to music, his own opera *Mefistofele* was a failure when first staged. The ageing Verdi did not take kindly to the poet's comment but forgave him when he said he had been misquoted.

The composer was at La Scala for the first night of his new opera - as was Boito - on February 5, 1887. Apparently Verdi was much too nervous to conduct it and instead was satisfied to be part of the excitement around him. It was a great success, though some pundits claimed the cast was weak except for the French singer Victor Maurel, who was described as the 'only true artist in the cast'. The emotions expressed at the final curtain were, according to one onlooker, indescribable with many weeping openly in the theatre. Afterwards, Verdi's carriage was dragged by the ecstatic citizens of Milan to his hotel where he was toasted and serenaded.

It was safe to presume that neither the Gaiety Theatre nor the surrounding streets would experience such euphoria after the DGOS's opening performance; indeed the reception for patrons prior to curtain rise was quite sedate as they sipped their drinks in the dress circle bar. As for the performance, it was warmly received though without any wild enthusiasm, which was understandable in the circumstances. It can be presumed that the music was new to the majority of the audience and apart from the "Credo", sung by Iago, and the "Willow Song" by Desdemona, little else would be familiar. The press critiques were curiously varied, from a production of excellence to the reason why the work wasn't universally popular. The honours of the evening went to soprano Ruth Packer as the heroine Desdemona, her singing in the dramatic last act being widely praised. While one reviewer lauded the performance of Parry Jones as Otello, a colleague felt he lacked passion in his acting. Baritone Edmond Dunlevy's sinister Iago fared much better, though he was said to 'have overplayed his hand.'

Everyone agreed that *The Flying Dutchman* was another major undertaking and this was underlined by the society ensuring extra rehearsals for the chorus. The production would provide a new and important musical experience for audiences starved of Wagner's works. The opera had been inspired by a voyage undertaken by the composer in the summer of 1839, bringing him from Konigsberg to London. The ship was caught in a terrible storm and tossed up onto the Scandinavian coast. The dazzling light of the storm and the roar of the sea made a powerful impression on Wagner, conjuring up an image of the condemned Dutchman aboard his spectral ship sailing the seas in desperate search for salvation. If Giuseppe Verdi had enjoyed a momentous first-night with *Otello,* it was somewhat different in the case of Richard Wagner - *the Dutchman* ran for only four nights after its Dresden premiere in January 1843. The composer wasn't too crestfallen as a year before his new opera *Rienzi* had been a big success in the same theatre.

Verdi had genuine admiration for Wagner, despite the fact that in some quarters his own operas were claimed to be inferior to the German's. In the Dublin of the forties his operas were little known, yet the society was encouraged three years previously by the warm response to *Tannhauser.* On this occasion Aileen Walsh was one of the sixteen chosen to sing in the female chorus and became increasingly aware of the importance of the production when informed by conductor Arthur Hammond that there would be four full weeks' rehearsals. She counted herself lucky to be among the chorus of sixteen for normally one had to wait for some time to be allowed sing in certain operas. She remembers that the voices blended well and Wagner's music presented few problems. The male choristers were, on the other hand, experiencing difficulties in mastering the music, so much so that a few weeks before opening night Arthur Hammond asked three of the women choristers to assist the men.

'It meant we came down an octave,' says Aileen Walsh, 'but between us all - and that includes chorus mistress Julia Gray and Arthur Hammond - the men improved.'

The role of the Dutchman was being sung by baritone Robert Parker, who was by now very much a veteran - he had sung with British touring companies in the early thirties. As Senta, Mary Cherry, an Argentine soprano, impressed the critics. She was making her Dublin debut and her incisive dramatic singing was noted by Joseph O'Neill *(Irish Independent)*, who picked out the female chorus as outstanding in the "Spinning Chorus". And like his fellow reviewers, singled out Dermot Browner's important contribution as Daland, the Norwegian captain whose ship is caught in the raging storm. Browner lives nowadays in Florida and has happy memories of the production. 'I know I was surprised to be cast in the part as I was inexperienced in opera. Frankly, I found Wagner's music difficult to sing and it took me some time to master it. But the critics were kind and said I performed well. It was obvious to us all that Robert Parker was past his prime as a singer, yet by sheer acting ability he got through the evening. He was a true professional.'

Dermot Browner was born in Dublin in March 1916, the only son of JC Browner. He was twenty-six when he started his vocal training and before long was winning cups and medals at the Feis Ceoil. In 1944, he made his operatic debut with the Dublin Operatic Society and three years later achieved a personal ambition when he sang Mephistopheles in *Faust,* a role in which he had long admired his father.

'I could not hope to emulate him as an actor for he was truly superb,' he recalls. 'Instead, I was happy to rely on my own interpretation.'

He did not pursue a singing career in Ireland but went to America to take up a business appointment and stayed on for thirty years instead of the intended year. A regular visitor home, he usually stays in Dublin with his sister Kitty Browner who has fond memories of both Dermot and her father in opera.

'I saw my father as Mephistopheles shortly before his death and to me his voice was as good as ever,' she said. 'We were raised in a musical home and I do recall him accompanying himself on the piano in the mornings. It was a pity that none of his records really did him justice. We were all very proud of course when Dermot sang his first Mephistopheles.'

Their cousin Alison Browner, the Dublin-born mezzo-soprano, would also sing a leading role with the DGOS in the 1990s, as well as with the Wexford Festival. She is also a concert artist of note and in demand internationally. Alison's Covent Garden debut in the `80s was a profound success.

Meanwhile, lack of money in September `46 ruled out visits by the society to both Limerick and Cork, which was a genuine source of regret to Comdt. O'Kelly. It was agreed however to accept an invitation to present a short season of opera at the Hippodrome, Belfast. An extra performance was staged for troops back from the war. This meant that after *Faust* had ended the stage would be got ready for the midnight presentation of *La Traviata.* To Comdt. O'Kelly, it began to look like 'round-the-clock' performances with matinees, evening and late night stagings. The success of the venture did afford him undoubted satisfaction.

The spring season of `47 at the Gaiety bore a familiar look as the programme featured A*ida, Rigoletto and Carmen.* While Gwen Catley was back to repeat her beguiling Gilda, her father on this occasion was sung by Leyland White who proved himself a convincing Verdi exponent. James Johnston sang his much admired Don Jose in *Carmen,* his final scene with Patricia Black (in the title role) being intensely dramatic. There was an enjoyable *La Boheme,* distinguished by English tenor Walter Midgley's excellently sung Rodolfo and Blanche Turner's moving Mimi.

There were from time to time some mishaps. In act three of *Boheme,* for instance, there was an unusual snowfall and this raised a laugh among the audience. On other occasions it was obvious that the principals needed quicker prompts from the wings but sometimes were inexplicably delayed. Once to Comdt. O'Kelly's disbelief, a soprano was still arranging her costume as she hurried from her dressing-room believing she had mistimed her entrance. O'Kelly quickly showed his displeasure. And later on there was an embarrassing moment when a Welsh tenor lost his voice in the final bars of the love duet at the end of act one of *Boheme,* leaving the hapless soprano to sing her way into the moonlight alone.

By now Verdi's *Aida* had become a popular part of the society's repertory and it opened on patron's night with a gala performance. The Covent Garden tenor Frank Sale was a convincing Radames and both Patricia Black (Amneris) and Ruth Packer in the title role sang with conviction in act two. Conducted by J M Doyle it was regarded as an excellent production. Expectations were high regarding the new staging of Mozart's *Don Giovanni* but generally there was disappointment expressed about Leyland White's Don, vocally in particular, and Walter Midgley's Don Ottavio. 'The tenor's singing of "Il mio tesoro" lacked 'a graceful flow and variety in the voice', stated the *Evening Mail.* Ruth Packer as Donna Anna and Owen Brannigan (Leporallo) emerged with the honours of the evening. But in the society's view the year had been successful artistically and box-office receipts were again satisfactory.

Offer from Paris

It was no surprise early in 1948 when Dr Larchet, president of the society, accepted the offer of a production of Debussy's *Pelléas and Mélisande* by principals of the Opéra-Comique. With his French influences and interest in the country's composers, he recognised the singular honour being conferred on them. The question whether Irish audiences were as yet ready for such an eclectic work did not apparently enter the equation. To Dr Larchet and his colleagues it was a welcome step out of what could be described as 'operatic insularity' and musically they saw it as a visit of overwhelming significance.

The production promised to be the highlight of the spring season and the society planned to make the first of the three performances on May 4 a gala occasion and one, for the first time, with an international dimension. More knowledgeable opera buffs would be secretly hoping for no repeat of the behaviour that marked the premiere at the Opéra-Comique in April 1902; nor indeed was this likely. The novel style of the music had then outraged the first-night Parisian audience and they laughed and hissed at the final curtain. The critics went on to savage it, though some gifted young composers, Ravel among them, supported Debussy, as did the influential critic of *Le Temps*. Criticism ranged from 'too refined' to the opera being set in a 'dream world'. 'The most subtle and atmospheric opera ever written,' was the verdict of a few others.

Not surprisingly the opera was considered a failure; Debussy would never again write another. He had spent eight years on *Pelléas* and *Mélisande* fervently believing he had found in Maeterlinck's legendary drama the perfect material for what he wanted to express in music. Set in the imaginary kingdom of Allemonde, the story is woven around Golaud's love for the youthful Melisande; she in turn falls in love with Golaud's half brother Pelleas. Feeling betrayed, Golaud kills Pelleas leaving behind a despairing Melisande with no further will to live.

The opera has five acts and is regarded as over-long, appearing perhaps even more so because of its dream-like and static quality. Undeniably, it would be a severe test for those Irish operagoers accustomed Verdi choruses and arias or the lilting melodies of Balfe and Wallace. Nevertheless, the evening of May was colourful in South King Street as the first of the guests arrived for the opening night's performance; they included government ministers, members of the diplomatic corps, religious heads, civic leaders and numerous others. It was the sort of scene that injected opera-going with a touch of style and elegance.

The President of Ireland, Sean T O'Kelly, and Mrs O'Kelly were warmly greeted in the theatre foyer by Dr Larchet and his wife Madeleine, with the latter presenting the President's wife with a bouquet of crimson and gold tulips. The presidential box was bedecked with royal blue and yellow draperies.

Despite the unknown nature of the opera and the cast, an undoubted air of expectancy hung over the theatre, partly due no doubt to the magical name Opéra-Comique. The pre-publicity had urged music lovers on no account to miss the production. Adding to the interest was the fact that the Radio Eireann Orchestra was in the pit and would be conducted by the distinguished musician Roger Desormiere.

The orchestra had been established in February of that year and comprised a mixture of Irish and continental players led by the Italian violinist Renzo Marchionni. Its numerical strength was now sixty- two and in future when it performed for DGOS seasons this would be acknowledged in the published programme, and in the words, 'held in conjunction with Radio Eireann'. Up to then the society used an ad hoc ensemble which was not entirely satisfactory. In Comdt. Doyle's view the availability of the RESO was essential if the society's musical standards were to be raised to an international level and in order to accompany visiting operatic companies.

The occasion was not lost on the newspapers, with at least one report comparing the colourful scenes in South King Street with pre-war days. 'Many men wore evening dress and the ladies came in some of the most luxurious frocks,' it stated, and added there was no mistaking the fact that Paris had come to Dublin. The only thing missing in South King Street last night was a French band playing the "Marseillaise". It was noted also that there were many onlookers in the street to watch the guests arriving. An attractive souvenir programme was published to mark the occasion and Comdt. O'Kelly recruited some of the chorus members to sell it in the theatre. Among them was Mona Brase, daughter of Col. Fritz Brase. She had joined the chorus the previous year and *Tosca* was her first introduction to opera. 'I shall never forget that moment when, standing in the wings, I heard the sinister opening bars as the curtain went up,' she told me later. She thought it a great experience also to see and hear the star singers so close at hand and to meet them off-stage. On this occasion she was selling programmes in the parterre. Later on in the evening she stood at the back of the stalls to see the opera. At first the music didn't mean much to her, partly because it was absolutely new, and also the action on stage was slow-moving. In subsequent performances she found, however, that the music grew on her and she could appreciate it.

For Aileen Walsh, seated at the back of the parterre, Debussy's music was a novel experience and took some time to adapt to, and the static nature of the opera itself could be puzzling. Anyone she thought used to operatic excitement was in the wrong place. Yet the singing by the principals was so expressive that gradually the whole thing gripped one and the climax was particularly moving. The reaction of the audience was, she felt, unusual: 'It was polite, even restrained, suggesting perhaps their puzzlement at the new musical scene style.'

Critic Joseph O'Neill *(Irish Independent)* pulled no punches next morning, when he stated: 'To a Dublin audience nurtured on ballad operas, and accepting Puccini works because of his occasionally lively arias and effective ensembles, this Debussy opera was not easy to accept. The audience seemed rather lost at the early stage. As the curtain rose, the fully booked dress circle had only half of its seats filled. Never were latecomers to an opera more offensive, because the music of the acts is continuous in spite of the changing scenes and there were at least fifteen minutes interruption to the first act caused by banging of seats and the shuffling of those who apparently thought they would be in plenty of time for the first big solo. As the intensity of the dramatic situation rose, however, the audience was undoubtedly gripped in the Debussy spell. From the vocal point of view, the chief attraction of the production was the splendid singing of Henri Etcheverry in the part of Golaud: his forceful baritone voice carried a wide range of expression and there was, too, a lovely tone colour to his singing. As Pelleas, Jacques Jansen's performance in the second scene of Act Four was profoundly moving. Irene Joachim was the mysterious Melisande and her singing always conveyed the troubled nature of her mind.'

Looking back on the performance, harpist Sheila Larchet says it was a remarkable occasion, not only because her father Dr Larchet was excited about Opéra-Comique's debut in Ireland but for opera-goers to see Roger Desormière conduct the RESO. 'For me it was an unforgettable experience. Naturally he was an expert on French music and I remember that rehearsals were different to any others. He was a perfectionist and was able to create the exact mood to ensure a totally idiomatic performance of Debussy's powerfully moving opera. The atmosphere was unique and all of us I think in the pit felt it.'

She was aware at the time that reaction was mixed but in her view this was to be expected as operagoers were seeing an entirely new style and it would take some time to get used to. 'But I consider the work a masterpiece. My father was pleased that the Dublin Grand Opera Society was able to stage it at the Gaiety with an Irish symphony orchestra. He always talked about the visit.'

The introduction of continental singers by the society to Dublin was especially pleasing to Comdt. Bill O'Kelly and the response of the audience encouraging. He felt they were on the right road and that in time more expansion could be possible. In his view there was no doubt that the society's patrons welcomed this kind of progress.

If the spring season had been dominated by the visit of the Opéra-Comique principals, the winter season was notable for a splendid production of *Tosca*, Joan Hammond sang the title in a manner that underlined her steady progress as a Puccini exponent. It was a big year for her, for besides appearing with the DGOS she was making her Covent Garden debut as the *Trovatore Leonora*, and her record of "O My Beloved Father" was still selling thousands of copies. The Cavaradossi on this occasion was the Dutch tenor Franz Vroons who quickly endeared himself to Gaiety audiences by his assured singing. His voice had an exciting ring to it, was rich in timbre and very expressive; his acting was convincing and never forced. Together on stage, Vroons and Hammond made a formidable duo as well as credible lovers.

Stanley Pope's Scarpia did not measure up to their standard and his act two confrontation with Tosca was adjudged dramatically weak. Harry Powell Lloyd directed with assurance and undoubtedly would be invited back again by Comdt. O'Kelly. There was an enjoyable *Rigoletto* with Edmond Dunlevy in the title role acting and singing with panache and being well supported by Audrey Bowman *(Gilda)* and the promising Canadian tenor Kenneth Neate as the Duke. This was followed by a tepid performance of *The Marriage of Figaro*, described by the *Evening Mail* as lacking in sparkle and visually having a faded look.

The production of Carmen compensated, with Franz Vroons proving an exciting Don Jose. 'His singing of the "Flower Song" was magnificent', commented the Evening Mail, 'and this was reflected in the enthusiastic reception accorded to him.' Indeed, to this day there are DGOS oldtimers who love to recall his performances in the Bizet opera. He was helped by the incisive conducting of a newcomer to Dublin, Vilem Tausky; he was to prove a valuable acquisition by the society.

Grand Opera in Butlin's Holiday Camp, Mosney? To the more fastidious opera buff it must have seemed absurd in July of that year. What was the

Prof. John F Larchet: DGOS's first president.

The full company of the Dublin Grand Opera Society on the Gaiety Theatre stage on the final night of the first season, May 1941.

CONDUCTOR J M DOYLE:
The society's first musical director.

VILEM TAUSKY:
The inspiring Czech
conductor.

JOAN HAMMOND

JAMES JOHNSTON

MAY DEVITT

Stalwarts
of the
Early Years

PATRICIA BLACK

RENEÉ FLYNN

JULIA GRAY

JOHN LYNSKEY

JOSEPH MCLAUGHLIN

NAPOLEONE ANNOVAZZI and Lt. Col. Bill O'Kelly...sharing a joke.

MAESTRO BOTTI (left) and veteran tenor Beniamino Gigli together in Dublin.

TITO GOBBI:
As Scarpia, one of his greatest operatic roles.

JEANNIE REDDIN: Splendid chorus
mistress

CONDUCTOR GIUSEPPE MORELLI:
Master of Italian repertoire.

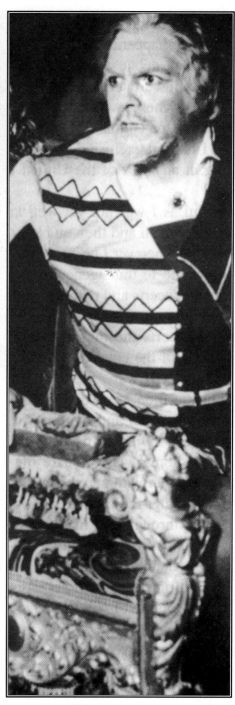

As Otello (above) and (below) Germont in
'Traviata'.

Soprano Rita Lynch (right) Greeted in Chicago by her concert fans.

Moira Griffith: A star in the forties with DGOS.

SOPRANO CATERINA MANCINI (left) and mezzo Ebe Stignani who together sang in a memorable 'Norma' for the DGOS.

VERONICA DUNNE: Acclaimed debut for society

PLINIO CLABASSI: An outstanding bass.

Long-serving DGOS Secretary Berti Timlin (right) with chorus members.

JAMES J O'CONNOR: Rallied the patrons for society.

J F MACINERNEY (left) a devoted society man, with Loris Gambelli bass.

VIRGINIA ZEANI: Her performances as Violetta and Lucia are vividly remembered.

The much talked of Hamburg State Opera sets for 'The Barber of Seville' broke new ground in Dublin.

MARGHERITA RINALDI: From La Scala to sing star roles for the DGOS

ANNA MOFFO...delighted fans in 'Don Pasquale'.

GIANNA D'ANGELO: Thrilling coloratura voice.

THE GREAT GIAN GIACOMO GUELFI:
A voice to remember.

..as was that of Luisa Maragliano (left) who
partnered him in 'Nabucco'.

The legendary Magda Olivero, the star of 'Adriana Lecouvreur' and (below) pictured with the DGOS cast of the opera (second from left, front row).

1962 - Town Hall, Dundalk: Paolo Silveri & Giuseppe Forgione in joyful mood.

1967 - Town Hall, Dundalk
Reception (left to right)...Frank Aiken, Maestro Napoleone Annovazzi and famed mezzo Viorica Cortez.

1966 - Operatic Concert, Armagh.
Zenaida Pally, Romanian mezzo signing autograph for Frances O'Gorman.

society really at? But to Comdt. O'Kelly it was, one can only presume, as natural as singing in his bath. He had always liked bringing opera to the people and he saw Mosney as a bold experiment, though he must have wondered if he could really balance the books.

And as an army officer he could only have seen it as 'Operation Mosney' as musicians, principals, back-stage crew and choristers prepared to take over the camp for one week, beginning on Monday July 12. The camp management agreed to let the society have the theatre and at the same time hope that the resident campers would confine themselves to the ballroom lured by bigger prize money. To boost attendances at the opera, it was planned to run special trains for patrons and their friends, returning to Dublin after the performance. Interest was soon considerable and seemed to justify the society's faith in the venture.

Faust and Rigoletto were the operas chosen and to chorus mistress Jeannie Reddin they were well cast. James Johnston was Faust and the other principals were, Margery Field (Marguerite), Patricia Black (Siebel), Bruce Dargaval (Valentine) and Harvey Alan (Mephistopheles).

Cast-wise, *Rigoletto* also bore a familiar look, with John Lynskey singing the title role, Patricia Black as Maddalena, Joan Butler as Gilda and English tenor Ivan Dixon as the Duke of Mantua. Dermot Browner was Sparafucile. Terry O'Connor was leader of the orchestra, mainly made up of freelance musicians. Sometime before, Comdt. O'Kelly and conductor J M Doyle had inspected the holiday village theatre and deemed it suitable for opera.

'We in the chorus were really looking forward to the week', recalls Mona Brase. 'For one thing, we would have our days mostly free to enjoy ourselves. We were accommodated in the chalets and the food was satisfactory.'

For Maura Mooney it was a special week. With her husband Gerard also in the chorus they had decided to bring along their two small children and before the week was out one had won first prize as the youngest camper. To Maura Mooney it was fun, though they were called on more than once to rehearse.

Mona Brase says there was just one misshap during the week and tragedy was averted by the alertness of Comdt. O'Kelly. He dived into the pool as one of the women in the chorus slid too fast down the shute into the water and got knocked out and almost drowned.

Vilem Tausky

December 1948. Vilem Tausky has conducted his last performance of the winter season at the Gaiety Theatre and since it is close to Christmas, is anxious to get back to his wife Peggy and young family in London. Comdt.O'Kelly has paid him his fee for the season, which is moderate by today's standard, but the conductor doesn't mind - he has money in his pocket and the chairman has already asked him back for the spring season of the following year. They are by now firm friends and O'Kelly arranges to drive him later in the day to Dun Laoghaire to catch the boat for Holyhead. Meanwhile, the genial conductor has planned a shopping spree and plans to play Santa to his wife and children.

Since his arrival in Dublin he has admired the well-stocked shops and bright windows which he knows is in sharp contrast to London where food rationing still exists. Dublin appeals to him: it is compact and easy on a pedestrian and the shops are within easy reach. The people are friendly and the banter among traders in Moore Street never ceases to amuse him. Today he visits shops in Henry Street and proceeds to fill bags with bread, chickens, peas, meat and a variety of other products, including sweets and biscuits. For some time he has known the scarcity of money but he is now reassured as he picks off pound notes from his wallet to pay for the food. Later on as Comdt. O'Kelly drives him to Dun Laoghaire, he hears him say, 'By God, Tausky, you're not half good to yourself. You'd feed an army on all that stuff in the bags there.' They shake hands and O'Kelly wishes him a merry Christmas and says he looks forward to seeing him again in the spring. For the first time in his life the conductor feels like Santa Claus.

These are among the memories he recalls when I meet him in December 1997 at his apartment, Raven Green Lodge, Ealing Broadway, London. For someone of eighty-seven years he is unusually alert and in good health and occasionally his smile lights up the quaint sitting room, with its grand piano and shelves of books and music scores. He is alone here for his wife Peggy passed away a few years before. His life has been monopolised by music and he still goes to concerts and operas and may give talks to gramophone societies or other groups. In a soft voice he will tell you seriously, 'All I can hope to do now is to pass on my knowledge to the younger generations. I am happy to do that.' I ask him where he would like to begin his story. He relaxes in his armchair as if he has just left aside his baton after a concert performance. 'I wanted to conduct an orchestra since I was seven years old,' he says. 'But of course I had to wait like everyone else of my age.'

* * *

Vilem Tausky, Moravian-born, was brought up in a musical home; his mother, extremely good-looking, was trained at the Vienna State Opera and sang there in productions conducted by Gustave Mahler and for years kept the scores with his markings on them; his father was a medical doctor who in his spare time loved to play the piano and sometimes accompanied his wife at concerts and musical soirees. At his parents' wishes young Tausky was sent to Brno University to study law and at the same time enrolled at the Janacek Conservatoire in the city. 'I was proud to become one of Janacek's pupils and study composition with him,' he recalled. Sadly, for me, he died only eight months later. He was a father to his students and a great loss.'

Tausky was eighteen and by now a Czech citizen and still anxious to make music his career. His opportunity arrived fortuitously when a repetiteur at the opera house became ill and he was asked to replace him. The management was impressed enough to ask him to return for other productions. He was asked to conduct performances of Puccini's *Turandot* with Zinka Milanov (then Zinca Kuncova) as one of the house's staff conductorsgot ill. Tausky says his most daunting engagement arrived when he was given the great Russian opera *Boris Godunov* to conduct with none other than Fyodor Chaliapin in the title role.

He was upset when some people warned him that Chaliapin was difficult and 'won't sing a note for you at rehearsal.' To a conductor of only twenty-one years it was alarming news. He was dispatched to the singer's hotel in Prague to discuss his musical approach. He was nervous but to his relief the Russian bass didn't turn out the monster that people suggested. 'He was cordial to me and quietly went through the score, making helpful comments on occasions. I told him that the people of Brno were excited about his coming to sing there and he seemed pleased to hear that.'

Tausky grasped his opportunity and still could hardly believe his good fortune. Conducting Chaliapin in his greatest operatic role was something he had never thought possible. It was a feather in his cap and he went on to conduct operas by his favourite composers, Janacek, Dvorak and Smetana, as well as the standard Italian repertory. And his new operetta *The Girl in Blue* was successfully staged at the opera house. It was now late into 1939 and the war clouds had gathered. Like other Jews, he decided it was time to get out of Czechoslovakia and one morning he caught a train for Paris. It was to prove a harrowing experience when Gestapo officers came on board and quizzed passengers' identity. 'I remember that moment vividly,' Tausky recalls. 'I held my breath when asked for my passport. I tried to look casual and was relieved when it was handed back to me. I counted myself extremely lucky.'

In France, at the outbreak of war, he joined the Czech resistance army and in 1940 crossed the Channel to England where he again donned army uniform, but instead of fighting he founded and conducted a Czech military band, visiting factories and bases all over Britain. In 1945, when he joined the Carl Rosa Opera Company, he conducted performances in uniform, something new to him.

Tausky had come to know many of the most prominent artists of the post-war era, including James Johnston, Eva Turner, Joan Hammond, Blanche Turner and the baritone Otakar Kraus whom he had known since his days in Brno. 'I accompanied Otakar on the piano for his audition for the opera house. His greatest asset was his superb acting.'

By this time Arthur Hammond, a regular conductor for years at Dublin seasons, had joined the Carl Rosa as musical director and he recommended the Czech conductor to Comdt. Bill O'Kelly. 'I found I could do business with this Irishman,' recalls Tausky. 'We agreed a fee and he outlined the programme for the season.' I could see that he had a good grasp of the operatic scene and knew the people he wanted.'

After the wartime austerity of London, Tausky found Dublin a pleasant relief. Most of the people he met in St. Stephen's Green or Grafton Street seemed well fed and the children didn't appear to be starving. He stayed in a guesthouse run by a Czech-born couple within a walking distance of the Gaiety Theatre. It didn't bother him that the DGOS chorus was amateur for he had already worked with amateur choruses in Britain. He was impressed by the managerial skills of Bill O'Kelly and it was obvious to him that it was a fairly smoothly run machine, although the chairman had told him they were short of money and the budgets were small. It was a friendly society and he was made to feel thoroughly at home; once he dined with Comdt. O'Kelly at his home and also was entertained on another occasion by Dr Larchet.

Among the operas he was asked to conduct on his return in May of 1949 was Verdi's *A Masked Ball* which the society was staging for the first time. By the time he arrived he expected the chorus to be well drilled and ready for rehearsals with him and the principals. He realised it was all somewhat rushed and frantic at times and depended on how well the principals knew their parts and the budget available to the producer to stage the work. He had discussed the problems with his fellow conductor James Doyle and they agreed that more time was needed to co-ordinate the different strands of the production. Achieving visual satisfaction, for instance, was important, though on the money available they could hardly hope for big, spectacular stagings. The presence of the Radio Éireann Symphony Orchestra in the pit ensured high musical standards. The choice of *A Masked Ball* was generally welcomed, even if its music, apart from the baritone aria "Eri tu" was not well known to the public. Verdi's name was enough to guarantee extra box-office sales.

The work itself had a troubled history and due to political pressure the locale was transferred from Sweden to Boston, USA. In the original libretto Scribe's story told of the assassination of Gustave 111, king of Sweden, but the Italian censor of the day had an objection to royal assassinations so Gustave became Riccardo, governor of Boston and the conspirators were re-named Samuel and Tom, names which seemed incongruous in so Italian an opera. Despite the place and name changes, the music remained untouched and contains some of the composer's finest melodies, in addition to a greater variety and flexibility of orchestral colour. The premiere was scheduled for Rome in February 1859. Verdi attended rehearsals and expressed satisfaction with the principals.

Once again he was to experience the thrill of a brilliant first night and the ringing shouts of "Viva Verdi!" He could not have anticipated however the passionate anti-Austrian feeling his opera stirred up and he was genuinely puzzled. No such feverish reaction was expected at the Gaiety Theatre opening that May. The society had made it a gala occasion with president Sean T O'Kelly and his wife in attendance. Behind the scenes, however, there was a crisis.

For most of that day, May 3, soprano Audrey Bowman, who was singing the role of Amelia, was feeling ill and receiving medical attention. It was feared in the afternoon that with her rising temperature she would not respond, and since it was too late to fly in a replacement, the society was forced to think about cancelling the opening night's performance. To everybody's relief, however, Miss Bowman rallied and by late afternoon felt she would be able to go on. The decision was left entirely to herself. It says much for her determination and professionalism that the audience did not suspect she was unwell. At the final curtain Dr Larchet came on stage and explained the soprano's ordeal and thanked her for her courage. 'I must pay tribute to her,' he said, for without her bravery we would most certainly have had to cancel the performance.'

The society's president was joined on stage by Comdt. O'Kelly who also commended the soprano and said that as a mark of their appreciation he was delighted to present to her a memento of the occasion - a landscape painting by an Irish artist. It was considered a successful performance, thanks not only to Audrey Bowman but to Kenneth Neate's splendid singing as Riccardo and Melvin Bartell's portrayal of Renato. The majority of the critics praised Vilem Tausky's handling of the score and the skilful response he drew from the Radio Éireann Symphony Orchestra. 'The conductor brought to Verdi's rich musical score that keen ear for detail and instinct that is his hallmark,' observed the *Evening Herald*.

Vilem Tausky also conducted the performances of *La Traviata* that season with Audrey Bowman singing Violetta and Kenneth Neate her lover, Alfredo. 'The tenor sang with a fine youthful fervour,' commented the *Evening Mail*. He was also said to have 'cut a dashing figure' in a costume of scarlet and mustard yellow. There was another 'first' when the society presented Mozart's comic work, *Il Seraglio* ('The Harem'), or to give it its full title, 'The Abduction from the Harem'. Despite its novelty, it was slow to attract operagoers and the production did not entirely please the critics.

This was surprising for with its Turkish setting and hilarious plot involving some highly amusing characters, none more so than the roguish, ill-tempered Osmin, Mozart's opera usually provided lively entertainment. It was premiered in Vienna in 1782 and was considered a huge success, both artistically and commercially, and thereafter was presented successfully in the main German cities during the composer's lifetime.

Irish Press critic Robert Johnston was one of the few who regarded the DGOS production as memorable, partly because of its effective settings and costumes, but most of all for Owen Brannigan's brilliant portrayal of Osmin. He had also praise for sopranos Margaret Ritchie and Ingrid Hageman in the roles of Constance and Blonde. And there were pleasing performances by the English tenors Richard Lewis and John Kentish as Belmonte and Pedrillo. In Johnston's view, the society showed courage in staging the work and hoped that in time it would present all the Mozart operas.

Faust, as expected, packed the Gaiety for all performances, confirming once more its enduring popularity with Irish audiences. James Johnston, in the title role, grabbed the headlines not only for his superb performance in the title role, but also for the way he managed to keep to his hectic schedule. For after the Gaiety performance of *Faust* he flew back to London next morning to sing the Duke in *Rigoletto* that evening at Sadler's Wells, and the next day returned to Dublin to sing Pinkerton that weekend. The truth was that the popular tenor found it almost impossible to turn down offers. He was once known after a strenuous performance in the opera house, to catch a taxi immediately afterwards to perform at a private concert in a London mansion where he could expect a considerable fee. He still believed that singers were often undervalued and underpaid and perhaps this was true in the Britain and Ireland of the forties, so he did not hesitate to accept additional work where he found it.

Comdt. O'Kelly did not complain and regarded Johnston's exemplary loyalty to the DGOS as an extension of their own personal friendship. To the chairman the ebullient tenor was the ideal professional, combining temperament with vocal mastery that made him indispensable to the society.

Privately, O'Kelly was relieved to see the 1940s pass. Later he would say they were among the most difficult years encountered by the society, for it was always a question of survival; yet he and his colleagues could point to positive achievements and tangible progress. Forging links with the continent was important and held out promise for the future. Like Dr Larchet he wanted to provide the opportunity for Irish audiences to hear Italian, French and German artists sing in their own languages and individualistic styles. He felt the more informed operagoer was hoping this would materialise.

To Dermot Kinlen, a present day Irish high court judge, the forties cast a magical spell and in operatic terms opened up for him new vistas. He was only seventeen when he became a DGOS patron member and was glad to avail of the concessions on offer. He remembered his father telling him stories as a boy about the people in the Gaiety 'gods' and how they sang arias at the interval from the Irish ballad operas and were cheered for their efforts. Gradually he himself was smitten by the 'bug' and attributed this to the impact opera made on him emotionally and musically.

'I considered it a fantastic experience, combining spiritual, musical and dramatic elements. To my young mind it was the greatest art form in the world. Spellbound, I listened as a youth to our own singers, James Johnston, 'Patty' Black, May Devitt and Renée Flynn bring operas alive and generate excitement. It was John Lynskey's Rigoletto however that had me in bits and the audience around me visibly moved and in tears as he agonised over the abduction of his daughter Gilda. I remember I went home in a high state of emotion and could scarcely get a wink of sleep. John's acting was so realistic that he was the hunchbacked jester. I could not take my eyes away from him. So for my generation the forties meant discovery, meeting and falling in love, as it were, with something called 'Opera'. I am still in love with it. We owe a lot to the DGOS for providing that opportunity and of course too, the Dublin Operatic Society. I have remained a patron member despite changes in the DGOS's amateur status.'

Monica Condron joined the DGOS chorus as a teenager in the late forties but before that had attended numerous performances at the Gaiety. Her mother was a first cousin of May Devitt's and from the age of ten had been brought along to see the soprano as Butterfly, Violetta, Mimi and Juliette and thought she was wonderful. Since the storylines were sung in English they were easy to follow and this was a great advantage for her generation. She harboured an ambition to be a principal singer and took lessons from Sydney Russell and Julia Gray. Later when she auditioned for Russell, he said to her frankly, 'There's something there, girl, but I don't think you'll ever make an opera singer.' She must have looked a bit crestfallen, for he was quick to add, 'If you're prepared to do a bit of work you could sing operetta.' She followed his advice and did sing with the Rathmines and Rathgar Society, and at the same time remained in the DGOS chorus and gradually was cast in small parts. 'I hated not being on the stage,' she recalled. 'I simply loved singing. The chorus was great and like one big family. I do remember Vilem Tausky's arrival and the way he achieved results by his quiet approach. I considered him a first-class musician, especially in the Verdi repertoire.'

From the outset she was struck by the personality of Comdt. Bill O'Kelly and his leadership qualities. He was 'Mr Opera' and she could see why the society had proceeded from strength to strength. He knew everyone in the chorus by name and occupation and expected loyalty to the society. 'You took him as you found him. I mean he could be abrasive and a bit blunt at times but as one got to know him he was easy enough to handle.'

Florrie Draper, one of the best known members of the society, says she became hooked on opera in the early forties. Her mother, May Fitzgerald Draper, was a violinist and in 1940 was leader of the orchestra for a short season by the Dublin Operatic Society at the Gaiety Theatre, although she wasn't playing in *The Magic Flute*, one of the four operas being presented that spring. After soprano Joan Hammond, who was singing Pamina, complained to George Sleator that in her view the orchestra was inadequate he immediately asked May Draper to take over a leader of the strings. Since she was unfamiliar with the music she sent her daughter Florrie into the Gaiety to collect the opera score.

'I was twelve at the time,' recalls Florrie, 'and when I arrived in the theatre the singers were on stage rehearsing. There was this large woman and I thought her voice was wonderful, the best I'd ever heard. Someone told me in a whisper that she was Miss Joan Hammond. Later on when my mother was playing for the DGOS season I did the walk-on part of the Page in *Tannhauser*, holding Miss Hammond's train. From that moment the stage fascinated me and I became hooked on opera. I was an angel in *Faust* and was in the ballet troupe in *La Traviata*. I thought the whole thing was magical, a fairytale. And when I began to study at the College of Art I kept up my interest and eventually joined the chorus and from there to the wardrobe department. I never got a penny for my work but I didn't mind; I just loved being part of the scene and making friends.'

For Moira Griffith the forties had been eventful and by the last few years of the decade she had met her husband-to-be Noel Reid. This had come about when she deputised as DGOS chorus mistress for a short time. 'Noel was in the baritone and bass section,' she recalls, 'and we got to know one another at rehearsals. I enjoyed working with the chorus and most of the time concentrated on getting more light and shade into their singing, as well as a better blend. There were numerous solo voices, some bigger than others, and while it was easy to teach them the notes it was more difficult to get the required blend. Conductor Jim Doyle was annoyed with me once for being so painstaking and said, "If they can sing the notes, that's enough for me."

Maura Mooney, who was a chorister since 1940, thought there had been a good improvement and this was shown when they sang the big Verdi operas. She still liked the way in which everyone mixed so easily together, i.e. the chorus and the principals, and there was none of the 'them' and 'us' attitudes about, so the society remained dedicated and friendly. 'I would have been lost without it - and that went also for my husband Gerard,' she mused.

To Aileen Walsh, every big production provided a tough challenge and tended to keep members on their toes. Working with new conductors and producers also injected fresh enthusiasm and this she thought was very noticeable when both Vilem Tausky and Powell Lloyd came to them. 'I think we were fortunate to have Vilem Tausky on the musical side for he was very knowledgeable on all aspects of music, especially the Italian operatic repertoire.'

There were times, of course, when everything did not run smoothly. Sean Kelly recalls a final rehearsal in the Phoenix Hall when some of the foreign musicians in the Radio Éireann Symphony Orchestra were refusing on petty grounds to continue playing, having complained bitterly to Vilem Tausky about the discomfort and the cold. One of them in the string section told the conductor he felt sick and could not continue. Tausky replied impatiently, 'Before we continue further, is there anyone else feeling sick?' A voice from the brass said, 'Yes, me.' Without raising his voice the conductor replied, 'It doesn't matter how many of you are feeling sick, I'm continuing with rehearsals, even if we have to use two pianos.'

Looking back, Vilem Tausky says that although the society was an amateur one, it was a first-rate one because it employed good professional singers and the chorus masters were very able. He felt Comdt. O'Kelly and his colleagues knew what they wanted. 'I was happy to be asked back for two seasons each year. At the time it gave me a sense of security and these seasons were relatively short, so I could continue with my engagements in Britain.'

The chairman Comdt. O'Kelly saw the forties as an era of progress and hope. Their seasons had become a welcome part of the Dublin entertainment and musical scene and no longer was the society spoken of as the Dublin Grand Opera Society but more affectionately as the DGOS. With the ending of the war they set about improving standards but this had posed a financial challenge which happily was met by subscriptions from an increased patrons' membership and more money from the higher-priced seats. It was now relatively safe, he said, to add to their repertory operas new to the audiences and it made it possible to engage first-class singers from overseas. The successful agreement negotiated with Radio Éireann meant that in future the society's productions would have the invaluable advantage of the RESO. Dr Larchet felt progress continued to be made but the society must not lose sight of restoring Dublin to the eminence it once had on the European scene.

Stars from Hamburg

Inviting the prestigious Hamburg State Opera to perform in Ireland in the spring of 1950 was nothing short of a master stroke by the Dublin Grand Opera Society. It meant not only an auspicious start to the new decade but a vote of confidence in the Irish opera-going public. And it came about through Comdt. O'Kelly's friendship with the German Legation in Dublin and the fact also that the Hamburg company was itself anxious in the post-war era to re-establish its overseas connections.

Earlier in the year, O'Kelly and Michael Dinnigan, the society's vice-chairman, visited Hamburg for talks with Gunther Rennert, the Intendant of the opera house there and in an amicable atmosphere the question of fees, travel and transportation of sets was ironed out to each party's satisfaction. Rennert was a powerful force in opera in Germany having worked in Berlin and Frankfurt before taking over the reins in Hamburg in 1946. Taking part in the discussions also was Arthur Gruber, music director of the Hamburg company, who was concerned about the orchestral accompaniment standard in Dublin.

To Comdt. O'Kelly the visit by the Germans marked a definite step forward in the society's activities as well as taking on board a most ambitious, if onerous, sponsorship. Undeniably it meant added responsibility for them but with everyone's support, particularly that of their loyal patrons, the chairman felt confident. The German government in Bonn had also pledged some monies and the Irish government was solidly behind the visit.

As music director in Radio Éireann, Fachtna O Hannrachain recalled that he personally was enthusiastic and had talks with the DGOS about the orchestral requirements. He immediately appreciated the important significance musically of the Hamburg visit and knew from experience that the RE Symphony Orchestra welcomed any opportunity to accompany an internationally renowned company.

Lt. Col. Doyle, the society's musical director, had conducted Mozart operas in Dublin and was now more than pleased to find the Hamburg company bringing with them *Don Giovanni* and *Cosi fan tutte*; it would be the first time for *Cosi* to be performed in its entirety in Ireland. Apart from the wide public interest the visit of all-German casts was arousing, he believed they as an opera company would benefit artistically from the experience of hearing a team of artists direct from one of the post-war Europe's leading opera organisations.

The society's president Dr Larchet worked tirelessly behind the scenes to ensure the success of the visit. He exerted influence in government and diplomatic circles and in this respect could be most useful to Comdt. O'Kelly who tended to favour a more direct approach. Between them they ensured that few strings were left 'unpulled'. Likewise, solicitor James J O'Connor, chairman of the Patrons Members Committee, felt the society had been honoured by the Hamburg people and he appealed for a significant rise in membership to help defray costs. The society, he stressed in a circular letter to all their members, was engaged in a good national and cultural work and had earned recognition and appreciation from all who had attended their productions.

O'Connor, who was considered somewhat eccentric and undoubtedly 'a character', thought nothing of keeping ticket queues in line outside the Gaiety and could be cross if anyone dared 'step outside the line'. He epitomised the voluntary spirit at its best in the society. There were times when he tended to get under the chairman's skin, but O'Kelly tolerated his idiosyncracies because of his exemplary enthusiasm in the cause of opera.

Obviously realising the importance of the occasion, the newspapers ran illustrated features about the Hamburg State Opera, giving details about its history and 'biogs' of the artists. One of the most photographed was the pretty Annaliese Rothenberger, who was in her mid-twenties and said to be a gifted actress-singer. She was playing Despina, the maid, in *Cosi fan tutte*. Martha Modl (Dorabella in Cosi) was coming with a big reputation having achieved much success in German opera houses as well as at Covent Garden, where her Carmen was greatly admired. Clara Ebers, singing Donna Anna in *Don Giovanni*, was stated to be in demand throughout Europe, as was Elfriede Wasserthal, the Donna Elvira in the same opera.

The male principals were no less talented. Matthieu Ahlersmeyer was perhaps the best known, being described as 'a great character actor and baritone'; he was taking the title role in *Don Giovanni* and had featured in a film version of *The Marriage of Figaro* in Germany. Partnering him as Leporello was Theo Herrmann, who was already a distinguished concert artist. He would also sing Alfonso in *Cosi fan tutte*. The two chief tenor roles in the productions were being sung by Berlin-born Walter Geisler. He had studied in Berlin and emerged as one of his country's finest Mozartian stylists.

As the opening night of this eagerly-awaited season loomed, the society ran into unexpected trouble regarding tickets. Opera fans, claimed one report, 'were in a state of revolt'. The Gaiety was entirely booked out for the Hamburg performances with many people queueing in vain for tickets. The more irate fans blamed what they called the 'present system of preferential booking for patrons', thus leaving a shortage of tickets for the general public.'

For the first time in Dublin operatic circles the word 'black-market' was being loosely bandied about. 'Two citizens whose integrity is beyond doubt,' reported the *Irish Press*, 'told of standing in a queue, and coming away empty-fisted. Before them two individuals had bought £50 and £27 worth of tickets each. As in the Sunday cinema racket, disappointed bookers are now awaiting an offer of tickets at fancy prices from vendors who have graduated to the more discriminating role of Grand Opera "fixer-uppers." '

It was left to James J O'Connor, chairman of the patron members, to try to sort out the confusion, or to be more precise, the unprecedented anger being expressed by opera buffs. He said the society appreciated the difficulties facing the public and their annoyance with the patrons' system, but the fact remained that patrons, paying their subscriptions of three guineas annually, must be catered for and given priority. It was they in fact who helped to make the Hamburg visit possible.

O'Connor did admit though to having heard the rumours of 'black-market' ticket sales and emphasised that they in the society deplored any such practice. 'We would indeed be grateful if anyone can supply us with a proven case,' he said. 'In the meantime, we do not think we would be justified in stopping the present system of booking for opera.'

One particular journalist it seemed wasn't entirely satisfied with his explanation about the apparent buying in of tickets in lots amounting to up to £50. He said he knew of staffs of certain large firms in the city who paid a colleague a day's salary to go and queue on their behalf and purchase tickets in bulks of twenty-eight seats. The moral in his view amounted to pitching one's tent outside the Gaiety Theatre when booking opened and take a chance with the law.

Comdt. O'Kelly, meanwhile, had other matters on his mind. Since the society was sponsoring the Hamburg company's visit he decided it was perhaps reasonable to ask a few of their well-off patrons and friends to put up some of the visiting crew and artisits. Apart from saving the society money, it ensured that the artists themselves were in delightful homes and tasting typical Irish hospitality. With this in mind, he called on the McDonnells at their lovely house off the Monkstown road, near Dun Laoghaire.

'When Bill O'Kelly called, he asked me if we had any spare rooms,'

Margaret McDonnell recalled, 'and when I told him we had, he said the society was having difficulty in getting accommodation for all of the German singers and they would be most grateful if I could accommodate two or three of them. I discussed his request with my husband Colm and since both of us were patrons and regular opera-goers, we agreed wholeheartedly.'

'Dalguise' stands on its own grounds and is nearly one hundred years old. The music room can seat up to ninety people and Margaret McDonnell describes the house as late Georgian and early Victorian. They moved into it when they married in the early 1940s. It was, she remembered, Bill O'Kelly who first invited them to become patron members and over the years they had become good friends.' Bill was very determined and if he wanted anything for the DGOS he got it; but of course in the nicest and most persuasive way!'

A native of Co. Waterford, her vivacious manner and generous spirit made her popular in musical circles and she has proved an enthusiastic fund-raiser for the society. Margaret McDonnell was the kind of woman who embodied the spirit of the DGOS and inspired those about her. She was continually trying to recruit new patron members 'I had to do something,' she once told me. 'We had no money in the society; it was up to us all to get some.'

One afternoon in April she welcomed to 'Dalguise' Bill O'Kelly and the artists from the Hamburg State Opera. They were Annaliese Rothenberger, Lora Hoffman and Martha Mödl, all three in the cast of *Cosi fan tutte*. Margaret remembers that Rothenberger was a real personality - and the prettiest of the three. After afternoon tea, she showed them their rooms and they looked pleased. Later on if she happened to have an afternoon free she brought the singers to County Wicklow for walks and afternoon tea. At other times, they expressed a wish to go shopping and were pleasantly surprised by the wide variety of goods available in both the food and clothes lines. Since the weather was fine and sunny the singers occasionally rehearsed on the green lawn, outside her house. 'It is the first time,' thought Margaret McDonnell, 'that scenes from an opera are being rehearsed on my lawn.' Once an uncle of hers was visiting the house and as he watched the singers, he turned to her and remarked with a smile, 'D'you know, Margaret, this is the first free opera I've ever attended, and it's great.' Sipping her coffee, she said, 'I should be charging you for the privilege!'

She was intrigued by the manner in which Bill O'Kelly controlled the singers. If he happened to drive them back after their night's rehearsals, he directed them to retire early to bed, as there were more rehearsals in the morning. At such moments Margaret McDonnell thought he sounded like a sergeant-major but she forgave him as she knew he had the welfare of the artists at heart, though one or two of them were mature and hardly needed to be told when to go to bed. For her part, she always ensured they had supper and a chat.

She and her husband Colm loved the society's gala nights, which injected gaiety and colour to opera-going, and it was no different for the first night of *Cosi fan tutte*. As usual they occupied a box and before curtain up had drinks with friends in the dress circle bar. Never before had they looked forward to an opera with more relish and sense of expectancy. 'I'm sure it was because most of the cast was staying with us,' recalls Margaret, 'and they used to ask us when we were going to hear them sing. They took their work seriously, but once it was over they could enjoy themselves.'

Seeing Annaliese Rothenberger in costume and make-up surprised her for a moment and she could hardly believe it was the girl who was staying in her house. She was greatly taken by her clever acting as the little mischievous maid and her singing was a pure delight. As she told me later, she found all the artists splendid and it was one of her happiest nights at the opera. She preferred *Cosi fan tutte* to *Don Giovanni*, perhaps because of the comedy and the very amusing plot, and Theo Herrmann's Alfonso was a delight and she also remembers how beautifully tenor Walter Geisler sang in both operas.

When conductor Arthur Gruber announced at the final curtain that the company was privileged to give the Irish premiere of *Cosi fan tutte*, there was an enthusiastic round of applause from the packed audience. Earlier, on his arrival in Dublin, director Gunther Rennert had said it was the first time since the war for a complete cast of a German opera to visit another country. It was plain that the visit was bringing a great buzz to the Gaiety and the only disappointed ones were those who couldn't get tickets at any price.

The society was fortunate at this time to have as its chorus master the outstanding German musician Dr Hans Waldemar Rosen. During the war he was held prisoner of war in England and afterwards on his release was advised by an English conductor to 'try Ireland for a living.' He was almost penniless and for a while lived in a Dublin hostel. To make ends meet, he began to teach music and when Jeannie Reddin left the DGOS for a time to accompany soloists on tours abroad, she recommended Waldemar Rosen to Dr Larchet as a possible replacement. She was thrilled when the society agreed to give him the job.

He was now extremely useful to the society during the visit of the German artists and apart from his skills as a chorus master, he often acted as an interpreter. He expressed some amazement at the DGOS's unusual set-up, especially the amateur chorus and in his opinion they lived two lives. As he explained, 'They shed their everyday existence when entering the realm of music. The only reward which they get for all their hard work is the noble enjoyment of great art. Standing side by side on stage with great singers from all over the world they know their responsibility and their genuine enthusiasm helps them to achieve what seems impossible on the continent.'

He was further surprised to learn that the choristers paid a small sum of money to the society to be one of the chorus. They endured the impatience of chorus masters, tiring rehearsals after a full day's labour, and even stood and waited in endless dress rehearsals on Sundays until late into the night. The whole thing was to his mind incredible and he admired their loyalty to the society. Choristers I talked to, like Aileen Walsh, Florrie Draper and Monica Condron thought that Waldemar Rosen had a very good way with a chorus and they valued his communicative skills. 'He knew his music superbly,' remarked Miss Walsh. 'We were lucky in those days to have people like Julia Gray, Jeannie Reddin, Moira Griffith and then Waldemar Rosen. The fact is you learned something new from each new chorus master or mistress.'

The critics gave very favourable coverage to both *Cosi fan tutte* and *Don Giovanni* and there was no doubt that the company's visit was a big success in every way. John J Finegan *(Evening Herald)* thoroughly enjoyed Cosi - his opening paragraph said it all: 'I'll cheerfully burn my boats by saying that in any experience of twenty-five years, last night's performance of Mozart's *Cosi fan tutte* at the Gaiety was the finest all-round one of opera I've seen in Dublin. Not even excepting *Don Giovanni* last week.

He was impressed by Gunther Rennert's skilful direction and the stage sets designed by Alfred Sierckle, which he described as 'highly imaginative'. He was taken by both the acting and singing of the well-balanced cast, in particular Annaliese Rothenberger, Walter Geisler and Lore Hoffmann. Finegan recalled for his readers a time when the opera's theme of woman is fickle was regarded as morally shocking and resulted in the work being put on the shelf. He wondered now what all the fuss was about, since the theme was seen as an exhilarating comedy.

There were also 'rave' notices for the production of *Don Giovanni*. Joseph O'Neill *(Independent)* summed up: 'The large audience saw the advantages of opera presented by a "house" company, over a presentation where the principals are drawn from different companies and lack co-ordination. Here the conductor Arthur Gruber had a team of eight singers who had a thorough understanding of each other, and a responsive orchestra, led by Nancie Lord, to complete his forces. The result was a performance of high artistic value.'

In O'Neill's view, the vocal performances were outstanding. The lyric singing of tenor Walter Geisler moved the audience to such enthusiasm that he had to repeat the aria, "Il mio tesoro". Matthieu Ahlersmeyer gave a tour-de-force performance as the Don and Elfriede Wasserthal was in wonderful voice as Donna Elvira. Robert Johnston in the *Irish Press* thought it was 'a great occasion' and that the singing was of such a standard as 'we have never experienced before in Dublin'. Each singer was ideally cast and all were blessed with rich Mozartian voices.

Johnston commented on the great reception accorded the cast and the fact that Comdt. O'Kelly thanked everyone concerned at the final curtain, and went on to introduce the director Gunther Rennert who in a brief speech paid tribute to the audience for its reception of the cast. Clearly the visitors were overwhelmed by the sheer warmth of the response they found in Dublin and by the time they were packing their bags to return to Hamburg had intimated to Dr Larchet, who had entertained the principals at his home in St Mary's Road, that circumstances permitting they would like to return to Ireland.

Sheila Larchet had found their visit an important musical experience and enjoyed every moment playing for them. Arthur Gruber, in her view, was an inspiring conductor of Mozart's music. 'He knew what he wanted from the orchestra - and he got it. I mean, everything blended so beautifully, the singing, the music, the whole atmosphere around each opera was realised and came across. I was so happy when they brought the Mozarts for we knew we'd get musical perfection.'

It was proving a tremendous spring season. It had opened with a performance of Verdi's *Aida*, and apparently an excellent one at that, with American soprano Doris Dorée winning acclaim in the title role. One newspaper critic considered it the best *Aida* cast he had heard in Dublin and was notable for its impassioned and controlled singing. The Italian tenor, Emilio Marinesco, was a most impressive Radames and his "Celeste Aida" received prolonged applause - he was singing in Italian, the rest of the cast in English. Patricia Black proved a convincing Amneris - by now one of her best parts - and the ever reliable Bruce Dargaval gave a powerful portrayal of the King of Ethiopia. The whole performance was said to have deserved the rapturous applause accorded it.

Vilem Tausky was back to conduct the new production of *A Masked Ball* and in all the reviews of the opening night's performance he figured as one of the stars. Robert Johnston *(Irish Press)* described his conducting of the orchestra as masterly and his reading of the Verdi score as inspired. Sharing the honours with him was soprano Doris Doree as Amelia whose voice was equal to all the demands made on it both vocally and dramatically. The *Evening Mail* summed up: 'Miss Doree's voice had a purity of quality and an expressiveness surpassing anything we had yet heard from her. She got excellent support from Kenneth Neate (Ricardo) and Bruce Dargaval (Renato), while Patricia Black's Ulrica had unerring conviction.'

In conversation with Vilem Tausky, he told me this was a particularly productive period in the history of the DGOS and he was impressed by the fearless way it tackled the big operas. 'I believe Bill O'Kelly and his colleagues were correct in their policy for to keep endlessly to the "Fausts", "Carmens" and "Trovatores" without venturing further afield would have served no purpose. I thought the chorus, for example, was improving all the time.'

Tausky had become a friend of Fachtna O'Hannrachain, Radio Éireann's music director, and from time to time was given concert engagements. This income from Ireland, he told me later in London, was important to him. He was coming for both the spring and winter seasons and although the fees he was getting from Comdt. O'Kelly weren't unusually high, they were at least on a regular basis. He was already engaged for the 1950 winter season to conduct the society's first production of *Don Carlo* and Bizet's *Carmen*. The Verdi work would be a big challenge for the society and he had had talks about the production with Dr Larchet and Comdt. O'Kelly who were both enthusiastic about tackling the opera, and the casting was almost completed.

A Meeting in Rome

The overwhelming success of the Hamburg State Opera's visit acted as a major spur to Comdt. Bill O'Kelly, Dr Larchet and the other DGOS committee members and strengthened their resolve to expand the operatic frontiers. They learned at this time from their good friend at the Italian Legation in Dublin, First Secretary Prince Luigi di Giovanni, that the Italian government's cultural ministry was providing a special subvention to impresarios and agents to cover the fees of Italian artists engaged abroad. It amounted to a package deal, as it were, with, say, the DGOS hiring an impresario in Rome or Milan to work for it. He compiled the package, submitted the cost to the society, with the impresario paying the artists from his government subvention. Comdt. O'Kelly was quick to recognise the scheme's merits and in the middle of 1950, accompanied by his vice chairman Michael Dinnigan, he travelled to Rome armed with names and addresses of likely agents.

They were fortunate to be introduced to Cardenio Botti who ran an agency at Via Novembre in partnership with a colleague, Renata Gaede, called O.P.E.R.A. and supplied not only singers, producers, conductors and designers but also organised festivals, recitals, concerts, operatic tours, ballet performances and auditions. Comdt. O'Kelly was told that Botti had a reputation for integrity and honesty and was most careful about the artists he took on and the events he was prepared to organise. From the start, O'Kelly and the shrewd Signor Botti hit it off well together and the DGOS chairman would say later that he was the kind of man with whom he could do business, so that before he and Dinnigan left Rome they were confident a deal could be worked out to everyone's satisfaction.

Cardenio Botti was scarcely the type of individual one would readily expect to be an impresario. For one thing, he was an outstanding musician, at once gifted and versatile. He completed his studies at the St. Cecilia Conservatoire in Rome and went on to compose as well as conduct operas and symphonies. He also revealed a natural flair as an organiser and manager of cultural events and before long was appointed director of the Teatro Massimo in Palermo and later of the Carlo Felice in Genoa. In time, he would become director of the organisation for the co-ordination of great Italian Opera Houses. A studious man, he was of a serious disposition and had made it quite clear to both O'Kelly and Dinnigan what he expected of the Dublin Grand Opera Society. He had also indicated to them that he saw no particular difficulty in negotiating a subvention provided his own terms were met by the society. Back in Dublin, O'Kelly found that the committee was enthusiastic about the plan, particularly so Dr Larchet, who was a strong advocate of Italian opera, believing it was tailor-made for the Irish operatic temperament. He saw it also as an opportunity for opera lovers to hear perhaps some of the finest voices in Italy on their own doorstep.

In subsequent visits to Rome, Comdt. O'Kelly and Michael Dinnigan occasionally met the young Irish soprano Veronica Dunne who had been studying there since 1946 and being fluent in Italian, she sometimes acted as their interpreter. She also introduced them to singers and their teachers and people in operatic circles. 'I met Maestro Botti with them and came to the conclusion that he wouldn't send trash over to Dublin because his reputation was at stake. What he would do was bring over tradition and good singers, conductors, directors and designers. He knew his job and had been trained in Milan with one of the leading agents there. Afterwards he decided to set up his own agency in Rome and was doing extremely well. As far as the DGOS was concerned, Botti was the right person in the right place and the society was bound to benefit from his experience.'

It was expected the society would be able to avail of the subvention scheme from the 1951 spring season onwards and the committee was anxious to call the season a festival of Italian opera. Although Maestro Botti would compile the package, Comdt. O'Kelly let it be known that he would travel to Rome or Milan to audition singers. Dr Larchet attributed the society's artistic progress to two factors, the availability of the Radio Éireann Symphony Orchestra as well as the Gaiety Theatre; but there was now a third factor - the hard-working, amateur chorus - that tended to worry him. With the signing of the Italian 'package deal' there would be a bigger onus thrown on each chorister, especially in respect of learning languages, and he hoped it would be able to cope. As always, he was reassured by the chairman's optimism and to Dr Larchet himself the chorus had coped well in recent years learning operas in Italian, German as well as English. Yet he knew it was asking a lot of them.

True to his word, Comdt. O'Kelly engaged Veronica Dunne to sing in the spring season of 1950 as Micaela in *Carmen*. It would be her operatic debut and she was in good company. Two outstanding tenors, Frans Vroons and Kenneth Neate were alternating in the role of Don Jose, with Patricia Black in the title role, and Bruce Dargaval once more as Escamillo. 'I was quite excited about my debut with the society,' recalls Miss Dunne, 'for I knew most of my family and friends would be present in the Gaiety. Although I had been studying in Rome for four years, I had kept in regular touch with home and the musical scene in Dublin. I was hoping that too much wasn't expected of me - I was still in the learning stage as an opera singer.'

The young soprano need not have worried. The critics apparently saw a lot of potential in her performance and an intelligent summing up was made by Joseph O'Neill in the *Irish Independent*: 'One of the satisfying things about this presentation of Carmen was the performance of Veronica Dunne, a young Dublin singer in the part of Micaela. She sang her music splendidly, and the rich quality of her voice was heard to great advantage. There is a fine resonant tone in her singing, and her first appearance in grand opera has been a considerable success.'

Conductor Vilem Tausky remembered her debut when I talked to him later about that '50 season. 'I suspected at the time she was a little nervous,' he said, 'but she showed secure musicianship and I had no need to help her or anything like that. I knew she was only beginning her career and I must say I was impressed by her soprano voice. It was sweet-toned and well placed. The audience was very generous to her in their applause and that is a big help for any young Micaela. I had little doubt she would go on to make a successful career for herself.'

It was one of the conductor's happiest seasons in Dublin; his close friend Otkar Kraus was singing Germont in *Traviata* and Marcello in Boheme and after performances they sometimes dined together with friends in city restaurants. They had plenty to talk about, chiefly their days together in Brno in Moravia and their admiration for Janacek's music. They were by now settled in London where Kraus was making a big name for himself in opera. Veronica Dunne, meanwhile, was quite happy with her DGOS debut and felt she hadn't disappointed either her family or her friends. In Italy, she was studying roles such as Butterfly, Mimi *(Boheme)*, Norina *(Don Pasquale)* and others and hoped she would be given the opportunity some day to sing them in Dublin.

Rome was proving a real education for her. She attended performances of *Boheme* with Magda Olivero as Mimi and made notes of the diva's stage movements and expressions; and on another occasion she was thrilled to hear Tito Schipa in Massenet's *Werther* and afterwards as he signed her autograph he enquired what she was doing in Rome and she told him she was a student. He had superb vocal technique, graceful and effortless, and when she asked him how long it would take to master vocal technique like that, he smiled as he said, 'My dear girl, I am over sixty and I am still learning. Every day I learn more and more. You must keep at it.' Having come from post-war austerity in Ireland, she found little relief in the even worse austerity of Italy where poverty was rampant and food scarce. She did not complain as it would be a reason for her father to tell her to return home and she did not want that. She felt insulated staying in a convent in Rome where she was carefully protected by Irish priests, especially Monsignor Hugh O'Flaherty, a kindly man, who had gained an international reputation for his courage during the war. He was to become known as the Pimpernel of the Vatican for his skilful efforts in concealing Allied POWs from the Nazis.

Veronica Dunne was blessed with a ready Dublin wit and used to joke that it was probably a wise thing for her to be hidden away in the convent. As she said, 'Can you imagine how easy it was for all those green Irish girls in Rome to get into trouble surrounded by all those sultry-looking young virile Romans? I mean, I thought you had to have an operation to have a baby.'

She was fortunate in her choice of singing teacher, for the elderly Contessa Calcagni enjoyed an illustrious reputation and she had no shortage of very talented pupils. The soprano's lessons began at 8 o' clock in the morning and at 11 o' clock she was handed over to a repetiteur who carefully took her over operatic roles. Sometimes in the evenings she was able to attend performances and on one occasion attended the Verdi *Requiem*, conducted by Arturo Toscanini, in the Argentina Theatre. The tenor was Gigli, the soprano Maria Caniglia and the mezzo, Ebe Stignani. She had a habit of getting famous singers' autographs and when Gigli recognised her Irish brogue, he smiled and said, 'Ah, La Sheridan. What a wonderful singer and what a marvellous Butterfly. I can hear her beautiful voice.' Signorina Stignani reminded the tenor that she had once heard Sheridan as Butterfly at the San Carlo Naples and that it was an unforgettable experience.

To Veronica Dunne meeting celebrities like Gigli, Caniglia and others and seeing their artistry at close hand, was all part of her musical education. ' I loved the atmosphere around them and I secretly longed to be part of it. But I was realist enough to know that you had to work awfully hard and have a bit of luck to get even half way up the ladder. I had read about their careers and the sacrifices they had to make for their art and I had no illusions. I was in no hurry to leave Rome until I believed the time was right. I was aware also that there were very few opportunities for young singers like me back in Ireland, so study suited me for the time being. I loved everything about Rome, its culture and its people and their deep love of music. I was not afraid of hard work, nor would I give in to distractions.'

It would be nearly another two years before she sang with the DGOS, but that didn't worry her. Looking back, she says, 'I had no objection to the Italians taking over the spring season with Maestro Botti's package. I knew I would be part of it very soon. I was delighted with the prospect, for I had trained in the Italian tradition and I always considered it a positive move on the part of the society to link up with Italy. I saw a new tradition begin in Dublin with Italian opera being almost entirely sung in the vernacular and many Irish opera lovers I know welcomed that.'

It pleased her that a new era was about to begin and she felt that Irish singers like herself would benefit. 'We would be working with new conductors, directors and chorus masters and so a challenge was being created and a new atmosphere. As I said, I was happy about developments and Bill O'Kelly knew that, and so did Maestro Botti.'

Serafino di Leo was a name new to Dublin in the society's winter season of 1950. Her career to date had been colourful. The Marchesa was singing at La Scala when World War II caught up with her and her 'adventures' included six months in a Fascist prison. After her release, she joined the partisan movement and contacted American Allied forces (she was of American descent) to whom her knowledge of Italian dialects was seemingly invaluable.

During her liaison with them she made eighteen parachute descents at night behind the Italian lines, and each time it was claimed succeeded in returning safely with some vital information. On the occasion of her first parachute descent she fainted and was for some time unconscious before she decided that this was not the place or the time for such a display of feminine nerves.

An elegant and attractive woman, Signora di Leo retained as a memento of those stirring days a light blue evening skirt made from the lining of a tent. And she always wore a gold bracelet given to her by Sicilian partisans and inscribed by them during the war. She was accompanied on her arrival in Dublin by her husband, British Army officer Major Fitzpatrick-Cooke of the Royal Inniskillings, whom she met during the conflict.

After the war she had resumed her career in Italy and elsewhere and was engaged by the DGOS to sing Elizabeth de Valois in *Don Carlo*, and Santuzza in *Cavalleria Rusticana*. She was acknowledged as an outstanding Tosca and a fine Verdian exponent. Vilem Tausky remembers her as 'a purposeful woman of strong personality and possessing an unusually fine soprano voice.'

It was understandable that the society should choose to stage the Italian version of *Don Carlo* - it was shorter than the Paris version that ran to five acts and which was premiered in March 1867 and though not regarded as a huge success, went on to run at the Paris Opera for forty-three nights during the season. Based on Schiller's play *Don Carlo*, the work had been commissioned for the Paris Exposition of 1867.

Verdi, who wasn't entirely satisfied with the original version, revised it later and after a run in Bologna was staged at La Scala. He had made several changes, wrote some new music, and deleted the whole of the first act, though he did salvage Carlo's aria. The new four-act *Don Carlo* did not meet however with the full approval of the critics, some claiming it was less satisfactory than the original.

It was still considered over-long and posed a problem for the DGOS. Operagoers at the time liked the final curtain to come down around 11 o' clock at the latest and became restless when it ran for any length beyond that. It was reckoned that the opera would not end at the Gaiety until at least 11 o'clock, so would the first-night audience remain for the fourth act? To their credit the great majority of them did and counted themselves fortunate, for Serafino di Leo gave a wonderful account of her big aria in the finale.

The society's enterprise in staging the work was abundantly rewarded by the tremendous reception it received from the audience. Charlie Dunphy, who had joined the chorus in that year, said a lot of the success was due to Vilem Tausky's musical skills, as well as the singing of the strong cast. When I asked him if the production lacked the visual splendour that it required, he recalled that the set designs were more than adequate. Looking back, he said 'I believe it was an exciting Verdian night and Bill O'Kelly was justified in putting it on. And I think also that Powell-Lloyd, as director, did a very good job.'

The cast, for the most part, was experienced, with Roderick Jones entirely reliable as Rodrigo, Harold Blackburn a commanding Grand inquisitor and Bruce Dargaval bringing nobility to the role of Philip II of Spain. Most of the critics agreed that tenor John David as Don Carlo was perhaps the weak link, both vocally and dramatically. Patricia Black won praise for her singing of the magnificent aria, "O Fatal Beauty". The big chorus was singled out for its impressive singing in the spectacular second act.

Serafina di Leo, who had made such an immediate impression in *Don Carlo*, was equally outstanding as Santuzza in *Cavalleria Rusticana*, dominating the stage by her convincing acting and singing. Young Irish tenor James McKenna was making his debut with the society and, from all accounts, it wasn't altogether auspicious. Josephine O'Hagen's Lola impressed most of the critics, but the chorus came in for some harsh criticism for sounding 'thin' in the famous "Easter Hymn".

The season was not without drama. James Johnston missed out on performances of 'Cav' & 'Pag' when he contracted a severe sore throat. James McKenna replaced him in 'Cav' but the society was obliged to ask Sadler's Wells Company to release Arthur Servant for the role of Canio in *Pagliacci*. There was more drama when he made his way to Northolt Airport to catch a plane for Dublin. 'Sorry,' he was told, 'there are no seats available on the afternoon flight.' Getting rather desperate, the singer explained his position to a passenger waiting to join the 3.30 plane from London and he agreed to surrender his seat on the flight, the last out of London for the day.

I have found that whenever DGOS oldtimers recall memorable performances they invariably include the 1950 *Tosca* high among them. Superlatives like 'remarkable' and 'definitive' are not unusual, and one critic at the time went so far as to claim it was the 'most complete performance' of the opera he had ever heard. Its principals were the Czech baritone Otakar Kraus, and soprano Gre Brouwenstijn and tenor Franz Vroons, both of the Royal Netherlands Opera. And for Irish operagoers it was a source of considerable pride that this *Tosca* was being conducted by Lt.-Col J M Doyle who had given such sterling service to the society over nearly a decade. There is a photograph of him in the *Irish Independent* of the day with the singers and he cut a fine figure in his evening dress. The Irish singers in the cast were Martin Dempsey, Joseph Flood, Brendan Cavanagh and Maura Mooney as the Shepherd Boy. And they like the principals sang in Italian, which prompted an evening newspaper critic to remark, 'Some of the Irish artists singing in Italian seemed to lose the self-consciousness that can diminish a portrayal.'

'It was impossible not to be carried away by the beauty and power of the three main singers,' commented John Finegan in the *Evening Herald*. 'Miss Brouwenstijn has youth and freshness. The big aria "Vissi d'arte" had an artistry that brought a spontaneous salvo of bravos at the conclusion. Vroon's fervour and vocal artistry and Kraus's powerful acting also brought enthusiastic audience reaction. Harry Powell-Lloyd's direction was most assured, notably in the final act. Everyone agreed it was a fitting finale to what had been a season well above the ordinary.

The 1951 season promised not a few more gold nuggets. The return visit by the Hamburg State Opera was again arousing excitement in musical circles, particularly as the company was bringing Rossini's *Barber of Seville* and Mozart's *Il Seraglio*, and Brounwenstijn was returning to sing her famous Tosca. Furthermore, Vilem Tausky was conducting a new production of *La Traviata* with the Italian soprano Rosanna Giancola singing Violetto. It was soon evident to the Gaiety's backstage staff that the *Barber* set was not only unique but would take a long time to build on the stage. 'We worked all night putting it up,' recalled George McFall, 'and it filled the stage. It was three storeys high and you could step from the top floor onto what we called the fly gallery. I had never seen anything like it and said so to our stage director Pat McClellan. The only trouble was that it would take two days to dismantle, so I asked him "What's going to happen when they perform *Traviata* on the night after the *Barber*?"'.

To chorus member Charlie Dunphy the set was ingenious and capable of accommodating thirty people on its top floors. He had never seen Dr Bartolo's house of that size. Like George McFall, he wondered how the society was going to get around the problem of following the *Barber* with *Traviata*.

The set had been designed by the Hamburg Company's Alfred Siercke and sliding panels opened the central hall door, and first and second storey rooms at either side. A central staircase figured with considerable effect in the general movement of the characters. The audience would no doubt find the design revolutionary, for in the past they had been accustomed to see only a section of Dr Bartolo's house but Siercke afforded a view of the entire façade. There was a magical effect when lights were turned on in the rooms and one glimpsed characters moving from one to another or from floor to floor.

Apart from the set design, there were other aspects of the production that thrilled the capacity audiences. It was being sung in German for one thing, and Dr Bartolo was presented as more comedian than gouty, grotesque figure, a natural schemer sporting no eccentric make-up. Adolf Meyer-Bremen was brilliant in the role. 'This opera is a comedy,' commented one reviewer, 'but last night the comedy was emphasised to such an extent that seasoned opera fans gasped. A Broadway musical could not equal the breathless speed and precision with which the new *Barber* was given, and the setting is a remarkable example of inventive genius.'

Although the cast as a whole won over the critics, it was clear that Annaliese Rothenberger's beguiling Rosina captured the hearts of the audience. A natural actress as well as a stylish singer, it was her infectious humour on stage that received most comment. The soprano had first made her mark at Mannheim, when at a concert her Mozart performances were noticed by Gunther Rennert who almost at once brought her to Hamburg. Now she fitted easily into his idea of a *'German Barber'*. And there were other outstanding portrayals by Horst Gunther as Figaro and Fritz Lehnert's lyric tenor as Count Almaviva that enthralled operagoers. Arthur Gruber was back in Dublin to conduct the Radio Éireann Symphony Orchestra.

To Norris Davidson, who had introduced the Rossini opera to Radio Éireann listeners, it was a milestone in the history of the Dublin Grand Opera Society. He had been sometimes disappointed in the past by the mundane stagings of productions in the Gaiety Theatre, but the Hamburg people had shown what could be done with money and imagination. It was an example to everyone, especially the teamwork displayed by the Hamburg casts. 'To say that I enjoyed the *Barber* would be an understatement; I can still see Dr Bartolo's house before me, his rooms, the staircase, everything. How could I ever forget it!'

The *Barber* was undoubtedly a difficult act to follow, no matter how good the production, and few people could deny that Mozart's *Il Seraglio* was anything but first-rate in every way. Director Gunther Rennert adhered to the style of the period and in Theo Hermann had an Osmin who really delighted audiences. As one veteran critic remarked, 'Hermann is remarkable, he can convey a whole comic situation with a twinkle of an eye.' Once again audiences took to Annaliese Rothenberger and her performance as Blonde, but it was Clara Ebers, as Konstanze, who made the biggest impression, her first act aria winning unstinted applause.

When it came to staging *La Traviata* it seems that Comdt. O'Kelly was at one point in favour of taking down the *Barber* set and putting it back the next day but the Germans wouldn't hear of it and argued that because of its size and solidity it must remain, otherwise they would make an issue of the matter. A compromise was arrived at; it was decided to cover most of the set with black silk drapery and perform *Traviata* with the minimum of props and scarcely any scenery. Charlie Dunphy remembers that it was akin to putting on an opera in the National Concert Hall today and the audience hadn't minded and appeared to enjoy it. 'I think the music is so good in the piece that it can be staged anywhere.'

Florrie Draper, who sang in the chorus, recalls that when it was suggested that the *Barber* set be taken down for the night the Germans became very cross and wouldn't hear of it. She was present when they exchanged some words with Bill O'Kelly and when he saw how determined they were he agreed to leave it on stage. She used to call the *Barber* set the doll's house but after seeing Bill O'Kelly involved in the row with the Germans she thought twice about joking about it. He wasn't amused when people came up to him and casually remarked, 'Bill, isn't that *Barber* set smashing?' On one such occasion he seemed to lose his patience and shaking his head, retorted, 'I don't ever want to see that bloody thing again.'

The society had a very big chorus at the time and she wondered how they were going to be accommodated on the limited stage space. 'The funny thing is that we were,' she recalls, 'and no one seemed to notice how we were wedged in. They cut out the ballet altogether and the chorus looked more static than they should. I still think it was better than hauling down that *Barber* set which was as solid as a rock.'

George McFall says that it took two days to take it down and this was done under German supervision as it would be used again in Germany. It wasn't a good idea, he thought, to follow the *Barber* with *Traviata* as it posed problems for everyone. It might have been a better idea to hold a concert instead. But he had to agree that it was an amazing set, a work of real ingenuity.

Whatever about the backstage problems, the Hamburg State Company enjoyed their stay in the city. Mona Brase was able to converse with them in fluent German and recalls she accompanied some of them on shopping sprees as there were still lots of goods they couldn't buy at home. She herself had noticed in the Gaiety the gasps from the audience when they first saw the *Barber* set, and the excitement that prevailed, but in Germany people didn't react always in that way. It was, she believed, this spontaneity and enthusiasm that thrilled the Hamburg visitors.

Comdt. O'Kelly was never the one to let a problem get in the way of progress. His motto was to press ahead and in this philosophy he was supported by Dr Larchet, Bertie Timlin and Michael Dinnigan, though by the latter trio in a more cautious way. They had already their plans made for the '51 winter season and it would be innovative insofar as the society was staging Verdi's *The Force of Destiny* for the first time.

As in the case of *Don Carlo*, they turned to Vilem Tausky to conduct the work. 'Bill O'Kelly told me he had been hoping to do the opera for some time,' the conductor recalls, 'and felt that since it hadn't been done in Dublin for years, now was the time. I knew he loved Verdi's operas and he was pleased I was available for the dates he wanted.'

The great composer had written his new work expressly for the Imperial Theatre of St Petersburg and was present for its premiere on November 10, 1862. Although it was greeted with enthusiasm and was a critical success, Verdi himself was not entirely satisfied and made changes for the La Scala production of 1869, which he himself directed. It is usually played in four acts and set in Spain and Italy in the eighteenth century. Regarded as brilliant musically, the plot is complicated and on the dark side and not without violence. It does provide though some compelling roles for the principals.

The Italian tenor Corrado D'Ottavi sang Alvaro who is in love with Leonora, portrayed by soprano Kyra Vane. The tenor's ringing high notes and secure middle register made him a good choice for the part, while Roderick Jones was a suitably vengeful Don Carlo, and Betty Sagon convincing as the gypsy girl. Bruce Dargaval was authoritative as the Franciscan Prior, and Martin Dempsey and Joseph Flood filled the smaller roles convincingly. Vilem Tausky came in for some very favourable mention, in particular by Robert Johnston in the *Irish Press*, who liked the way the Radio Éireann Symphony Orchestra performed the overture.

That the production had been well rehearsed was reflected by some members of the press being permitted into the Gaiety in the afternoon to note the proceedings. Comdt. O'Kelly and Bertie Timlin were also in attendance. 'To the uninitiated it was a mixture of beautiful singing and threatened mayhem,' said one report. And it continued, 'The opera is a succession of luscious melodies and obviously the company is delighted to be doing the opera and is most enthusiastic. But unfamiliarity with the work resulted in the need for welding well-rehearsed sections into a harmonious unit. When the conductor Vilem Tausky was satisfied with the singing the director Powell Lloyd was not willing to accept the movements on the stage. And so there were stoppages, repeats, lectures, sudden calls for lights, changes of props and even gunfire.

'When the guns - or the requisite apparatus for the reproduction of explosions - were unavailable immediately, the conductor proceeded to give a vocal imitation between waves of his baton. This exhibition of versatility delighted everyone present. The tenor part is sung by a young Italian who is bursting with vitality, and has a voice of amazing power. He bounced around the stage like a rubber ball and interspersed long sentences in Italian with "Thank you"'.

Talking with choristers of the time such as Maura Mooney, Aileen Walsh and Charlie Dunphy, they said they often wondered at rehearsals whether the opera would come together at all on opening night. 'I remember it was often chaos,' said Miss Walsh, 'but in some miraculous way it did and we tended to forget the chaos and crises that had gone before. I'm sure Bill O'Kelly and the others felt the same way. We were lucky I think to have conductors like Jim Doyle and Vilem Tausky who didn't let problems come in their way. But it was incredible how some of the operas actually went on.'

Some of the visiting artists became deservedly popular in Dublin and Cork. Bruce Dargaval made many friends by his singing, outgoing personality and Welsh wit. Originally he was a steel worker in Neath, South Wales, and gave it up to become a professional singer at the age of twenty-four. His opera career began with the Carl Rosa Company in the 1930s, but the slump in opera brought him to musical comedy, revue and even variety. Just before the war, when he was at Sadler's Wells, Gigli heard him and pressed him to go to Italy for training, but the war intervened. Later on he sang at Covent Garden, where his Escamillo was highly regarded. Freelance work appealed to him and he liked nothing better than to sing in Ireland. Verdi was his favourite composer. 'You've got to have a voice to sing him'. And his favourite conductor, Thomas Beecham - 'He is a demon for discipline, but he knows exactly what he wants, and sees that you give it to him.'

Irish singers were making an important contribution in smaller roles, especially Brendan Cavanagh, Joe Flood, Martin Dempsey, Patricia Lawlor -

who sang an excellent Siebel *(Faust)* - and Josephine O'Hagan. It is worth noting too that Sam Mooney, the popular Dublin baritone, once came to the society's rescue in the winter season of `51 when Ernest Davies, who was singing Ferrando in *Trovatore*, became suddenly ill. Mooney took over without a rehearsal and acquitted himself admirably.

Silveri's Arrival

Rome, April 1998. Monteverde is a picturesque residential area standing high above this ancient city of cathedral spires, myriad apartments and busy streets. It is a warm, sunny morning as I linger by the roadside and take in the panoramic views beyond. Nearby is Ugo Bassi, a quiet avenue of pretty private houses, and on the black iron gate of No 3 is a plaque that reads, 'Villa Silveri-Cirinco'. Bathed in sunshine, it stands on its own ground, looks attractive and is topped by a neat dome. Like a pilgrim I've come to meet Paolo Silveri, the legendary Italian baritone.

Momentarily at the door I'm greeted by a young man of oriental appearance who leads me into the hallway where a small life-size bronze figure of Rigoletto is perched on a plinth, and from here to the dining room, quaint and spacious, and dominated by a mahogany table and antique chairs. Sitting in an armchair close by is a grey-haired woman, perhaps in her late seventies. Obviously she has been expecting me. As we shake hands, she says softly, 'I am Delia, Paolo's wife.'

From the adjoining room comes the sound of a piano being played and a singing voice. 'Paolo has pupils this morning,' Signora Silveri says, 'but he will be with us shortly.'

We talk about his long career and she points proudly to the photographs on the walls that show him in costume for some of his most celebrated roles. What are her own favourites? 'There are so many,' she answers with a smile. 'I like them all but maybe Rigoletto a bit more; I really don't know. Paolo says he has sung it five hundred times; can you imagine that? I believe him for he is happy to sing it.'

At that moment he enters the room and I stand up to shake his hand. He is barely recognisable from his photographs; he is frail, moves slowly and looks tired. We chat about Dublin and he enquires about his old friends and is visibly saddened when he hears some of them have passed on. 'I would like to go back there once more,' he reflects. 'I think I would like to see the Gaiety Theatre again.' I can see he is sincere. We talk about the house and he tells me his wife and he have lived in it since their marriage in 1941. It belonged to Delia's father, the well-known bass Giulio Cirino and his family.

'We live in part of the house when we marry first,' she says, 'and we stay ever since.'

It is by now early afternoon and soon we are conveyed by their chauffeur to one of their favourite restaurants and stay there for nearly two hours. Earlier Paolo has complained of a cold but is cheered by the cuisine and goes on to show how good a raconteur he can be. He expresses surprise though later when I suggest that perhaps coaching singers may be too taxing. All he will say is, 'Coaching young singers is my life.'

It has been a delightful interlude, one that has provided me with a precious insight into the lifestyle of a great artist in retirement, yet remarkably still involved with another generation of singers. Back in the villa, he invites me to join him in his compact music room where we can listen to some of his greatest recordings. Most memorable perhaps of them all are the excerpts from his Covent Garden performance of *Boris Godunov* which he sang in English. One suspects it affords him immense satisfaction. I hear him also sing arias by Verdi, Bizet, Mozart and Puccini and the evening ends musically with *Rigoletto*. It is his favourite. He follows every note of his own voice as though anxious to relive the performance.

Signora Silveri arrives with drinks on a tray and as we proceed to sip them his recollections return to the first time he sang for the Dublin Grand Opera Society. For a man who will be eighty-five years old that coming December his memory is good and he seems pleased to remind me of his first visit to Dublin to sing Figaro in *The Barber of Seville*. I listen enthralled.

* * *

It was the winter season of 1952 and it looked exciting as it featured Italian, British and Irish artists. Furthermore, Dutch tenor Franz Vroons was returning to sing Don Jose in *Carmen*. There was no doubt, however, that the society had pulled off a coup in engaging Paolo Silveri and it came about through the friendship between the Italian Ambassador to Ireland, Prince De Giovanni di Santa Severina and Prince Caracciolo, who was living in the country and was a great opera lover. Maestro Botti and Comdt. Bill O'Kelly were also in on the discussions.

Silveri, who was approaching forty, was by now well established in his career. Although he had started out as a bass he made his debut as a baritone - the elder Germont in *La Traviata* - and showed early promise of becoming an outstanding Verdi exponent. During his ten years in the army he found time for vocal study in Rome, and in May 1943 sang with a cast in *Aida* that included Maria Caniglia, Beniamino Gigli and Gino Bechi.

He admitted it had been a struggle, for some impresarios refused to accept he was a baritone and wanted to cast him in bass parts. He turned down all their offers. Delia, his wife, was proving by his own admission a wonderful help. She was an accomplished pianist and assisted him vocally and in interpretation. He felt he had arrived when he sang with Gigli in *Ballo in Maschera*. 'I remember that after my big aria "Eri Tu" the audience clamoured for an encore but I did not respond to their wishes, as I was afraid of offending Gigli. At the final curtain, as we moved forward to take a bow he was a little behind me and began to step back and pull the two edges of the curtain together so that I was alone. This was answered by thunderous applause. It was a grand gesture on his part.'

When Silveri toured Britain after the war with the San Carlo Company of Naples he again sang with the great tenor in performances of *Boheme* and *Pagliacci* and recalls that he felt somewhat embarrassed when his newspaper reviews surpassed those of Gigli. On reflection, he says it must have been difficult for him to accept. He would have felt the same way in Gigli's shoes.

Britain was good to him. Opera fans loved his beautifully-controlled and sonorous voice, but perhaps just as much, his infectious personality on stage, for by now he was accepted as an outstanding actor-singer. After the success of his *Rigoletto* he reached a new pinnacle of popularity and was offered a contract by Covent Garden management. Amazingly, he was to sing most of his performances there in English, which was the policy of the 'house' at that time. And in doing so he became the first Italian to sing roles such as Rigoletto, Count di Luna, Marcello, Germont and Escamillo in that language. Making operatic history afforded him the utmost satisfaction.

In conversation Silveri can easily become emotional, whether it is recalling happy events involving his wife and children, singing with Gigli or di Stefano in Parma or Arena di Verona, or receiving tumultous applause for a well-sung aria. He makes no secret of the ambition of every young Italian singer: it is simply to get their first engagement at La Scala, Milan. He was aged thirty-six before the hallowed doors were opened to him.

Although he was contracted to sing four performances of King Alfonso in Donizetti's opera *La Favorita*, it was as Count di Luna in *Trovatore* that the baritone actually sang his first performance there. It came about at short notice when his friend and colleague Gino Bechi took suddenly ill and he was pressed into singing the part. His debut was a tremendous success. He was overwhelmed by the applause. As he would say later, 'After that, the doors of La Scala were flung open to me.'

He could be generous-minded in respect of colleagues. Once when he could not sing in *La Forza del Destino* at Arena di Verona he recommended a young baritone, Aldo Protti, as his replacement and was delighted when his choice was justified. The tenor Mario del Monaco was to become one of his closest friends and according to Silveri, some of his greatest performances were with the tenor. In his villa in Rome is a drawing of del Monaco, and in conversation Silveri likes to refer to his friend and the occasions they sang in *Otello, Andrea Chénier, Tosca* and *Trovatore*. One quickly got the impression talking to him that he made more friends than enemies in his days as a singer.

Prior to his debut for the DGOS in 1952 it had been an extremely busy time for him. He had sung at the Rossini Festival in Pesaro and later on in Tosca in Turin. He admits today it was a hectic schedule and sometimes he was obliged to insert certain clauses in his contracts so as to ease travel problems or avoid a clash of dates. He was in London in November of `52 recording during the daytime for Columbia Records and singing in the evening at Covent Garden. By now he was engaged to sing in four performances of *The Barber of Seville* in Dublin, beginning on Tuesday, December 2.

On the previous evening he was scheduled to sing a Verdi role at Covent Garden and almost missed making the theatre because of fog. When he set out the weather was murky and the taxi was able to make its way, but gradually a dense blanket of fog descended and soon the driver refused to continue with the journey. He advised the singer to get out and find the underground. 'I tried to do so but then lost my bearings and became totally disorientated,' he recalled. 'I started to panic and call out, "Where am I? Help me!" in the hope that someone would come to my assistance. At last someone did arrive, a policeman who took me by the arm and guided me to the underground station where I was able to find my way to Covent Garden.'

Worse was to come. He was informed in his hotel the following morning that all flights to Dublin were cancelled because of the fog, and since he was due to go on stage that evening as Figaro, he became a little frantic. He telephoned the Italian legation in Dublin about the position and asked them to get in touch with the Dublin Grand Opera Society. His words were, 'If I can get to Dublin I will sing, but I cannot see past the fog at the moment. I will do my best to come to Ireland, I assure you.'

It was one occasion when his wife Delia was not with him as she was taking care of their children in Rome. Normally she was good in a crisis and able to ease his anxieties. He arrived at London airport in an agitated state and the tedious hours of waiting did not help. More than once he despaired of getting a flight and was on the brink of telephoning the Italian legation in Dublin when a man, seeing his unease, came up to talk to him. The singer quickly explained his dilemma and to both his relief and surprise the man, who happened to be a pilot, offered to try to fly him across the Channel in his two-engine plane.

'I was aware of the risks involved for both of us,' Silveri recalled, 'but I was so anxious not to let the Dublin opera society down that I said "yes" to the pilot. I offered to pay him but he said a ticket for the opera in Dublin would be enough. Naturally I was nervous; nervous for myself, Delia and my children, and the pilot beside me. You can imagine my pleasure and great relief when we touched down at Dublin airport. I cannot tell you how happy I felt at that moment.'

It was just after 6pm when they had landed in Dublin. Soon he was whisked away by taxi to the Gaiety Theatre where Comdt. O'Kelly, Bertie Timlin and their colleagues awaited him. They listened in almost disbelief as he recounted his experience. They brought tea and sandwiches and more than once O'Kelly asked him if he was feeling alright to go on. Silveri, big and broad-shouldered, assured him he was feeling good.

Looking back, he says he was young and energetic and not worried. 'I was no longer agitated, I was relaxed with new friends. I wanted so much to sing for the people of Ireland.'

As he made up in his dressing room, he had a brief visit from an official of the Italian legation who enquired about his flight experience and wished him luck with his performance. Silveri knew little or nothing about Dublin except from what he had heard in Covent Garden. A few of the singers there had sung in Dublin and told him they enjoyed the experience and assured him he would find the audience friendly. By now he felt more at ease though the thought of the flight sometimes came back to him and he still counted himself very fortunate.

That evening he showed no signs of stress on stage as he sang the village barber Figaro. After his "Largo al Factotum," there was prolonged applause and he felt the performance by the cast around him was very good. Playing Basilio was his fellow countryman, the bass Plinio Clabassi and he was pleased that he, too, got a great reception from the audience. The papers next day praised the production and regarded it as one of the best *Barbers* seen in Dublin for a long time. The *Irish Press* heading read: PAOLO SILVERI A BRILLIANT BARBER.

'The artist of the evening was Paolo Silveri,' stated the paper's critic Robert Johnston. 'He enchanted everyone with his fine voice, extraordinary technical accomplishments and his acting. There were other fine performances by Plinio Clabassi (Basilio) and Arturo la Porta (Bartolo). Bruno Nofri proved himself an inventive director.'

Paolo Silveri was impressed by the genuine friendship shown to him and by the warmth of the Gaiety audience. When he dined next day with Comdt. O'Kelly and Maestro Botti they discussed the possibility of his return to Dublin in the following spring to sing in *Rigoletto*. 'I tell them I am happy to come back to Dublin if I am not too busy,' the bartione recalled. 'At this time I have many engagements in Europe and south America.'

Giuseppe Morelli conducted the Rossini opera and came in for very favourable comment. He had been invited to Dublin by Maestro Botti and had a distinguished musical background. Born in Rome in 1907, he had trained as a conductor at the National Academy of St Cecilia under the direction of Maestro Molinari and later went on to conduct operas in Italy and the rest of Europe.

He lives in an attractive apartment block within a short distance of the Olympic Stadium in Rome and like Paolo Silveri, he still coaches singers. On his grand piano is a small bronze statue of Wagner and on shelves around the room are books, masks, music scores, LPs, and antiques he collected on his tours, and small ornaments. Paintings hung on the walls and were a mixture of landscapes and portraits.

Although frail, Maestro Morelli is recognisable from photographs and has retained his sense of humour. Over coffee he tried to remember his early years conducting in Dublin, and names like Silveri and Clabassi and Nofri clearly struck a chord. But it was the society's chairman Comdt. O'Kelly who seemed to have made the most lasting impact. He called him the 'Miracle Man' which was the first time I had heard anyone use the phrase. When I asked him the reason, he replied weakly, 'Nothing is impossible to Bill O'Kelly, nothing in the world. I like going to Dublin, I like your Irish whiskey.'

He asked about the Gaiety Theatre and if Italian opera seasons were still presented there by the Dublin Grand Opera Society. For a man of ninety-one his curiosity had not waned and he recalled with a smile Paolo Silveri's Figaro. 'Fantastic' was the word he used. It was a word I had heard Silveri and others use in different contexts. Silveri used it to imply a remarkable person as opposed to a performance. Morelli remembered the DGOS chorus as very big and very good. You got the impression that opera in the Dublin of the early 1950s was a big friendly event which he was happy to be part of. From all accounts, the popular bass Plinio Clabassi shared the same view for he was enjoying himself no end, between singing, going to soccer matches and accepting invitations to parties. The chorus members in particular held him in high regard, as they did Maestro Morelli.

It was proving a splendid year for the society. Clabassi sang a commanding Ferrando in *Trovatore*, the English mezzo-soprano Constance Shacklock was acclaimed as Carmen, opposite Franz Vroon's Don Jose, and the veteran Welsh baritone Bruce Dargaval was back to sing Escamillo in *Carmen*. There was considerable interest among Irish operagoers in that season's *L'Amico Fritz* for Veronica Dunne was partnering the talented Italian lyric tenor Alvinio Misciano in Mascagni's romantic comedy cleverly woven around the lovers Fritz and Suzel. Written a year after the composer's acclaimed *Cavalleria Rusticana*, the work is notable for its tuneful melodies and the "Cherry Duet" sung by Fritz and Suzel.

Misciano owed the success of his early career to Paolo Silveri. They first met while in the army in Italy and were officers in the same unit. At the time Misciano had a baritone voice and one day called on Silveri to hear him sing. 'As soon as I hear him I know he is a tenor and I tell him so,' he recalled. 'I take him for some lessons and before long he is able to reach the top notes in the tenor range that he never believes he possesses. The colour of his voice changes and gains the beauty and polish of a true tenor.'

The young tenor, who was born in Milan, went on scholarship to the Teatre dell' Opera and made his debut in Rome in 1946. By the time he sang Fritz for the DGOS he was just about the right age to play the landowner. His lyrical voice blended well with Veronica Dunne's agile soprano and they acted convincingly. 'Alvinio was lovely to sing with,' Miss Dunne recalls. 'His voice suited Mascagni's music, so he was ideal for the part.'

Earlier in the `52 spring season she had sung Norina in Donizetti's comic masterpiece *Don Pasquale* and was less fortunate with the choice of tenor. Ivan Cecchini, as Ernesto, sang in Italian and the rest of the cast in English; his acting was wooden and vocally he lacked the lyric beauty that the part requires. The rest of the cast fared much better, with Ronald Stear a 'magnificent' Pasquale and Bruce Dargaval excelling as the genial Malatesta.

It was another successful evening for Veronica Dunne. 'Her acting had all the playfulness and guile that the character of Norina demanded,' noted the *Evening Mail*; while other reviews emphasised her flair for comedy and easy bel canto phrasing. Except for the performance by the tenor Ivan Cecchini, she has satisfying memories of the production, particularly Vilem Tausky's pacing of the music which she thought inspired.

In that 1952 spring season she also sang her favourite role of Mimi in *La Bohème* before a packed 'house' and in Italian. Her Rodolfo was the Italian tenor Giuseppe Zampieri, who cut a romantic figure as poet and lover, and sang with a beautiful, ringing tone. His fellow countryman, the baritone Giulio Fioravanti, also won praise for his portrayal of Marcello, while Sandra Baruffi revealed a richness of vocal quality as Musetta. It would appear that everyone, including the chorus and producer (Sydney Russell) shared in what one evening music critic described as one of the best *Bohèmes* he had witnessed in forty years of opera-going in Dublin.

TRIUMPH FOR DUBLIN SINGER IN BOHEME proclaimed the *Evening Mail*, and from all accounts, it was an accurate summing up of Veronica Dunne's Mimi. The critic stated that she 'added lustre to the part and her singing and acting showed a maturity surprising in one with so little experience of grand opera.' The *Evening Herald* noted, 'The Clontarf girl was portraying Mimi, the little dressmaker for the first time; she brought to the role the very ecstasy of youth. The notes were beautifully shaped, the Puccini melodies lay easily on the clear, spring-like voice. This was a Mimi of heart-touching quality, notably in the "Farewell" aria of the third act.'

The only jarring note came in the paper's final comments about the production: 'There was new scenery. The garret and the gateway to Paris were the most effective sets. The square near the Café Momus looked, however, like a medieval German town - it certainly wasn't Paris. The snow-making apparatus at the start of the third act was unsound: the flakes fell like feathers from pillows torn open by a naughty child.'

At the final curtain, it seems, there was 'terrific enthusiasm displayed,' with the principals being recalled repeatedly, and Veronica Dunne being showered with bouquets. The Italian artists must have thought for a moment they were in Naples or Venice. 'I shall never forget the applause I received,' she said. 'The cheers still ring in my ears to this day.'

Invitation to Munich

Opera connoisseurs could not have hoped for better news. The announcement early in 1953 that the Munich State Opera had accepted the DGOS's invitation to perform in the spring season of that year was almost too good to be true, although everyone agreed that after the success of the Hamburg visits anything was possible. Perhaps Maestro Morelli was correct after all - the chairman Comdt. O'Kelly was indeed some kind of miracle man.

The German company could look back on a three-hundred-year-old tradition, dating to 1653 when the first performance of an opera took place in the Bavarian capital. There followed performances of new works by the great Amadeus Mozart, including *Idomenio*, which were composed especially for the Munich stage. When in 1945, all cultural life seemed to have come to an end at the same time as the military and economic collapse, no one could have guessed that within a short time the nucleus of a new company would be in place.

Fortune had played a part in the recovery. With their own opera house destroyed in the Allied bombing campaigns they were lucky to be able to find a home in the Prinzregent Theatre which had only suffered slight damage. As early as November 1945 the company was able to present Beethoven's opera *Fidelio* and by the early 1950s it was again one of the strongest in Germany.

Persuading the company to visit Dublin took some time. The society found a genuine friend in Dr. Alfred Koll, secretary of the German Legation in Dublin and he opened doors for them in Bonn and Munich. Comdt. O'Kelly, Bertie Timlin and Fachtna O'Hannracháin, music director in Radio Éireann, travelled to Munich in the late autumn of 1952 for talks with the opera company's director Prof. Rudolf Hartmann, Prof. Robert Heger, the distinguished conductor, and stage director Ulrich Reinhardt. The Germans quickly outlined the guarantees they wanted.

'I was invited along by Bill O'Kelly to answer questions about the Radio Éireann Symphony Orchestra and to satisfy them that musically it was up to requirements,' recalled O'Hannracháin. 'It was plain that they didn't want a scratch orchestra accompanying their singers and I agreed with that. I was able to tell them the orchestra had played for the principals of Opéra Comique as well as the visiting Hamburg State Company and that eased their worries. Prof. Hartmann was the hardest to satisfy and though friendly, he was a tough negotiator. I remember we were brought to an opera performance for the purpose I suspected of showing us the high musical standards of the Munich company.'

O'Kelly was in turn quizzed about the Gaiety Theatre, the size of its stage, the backstage amenities and the staff. Bertie Timlin was able to assure the Germans that the company would be well supported by the Irish public and that their productions would probably be a sell-out at the box office. It was left to O'Kelly and Timlin to finalise the financial arrangements and the fees involved. It was a package deal with the Munich company bringing with them the principal singers, stage sets and costumes.

'The deal was clinched before we left Munich,' says Fachtna O'Hannracháin. 'I've no doubt it helped a lot that the Hamburg people had been so well treated on their visits to Dublin and Munich knew about this. Nevertheless, it took some hard bargaining on Bill O'Kelly's part but I could see they respected his determination and enthusiasm. He was a realist and knew what was needed and how to achieve it. He impressed people by his sincerity and obvious organising skills. Although we begged to differ on occasions, I got on well with him for behind his somewhat abrasive exterior there was a good-natured man.'

During their visit it struck him forcibly that the chairman was running the society his way but he himself believed it was the only way it could be done in opera. He was able to inspire and cajole people and though they might argue he was autocratic few could deny his leadership skills which undoubtedly helped to hold the DGOS together. He made a good impression on the Munich people who were pragmatists and in no way swayed by Irish blarney.

Meeting the expenses of the Munich company posed problems, but they were overcome by aid from the German government in Bonn, the Arts Council of Ireland and from the society's own contribution, which came from patrons' subscriptions and box-office takings. The Italian subvention took care of the operas featuring that country's artists. Around this time James J O'Connor, chairman of the society's patron membership, was ensuring that numbers increased annually and he made repeated appeals for new members, emphasising strongly that visits from German companies especially could not be possible without financial guarantees. The response he got was usually very good.

It promised to be a momentous season comprising seven operas, two of which had already caught the public's imagination and there was a clamour for tickets. These were *Tristan and Isolde*, being staged by the Munich company, and the DGOS's presentation of Verdi's *Rigoletto* with Paolo Silveri in the title role. *La Bohème* would be sung in German for the first time in Ireland and this put an extra onus on the chorus mistress of the time, Moira Griffith.

It helped that she had learned German at school and also that Noel Reid, her fiancé, was fluent in the language. He was a chorus member and between them they worked out a phonetic system of teaching the lines. It was still difficult to master all the lines, said Florrie Draper, and she remembers writing them on slips of papers and memorising them at bus stops and at home. The two female choristers who came from Munich to help them out did not seem to know the Puccini score and like everyone else worked from the music score. After a while some of the more witty choristers had privately nick-named them 'Gert and Daisy'.

The majority of the critics expressed disappointment about the production and clearly did not take to Puccini's opera being performed in German. Phrases such as 'lack of emotion', 'sound singing but little passion,' and 'an unmoving act one love duet' indicated that there was an untypical coldness about the performances. One evening newspaper reviewer summed up, 'The German phrases did not rest comfortably on the Puccinian notes.'

The *Barber of Seville*, in the same season, was more to the audience's liking and was performed in true Italian style and conducted with loving care by Giuseppe Morelli. There were at least two outstanding portrayals, Giuseppe Forgione's barber and Plinio Clabassi's singing teacher. The whole thing was played with a style and verve that roused the audience to genuine enthusiasms.

As always, *Madama Butterfly* drew packed 'houses' and they gave a hearty reception to Alvinio Misciano's Pinkerton and the Cio-Cio-San of Elena Rizzieri. The tenor had endeared himself in a comparatively short time to the Irish opera-going public by his polished lyrical singing and winning stage presence. He also mixed easily with the choristers, something that Comdt. O'Kelly always encouraged the principals to do. He wanted on no account the 'us' and 'them' attitude. Whatever about the Germans, the Italian artists were good social mixers and wanted to enjoy themselves in Dublin.

The choice of Wagner's *Tristan and Isolde* could hardly be surpassed. Since its premiere in Munich in June 1865, it had enjoyed universal appeal, its magnificent Prelude and Liebestod becoming very popular outside the opera house as concert pieces. And its Celtic theme, which Wagner had found in the thirteenth-century German poem by Gottfried von Strassburg, has also a direct Irish link; indeed the great work opens with Tristan taking Isolde, daughter of the King of Ireland, on his ship to be married to his uncle, King Marke of Cornwall. Musically, the highlight of the opera is the moving love duet in act two. To Thomas Mann it was one of the most inspired love stories ever written. In Dublin the opera was being conducted by Robert Heger, the leading conductor of the Munich State Opera; he was a musician with a wealth of Wagnerian experience and was said to bring to the composer's works an 'unerring sense of style and interpretation.' The principals had already sung the work on numerous occasions in Munich.

It was ten years since the society last staged a Wagner opera, and that was *Tannhauser* in 1943. *Tristan and Isolde* had not been staged in Dublin since before the first world war when it was sung in the old Theatre Royal by the Quinlan Opera Company with Agnes Nicholls and John Coates as the lovers; Sir Thomas Beecham conducted. Expectations were naturally high among music lovers that the Munich company would do more than justice to Wagner's masterpiece and there was no surprise when it was announced that the Gaiety Theatre was booked out for opening night.

It was fitting also that it was chosen to open the season on Monday April 20. The *Evening Herald* headed its review, 'NIGHT OF GREAT SINGING' and the introduction read: 'Wagner is conspicuous by his absence from the opera season here and consequently it is not without reason that the city's opera lovers have been looking forward eagerly to hearing (the majority for the first time) *Tristan and Isolde* performed by a company steeped in the Wagnerian tradition.

'Last night's performance will surely be remembered by many as being the outstanding event of its kind for years. The singing of all the principals was magnificent, the characterisations were brilliant studies, and the settings were faithful to the composer's intentions; indeed Ulrich Reinhardt's direction reflected the atmospheric mood superbly. After a rather dull start to the Prelude, the Radio Éireann Symphony Orchestra warmed up to give a very impressive response to Robert Heger's conducting, the strings in particular, would have been a credit to a larger- and better-known ensemble.'

The staging was also praised by the *Irish Times* as well as the lighting and costumes. As the lovers, August Seider (Tristan) and Erna Schluter (Isolde) were admirably matched, both in physique and voice and their singing displayed a wide range of emotions, particularly in the big love duet in act two. The supporting cast, in particular Ira Malanuik for her study of Brangane, was excellent. The conductor Robert Heger produced some magical effects, notably in the Prelude and in the passage depicting Tristan's rush to answer Isolde's signal.

Robert Johnston in the *Irish Press* regarded the orchestral accompaniment as the main glory of the evening although August Seider's singing as Tristan was of exceptional quality. He expressed some reservation however about his performance in the love duet. 'Seider's voice here had more caution than fervour, more tension than rapture. But it served him better in the death scene where he rose to a height of intensity for which he had to call on vocal reserves. His last meeting with Isolde was indescribably moving.'

Playing in the wind section of the orchestra, Gerry Larchet found the occasion unforgettable. 'Looking back, I remember thinking how privileged I was as a young musician to be performing Wagner's music under a conductor of Robert Heger's stature. He was in his late sixties when he came to us, if anything it added to his authority on the podium. He was demanding as well as inspiring and he never allowed orchestral volume to drown out the singers. It was his skill in shaping the music that made you admire him, his use of tempos and the way he coped with the great dramatic climaxes in the music: it was a new experience for me. I remember one newspaper critic asking why the orchestra couldn't play up to this standard more often and of course the answer was that Professor Heger wasn't always the man with the baton.'

To young Larchet, it had been a unique occasion and he was able to sense it in the theatre, in the tangible silence that preceded the playing of the Prelude. As usual, his parents invited the Munich principals for drinks to their house, 8 St Mary's Road, and Gerry Larchet has no doubt that Robert Heger was among the guests. 'My father was always at his best entertaining musicians; he empathised with them and talked about the Irish music scene which he found most of them wanted to learn about. For his part, he would want to learn more about music in post-war Germany. He enjoyed meeting these people and could relax with them. 'In a way I suppose it was good public relations for the society, though my father wouldn't see it in that way but rather as promoting friendship.'

Harpist Sheila Larchet always welcomed the opportunity to perform with outstanding conductors, contending that they usually inspired musicians to rise above themselves. It was no different in the case of Robert Heger. She agreed he had had an extraordinary effect on her. 'I mean, when he was conducting *Tristan* I got this feeling that it was Richard Wagner himself who was up there, for he had this incredible insight into the composer's music and created a mood that merged stage and pit in one unit. He was able to shape the music to convey every nuance. It reminded me so much of Roger Desmoriére's conducting of *Pélleas et Mélisande*, though of course Debussy and Wagner's music is entirely different.

An unexpected crisis hit the society during the run of *Tristan and Isolde* and once more Comdt. O'Kelly spent most of the day trying to solve it. When soprano Erna Schluter contracted a throat infection every effort was made to get a replacement but without success. Rather than disappoint the hundreds of people who were coming to the Gaiety to hear the opera, the DGOS committee decided not to cancel the performance but instead put on the last act of *Tristan* omitting the role of Isolde, and devote the rest of the evening to a celebrity concert by Munich singers not engaged in the Wagner work.

Most of the audience were happy to remain for the concert and the management announced that on production of their half-tickets they would get priority booking for the extra performance of Tristan on Sunday, May 3. A replacement for Erna Schluter was flown in from Germany next day; she was the experienced Wagnerian soprano Paula Baumann and, according to the critics, she surpassed expectations as Isolde. 'She had a voice of really beautiful quality, exquisitely pure on top with extraordinary flexibility and easy natural projection,' the *Irish Times* stated.

There was an interesting sequel to the performance of *Tristan and Isolde*. Radio Éireann had broadcast the opera in full from the Gaiety Theatre on the Dublin wavelength, while at the same time providing an alternative programme on the Athlone transmitter. It was a major undertaking and was welcomed by opera lovers unable to get tickets for the performances. The *Irish Times* radio critic wrote on the subject and while lauding the station for relaying the opera, asked: Is the 240 metre transmittor powerful enough to carry a programme adequately?

Evidently, the critic argued, Radio Éireann had already some doubts on the subject, because during one of the intervals in *Tristan* listeners were informed that if their reception was not up to the mark they should send a postcard to the station. At 7pm the transmission was coming through reasonably well, but throughout the first act it disimproved steadily and by the time they had reached the magical scene in Isolde's garden the lovers had to compete with an Italian recording of *Pagliacci* emanating from somewhere in the studio.

By the time the last act arrived the critic must have been beside himself with frustration. He wrote: 'The final act which ended at 11.30 barely penetrated a foreground of noise created by what sounded like a conversation conducted in French language through a mask of bubble gums. The effect would have its funny side had it not been so infuriating for those who wished to listen to Wagner exclusively.

'During the season there are to be more direct relays of opera from the Gaiety. If something is not done immediately to improve the Cork-Dublin transmitter one can only recommend those who have a partiality for opera to avoid Radio Éireann on pain of endangering their sanity.'

Norris Davidson had given the introductory talks about the opera's storyline before and between the acts and deliberately kept them short. Compared with the quality of transmission today it was only just about adequate, he recalled, and in his experience the broadcast rarely, if ever, sounded as good as the actual performance in the theatre. In those days there were only two wavelengths, Dublin and Cork, and sometimes listeners in Cork received their regular programmes while on the Dublin wavelength an opera, full or in part, was relayed. There were complaints from some listeners that the opera ran too long and interfered with their regular listening.

'I remember getting a letter on one occasion from an irate listener deploring opera broadcasts and asking how long she must suffer them. I cannot say what they thought of *Tristan and Isolde* running until 11.30, but I've no doubt it maddened some listeners. From time to time, I did receive complimentary letters myself, saying how much they enjoyed my introductions to the different acts.'

Davidson, who was blessed with a smooth and sonorous voice, first got the opportunity to act as opera link-man on radio in the late 1940s, mainly because he got his timing perfect; before that the announcer doing the job was always getting her timing wrong and the National Anthem might blast off before she finished introducing the opera. He did his first broadcast from the Gaiety Theatre and the opera was broadcast live. The technical side did not concern him: his task was solely to introduce the operas. He got no extra remuneration for doing this as it was taken as part of his normal work schedule at the station.

Looking back, he says the conditions in the Gaiety in those days were not good for broadcasting as soundmen were experimenting with microphones. At one time they hung two in front of the stage to pick up the voices and this wasn't always satisfactory. For the most part they concentrated only on the voices and tended to ignore the orchestra, so that there was often an imbalance in the broadcast of the production.

Davidson found Bill O'Kelly helpful and always very pleased when an opera was broadcast. 'I think he felt these broadcasts were making opera more popular and he was probably correct in that assumption. He was the driving force behind the society and had his finger in every pie, as it were. There were similarities between O'Kelly and Dr Walsh whom I got to know when I was doing broadcasts from the Wexford Festival. They were both motivators though Walsh wanted things done solely his way - Bill O'Kelly at best was prepared to listen to others.'

As Radio Éireann Director of Music, Fachtna O Hannracháin chose the operas to be broadcast but he felt that some of the productions were inadequate and this did not help in broadcasting them. Small parts were not always well filled and it struck him that the society was more concerned about the singing than about improving the staging of the operas. More rehearsal time was needed, especially with the orchestra. Since Radio Éireann was giving the orchestra free he believed the station was entitled to a higher standard of production.

O Hannracháin admits that he was sympathetic to the DGOS and appreciated the value of opera as an art form and the pleasure it afforded people. The relations between himself and the society were cordial and this extended to their discussions in the station itself. 'At the time I saw it very much as an amateur society, working on an inadequate budget which militated against achieving higher production standards. I was disappointed that the government did not match the Italian subvention pound for pound for that would have meant a great deal to the society. As it was, they were doing a good job in the circumstances and the seasons were hugely popular with all sections of the community. We were happy to be part of that scene, though a few people in Radio Éireann didn't share my enthusiasm.'

A Memorable Jester

Paolo Silveri stayed in the Shelbourne Hotel that May of 1953, prior to his appearance in *Rigoletto*. A big, handsome man, sallow-skinned and dark-haired, he easily attracted attention in the hotel foyer or in the street but he seemed unperturbed and took it all in his stride. The truth was that he enjoyed the limelight as much as the applause at final curtain, and he loved people and valued their friendship, though he did not suffer fools gladly. He was regarded as one of the most intelligent artists to emerge from post-war Italy, a musician as well as a singer and a composer to boot - at least one of his songs was sung by Mario Lanza.

Yet Silveri admitted to me in Rome that he was scarcely prepared for the reaction that followed his success as the jester in *Rigoletto*. Apart from the tremendous scenes of enthusiasm in the Gaiety Theatre, he was now the focus of renewed attention. In the Shelbourne foyer he was approached by well-wishes for his signature, others wanted to shake his hand and congratulate him, while more ardent music lovers longed to talk to him about his career and the other singers he had met or sung with.

'I did not mind,' he says. 'Why should I mind if people want to be friendly? They liked my Rigoletto, that was enough for me. I was happy for them and Dublin was good to me.'

He was invited to house parties and to public functions, and he was sought for charity concerts. Jeannie Reddin accompanied the baritone at one of them in the Gaiety Theatre and found him both charming and interesting. 'As a personality, Paolo was larger than life and he had those extra qualities that singers need. He was a natural actor on stage and an absolutely great artist. I regarded him as a first rate musician and an outstanding Verdian singer. He was devoid of pretension and had a ready sense of humour.'

Silveri and Comdt. O'Kelly got on well from the beginning and provided the baritone was approached the right way he usually agreed to a request for a newspaper interview or an appearance at a charity function. O'Kelly however would in no way have him exploited. This held true in the case of all his guest artists. And he was the first to admit that Silveri was one of the biggest stars, if not the biggest, that the society had engaged, and he made no secret of his unbounded admiration for his *Rigoletto*.

It was nine years since Silveri had made his debut in the role. It was a day he was never to forget. 'I became spellbound by the tragic jester,' he was to say later. 'Since then I have played it countless times and each time I put on the make-up and the costume I am filled with the same indescribable emotion. For Rigoletto experiences all human emotions: love, tenderness, sorrow, hate, revenge and all of these must be expressed by the voice.'

For a big man he could move with agility on stage and make the most of a dramatic situation. 'He was a superb actor,' recalls Charlie Dunphy, who sang in the chorus of the Gaiety production. 'Watching him perform was a riveting experience. You tended to watch no one else on stage when he was singing the part,' said Jeannie Reddin. 'He had this hypnotic effect on one.'

It was a reunion in Dublin for Silveri. He was delighted to be singing with Alvinio Misciano who had made such good progress since their days together in the Italian army. He felt the role of the Duke of Mantua was ideal for his tenor voice and personality. During the previous nine years his Dukes included Richard Tucker, Jussi Bjorling and Giuseppe di Stefano. It was an excellent reflection on the musicianship of Lieut.-Col. J M Doyle that he was chosen to conduct these *Rigoletto* performances and the critics were to praise his handling of the wonderful Verdi score.

Predictably, the night belonged to Signor Silveri. The *Evening Herald* caught the mood in its introduction: 'The cheers which greeted the performers at the final curtain on Saturday night were thoroughly deserved, as the work was presented with great verve and ability. Paolo Silveri is a great baritone and a great Rigoletto. Here was no mouthing idiot but a clever jester, ruthless and cunning, who knew how to please his master. The grand, rich voice rose to heights of intensity in the dramatic scenes, never losing its ringing tone, and then almost cooing in the tender passages with his luckless daughter Gilda.'

'Silveri's was a triumph of operatic artistry', observed Joseph O'Neill *(Independent)*. It was noticeable that the rest of the cast fared well, notably Plinio Clabassi as Sparafucile, Erina Valli (Gilda) and Alvinio Misciano. Around this time Brendan Cavanagh was displaying flair and musicianship in small parts and his acting was always convincing. Joseph Flood, another Irish singer of talent, was Marullo, and the Italian mezzo Gianella Borelli sang Maddalena.

Norris Davidson had witnessed the performance from a seat at the back of the dress circle and believed it was another milestone in the comparatively short history of the society. He had already greatly enjoyed singers like Joan Hammond, Otakar Kraus, Franz Vroons and the German artists, but Silveri's Rigoletto in his view was different. Irish audiences were hearing a performance that could have graced any stage in the world; it was Italian singing at its best. 'I'm sure it was what Verdi himself had in mind, an almost perfect combination of singing and acting. I remember I was moved and I couldn't say that was always my reaction to opera houses.'

The year ended successfully for the society. It marked the welcome return of the Hamburg State Opera and their great director Gunther Rennert. 'He was a genius in the use of curtains and back-clothes to create atmosphere,' remarked one morning newspaper critic, although he found the German staging of Mozart's *Don Giovanni* perhaps too sombre. For example, James Pease, as the Don, wore a dark, almost black costume, that gave him an unnecessary aura of evil. But Pease acted and sang extremely well and in Toni Blankenhein (Leporello) he had a splendid partner.

It was the third visit by the company in five years and in musical circles this was considered unusual, for it was generally thought they would not be coming to Ireland so soon after their previous visits. Essentially the company's aim was to foster both educational and cultural links between the countries and it was also seen as a tribute to the warmth of the Irish people.

The production of Mozart's *Il Seraglio* was critically acclaimed, with a notable performance by Theo Hermann as Osmin, the keeper of the palace and harem. His big, rich bass voice and flair for comedy made him the star of the evening though Annaliese Rothenberger, as Constance's maid, was close behind. The *Evening Mail* commented, 'The only flaw in the work was that the opera, which has long stretches of spoken dialogue, was performed in German and the audience missed many of the points of the conversational passages.'

The society was presenting Smetana's *The Bartered Bride* for the first time and though it was an unknown work in Dublin, it opened the season. The storyline centres around a Czech village romance and Smetana's music is irresistible with lively dance rhythms and catchy melodies. The *Herald* critic, John Finegan, felt the spoken dialogue was a blessing, in that it helped to make an unfamiliar plot easy to understand. His one main criticism centred on the large chorus of seventy which though singing admirably, tended to crowd the stage so that movement was lethargic and grouping difficult.

The opera, it seems, was well cast with Irish soprano Dolores Burke and Welsh tenor Rowland Jones convincing lovers. I liked one critic's final paragraph, 'The settings are irreproachable, the Czech atmosphere unmistakable. All hail to the unrecorded designer!' In the *Irish Press*, Robert Johnston was somewhat sceptical about the opera, expressing doubt that it would achieve any lasting measure of success in Dublin in the long-term.

New guest artists came and went, not all of them making the required impression. There were, however, quite a few exceptions. A young Maltese tenor, Oreste Kirkop, who resembled the early Mario Lanza, sang well as Rodolfo and showed decided promise as a Puccini singer. His acting also caught the eye. The more experienced Constance Shacklock was back that season to sing an impassioned Carmen partnered by Franz Vroons as Don José. 'Miss Shacklock has added to her portrayal,' commented J J Finegan, 'several touches since we last saw her, touches that further emphasise the earthiness - call it vulgarity, if you like - of the fascinating gypsy. She clawed, she violently threw things about. Then in the last act, in the face of death, the actress splendidly brought out the courage of Carmen.'

Comdt. O'Kelly, meanwhile, continued to try to recruit Supers, or those prepared to carry spears, be slaves or soldiers or revolutionary rabble, and not be asked to sing a word. As these were seen as thankless 'roles' it wasn't at all easy to find recruits. However, a young civil servant Tony O'Dalaigh, who had arrived in the city from his native Co. Cork in 1951, answered O'Kelly's call and joined the ranks of the 'Supers'.

'I was thrilled to be one of them and be on the stage with international stars,' he recalls, 'and it didn't worry me that I hadn't to sing. Walking across the stage in *Trovatore* or *Aida* seemed not only fun but a privilege. We carried out the director's instructions as best we could but there could be problems, as when Supers failed to turn up and one's friends had to step in and try to follow instructions. Sometimes the numbers were reduced if we couldn't get enough Supers.

O'Dalaigh concluded there was little real production as we know it today and, instead, improvisation was the name of the game. He was once amused when a director tried to persuade a soprano, singing Tosca, to make her entry from a certain side of the stage. She protested that she had never entered from there before. In his own case, he was delighted to be getting valuable insights into opera. Sometimes he and the other young Supers went up into the 'flies' to watch scenes and climbed down when their own turn came to go on stage. It was exciting and there was some glamour and mystery about it all. As a theatre lover, he found the dramatic side of opera very stimulating and in time he would come to appreciate the music. It was a time of mass opera-going when queues formed to snap up tickets, particularly when it was announced that Silveri or other stars were in the casts.

'The whole thing grew on me,' he says. 'We talked about performances and the performers with real enthusiasm and opera opened up a marvellous new world for me. I had come from a small place in the country and you can imagine my feelings as I mixed with these foreign stars.'

Everything indicated that the year 1954 would be just as rewarding as any of the previous seasons. The society was able to announce that Paolo Silveri was returning to sing the elder Germont in *Traviata* and also Scarpia in *Tosca*, one of his greatest operatic roles. Furthermore, he would alternate in the part with the outstanding Tito Gobbi who was making his Dublin debut. It caused a stir, too, that Rina Gigli, daughter of the great Beniamino, was to sing the title role in *Madama Butterfly*.

Music lovers had an additional treat when Gigli himself came to Dublin in April `53 to sing in a matinee recital at the Theatre Royal, which in those years was being described as 'that marvellous palace of entertainment.' Predictably, the renowned tenor played to a capacity house and did not spare himself, singing fourteen songs in the programme and an incredible thirteen encores. For the occasion, the management had put in one hundred and twenty extra seats on the stage.

It was hoped that the tenor would return that May to partner his daughter in *Madama Butterfly*, but alas engagements did not permit the unique partnership. There was as expected unusual interest in her debut at the Gaiety and the theatre was packed on opening night, May 4. Her performance was well received, though not ecstatically. Oldtimers I talked to told me they found her voice lacking in volume and in the act one love duet failed to match James Johnston's ringing high notes. She sang the part in Italian while the rest of the cast and chorus sang the opera in English.

Everyone agreed though that Signorina Gigli was a first-class actress and conveyed both the joy and agony of the part. As the *Evening Mail* critic put it, 'If the rapture of the love duet eluded her she managed to convey in full measure the dramatic aspects of the role, and the death scene was most moving.

The soprano's Violetta appeared to make a better impression and in her scenes with Paolo Silveri, she sang most expressively. At the time the baritone was a friend of her father's and he welcomed the opportunity to sing with his daughter. 'I have happy memories of *Traviata* and I liked very much Rina's performance,' he told me. 'I think she enjoyed Dublin and the Irish audience.'

Tito Gobbi was at the peak of his career when he arrived to sing Scarpia. A superb singing-actor, he had by now under his belt more than thirty principal roles - he would eventually top the hundred mark. He was known to devote a lot of study to a new role and admitted that before he sang his first Macbeth in Italy he spent a long time thinking about the make-up he would use. In the case of Scarpia, it was the same approach, down to the exact kind of costume he would wear.

'One reason why I love *Tosca*,' he said, 'is that it becomes a new opera with every change of the name part. I have had the privilege of partnering some of the finest Toscas in the world, and every one was subtly and fascinatingly different.'

He first sang Scapria in his early twenties in Rome. He reckoned the character was a man in his forties but when someone told him that in the part he walked like a man in his twenties he became upset. Irish audiences had heard about Gobbi's successes and packed the Gaiety for the first night. It was a gala occasion graced by the President of Ireland, Seán T O'Kelly and his wife. Apart from Gobbi, the cast included Alvinio Misciano as Cavaradossi and the soprano Maria Boi in the title role. Giuseppe Morelli was the conductor.

The papers the next morning concentrated almost exclusively on Gobbi's portrayal of the evil chief of police. One critic found it 'too overpowering, especially the act two confrontation between Scarpia and Floria Tosca,' and added, 'This was extraordinarily vivid acting, supported by a wealth of glorious singing.'

Independent Newspapers had a fine tradition for producing excellent music critics and Mary MacGoris was soon to display an exemplary eye for musical and dramatic detail, and from the middle 1950s onwards she became the most important voice on the newspaper scene. Summing up that season's *Tosca*, she noted, 'It was the powerfully controlled voice of Tito Gobbi - a voice that easily rode over the trombones at the end of act one - that struck me most forcibly. It was used subtly to suit every turn of the dramatic situation and the singer invested Scarpia with a blatant evil which made credible the chief of police before whom all Rome trembled - "Tutte Roma Tremava".

Paolo Silveri's portrayal of the part - he sang one performance, on May 19 - was no less riveting. In conversation, he reminded me that it was one of the roles that set him on the road to fame. From the outset, he was totally conquered by it, fascinated by the character's sinister, twisted and malevolent nature, comprising love, hate, treachery and contempt which vied with a conflicting intellect.

Scarpia's personality was, he told himself, the very opposite of his own, so for that reason he felt it made the role psychologically difficult for him to portray but in time he mastered it. Operagoers in Dublin were divided about his and Gobbi's interpretations and some oldtimers told me they had attended both performances. 'I adored Silveri's Scarpia - if that's the right way to put it,' Jeannie Reddin assured me. 'I do believe it was the definitive portrayal.' Chorus members, who sang in both performances, told me that if Gobbi's portrayal was more subtle perhaps, Silveri's was better sung.

Aileen Walsh was still convinced that neither of their portrayals equalled that of the Czech baritone Otakar Kraus whom she regarded as 'frightening' in the part. 'I'll never forget the way he stalked Tosca in act two, and the evil in his eyes.' Veronica Dunne was inclined to agree with Miss Walsh about the merits of Kraus's Scarpia without however passing judgment on either Gobbi or Silveri.

Verdi's *Force of Destiny* was a particular favourite of Comdt. Bill O'Kelly's and in that season he knew the society had a cast to do it full justice. Maestro Botti had been able to engage the brilliant dramatic soprano Caterina Mancini to sing the role of Leonora and she was to make a resounding impression. It is a performance that Tony O'Dalaigh vividly remembers for its magnificent singing. 'The society was bringing some great singers to Dublin at this time and the word went round that they had to be seen, so naturally the queues formed in South King Street.'

The society which sometimes was accused of being too conservative in its choice of operas, surprised music lovers in that season by staging the first performance in Ireland of *Cecilia*, a new opera by Mgr. Licinio Refice who arrived in Dublin to conduct it. The opera tells the dramatic story of Saint Cecilia, patroness of music, who was martyred for the Faith. The DGOS chorus was augmented by the Dublin Cecilian Singers. Plinio Clabassi made the biggest impact as Bishop Urbane and was in brilliant voice.

The work received a polite reception with one evening newspaper reviewer remarking, 'I am sure further performances will see an improvement on the first night when the orchestra by its volume of sound tended to drown out most of the singers.'

The season had featured six operas and some star-studded casts. Taken against the exorbitant costs of presenting opera today, the DGOS certainly struck a bargain in those days with the Maestro Botti Agency in Rome. The society got the complete package for the equivalent of £6,000, though they had to meet the artists' air fares. In turn, Botti was paid a subvention by the Italian government for the purpose of paying the Italian singers, conductors and producers. It is hard to see how the deal could have been bettered and the DGOS could consider itself most fortunate. Presumably fees paid to artists greatly differed according to their reputations; for instance, Signors Silveri and Gobbi would have received far more than, say, Alvinio Misciano and Rina Gigli, though I expect that singers like Plinio Clabassi and Caterina Mancini ensured the journey to Dublin was well worth their while financially.

The `54 winter season was notable for the return of the Munich State Opera with *Fidelio* and *Hansel und Gretel* as well as artists from Sadler's Wells, Glyndebourne and Covent Garden. Among them were Amy Shuard, Patricia Johnson, Olwen Price, Paul Asciak and William Edwards. There was a bright opening to the season with a well-produced *Bohème* by Harry Powell-Lloyd and Veronica Dunne was back once more in her favourite role of Mimi. She was partnered by the English tenor Walter Midgley as Rodolfo and the Welsh baritone Roderick Jones was Marcello. And there was a glamorous Musetta, Betty Fretwell, who displayed a voice of excellent quality.

'For Veronica Dunne it was a most successful evening,' commented the *Evening Herald*. 'As Mimi she sang with exquisite ease, and inflected the part with much feeling.'

The history of Vincenzo Bellini's *Norma* is peculiar. A disaster on its opening night at La Scala in December 1831, it redeemed itself at the second performance when it won critical acclaim and proceeded to become an international success, particularly with Covent Garden audiences who 'raved' about Malibran in the title role. When the DGOS staged it for the first time at its spring season of 1955, it aroused surprising enthusiasm for a little known work, this being mainly due to the stellar cast headed by Caterina Mancini (Norma) and Ebe Stignani (Adalgisa).

'A wonderful night,' recalled Aileen Walsh, who sang in the chorus. 'And whenever I hear the opera mentioned I hear again Mancini and Stignani in the duet "O Mira Norma". I remember they sang amid total silence, followed by a spontaneous outburst of applause. They were fabulous together. Stignani was an extraordinary artist, for when she sang for us in `52 she was over fifty years of age, yet if you closed your eyes you'd think it was the voice of a twenty-five year old woman. Seemingly she was married to a wealthy businessman, so was able to choose her engagements and take care of her voice.'

In her opinion, Dublin hadn't heard voices like these up to then singing opera in Italian; they were big, opulent voices that were artistically used and in this respect Mancini's was exemplary. There was beauty in her soft singing as well as in her dramatic outpourings. That `55 production would be remembered as one of the highlights of the decade. Other choristers like Florrie Draper, Maura Mooney and Monica Condron endorsed Aileen Walsh's viewpoint, attributing its success also to the over-all balanced cast and Alberto Erede's superb conducting of the Radio Éireann Symphony Orchestra.

Were it not, however, for Bellini's glorious music, the plot itself might be considered off-putting by more sensitive opera buffs. It concerns Norma, the High Priestess of the Druids at the time of the Roman occupation of Gaul. She had forsaken her vows and secretly married Pollione, the Pro-Roman Consul, who however is now in love with Adalgisa, another priestess of the temple. Angry at discovering Pollione's faithlessness, Norma declares war against the Roman invader. The climax is as harrowing as anything in opera as Norma and Pollione are re-united in death.

The opera, by all accounts, was intelligently staged and directed by Elizabeth Woehr, with impressive sets and costumes. The *Irish Independent's* heading, BEAUTIFUL MUSIC IN THE HEROIC STYLE, emphasised the vocal dynamics, remarking, 'It is not difficult to understand why Bellini's opera is not very often performed when one considers the standard of singing required. The performance given by the DGOS gave us singing in the heroic mould, and while Caterina Mancini deployed all her artistry to the role of Norma, the most magnificent singing of all came from the famous contralto Ebe Stignani. The sheer beauty of this smooth and radiantly youthful voice was enhanced by effortless musicianship.'

In that spring season the distinguished soprano Maria Caniglia was making her DGOS debut and as one of Gigli's notable operatic partners, the more knowledgeable were looking forward greatly to her performances as Floria Tosca, a role in which she was by now world renowned. Her Cavaradossi was the American tenor Giovanni Millo, a plump figure, but so too was Signorina Caniglia. While she did not disappoint either vocally or dramatically, there was one amusing episode that had some of the audience tittering. It occurred as Cavaradossi is brought back from the Scarpia's torture chamber, his white shirt bloodstained, and as Tosca proceeds to take him in her arms and they stagger over to a couch - the venerable old one used in countless productions - and plonk down on the seat, one of the legs gives way under their combined weight and they roll gently onto the floor. But as one chorister told me, 'Fair dues to them both, they kept singing as though nothing had happened, but it did rather spoil the drama.'

Veronica Dunne figured prominently in the winter season of `55. She was perhaps unfortunate to be singing Marguerite in what was described as a visually unattractive staging of *Faust*. As one critic put it, 'Marguerite's garden was more like a churchyard than a private residence's approach and the church interior was as bare and forbidding as a prison cell.' A colleague was equally unimpressed: 'Siebel's bouquet was composed of nondescript blooms; the garden did not boast of even a blade of grass, and the whole opera was played in a dull light which lowered to dimness on any whim and cast unbecoming shadows on the singers.'

In view of their melancholy surroundings the principals could hardly be blamed if they failed to give of their best, added another critic. Indeed, the reviews were mixed, only Michael Langdon as Mephistopheles winning full approval for his singing and powerful acting; Brychan Powell's Faust was described as colourful and over-cautious, while William Edward's Valentine fared no better. The women Veronica Dunne (Marguerite) and Celine

Murphy (Siebel) did noticeably better without making a big impression. Strangely, more than one reviewer remarked on the lack of volume in Miss Dunne's voice; up to this it had seemed fully adequate in the Gaiety Theatre.

She was to make a much better impression as Nedda in Pagliacci and received excellent notices. 'The pathetic Nedda was sung with touching sincerity by Veronica Dunne,' stated the *Evening Herald* critic, 'and she acted with great effect in the closing scenes - a considerable test for a soprano's dramatic powers.' The Italian tenor Antonio Annaloro sang the role of Canio in his native tongue and was said to have brought tremendous feeling to "Vesti la giubba", described as one of the highspots of the evening.

For one night only, Saturday, November 26, *Pagliacci* was performed before *Cavalleria Rusticana*, mainly to give the clown Tonio the opportunity to ring up the curtain on the refurbished Gaiety itself, where the pit had been extended and the famous 'gods' gallery taken away. There was enthusiastic applause from the capacity audience when baritone William Dickie in conventional evening dress came before the curtain to sing the Prologue. Choristers like Aileen Walsh and Maura Mooney remember there was a real buzz in the theatre and the magnificent singing by English soprano Amy Shuard as the unhappy Santuzza invested *Cavalleria Rusticana* with considerable drama and passion.

Miss Shuard's portrayal of Butterfly was also greatly admired that season. Summed up one critic: 'The soprano did justice to this great role. Her voice, rich and sensitive, has both power and pathos, and her acting throughout had that clear suggestion of the tragic that can lift Butterfly from the category of the sentimental schoolgirl into the realm of 'noble womanhood'.

The year had a most successful climax for Veronica Dunne. In Powell Lloyd's production of *La Bohème* she excelled as Mimi, undoubtedly the best role in her repertoire. She had already sung it at Covent Garden in the presence of Margaret Burke Sheridan, who had given her some friendly 'tips' on how to approach the part. Her Rodolfo in Dublin in the winter of `55 was the English tenor Charles Craig who was highly rated. Miss Dunne counts him as among her finest Rodolfos. 'I've no doubt about this,' she told me. 'Charles had a magnificent tenor voice and I had to work hard to match him in the big love duet in act one.'

It was a strong all-round cast, with Peter Glossop playing Schaunard and Ronald Lewis as Marcel. The conductor was Bryan Balkwill. Veronica Dunne was now married to the Dublin businessman Peter McCarthy and she admits that with her young family, commuting to London and elsewhere wasn't easy.

Escape from Bucharest

When the raven-haired Virginia Zeani arrived in Dublin for the first time in April 1955 she was twenty-six, shapely and a striking young woman. DGOS choristers remember her as exceptionally attractive, intelligent and having a bright personality. When I talked about those years with Paolo Silveri in Rome in the nineties, he had no hesitation in pin-pointing his first meeting with Zeani. It was in November 1954 in Sicily, at the Teatro Bellini in Catania. She was singing Violetta in *Traviata* and he was the elder Germont.

'I was immediately struck by her beautiful looks,' he said, 'and by her vivid and moving interpretation of Violetta. I was satisfied she had a great career before her.'

Virginia was Romanian, born in the village of Solovastru in the year 1928. At the tender age of four she discovered she could sing and regarded singing as natural as washing her teeth. When her parents, who were not well off, asked her to do errands she sang the requests. At the age of seven she was brought by them to an elementary school in Bucharest and in subsequent years her cousin began to take her to the opera. *Madama Butterfly* proved a turning point for her.

'I was hearing the opera for the first time and at the final curtain I was inexpressibly moved and cried and cried to myself. When I went home I said to my mother, "I am going to be an opera singer, it's the only music I ever want to sing Mum, because I adore it." I had this ambition inside of me and it overshadowed everything else, even my academic studies. My mother listened to me but did not try to discourage me. I am sure she felt I already knew what I wanted to be in life.'

She was thirteen when she began vocal studies in Bucharest with the Romanian singer Lucia Anghel who coached her as a mezzo-soprano for the next two years. After that she went to the famous Russian-born soprano Lydia Lipkovska, a bel canto specialist who had sung with world artists, including Titto Ruffo. Virginia felt fortunate to have got this opportunity, and by the age of nineteen she was singing soprano. It was Miss Lipkovska who advised her to try to pursue a career outside the country, but Romania being Communist it was not an easy course to take. Fortunately, she says, she had a friend - a secretary in the Italian Consulate - and she secretly promised to help her escape. She remembers it was a tense and unnerving time for her as she waited with friends who were also getting out. The worst moment was bidding farewell to her weeping parents - she was their only child - and leaving the house with only a small suitcase. Eventually she made her way to Milan armed with names and addresses of people she was told to contact. She was assured that the city was the music capital of the world. She was by now nearly twenty and determined to make the most of her opportunity. There was no shortage of outstanding voice teachers and she sought advice about the most suitable one for her. The name of Aureliano Pertile, the preferred tenor of Toscanini's era, was suggested and she was fortunate enough to be taken on by him.

'I was so happy at this time of my life,' she recalls. 'Here I was with a great teacher and I loved everything about Italy, the climate, the people's love of singing and the warmth of the people themselves. I remember, too, how excited I was when I made my debut as Violetta in Bologna and went on later to sing Lucia, Gilda, Mimi and Adina in *L'Elisir d'Amore*. I felt so much improvement in my voice, thanks to Signor Pertile's gifts as a coach.'

When she was singing Violetta in Rome she was contacted by Maestro Botti who offered her roles in Dublin and she accepted without undue hesitation because of the singers in the casts, among them Paolo Silveri and the tenor Antonio Galie. Although the fees were only moderate, she was singing leading roles and this was important for an inexperienced young soprano like herself. 'I was anxious to learn and become a better actor. I could not do this without constant work in the opera house.'

The Dublin of the fifties, with its leisurely pace and friendliness, appealed to her instantly and soon she felt she had joined one big family of singers, conductors, producers and chorus. She was fascinated by the dedication and enthusiasm of the amateur chorus members, something she had not experienced before. Maestro Botti introduced her to Comdt. Bill O'Kelly who expressed the hope that her stay in the city would be very happy. 'I remember him as a small, stout man, friendly, and very involved with everything about the opera. He said he had heard very good reports about my Violetta in Italy.'

It was, however, the role of Mimi that she was singing in the spring season of `56 with Paolo Silveri as Marcello and Antonio Galie as Rodolfo. She was described by one critic as probably the most attractive Mimi ever to appear on the Gaiety stage, and added, 'Miss Zeani invests the little seamstress with character and spirit; she moves and acts beautifully, but her voice though strong is inexpressive and not very well controlled.' The majority of the critics though preferred her as Manon in Massenet's opera where she was partnered by the excellent tenor Alvinio Misciano. Commented Mary McGoris (*Independent*), 'Virginia Zeani builds up the part from the start to such purpose that we are quite prepared to shed tears at her untimely end.'

NIGHT OF WONDERFUL SINGING proclaimed the heading in the *Evening Herald*, with its critic stating, 'Virginia Zeani gave lustre to the performance as Manon. In her superbly controlled singing - colourful, dramatic and full of fervour - she brought the part fully to life.'

The soprano had already caused a stir and she was quickly becoming the darling of Gaiety audiences. Her biggest moment arrived when she sang in *Traviata*, the last production of the season. Margaret Burke Sheridan was back in her favourite box after an absence of some months, and it was soon evident that she adored Virginia Zeani in the role of Violetta. As the young soprano took her bow at the end of the first act the diva rose and applauded her, raising her voice at the same time to shout 'Brava!' And at the final curtain she went on stage to present her with the fan that she herself had received from the renowned Nelli Melba years before at Covent Garden. It was a poignant moment for everyone on stage, and there was silence when Miss Sheridan said, 'I never heard anybody that I wanted to give the fan to before, but this girl has so many qualities - temperament, voice, acting ability.'

They shared at least one thing in common - both were friends of Aureliano Pertile. He had partnered Miss Sheridan in some of her best recordings - in particular the act one love duet from *Madama Butterfly* - and was then coaching Miss Zeani to sing new roles. In conversation with the soprano, she counts the Burke-Sheridan gesture as among the most unforgettable of her career. 'When I had earlier told Signor Pertile that I was to sing in Dublin, he reminded me of Margaret Burke Sheridan and their engagements together. I felt I knew this elegant woman before I set out for Ireland.'

That spring season was also notable for the deep impression made by the American soprano Gianna d'Angelo. Like Virginia, she too was young and beautiful with a voice of gold. Born in Hartford, Connecticut in November 1934, she was Juilliard-trained, completing her studies in Italy with Giuseppe de Luca and Toti dal Monte. Eager to gain experience, she jumped at the invitation by Maestro Botti to come to Ireland. Everyone agreed in the DGOS that she was stunning in appearance, slender and delectable. 'Yes, every male chorister from twenty to forty was secretly in love with her,' mused one young chorus member. 'And she had youth and charm to back it up.' To Maura Mooney, she made a big impression at rehearsals. 'Gianna had this lovely coloratura voice that you could listen to all day. It was silver in texture and magical in the ears.' Florrie Draper said it was a period when the society was beginning to engage women who looked like film stars. 'I mean, Zeani and d'Angelo could have stepped on any Hollywood film set. They certainly brought colour to the scene and I think audiences appreciated it, and didn't it give the men something to admire, too? It was not long before d'Angelo had the audience in the palm of her hands. Her exquisite Gilda, opposite Silveri's Rigoletto, was acclaimed, especially the way she used her agile voice in "Caro Nome"'. 'Here was really beautiful soprano colorature singing,' commented the *Irish Times*. 'This was the peak of her performance.'

Paolo Silveri has told me that the soprano was probably the youngest Gilda he sang with and he does remember vividly those performances in Dublin of that May of `55. It was, however, her Lucia in Donizetti's opera that sent the Gaiety audiences into raptures. To Florrie Draper, d'Angelo's Mad Scene was mesmerising, while Aileen Walsh remembered that she moved gracefully on stage and sang like a thrush. Monica Condron can still vividly recall the soprano's youthful, even fragile look, and the purity of her voice. 'The audience really took her to their hearts and at this time she was being greeted with real enthusiasm. I think her age had something to do with it, as well as her appearance.'

During the run of *Lucia,* Gianna d'Angelo confided in Florrie Draper, who was by now in the society's wardrobe department, that her father was dying in America and she was worried. But she surprised Miss Draper by asking her that if a telegram arrived for her before the first night of *Lucia* not to tell her about it. She regarded it as an unusual request but understandable perhaps in the circumstances. Later, a telegram did duly arrive stating that her father was dying. 'I advised her to take but one curtain call and that I'd have a taxi standing by to take her to the airport as quickly as possible. I had her clothes ready and packed. It worked like a dream for her. Gianna was at her father's bedside when he eventually died.'

In the case of the Italians, Caterina Mancini and Ebe Stignani, it was the quality of their voices that enthralled audiences. They produced a big sound that filled the Gaiety, yet such was their superb technique that they combined flexibility with tonal colour and dramatic conviction. Together in that season's *Il Trovatore* they caused a virtual sensation, with Stignani's Azucena - the old gipsy woman obsessed with revenge - really raising the temperature. 'I don't wish to hear the opera better sung,' recalled Tony O'Dalaigh, an avid admirer of the singers. He also thought that Mancini's Leonora went right to the heart with the soprano displaying consummate artistry. It was considered a memorable *Trovatore,* conducted with authority by Giuseppe Morelli, a deft hand at inspiring an orchestra. Paolo Silveri had sung with both Stignani and Mancini in Italy and considered them natural Verdian singers. As he said, 'They sing the music as Verdi wrote it and sing it magnificently.'

Renato in *Un Ballo and Maschera* was one of the baritone's most celebrated roles and in Dublin he sang it opposite Mancini's Amelia. This was, from all accounts, another compelling Verdi occasion, enhanced by the fine performance of Antonio Galie as Riccardo. Oldtimers, while admiring the tenor's well-focused tenor voice, thought he played 'a little to the gallery' but they didn't hold that against him. As one of them told me, 'Make no mistake, Galie had all the notes and could act a bit too.'

The season, despite the excitement generated by nearly all of the productions, was clouded by the unexpected death of Antonio Manca Serra, one of Italy's leading baritones. On his arrival in Dublin he appeared in good spirits but later in the day he complained of feeling unwell and some hours later died of a heart attack in his hotel room. Aged thirty-three, he had built up a growing reputation in Italian opera houses. He had first sung at the Gaiety Theatre two years previously in *Lucia di Lammermoor* and *La Traviata*.

To Paolo Silveri, in particular, it was a big shock as he knew him and had followed his career with interest. 'Antonio had a grand voice and a big future,' he recalled. He himself was one of the Italian artists who sang at the Requiem Mass for the deceased baritone in the Franciscan Church, Merchants' Quay. In fact, he sang a requiem of his own composition and tenor Antonio Galie sang "Ingemisco" from Verdi's *Requiem*. The organist was Maestro Morelli.

There was a shock in store for the audience at the last performance that season of *Rigoletto*. At the final curtain, amid thunderous applause, Paolo Silveri, who had sung the hunchbacked jester, smiled and in typical fashion blew kisses to the audience. Eventually he began to speak and in a wavering voice announced sadly that this was the last time he would appear on stage in an opera, that his career had ended. He could not explain, he said what had induced his decision, though he promised that if one day he should change his mind and return to the stage, it would be to the Gaiety Theatre. The audience reacted quickly. They began to applaud and it went on for a long time. Waving for the last time, he walked alone from the stage.

He admitted later he had felt exhausted after the performance of *Rigoletto*, utterly spent. Maureen Lemass, a patron of the society, was sitting beside her mother Lucy, and both were ardent admirers of Silveri and they like everyone else had been caught up in the excitement of the occasion. They did distinctly remember, however, that the baritone cracked on a note halfway through the performance and seemed for a moment in some distress but carried on to finish the opera. None of the audience appeared to notice it happen, or if they did, ignored it.

'Paolo Silveri looked distraught to me at the final curtain,' says Maureen Lemass. 'Listening to his words almost made me cry. People around me were visibly moved and obviously shocked by his unexpected announcement. Turning to my mother, I said 'I hope he changes his mind soon.'

John Allen had joined the DGOS as a Super two years before and would shortly graduate to the chorus in the tenor section. He considered Silveri's a superb portrait of the jester, but it struck him around this time that a pronounced wobble had come into his voice on sustained notes and he wondered if he was coming to the end of his career. Yet it was ironical that the critic Mary MacGoris in her review of Silveri's Rigoletto earlier that season commented that he gave a magnificent performance, histrionically convincing, artistic and deeply moving, vocally noble and expressive. His interpretation throughout was faultless and his singing ranged widely in colour from the rage and wild pleading of "Cortigiani" to moving tenderness in the duet "Piangi."

In my discussions with the singer at his villa in Rome, I asked him more than once what prompted him to announce his retirement on that May evening and he was inclined to put it down to exhaustion. 'I just felt very, very tired.'

If the spring season tended to be regarded by now as the glamour one, Lt.-Col. O'Kelly and his colleagues ensured there were also ample gems to satisfy fans in the winter season. In that `56 season the society was presenting Verdi's *Simon Boccanegra* for the first time and O'Kelly had asked James Johnston if it was possible to get Charles Mackerras to conduct. The Australian-born conductor, who had just turned thirty, enjoyed a growing reputation and later intimated he would like to come to Dublin if he could fit in performances between his concert dates. Eventually a schedule was worked out, opening the way for his debut with the society.

O'Kelly had attended the British premiere of the Verdi work at Sadler's Wells in October 1948 and was impressed not only by the splendour of the music but the outstanding performance by James Johnston as Gabriele Adorno; indeed, the cast for Dublin mainly consisted of Sadler's Wells artists, with Roderick Jones singing the title role, long considered to be one of the composer's finest character creations. Amelia, the woman in love with Adorno, was being sung by Victoria Elliott, another 'Wells' favourite, and the excellent Howell Glynn was cast as Fiesco. The setting is Genoa in the fourteenth century and not unlike other Verdi operas, was revised and in this case the magnificent scene in the council chamber was added. Because of its sombre nature, the premiere in Venice in March 1857 was not an unqualified success and the opera has taken some time to achieve universal popularity. It has helped that some of the greatest baritones have taken the noble role of Boccanegra into their repertoires.

The Dublin production of that year was, according to the critics, well-balanced and distinguished by some impressive singing, and although the Gaiety was not entirely full it was well supported. James Johnston repeated his Sadler's Wells success as Gabriele Adorno and in Victoria Elliott he had a convincing partner, while Roderick Jones's study of the complex Boccanegra possessed considerable depth and his secure, resonant baritone coped well with the great climaxes.

When I contacted Sir Charles Mackerras in the late spring of 1998, he had just returned from the Metropolitan, New York, where he had been successfully conducting Janacek's *The Makropoulos Case* - he is an acknowledged expert on the composer's work - and he was already looking forward to conducting *The Marriage of Figaro* at the Salzburg Festival that summer. For a man of seventy-three, he is sprightly and retains his energy and enthusiasm. He remembered, of course, his first engagement with the DGOS, though strangely he had no particular memories of *Simon Boccanegra*.

He confirmed it was James Johnston who had recommended him to Bill O'Kelly. British singers, he knew, liked coming to Dublin and the DGOS had a good name. 'I soon found out that the atmosphere was informal, and there was a marvellous pub which served superb draft Guinness, which was approachable through a back door, so that performers very frequently used to drink in the back bar of the pub in costume.'

To Mackerras, the singers in the chorus varied a great deal in talent and in punctuality and attendance. It was certainly true that the dress rehearsals and performances used to have double, if not more, numbers than they had rehearsals, and consequently principal singers found themselves at the performances suddenly having to push through vast numbers of chorus members which at the rehearsals had not been a problem.

The Radio Éireann Symphony Orchestra tended at the outset to fascinate him. 'I remember at the time it was quite good, although very variable. It did not have a homogenous style because so many of the players were of different foreign origin. For example, the four horns led by a Frenchman were all of different nationalities and all played in different styles. There were very few Irish in the orchestra and I think that it mostly was made up of older Italians, Germans, French and Slavonic players.'

Recalling his working relationship with Bill O'Kelly, he felt he could be difficult at times but he was also immensely appreciative of good performances and good singing. 'I would say that as an opera entrepreneur he did an excellent job under difficult circumstances, and that all in all his heart was in the right place.'

The Carney twins, John and Tom, joined the chorus in `56 and would go on to make a significant contribution to the society's work. 'I had no idea how much time it would take up,' recalls John Carney. 'In fact, I didn't see it as a question of personal sacrifice - I was smitten by the whole experience, theatrical as well as musical.' His brother Tom's immediate reaction was one of fright. 'We were more or less thrown in at the deep end as my first opera was *Idomeneo*, sung in German by a cast from Essen. We were also in *Carmen* and *Boccanegra* that winter season. I can still hear Jimmy Johnston's tenor voice soar over the orchestra in *Boccanegra* and I wondered if he realised how good he was at the time.'

To John Carney, Johnston could be very helpful to the chorus. 'I remember we were rehearsing *Boccanegra* and in the big council scene there are two factions and they ended up having a hoist on stage. We were rather timidly making shapes to fight when Jimmy turned to us and declared, "Will ye for God's sake fight lads!"'

And Tom Carney recalled also an incident in the same scene of the opera as the plebeians and the patricians sing angrily across the council chamber at each other, with Boccanegra finally pleading for peace between them. 'The rehearsal at this point was going badly and we couldn't get the musical timing right and conductor Charles Mackerras seemed to be getting frustrated. Worse, the musicians in the pit were doing crosswords and throwing paper aeroplanes. Mackerras put down his baton and said to them, "Gentlemen, those people up there have no music, you have music before you, just take it easy."'

The brothers' impressions of Bill O'Kelly were favourable and he was among the first to extend a warm welcome to them. To John Carney, he was an extremely good manager of people and as a result the atmosphere in the chorus was harmonious. Both of them had enjoyed themselves in that first season and pledged to carry on.

Dympna Bugler joined the chorus on the same day as John and Tom Carney. She sang in the church choir in Rathfarnham and one day met Paddy Diffney, who was a member of the DGOS chorus, and he told her they were urgently in need of new members. 'Paddy asked me to join and I agreed, and since I knew John and Tom Carney I asked them to come along with me. I remember saying to myself after the first rehearsal, "Gosh, this is going to be exciting." Seeing Julia Gray in bare legs in the middle of winter and a fag in the side of her mouth was something, but could she play the piano! - she could make it sing, and what a good chorus mistress she was.'

Dympna was working at the time in an insurance office and with rehearsals taking up more and more of her time she had little time for a social life outside of opera. She was impressed by the calibre of the women in the chorus, especially Monica Condron, Kitty Vaughan, Ann Bishop, Rita Cullen and Maura Mooney. 'All of them were good musicians and Maura Mooney was my mentor, and if I did something wrong Maura would say to me, "Sing it this way". I think Bill O'Kelly was lucky to recruit John and Tom Carney as they were very dedicated, as were others like Charlie Dunphy and Gerard Mooney, Maura's husband.'

Before long, Dympna Bugler would marry Tom Carney, while his brother John met his wife-to-be, Bridget Finucane, in the chorus.

Adèle's Romance

Adèle Leigh was coming to Dublin in that winter of 1957 to sing Mimi in *Bohème* and Susanna in *The Marriage of Figaro*. A striking and beautiful young woman, she was a principal at Covent Garden since the early fifties and between engagements there sang with success in both opera and operettas on the Continent. It wasn't, she assured me, her first visit to Dublin; that had come about in unusual circumstances.

'When I joined Covent Garden we used to do spring tours of the provinces and food-rationing was still in operation in Britain. I remember we were visiting Liverpool and for some inexplicable reason I got this craving for sugar. I think I missed sweets and things like that. Someone in the company said, "We're not far away from a big box of chocolates," and when I asked where, this person replied, Dublin. So we devised a plan that immediately our operatic performance ended we'd rush off and catch the night boat to Dublin, and we did just that. On arrival there at seven in the morning, the first thing we did was tuck into a large breakfast of eggs, sausages, bacon and black puddings, the lot, all the things we couldn't get in London.

'After that we went into a dozen sweet shops in O'Connell Street and Henry Street and packed up with sweeties. It was marvellous and I can still remember the smile on baritone Jess Walters' face and his wife Amy's. I fell in love with the place on my first visit and later on when Colonel Bill O'Kelly asked me to sing for the DGOS I was thrilled to do so. It seems he had seen some of my performances at Covent Garden and liked them.'

She stayed at the old Jury's Hotel in Dame Street on her arrival in Dublin for *Bohème* and *Figaro*. She noticed that among her colleagues was this tall, handsome young man, a gorgeous creature in her teenage eyes, and she said to herself, 'Oh I fancy that man.'

It struck her that he looked a shy young man. Some days later Christopher West, who was producing the *Figaro*, and John Copley, an aspiring director, invited her to Jammet's restaurant for lunch. As she had been there before and adored the food, she said to West, 'Oh, that's a lovely idea. Coming from Britain, I think we were all a bit hungry and appreciated fine food.'

By now she knew the name of the young man she had fancied to be the bass James Pease, who was said to be American-born. When she walked into Jammet's she found to her surprise that he was seated at a table in the corner beside Christopher West and John Copley. She learned later they had both arranged it that way. The meal was fun and to her delight found she shared the same sense of humour and interests as James Pease. 'We had a good deal in common,' she mused. 'I mean, we were both beginning our international careers and eager to do the best we could. Making conversation with him was easy and we had plenty to talk about. We were to see a lot of each other in Dublin, for between rehearsals we often dined together in restaurants or took walks around the city.'

To Adèle Leigh, the DGOS chorus was more than competent. 'I think they sang so well I believed, before I was told, that they were professional.' She counted the Dublin engagement as a kind of holiday and it didn't worry her that the fees were very low. It was a friendly society and it engaged very good principals. For example, James Pease was singing Figaro and also Colline in *Bohème*, so it was a busy time for both of them. 'I think meeting James in such romantic circumstances was a help and I tried not to make it a distraction. And it was great that Christopher West was directing both operas, as I considered him very talented.'

Her Mimi was enthusiastically received by both audiences and critics. Charles Acton in the *Irish Times* could be acerbic but on this occasion, commented, 'I could not ask for a better Mimi then Adèle Leigh. She has everything the part requires - appearance, acting really lovely singing. By the time Mimi dies, one can but share Rodolfo's broken heart.'

The part on this occasion was sung by William McAlpine who was described as a first-rate Rodolfo with a purity of tone ideal for Puccini's music. James Pease made his mark as Colline and sang a very moving farewell to his old coat. Robert Johnston *(Irish Press)* was convinced that this was no routine performance of the opera but one exceptionally well sung and acted. He attributed a good deal of its success to conductor Warwick Braithwaite.

To Adèle Leigh the Gaiety was an adorable little house really suited to operas like *Bohème* and *Figaro*. She had particularly happy memories of Mozart's opera as it was the first she had sung at Covent Garden and then it was as Barbarina, and later she sang Cherubino, and then Susanna. It had helped that she had begun her career as an actress as this afforded her clearer insights into characters and how they should be played. That season she made a big impact at the Gaiety and found a champion in Charles Acton. 'During the whole evening I completely lost my heart to Miss Leigh,' he wrote, 'and she afforded me the greatest pleasure.'

It was a formidable cast of principals, with the gifted Welsh bass-baritone Geraint Evans singing the Count, while James Pease got good notices for his

Figaro, though one critic found him too restrained in the aria, 'Non piu andrai'. A lot of credit for the success of the production was given to director Christopher West and conductor Bryan Balkwell. Mary MacGoris warned *Independent* readers: 'Anyone who misses this *Figaro* will miss the best operatic production in Dublin for several years and one of the most enjoyable performances of this opera it can be possible to see.'

Adèle Leigh was thoroughly enjoying herself and her romance with James Pease was, she could say, proceeding gaily. And the reaction of the Gaiety audiences greatly pleased her; they were more spontaneous than their Covent Garden counterparts and responded more readily to comic situations, irony and wit. She felt she could not thank Bill O'Kelly enough. He had permitted her to sing Mimi as up to then she usually sang Musetta in the Covent Garden productions. The only drawback in Dublin was the hectic schedule between rehearsals and getting an opera on stage and in her view it was all too rushed. She had made friends and these friendships she told me later, were to endure. She and Veronica Dunne, for instance, had a happy reunion - they had sung together in Gluck's *Orfeo and Euridice*, in what was tragically to become Kathleen Ferrier's last performance before her untimely death from cancer.

Barbara Howitt was the Marcellina in *Figaro* and like Miss Leigh has, she says, fond memories of Dublin. 'I remember the occasions always being happy and full of laughter. For one thing, the proximity of Neary's bar to the Gaiety stage door with its oysters and Guinness probably eased our paths through long rehearsals. And I remember, too, the chorus being very competent and with beautiful Irish voices. I suppose we weren't too worried about rehearsal time as the other UK singers like myself were singing roles we already were very well versed in at Covent Garden. It was a warm and heartening experience to sing in Dublin and we all enjoyed it.'

It was the extreme warmth of the audience and their appreciation of the artists that struck her most of all. One avid opera buff who happened to be the head brewer of the Guinness firm at the time, invited the *Figaro* cast to a reception in the brewery where they were entertained by the directors. That Christmas, to her great surprise, she had a telephone call from Park Royal in London, the Guinness HQ, asking her when they could deliver her Guinness and in due course a lorry solemnly drove up to her flat with a barrel, which the driver carried up in his arms to her first floor flat and tapped it for her. 'I can tell you it was quite a conversation point at Covent Garden for some time.'

There was a happy ending to Adèle Leigh's romance for she and James Pease were married in London six months later. 'James proposed very quickly to me,' she recalls, 'and the wedding later had a fairytale air about it.

And I had already told Bill O'Kelly that both James and myself would love to return to sing with the society.'

That season's production of Offenbach's *The Tales of Hoffmann* caused Bill O'Kelly and the DGOS committee more problems than they could have imagined. When Anne Bollinger was struck down with an attack of `flu a late replacement had to be found to sing the role of Antonia. At this time Veronica Dunne was alternating in the part with Joan Sutherland at Covent Garden and Colonel O'Kelly contacted Miss Dunne's agent Joan Ingpen and urgently enquired if she was available on the Dublin dates. Ingpen confirmed that she was.

'I was sitting at home that weekend in Dublin,' recalled Veronica Dunne, 'and Joan Ingpen telephoned me to say she was looking for the same fee that Anna Bolinger was going to get for signing Antonia. Apparently Colonel O'Kelly took strong exception to this and said he couldn't pay the full fee demanded, only £30. Joan argued with him that since I was singing the same role it was only fair I should get the same amount, which I believed to be £90. Joan's insistence paid off, but later on Colonel O'Kelly did not mince his words to me as to what he felt about the episode.'

It would be another five years before she was invited back to sing again for the society. Talking to her, she says she has no regrets about taking the stand she took. In her view, she was standing up for the rights of singers who otherwise might be treated as second class artists. As for her performances in *Hoffmann*, she was highly praised; indeed Mary MacGoris *(Independent)* noted, 'Our Miss Dunne covered herself with glory - she was completely convincing as the loving but song-struck Antonia; she looked absolutely delightful and she gave us consistently the best singing of the night. Barbara Howitt as Nicklausse also sang excellently with warmth, colour and vitality.'

It was a production, however, that nearly came unstuck at the last minute for James Johnston, who was to sing Hoffmann, was hit by a sudden bout of `flu and the society had once again to find a last-minute replacement. Welsh tenor Edgar Evans was contacted at Covent Garden and within a few hours caught a plane to Dublin and had only fifteen minutes to make up before he went on stage as Hoffmann. In the circumstances he acquitted himself well, singing with both feeling and assurance.

Oldtimers will tell you there was always an air of expectancy in the Gaiety when the DGOS staged an opera for the first time. 'I think this was true of *Norma* in `55 and *Don Carlo* in 1950,' recalls Aileen Walsh. 'We all liked to see the society breaking new ground. And there was a buzz in the winter of 1957 when we were doing Puccini's *Turandot* for the first time for we knew it was a spectacular opera.'

Six months before he died Giacomo Puccini had told his librettist Giuseppe Adami, 'I think about *Turandot* every hour and every minute, all the music I have written before seems a joke and is no longer to my taste.'

He died in 1924 without finishing the work. His fellow countryman, the composer Franco Alfano, completed the score and the opera's premiere took place at La Scala in April 1926. The story is set in Peking and centres around Princess Turandot who has vowed she will only marry a suitor of noble blood who can solve her three riddles. As the 'ice lady' she wins little sympathy - all that is reserved for the devoted Liu, the most touching character in the opera.

Aware of the visual grandeur demanded, the society spent extra money on costumes - described by one veteran critic as sumptuous - and stage sets, and on the opening night the audience had something colourful to view. Sylvia Fisher, the Australian soprano, was entrusted with the taxing role of Princess Turandot and, from all accounts, coped well dramatically, though in the higher ranges her voice was stated to be 'under strain'. Walter Midgley, as Calaf, fared somewhat better and his 'Nessun Dorma' was greeted with enthusiasm. The words of one evening newspaper critic were reassuring, 'Nearly every seat was occupied for *Turandot* which was a surprising thing, for usually there is no surer way of emptying the Gaiety than putting on some unfamiliar opera, even when the name Puccini is attached.'

If the society had been pleased with the box-office response to *Turandot*, it was clearly disappointed in the case of Giordano's *Andrea Chénier* which it was also staging for the first time. And none more so than Dr Larchet who had helped persuade Maestro Botti and Colonel O'Kelly to present it. The work was already gaining in popularity in leading opera houses and Larchet believed it was time that Dublin audiences heard it. Set in the time of the French Revolution, it is noteworthy musically for its stirring choruses, arias and flowing melody. Tenors continue to be attracted to the role of Chénier, as baritones are to Gerard. The society was satisfied it had in Caterina Mancini, Antonio Galie and Giulio Mastrangelo the ideal set of principals. As in the case of *Turandot*, additional money was provided to ensure that the revolutionary mood was reflected in the sets and costumes. There was, however, a disappointing attendance on the opening night in April, with empty seats in the stalls and dress circle. Dr Larchet did not appear too disappointed. Confronted by an evening newspaper columnist in the bar afterwards he said calmly, 'The Dublinman is reputed to know what he likes. I think it would be more correct to say that he likes what he knows.' Pressed if the society would continue to put on operas unfamiliar to Irish opera fans, the society's president replied, 'We blazed the trail with Tosca and in a few years time I confidently believe that *Chénier* will be equally popular.'

In his review in the *Evening Herald*, critic Brian Quinn touched on the question: 'The only excursion from the usual repertoire being made this season by the DGOS is Giordano's *Andrea Chénier* was given a first performance last night. The Gaiety was not completely full. Perhaps the fact that the composer died in 1948 made him sufficiently modern to scare away some people. They need not have worried. Giordano, as a composer of rich melody and an inventor of dramatic situation, is only a step below Puccini (who overshadowed him and that is no mean place in Opera's Hall of Fame). He singled out Caterina Mancini as the star of an exciting evening in the theatre and said her duet with Antonio Galie in the final act was the undoubted highlight. He praised the chorus for its assured singing in such exalted company.

It was proving an interesting decade for operagoers. The prospect of seeing a Japanese soprano as Cio-Cio-San in *Madama Butterfly* enhanced box-office takings and patrons were not disappointed, for Miki Koiwai gave 'a vivid interpretation, at once dramatic and beguiling.' Antonio Galie was a splendid Pinkerton and Giuseppe Forgione's well-sung and sympathetically acted Sharpless further confirmed the view that he was one of the most talented baritones on the current scene. Musically, much of the success was attributed to Franco Patané, one of the finest operatic conductors of this era.

Norris Davidson continued to provide enjoyment for Radio Éireann listeners with his informative and polished introductions of DGOS productions recorded at the Gaiety Theatre. Few, if any, were broadcast live anymore, except perhaps from the Wexford Festival, and according to Davidson this policy worked best. 'It gave us time to edit the tapes and choose the best recording. Technically, there was a big improvement, though I still found that broadcasts seldom, if ever, came up to the standard of the performance you heard in the theatre. However, I got letters from people who enjoyed opera on air. In my brief talk about each act I tried to give them an indication of what was taking place on stage.'

Both Bill O'Kelly and Dr Larchet continued to be enthusiastic about the broadcasts and believed they increased the popularity of opera and the work the DGOS was doing. Davidson was intrigued by the reaction of the visiting guest artists. At this time the Peter Hunt Recording Studios were located in St Stephen's Green and Hunt used to record the operas and the singers came in to listen to themselves on tape. He was present on a few occasions when Italians became furious at what they heard. 'I don't know what they expected but they did not hide their feelings; others would listen and smile to themselves and be pleased with their performances. Peter Hunt sold quite a number of tapes and I don't think Radio Éireann was particularly concerned about it.'

Davidson was not surprised by the society's progress as people were very enthusiastic, though he wondered if there were by now too many committees. 'I suspect that Bill O'Kelly wanted it that way for fund-raising purposes and the structures were working for him. I could not understand how they were achieving so much on such a shoe-string budget, it was incredible really. But as long as they had Louis Elliman's support and that of Radio Éireann and the Symphony Orchestra and, of course, the large amateur chorus they could carry on. The government through the Arts Council should have been able to give them far greater financial backing. It was absurd the way the society was forced to exist.'

The fact was that for the most part it existed on voluntary input, on people who were prepared to sacrifice their time to help out the society. Patrons' subscriptions were collected in this manner, and joint honorary treasurers Prince Caracciolo and Clem Morris shared the task of keeping the accounts, while others who lent a hand were Aileen Walsh, by now on the management committee, Tom McMahon, John F MacInerney, Thomas Doyle, S.C., and Gerard Mooney. And secretary Bertie Timlin, who was exceedingly thorough at his work, was now being assisted by Monica Condron. Few amateur organisations at the time could boast of such a selfless team.

Martin McCullough tells the story that when he was a joint treasurer a few years previously, he and his wife Mary were involved in the distribution of hundreds of patrons' tickets, a task given to them by patrons' chairman James J O'Connor. McCullough was in business with his father, who himself was very supportive of the DGOS. Despite his dictatorial ways, he found it fun working for Colonel O'Kelly because 'you knew he had his heart in opera.' But he seemed to have little regard for money so it was left to people around him to find it the best way they could. 'As far as I could see, Bill ploughed on in his efforts to get the operas on stage. He was grateful though for the voluntary work being done and conveyed that impression to me.'

McCullough usually collected the patrons' tickets for the operas from the Gaiety Theatre and brought them home and with his wife Mary spread them out on the dining room table alongside the applications which came in from all kinds of people, ranging from those with hearing problems to artificial limbs. Understandably these people wanted certain seats in the theatre. It could be a painstaking task sorting them all out. Not that James O'Connor was not grateful.

'In one way we were O'Connor's lieutenants,' added McCullough, 'and when we had finished our job he would arrive at the house with a box of chocolates or a bouquet of flowers for Mary. It was typical of the man. We were, we knew, only two of the numerous people happily doing chores for the society with no thought of payment. On reflection, I don't know how people were persuaded to give up their time. But I never heard anyone complain and that I suppose speaks for itself.'

There was another story he recalled that was also typical of James O'Connor. At the time people like Noel Purcell, Maureen Potter and Jimmy O'Dea had the free run of the Gaiety, as had Margaret Burke Sheridan, and one evening she breezed into the theatre shortly before the rise of the curtain on *La Traviata*. She went up to James O'Connor and asked for a ticket. He told her the house was full but she persisted. Turning to the diva, he said, 'If you behave yourself I'll see what I can do.' He handed her over to a steward and a seat was found in a box for her. Before long, however, she started to wave to people and distract others and speak out loudly. The upshot was that O'Connor remonstrated with her at the interval and with that she got into a huff and sailed out into South King's Street. Having a sudden remorse of conscience, James O'Connor hurried into the dress circle bar and bought the biggest box of chocolates on sale and trotted off after Miss Sheridan. When he caught up with her he apologised, and handing her the chocolates, remarked, 'No hard feelings, please mam.'

He was involved himself in an episode that wasn't as amusing as O'Connor's box of chocolates. Usually the President of Ireland Sean T O'Kelly was asked to nominate a suitable date for him to attend the society's gala evening performance and a member of the management committee would be asked to go to the President's residence in the Phoenix Park to finalise the matter.

'I went there as requested,' recalled Martin McCullough, 'and I was chosen because he was married to my aunt. We chatted about the season and he was quite genial and said he was looking forward to the gala performance, asking at the same time about Colonel O'Kelly and Dr Larchet and others. You can imagine my surprise a few weeks later when he telephoned and asked to see me. He sounded agitated. I wondered what on heavens was on his mind. When we met, he came to the point quickly. He said he had gone to the trouble of attending the gala night in full tails with starched collar and bow tie - wearing the full regalia in other words. However, when he and Mrs O'Kelly arrived in the theatre they were welcomed by Dr Larchet, Bill O'Kelly and myself attired in dinner jackets and he didn't think that was good enough, and I remember he added crossly, "If I'm going to get into this hard-boiled suit of mine, the most uncomfortable thing that any man could be asked to wear, and you fellows line up in soft jackets, you can go back and tell Bill O'Kelly that he and his welcoming committee have got to wear full dress next time." In a word, it was the President of Ireland giving me orders.'

To McCullough it was all part of the opera scenario that at times could be both unpredictable and funny. They were living through an economic depression in Ireland and he felt that opera enlivened people's lives, bringing much needed colour and excitement. He regarded the social side of the scene as important also and knew that foreign artists loved to be entertained with true Irish hospitality. Most of them came on their own and apart from their Gaiety engagements, did not know the Irish. After a while, though they were being invited to supper parties and enjoying themselves, Mary McCullough said people were being introduced to Italian cuisine and some Italian restaurants came into their own, especially Nico's in Dame Street. 'I think that opera-going and enjoyment became synonymous and we all had a good time. Different people gave post-opera parties and suppers and if you were lucky star singers sang for the love of it. They were wonderful times.'

Dr Dermot O'Kelly had been invited to become a patron member by James J O'Connor and soon he was being asked to act as steward in the Gaiety, showing people to their seats. As a medical man, he noted that dampness tended to affect some of the guest singers' voices but otherwise he regarded them as a healthy bunch, though he had concluded privately they were all hypocondriacs. He remembered once being called to an Italian tenor's dressing room when he complained of a small lump on his right side and anxiously wanted to know the treatment for it. 'I could see immediately it was nothing but a lump of fat and I advised the fellow to go easy on pasta in future.'

Like the McCulloughs, the O'Kellys also enjoyed the social side, whether this was entertaining friends at post-opera suppers or accompanying them to city restaurants. The Lovatt-Dolans, John and Elizabeth, were also patrons and friends of the McCulloughs and they too enjoyed the social side of the scene. 'I remember that Italian cuisine began to get really popular,' recalls Elizabeth, 'and indeed some people also learned the Italian language so that their party-going would be even more enjoyable.'

By now Prince Caracciolo and his wife Mary - known to her friends as "Boodie" - and their family had settled into their lovely new home, The Park, Rathfarnham, and already their post-opera suppers were among the most enjoyable on the social scene. With his Italian background, the Prince, known affectionately as 'Freddie', went out of his way to make the Italian guest artists feel at home. Paolo Silveri told me he has happy memories of the Prince's generosity, so has Giuseppe Morelli. The Caracciolos had become part and parcel of the DGOS seasons and "Boodie" Caracciolo was a charming hostess.

There was an air of old-world chivalry and courtesy about Prince

Caracciolo. Born in Civitavecchia, he spent most of his young life in Rome. He was, as it were, the young-man-about-town, gallant and daring; he was a boxer, a daredevil, a fast motor-bike fiend. He even secured a pilot's licence which was in fact to lead him into the administrative end of K.L.M. airlines. It was in this arena that he first encountered by chance his wife-to-be, the beautiful Augusta Purcell-Fitzgerald, and in July 1938 they were married at Brompton Oratory, London. Later, they returned to settle down at the Island in Co. Waterford, where the prince turned at once to breeding horses - his first stallion was appropriately called "Ernani".

Freddy Carracciolo was an authority on Italian operatic repertoire and since his arrival to live in Rathfarnham had helped to compile articles for the DGOS programmes. He was always conspicuous at the opera, with his splendid brocade waistcoat and opulent velvet dinner jacket. He had style and he was the man for the celebratory occasion. He did not try to understand Colonel O'Kelly; instead he went along with him, whispering in his ear about up-and-coming Italian singers and conductors or sopranos he had heard in opera in Rome. The Colonel listened to him and together in Rome they sometimes went to operas to hear young artists. Dr Dermot O'Kelly says that Freddie Caracciolo was said to be a very good judge of a singer's worth and potential. 'I think everyone knew this and respected his knowledge.'

When the prince became chairman of the society's patron members he worked hard to increase the membership, something that Col O'Kelly was not slow to acknowledge, for behind his sartorial style Carracciolo was a realist and was aware that the DGOS was working on a paltry budget. Sometimes he wondered how they managed to stage the spectacular operas with so little money available.

Virginia Zeani's Lucia

Virginia Zeani was returning in the spring of 1958 to sing Lucia in Donizetti's popular opera, having unavoidably missed the previous year. She was by now married to the famous bass Nicola Rossi-Lemini and he was also coming to Dublin for a concert engagement at the Gaiety Theatre. They had first met in Florence in 1952 but it would be another four years before they met again. On this occasion it was at La Scala in Handel's *Giulio Cesare*, when he sang Cesare opposite her Cleopatra in a acclaimed production that included in the cast Franco Corelli and Giulietta Simionato.

'Nicola and I became friends and lovers,' she recalled, 'and before long he asked me to marry him within a week. I said three months and he agreed. I admired him so much as an artist, his Boris Godunov was the best I'd ever seen, so was his Don in *Don Giovanni*; everything he did was exceptional. Singing with him on stage was a great experience as he was a wonderful actor-singer. Off-stage, he was generous, warm-hearted and fun. We were so happy together, so much in love.'

As a performer Virginia Zeani was adored by the Dublin public, as much for her sultry looks as for her luminous voice. That spring of `58 she scored a personal triumph as Lucia. 'The soprano's night' proclaimed the critics. Brian Quinn told *Evening Herald* readers he was particularly enchanted by her performance and said she dominated the opera by the sheer radiance of her voice. He regarded her Mad Scene as 'riveting'. When I talked to the soprano herself about the production she said it was a magical evening, thanks in no small way to Giuseppe Morelli's conducting and Bruno Nofri's directing. As for the cast, she remembered the fine performances by Antonio Galie, Carlo Meliciani and Ferruccio Mazzoli. She had come to have tremendous admiration for the Gaiety audiences. 'They were very kind to me, so generous in their applause, and they liked my Lucia so much.'

How Maestro Botti and Colonel O'Kelly had managed to persuade the soprano to come to Dublin remains a mystery, for by now her career was peaking and she was in demand in most of the leading opera houses. It certainly wasn't the money, as the fees paid to guest artists were comparatively small, though one imagines that Zeani was among the best paid at this time. When she sang the role of Blanche De La Force in the world premiere at La Scala of Poulenc's *Dialogues Des Carmelites*, she attracted a great deal of attention. She had been personally chosen by the composer Francis Poulenc.

She was particularly thrilled that her husband was able to sing in Dublin as this had been her wish since they first married. 'I had told Nicola a lot about Ireland, its lovely scenery and above all, the lush green of the land, as well as the friendliness of the people, so that he had a pretty good idea of what to expect.' The recital on Saturday, May 3, was a success; in his rich, noble bass he sang songs and arias by Gluck, Brahms, Mussorgsky, Verdi and Mozart, displaying an outstanding vocal technique and artistry. 'He was a handsome man and a fine musician,' recalls Jeannie Reddin, who always enjoyed accompanying the stars. She had accompanied Ebe Stignani in London's Festival Hall and toured with Joan Hammond.

'Ebe Stignani was humility personified,' she says, ' and despite her fame she never acted the prima donna. And I do remember playing for Annaliese Rothenberger in a Radio Éireann concert broadcast when she came here with the Hamburg State Opera, and she too was charming and easy to work with.'

Not surprisingly the visiting singers liked to socialise and be offered invitations to post-opera suppers and week-end parties. Virginia Zeani became a friend of 'Boodie' Caracciolo's and enjoyed, she says, some delightful evenings at their home. She was also invited to Russborough House, the residence of Sir Alfred and Lady Beit and was astonished by the range of art on display.

That spring season was proving eventful for a variety of reasons. It was clouded though on the eve of its opening by the death of Margaret Burke Sheridan in a Dublin nursing home. Opera paid its own tribute to a woman who had become part of the Dublin social and musical scene in the preceding decade. Prior to the rise of curtain on the evening of April 17 on Puccini's *Manon Lescaut* at the Gaiety the entire cast, chorus and audience stood in memory of the soprano. The society's president, Dr John Larchet, spoke of her rise to glory in Italy to become a renowned prima donna and this in a relatively short time. Unfortunately she retired much too early in her career, but she would be remembered by some very worthy recordings she left behind. Colonel O'Kelly felt that music had suffered a great loss by her death and he could say that Margaret had always been a good friend of their society and an inspiration as well.

Ebe Stignani and Gloria Davy sang at her Requiem Mass at the University Church, St Stephen's Green. Her tomb in Glasnevin Cemetery is inscribed with the brief epitaph the diva would no doubt have chosen herself:

'Margherita Sheridan, Prima Donna.' Mary ('Boodie') Caracciola, who was her friend and executrix, was to say of "Maggie from Mayo": 'The sunshine of Italy was in her eyes; the age-old sorrows of Ireland were in her voice, rich with the deep beauty of her native land.'

It was Miss Sheridan who had suggested to Colonel O'Kelly that the society break new ground and perform *Manon Lescaut* for the first time - she herself had sung the title role with acclaim in Italy. Maestro Botti had assembled a strong cast, headed by Italian soprano Elisabetta Barbato who had already sung the title role with success at La Scala. She was said to have 'a flexible and opulent voice.' Tenor Umberto Borso was returning for the second time to sing Des Grieux. He had made his operatic debut four years previously at the Teatro Sperimentale of Spoleto in *La Forza del Destino* and his voice was notable for its fine dramatic ring, good range and he was lauded by the critics who predicted a very bright future for him. The distinguished Alberto Erede was the conductor; he had been in Dublin the previous September to conduct the *Verdi Requiem* for Our Lady's Choral Society and impressed the critics. Born in Genoa in 1908, he went on to conduct at the Metropolitan Opera House, La Scala and Glydebourne, and had recorded with Tebaldi, del Monaco, Stignani and Mancini.

Whether Margaret Burke Sheridan would have given Bruno Nofri's production of *Manon Lescaut* her full approval no-one will ever know, but the critics for the most part gave it a vote of confidence without extolling its virtues, though it was clear that Umberto Borso stood out. 'Heroic and passionate, he gave Puccini's inspired music its full value,' stated one evening newspaper critic. He found Signora Barbato's powerful voice, however, lacking in colour and shade, and baritone Giuseppe Forgione's portrayal of Lescaut 'too gentlemanly for such a rogue.' Alberto Erede made a marked impression, not only on the critics but on some of the Radio Éireann musicians. 'Maestro Erede conducted with wonderful insight into Puccini's score and made the music flow,' commented one critic. Sheila Larchet, harpist in the orchestra, thought Erede inspiring. 'I felt how fortunate the society was in having conductors of his calibre who understood the music and what Puccini intended.'

As a festival of Italian opera, there could have been few complaints. The production of *Ballo in maschera* pleased audiences with Caterina Mancini and Antonio Galie being as convincing as ever - in the eyes of the Dublin public the pair could do no wrong. And they were ably supported by newcomer Gioi Giovannetti as the Page, Oscar, displaying a lovely fresh-toned soprano voice, and Carlo Meliciani who sang with conviction as Renato. Conductor Giuseppe Morelli ensured a satisfying musical experience. Talking to him at his Rome apartment, he expressed admiration for Galie who nowadays coaches singers. To Morelli, the tenor had a commanding stage presence and knew how to endear himself to an audience. 'He was an expressive singer in true Italian tradition and musical, too. I had no worries when he sang for he was an artist.'

One of the biggest talking points of the season was undoubtedly the Dublin debut by Italian baritone Aldo Protti. The power of his voice surprised chorus members like Tom and John Carney and Dick Hanrahan. Another was heard to ask, 'Do you think Protti's voice is too big for the Gaiety?' The answer was 'no' of course but that season he did manage to electrify audiences; indeed, one critic was to comment, 'Signor Protti's performance was so electrifying that whenever he was not on the stage the opera seemed to sag.'

If the voice lacked polish, it lacked little else and it coped effortlessly with Verdi's music. It was the kind of voice that appealed to Colonel O'Kelly and produced an exciting sound that tended to rouse audiences. To O'Kelly, Verdi must excite, stimulate and be musically rewarding, so he always welcomed what he liked to describe as 'a Verdi voice' and he knew that Italy had more than its share. Renata Ongaro was making her Dublin debut as Gilda and arrived with an impressive record. The summer before she had scored a personal success at Arena di Verona as Gilda and since then had recorded *Lucia di Lammermoor*. Her Rigoletto at Verona had been none other than Aldo Protti. She did not disappoint her Dublin audiences and, if anything, emerged as one of the young stars of the season. Except for Ermanno Lorenzi's rather bland Duke of Mantua, it was regarded as a splendid *Rigoletto*.

So a season that had begun with rumours in the newspapers that it might have to be cancelled because of under-funding turned out to be successful after all in most respects. Yet some questions were being asked about the society's precarious financial position and these were not fully answered in a piece in the opera programme by Colonel O'Kelly, headed, 'CAN WE CONTINUE?'.

The chairman admitted that the presentation of opera in Dublin at that time was one of the most difficult tasks that any organisation could undertake and it was only possible when undertaken by an amateur organisation such as the Dublin Grand Opera Society with, of course, the wholehearted co-operation of the Radio Éireann authorities. Their main sources of income were their share of the box-office takings, the patrons' subscriptions, as well as limited guarantees against loss from Bord Fáilte and the Arts Council. The seasons by the Germans and Italian companies were made possible by grants to these companies by their respective governments.

It was the ambition of the society management to reach the stage in the near future when each season would hopefully pay its own way through box-office takings and the limited guarantees against loss, as at present. There was however no hope that they could make any progress in reducing the debt which had been incurred by the society over the years since its formation and which at times seriously threatened its future. To reduce it from box-office takings of future seasons they would have to agree to drastic reduction in the standard of productions. It would also entail confining the society's activities to the well-known and popular operas.

'One way out of the problem,' he wrote, 'is in the absence of grants or subsidies to double the present number of patron members. If the figure totalled one thousand active members this would result in a welcome improvement in our financial position. Many people might say that it should not be difficult to have one thousand patrons, but in fact we are very far short of that figure. The people of Dublin should look upon the society as their society. If it ceased its activities it would leave a serious gap in the capital's musical activities. So we appeal for people to become patrons and help to keep that operatic heritage alive.'

Donnie Potter had joined the society in the mid-fifties and was by now on the patrons' committee. There seemed to him to be a financial crisis each year and it took considerable optimism on everyone's part to ensure that the society didn't go under. It was seriously underfunded and that was the real problem and the cause of continuing uncertainty. For its survival it depended largely on revenue generated by the box-office, patrons' subscriptions, a small Arts Council grant and some financial assistance from Bord Fáilte. The society's spring season of Italian opera was still however being helped by a subvention from the Italian government.

'What we most needed was a decent Arts Council grant,' says Potter, 'but that wasn't forthcoming. I can remember in the fifties going on a deputation to a bank for an overdraft of £2,000. Bill O'Kelly, Prince Caracciolo and Tom McMahon were also part of it, and after lengthy discussions with the manager we were getting nowhere, so Bill led the walk-out of the group. 'I wouldn't let that fellow manage a huckster's shop,' were his parting words to us. It was all a little desperate and humiliating and at times we approached politicians to try to help influence the Arts Council to increase their grant. I don't think people in authority realised the contribution the society was making to enhance the musical life of the capital; if they did, they were ignoring it.

There was meanwhile more than ordinary interest in the engagement of the American soprano Gloria Davy to sing the title role in *Aida* in the spring of `58. She would be the first coloured artist to do so in Dublin.

Sultry and stunning in appearance, she arrived with a growing reputation and attracted the newspapers who sought interviews with her. She was Brooklyn-born and as far back as she could remember wanted to become a singer. As she said, 'I had always the feeling that I must sing, there was absolutely no other career, even remotely in sight. If I hadn't become a singer I'd probably have studied the piano. My family believed in my talent and that was the most important thing to me, and they paid for me to go to the New York High School of Music and Art.'

At the age of sixteen she won the much-coveted Marian Anderson Study Award, a money prize which she used for training at the Juilliard School, New York. A year later came her professional debut in a song recital at the Town Hall, New York, and she was just twenty-one when she made a musical splash as a replacement for Leontyne Price in a touring production of *Porgy and Bess*. It was while she was appearing in the show in Milan that she attracted the interest of maestro Victor de Sabata who offered to coach her as Aida. She said she owed everything to him, in particular her appearance as Aida at the Met. Aged twenty-five, she was tall and graceful and looked perfect for the part.

Her failure to dazzle the critics was difficult to fathom, for oldtimers I've spoken to found Miss Davy's Aida vocally and dramatically convincing, though she was naturally overshadowed by the powerful Amneris of Ebe Stignani and Ferrucio Mazzoli's regal Ramfis. Most reviewers agreed on her grace and dark beauty and her striking stage presence, but found her voice scarcely heroic enough for Aida's music and in some passages lacking both range and sufficient colour. I do remember attending a concert she gave at the Savoy Cinema, Limerick some days later when she was quite superb in Verdi, Puccini and Mascagni arias and duets. Maybe it was wrong to judge the soprano on a single season in Dublin.

Soprano Joan Sutherland by contrast made an unmistakable impact that winter of `58 as Donna Anna in *Don Giovanni*, a production that undeniably is remembered by many of the DGOS. It featured Geraint Evans as the Don and at least one critic described his portrayal as irresistible, Irish tenor Dermot Troy as Ottavio and Martin Lawrence as Leporello. There was general agreement that Miss Sutherland's performance had hints of star quality and that she had an excellent career before her. To John Allen, who was singing in the chorus, it was an important occasion. 'We were seeing the breakthrough not only of Joan Sutherland, who was a stunning Donna Anna, but also Dermot Troy whose "Il mio tesoro" captivated the audience. I didn't realise at the time that he was deaf in one ear and so was puzzled why he sang the aria "Dalla Sua Pace" flatly in some spots. Geraint Evans was singing the Don for the first time and it was apparently testing himself in the role; he would drop it later for Leporello. It was a very good *Don Giovanni* and Dublin was seeing young singers who would soon go on to attain operatic glory.'

It was a gala occasion and from all accounts, more colourful than usual. It certainly included more government ministers and they were welcomed in the theatre's foyer by Dr Larchet and his wife, Lt.-Col. Bill O'Kelly, Prince Caracciolo and Tom Doyle, S.C., chairman of the DGOS Patron Members' Committee. It was stated that many of the audience were in formal dress and that boxes were banked by flowers. *Don Giovanni* was the best booked opera of that winter season of `58, partly because Dermot Troy was making his debut with the society.

Born in Tinahely, Co. Wicklow, in July 1927, he had already sung at Glyndebourne and at Covent Garden, in the latter house as Vasek in *The Bartered Bride* and David in *Die Meistersinger*. He was settled in London with his wife Eithne, and really made his mark in the Covent Garden production of Berlioz's Les Troyens when his singing of the sailor's aria was noted by the critics. Soon he would be going to the Mannheim Opera where he had successfully auditioned. His lyric tenor of lovely timbre was ideally suited to Mozart's music but was disappointed that Covent Garden management did not ask him to sing Tamino in *The Magic Flute*.

Norris Davidson was a lover of Mozart's operas and told me he regretted that the DGOS had not by then invited Dermot Troy to sing Tamino. He had liked the tenor's stylish singing as Ottavio and it had recorded well; indeed the broadcast of *Don Giovanni* had been particularly well received by listeners not only because of his being in the cast, but the quality of the recording itself was good. The audience's enthusiasm had also come through in the broadcast and the Radio Éireann Symphony Orchestra under Bryan Balkwill had sounded extremely good.

There was a mixed reception that winter season of `58 for *La Traviata*, directed by Bruno Nofri, though Attilio D'Orazi was a decided success as Germont, his warm-toned voice and convincing acting being ideal for this sympathetic part. Strangely, tenor Renato Cioni did not please the critics, with one of them accusing him of 'singing out of tune.' Cioni would go on later to sing opposite Callas in the same opera.

Poor Butterfly. As if her dilemma in Puccini's opera is not agonising enough, it seems sheer bad luck when the soprano portraying her has to quit after the first act or just when she and Pinkerton have pledged their love in one of opera's most passionate duets. Cuban soprano Dora Carral underwent the ordeal on the night of December 9 when she began to lose her voice as a result of flu. Colonel O'Kelly, who as usual was on hand backstage in case of problems, immediately knew he would have to find a replacement. He was aware that the Italian soprano Ofelia di Marco had sung Butterfly in Italy and now was in Dublin to sing for the society in *Traviata*. He decided to contact her.

The soprano had not long arrived back at her hotel following rehearsals and was feeling a little tired and hungry. But she unhesitatingly responded to the call and was ready to go on stage in act two inside of thirty minutes. To Colonel O'Kelly's relief everything went without a hitch. But who would take over the role two nights later? At this time Paolo Silveri was in charge of a number of Italian artists and announced he had engaged a soprano in Milan and she would arrive in Dublin on the next day.

Colonel O'Kelly's casting problem wasn't over. The replacement for Miss Carral was found to be unsuitable and she was told to pack her bags for Milan. O'Kelly instead asked Joan Hammond, who was in Dublin to sing Tosca, to take on Butterfly as well and she agreed. The soprano was staying with the McDonnells, Margaret and Colm, at their home, "Dalguise", on the Monkstown Road. To Margaret McDonnell the soprano had a great zest for life and she enjoyed having her in the house. Staying there also was her piano accompanist Ivor Newton and at this time they were rehearsing the role of Tatyana in Tchaikovsky's *Eugene Onegin* which Miss Hammond was due to perform shortly in England. At this time the McDonnells had a young girl Susan working for them and she had expressed a desire to enter the convent. Being a feast day she went to Mass and on her return Margaret McDonnell asked her to leave extra towels in the bathroom as Joan Hammond would be using it that morning. Once in the bathroom, the girl began to sing "Hail Queen of Heaven" and as she did so Miss Hammond left her music rehearsal in the adjacent room and said to her, 'Too much competition, girl. I'll have to leave.'

With that, Margaret McDonnell hurried up the stairs and asked Susan to stop singing. 'The thing was that Susan hadn't a note', she recalled. 'Anyway, Ivor Newton came down to the dining room after a while and asked if we were having coffee. Susan was wearing her blue ribbon and medal to mark the feast day and Ivor said to her, "You must be one of the waifs?" to which Susan replied, "Oh, no sir, I'm a child of Mary."'

Joan Hammond found the story amusing, though in more serious moments the famous soprano was showing increasing interest in Catholicism. 'Joan was like one of the family,' said Margaret McDonnell, 'and I think it used to fascinate her when she heard members of my family say to me, "Mum, we're going to Mass". Someone in the house always seemed to be going to church. One day out of the blue, she said to me, "D'you know, Margaret, I'm becoming interested in your church and some day I may well decide to be one of you." After a while my husband Colm began to give Joan religious books and she talked to him about them. I think she was very much touched by the faith among Irish people and their devotion to the Mass and the Sacraments, and she also found that people seemed to find contentment in prayer.

'Some months later she telephoned me from San Francisco to say she'd made up her mind and wanted to join the Catholic Church. I said I was very happy to hear the news and so was Colm and that if she wished I could arrange for her to be baptised and confirmed in Dublin. I remember she was very happy about that and intimated she'd stay with us for a week or so. It was a happy day for all of us when Joan was received into the Catholic church and I knew my friends in the DGOS shared her happiness.'

Silveri's Otello

Villa Silveri-Cirino, Rome.

It is a pleasant April evening in 1998 and I am back at Paolo Silveri's home to find answers to questions that are still a lively topic of conversation among an older generation of DGOS members and opera buffs generally. They concern the singer's surprise switch from baritone to tenor in 1959, to sing the title role in Verdi's *Otello* at the society's spring season. Does the famous baritone realise the risks involved? What prompts the change? Who is behind the decision? Why does he cease singing tenor almost immediately after his Dublin Otello? He is not surprised by my questions, if anything he looks prepared for them. As we sit, Paolo, his wife Delia, and myself by the long mahogany table in the quaint room and begin to recall the past it does not seem at that moment far away. I know by now that Paolo is an emotional and sensitive individual, that before I can ask for answers I must examine factors that have affected him as both singer and person.

It began in Dublin in the spring of 1956 with the sudden death of his colleague Antonio Manca Serra and is exacerbated more than six months later when another friend, the brilliant young conductor Guido Cantelli, is killed in an air crash en route to America, a flight that Silveri is scheduled to be on but misses his connection from Rome airport to Milan to link up with Cantelli. Silveri is deeply shocked. For months afterwards he confines himself to teaching his score of pupils at his home, refusing offers to sing Rigoletto, Scarpia, Count di Luna and other roles synonymous with his name. He admits to me he has lost confidence and fears if he does return to the stage he may die of a heart attack. He sometimes feels tired and suffers from palpitations. But he maintains his contacts with the DGOS and some of his mature pupils sing in productions for the society. When Lt.-Col. Bill O'Kelly and Bertie Timlin visit Rome they invariably call at his home and it is here in late 1958 that *Otello* is mentioned for the first time.

'One afternoon I am at the piano coaching my pupil to sing Desdemona,' he begins in a soft voice, 'and when we sing together the love duet in act one of the opera I think it sounds good. Signorina says we should surprise Bill O'Kelly next time he comes to my house, so when he arrives and wants me to sing I give him "Esultate" from act one of *Otello* and then Signorina and myself sing the last act together. After that, he is very excited and pleads with me to sing role of Otello in Dublin in the spring season. I am not sure, and when he asks me to sign contract I tell him it is not a question of money. Do I go back to the stage? Am I ready to sing Otello? I tell myself I am only feeling the part and getting to know it for my voice. Delia, my wife, is not sure I sing tenor part, but Bill O'Kelly insists I am ready and before he leaves the room with Bertie Timlin I promise I will sing Otello and he shakes my hand and thanks me. I do not know if I have done the right thing. I remember I have promised the audience in Dublin that if I sing again I will sing for them in the Gaiety Theatre. I feel happier now.'

'I leave the decision to Paolo himself,' says Delia, giving a reassuring glance across at her husband. 'I know he will sing Otello well if he wants to. I tell him I will be by his side in Dublin; that is the way it has always been - me by his side at the opera.'

* * *

The news that the great man was coming to Dublin to sing his first tenor role was met with a mixture of expectancy and scepticism. Opera buffs who had been in raptures about his Rigoletto, Renato, Figaro, Germont and Count di Luna could not accept that he could switch to tenor; others were curious about his odd decision but felt he wouldn't sing Otello unless he was able for it. Predictably, the queues formed early in South King Street for tickets and it soon looked like the four performances would be entirely sold out before the doors opened. The baritone's popularity was undiminished. It was bound to be a unique operatic occasion.

Colonel O'Kelly ensured that enough money was provided to do justice to Verdi's spectacular opera. It would be directed by Bruno Nofri who had in his time directed more than one hundred and sixty operas. Born in Milan in 1908, he had his early training as an assistant producer at La Scala and by the late 1930s was a well-known name in Italian opera. To George McFall, a member of the Gaiety backstage staff, he was a genius at sorting out sets and costumes when they arrived from Italy. He could not fathom how Nofri was able to distinguish between what was needed for each different production. 'The man had an eagle eye and in no time at all every item was perfectly in place. He worked quietly and calmly, an extraordinary man for detail.'

Franco Patané, the conductor, was considered one of the most gifted in his field and had conducted nearly all of Verdi's operas, including *Otello*. His son Giuseppe was also conducting for the DGOS that season. Born in Naples in 1932, Giuseppe had a remarkably wide repertoire for a young man, comprising no fewer than eighty-four operas. His professional career began at the age of seventeen. The cast was carefully chosen with Ofelia di Marco singing the role of Desdemona. Since her debut in Spoleto her career had taken off and she had sung with notable success in Rome's Caracalla Baths. Singing Iago was Alfro Poli who was equally well known in films as he was at La Scala or Rome Opera. A handsome man with a sonorous baritone voice, he counted Iago among his most popular roles. Brendan Cavanagh was proving indispensable to the society in comprimario parts, being secure musically and a good actor; he was cast as Roderigo.

Paolo Silveri and his wife Delia were booked into a city centre hotel and the baritone soon realised the extraordinary level of interest in his Otello as friends telephoned him with their good wishes and in the streets people sought his autograph and in the hotel foyer he was approached for a word. 'I am back among friends,' he recalls, 'and I feel happy that everyone wants me to sing well as Otello. Bill O'Kelly tells me the tickets sell well and I feel I have to sing well to please everybody. It is strange for me to come back to Ireland as tenor for they know me only as baritone. I tell my wife they will understand why I want to sing fantastic role of Otello.'

He had by now mastered the part and the rehearsals were devoted to working with his director and the rest of the cast. The opening night was scheduled mid-week with a dress rehearsal on the preceding Sunday, as the DGOS chorus was available as was the Radio Éireann Symphony Orchestra. There was a shock in store for Silveri when he arrived in his dressing room in the form of a nasty letter. It is totally unexpected. 'I feel very upset when I read it,' he recalls, 'for it says, "Silveri, you are nothing as a baritone, now you want to be the best tenor." I suspect immediately it has come from a bad and jealous colleague in Italy. I do not understand; I ask myself why should this happen to me.'

He had a four days' wait to opening night. He admitted to me that he felt nervous and the letter incident had not improved his state of mind. Worse was to follow. On the first night itself he felt in some distress; earlier that morning a boil had broken out under his right arm and a doctor was called to lance it but it continued to cause him discomfort so he rested for some four hours in his room. When he got up in the late afternoon and rang the hotel staff for a large steak, topped with two fried eggs, he was told he could not have it until later; instead he had to be satisfied with tomatoes, sandwiches and coffee. By the time he arrived with his wife at the Gaiety dressing room to make up he was by his admission not in the best of spirits.

There was no doubting the importance of the occasion. The Gaiety was packed with every box occupied; there was standing only for a limited number of people. For weeks the production had been a talking point among opera-goers and many failed to obtain tickets. 'There was a great buzz in the theatre itself,' says Donnie Potter, 'and I would say typical of a big opening night. It wasn't every day after all that one of the world's greatest baritones switching to a tenor role. As Silveri was very popular I expected, come what may, he would have the audience on his side.'

As he made up in his dressing room, the singer's wife was there to assist him and she prayed silently that all would be well. She remembered his anguish over the previous two years because of the death of his friends and she hoped he had got over it. She had to admit it hadn't been the best preparation for Otello. She would stand in the wings as Paolo sang the part; he always liked her to be close at hand. Yet she knew that the moment he began to sing the part he would forget everything else and be Otello; that was the way with Rigoletto, Renato, Figaro and the others.

The performance went better than he had expected and the audience gave him tremendous reception at the final curtain with shouts of 'Bravo! Bravo!' ringing round the auditorium. Soon some of the audience was standing and applauding enthusiastically; all the time Silveri looked visibly moved. Back in his dressing-room he tried to catch his breath. It was clear at that moment that singing the role had taken a good deal out of him, but later he told me, 'I am happy to sing it because it shows me I would have done better if I had not hurried myself and, instead, waited for another six months.'

The critics, for the most part, were generous in their praise of his performance. 'SUPERB PRODUCTION OF OTELLO' proclaimed the *Irish Independent* with Mary MacGoris stating that obviously a lot of hard work had been put into the production with the result that it measured up to the greatness of the work. 'Paolo Silveri's Otello was striking in its tremendous artistry,' she noted, 'and he gave us convincingly the noble Moor led to destruction no more by the machinations of evil than by the flaw in his own nature. His voice now changed to tenor, has certainly the power and weight for this taxing role, and he used it expressively and passionately phrasing with impressive intelligence and satisfying skill.'

Miss MacGoris went on to describe Ofelia di Marco as 'an exquisite Desdemona, her voice having a lovely sweetness as well as strength, and its effortless quality brought out all the poignancy of the music.' And she was evidently impressed by Alfro Poli's Iago which she stated was subtle and in the very best operatic tradition. 'Flamboyant and ingratiating by turns, he conveyed an inescapable aura of wanton evil and his splendid singing was notable for its beautiful style. The Radio Éireann Symphony Orchestra was quite superb under the direction of Franco Petane who swept the performance on with a magnificent feeling for the drama and the tenderness of the marvellous score.'

Brian Quinn *(Herald)* shared MacGoris's enthusiasm, and added, 'It was indeed a triumph for Paolo Silveri. There was artistry in every move and gesture. One forgot Silveri, so complete was his absorption into the character of the Moor. The chorus gave its best ever performance and the stage sets were also first-class. It was a night of opera to remember.' Charles Acton in the *Irish Times* echoed Quinn's praise of the chorus, stating it sang better than ever before; indeed it had excelled throughout the whole season. He thought that in this Otello the centre of gravity of the opera had shifted back from Iago to Otello, and this in spite of Alfro Poli's outstanding interpretation of the part. The main reason for the shift was the dramatic stature of Paolo Silveri's Otello. The noble Moor was great from beginning to end in his portrayal of the part and his dominance of the stage was complete.

'When a baritone of Mr Silveri's fame makes his debut as a tenor - even if in the relative obscurity of Dublin - he must be anxious about it,' added Acton, but there was no sign of it last night in his acting, though it is unlikely that his excessive vibrato, a certain hardness of quality and a lack of piano, were due to such anxiety. I do not feel it would be right at just this moment to assess his future as a tenor.'

I liked the way the *Evening Mail* evoked the occasion: 'The storm with which the opera opens was splendidly conveyed both musically and visually. The lightning, the rolling clouds, the turbulent waters, the terrified people - all were brought vividly before us, while Franco Patane steered the orchestra through a stirring rendering of the perfectly appropriate score. When Paolo Silveri made his entry in the part of the tragic Moor, there was a spontaneous burst of applause from a section of the audience, which was taken up by others. He is, of course, a great favourite and this unusual reaction was excusable on such a remarkable occasion; at the same time it was a pity to spoil the spell of the moment on stage. Silveri is, of course, gifted with acting ability quite above the general standard of tenors and he painted a vivid picture of Otello and the gradual poisoning of the noble mind by the villainy of Iago.'

As was the case with his colleagues, the critic had no doubt about Silveri's vocal performance. 'As a tenor, Silveri was equal to the demands of the music. He took the high notes with ease, yet with a certain suggestion of baritone quality.'

Discussing the production with former DGOS chorus members was revealing insofar as the majority of them felt that Silveri was unwise to take on the tenor role of Otello. Aileen Walsh, who was then in on the management committee and joint treasurer with Prince Caracciolo, thought it was a mistake and for the first act she had gone up to the upper circle of the Gaiety where she stood with her hands clasped for fear he might crack on the top notes and was terribly relieved when he hadn't. 'I agree, though, Paolo acted the part magnificently but the voice to me hadn't the clarion ring needed for the role.' Mary Troy thought there was a baritonal ring to his voice and while this was acceptable, he sometimes sounded forced in the top register and under some strain. She preferred to remember him as the glorious baritone in Verdi's operas. John Allen, also a member of the chorus on the occasion, says his most vivid memory was seeing Silveri's wife kneeling in the wings praying no doubt that her husband would get through the role, for the man in Allen's view was nearing the end of his career and it must have been a horror event for him. The wobble was still evident in the voice. 'I'll always remember the spectacular opening chorus to the opera and the applause of the audience; but, no, it was not for us they were applauding but the entry of Silveri. In those days the claque worked in the Gaiety, for the off-duty singers were in the audience and always led the applause. As for Silveri, the vocal range was there and if he had tried to sing the part five years before he could have done it, as there are baritonal notes in it. He was a very high baritone but singing Otello, I felt, his voice was strained and it was unsteady; others noticed this also and remarked on it to me.'

Tom Carney, who had been hugely impressed by Silveri's Renato and Rigoletto, was astonished he was singing tenor, though he had no doubt that dramatically he would have no problem with Otello. 'I felt on stage that he hadn't the vocal dynamics for the part and frankly I was disappointed and wondered if he should ever have attempted it. But Paolo was a very likeable person and few would care to criticise him in public.'

Dympna Carney had adored Silveri in his great Verdi characterisations but on his occasion as a chorus member, she cringed when he sang "Esultate!" in the first act. She feared he would break down during the performance. In Veronica Dunne's opinion, it was a mistake on his part to sing Otello. It was also very risky as his voice was not there for so demanding a role; he was a high baritone - and a magnificent one at that - and should never have been persuaded to sing anything else. Paddy Brennan, who was a Super in the production, found Silveri's tenor voice alien to his ears. Up to then he had been accustomed to tenors like Umberto Borso who was in effect the 'house tenor' and if anyone was to be asked to sing the Moor it should have been Borso. 'I do feel that Silveri was less than happy with his own performance for missing on this occasion was the smiling good humour so typical of the man; instead you got an untypical look of anxiety.'

To Brennan, the famous baritone 'lived' the part of Otello as he had seen him do in the case of Rigoletto which had made an incredible impression on his young mind. 'Paolo was one of the first singers to make me realise that opera wasn't just about putting on a costume and standing there waving your arms; he was actually the character he was singing.'

Later on in Rome during our discussion on *Otello*, Delia Silveri confessed to me that she was happier when Paolo sang baritone. Singing Otello made her husband tired and she feared for him. She was relieved when he returned to sing his favourite baritone roles. When I asked Silveri himself why in actual fact he did not again sing tenor on his return to Italy, he said he had made a promise to his daughter Silvia that he would sing Rigoletto opposite her Gilda and now he was to achieve that personal ambition. She would make her debut in the role with the Budapest State Opera.

In his own autobiography, published in Italy, Silveri revealed that on his return home after *Otello* in Dublin, he was offered tenor roles at La Scala (Don Jose) and in Germany (Tristan, Samson and Siegmund) and had no hesitation in turning them down. 'I did not want to study these parts at this stage of my career. Instead, I go back to sing Scarpia, Nabucco, Macbeth, Rigoletto and Escamillo. I am happy again.'

If Silveri's Otello had tended to dominate that `59 spring season there were other operatic gems worthy of attention. The young American soprano Anna Moffo caused a sensation as Norina in Donizetti's comic masterpiece, *Don Pasquale*. Displaying a voice of lovely timbre and agility allied to first-rate acting ability, she quickly became the darling of Dublin audiences. Her personal beauty matched that of either Zeani or d'Angelo. John O'Donovan, the *Evening Press* critic, commented, 'Anna Moffo is phenomenal; a ravishing black-haired beauty, radiant with Southern vivacity, and yet with a voice and a sense of style that we have been led to believe can only be found in women of forty with figures like Falstaff.'

O'Donovan's colleagues were also bowled over by the soprano's performance. 'Miss Moffo has a gorgeous coloratura,' observed the *Evening Mail*, 'even in quality throughout her range, with no shrillness in the higher register. And she has good looks, a delightful personality and is a complete actress.'

Chorus members could always be relied upon for an intelligent assessment of guest principals. 'The perfect Norina,' concluded Aileen Walsh. 'I could listen to her sing every hour of the day.' Maura Mooney believed Moffo's voice suited Donizetti's music to perfection, and Dympna Carney.agreed. She also was delighted by the performance by Attilio d'Orazi as Malatesta in the opera. 'He was becoming a firm favourite with audiences and the choristers for his grand personality.'

Whenever that *Pasquale* is recalled, I have found that choristers are eager to mention the name of Salvatore Gioia, a young lyric tenor from Sicily who was singing Ernesto and whose voice blended beautifully with that of Anna Moffo's. He had made his debut three years before at Spoleto in Cimarosa's opera *Matrimonio Segreto* and had a rising reputation as a Rossini, Donizetti and Bellini exponent. 'There were echoes of Tito Schipa about the quality of his voice,' said Tom Carney. To John Allen, he was a most convincing Ernesto and sang Donizetti's music with fine phrasing and seamless legato.'

Audiences were certainly in for a treat that season as Gioia also sang the lyric role of Almaviva in Rossini's *Il Barbiere di Siviglia* to enthusiastic applause. Mary MacGoris was however irritated by the tenor's habit of 'addressing his remarks to the conductor's eyebrows.' Attilio d'Orazi enjoyed himself enormously singing Figaro and had the audience wholly on his side. His penchant for comedy stood him well in the role and he sang stylishly. With Franco Patane on the podium and Bruno Nofri directing, this was a high-class *Barber* and it was enhanced further by the presence of Margherita Rinaldi as Rosina. Discovered at the Spoleto competition where she won first prize, she made her debut in *Lucia di Lammermoor*, winning very favourable praise from the critics and it came as no surprise when she was called to La Scala. Judging by her Rosina, the young soprano was blessed with a lovely coloratura voice and impressive stage presence. More would be heard of her in Dublin where she was already being talked about in music circles.

It was Dr Larchet who had suggested to Bill O'Kelly that the society stage the Irish premiere of Giordano's *Fedora* which had first been performed in Milan in November 1898 with Enrico Caruso singing the role of Count Loris Ipanov. The opera was a great success and the composer's most successful work after *Andrea Chénier*. Set in St Petersburg, it recounts the fate of the Russian Princess Fedora, who in her quest to avenge the death of her lover, leaves a trail of destruction and ends up poisoning herself.

Interest in the work in Dublin was only moderate and on the first night, December 12, the Gaiety was far from full. It was also noticeable that tenor Augusto Ferrauto had pitch problems and more than once he 'wandered off the note,' something that annoyed Bill O'Kelly who as always was seated in the wings. Next day he decided to seek a replacement - Guiseppe Savio - for Ferrauto who on that day was on the next flight back to Italy. Apart from the tenor's poor performance, the rest of the *Fedora* cast won critical acclaim, particularly Nora de Rosa in the title role; she displayed fine dramatic power and sang strongly. Baritone Antonio Campo stood out as Siriex and mezzo-soprano Celia Alvarez Blanco was an excellent Contessa. In his parting comment in the *Irish Times*, critic Charles Acton, stated, '*Fedora* is an opera and a presentation that I recommend while we have the chance to see it, especially as it was very disappointing, indeed, to see a number of empty seats. Is the Dublin opera public really so very highbrow in its approach to novelty? What one wonders would be the effect on them of an opera properly of our century, of *Peter Grimes, Les Carmelites, Die Kluge*? Is it utter timidity or lack of interest in the unfamiliar romantics? Certainly it must be very discouraging for the DGOS, whose average standards seem to be continually rising and who are now thoroughly worth every opera lover's support.'

While it was a valid comment and worth airing the fact remained that opera-goers in the Dublin of the time were conservative and cautious about parting with their hard-earned money unless they felt they were going to get full value. True, tickets were comparatively cheap, yet times were bad, jobs scarce and there was a fine choice of alternative entertainment available. While both Dr Larchet and Bill O'Kelly were naturally disappointed by a lack-lustre response to a work like *Fedora*, they believed it was the society's duty to explore these lesser known operas. But with the society strapped for money it was a high-risk policy.

The society broke new ground in the `59 spring season when Salvatore Allegra came to Dublin to conduct his opera *Ave Maria* which had already been seen at La Scala and the Rome Opera. A two-act work, the story is slight and centres around a pious old peasant woman who is troubled about her son who has been led astray by an unscrupulous woman and is praying hard for him. But he stubbornly sticks to his ways until brought to his senses when he pushes her roughly aside and she dies as a result of a fall - to the strains of "Ave Maria" penetrating into the cottage from the valley below.

The society was disappointed when Archbishop Charles McQuaid was unable to accept an invitation to attend the opening night's performance. There were, nonetheless, quite a number of clerics in the packed theatre and a definite sense of occasion was evident. The critics did not go overboard about the work. 'It has its dull moments,' noted the *Evening Mail*, 'the overture is singularly uninteresting - but it is on the whole a melodious and satisfying example of its kind.' There was praise for Inez Bardini's portrayal of the tormented mother, and her singing had the emotional intensity the part required. I liked one reviewer's final paragraph: 'Staging and costumes were excellent, possibly a bit too lavish - the old woman's cabin had the dimensions of a baronial hall.'

Signorina Bardini sang Santuzza in *Cavalleria Rusticana*, which was staged with *Ave Maria* and scored as a personal triumph, with Umberto Borso giving an incisive performance as Turridu, displaying a voice of range and power to meet all the demands of the part. The chorus was stated to be in particularly fine form in the great Easter Hymn. Interviewed after the first-night of *Ave Maria*, Salvadore Allegra expressed satisfaction at the warmth of the Dublin reception for his opera and hoped that the society would stage his others such as *Medico Suo Malgrado* and *Romulus*. He was particularly pleased by the Radio Éireann Symphony Orchestra's accompaniment.

In that year's winter season *The Marriage of Figaro* was revived, with Adèle Leigh and her husband James Pease among the guest principals. To Miss Leigh, Dublin was a city of romance as she had met her husband James there. 'We dined together in Jammet's,' she recalled, 'and the food was as wonderful as ever. And our friends were in the cast, Jess Walters, Patricia Bartlett, Johanna Peters and David Kelly, and we all enjoyed ourselves just as before.' When I talked to conductor Charles Mackerras, he thought this particular *Figaro* was one of the best he had conducted and that Adèle Leigh and James Pease were splendid Mozartian singers. 'The thing is you must have the right voices for Mozart and I think we had them in that production.'

Miss Leigh did not particularly like singing opera in English but because it was Dublin, where it was the policy in the winter seasons, she was happy to go along with it. She sang Micaela in *Carmen* and as far as she can recall the role of Don José was sung in Italian by Umberto Borso. Ken Neate was back in Dublin to sing Faust with an all French cast. Italian mezzo Mafalda Masini sang Azucena in *Il Trovatore* as well as Carmen. Christopher West directed both *Carmen* and *The Marriage of Figaro*.

Arias in the Morning

Arias and duets in the morning? It sounds daft in today's programmed world but in the spring of 1960, when life was more leisurely, there was time for such indulgence. And it came about on this occasion because of the sheer enthusiasm of opera fans who took their place in the queue in South King Street long before the Gaiety booking opened at 10.30am. Indeed, many would have begun queueing on the afternoon before with stools and flasks of tea and throughout the night some of them would be relieved by friends who kept their places for them. 'They were a cheerful bunch,' recalls Donnie Potter, 'and while some of them dozed off to sleep, others joked and laughed undaunted by the lengthy wait.'

In Tony O'Dalaigh's view it was the exotic thing about Italian opera that was causing the clamour for tickets and the prospect of seeing stars such as Zeani, Rinaldi, Borso, Clabassi and Piero Guelfi in their favourite operas. They were proving a tremendous attraction and everyone wanted to hear them.' He himself often booked for friends and came away sometimes with two hundred tickets for distribution to his own particular group.

The Gaiety management decided one morning to throw the doors of the theatre open at 8.30, evidently taking pity on those fans who had queued all night, and asked them to take the parterre seats. There was another surprise in store when John F McInerney, a DGOS officer, arrived and proceeded to give an illustrated talk on some of the operas to be staged during that season. He was loudly applauded before he got down to the serious business of playing arias and duets from *Tosca*, *Turandot* and *Falstaff*. As a further friendly gesture, the management distributed cups of hot coffee and in case morning fatigue was setting in, a member of the Rathmines and Rathgar Musical Society played recorded excerpts from the society's current production of *Naughty Marietta*. By the time the booking opened with three times the normal staff, the fans seemed reluctant to leave their seats and entertaining fare.

The DGOS showed enterprise when it decided that spring to start what it described as a 'First Nighters' Club'. A raffle, entitling the winner to free seats, would be held on the first night of each of the six productions.

Programmes would be numbered and the winning number posted in the Gaiety foyer at the end of the performance. It was Colonel O'Kelly's idea. For some time he had been puzzled by the number of empty seats at first nights particularly and had discussed the question with his management committee. It was hoped the First Nighters Club would remedy the situation. 'We've lost money due to this attitude in Dublin,' he was quoted as saying, 'and it's one of the reasons why there is so much red ink used in making up the opera accounts. It's the sort of situation you're not likely to find on the Continent.'

It was customary prior to each new season to hold a press reception in order to announce programme details and at the same time attract maximum publicity. In a convivial atmosphere, critics and newspaper columnists mingled with members of the society, among them Dr Larchet, Col. O'Kelly, John F MacInerney, Prince Caraccioli and Bertie Timlin. Usually the principals in each of the operas were in attendance for interviews and photographs. 'Bill O'Kelly liked to conduct his usual review of the troops,' Terry O'Sullivan, the popular *Evening Press* columnist, used to joke. 'Bill knows everyone by name from a soldier to a general.'

Since the society had scarcely a penny to spend on publicity these receptions were very useful. 'The publicity we got was invaluable to us,' recalled Donnie Potter, 'and helped in no small way to sell tickets. If we had to pay for the space it would have cost us thousands of pounds.'

It was a major festival season of Italian opera, in fact the sixth - and Bellini's melodic *La Sonnambula* was being presented by the society for the first time. Gianna d'Angelo had been engaged to sing the role of Amina as well as the title role in *Lucia di Lammermoor* but had to cancel her engagements at short notice. This upset Paolo Silveri who was deputising for the indisposed impresario Maestro Botti and had engaged the singers. He was particularly annoyed by the soprano's telegram, which stated, 'I am sorry. I cannot and am not coming to Dublin. I am singing in Lisbon at this time.'

Signor Silveri threatened to sue her for breach of contract. 'A contract to us is like law,' he said, 'and cannot be broken unless by mutual consent.' Gianna d'Angelo, for her part, denied she had broken any contract and said her agent intimated she would not be required in Dublin for that spring season. Meanwhile, the society was faced with a more serious problem when the Italian government cancelled the subvention for that season for economy reasons. It was a grave problem and Colonel O'Kelly explained to the newspapers that they intended carrying on and all six operas would be presented. Paolo Silveri, in a typical gesture, announced he was prepared to bridge the financial gap between the financial resources of the DGOS and underwrite the cost of bringing the Italian singers he had already engaged to Dublin. At the same time he contacted each of the singers and explained the crisis that had arisen and appealed to them to stand by the society. The response was heartening and apart from d'Angelo, everyone agreed to sing. Her part in *Lucia* was given to Margherita Rinaldi and in the first two performances of *La Sonnambula* her place would be taken by Virginia Zeani.

Zeani's career was by now at its height. She had become a firm favourite at La Scala where her roles included Butterfly, Lucia, Violetta and Adina. She had also figured in a famous Scala production of *The Tales of Hoffmann* in which she performed all four female parts opposite the four villains of her husband Nicola Rossi-Lemeni. Her French repertoire also included roles in *Manon, Thais, Werther* and *Faust.* In that 1962 spring season the popular soprano displayed a new maturity vocally - her acting had always been extremely convincing. Although one morning newspaper critic found her voice 'too rich and sombre' to impersonate a simple village maiden in *La Sonnambula*, other reviewers thought she carried the role of Amina with her usual aplomb.

Zeani was steeped in the bel canto tradition and told me she counted Amina as ideal for her voice, though she was perhaps better known as Elvira in *I Puritani*, Norina *(Don Pasquale)*, Lucia and Adina *(L'Elisir d'Amore)*. But she was a versatile artist and La Scala had mounted two important works for her - Verdi's *Alzira* and Rossini's Otello. 'I was able to cope with many different roles because my technique was good,' she said, 'and I hoped in time to sing Tosca, Desdemona, Charlotte in *Werther* and Tatyana in *Eugene Onegin.* I wanted new challenges to keep my career interesting.'

Opera fans were undoubtedly getting full value for money, as Margherita Rinaldi's performance as Lucia filled the Gaiety to capacity and aroused great enthusiasm. Choristers like Dympna Carey, Aileen Walsh and Joan Rooney adored her in the part and remember her moving Mad Scene as though it was performed only yesterday. 'She combined beauty and voice,' mused Paddy Brennan, 'and was a truly remarkable performer. She made a great impression on me from the beginning; she possessed a radiant and limpid voice. Her Lucia was both beautifully sung and acted and her characterisation was always true, it was a joy to be on the stage with her.'

Lucia di Lammermoor proved one of the biggest commercial and artistic successes of the season; in fact, the Tuesday night performance broke the Gaiety's box-office record with receipts somewhere between £600 and £1000, and so pleased was the theatre's owner Louis Elliman that he invited Colonel O'Kelly, John Larchet, Bertie Timlin and other DGOS committee members into his office where he proceeded to open a bottle of champagne. It was not the first time that Elliman had celebrated record box-office receipts and as a showman, he never let the occasion pass without toasting the achievement. To Bill O'Kelly, Elliman's support remained one of the prime factors in the society's success and he never tired of stating the fact at press receptions.

When it was announced that the baritone Enzo Sordello was to sing the role of Ford in *Falstaff*, it tended to heighten the interest in the production. No doubt opera buffs remembered that he was the singer who clashed with Maria Callas at the New York Met and by the time he arrived in Dublin for rehearsals he was recognisable from his photograph in the world's newspapers. He was quizzed by Irish reporters who wanted to know if he had actually kicked the diva in the shins. Sordello would not be drawn. 'I am here to sing in *Falstaff*, not to answer your questions about *that* woman.'

Since the famous 'incident' with Callas had occurred in the mid-fifties, Sordello naturally wanted to forget it ever happened, but wherever he went it was dragged up by the press. And it had come about when they were singing in *Lucia di Lammermoor* and in an act two duet he sustained a high note longer than perhaps he should have, so that Callas became furious with him and complained to Rudolf Bing the Met's general manager. After the performance she was reputed to have said to Sordello, 'You'll never sing with me again'; and to Bing she issued the ultimatum, 'It's Sordello or me.' To placate the diva, Bing went ahead and terminated Sordello's contract. It was claimed at the time that she was under severe pressure and 'took it out' on the baritone.

He settled easily into the Dublin scene however and became well liked by chorus members. His voice was rich, vibrant and expressive and he emerged as one of the stars of the production. Piero Guelfi, as the fat knight, proved a splendid actor-singer and his natural flair for comedy stood him well in what was being described as a first-class production of Verdi's masterpiece. 'I really enjoyed singing in the opera,' recalled chorus member Dick Hanrahan, 'not only because of Piero Guelfi's performance but because the cast was so well balanced and I think we in the chorus didn't do badly either - or so the critics claimed.'

Guelfi was a good social mixer and made friends in the chorus. He was intrigued by the Guinness pint drinkers in the pubs near the Gaiety and the rounds system tended to baffle him. Unlike most of his countrymen who found Guinness somewhat heavy for their taste, he came to like a pint or two of the stuff. 'I used to drink with Piero in Neary's,' recalled Jimmy Brittain, 'and he'd laugh and say that stout was good for his voice. I told him this was an accepted fact in Ireland for years, though John McCormack preferred champagne. I made good friends too with Plinio Clabassi and Ferruccio

Mazzoli and they enjoyed Dublin wit and stories. They were great days to be part of the DGOS chorus.'

Paddy Brennan remembered that Clabassi was a real favourite with both Supers and choristers and was also a passionate soccer fan; in his day he came close to becoming a professional player and retained a love for the game. The big bass was told about the intense rivalry between the Dublin teams Drumcondra (Drums) and Shamrock Rovers (Rovers) and the capacity crowds their local clashes attracted. 'We decided to bring Plinio along one Sunday to see them in action. He enjoyed his trip to Glenmalure Park, except that the excitement of the game left him almost voiceless. He liked to roar and scream like the fans around him. I remember he was supposed to sing at a concert that evening and Bill O'Kelly was enraged and tore strips off one of his own sons for joining Plinio with the rest of the lads at the game.'

Usually the group, which consisted of both Supers and chorus members, as well as Italian singers, assembled on Sundays, if free, at Jury's Hotel in Dame Street and set off from there to a match. On other occasions the choristers and the Supers made up a team to play members of the Radio Éireann Symphony Orchestra who would be strengthened by personnel from the broadcasting station. Friendships were forged and camaraderie enhanced. Plinio Clabassi had a hand in organising rehearsals so that they would be free for a few hours to play or attend a game. But it wasn't always easy to try to fit in the sporting side.

Irrespective of what went on around him, either soccer games, post-opera supers or late night parties, Colonel O'Kelly never once lost sight of the main goal - the presentation of opera. Nothing, in his view, must get in the way of aiming for excellence, though he was no spoil-sport by any means. He usually contributed his party piece. He was especially proud that season to have engaged the outstanding American soprano Lucille Udovick to sing the title role in Puccini's *Turandot*. Udovick was already a big name in Italy where she had perfected her vocal art and now resided. She was in demand at La Scala and other leading European houses. And she had already recorded the role of Turandot with Franco Corelli (Calaf), Plinio Clabassi and Renata Mattiolo (Liu). She was once described by an American critic as 'an attractive, facially animated actress of appropriately operatic proportions and blessed with a rich dramatic soprano voice.' She was to make an immediate impression in the Gaiety, excelling both vocally and dramatically.

'Udovick is obviously one of the historic Turandots,' stated Charles Acton in the *Irish Times*. 'With a fine voice that commands us across the fullest orchestra, an icy authority and distant beauty that was only in part created by production and dress, she had the rare power to melt suddenly and humanly - to show that Puccini's strange creature was possible and credible.'

Seemingly, Umberto Borso's Calaf was a real match for her and his "Nessun dorma" drew prolonged applause from the crowded 'house'. His was by no means a volcanic voice in the del Monaco mould but rather a well-focused, expressive instrument with ample tone, colour and flexibility. Borso's Calaf remains one of the best heard in Dublin of any era.

Bruno Nofri's production was described as spectacular and Franco Patane's conducting of the RESO as 'nothing short of inspiring'. Critics praised the chorus as well as the National Ballet dancers. I should add that this *Turandot* is often recalled by oldtimers and chorus members who vividly remember Lucilla Udovik's performance. 'It was thrilling,' says Aileen Walsh, 'and what a voice!' 'She wasn't far behind Eva Turner in the part', said Florrie Draper, while Joe Black used to joke that there was no melting this ice lady's heart. By now Paddy Brennan had graduated from Super to the chorus tenor line and sang in *Turandot* and it still remains one of his greatest memories. 'I can recall the sheer spectacle of the production and the incredible number of Supers - sixty plus, I think - and the huge chorus, and it was the first time that the Gaiety stage was used to its full depth. As for Lucille Udovick, she was an ample lady with a voice to match. Franco Patane was wonderful on the podium.'

The seventh Festival of Italian Opera opened in the spring of 1961 with an acclaimed production of Verdi's *Aida* with Claudia Parada in the title role. A native of Chile, she had come to Italy in the fifties to further her career and since her last appearance in Dublin (Leonora in *Trovatore* in 1959) had substituted for Callas at La Scala. She received some outstanding notices for her Aida at the Gaiety, as did Myriam Pirazzini for her stirring Amneris, her last act being especially noted when she is beset by remorse. Angelo Bartoli's Radames was credible throughout and vocally he was equal to the demands of the music; his "Celeste Aida" was enthusiastically received.

Unfortunately Bartoli's voice gave way in the fourth performance and he was unable to continue after the Triumphal Scene in act two. A messenger was rushed to the hotel where Umberto Borso was staying and he was summoned to the Gaiety to finish the performance. There is an intriguing sequel to the episode. A small group of DGOS members attended a recital in Birmingham in 1995 by the brilliant mezzo Cecilia Bartoli and afterwards went backstage to congratulate her. She was surprised to learn that her father Angelo Bartoli had sung a leading role in Dublin, and had become indisposed. And she was amused when asked, 'We expect you to come to Dublin in the future to finish that unfinished performance by your father!'

Singing Amonasro in *Aida* was Piero Cappuccilli who was by now building up a tremendous name for himself. Since he made his debut in 1957 he had sung in most of the leading European opera houses and was called to the Met. to sing Germont, following the sudden death of the charismatic American baritone Leonard Warren. In 1960 he had sung the leading roles in recordings with Callas of *Lucia di Lammermoor* and *La Gioconda*, and in *The Marriage of Figaro* and *Don Giovanni* under Giulini with Sutherland, Schwarzkopf, Sciutti and Taddei.

Born in Trieste in 1929, he loved sport as a youth and wanted to excel in some aspect of it. But he chose architecture as a career and planned to enrol at the local university, though at the same time his grandfather and uncle - both avid opera lovers - prevailed on him to take up singing as a career. They had heard him sing Tosti songs and were impressed by the natural strength, vibrancy and resilience of his baritone voice. At one stage his uncle's forcefulness tended to irritate him. 'I had never seen an opera in my life,' he recalled, 'and didn't appreciate what all the fuss was about my voice.'

Eventually, to please his in-laws, young Cappuccilli agreed to audition at the local opera house and amongst those present was Luciano Donnaggio, a first-rate bass in his day and who was now about to take on pupils. He agreed, but after six months tired of the routine of singing lessons and stayed away to concentrate on his architectural studies. He made no secret of his doubts about opera as a career, telling friends that it was an overcrowded profession in Italy. Puzzled by his absence, Signor Donnaggio contacted his former pupil and tried to convince him there was a very bright future for him in singing and offered on his return not to charge him a fee.

Cappuccilli says he was taken by his teacher's sincerity and resumed his singing lessons and they were to last for five years. He went to Milan where he auditioned for Maestros Campogalliani and Confalonieri, both coaches at the singing school of La Scala. Their reaction was more than enthusiastic - they in fact invited him to attend their evening classes. He went on to win various competitions, including one for Young Opera Singers organised by the Italian Operatic Concert Association, and his success led to an invitation to appear as Tonio in a performance of *Pagliacci* at the Teatro Nuovo, Milan in 1957.

The critics immediately spotted his potential and predicted a bright future and inside a few months, he got engagements in Reggio Emilia and Florence; his first engagement outside of Italy was at the Athens State Opera where he sang Count di Luna in *Il Trovatore*. Soon he began to be hailed as a genuine interpreter of Verdi's music and more offers poured in for him to sing in *La Traviata*, *Rigoletto*, *A Masked Ball* and *I due Foscari*. 'I adore Verdi,' the singer would say later. 'He just suits my voice and I never encounter any difficulties when singing his roles, which although extremely demanding are nevertheless well-written for the voice.'

Veronica Dunne had no doubt about the merits of his voice. 'It was made of steel,' she said. 'During those years in Dublin he was to become one of my favourite baritones. Although a small man in stature, he was strong and wiry and there was real strength and resonance in his voice and he could lift the Gaiety roof. I will say one thing for the DGOS, it was bringing over some star singers and audiences could be grateful for this.' Paolo Silveri told me that he himself was responsible for engaging Cappuccilli and that he came to Dublin for a very small fee.

The return of Lucille Udovich in the spring of `61 to sing the title role in *Norma* for the first time in Dublin was a real cause for celebration and, as a consequence, booking was heavy among those who hadn't forgotten the soprano's Turandot. And singing the part of Adalgisa was Myriam Pirazzini, who had already sung Amneris for the society. Umberto Borso was cast as Pollione, a role well suited to his vocal gifts. It was six years since the society had staged *Norma*, when the protagonists were the great Ebe Stignani and Caterina Mancini.

It was soon apparent that Udovich and Pirazzini were also ideal for this dramatic Bellini opera and both were lauded by the critics, none more so than by Mary MacGoris *(Independent)*. 'The most electrifying moments in the whole gripping performance came in the duets and trios between Udovich, Pirazzini and Borso,' she stated. 'The only thing lacking in Udovich's ardent Norma is her inability to produce a flexible coloratura and a melting *mezza-voce*, otherwise it was a towering performance and the soprano displayed many of the qualities the role demanded.'

The season was also notable for the first production by the society of Cimarosa's *Il Matrimonio Segreto*. Although the composer may not have had the melodic gifts of either Bellini, Rossini or Mozart, his music has abundant grace and style and entertainment value. The DGOS production was visually striking with attractive sets and beautiful costumes and inventive direction by Carlo Acly Azzolini.

'It is to be hoped that no one who has the faintest interest in opera will miss *Il Matrimonio Segreto* at the Gaiety,' observed one critic, 'It is possibly the best and certainly one of the most delightful performances the society has ever offered us.'

While the theatre was not filled for the performances, the opera was an undoubted artistic success, thanks to the accomplished cast that included Margherita Rinaldi, tenor Salvatore Gioia and Mafalda Micheluzzi. The conductor was Napoleone Annovazzi who was totally in sympathy with Cimarosa's work and was said to have 'coaxed some polished playing from the Radio Éireann Symphony Orchestra.' Much more would be heard of Maestro Annovazzi in Dublin in the years to come.

Charles Mackerras was returning that winter of `61 to conduct *Carmen*, *Madama Butterfly* and *Faust* with casts made up mostly of English and Welsh singers. The Irish interest centred in Bernadette Greevy whose lovely contralto voice was attracting a good deal of attention. She was singing Siebel in *Faust* and she did not disappoint her admirers; indeed, so impressive was her performance that it prompted Mary MacGoris to comment, 'So good was she that there was a case here for including the charming third-act Cavatina, known in English as "When all was young and pleasant", even though it is seldom sung anymore nowadays.'

Charles Mackerras has some vivid memories of both *Faust* and *Carmen*. 'There were all sorts of incidents actually in both operas,' he recalled, 'and I remember that the producer Michael Geliot had a terrible row with Bill O'Kelly over the fact that Michael had produced the church scene in *Faust* inside the church and Bill thought that it was blasphemous to have the Devil in church. It is true that Gounod's version probably had Marguerite trying to enter the church from outside and being prevented by Mephistofeles, but of course the scene is normally produced as inside the church, even in Catholic countries such as France and Italy.'

Whenever I myself have talked to chorus members about the season, they have invariably recalled the 'organ episode' and their versions differed in small details. All were agreed though that Mackerras stopped the performance at one point and that after the final curtain the rumours spread that Colonel O'Kelly took the conductor aside and rebuked him.

Mackerras had a quite philosophical explanation, or so it appeared to me in our conversation. As he put it, 'The incident with the organ was, as far as I remember, to do with the fact that the cable of the electronic organ had somehow got ruptured and that when the player started to play it, nothing happened. The Marguerite Ana Raquel Satre was extremely thrown by the fact that the organ did not come in and so failed to come in herself, with the result that the performance more or less ground to a halt and I was forced to stop until the cable could be re-attached, after which we did the scene again without any difficulty. I believe that Bill O'Kelly was annoyed that I had stopped in the middle of the scene, but I cannot remember that he complained about it to me, because in point of fact I had no other choice.'

Tom Carney was one of the off-stage chorus in the scene and as he watched the backstage closed circuit television he was able to pick out Charles Mackerras, and after the orchestra stopped playing, he turned around to the audience to tell them that something was wrong and would be corrected as soon as possible. 'I think we were all bemused at what was happening and it seemed some time before Mackerras resumed conducting.'

According to Charlie Dunphy, also in the chorus, the organ seemed badly out of tune and was playing in a different pitch to that of the orchestra, so something had to be done. 'It's a long time ago,' he said, 'but I imagine there was an electronic fault which sometimes happened in the case of these organs, or else the instrument wasn't tuned properly. I think that Charles Mackerras had no other option except stop the scene; I had seen opera performances being stopped in my time for various other reasons. Once a beam fell from the proscenium arch and the conductor then called a halt 'to the proceedings'.

Norris Davidson told me that Radio Éireann was well aware of such eventualities and it was one of the reasons why the DGOS productions were recorded more than once and carefully edited for broadcasting, omitting of course any stoppages or disasters. Fortunately, he said, such things didn't often happen, though he could recall a few. Once the Gaiety curtain was brought down too soon on *La Bohème* and the orchestra was left to 'fill in the time'. He was philosophical, however, and felt that things could go wrong in the best planned productions.

Indeed, at the third performance of *Faust* that winter season the Gaiety gremlins were again at work. As Charles Mackerras was to recall, 'At this particular performance Ana Raquel Satre was singing the aria by the window at the end of act three and although the false window had no glass in it, it was obvious that the window would not open without the aid of some other person other than the singer. A stage hand was told to open the window without his hands being seen, and in the darkness his hands went up the soprano's dress instead of up the wall. The audience - and we who were watching her sing - could not understand why she sang the aria so badly and looked as if she was flapping her hands in anger rather than singing about her love for Faust. The fact was that she was trying to slap the unfortunate stage hand so that he would take his hands away from her legs. In the meantime the window remained firmly shut.'

Apart from the gremlins, it was an enjoyable season with Dublin-born Peter McBrien making his debut as Dancairo in *Carmen* - he also had a small part in *Faust*. He had been recommended to Colonel O'Kelly by Robert Johnston, the *Irish Press* critic. After the audition he was told by the Colonel he had the part and before he left the room the contract was signed. To McBrien, the DGOS chairman was forthright and earthy and his heart was obviously in opera. He himself had studied violin and wanted to make it his career, but at the age of nineteen he won a vocal scholarship to the Royal Irish Academy of Music and began his studies with Professor Viani and later on was coached by Michael O'Higgins. By now he was a member of the Radio Éireann Singers, directed by Dr Hans Waldemer Rosen and being married, was happy to stay in Ireland, though Michael O'Higgins believed he had a future in Germany. He possessed a flexible and strong baritone voice that sounded first-class in Italian, German or Russian opera.

If *Madama Butterfly* failed to please the critics, it was a different story in the case of *Cosi fan tutte*. The performance apparently evoked 'much of the charm which pervades the opera and Michael Geliot's production did not clash with the music.' Sung in English, the cast sang stylishly, notably Margareta Elkins (Dorabella) and Patricia Bartlett (Fiordiligi), while Elizabeth Robinson was said to 'have caught the insouciant spirit of Despina to perfection.'

The society had sometimes been accused of failing to exploit the potential of Irish singers, but this was not altogether true. Tenor Edwin Fitzgibbon was showing promise and had impressed Paolo Silveri at his audition. After his early studies at the Royal Irish Academy of Music, where he sang baritone, he went to the Royal Manchester College of Music and completed his studies under Frederick Cox, the principal, but this time as a tenor. His performance at the college as Cavaradossi in *Tosca* greatly impressed the critics of the *Guardian* and the *Daily Telegraph* and both hailed him as a discovery.

Back in Dublin, he sang regularly on radio programmes and Colonel O'Kelly intimated to him that the society was prepared to use him when the right parts came along. The question was whether the singer was prepared to go professional as he appeared to have a good future in the civil service; it was the age-old conflict between security and professional insecurity. Fitzgibbon did enjoy singing and was encouraged by what people were predicting about him. It was not an easy choice for him.

With growing uncertainty surrounding the future of the Italian government subvention, the society was seeking funding from private individuals as well as business firms, mainly to guarantee against production losses. More than forty names were listed in the winter season programme and these included Sir Chester Beatty, Sir Alfred Beit, Hector Grey, Dockrell's Ltd., McConnell's Advertising Services and Murray's Car Rentals. And later in his annual report for the year (1961) honorary secretary, Bertie Timlin, stated: 'Our financial strength largely derives only from the subscriptions of patron members and from functions organised by the committees. If these are not sufficient our commitments are jeopardised and long-range planning becomes a gamble. We are then dependent on our guarantors who guarantee our productions to a degree against loss, Bord Fáilte and the Arts Council to make our overdraft more acceptable to the bank directors - and subject to suitable guarantees from us.'

The society's application to Bord Fáilte, he said, for a guarantee against loss on their spring season was granted by an offer of £500 and it was only after much effort and persuasive argument by their own management committee that the guarantee was increased to £1,250. And they were not helped when the Italian government found it necessary earlier in the year to cut the subvention allocated to foreign countries, including Ireland. That meant that in order to present their spring season they were obliged to increase their own financial commitment by an advance of a further £500.

Patron members, it seemed from the report, were unhappy about the winter season which consisted of four operas sung in English, and compared the season unfavourably with the spring season, but it was overlooked that the winter season was not subsidised from any source and the security the society had was the Arts Council guarantee against loss, which because of its limited finances was considerably less than that of Bord Fáilte Eireann.

Bertie Timlin could state, however, that the society was slowly emerging from the slough of financial back debt and was in fact about £1,500 better off than at the same time last year. This was mainly due to their guarantors, patron members and their committees, particularly the Ladies' Committee which though almost anonymous had made practical contributions since it was formed. As can be seen from the report the society continued to depend on the goodwill and generosity of friends and business firms and their patron members and was grateful when Margaret McDonnell and the ladies in her committee came forward with a cheque, the proceeds of a successful function or other. What was required more than ever before was a realistic grant from the Arts Council, otherwise the society would continue to struggle into another decade.

Memories of 'Nabucco'

It is early May 1962 and chorus members are rehearsing in rooms with sliding doors, a piano, a table and some chairs. It is a casual-looking scene but chorus master Riccardo Bottino goes about his work earnestly; up to this stage Julia Gray had coached the chorus members but usually an Italian took over sometime before opening night. The DGOS chorus is augmented by choristers from Cork and Belfast. The opera being rehearsed is Verdi's *Nabucco* and never before staged in Dublin. Its background is fascinating, if only because it will change the course of Verdi's life. Saddened by deaths in his family and the failure of his second opera, *Un Giorno di Regno*, he is in no state of mind to write a new work and has no intention of doing so. But he is strongly persuaded by Signor Merelli, director at La Scala to read Solera's libretto, set in Babylon and Jerusalem, and come up with a musical score. He finally relents and by the spring of 1842 *Nabucco* is ready for rehearsal. Soon the rehearsals are generating extraordinary excitement, particularly the magnificent third act chorus 'Va pensiero' which in the Austrian-ruled Milan, arouses strong patriotic feelings as the Milanese see themselves as Jews suffering under the Babylonian yoke. The whole La Scala Company is predicting a stupendous success even before the rise of the opening night's curtain.

The reaction at rehearsals in Dublin is not dissimilar though, of course, there is no hint of patriotic fervour except suppressed excitement. 'We know we're on a winner,' says Paddy Brennan. 'We have not only a very strong chorus but a tremendous cast. We have a wonderful Nabucco in the Italian baritone Gian Giacomo Guelfi, a role which we hear he has been singing with great success in Italy. He is a towering man with a voluminous voice that has also lots of shading and colouring. And everyone is raving about Luisa Maragliano's Abigaille. As an artist, she generates excitement from her first note.'

Dympna Carney agrees and finds her dress rehearsal performances electrifying. She cannot wait for the first night. It's Guelfi's voice that 'bowls over' Tom Carney. Listening to the baritone, he gets the impression he has a microphone stuck in his throat. But it is not a rough voice, he sings expressively, and there is polish to it. He says it is a big choral work and learning the chorus parts hasn't been easy. Dick Hanrahan predicts a big first night success, so does Joe Black and Jimmy Brittain. Aileen Walsh is thrilled that the dress rehearsal has gone so well, so are Florrie Draper and Monica Condron. John Carney feels that Irish audiences will love the great choruses and the spectacular side of the opera. Charlie Dunphy is impressed by Maestro Annovazzi's control on the podium and the playing by the orchestra. Everyone agrees that it will be one of the society's biggest nights and the opera will come as a marvellous surprise to those who have heard only radio plays of the chorus 'Va pensiero'. There is more to it, says Mary Troy.

*　*　*

As the opening night, Thursday May 10, loomed word had already reached opera fans that Nabucco was not to be missed on any account, so that when Gaiety booking opened the queues were longer than usual; the rest of the programme included *Trovatore*, *Bohème*, *Traviata*, *Lucia di Lammermoor* and the triple bill comprising *Gianni Schicchi*, *Suor Angelica* and *Medico Suo Malgrado*. Interest was added by the fact that the society was celebrating its 21st anniversary and at the Royal Hibernian Hotel on Saturday, April 21 the occasion was toasted.

Indeed, the influential Maestro Botti was happily back after his illness to toast the society, and told the large gathering that included the Italian Ambassador Baron Vittorio Winspeare that the Dublin Festival of Italian Opera was by now one of the most important in Europe. Replying to the toast, chairman Colonel O'Kelly talked of the society's achievements and said they had surpassed all their expectations. The first season in 1941 had cost £900 to mount and, in comparison, the 1962 season was costing an estimated £31,000. More toasts were proposed by Thomas A Doyle, S.C., a member of the DGOS management committee and the society's president John Larchet, who like Col. O'Kelly, referred to the great progress made by them against the odds. No one, he said, could have imagined in the early forties that they would twenty-one years later be hearing some of the outstanding operatic voices in the world.

It was going to be also a colourful season in that spring of '62, for the society was importing in the Botti 'package' the settings and costumes from Rome and the wigs from Palermo. There was general satisfaction that Maestro Annovazzi was coming back to conduct a number of productions including *Nabucco*. He had been first contacted by Colonel O'Kelly when he was conducting performances by the San Carlo Company in London two years previously. 'I received a telephone call asking me if I could come over to Dublin urgently to meet him there. It appeared that he was having some contractual problems with a conductor who had been previously engaged. Unfortunately my own contractual commitments prevented me from leaving London at that moment and my first acquaintance with Dublin and the DGOS did not come until the following spring of 1961.'

Annovazzi was small in stature, urbane in manner and bore a studious appearance. Although born a Florentine, he completed his musical studies in Venice and began his conducting career at Riga in 1935, and in the post-war era was soon in demand in European and North American opera houses. His successes in Lisbon and Barcelona particularly brought him a higher profile and he was undoubtedly a 'capture' for the DGOS. Furthermore, he and Col. O'Kelly hit it off exceedingly well from the start, their opposite temperaments blending surprisingly well. Dr Larchet admired Annovazzi as a musician and regarded him as one of the most knowledgeable he had encountered. He felt he would be of inestimable value to the society.

During the final rehearsals of *Nabucco* the conductor made a marked impression on the chorus members. To people like Florrie Draper, Aileen Walsh, Dympna Carney and Monica Condron, Maestro Annovazzi understood singers and possessed a deep insight into opera. 'I enjoyed working with him,' says Dympna Carney, 'and although he was musically demanding he was very fair and courteous. I think we all agreed he brought something extra to music. Looking at him on the podium, you felt that nothing could go wrong. He seemed to know every principal's part and was not slow to cue singers either.'

The Gaiety was full for the opening night of *Nabucco*. Donnie Potter would say there was a special atmosphere in the house, one of unusual expectancy. 'At this time stories had been coming out of rehearsals that the cast was great and the chorus was bigger than ever before. I don't think I ever saw the chorus members so excited about an opera.' Norris Davidson says they planned to record all four performances of *Nabucco*. He was amused by the fact that in one or two of Radio Éireann's sponsored programmes of the time the presenters played the chorus 'Va pensiero' nearly thrice a week. It seemed that listeners were crazy about it and inevitably the presenters emphasised that it would be heard during the DGOS's spring season.

Prince Caracciolo edited a special programme to mark the 21st season and it carried a message from President de Valera which stated briefly, 'Heartiest congratulations to the Dublin Grand Opera Society on its 21st anniversary. May its splendid work for the opera in Dublin bear an ever-increasing abundance of good fruit.' Colonel O'Kelly also penned an article about the society and recalled the contributions made in the early years by such as James Johnston, John Lynskey, JC Browner, May Devitt, Patricia Black,

John Torney and others.

Interestingly, one of the most notable links with the foundation year 1941 was chorus mistress Julia Gray, one of the best-loved characters in the society's history. She was still hale and hearty in that year of 1962 and as everyone agreed, no one could play the piano like Julia - and she was of course a first-class coach of the chorus. As Aileen Walsh liked to remark, 'You'd go a long way to find someone to surpass her.'

From an audience's point of view the story of Nabucco, the conqueror, whose Assyrian armies have overrun the kingdom of Judea, and who dares to call himself God, is matched in every respect by the music. And from the magnificent opening chorus, when the High Priest Zaccaria exhorts the Jews and Levites to have courage, there is a nobility of Biblical proportions. Dramatically the highpoint is the arrival of Nabucco, as is also his final humiliation later and impassioned plea for forgiveness.

Anyone who was at that opening night in the Gaiety will I have no doubt, retain vivid memories of the performance. I can still hear the Radio Éireann Symphony Orchestra play the captivating overture that in a way paints the whole musical canvass, with Maestro Annovazzi as assured as ever. As the High Priest Zaccaria, Ferruccio Mazzoli's powerful bass voice projected into every corner of the theatre, and when he is joined by the chorus, the whole majesty of Verdi's opera comes alive on stage.

We are told that at the La Scala premiere of the work the audience 'was sent into a state of delirium by the third act chorus "Va pensiero" and insisted on its being repeated, but a law was in force in Milan forbidding encores, as they were too frequently turned into demonstrations against Austrian rule.' We were more fortunate in the Gaiety on the May night in `62 as the chorus responded to the tremendous enthusiasm of the audience and repeated the chorus. As the voices rose in unison to transcend the orchestra I shall never forget the silence and, at the conclusion, the rapturous reception. The applause appeared to go on forever.

There were other memorable moments of course provided by Gian Giacomo Guelfi's portrayal of Nabucco and Luisa Maragliano's astonishing performance as Abigaile. Many opera buffs were loathe to leave the Gaiety that night and for a long time after the final curtain sipped their drinks and discussed the evening's excitement. Not a few planned to attend another performance of the opera if she could get tickets. I joined some others in the foyer and awaited the arrival of Guelfi, as more people than usual wanted their programmes autographed. After a while, he strode down the stairs accompanied by his wife and some colleagues, cutting an impressive figure. A big man, he smiled at the onlookers and began to sign their programmes; others shook his hand warmly and congratulated him on his singing. He seemed to have little English. Soon he and his party were gone leaving behind a cluster of opera buffs still talking about Guelfi, Maragliano, Mazzoli and perhaps most of all the genius of Giuseppe Verdi.

The newspaper headlines told the whole story. 'GREAT SINGING BY GUELFI' proclaimed the *Evening Herald*; 'NABUCCO CHORUS WAS MAGNIFICENT' *(Irish Press)*; 'NABUCCO MAKES OPERA MEMORABLE' *(Irish Times)*; 'OUTSTANDING SINGING IN VERDI OPERA' *(Irish Independent)*. In her *Independent* review, Mary MacGoris thought that 'care obviously had been lavished on the performance and the casting and the two main characters were outstanding. Gian Giacomo Guelfi had used his magnificent voice, vital and beautiful, with considerable artistry; his performance would have been even more effective if he had unleashed its power more often in the scenes of early pride and final triumph to contrast with the moving singing in his period of madness and imprisonment.'

In Abigaille, Luisa Maragliano had a role that suited her style to perfection. The formidable difficulties of its extraordinary range, she surmounted with ease; while the vibrant quality of her voice and her fine dramatic sense gave full value to its chief emotions of anger and hatred. To Miss MacGoris, however, it was a 'grave artistic error to repeat "Va pensiero", especially as it was done well after the applause had ended and needed loud off-stage hisses to silence the High Priest, who had already begun to discourse.

Charles Acton, in the *Irish Times*, thought the chorus was splendid, and added, 'Heaven forbid that we should return to opera encores, but this one last night was fully justified. Robert Johnston *(Irish Press)* made no reference to the encore; instead he wrote of the DGOS chorus's achievement in the opera and their splendid singing throughout. Like everyone else, he praised Gian Giacomo Guelfi's Nabucco as a portrayal of immense power and Luisa Maragliano's exciting Abigaile. He also singled out Ferruccio Mazzolli and the two lovers sung by Paola Montovani and Angelo Marchiandi.

Brian Quinn, in the *Herald*, had some kind words to say about the chorus but 'hoped the encore episode would not be repeated.' He thought that Gian Giacomo Guelfi dominated the performance, displaying a voice of remarkable power, scope and range, and that Paola Mantovani made a profound impression as Fenena, as did Luisa Maragliano as Abigaile.

Despite the criticisms about the encores, "Va pensiero" was repeated in subsequent performances. 'We seemed to have no other option,' says Paddy Brennan, 'for audiences would not let us continue unless we sang it again. I know that *Nabucco* became the talk of Dublin and everyone wanted to see it.' John and Tom Carney, as well as Dick Hanrahan were inclined to see the production as a landmark in the society's history and believed it opened the way to the staging of other big choral works. While they conceded that the Gaiety stage was restricted in size and depth it was big enough for most operas provided the director and designer were skilful enough. Singing *Nabucco* was a tiring exercise, recalls Dympna Carney, and one had to try to relax for some time afterwards. To Jimmy Brittain and Charlie Dunphy, it was a very exciting occasion and showed everybody why *Nabucco* had achieved world popularity.

It was to prove a compelling Verdi season with Piero Cappuccilli again showing how outstanding a Verdian baritone he had become, bringing style and vigour to the roles of the elder Germont in *Traviata* and Count di Luna in *Trovatore*. His characterisations were well drawn and he thrilled the Gaiety audiences in the big set pieces. The sets for *Traviata* were by Sormani of Milan and the cast, particularly tenor Umberto Grilli, was of a uniformly high standard. Maestro Annovazzi's conducting of the RESO was noteworthy. The critics as a whole had been impressed.

The season had opened with *Trovatore* and it was generally agreed that mezzo Lucia Danieli, as the gypsy woman Azucena, equalled Cappuccilli for vocal dynamics and artistry. Born in Vicenza, near Venice, she quickly came to the forefront in Italy where her Amneris and Azucena were admired at La Scala and the country's other leading opera houses. She was making her Dublin debut.

Both Piero Cappuccilli and Umberto Borso - who was singing Manrico - were stated to be perfectly cast and made a significant contribution to what was regarded as a splendid production, although at least one critic found the sets far from impressive and some of the costumes even ugly to look at. There was a tendency among some critics at this time to harp on tiny production details and flaws while overlooking some of the bigger virtues.

Sometimes the result could be amusing, if not occasionally hilarious. For example, *Irish Press* critic John O'Donovan's description of the big trio in act one of *Trovatore*: 'I can look at Murillo without flinching, but when Leonora in Mediterranean blue, the Count in Robin Hood green, and Manrico in Soviet red lined up for their trio, I hastily pulled down my eyelids and refused to raise them until my neighbour gave me the all clear.'

Gianni Schicchi, it seemed, proved best of the triple bill and according to most reviewers was well performed, with baritone Scipio Colombo outstanding in the title role, being 'right inside the part of the wily old rogue.' As his daughter, Valeria Mariconda, a young soprano from Tuscany, sang beautifully while Angelo Marchiandi, from Genoa, proved 'a spirited tenor.' Edwin Fitzgibbon, who had appeared earlier in *Nabucco*, was singled out for mention in a production where the teamwork was excellent.

Strangely, *Suor Angelica*, which has enjoyed great success in more recent years, did not impress the critics greatly in that `62 season, nor the third opera in the triple bill *Il Medico Suo Malgrado* which was described as 'terribly slight,' though Scipio Colombo and the bass Giorgio Onesti stood out in the cast. Maestro Annovazzi was certainly being kept busy and was rewarding the society's faith in his musical skills.

According to Geraldine O'Grady he was an outstanding operatic conductor. He breathed and lived the music and she used to think he had the face of somebody who loved music and it was written all over him and his musicianship was undeniable. During an actual performance he sang every word and note and so was a superb guide to singers. Although he projected a quiet personality, musically he was demanding and more than once in rehearsal he emitted a few yells when singers got it wrong or a musician's concentration lapsed. Most of the time his irritation was justified. As he was a good communicator, he was able to get through to everyone what he wanted.

Two years previously she had joined the orchestra as leader and enjoyed playing at the DGOS opera seasons, even if they were very different from her symphonic engagements with the orchestra. She had been deeply moved by the performances of *Norma* and in that `62 season both *Nabucco* and *Traviata*. There was little to choose between the individual performances by Gian Guelfi and Piero Cappuccilli, though she would never forget Cappuccilli's opening bars of 'Provenza' in *Traviata*. 'I could hardly play with the emotional impact on me. It was one of the first times a voice made me almost forget I was playing.'

To Geraldine O'Grady there were some drawbacks playing in the Gaiety. The pit itself could be freezing and it was there she got her first attack of fibrositis on her neck and shoulders and it stayed with her ever since. For some reason the place always seemed cold in March and April and opera rehearsals could be a chore, with draughts of cold air coming from the back stage. Furthermore, since most dress rehearsals were held on a Sunday she seldom got the day off. 'I don't think I ever had Easter Sunday off during my four years leading the orchestra. And it was a hectic schedule, too, with scarcely time for lunch.' Musicians hadn't the same rights then as they enjoy nowadays and often she felt they were being exploited.

Ironically, though, she never felt tired, mainly because she was exhilarated by the music itself. And an exciting performance she would feel heady and usually tried to relax over a chat and a late night meal. And it was enjoyable playing the music of different operatic composers. A Mozart opera was the most difficult to accompany and one could never relax one's concentration for a moment. The appeal of the Italian repertoire was contained in the lovely melodies and the opportunity it afforded artists to show off their voices. There were times when the atmosphere in the Gaiety could be electric and the audience on a high; at other times it could be amusing. As when they were playing for the triple bill that season. 'I can recall there was a donkey in *Suor Angelica* and at the interval between Gianni Schicchi and they were preparing the stage, which at the time was old and full of cracks. Anyway, this musician was smoking a cigarette and the next thing the donkey did his No 2 and it all poured down on top of his bow tie and tuxedo. Obviously the animal had a gastric upset and here I was witnessing it all. What could I say or do? Next moment, the violinist dashed to the nearest door and since it was the ladies there were shrieks from the inside. It was no use, he had to be sent home in a taxi for a clean-up. 'I remember we played on without him. But oh, what a smell it had been.

The society was still in celebratory mood during that winter season and fittingly mounted Wagner's *Tannhauser*, as if to answer those critics who felt it was shamefully neglecting the composer's great works. It had been nearly twenty years since *Tannhauser* was last performed. A feature of the revival was the engagement of Irish singers, Edwin Fitzgibbon, Jimmy Brittain, Gerald Duffy and Joseph Dalton, as well as newcomer Mary Sheridan to sing the shepherd boy.

'I think we all looked forward to the opera,' recalled Tom Carney, 'for Wagner's music had a special quality that appealed to the chorus. I do remember that the orchestra played exceptionally well and there was warm applause for the overture. The German principals were all very good, especially Alexander Lorenz's Wolfram and his "O Star of Eve" was beautifully sung.'

Tibor Paul and the Radio Éireann Symphony Orchestra emerged triumphantly from the performance and accompanied the singers in admirable fashion. Mary MacGoris described the singing as 'extremely artistic, rising in the second and third acts to magnificence.'

Mozart's *Don Giovanni* was also revived that season with Tibor Paul again conducting the RESO. It was, from all accounts, a more workmanlike than inspired opening performance, failing as Brian Quinn (*Evening Herald*) stated to 'add an extra dimension to one's experience of opera.' The cast impressed, particularly Edith Mathis, as Zerlina, and Carlos Alexander in the title role of the seductive Don. 'He was suave and assured and sings well,' summed up one veteran reviewer.

Undoubtedly it had been a memorable anniversary year and it was fitting that a presentation was made to both Dr Larchet and Colonel O'Kelly for their contribution to the work of the society. Each was presented with a gold and silver cigarette case. Bertie Timlin could always be relied upon to make his annual report an accurate and entertaining account of the society's activities. When the music, for instance, of *Don Giovanni* was not available in time for the Gaiety performance, conductor Arthur Hammond, an old friend of the society, came to its assistance.

Timlin also recalled the *Tannhauser* performance, stating, 'During one of these performances, the Pilgrims' Chorus having finished, the German producer happened to stroll into the Gaiety green room where he saw, relaxed and comfortable in a chair, a reverend Franciscan who was discussing the opera with one of the principals. The producer, horrified by a pilgrim's laxity, grasped him by the habit and exploded, "Upstairs man, and change that robe immediately!"'

Giuseppe di Stefano

They refurbished the Gaiety's No 1 dressing room for his arrival. He and his entourage were booked into three suites in the Royal Hibernian Hotel for the duration of his stay in that June of 1963; while the DGOS itself dug deep into its meagre resources to ensure that Giuseppe di Stefano, celebrity, recording star and longtime La Scala partner for Maria Callas would be able to fulfil the engagement. His fee of £1,500 a performance was creating a society record but Colonel O'Kelly and his management committee reckoned it was worth the risks involved.

Anyway, Dubliners loved film, theatrical and opera stars and in the latter category few equalled Signor di Stefano. His extrovert personality, handsome appearance and his liking for cigars, gambling and champagne lent him a more worldly dimension than most of the famous artists of the day. At the age of forty-two his diary was pretty full and his engagements in the following months included *Tosca*, to be recorded in Vienna for Decca with Leontyne Price and Giuseppe Taddei with Herbert von Karajan conducting; it was the opera he was to sing in Dublin. That he was bringing his Rolls Royce along with him invested his visit with that extra touch of glamour. Every other production that spring season appeared to be dwarfed by *Tosca*, for Scarpia would be portrayed by Gian Giacomo Guelfi, so the prospect of hearing two great voices in the same opera lengthened the ticket queues in South King Street. The popularity of Italian opera had reached its zenith and fans could look forward also to Cappuccilli as Rigoletto, Dino Dondi in the title role of *Macbeth* and Margherita Rinaldi in *La Sonnambula*.

Understandably, the newspapers concentrated on di Stefano's life and career as well as his stage and recording partnership with Callas. There is little doubt that his rise to fame was meteoric. Born in Motto Sant Anastasia, a village in the Sicilian provinces, in 1921, his entry to La Scala was amazingly rapid, in fact just a year after he had made his debut at the Teatro Municipale in Reggio Emilia in April 1946. His smooth and liquid tenor voice made him an instant favourite in lighter lyric roles, and when he sang Elvino *(La Sonnambula)* and Des Grieux *(Manon)* at the Rome Opera he was immediately hailed in the same breath as Tito Schipa. Although he was no actor, his graceful stage style, good looks and exquisite phrasing made him almost unrivalled in his sphere.

It was his link-up with Callas, however, that lent him celebrity status. They first sang together in *La Traviata* and shortly afterwards in Mexico in *I Puritani*. It was on his own admission a unique experience. 'She gave the same passion as a man could,' he recalled. 'What was astonishing to me was the coloratura in *Puritani*. I had never heard it sung like that before.'

Callas, for her part, made no secret of her admiration for the singer and that she wanted him to record with her. Their voices blended beautifully, especially in the recording of *Puritani,* but there were inevitable clashes of temperament and Irish newspapers featured them from time to time. One such was the occasion in 1955 when di Stefano walked out of rehearsals of *Traviata* and Callas, angered by his behaviour, accused the tenor of lack of respect for her. 'I was having trouble with pitch,' was his weak excuse.

Dublin's opera fans accepted the Callas - di Stefano outbursts as simply a part of the world operatic scenario and were concerned only with hearing the tenor in some of Puccini's most mellifluous music. 'His coming was creating both curiosity and excitement among us all in the chorus,' says Mary Troy. 'I could hardly believe I would be sharing the same stage with him. I didn't care what anyone said about him, I just loved his voice. He was fabulous and everyone seemed to know him by his records.'

'I do agree that everyone was a bit excited about him,' recalls Joan Rooney. 'I could hear others in the chorus talk about his records and everyone wondered if his voice would be the same. His name was magic; I mean baritones can be great and Silveri, Guelfi and Cappuccilli were certainly that but a star tenor is something else. I couldn't wait to hear him sing.'

To Aileen Walsh he was the most glamorous singer to be engaged by the society. 'We all had read about his La Scala appearances and the wonderful triumphs he enjoyed singing with Callas, so it was no surprise that he was the biggest talking point in our spring season.' To Geraldine O'Grady, di Stefano was a handsome man with a particularly beautiful lyrical tenor voice. 'I think he was born to sing bel canto and those sweet Tosti songs.' Monica Condron said that since most people had not heard di Stefano sing in opera they were inclined to judge him solely by his records. She hoped they wouldn't be disappointed.

The male choristers were also curious about the tenor's arrival. Tom and John Carney remember the subject being discussed and people asking whether the tenor was by now a little over the hill, this despite the fact that he was only forty-two. Dick Hanrahan had followed his career and played his records and reckoned the society had done very well to get a singer of his stature. 'Frankly, I was baffled how they managed to get him to Dublin.' To

Jimmy Brittain, di Stefano's was one of those natural and beautiful Italian tenor voices that could charm without effort. His Neapolitan songs were very appealing and he hoped that singing heavier roles would not darken and spread the voice. Norris Davidson recalled that Radio Éireann had received more enquiries than usual about the broadcasting date of the opera from the Gaiety. 'I was surprised by the wide interest, especially from people who weren't exactly opera-goers. I could only deduce that he had many admirers in Ireland and the DGOS did extremely well in engaging him for *Tosca*.'

Maureen Lemass, a patron member, admired di Stefano for his supreme artistry and style and looked forward very much to hearing him sing. Tony O'Dalaigh was no longer a Super but his interest in opera if anything had increased and he usually joined the Gaiety queue to book hundreds of tickets for distribution to his friends. It was the pool system and it worked very well. For years he had been an avid admirer of di Stefano's and regarded him as one of the really great tenors of his generation, although he believed that Cavaradossi was not his meat. He considered his voice more suited to the bel canto repertoire and *I Puritani*. But that would in no way keep him from the Gaiety.

It was a typical June day when di Stefano and members of his entourage booked into their hotel. Some hours later reporters and photographers were waiting in the foyer for him and before long he agreed to talk to them. It was all very informal and he answered questions in an easy, casual manner. Yes, he had met Irish people in his travels, especially in America, and was taken by their gaiety and love of song. And he had long admired the art of John McCormack and the way he sang songs like 'I Hear You Calling Me'. When a young reporter quizzed the tenor about his temperament and occasional tantrums, he smiled and admitted he could be temperamental but 'only for the sake of his art.' Once, he said, he was due to sing arias at a function in Chicago attended by Queen Elizabeth of England but cut his programme short when he saw her sipping her coffee during his second song. 'If she was drinking coffee, then she hadn't enough interest in my songs or singing,' he explained.

There were rumours circulating around Dublin that he was being paid astronomical fees, but when he was quizzed again by the reporters he shook his head and said that it was a matter between his agent and the Dublin Grand Opera Society. As the cameras clicked, he made it plain there must be no photograph taken before his performance, neither in the Gaiety nor in his dressing room. Later that afternoon the tenor was due at the theatre and Paddy Brennan remembers he and other chorus members were waiting expectantly for his arrival. 'We were standing over near the stage door when he arrived accompanied by his chauffeur. He was smoking a cigarette from a holder and his coat was thrown loosely over his shoulders in typical Italian style. Bill O'Kelly greeted him in a mixture of Italian and English and struggled to make himself clear. 'I can still see di Stefano standing there nodding, obviously taking it all in as Bill tells him that all the tickets have been sold for the Tosca performances while people nearby are queuing for standing room only. To my surprise, di Stefano in the broadest of American accents says, 'I hope they enjoy the show'.

A frequent visitor to the Gaiety in those days was the tall, white-bearded Noel Purcell, film actor and variety star. Soon he was complaining he could not get a ticket for *Tosca,* one of his favourite operas. When Bill O'Kelly heard about Noel's dilemma he suggested that the only way he could see the performance was to be actually part of it. 'You're going to play the Cardinal,' he said to him one evening in the Gaiety green room. 'I can't think of anybody better qualified.' The jovial Purcell shook his head and with his long arm on O'Kelly's shoulder, replied, 'If you say so, Colonel. Come to that, I don't think I'd make a bad Pope either!'

Some people in the Gaiety queue dashed forward when they spotted di Stefano that afternoon and sought his autograph. He obliged a few of them before he was led away to his dressing room, which was fitted with new plush red carpets and printed linen covers on the furnishings. Bill O'Kelly was beaming, for not only was the tenor's visit a great prestige boost for the society but record box-office receipts were guaranteed, amounting in all to £1,170 on the first night but since the tenor was receiving the princely sum of £6,000 for his performances every penny at the box office was needed. He remained a big talking point, especially his gleaming Rolls Royce that was attracting a lot of attention in Dawson Street.

On Saturday evening, June 8, people gathered in South King Street to watch the opera buffs arrive for opening night. It was a distinguished gathering of diplomats, public representatives, and patron members - many of them elegantly dressed - and rank and file opera lovers. The foyer was crowded, an animated scene as people tried to be heard above the chatter. Everywhere there was an unmistakable buzz; the society had come a long way from the poorly attended *Tosca* in the forties. Dr Larchet, Prince Caracciolo and John F MacInerney were in the foyer to greet special guests and Dr Dermot O'Kelly and the other stewards were in the 'house' ensuring everyone found their seats.

It was one of those evenings when the occasion seemed bigger than the opera itself. It was the people's opera, though, and class was forgotten as the moment drew near for curtain rise. As a young journalist I had been fortunate to get a single ticket in the parterre and like everyone else was impatient for the opera to begin. And when it did, and Giuseppe di Stefano sang his first big aria in the Church of San Andrea Della Valle, Rome, we were listening to a familiar voice, one totally recognisable from his records, at once eloquent, silver-toned and effortless. Although it had darkened from his young days, the beauty of tone was still there as well as his subtle artistry.

Di Stefano gives the impression that he has walked straight from his Rolls Royce to sing the part, such is his casual air. But of course it is deceptive for it tends to conceal his consummate artistry. Later on the powerful voice of Gian Giacomo Guelfi, allied to frightening dramatic intensity, dominates the opera, though di Stefano emerges in the final act to send the house into raptures with his beautifully sung 'E lucevan le stelle.' And the typical di Stefano voice, caressing and seductive, is heard in his lovely duet ('O dolci mani') with soprano Marina Cucchio.

When the curtain finally comes down the applause is resounding and prolonged, as though the full 'house' wants to vent its pent up feelings. The principals take their bow again and again as Maestro Annovazzi and the RESO stay in their places. Colonel O'Kelly is as always somewhere back stage, no doubt proud of one of the greatest occasions in the society's history. It didn't seem to matter at that moment that soprano Signora Cucchio wasn't quite on the same level as di Stefano and Guelfi. The vast majority of those present had after all come to hear the tenor and at least those around me seemed satisfied enough, although one sturdy Kerryman thought he was 'much better on record'. The debate would undoubtedly go on and it was all part of the vibrant operatic scene of the time.

'It was a magical night,' recalled chorus member Mary Troy. 'Di Stefano's voice came up to all my expectations. He made Guelfi sing his heart out.' To Joan Rooney, the tenor used his voice exceptionally well and was supremely well cast as Cavaradossi. 'I thought he was terrific,' remarked Tom Carney. 'His voice was polished and his soft singing and phrasing remarkable. His coming was a landmark for the society. He was a superstar.' In Aileen Walsh's view, people came to hear his golden voice and most of them were not disappointed, though some felt his voice had gone off a little.'

For Donnie Potter it was a peculiar occasion. He was at the time ill in hospital and was actually allowed out for the evening to see the performance. 'I was invited into Mrs Sean Lemass's box and so had a good view from there. Although di Stefano was a big star when he came to Dublin, I felt on the night he was overshadowed by Guelfi's Scarpia. For all that, it was a memorable occasion for all of us in the society. Ticket prices had been increased but no one complained - they got more than their money's worth.

To Dympna Carney, di Stefano seemed unassuming and got through his work like the professional he was. It was the entourage around him which was treating him like a god. He was the star and a beautiful singer and people remember his Gaiety performance to this day. Nonetheless, it was Guelfi who stole the show with his compelling Scarpia. Mary Sheridan recalls that she felt the excitement in the theatre on the occasion. It was in the air and one knew that star singers were on stage. Florrie Draper had helped to recruit Supers for the opera and says she had no trouble whatsoever. 'Everyone wanted to be on stage with di Stefano. He was a dream performer but he could swear like a trooper and was always complaining about things going wrong. I remember he was adamant that no one should stand on the wings as he sang. He acted like the star he was. I enjoyed his singing performance, and so did my friends.'

Since the fifties members of the St Cecilia Gramophone Society in Dundalk regularly attended the DGOS seasons at the Gaiety, among them Frances O'Gorman who on her own admission, was 'mad about music'. Usually the society hired special buses for the spring season and the road journey never once seemed long as they talked and argued about the merits and otherwise of their favourite singers. Most of them had programmes signed by the Italian guest stars.

Giuseppe di Stefano had been Frances O'Gorman's idol for years and she had collected most of his LPs and reckoned he was one of the most beautiful lyrical tenors in the history of opera. When it was announced he was to sing in Dublin there was, she remembered, a clamour for tickets and this extended to Dundalk. She did manage to book for two of his performances. ' I really hate to say this, but at the first one on June 11, I was terribly disappointed in him. There were only occasional flashes of what I had come to expect, and for most of the time he appeared to stroll through the performance as if he was sleepwalking. However, three nights later it was a different matter altogether. I had travelled from Dundalk with members of the Gramophone Circle and all of us were looking forward to the evening. Would I, I secretly wondered, have my dream shattered once more? I'm happy to say that such was not the case. In a word, he was simply marvellous as Cavaradossi. And to cap it all, I was invited with a few of my friends to visit him in his dressing room where he autographed my LPs and gave us signed photographs of himself. He told us also he had enjoyed playing on Irish golf courses.'

For a while afterwards Frances and her friends waited in the theatre foyer and eventually the tenor strode down the stairway, stopped several steps from the bottom and to everybody's delight began to sing 'Arrivederci Roma'. When he had finished singing, they cheered and applauded him and it was yet another golden operatic memory for her.

At least two critics, Charles Acton and Robert Johnston drew attention in their reviews to the fact that soprano Marina Cucchio laboured under a cold and obviously it affected her singing and probably her acting as well. She was replaced in later performances. Acton was greatly impressed by the tenor's performance, the beautiful quality of his voice, his exemplary phrasing, the way he obeyed the composer's marks, and he was a rarity among opera tenors as he was content to sing and not just to make his voice ring off the walls. To Robert Johnston, di Stefano provided real pleasure to opera purists and his *mezzo voce* was admirable. This aspect was also touched on by Brian Quinn *(Evening Herald)* who said that the most abiding memory of the tenor's performance was the effortless way he floated his top notes across the footlights and into the auditorium: they were things of rare beauty. Other critics referred to the tenor's entirely natural talent and the rich, sensual and virile timbre of his voice and his stage presence. These virtues were guaranteed to endear him to audiences and undoubtedly attributed greatly to his success.

It was his lifestyle, though, that also proved a talking point in Dublin. The Irish like men who enjoy a drink, a flutter on the horses and perhaps a good game of poker. Di Stefano came into this category and stories began to circulate from his hotel of the late night poker sessions with friends, including the film star Peter Finch who was sometimes 'tired and emotional' and no expert at the game. Donnie Potter would say the Italians liked card games and he played with them at Nico's restaurant. But di Stefano was playing for fairly big stakes.

Maestro Annovazzi happened to drop into his hotel after a performance of Tosca and found him sipping a Scotch, smoking a cigar and preparing for a poker session. 'Will you join us, Maestro?' asked the tenor smilingly. Annovazzi nodded his head and looked at the tenor in a curious way. 'Your voice, Pippo,' he said, 'it will not last, you know, if you continue to treat it like that. And you must not stay up late every night.'

'You must not worry for Pippo, Maestro,' di Stefano replied, with a friendly hand on the other's shoulder, 'Pippo has no fears. If my voice fails me I go back to my little village in Sicily and settle down and sing no more.'

To his friends, the tenor was affectionately known as 'Pippo' and his warm-hearted personality made him friends easily. Maestro Annovazzi was of course deadly serious and could be a disciplinarian. It was known that some Italian artists avoided being seen drinking and smoking in his presence.

If di Stefano left Dublin on June 18 in high spirits, the same could probably not be said about another outstanding Italian tenor, Ferruccio Tagliavini who gave a recital at the Gaiety accompanied by Jeannie Reddin.

Frances O'Gorman and her mother travelled from Dundalk to be present and were saddened to find so many empty seats in the theatre. They had both admired his singing and possessed his records.

Unfortunately the recital was delayed by the slamming of doors in the dress circle as people straggled into their seats from the bars. To Frances O'Gorman, it was downright bad manners. 'I was embarrassed and felt this was no way to treat a brilliant singer. It could not have been a very enjoyable occasion for him.' As soon however as he sang Tosti songs and arias by Massenet and Cilea she forgot what had gone before and enjoyed his performance enormously. He had an appealing presence and his voice was lyrical and warm in timbre. He deserved a packed house. She suspected though that people's money had been spent on tickets for di Stefano's *Tosca,* so on this occasion Tagliavini had to take almost a back seat. She had sympathy for him.

The di Stefano saga was not quite finished. It is said that when tenor Umberto Borso, a firm favourite with Irish audiences, saw at first hand the way the red carpet was pushed out for di Stefano he took umbrage and vowed never again to sing in Dublin. He was especially irked by the talk of di Stefano's fees for in comparison to his own they bore no resemblance. Whether he confronted Colonel O'Kelly on the question no one seems to know, but at least one chorus member says Borso was angry and let it be known to some of his Italian colleagues.

The sight of di Stefano in his plush dressing room must have been especially galling for Borso, as he had to make do for years with dressing rooms in a poor condition. He would be a loss; his Radames, Manrico and Riccardo were but a few of the parts that stay in the memory. He did however see out that spring season of 1963.

Pavarotti as the Duke

Luciano Pavarotti. To the vast majority of Irish opera lovers the name did not register in that early summer of 1963. As far as they were concerned the only tenor in the news was Giuseppe di Stefano. But Colonel O'Kelly believed that before long Luciano Pavarotti's name would be well known in the operatic sphere. He had engaged him to sing in that season's *Rigoletto*, having first heard him in Loreto in Italy.

One Sunday the Colonel found himself in Rome with impresario Maestro Botti and with not a lot to do - the previous day they had completed auditions in the city. 'Maestro, is there any opera worth seeing anywhere tonight?' he asked Botti, who shook his head as if to indicate nothing of importance. O'Kelly persisted and Botti told him there was a performance of *La Traviata* in the town of Loreto in Perugia but that was some distance from Rome. 'Never mind,' said the Colonel, 'let's go and look for ourselves.' He had often relied on his instincts and discovered a talented tenor or soprano.

He had to admit though that the *Traviata* was pedestrian and the production dull and unimaginative. Vocally it was undistinguished except for the tenor's performance as Alfredo and had to check the programme for his name: Luciano Pavarotti. He was tall, thin and had an easy ringing top to his voice and an attractive tonal quality. Since Maestro Botti was slow to commit himself, his response wasn't enthusiastic when O'Kelly suggested that Pavarotti would make an acceptable Duke of Mantua for them. He got his way and before he left for Ireland that week it was agreed to sign the tenor on the dotted line.

Pavarotti was in his late twenties and from a musical background - his father was a baker and also blessed with a tenor voice. Young Luciano was twelve when he was brought to the local Modena theatre to hear Beniamino Gigli in concert and for the next two hours his eyes were transfixed to the stage. Although Gigli's voice was familiar to him through his father's almost worn-out records, he was thrilled to be close to the great tenor and to hear him sing. To get even closer to his idol, he rushed round afterwards to meet him and said, 'When I grow up I'm going to be a tenor too.'

Gigli, by now in his fifties, looked at the sturdy boy before him and remarked, 'Bravo. But you will have to work hard, and realise that every time you sing you start all over again; you never stop singing.' Pavarotti was to say later on, 'I can't tell you what an impression that made on me. Beniamino was world-famous, acknowledged by everyone to be one of the finest singers of all time; yet he was still working to improve his artistry, still studying. I think about that every day, and I hope I am the same, that I will always keep the desire to become better.'

Eventually he discovered he had a good tenor voice and told his parents he wanted to be an opera singer. His self-confidence seemed justified for early in 1961 he entered a singing competition and won first prize. The prize was the role of Rodolfo in *Bohème* in Reggio Emilia, which is about twenty-five miles from Modena, and there he joined a company of singers, all hopeful but penniless. The opera was directed by Mafalda Favero, a famous singer in her day and young Luciano says he learned some stagecraft and movement from her.

He was very nervous though before the actual performance mainly because of his fear of conductor Maestro Molinari-Pradelli who had given him a tough time in rehearsal. But he sang well and felt very good after the audience loudly applauded his 'Che gelida manina.' On the way home his father cautioned him. 'It was very nice Luciano, very nice, but you still don't sound like Gigli and Schipa. You must work harder.'

He was more encouraged by what the *Nova Gazette di Reggio Emile* had to say: 'The tenor Luciano Pavarotti sang with estimable good taste and with vivid musicality, likewise displaying vocal equipment both penetrating and flexible. He was liked more than his colleagues.' By this time he had fallen in love with a young teacher and they were married in September 1962. She had no doubt he could make a living from singing. 'If I don't I'll go back to selling newspapers,' he joked his pretty, dark-haired young wife.

He sang a few more *Bohèmes* in Lucca but he feared they had not gone as well as his first Reggio Emilia. He was astonished to be visited after one performance by another of his idols, Tito Schipa, and the veteran tenor assured him that his voice was beautiful. 'You should sing just as you are singing and don't listen to anybody,' he advised. 'Do not push your voice to sound like anyone else.'

In May of `63 Luciano got the break he needed. Before he was due to sing in Dublin he was engaged to sing Pinkerton for Northern Ireland Opera Company. A number of opera fans from Dublin and Dundalk attended the performance of *Madama Butterfly* at the Opera House, Belfast. Frances O'Gorman and her Gramophone Society friends from Dundalk remember enjoying the performance and afterwards meeting the young tenor. Looking back, she says he had one of the most charming voices she had heard for a long time. And off-stage he had a warm and genial personality and good sense of humour. They decided to book for the DGOS Rigoletto in May of that year.

Maureen Lemass and her DGOS friends were impressed by Pavarotti's Pinkerton, especially his range and ringing high Cs. As in the case of Frances O'Gorman, they too felt he would make an ideal Duke of Mantua. En route to Dublin the tenor joined other Italian artists from Dublin to sing in a celebrity concert at the Town Hall, Dundalk. The annual concerts were organised by Father Shields and the Gramophone Society committee and usually there was a clamour for tickets and the hall would be sold out long before curtain up. Apart from Pavarotti, the other performers were Plinio Clabassi, Anna di Stasio, Loris Gambelli, Ernesto Vezzosi and Margherita Rinaldi. The accompanist was Maestro Annovazzi and it was customary for Colonel O'Kelly, Bertie Timlin and other DGOS management committee members to attend.

Frances O'Gorman recalled that Luciano Pavarotti created an excellent impression in such arias as 'Che gelida manina', 'La Donna e mobile' and in the love duet from *Madama Butterfly*. That week-end he slipped into Dublin a virtual unknown. Chorus members could be forgiven for treating him like any other young Italian artist; indeed the main interest in *Rigoletto* was in Piero Cappuccilli's portrayal of the jester and in Margherita Rinaldi's Gilda.

The chorus members were usually fairly good judges of young singers with potential, but in the case of Pavarotti I found that Tom Carney's words seemed to sum up the general reaction. 'We didn't take a great deal of notice of Pavarotti at rehearsals,' he said. 'I did get the impression though that he was on his way up. He was a quiet personality then, making his way socially and musically.' John Carney felt his voice projected easily and he had no trouble at all singing the Duke of Mantua's music. To Monica Condron, he was musical and approached his music seriously. 'I would imagine he was ambitious and eager to get on, though in those days he appeared somewhat shy. Of course he was, singing with the society for the first time and didn't know anyone really. Bill O'Kelly mixed with the guest singers and tried to make them feel at home. He encouraged the chorus members to talk to them and have a cup of tea with them.' Aileen Walsh said they were always delighted to get singers on the way up. For one thing, they didn't cost a lot and sometimes you got a real discovery. Joan Rooney remembers Pavarotti as tall and good-looking and a natural tenor but she saw nothing that indicated he would one day be a superstar.

Paddy Brennan recalls that Pavarotti studied the role of Riccardo in *A*

Masked Ball with Umberto Borso, but unfortunately he was never to sing it in Dublin. 'Borso was an excellent Riccardo so Pavarotti was in very good hands. Because of the fuss being made about di Stefano, I think that Luciano had little hope of capturing the limelight, but he had the notes for the Duke of Mantua and you could spot the potential in his voice. He had a long way to go, however, before he would be in any way convincing as an actor.'

That season's *Rigoletto* is remembered as superb. Donnie Potter felt that Cappuccilli, Rinaldi and Pavarotti made a fine trio of principals. But the opening night took place with some tension behind the scenes. The Pope of the time, John XX111 was gravely ill and expected to die. Colonel O'Kelly was on tenterhooks all day because the custom in Ireland at the time was that if His Holiness died during the day, performances must be cancelled; if he died after the first interval, the performance would be completed, and the following day's performances cancelled.

Another problem was that in the event of cancellation the society would have to return the ticket money but would still have to pay the singers' fees. In the circumstances, Col. O'Kelly did not think it improper to let *Rigoletto* go ahead despite the fact that the Pope had died. He had somehow managed to keep the news from everyone until the curtain rose. At the interval, though, an announcement was made about the Pontiff's death. Pavarotti would say later that the company knew all evening that the Pope had died.

The critics generally picked out Pavarotti as promising though Charles Acton in the *Irish Times* commented, 'The tenor seemed to have a hard unsympathetic voice of very little variety.' Mary MacGoris was more impressed. 'He was extremely convincing. As the all-powerful amoral Duke his voice is clear, strong, agile and efficient, if a trifle slightly produced, though he should remember that "La donna e mobile", the well-known aria, is a careless song however difficult to sing.'

It was Geraldine O'Grady's last year with the orchestra - she would embark on a solo career later on. She found Cappuccilli's *Rigoletto* a tremendous portrayal of the troubled jester and that Pavarotti's performance was in a way overshadowed. She thought he sang confidently and showed considerable musicianship. Jimmy Brittain, a concert tenor and chorus member, often sang Neapolitan love songs and had no doubt that Pavarotti would go places. 'I found his singing very expressive and when he went for a high C it sounded unforced. I wasn't surprised later on when his career took off.'

The society that spring was presenting for the first time Verdi's *Macbeth*, based closely on Shakespeare's play. The title role was being sung by Dino Dondi, a native of Bologna, where he was born in 1925 and one of the best known Verdian baritones in Italy. It is interesting to note that Piero Cappuccilli has described the role of Macbeth as the most demanding, and rewarding, of all early Verdi roles and he admitted he waited eighteen years to tackle it. In Cappuccilli's opinion it is emotionally draining because of the character's complexity and the variety of dramatic situations he finds himself in.

Lady Macbeth was being sung by the Argentinian soprano Sofia Bandin; her debut was made in the famous Colon Theatre of Buenos Aires. She was by now an accepted interpreter of the Verdi part. Singing Banquo was bass Plinio Clabassi, an established favourite with Irish audiences. Edwin Fitzgibbon was singing Malcolm, one of the tenor roles in the opera. Much was expected of the chorus for in this respect the demands on them were exceptional.

Patrick Somerville was chorus master. He was a Dubliner, born in Harold's Cross and first became interested in music on joining St. Patrick's training college for teachers where he worked with the choir and eventually started his own quartet. Later on he was 'roped' into the O'Connell's Musical Society as musical director and remembers that Austin Gaffney was an inspiration to the members. However, it was Monica Condron who had invited him into the DGOS. They first met when he directed the Dublin Light Opera Company in Wallace's *Maritana* and she was singing the title role.

He had known Bill O'Kelly years before when he commanded his L.D.F. unit and at one stage Bill had considered starting a choir from the hundreds of men but it came to nothing. He got on well with Comdt. O'Kelly and admired his leadership qualities. 'I found him fair but if you stepped out of line you would hear all about it.' The standard of the DGOS chorus surprised him - it was made up of some very good singers and they were serious about what they were doing. His own wife Chris, an excellent pianist, was the accompanist in rehearsals.

Before rehearsals started, he remembered Prince Caracciolo bringing along a recording of *Macbeth* and everybody was enthralled by the opera. 'Listening to the music, I found it stirring with some magnificent choruses and great arias for the principals', Somerville recalled. 'Prince Caracciolo was very supportive and talked to me about the opera itself and when he had first heard it in Italy. I could see he was fond of it. It was being sung in Italian and as far as I could gather the chorus members were enjoying the rehearsals and the attendance was good. I felt deflated when people sometimes stayed away. The ladies loved singing the witches part and I'd joke them and say it came naturally to all of them.'

Sometimes Colonel O'Kelly sat in at rehearsals to satisfy himself that everything was proceeding smoothly. To Somerville, he was a genuine Verdi admirer and he got the impression that if Bill had the time he would have loved to sing in the chorus of Macbeth. He himself never tired of listening to Plinio Clabassi; it was a powerful bass voice and Verdi's music brought the best out of him. During the final weeks of rehearsals Maestro Riccardo Bottino took over as chorus master.

Somerville says that this never worried him; if anything he welcomed Bottino's coming and found he gave some very useful tips to the choristers. He accepted he was a full-time professional chorus master and his experience could be vital in a big choral work like *Macbeth*. He was surprised, however, when a fellow Italian once asked the men in the chorus not to enunciate the words at all, stating that no one wanted to hear the words but rather the sound. 'That all struck me as very strange for I spent most of my teaching life trying to get words across.'

The performances of *Macbeth* did not exactly fill the Gaiety but the production was well received by both audiences and critics, though Brian Quinn (*Evening Herald*) found the pace of the early acts ponderous and the later battle scenes bordering on the comic. He had no real complaint with the singing. Dino Dondi was very impressive in the title role and as an actor he was compelling. He was matched by Sofia Bandin's Lady Macbeth and Plinio Clabassi was a towering Banquo. Edwin Fitzgibbon had fared well as Malcolm and Carlo Menippo was a convincing Macduff. The sets evoked the right mood with those for the banquet scene quite sumptuous. Most of the critics praised Maestro Annovazzi's conducting.

In conversation with choristers about past performances, I have found that this `63 *Macbeth* figures high in their memories. John and Tom Carney agreed that the opera took a good deal of preparation but it was very rewarding singing Verdi's music. Dick Hanrahan and Jimmy Brittain thought the same. Singing the witches' music was a new experience for Florrie Draper and Mary Troy and they regarded it as challenging. To Miss Draper, it had to be excellently sung because it evoked the terribly dark mood of the opera. Strangely, though, it would not be staged again by the society for another sixteen years. Perhaps the Colonel considered it that bit sombre for Verdi fans more attuned to *Rigoletto, Traviata and Trovatore*.

It was a vintage season in every way. The social side was swinging, with Nico's restaurant crowded after almost every performance and if patrons were in luck they would hear Italian guest artists singing Neapolitan songs to piano accompaniment. Prince Caracciolo and his wife 'Boodie' continued to host lively parties at their home in Rathfarnham, being generous in their invitations to visiting guest singers as well as members of the society, while in lots of other houses people held convivial post-opera suppers. In Lovatt-

Dolans' there would usually be music with John Lovatt-Dolan accompanying singers on the piano.

'The social side still continued to be a very integral part of the spring season especially,' recalled Martin McCullagh. 'The Colonel loved to see patron members and their friends enjoying themselves and I know very few people who didn't. Opera in those days brought a sparkle and life to the music scene that is perhaps missing nowadays.'

Margaret McDonnell and the Ladies' Committee held enjoyable fund-raising functions and usually made a decent profit so that their contributions to the management committee amounted to a considerable sum by the end of the year. Colonel O'Kelly always expressed his grateful thanks, especially since the society was still in dire need of funds. And it rarely got what it sought from Bord Fáilte or the Arts Council and there was still uncertainty about the future of the Italian government subvention. Musically, it was another matter. Few could deny the pleasure the society's seasons were providing and the great voices Irish opera fans were being offered.

Acclaim for Benelli

Like Pavarotti, the young tenor Ugo Benelli arrived in Dublin in that spring of `63 an unknown to sing Elvino in Bellini's *La Sonnambula*. He made an immediate impression and was hailed as a discovery and a lyric tenor of remarkable promise. He was blessed with handsome dark looks, a slim figure and a winning personality. He owed his presence in Dublin to Colonel Bill O'Kelly.

They had first met in an agency office in Milan where the tenor was auditioning for pianist and composer Franco Mannino, the brother-in-law of Luchino Visconti. After he had sung his first aria the door opened and Colonel O'Kelly arrived with Maestro Botti and sat down on chairs to listen to him sing. 'I had no idea who these two men were,' Benelli recalls, 'but afterwards they introduced themselves and Bill O'Kelly said he would like to have me sing in *La Sonnambula* in Dublin. I noticed that Maestro Botti was hesitant, as though he had someone else in mind, but O'Kelly was insistent and said he would finalise the contract with my agent. I liked his direct manner and when he said it was just the voice the society was looking for I believed him.'

He felt indebted to O'Kelly. 'I was entirely unknown to him and although I had already sung roles in Italy and elsewhere he could have overlooked me, as Botti appeared to want him to do, and for days afterwards I remembered that.' He had married two years previously and his wife Angela was expecting their first child. He was aware of his new responsibilities and welcomed any offers of work. His career had progressed to his satisfaction and he was fulfilling a childhood ambition to be a singer. Although born in Genoa his parents had moved to Florence where they set up a hat-making business. He was seven years of age when his mother and aunt decided it was time for him to learn the piano and for the next few years he studied diligently. By the age of twelve he discovered he had a promising voice and people around him began to notice it also. A woman who lived above his family was fond of opera and one day gave him the music of arias from *Traviata and Fra Diavolo* and he tried to sing them. And another friend, who sang in amateur musicals, told him he had a beautiful voice and that when he reached eighteen she would introduce him to a singing teacher. She kept her word and before long he entered for a competition for a place at the La Scala Opera.

'I was told there were about two hundred and eight competitors but I decided to be daring and sang difficult arias from *I Puritani and La Sonnambula*. I suppose I was eager to show off my lyric tenor voice and ample range and had no fears. Eventually I was chosen with two other competitors - one was Fiorenza Cossotto - to begin my studies at the school. The opportunity came at just the right time for me to get instruction from famous old singers and producers on all aspects of singing and stagecraft.'

It was by now the late fifties. He had acquired an agent and was engaged to sing in Montevideo, South America. It was a short intermezzo by Mozart which the management used to stage between the first and second acts of the main opera and lasted about twenty-five minutes. It required, however, refined vocal technique and good breath control and he was pleased with his performance. His real debut was at the Liceo Theatre in Barcelona as Fenton in *Falstaff*, produced by Franco Zeffirelli, and he received promising reviews; he sang it again in Parma in that same year. He had already met his wife-to-be in Genoa where she was an interpreter and at first it seemed she wasn't keen to marry 'this young singer'; but when she and her mother attended his recital he deliberately changed a song at the end of the programme to make it sound more romantic. He remembers this made her cry so her mother said to her, 'Ugo made you cry, now you'd better marry him.'

'Angela was younger than me, very intelligent and had a critical mind. Since she too was taking singing lessons she was able to discuss my career with me. I was shy at the time but I do believe it was love at first sight. When this other girl introduced Angela to me I looked at her and immediately decided, "This is the girl for me."'

Angela Benelli recalls that her first meeting with Ugo was at their teacher's studio. 'I thought his voice was by far the best of all other students and never doubted he could be a professional singer. As I loved music and opera I had voice training for some years. I always trusted Ugo and never thought about the risks of marrying a young singer. He has been very sincere and trustworthy. I am a strong optimist and I seldom worried about his travelling for engagements and tried to telephone him as often as I could.'

The first opera she heard him sing was *L'Elisir d'Amore* in 1956 at Teatro Falcone in Genoa and the quality of his voice and his pathos captured her heart. She once had a difficult job trying to prevent him from signing for the Spoleto Festival where the producer Luchino Visconti wanted him to sing Alfredo in *Traviata*. 'I remember Luchino had personally asked Ugo to go there but he was very young and his *tenor di grazia* voice could have been spoiled by this role.'

After their marriage Angela and Ugo took an apartment in Milan; it was absolutely necessary, he told me, as the telephonic communications between Genoa and Milan were at the time inadequate and an obstacle to progress in his profession. They were happy days for them both, though in the operatic field the competition was keen and there were a lot of good voices around. 'I dreamed his career would take him to sing in La Scala and other prestigious opera houses,' said Angela. 'I had heard about Ireland and I was pleased he was going there to sing as it would further his experience.'

Before he set out for Dublin, he talked to Maestro Botti about the climate and the food and the clothes to wear. It did not worry him unduly that the fee offered him was small. He wanted the work and the satisfaction of singing with established professionals. On arrival in Dublin he didn't take a taxi from the airport, instead he travelled by horse and carriage having agreed a reasonable fare with the cabman. He was booked into the old Jury's Hotel in Dame Street. It was a wonderful place and some of his Italian colleagues were also staying there. The restaurant was downstairs where he breakfasted in the following weeks but avoided having dinner as it was too costly.

To the young Benelli, it seemed a luxurious hotel and he regarded it a novelty to be staying there. He was told that Bill O'Kelly had negotiated a special deal for singers with the management; it was a lively place also and he was intrigued by the Irish cabaret put on there. He was struck by the scarcity of cars in the city and some of the vehicles he saw in the streets were old American Fords. The traffic was light in comparison to Milan and the air fresher. It was the friendliness of the people that struck him most forcibly, the way they greeted each other or stopped in the street and talked and didn't appear afraid to talk to strangers. Angela, he knew, would enjoy the scene but being pregnant was unable to come with him.

He was able to relax because he knew the music of *La Sonnambula* and looked forward to his own DGOS debut confident that he would do well. He was introduced to Nico's restaurant and loved the atmosphere. 'I think Ruggero Nico was very grateful to us for going there and sometimes we sang for the important customers like government ministers and diplomats; in return, he provided us with free dinners. The food was very good and I can still remember the big, juicy steaks. Ruggero was a nice man and loved having singers in his restaurant.'

Chorus members took to Benelli from the first rehearsal. He had an easy sense of humour and was friendly. To Dick Hanrahan his musicianship was very evident and he used his lyrical voice stylishly, never forcing it. Aileen Walsh and Joan Rooney felt he fitted into the society's scenario like a glove.

Like everyone else they admired his comic flair on stage and he was made for romantic roles. 'Ugo was a charmer,' said Florrie Draper, 'and had the looks of a film star. Sometimes his singing reminded me of Tito Schipa's voice.' Dympna Carney said he knew his music before he arrived at rehearsals and his voice blended beautifully with that of Margherita Rinaldi.'

Benelli says he did not encounter either Luciano Pavarotti or Giuseppe di Stefano in Dublin as they were staying in different hotels and singing on different dates. He had met Pavarotti at a concert in Italy and remembered him to be big and friendly and was talking about a vocal competition he had won. It was the warmth of his personality however that tended to stick in the mind. The only time up to then that he had met di Stefano was in Cincinnati where he was singing in *Manon*. 'There was a story that he liked playing roulette and that he had lost all his money and was forced to fly back to Italy on a second class ticket. They say it was true.'

Despite the 'rave' press reviews *La Sonnambula* was a box-office flop that season, which was a mystery to both Dr Larchet and Bill O'Kelly. Benelli's honeyed tones and total credibility as the village youth Elvino won all hearts, including those of some veteran critics. To Robert Johnston *(Irish Press)* Benelli was a real find who in his opinion would grace world stages within a few years. 'The voice is pure and fresh-toned and he says more with a single facial expression, or a smile, than other artists double his age. Let's have him back in Dublin again - and soon.' Mary MacGoris told *Irish Independent* readers that it was a well-placed voice with an attractive quality, while Brian Quinn *(Herald)* stated he was one of the best lyric tenors heard in Dublin for some years.

'It was love at first sight between me and the audience,' Benelli said later. 'After that I began to be known and since I had good English I was able to thank people when they talked about my success. It made me feel good. The role of Elvino was perfect for my voice and I would sing it many times in my career.'

To the tenor the cast was outstanding and their brilliant performances, particularly by Rinaldi and Clabassi, helped in his success. He soon discovered that Clabassi was a gentleman. 'I had heard he could be detached in his manner towards young singers like myself and that made me feel uneasy, but after the last performance of *Sonnambula* he came to me in my dressing room and said with a smile, 'Ugo, you can speak with me. Your Elvino is very good. You will go far.'

Colonel O'Kelly expressed delight at his successful debut and said he would have him back. Young Benelli saw him as a fatherly figure running a large operatic family. He admired his sincerity as well as his managerial skills. He was to return home to Milan a happy man. 'Ugo was enthusiastic about the Dublin audience,' recalled his wife Angelo. 'As a young singer their support meant so much to him.'

Behind the glitter of the opera the financial position during 1963 remained, in the words of joint treasurer Tom McMahon, 'quite grave' with the result that he spent months on end endeavouring to raise funds. He approached the Arts Council, Bord Fáilte and some government ministers to put the society's case strongly before them. Eventually it resulted in the introduction and passing of a supplementary vote in the Dáil for £5,000 to be made available by the Arts Council to the society.

'We were desperate at the time,' recalls Aileen Walsh, joint treasurer with Tom McMahon, 'and the Dáil vote saved us from embarrassment. We had applied early in that year to Bord Fáilte for a guarantee against loss of £7,000 and a most disappointing offer of £750 was made, and in fact paid later to us. So it can be imagined with what trepidation we prepared for the spring season. But we always managed to pay our guest artists.'

Looking back, Donnie Potter again wondered if they were over-stretching themselves by presenting six major operas in the spring season, for if one or two failed to win box-office support the society was in trouble. Norris Davidson, meanwhile, was worried about something else. When Radio Éireann transferred from Henry Street shortly after the setting up of television at Montrose it was discovered that a lot of things went missing, including DGOS tapes and recordings. All branches of the arts had in fact been hit. He considered it a serious matter as considerable time had been devoted to recording opera and some of the performances were of historic value. No one in the radio station seemed to appreciate the gravity of the issue.

Since the sixties the standard of recording of Gaiety productions had been, he could say, greatly improved and the broadcasts were reaching a wider public. 'I think we were coming close to capturing the performance in the theatre itself, notably in the orchestral accompaniment.'

In spite of the financial constraints the society mounted another ambitious spring season in 1964, that included a revival of Verdi's *Otello, Chénier and Nabucco* and the galaxy of stars engaged would have done justice to any opera house in the world. Familiar names like Margherita Rinaldi, Gian Giacomo Guelfi, Anna Di Stasio and Loris Gambelli were again taking leading roles, as also was Luciano Pavarotti who would be heard as Rodolfo *(Bohème)* and Alfredo *(Traviata)*. And the elder Germont in that *Traviata* was the great Giuseppe Taddei, born in Genoa in 1916 and whose repertoire by now was said to number more than seventy operas. A recording star, he was equally at home in Mozart as well as in Verdi and was a most versatile artist.

Peter McBrien felt that this *Traviata* was one of the greatest Dublin has seen with wonderful performances by Taddei, Rinaldi and the young Pavarotti. He regarded Taddei as a supreme actor-singer whose artistry shone throughout. 'I didn't wish to hear a second act better sung. Margherita Rinaldi seemed to be inspired by his presence and her Violetta is still vivid in my mind. As for Pavarotti, he showed outstanding promise; his voice was easy-flowing and flexible and the higher up he went the better he sounded. In my view there was no mistaking his star quality.'

Mary Sheridan had a part in the opera and thought that Rinaldi scored a personal triumph as Violetta and she was also deeply impressed by Giuseppe Taddei's performance. She was delighted to be part of such a successful production and to hear Rinaldi's coloratura meet every demand of Verdi's music. 'The whole thing was so exciting that I remember almost every scene in the opera to this day.'

Paddy Ring sang Roderigo in *Otello* and one afternoon was going upstairs in the back of the Gaiety to get his costume when he heard a tenor warming up in his dressing room. 'I think it was number two dressing room which was shared by the principal tenor. I stopped in my tracks and listened to the voice. Whoever it was, was doing scales and singing top Bs and Cs effortlessly, but it was the sheer quality of the voice that attracted me. There was no question of technique or placing of the voice, it was just happening in the most natural way. It was a glorious sound in every way. As I listened, Mary Sheridan came by and I asked her his name. She looked surprised and remarked, "That's Luciano Pavarotti." When I heard him sing Alfredo and Rodolfo that season he confirmed my very first impressions on the stairway. True, he was no actor but the way he projected his voice and the warmth he brought to his singing bowled over a young tenor like myself.'

Mary MacGoris who had been enthusiastic about Pavarotti from the beginning, was again struck by his singing in *Bohème*. 'The outstanding voice in *Bohème* was that of tenor Luciano Pavarotti,' she noted in the *Independent*. 'It has an interesting quality and unforced strength and range; when he can cover the top notes more easily and acquire a more assured use of a promising *mezzo voce,* this singer should be fit for the big heroic roles. He sang, too, with musically-directed intelligence, using the voice to reinforce his acting in an acceptable portrayal of the romantic Rodolfo.'

Charles Acton in the *Irish Times* found the *Bohème* 'depressing', except for the Café Momus scene. He had changed his mind however about Luciano Pavarotti; whereas he had been lukewarm about his performance as the Duke in *Rigoletto* in the previous year, he now found his Rodolfo a different matter. 'Pavarotti's Rodolfo was acceptable,' he noted, 'and his voice and singing were lovely except for a tendency to force at the top with the consequent disruption of his phrases.'

Chorus members felt the tenor's voice had much improved in twelve months and he was singing with greater confidence. Jimmy Brittain said Rodolfo's music suited his voice to perfection and his first act in particular was worth going a long way to hear, Aileen Walsh and Joan Rooney agreed. Florrie Draper thought it was one of the best young tenor voices she had heard singing with the society and wondered how Bill O'Kelly was discovering them.

As expected the performances of *Nabucco* packed the Gaiety with opera fans eager once again to hear Gian Giacomo Guelfi sing the title role and Luisa Maragliano repeat her fiery Abigaille. 'Her thrilling voice and dynamic stage-work dominated the opening performance,' observed Mary MacGoris. 'Vivid but controlled, she soared where necessary over the orchestra and chorus, yet adapted herself perfectly to the demands of concerted pieces.'

All the critics agreed Guelfi's Nabucco had lost none of its power and dignity and that he made an excellent foil. The audiences were still looking for encores of 'Va Pensiero' and the chorus was obliging them, though one acerbic critic felt that on the first night their singing didn't warrant an encore. Tenor Enzo Tei gave an excellent account of himself as Ismaele in the opera and both Mary Sheridan and Edwin Fitzgibbon did well in other parts.

The colourful gala performance that season was reserved for *Turandot* with Italian soprano Carla Ferrario in the title role. She had first sung it in Palermo in 1963. Her repertoire also included Norma and her strong dramatic voice was gaining her increasing recognition. Calaf was being sung by Angelo Loforese, who had made his debut twelve years before as Turridu in *Cavalleria Rusticana* in the Teatro Nuovo, Milan.

Directed by Enrico Frigerio, the noteworthy features of the production were the sumptuous sets and the costumes from Rome. It is remembered as a workmanlike performance though inferior to the 1960 staging with Lucille Udovick. The revival of *Otello* after five years was more successful and according to chorister Paddy Brennan, was well cast and both vocally and dramatically contained some outstanding moments. The title role was sung by Italian tenor Pier Miranda Ferraro who had studied with Aureliano Pertile and in 1959 had recorded *La Gioconda* with Callas and Piero Cappuccilli. He made a big impression on Irish opera fans with the heroic quality of his voice and convincing acting.

Virginia Zeani was back to sing the role of Desdemona which she had sung in leading opera houses abroad. Her Lucia and Violetta were still vividly remembered at the Gaiety and her Desdemona was on this occasion convincingly sung and acted; indeed she was in luminous voice, especially in the tragic last act. While in Dublin she told me she renewed acquaintances with all her friends, notably Alfred and Lady Beit, Prince Caraccioli and his wife 'Boodie' and numerous other friends. As always, she marvelled at the verdant green of the land, the friendly Irish, and the remarkable DGOS chorus.

'I was always delighted to come back to Ireland when I could,' she said. 'I suppose it was more relaxing for me than slipping in and out of big cities and opera houses. I could sing and relax in Dublin and enjoy myself more. Nothing had changed since I was here in the fifties, least of all your lovely audience.'

It was voted a highly successful spring season and apart from the box-office receipts and the Italian subvention amounting to about £5,000 and a similar sum from the Arts Council, the subscriptions from the one thousand patrons came to a sizeable sum. The splendid programme compiled by Prince Caracciolo realised a profit of £250, in spite of sharp increases in printing costs, and the Ladies' Committee organised a masked ball during the season at the International Hotel, Ballsbridge, and this popular event brought in a further £350.

It was also noticeable that the number of guarantors from both the private and business sector was increasing and by now amounted to well over sixty. Business interests included Aer Lingus, P.J. Carroll & Co., Arthur Guinness Son & Co. Ltd., Russell & Royal Hibernian Hotel and Jury's Hotel. Their support was a hopeful sign but the reality remained that the Arts Council grant was still inadequate. 'We needed much more than we were getting,' said Aileen Walsh, joint treasurer. 'Filling the Gaiety every night was not enough in itself.'

The Wiesbaden Episode

In early April 1964 Colonel Bill O'Kelly visited the German Embassy in Dublin for talks with the Cultural Attache, Dr Gunther Beckers, about the possibility of Wiesbaden Opera coming to Dublin. They discussed various figures but O'Kelly was reluctant to commit the Dublin Grand Opera Society to any specific amount regarding expenses. Later he phoned Dr Beckers at the embassy and informed him that after a lot of thought the society could not sponsor the proposed visit by the Wiesbaden Opera.

Dr Beckers was, however, persistent and urged the DGOS chairman to re-consider his decision. He seemed anxious to forge new links with the society. The outcome was that O'Kelly agreed to recommend £500 per performance in an endeavour to make the visit possible. Dr Beckers did not think this was a realistic figure but agreed to put it before the Wiesbaden Opera's intendant. O'Kelly heard no more about the matter for sometime and assumed the visit was not taking place. In fact, he was in advanced negotiations with another overseas company to fill the bill.

He was surprised that June of `64 to receive a phone call from a member of the German Embassy staff acting for Dr Beckers, who was on leave. He was informed that a Herr Grosser, technical director of the Wiesbaden Opera, was arriving in Dublin inside two days to examine the Gaiety Theatre's stage equipment and amenities. Colonel O'Kelly told Dr Beckers' deputy that he was amazed to hear the news as the society had not signed any contract or discussed details of the visit. The deputy seemed surprised and said he understood the Wiesbaden Company was coming to Dublin and had received some funding from the German government.

A few days later Colonel O'Kelly met Dr Gresser in Dublin and told him of his surprise and that he knew nothing of the visit of Wiesbaden and of his amazement that matters had progressed so far without his knowing anything about it, in particular the financial arrangements for the visit. Grosser said he would be reporting to the intendant at Wiesbaden Opera when the company returned from annual holidays at the beginning of September.

Subsequently O'Kelly received a phone call from Dr Beckers that the Wiesbaden company's visit was on and he would be hearing from the company directly. But he did not hear from them directly, and since he was on his way to Rome to hold auditions, he cabled the Wiesbaden intendant asking him to meet him there for talks. When he reached Rome however he found a cable waiting for him to travel to Wiesbaden. Bertie Timlin was travelling with him at the time and both of them went to Wiesbaden for talks. O'Kelly told the intendant that the society could not afford more than £500 a performance and before he and Timlin left for home he assumed there was agreement.

Nonetheless, he was not entirely satisfied. He was thrown into confusion when he received a contract from Wiesbaden dated Oct. 7, in which the figure of 44,000 DM was mentioned. He phoned Dr Beckers at the German Embassy and informed him that he never agreed to such an amount and that the society could not meet it. On October 28, he wrote to Dr Grosser at Wiesbaden Opera, in the course of which he again expressed his surprise at the figure stated in the draft contract, and added:

> Whilst our society would appreciate the presence of the Wiesbaden Opera at the Dublin winter season, it is quite outside the resources of the society to provide this contribution. Had the society been aware earlier that the participation of Wiesbaden would involve such cost we would have been obliged with great regret to decline the visit, however attractive it would be.

> In view of our heavy financial loss on recent German seasons the society finds itself heavily in debt despite substantial State assistance. We have given careful thought to this problem, and as a gesture of our goodwill and our anxiety to present your distinguished company to our Dublin audiences, we are prepared to offer an inclusive contribution of £3,500 towards this presentation. We feel that you should be made aware that this offer will involve our society in a substantial increase in the debt which it has already incurred in its policy of presenting the best of European opera to Irish audiences. We would be very pleased to have agreement to this suggestion and would welcome an amended contract.

Dr Beckers in his reply to Colonel O'Kelly on November 3, stated:

> I have noticed that you are now prepared to offer a contribution of £3,500 towards the participation of the Wiesbaden Opera in the forthcoming winter season of your society. Since the Intendant of the Wiesbaden Opera has not yet defined his attitude regarding your contract amendments, I have to refrain from any comment in this matter.

At the society's management committee meeting of November 22 the contract was still not signed which appeared surprising since the Wiesbaden visit was due to take place in that month of November '64. It was agreed at the meeting that joint treasurer Tom McMahon, along with Thomas Doyle, S.C., and Colonel O'Kelly get in touch with the Wiesbaden Intendant as to the exact time limit for the signing of the contract and for payment of an agreed contract fee. The trio reported back within a week to confirm final agreement of the contract and that the German company would be arriving in Dublin later that month.

In retrospect, it was to say the least a most unusual way to go about business, understandable perhaps in the case of the DGOS because of its poor financial position, but uncharacteristic in respect of the German company. Nowadays opera visits are planned often two, even three years in advance so the DGOS's was rather an amateur approach and Wiesbaden's little better. As events transpired the company's visit was worth waiting for and the opening production of The *Flying Dutchman* was hailed as an unqualified success. The singing by the professional chorus was exemplary and undoubtedly an eye-opener for Irish opera fans. 'It was an immensely satisfying experience to hear such rich, perfectly blended voices,' noted one evening newspaper critic, recalling the famous sailors' chorus in act three. The cast were described as superb with Tomislav Neralic magnificent in the title role and was matched by Liane Synek's well-sung Senta. Teamwork was the key to success in the company's second offering, *The Seraglio* and visually the staging as well as the costumes drew favourable mention.

It was to prove a busy season for Veronica Dunne as she sang in the DGOS's production of *Der Rosenkavalier* and also in Bizet's *The Pearl Fishers,* both being presented for the first time by the society. Mary MacGoris derived much pleasure from the Strauss work whose sensuous and beautiful music had made it such a favourite on the Continent. 'The first Straussian thrill arrived when the rich soprano of Veronica Dunne as Sophie and the clear, appealing mezzo of Margarethe Sjostedt as Octavian, joined in the "Presentation of the Rose" duet,' she observed in the *Irish Independent*. 'From then on, the Society's considerable hardihood in presenting this difficult but splendid work was amply justified, a vindication reaffirmed by the exquisite final trio of Sophie, Octavian and the Marschallin.'

The Pearl Fishers failed to sparkle despite Bizet's gorgeous music, arias and duets. The production was described as dull with the first act particularly slow-moving. Welsh tenor Rowland Jones disappointed the critics as Nadir, though most of them agreed that baritone Raimund Herincx was an outstanding Zurga and Veronica Dunne was vocally impressive as the priestess Leila. Discussing *Rosenkavalier* and *Pearl Fishers* with her later on, she recalled her unhappiness at having to sing five performances on the trot. 'I was a young singer and though I had lots of energy at the time, I still felt it was asking too much of me. We also needed a lot more rehearsal time for Rosenkavalier ; it is a lovely, if demanding opera, and you've got to stylise it and that takes time.'

The spring season of `65 will always be remembered by operagoers as the 'festival of flowers'. Five thousand carnations - in colours of the Irish and Italian flags, orange and white and red and white, with the green provided by the stems - decorated the Gaiety Theatre for the first night performance of Verdi's *Ernani*. The flowers, worth about £300, were flown in from Italy as a gift of the San Remo Tourist Office through Dr Giuseppe Guaraldi, Italian State Tourist Office representative in Ireland. The flowers used to decorate La Scala Opera House usually came from San Remo. Colonel Bill O'Kelly described the San Remo gesture as wonderful and said it furthered the strong links between Ireland and Italy. And he was to say that the entire cast of principals in that opening performance of *Ernani* were from La Scala, a fact that the society was indeed proud to record.

It was being presented for the first time by the society. Set in 16-century Spain, the plot is drawn from the Victor Hugo play *Hernani* with the libretto by Francesco Maria Piave. It is said that Hugo regarded the opera as a travesty of his work, though it is generally held that Piave's compression of the play was expertly done. The opera was adjudged a decided success on the first night in Venice, March 9, 1844 and Verdi believed it would have been an even bigger success if the cast was stronger. It is notable for its full-blooded melodies and in Ernani, a banished nobleman-turned-outlaw in love with Elvira, it has a colourful leading character. In the Gaiety production he would be sung by Pier Miranda Ferraro while Plinio Clabassi was cast as Silva. Piero Cappuccilli was returning to sing the King of Spain. The singer was not only popular with audiences but with the society's members and chorus since 1961.

They saw him as a cool and unruffled character who did not betray nerves before a performance. He had a quick sense of humour and was considered 'a lady's man', as they put it quaintly in the Dublin of the time. His philosophy about singers was interesting. He believed they should lead 'normal, sane lives and not over-protect themselves.' The behaviour of some of his colleagues puzzled him, especially those who appeared to live normal lives but who, come the performances, were transformed into nervous wrecks with the result that their singing suffered.

Ernani is remembered by chorus members as tremendously exciting. To Paddy Brennan it was distinguished by the glorious singing of Cappuccilli. Cappuccilli was special, a Verdian baritone who got right inside the characters he was singing and whose voice met every challenge. It was something more than technique; he was able to evoke a diversity of moods and colour and shade the voice wherever necessary. He brought also intense feeling to his singing, something which gripped audiences.'

Choristers like Aileen Walsh, Dympna Carney, Joan Rooney and Mary Troy were astounded by the steely nature of the voice, its compelling power and range. 'For a small man,' said Mary Troy, 'you wondered where this powerful voice was coming from; I mean, too, his breath control and seamless legato - they all helped to make him a great singer.' Florrie Draper had loved his Germont in Traviata and his Count di Luna in *Trovatore*, but she felt his King of Spain surpassed them both. To Dick Hanrahan and Jimmy Brittain, Cappuccilli had not only a magnificent voice but off-stage he had a warm personality and could be 'a bit of a joker.' Everyone agreed that Plinio Clabassi's performance as Silva in Ernani was of the highest standard, dignified and beautifully sung. There were mixed views expressed by the critics about Marcella di Osman's portrayal of Elvira. Mary MacGoris summed up, 'Piero Cappuccilli sang with brilliant intensity as the hot-headed autocratic young king, and Piero Miranda Farraro, though he did not manage much in the way of legato, was fine in the martial outbursts with which the role of Ernani is studded.'

The sets were said to be excellent and the costumes colourful and this combination was most effective in the very attractive finale. It was noticeable that Maestro Annovazzi won a lot of kudos for his admirable conducting and he was by now deeply involved with the artistic progress of the society. Colonel O'Kelly regarded him as almost indispensable and engaged him regularly for both spring and summer seasons.

Meanwhile, the members of the St Cecilia Gramophone Society continued to hire a coach for the spring season at the Gaiety and as usual went out of their way to get autographs from the star singers. Frances O'Gorman had found Cappuccilli's performance in *Ernani* 'truly remarkable'. 'He had become my top favourite among the Italian guest singers. I mean he had a really splendid voice, was an excellent actor and also possessed that mixture of charm and dynamic presence that we call "star quality". We enjoyed ourselves tremendously coming to Dublin and hearing stars we would have paid a fortune to hear elsewhere in the world.'

She has kept many signed DGOS opera programmes as well as miniature photographs autographed and given to her by the guest stars. These include Anna Moffo, Gianni d'Angelo, Luisa Maragliano, Virginia Zeani, Umberto Borso, Paolo Silveri and Piero Cappuccilli. She felt herself privileged to meet so many stars and was on the Dundalk Concert Committee who invited them to sing annually in the local Town Hall. 'Who will ever forget these star-studded concerts? I was always intrigued by some of the singers strange eating habits. Before some of these concerts we joined them at "high tea" and after the event itself we had a terrific time at late night parties in the Ballymascanlon Hotel, so I had plenty of time to observe odd characteristics. One gloomy, tall baritone once sat down to a platter piled high with slices of bread and butter, polished them off and would not take anything else. This other singer, a tenor, had a huge apple tart - enough for six - and enjoyed every bit of it, accompanied by a large jug of milk, which drained! The strangest of all was the young lyric tenor on his first venture out of Sicily, who ate a large chicken by himself. Nothing strange in that, you might say, except that after he'd left the table, nobody could find the bones!'

The Dundalk concerts had first begun in 1953 and the Gramophone Society was to play host to some fifty artists up to the 1960s. Father Peter Shields could take the credit for much of their success, for his love of music, particularly opera, was obvious to everybody, recalled Frances O'Gorman, and he was able to speak to the visitors in Italian and this was much appreciated. 'I think his sense of humour also rubbed off on them and they enjoyed his company and his generous spirit. He would be given an award in due course by the Italian government.'

She was one of those opera fans who regularly queued in South King Street for tickets, and it was in such a friendly queue one day that she met her husband-to-be. 'I remember I was queueing for standing room to hear Paolo Silveri sing Otello and there was a terrific atmosphere around the Gaiety as Silveri was very popular with the fans and everybody that opening night was backing him to the hilt to make a success of the role. At that moment a fair-haired young man in a tweed sports jacket suddenly came over to me and asked me the time (later, I found out that he was actually wearing a wrist watch in good working order, but he pulled his shirt sleeve over it!) We chatted about our favourite operas and singers and ended up in two seats in the Upper Circle given to us by a friend. Later, we went for coffee to

Roberts, and thus began an "operatic" friendship that was to end in marriage in the very beautiful old church, St Nicholas of Myra, in Dublin's Frances Street.'

Frances and Michael McCarthy remain avid opera fans and in her case, Frances is also identified with the restored Shaw birthplace in Synge Street, Dublin, where she greets many visitors each year. 'I shall never forget those magical Italian opera seasons in the dear old Gaiety, and they'll always generate golden memories for me and, of course, for my husband Michael.'

Ernani was not the only great Verdi work performed in that spring of `65; the presentation of *Don Carlo* was being revived after fifteen years and greeted with enthusiasm. It is a production firmly etched in my memory for some memorable individual performances, particularly in the case of the bass, Raffaele Arie, who was singing King Philip of Spain. His magnetic presence combined with his subtly coloured voice and dignified acting touched a chord in me that I had not experienced in this opera before. His duet with Rodrigo (Giulio Fioravanti) drew such applause that conductor Maestro Annovazzi and the Radio Éireann Symphony Orchestra had to cease playing for a moment. Everything about the production - the fine sets and costumes and the singing of the chorus - lent the evening a special magic.

Paddy Brennan has also vivid memories of the occasion and of Arie's performance. 'I remember how chuffed Bill O'Kelly was when he first introduced the bass to us at rehearsals, as though to say, "Look, I've brought along another great one." It was true. He was a world name at the time and one of the outstanding basses on the scene. He wasn't terribly tall but like Cappuccilli he had a regal presence on stage and a darkly coloured and expressive voice. And he was a most intelligent and sensitive artist. I don't think Bill O'Kelly could really get over the fact that he was able to get him for the society. Another miracle on his part, you might say.'

La Bohème remained a favourite with the chorus because, as Paddy Brennan recalled, 'you never knew who you'd bump into in the Café Momus scene. Bill O'Kelly and Maestro Botti were always a fixture there and were attired in the most outlandish costumes. The chorus master might be seated in the café on some nights also, and if a star guest artist was free he might drop in to join the chorus. It was a morale booster for us all and integrated the company.'

Around this time they were joined by some professional choristers from Italy and these could be a big help in tricky musical moments. In the case of *Ernani*, for instance, they were very useful, sometimes shepherding the amateur chorus members round the stage or cueing them at vital dramatic points. To Paddy Brennan, their presence was highly important. 'We could not have sustained works like *Ernani* or *Don Carlo* without this professional support.'

Dympna Carney made the point that in the sixties the chorus, singing in numerous big productions, were often over-stretched. 'The truth was that you had to be a lover of opera or mad to be part of the chorus, I mean to commit oneself to such a workload. But we carried on gallantly because we all loved singing and being part of the exciting scene. True, there was bickering and the odd row and show of temperament, yet it was a wonderful outlet for a lot of people and a great way to get rid of stress. The tiring bits I found were the rehearsals themselves and you needed resilience and stamina to keep going; above all, enthusiasm. It helped, of course, that my husband Tom was part of the same scene and I knew he loved everything about it.'

Monica Condron, who by now had graduated to small roles in the different productions and was also assistant secretary, felt the whole scene became part of one - the singing, rehearsals, gala nights, fund-raising functions and meeting the guest artists, so one never thought of opting out. 'We were enjoying ourselves and didn't mind making sacrifices for the society. Bill O'Kelly was very grateful and so we felt we had a responsibility to him to keep the society ticking over. I don't regret a moment of my involvement.'

To Aileen Walsh, joint treasurer, the whole thing was time-consuming and as a teacher, she often wondered how she found the time but as in the case of Monica Condron, one season slipped into another and Bill O'Kelly, Dr Larchet and the others in the management committee expected the status quo to remain intact. 'I didn't seem to have time to think of anything else but opera and the financial crises that affected us from time to time.'

There were also some unsung heroes during those hectic spring seasons, in particular the Gaiety backstage staff and the society's stage manager the kilted Scot, Patrick MacClellan, who worked tirelessly and ensured that props were obtained for every new production. George McFall worked closely with him and said it was a gruelling job handling six major productions in a single season. 'Patrick never complained and worked terribly long hours and gave as good as he got to Bill O'Kelly. But Bill trusted him completely and if a special prop was needed Patrick would go off hunting to antique shops to get it. And if he happened to borrow a prop it had to be kept safely for its owners.'

Sometimes there were mishaps backstage and these might lead to a temporary crisis. Once McFall was amused during a performance of *The Tales of Hoffmann*, conducted by Maestro Annovazzi. Since the gondola did not appear on stage until act two, the backstage staff set it in place in act one and as Annovazzi came out of his dressing room at the interval between the acts to resume his place on the rostrum he happened to spot the gondola and immediately 'saw red'. As it was painted black and silver, he refused to start the performance until the colours were changed; in Italy these colours were synonymous with a funeral hearse and being superstitious, the conductor was adamant in his stand.

George McFall realised he had to act quickly or the performance was in jeopardy. 'No one could reassure Annovazzi that there was nothing wrong with the colours. I grabbed one of the chorus members' cloaks, he recalls, 'and threw it on the gondola and said to the conductor, "Now it's covered Maestro, can you go on?" As he looked at it, I added that I would have it repainted next morning. He was still nodding his head as he joined the orchestra.'

Veronica Dunne was making her last appearances with the society in the winter season of `65, in her favourite role of Mimi in *La Bohème* and as Elvira in *Don Giovanni*. She remembers this *Bohème* with affection as the Rodolfo was Charles Craig, one of the best Rodolfos of the day. 'Charles was fabulous and he did have a very impressive tenor voice, though I used to hate him for the way he used to get up to that top note and hold it in the love duet at the end of act one. I think he did it on purpose!'

The *Don Giovanni* won praise from the most discerning of the critics, with Forbes Robinson making a strikingly handsome Don and singing with subtle artistry. To Veronica Dunne, he was a polished actor and splendid bass and had a powerful stage presence. James Pease as Leporello was a good foil. She enjoyed the performance and got some excellent notices. Ann Moran, a young Irish soprano, showed promise as Zerlina.

The society, reflected Veronica Dunne, was giving opera a great boost in the sixties - a vintage decade in her view - and she was happy to be part of it, although she would love to have been given the opportunity to sing Butterfly as well as Desdemona in Verdi's *Otello*. She conceded that opera could be cruel insofar as certain roles escaped singers and it was the same in her case. She had the highest admiration for people like Bill O'Kelly, Dr Larchet, Bertie Timlin and others who had put so much into the society to ensure that Dublin would get the very best. How could anyone forget the wonderful performances by Rinaldi, Zeani, d'Angelo, Stignani, Mancini, Silveri, Cappuccilli and Gian Giacomo Guelfi in both the fifties and sixties? In her opinion, some of these performances matched the best in Europe.

While most opera pundits in Ireland felt that Mimi *(Bohème)*, Marguerite *(Faust)* and Antonia *(Hoffmann)* were perhaps Veronica Dunne's best-remembered roles with the society, Sir Charles Mackerras was of the opinion that her Manon in 1962, which he conducted, was very meritorious. 'I did indeed enjoy my performance of the opera with Veronica Dunne. It was my first experience of the opera and I remember that I admired her performance very much as well as her enthusiasm during rehearsals. The opera is very long and despite many cuts the rehearsals were inadequate, although I can recall that the performance of the principals, especially Veronica Dunne, was extremely good.'

Society in Crisis

It was to be a year of celebration. The society in 1966 was marking its silver jubilee and everything seemed poised for another memorable spring festival of Italian opera. President Éamon de Valera congratulated the society on its achievements. 'What the society has done for opera is worthy of the highest praise. All lovers of good music are in the society's debt.' And Dr Larchet, the elected DGOS president since its foundation, said that one must feel a sense of gratitude and satisfaction at what had been achieved. For instance, out of a repertoire of sixty operas, many of these were heard in Ireland for the first time, notably *Nabucco, Falstaff* and *Andrea Chénier.*

As more tributes poured in, a cloud unfortunately hung over the horizon and posed a threat to the society's future activities. The subvention from the Italian government, reckoned to be worth about £12,000, was in doubt because of a court scandal that had blown up in Milan where impresarios were accused of misappropriating subvention monies; furthermore, the new government in power was determined to end the subvention policy. To Colonel Bill O'Kelly and his management committee, the situation was serious and the chairman vowed that every avenue would be explored to try to get the Italian authorities to reverse its decision.

The death of Louis Elliman, managing director of the Gaiety Theatre was also a severe blow and Dr Larchet was to pay him a worthy tribute. Donnie Potter, a member of the society's management committee, recalled that Elliman had never once lost interest in the society's welfare and before every new season put £1,000 forward as a guarantee and indication of his optimism. Their long-serving honorary secretary Bertie Timlin was seriously ill and his work was now being handled by Monica Condron. She would say that the question of the Italian subvention had been discussed by the management committee as early as January of that year 1966, but when Colonel O'Kelly telephoned Maestro Botti in Rome he was assured that the application for a subvention would be successful.

O'Kelly was however still worried and Prince Caracciolo was asked to go to Rome to have talks with Botti. He reported back later that because of the change of government there was confusion about the availability of future subventions. In the meantime, O'Kelly said that no contracts had been signed with either Maestro Botti or the Gaiety Theatre management. By March 14 the crisis deepened. By now O'Kelly was in Rome and it was there that he learned the application for a subvention had been turned down. He immediately got in touch with the Irish ambassador who agreed to pursue the matter.

It was to no avail, and even the intervention of the Irish government through the Tánaiste got nowhere. In an act of desperation, Colonel O'Kelly proposed three courses: first, the cancellation of the spring season; secondly, to go ahead with the plans as they stood and hope for the best, in spite of the fact that the season would cost more than they could afford; and thirdly, to ask the Irish government to subsidise the society. And it also decided that Prince Caracciolo and John F. MacInerney, management committee members, should see Tim O'Driscoll, head of Bord Fáilte, to find out if the board would give the society a subsidy of £5,000. But O'Driscoll regretted they could not meet the request, though he was sympathetic.

Colonel O'Kelly was emphatic that if they postponed or cancelled the spring season it would be, in his view, the end of the society and he for one would not be prepared to re-organise it at a later date. However, he would let the final decision rest with the management committee. He did point out though that the cost of mounting the spring season would be in the region of £24,000 and that the income from the box-office, Arts Council, patrons members and their seventy guarantors amounted to £24,800, so he was inclined to the view that they should proceed with the season.

The newspapers, for the most part, were not aware of the full facts, although the dailies hinted that the number of presentations would probably be reduced. It was left to the *Sunday Independent* to mention the word 'crisis' for the first time, and that behind the scenes the DGOS committee officers, headed by Colonel O'Kelly, were caught in their worst dilemma for twenty-five years. There was a further setback when Maestro Botti notified them by telegram that 'he was not interested in organising the spring season.'

To O'Kelly this was the final straw. He acted quickly - probably too hastily as it transpired - and called on the Gaiety management to say there would be no DGOS spring season of opera. Later that day, he telephoned Tibor Paul, principal conductor of the Radio Éireann Symphony Orchestra, with the grim news. Paul could scarcely believe what he was hearing and told Colonel O'Kelly that in his opinion it was a disastrous decision and it would be impossible for him at such short notice to change the orchestral schedule. At the same time he pledged his maximum support if a season of English or Italian opera was undertaken.

Tibor Paul's pledge appeared to act as a spur to Colonel O'Kelly, for he changed course rather dramatically and began to make enquiries in both London and Rome about the availability of artists. By this time Prince Caracciolo had made contact in Rome with Signor Gino Menelao, an established impresario, about organising an opera season in Dublin that spring. He agreed to go ahead provided a sum of £19,000 was forthcoming. Colonel O'Kelly agreed to travel to Rome to finalise matters and at this stage it looked as if the season had been saved. Twenty-two performance would be staged at a cost of £19,000, while at the same time the society's management committee requested the Irish Arts Council to increase its grant.

Donnie Potter was not confident and regarded the loss of the Italian subvention as a real body blow. 'At this point I couldn't see any real future for the society, for even with the subvention we were struggling to make ends meet. Maestro Botti had served the society very well and was an honest broker and his resignation was another severe blow to our hopes. Knowing Bill O'Kelly's fierce determination and optimism, I was able to draw some comfort in the crisis. We also had government ministers on our side and from time to time they were able to get us a once-off grant of about £5,000 to guarantee against loss.'

Although Signor Menelao agreed to organise the `66 spring season, Potter felt that in the long-term he was not the impresario for the job. 'I had my doubts about him and felt that Maestro Annovazzi was the man to see the society into the seventies and beyond. He had a vision and understanding that was ideal for our kind of set-up and he had a genuine interest in the society. He was well equipped to prepare a "package" that would ensure we got first-class singers, conductors and producers. I conveyed my feelings more than once to Bill O'Kelly and before long he came round completely to my way of thinking.'

It was around this time that millionaire Sir Alfred Beit let it be known he was prepared to invest £1,000 in the society in an effort to ease the financial pressure. In some quarters this was regarded as a very generous gesture but Colonel O'Kelly suspected that Beit was seeking artistic control. Joint treasurer Aileen Walsh said she had heard about Bill O'Kelly's anxiety. 'He didn't want to relax control; it was his society and he prided himself in knowing all his "troops" by name, meaning of course the chorus. When the Beit offer came up for discussion at a management meeting it got nowhere, except that Sir Alfred was thanked for his interest and his willingness to help in the crisis.'

Monica Condron, who would shortly be installed as secretary following the death of Bertie Timlin, felt that Bill O'Kelly would in no way relinquish his powers, either managerial or as a selector of the operas. Any suggestion that Sir Alfred Beit might take over that latter responsibility made Bill naturally resentful, and understandably so. 'I'm sure that Sir Alfred meant well but he probably underestimated Bill's authority.'

Donnie Potter has no doubt that Sir Alfred was prepared to give £1,000 but with the stipulation that he would have a say in the choice of the operas. This did not fall in line with the views of the management committee and they reluctantly refused to accept the offer. Beit was the only one to come forward during the crisis of that year with any such offer. 'In our book, it was a considerable sum of money, enough to meet our bank overdraft, but we could see that if we accepted it might mean a split in the society.'

From time to time, the chorus members heard rumours of an 'impending crisis' and the 'loss of the subvention' but most of them were happy to leave any such problems to the management committee. 'I do remember there was a feeling in the society that something was happening,' recalls Paddy Brennan, 'and eventually we were all called together and informed that the subvention was actually lost. Up to this Bill O'Kelly, in typical style, had played his cards close to his chest and we weren't aware of the problems. Nonetheless, the ending of the subvention was clearly a turning point, though to most of us it was somewhat vague and our understanding was that Maestro Botti used to get money from the Italian government to pay the Italian artists, otherwise it didn't concern us. There had been talk in the previous year that Mario del Monaco was engaged to sing Otello in the spring of 1966 but that seemingly fell through.'

Despite the crisis, five productions were scheduled for that spring - *Don Pasquale, Tosca, La Traviata, Il Trovatore and Rigoletto*. And most of the visiting artists were popular and familiar names, including Attilio d'Orazi, Ugo Benelli, Piero Cappuccilli, Enzo Tei and Luisa Maragliano. A new name was added to the list, Renato Bruson, who was in the true tradition of first-rate Italian baritones. Returning also was Margherita Rinaldi whose name alone sold tickets at the Gaiety box-office.

Benelli says he was delighted to return to Dublin to sing Ernesto in *Don Pasquale,* the popular Donizetti comedy. By now he and his wife Angela and their two young children had moved from Milan to Genoa. 'I love the city because of its beauty and its climate', he says. 'The fog in Milan is not good for singers, Genoa is by the sea and better for the voice.' He was a rising star, getting more and more engagements throughout Europe and in North and South America.

He had promised Colonel O'Kelly he would come back, engagements permitting. 'I was still a young lyric tenor finding my way and had a wife and children, so I came to Dublin for the money and for the music. Bill O'Kelly had been good to me and I think he was happy with my Ernesto. It was one of my favourite parts.' He enjoyed the post-opera suppers and parties and continued to make friends. With his good English, he got to know people better than his Italian colleagues and was rather proud when taximen hailed him by name in the streets of Dublin.

Musically, it was turning out to be a highly enjoyable season. Napoleone Annovazzi, according to the majority of the critics, conducted a first-class *Rigoletto*. 'He moulded Verdi's long phrases, brought out the touches of colour and induced the Radio Éireann Symphony Orchestra to give a spring-heeled effect to the more conventional accompaniments,' noted Mary MacGoris in the *Irish Independent*.

As usual Cappuccilli electrified the audience by his acting and singing and injected the role of the jester with telling Verdian strength and no little subtlety. Oldtimers in the society and outside it still like to compare his interpretation with that of Paolo Silveri. If Cappuccilli's fine voice, with its controlled expressive range and power thrilled Verdi fans, Silveri's portrayal appeared in the eyes of many more thoughtful and moving, though no less compelling.

Dublin was that season hearing for the first time Renato Bruson as Count di Luna in *Trovatore* and he, too, gave an exciting performance. To Tom Carney, he had a splendidly smooth baritone voice, incisive and beautifully projected. 'You could see the potential in the way he sang "Il Balen" and there was no doubt about his star quality.' Dick Hanrahan, Jimmy Brittain and John Brady, all of whom sang in the chorus, recognised the richness in Bruson's voice, his dramatic power and fine phrasing. Dympna Carney believed it was a true Verdian voice, strong and flexible and she felt the baritone sang with deep feeling.

Bruson happens to be my own present-day favourite baritone. I like to remember his Nabucco in Arena di Verona as unforgettable and his final scene in Verdi's *I due Foscari* as one of the most sublime moments in opera. Likewise, his Boccanegra and Macbeth confirm how great a Verdian exponent he became since the sixties. When he visited Dublin, he was only five years a professional singer; but by March 1969 he would be singing Count di Luna at the Metropolitan.

It was fitting in that silver jubilee season of `66 that Margherita Rinaldi would be asked to sing Violetta in *Traviata* and as expected it proved a highlight, not only for her luminous singing, but also Attilio d'Orazi's memorable elder Germont. John Carney recalls the performance with pleasure, as do Paddy Brennan and Monica Condron. He was a versatile artist, equally at home in comic or tragic roles, and in Dublin he was a great favourite with audiences.

So a spring season that at one stage was under threat ended on a high note, although it must be remembered that because of the loss of the subvention two productions were not staged, *Aida* and *Adriana Lecouvreur*. Nor could the patron members have been entirely happy, as at the outset of the season they were asked to forego their free vouchers for seats. Generally, though, attendances were good and box-office receipts most encouraging.

Opera-goers were in for a pleasant surprise in the winter season of '66. Not only had Maestro Annovazzi been asked to take over the artistic direction of the society but he also managed to bring to Ireland talented Romanian singers for *Samson and Delilah, Mignon and Ballo* in *Maschera*. He had connections in the country's capital, Bucharest, having conducted operas regularly there, and though Romania was behind the Iron Curtain he was able to arrange visas through the Romanian Embassy in London.

'It was a master stroke on his part,' recalled Donnie Potter, 'for after the loss of the Italian subvention the society's morale was low, but with the arrival of the Romanians there was a buoyant mood of both expectancy and optimism. I never doubted that Maestro Annovazzi had both the musical and organisational ability we wanted.'

Bringing the Romanian artists to Ireland for the first time was a great achievement on Annovazzi's part, recalled Monica Condron, and they came at a time when a fresh infusion of talent was needed. Aileen Walsh remembers they weren't paid high fees and this suited the society as money was scarce. To the Carneys, Tom and John the timing of their coming could not be bettered. 'Here we were, getting outstanding new voices just when we wanted them,' reflected Tom Carney, 'and it was great for audiences as well.'

Dympna Carney had sympathy with the Romanians when they arrived in Dublin. 'I do remember they had few clothes with them and they were as poor as any of the poor Irish. I was inclined to pity them. And as they went off shopping in Grafton Street or Henry Street, I used to wonder what they'd use for money. I'm sure they were thrilled to get out of Communist Romania and taste the western way of life.' Florrie Draper thought they fitted in very well and she heard that Bill O'Kelly was charmed by their singing at the rehearsals.

The nine Romanian artists stayed in Jury's Hotel in Dame Street and it was said at the time that officials from the Romanian Embassy in London were 'looking after them' and that when they went shopping these officials accompanied them. The *Evening Herald* began to investigate the story, and claimed that the singers were being 'watched' for fear they defected and were never left on their own in public. 'ROMANIANS TOO BUSY TO

SIGHTSEE' was one *Herald* headline in which the reporter claimed that the singers' travels were 'confined to taxi runs between Jury's Hotel and the Gaiety Theatre.' The excuse given was that they wished to 'avoid chills in the December weather or sore throats.'

Marcel Ghibernea, First Secretary, Cultural Attache to the Romanian Embassy in London, told the newspaper he had come to Dublin to 'assist his compatriots on their visit to Ireland.' And he added that although the singers had not had much opportunity of meeting the Irish people as yet, they were enjoying their visit.' Some members of the chorus did feel that the Romanians were being discreetly watched and sometimes noticed they were accompanied to the Gaiety by officials. It was strongly rumoured at the time in fact that one of the artists was a member of the Romanian secret police and was the 'link man' in Dublin for the embassy officials from London. This view persists today in operatic circles.

When Bernadette Greevy had to cancel her appearance in the title role of *Mignon,* Colonel O'Kelly asked Maestro Annovazzi to try to get another Romanian to take her place. The maestro succeeded in engaging mezzo-soprano Viorica Cortez who quickly made her mark as Mignon, the noble girl taken by gypsies. The opera by Ambroise Thomas, was being staged for the first time by the society and had been inspired by Goethe's novel, 'Wilhelm Meister.' Premiered at the Opéra-Comique in November 1866, its music has grace and charm and it is considered Thomas's best opera.

Dublin audiences not only enthused about Viorica Cortez's brilliant performance but also that by tenor Jon Piso, whose musicality and expressive singing aroused real enthusiasm in the theatre. The critics liked the feeling he brought to his singing, as well as his gracious stage presence. 'Piso sings with intelligent lyricism and great heart,' summed up an evening newspaper reviewer. And a colleague stated that the society had scored an undoubted success with the opera. Piso also impressed as Riccardo in *Ballo in Maschera* and was matched in presence and vocal beauty by Elena Dima as Amelia.

The production that is most vividly remembered is *Samson and Delilah* with the Romanian principals Zenaida Pally and Ion Buzea. Pally, with her dark, seductive Mediterranean appearance, looked perfect for the role of Delilah, while Buzea was a colossus of a man, a real-life Samson, or as one newspaper put it, 'a great hunk of a man.' He was already a big name in European opera houses and was soon to confirm his reputation in Dublin. The critics were bowled over. 'From this performance of the opera,' noted Charles Acton in the *Irish Times,* 'it would seem that the DGOS struck oil when they went behind the Iron Curtain. The protagonists in last night's opera were the best I have heard in Dublin for many a long day.' Chorus members 'raved' about the performance. Maura Mooney told me it was the best Samson she had seen and that Pally and Buzea played the big love scene in act two as if they were real lovers. Florrie Draper felt that Pally was the most sexy Delilah she had ever seen and Buzea a kind of Valentino of the opera. 'Sparks flew alright,' she mused. 'But isn't that what the opera is all about anyway?' Aileen Walsh thought the whole production was exciting and the singing exceptional. You either play *Samson* and *Delilah* with passion or . you lose, she said, and in this case Pally and Buzea gave it everything. Maureen Lemass told me she would never forget the first night's performance. 'I do recall that Jon Buzea was stunning as Samson in both his acting and singing. What a stage presence! He and Pally were so credible that you believed they were right out of the Bible.'

In Paddy Brennan's view, the Romanians made a tremendous impact in that winter season of `66 and opened up a new era for the society. He remembered that one English critic went away thrilled by the *Mignon* and *Samson* as well as by the singing of Pally, Buzea, Cortez and the others. 'The truth is that the man couldn't have come to Dublin at a better time. Maestro Annovazzi had changed the course of the DGOS with one inspired stroke and for the next few years Piso, Cortez and the rest would thrill Irish audiences.'

It was to be Patrick Somerville's last year as a chorus master with the society. He counted *Mignon* as one of the best operatic performances he had seen, mainly due to Piso and Cortez. He also remembered it for another reason. A row erupted involving Piso and his Romanian colleagues in the cast and Patrick MacClellan, assistant director, when the latter decided to use dry ice as smoke in one of the scenes. 'I do remember Piso was furious and told MacClellan he didn't want it used. His colleagues joined in the protest and explained that it would be bad for their voices, but big Pat Clellan was having none of it. Of course he had his way and dry ice - which is only a vapour anyway - was used. At one stage I feared Piso would not sing.'

Somerville also enjoyed *Samson* and *Delilah* and recalled that tenor Ion Buzea sang the role of Samson attired in a lion's cloth, completely bare from the waist up. He was the most imposing man you could imagine - all six feet four inches of him - and from all accounts the women in the audience fell for him in a big way. 'I remember I was doing choral teaching in my school and one of the girls remarked that she had seen *Samson* and *Delilah* on the previous night and added with a laugh, "I'd like to see that Samson again!"'

To Somerville, the Romanians brought something new to the scene. They sang extremely well in French and the women in particular looked right for their parts and had voices to match. 'Bill O'Kelly told me he was very proud of them and I think he was happy to see them succeed outside of the Iron Curtain. Bill could be blunt but he had a lot of heart.'

Reading over the society's annual report for that year 1966, it again struck me forcibly that its future was unquestionably in jeopardy. I quote: 'Few realise the serious situation that arose after the loss of the subvention and how hard it was to make the right decision and one which would ensure the future of the society. The management committee generally felt that to shut the door without giving our patrons and public a chance to show their support was lacking in trust all round. After many meetings the decision to go ahead was made, but in doing so we envisaged a big loss financially and while our thanks are due to the Arts Council for a guarantee against loss of £5,500, we also had to find money from other sources. Our sponsors were also called upon and very willingly gave.'

The overall outcome was not nearly as bad as anticipated. A loss of £4,400 was reported on the spring season, leaving the society with a total debt of £15,000, which suggested that it was in the words of management committee member Dick Hanrahan, 'slipping back again', and he hoped a more sensible approach would be made to meet the debt. Everyone was agreed though that in the circumstances the society had done extremely well in putting on the season without the Italian subvention.

At a committee meeting in August of `66, Colonel O'Kelly declared, 'There will be no further Italian seasons unless we are granted a substantial subvention.'

Return to Cork

'I caught the opera bug in the spring of 1967,' admitted Harold Johnson, Cork-born chartered accountant who up to then had been more interested in straight theatre. A genial, outgoing Corkonian, he had seen the city go through a difficult time after the old Opera House was gutted by fire in 1955 and had played his part in ensuring that it would be replaced by a modern home for opera and music generally.

As a shareholder, he was interested in its future as a venue and hoped to see it provide the best in entertainment. Now after more than a decade without grand opera, the new Opera House was opening its doors to the DGOS and its presentations of *La Bohème, Madama Butterfly* and *Lucia di Lammermoor;* the casts, conductors and producers were nearly all international and as usual they would be supported by the large DGOS chorus. Undeniably the city was starved of grand opera and it was expected the productions would be greeted by full houses.

Nothing of the sort. Harold Johnson was present at Monday's opening of *Bohème* and on his own admission, was shocked by the smallness of the attendance - the theatre was less than half full. He had been deeply moved by the performance, especially the climax culminating in Mimi's death. Musically and theatrically, the production was an eye-opener to him and by the time he left the Opera House he had to confess he had caught the opera bug.

'I had no doubt in the world about it. I think it was the impact the music and drama together made on me and the superb singing by tenor Ettore Babini and soprano Maria Angela Rosati in the main parts, not forgetting either baritone Franco Pagliazzi, as Marcello, and Vittorina Magnaghi's Musetta. Maestro Annovazzi wove the whole thing together as it were with a magic wand.'

Despite the small crowd, it had been an exciting evening in the theatre and like everyone else he joined wholeheartedly in the applause at the final curtain, and it seemed to go on for at least five minutes. The review in the *Cork Examiner* next morning reflected the mood in the Opera House. 'The prolonged applause was a magnificent tribute to a magnificent company.

What a pity therefore that so few Cork opera-goers turned up for the performance. While the balcony was predictably full, the remainder of the house was half empty; this must make it disheartening to the artists to take the boards in such conditions.'

Harold Johnson returned the following night for *Madama Butterfly* and was even more moved than on the Monday, mainly because of the shattering performance by the Italian soprano Edy Amedeo as Butterfly. 'All I can say is that the acting and the singing left me almost speechless.' Again, the Opera House was less than half filled. He could only attribute it to poor advertising by everyone concerned. He was delighted to learn, however, that by Thursday night there was a clamour for tickets and the house was full to capacity for the rest of the week. He decided to do everything in his power to ensure that the DGOS was invited back to Cork to present a week's season every spring.

What Johnson did not know however was that the visit by the DGOS to Cork might never have taken place because the society and the management of the Opera House found it almost impossible to come to an agreement about guarantees. The majority of the members of the DGOS management committee were strongly in favour of the visit taking place but Colonel O'Kelly hesitated until such time that the Opera House manager Bill Twomey and director Gus Healy came up with acceptable terms. Both O'Kelly and Donnie Potter were worried about the amount they could lose on the visit and it was further agreed that the society would not be asked to meet the salaries of members of the Radio Éireann Symphony Orchestra.

While the society's week of opera in Cork was voted an artistic success, as a commercial proposition it was far from satisfactory. Subsequent minutes of management meetings reveal that for months afterwards there were arguments between the Cork Opera House management and the DGOS about certain costs to be met such as outstanding overtime payment for the backstage Opera House staff. Donnie Potter says that correspondence continued for some time and it was finally agreed that before another visit could take place a special committee should be formed in Cork to ensure that the DGOS incurred no losses on any future visit.

'We were being realistic,' Potter added, 'and made it known to the Opera House management that Cork itself must make a major contribution towards our costs. Bill Twomey and Gus Healy agreed to this but unfortunately another visit would not take place until 1971.'

To Harold Johnson, this was a great pity as it left the city once again starved of grand opera. At shareholders' meetings he persistently asked when could they expect the next visit by the DGOS. 'It didn't make sense to me at the time that the DGOS wanted to come and somehow Cork itself wasn't able to meet its modest guarantees.'

Members of the DGOS chorus have very happy memories of that 1967 visit, such as the warmth of the audiences, the receptions put on for them by the breweries and the overall sense of camaraderie the visit generated. Paddy Brennan says they all looked forward to Cork in that June and made a holiday out of it. Tom and John Carney felt it was good for the society to tour and it helped to inject a great team spirit. They were able to relax and in their free time visit scenic spots and have fun. Dick Hanrahan liked the Opera House as a venue and thought the acoustics there were excellent. 'When the theatre was packed, as it was for the final three nights of our visit, there was an exciting atmosphere and a buzz of excitement. The Italian artists told me they loved the theatre and Cork itself. It was friendly and I remember there were a few late night restaurants where we could dine.' To Florrie Draper and Maura Mooney it was akin to a week's holiday and like the other choristers were hoping that the society could bring opera there every year. 'I think we owed it to Cork,' said Miss Draper, 'as many of the opera-goers there could not come to Dublin to see our spring season presentations.' Aileen Walsh had no doubt that Colonel O'Kelly wanted to visit Cork regularly but he had to be cautious as the society just could not afford to lose money. 'I think that Bill was right in asking the Cork people to prepare the way for us and have certain guarantees in place. It was a pity though that four years went by from 1967 to 1971 without another visit.'

The highlight of that spring season of `67 in Dublin was of course the first ever staging by the society of Francesco Cilea's opera *Adriana Lecouvreur* with the 'divine' Magda Olivero in the title role. Both the composer and the soprano had been in the news in the previous year when the world celebrated the centenary of his birth with revivals of *Adriana Lecouvreur* with Signora Olivero singing in a number of anniversary performances. She was identified with the role of Adriana more than any other in her repertoire.

'Some of us in the chorus knew about her but not enough about her reputation,' recalled Paddy Brennan. 'At that time in the sixties few people travelled abroad to attend opera and mostly depended on gramophone records and radio broadcasts, so we really weren't aware of the true importance of "Divine Magda", as she was affectionately called. She was in fact a living legend. Freddie Caracciolo and John MacInerney would have known her, and Annovazzi knew her personally and was instrumental in getting her to sing for the society. Generally, though, Irish opera-goers didn't know about her and consequently there was no great rush to the box-office for tickets.'

There was in addition a resistance to little known operas and *Adriana*

Lecouvreur fell into that category, despite the fact that it was being described in press releases as an opera 'with passion to stir every heart.' The work itself is based on the life of the famous French actress Adrienne Lecouvreur (1692-1731) who won renown for her roles in plays by Corneille and Racine, as well as her friendship with Voltaire. Outside of Italy, however, Cilea's operas were slow to gain popularity, only *L'Arlesiana* and *Adriana* being staged; indeed, Cilea was cruelly dubbed the poor man's Giordano. Both composers, it will be remembered, worked under the shadow of Puccini, depending on powerful melodies to cover up some poor musical joinery in their operatic scores.

Quite apart from its 18th century setting, *Adriana* has much in common with Giordano's *Andrea Chénier,* in its compelling lyrical flow of melody which is basic to its appeal, needing a soprano and tenor prepared to 'knock the slates off the opera house roof.' Magda Olivero had made the role of Adriana her own and one that had played a crucial part in her illustrious career. Born in Saluzzo, near Turin, on March 25 1914, she was blessed with a natural voice and went on to make a career of singing, being especially noted for her Puccini roles. In 1941 she married an American industrialist and decided to retire from the operatic stage, a decision that shocked her friends and admirers. Irish soprano Veronica Dunne tells the story that her decision was precipitated by an experience singing in an opera conducted by Vincenzo Bellezza.

'When I was studying in Rome in the early fifties, at a time when Magda Olivero made her celebrated comeback, it was said that singing under Bellezza was partly to blame for her unexpected retirement; he was very deaf and allowed the orchestra to play too loudly, so that Magda sang herself out in no time and later had to resume her studies before contemplating a comeback. I am inclined to believe the story as it was circulated widely in Italian musical circles. I did hear that on her return she sang gloriously as Tosca and Mimi.'

Francesco Cilea was to play a major part in her comeback. In August 1950, by then in his eighties and sensing perhaps approaching death, he wanted desperately to hear Olivero sing Adriana as he remembered her in the part. He wrote to her and it was said that out of a sense of loyalty she agreed; not only that but visited his house and sang excerpts from his opera. Cilea, who accompanied her on the piano, was visibly overcome. 'You have gone beyond notes,' he told her. 'You have understood what I felt in composing opera and you have entered into the soul of Adriana in the same way as I did.'

In Paddy Brennan's view, *Adriana* was an opera that needed a legendary singer like Olivero to make it work. The tragedy was that opera-goers in Dublin found out too late of her greatness and did not attend her

JON PISO: The stylish Romanian tenor.

ANTONIO GALIE: Tenor of distinction.

GIUSEPPE GIACOMINI: Made profound impression.

BORSO: As Radames (above) in 'Aida'.

UMBERTO BORSO: (right) Dramatic tenor of note.

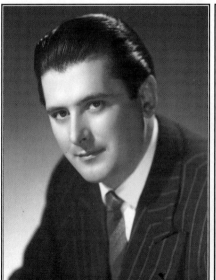

ALVINIO MISCIANO: Sang Duke of Mantua.

CHORUS master Giuseppe Giardina.

GIUSEPPE DI STEFANO: In relaxed mood, and (inset) as Cavaradossi in 'Tosca'.

FLAVIANO LABO (second from left) joins in a toast with Lt. Col. Bill O'Kelly (extreme right) and other celebrities.

Rehearsing in Dundalk: Maestro Franco Patané (piano), Giuseppe Forgione (baritone), and Michele Incenzo (clarinet). RTE Symphony Orchestra.

ALDO PROTTI: The Italian baritone with the hurricane voice.

CHORUS of 'The Queen of Spades' sang the opera in Russian.

HARPIST Sheila Larchet.

TENOR Brendan Cavanagh.

PIERO CAPPUCCILLI: A voice of steel.

UGO BENELLI: A star of bel canto.

LUCILLA UDOVICK: Sang magnificently.

LUCIANO PAVAROTTI...in Dublin for DGOS concert with Monica Condron (left), Aileen Walsh and Donnie Potter, DGOS chairman.

RUTH MAHER: A versatile performer.

SUZANNE MURPHY: A moving Violetta.

PEDRO LAVIRGEN: Spanish tenor

AURIO TOMICICH (right), in a scene from the DGOS's 'Puritani', and (above right) the popular Prince Caracciolo.

Outside the Café Momus in the '76 production of 'La Boheme': (from Left) Patrick Ring (Aleindoro), Hagint Vartanian (Mimi), Franco Bonanome (Rodolfo), Terry Reid (Musetta) and Peter McBrien (Schaunard).

ATTILIO D'ORAZI: (right)
a memorable Falstaff.

RENATO BRUSON: (above) Showed
rich promise.

LICINIO MONTEFUSCO...a baritone in the great Italian tradition.

The DGOS chorus in lively rehearsal for the 'La Boheme' in the 1987 Spring Season.

SOPRANO Adéle Leigh found romance in Dublin with American bass James Pease

PRODUCER Tom Hawkes.

PROF. Anthony Hughes.

DGOS Gala Nights...Donnie Potter (right) greets President Hillary and Mrs Hillary.

President and Mrs Childers (above) also warmly received.

Greetings (right) for President de Valera.

DARIO MICHELI: The gifted
producer/designer.

Together:
in Dundalk
Lino Martinucci (tenor),
Helge Bomches (bass),
Attilio D'Orazzi (baritone);
(front) (left to right)
Fr. Peter Shields,
Aida Abagieff (sop.)
and Maestro Annovazzi.

PADDY RYAN: Very innovative

HAROLD JOHNSON: Caught opera 'bug' in Cork.

ALBERT ROSEN: (right) Made big impact with DGOS.

MARY SHERIDAN: Soprano, a star in 'Turindot'

Nico's restaurant in Dame St, popular with opera buffs.

FRANCO BONANOME and Terry Reid met and married in Ireland.

performances in any numbers. They missed a unique opportunity. Critic Charles Acton waxed enthusiastic about the production and was grateful to the DGOS for staging it. He emphasised that the success of the opera largely depended on the prima donna in the title role and in this respect the society was fortunate to have Olivero. She had a worthy partner in Jon Piso and it would be a shame, he added, if there were empty seats in the theatre for Olivero's final two performances.

At this time a number of London's leading critics began to take an interest in the society's spring seasons. John Higgins of the *Financial Times* attended the first night of *Adriana* and came away very impressed. He reminded his readers that Olivero had sung the role four years before in Edinburgh and that it was by now a 'performance rather than an interpretation.' 'There is no mistaking the *grande dame* aspect. Adriana's red-robed entry into the Green Room of the Comedie Française may have a touch of one of Bea Lillie's wilder creations, but there is also a flicker of la divine Sarah. The famous quotation from *Phèdre* is delivered with enough bite to silence any rival and the death scene is carried off with superb melodrama, as Adriana collapses on a chaise longe, her hair in full flood around a chalk-white face.'

Dundalk opera buffs, meanwhile, continued to attend the glamorous spring seasons, led by Father Peter Shields of the Gramophone Society; he also helped to organise the annual concerts in the Town Hall with star DGOS guest artists. Frances O'Gorman counts the performance of *Adriana* as among her most vivid memories. It was a real experience, she said, hearing Magda Olivero singing her favourite role. 'She was not young at the time but she was every inch a prima donna, using her voice with musical intelligence and sensitivity. On the stage she looked divine, and the magic of her voice and presence made you see a young, extremely striking woman loving and suffering for that love. I count myself very fortunate to have met one of the really outstanding talents of her generation.'

'Magda was unforgettable,' recalls Maura Mooney. 'Funny thing is that she had a kind of hypnotic effect on me.' To Florrie Draper she was one of the very few real prima donnas to sing with the society. 'True, we had great singers but it would be wrong to call them prima donnas. Off-stage, Olivero was a lady, simple and charming, and without pretension.' For Maureen Lemass the diva's portrayal of Adriana was intensely moving. 'I just cannot convey in words her whole approach to the role and the incredible way she got inside it. It had to be seen to be believed. All I can say is that she lived the part and in the course of the performance became the embodiment of the famous French actress she was portraying.'

Maureen Lemass got to know Olivero on a personal basis and they went shopping and sight-seeing together. Later on they began to correspond and do so to this day. The diva thoroughly enjoyed her visit to Ireland, so much so that before she departed she promised Maestro Annovazzi she would return the following year to sing Tosca. That spring season of `67 was notable for some high-class individual performances. Viorica Cortez was an exciting Princess Eboli in *Don Carlo* while the young Italian baritone Silvano Carroli was greatly admired as Marcello in *Bohème;* he would go on to become a world star. Soprano Jolanda Meneguzzer, a La Scala favourite and a specialist in coloratura roles, made a sensational DGOS debut as Lucia. Jon Piso was back in Dublin to sing in both *Adriana Lecouvreur* and *Don Carlo* and it was evident that he had by now won the hearts of the Irish opera-going public. Other guest artists who made a good impression that season were tenor Bruno Rufo, who sang Radames in *Aida,* baritone Alberto Rinaldi, making his Dublin debut, and the Romanian bass Nicolae Florei.

Giuseppe Giardina was working with the society for the first time in that season and is fondly remembered by the DGOS committee members and choristers. He was named in the programme as chorus master and assistant conductor and was accepted as a splendid musician. Colourful, witty and articulate, he fitted into the Dublin of the sixties like a glove. Although born near New York, where he studied piano at the Juilliard School, he went on to obtain his musical diploma in organ and composition in Rome and was a pupil of the celebrated conductor *Tuilio* Serafin.

When I visited Giardina at his quarters in Via Del Boschetto, Rome in April of 1998, where he coaches young as well as established singers, he was happy to recall those halcyon days, as he called them, in Dublin. Since then of course he has spent twenty years attached to Rome Opera as chorus master, and he has enjoyed meeting Irish friends on their visits to Rome, among them Tom and Dympna Carney. He admits that it was the warmth of the Irish temperament, their humour and carefree spirit that drew him to Ireland - he once worked also at the Wexford Festival.

'I retain some of my nicest memories from my work in Dublin,' he says, 'for besides the music I got to know the city, I mean the cobbled-stone streets, Guinness brewery, Moore Street traders - where I bought fruit and vegetables - Trinity College, the Joycean heritage - it was all so delightful, as was working with the DGOS amateur chorus. I had worked with amateur choirs for twenty years and they sang because they wanted to sing; by contrast, a professional operatic chorus could be a frustrated lot as most of them wanted to be soloists. There were some fine voices in the DGOS chorus and their enthusiasm was infectious.'

He had been invited to Dublin by Maestro Annovazzi whom he described as a very good practitioner who knew the business intimately. Giardina suspected that one of the reasons the conductor gave him the job was because of his English. 'I think he believed I would be very useful to have in Ireland. He was able to persuade young singers to take roles with the society for little or nothing, convincing them they were getting golden opportunities. In fairness to him he created stars, among them Viorica Cortez, Maria Angela Rosati and others.'

He was pleased to be in Dublin for Magda Olivero's Irish debut as Adriana. Years before he had met her in Bari when she was singing the role in which she was unrivalled, even surpassing Renata Tebaldi's portrayal. He also admired Olivero's Fedora and Tosca as she invested them with incomparable dramatic depth. She was a serious artist who prepared parts in great detail. Once he remembered her coming out of her dressing room as if in a trance. He was entranced by her and though the voice wasn't the prettiest in the world there was drama in it, emotion and feeling. In others the voice can just be a sound but not with Olivero.

Giardina found that the DGOS chorus responded very well to his coaching, partly because he was communicating in English and could explain things in detail to them. 'They used to say that Giardina can make the stones sing and that naturally amused me. They were very receptive and though the men were outnumbered by the women, the balance was good. I'd sometimes join them in Neary's bar for a pint of Guinness, but I wasn't a pint drinker. Once I joined these eight choristers and they were working the round system and I pleaded to be left out as I could see myself passing out if I went more than two pints. I had no problems with Bill O'Kelly and he left me alone to prepare the chorus and enjoy myself afterwards. It struck me that both O'Kelly and Annovazzi were doing a good job and getting the best people possible from Italy and at the right price. It was a bit of a miracle really, putting on six operas without an Italian subvention and not a lot of money either from Irish sources. I don't know what Magda Olivero got for her *Adriana* but she seemed happy enough to sing in Dublin for the society.'

Choristers assured me that Giuseppe Giardina was one of the most popular chorus masters to work for the society. To Dick Hanrahan and Tom Carney, he was a first-class communicator as well as musician. John Carney thought he had a way with the chorus and was able to get the very best out of them. The female members enjoyed his colourful personality and sense of fun and all agreed he was a valuable asset to the society. Dympna Carney summed up, 'We respected him most of all because he knew his operas and their background and explained the meaning of every line to us. We knew exactly what we were singing.'

By the spring season of `67, Brian O'Rourke was principal clarinettist with the Radio Éireann Symphony Orchestra and remembers Magda Olivero's performance as Adriana as one of the highlights of the season. He admitted he was sometimes amazed by the high artistic standard attained despite the serious lack of orchestral rehearsals. In some of the operas the musicians were seeing the scores for the first time but were helped by the fact that the guest principals had sung the operas before. The coming of the Romanians, he felt, was a milestone and people like Piso and Cortez were very exciting performers and brought a buzz of excitement to the Gaiety. 'I remember that it extended right down the orchestra pit and the atmosphere generated in the house was electric. I especially admired the Romanians in the French repertoire and *Mignon* with Piso and Cortez was pure magic.'

Maestro Annovazzi, he felt, had enormous ability and knew the operas and the music in every detail. 'I know that some people claimed he was boring but I never subscribed to that theory; I mean they used to put a stopwatch on him and his tempi between one evening and another never fluctuated. His sense of pacing was impeccable and he knew the capabilities of the singers. Because of his calm temperament and musicianship he was able to handle crises and, of course, he was a godsend to inexperienced or young singers. I could see they revered him and he was also a wonderful man to cue them. Giuseppe Morelli was perhaps more inspiring than Annovazzi and certainly used up more adrenalin and was well liked and respected by the orchestral players, but I still preferred Annovazzi's artistry.'

Meanwhile, the voluntary input remained an important factor in the survival of the society, although for a few years leading up to 1967 there had been no fund-raising. Prince Caracciolo believed it was time to re-activate the women's committee and arranged for a meeting to be held at the Royal Hibernian Hotel. Among those present were Margaret McDonnell, Moyra Potter, Elizabeth Lovatt-Dolan and Carmel McHale. It was agreed that a ball would be held that autumn to raise funds for the society. An indication of how costs compared with today's can be seen at a glance. There was for instance no charge for the ballroom in the Intercontinental Hotel, the venue for the ball; the band though would cost £80 for six hours' playing. The tickets were a modest three guineas each, though each chorus member would be allowed to purchase two tickets at two guineas each. Dancers could have for example a cold buffet for twenty-two shillings per head, with five shillings extra for a hot dish.

The women's committee soon showed their mettle at fund-raising and their first venture, though small, raised near £80. This was a convivial supper at Nico's restaurant in Dame Street. Carmel McHale recalls that everyone worked hard to raise money and Bill O'Kelly and 'Freddie' Caracciolo gave them a lot of encouragement. Margaret McDonnell was also an inspiration and came up with some novel ideas.

The big artistic success of the winter season of `67 was Massenet's *Werther*, which was being performed for the first time by the society with Piso and Cortez in the leading roles. True to tradition, opera-goers left many seats empty in the Gaiety, mainly because the opera was unknown to most of them. *Evening Herald* critic Brian Quinn hoped the two remaining performances would pack the place, if only to hear Piso in the title role. The tenor, he noted, sang superbly throughout all three acts. One would have to travel far to hear his equal in the part. Singing in French suited Jon Piso, recalled Irish tenor Patrick Ring, a sentiment with which Paddy Brennan wholeheartedly agreed.

Polished Irish baritone William Young has happy memories of the production and Piso's captivating performance. The tenor's musicianship, he felt, was beyond question and his phrasing was exemplary. Sharing Piso's dressing room he saw the superstitious side of him. He himself was getting dressed in an opposite corner of the room and as he couldn't communicate with the tenor because of the language barrier, he began to whistle as softly as possible. Suddenly, Piso raised his head and looking across the room, exclaimed, 'No, no!' As he uttered the words a look of apprehension came into his eyes. When Young told his friends later, he was assured that Piso was a very superstitious person. On another occasion he was sharing a dressing room with the baritone Attilio D'Orazi and about an hour before the performance he would go on stage and for about twenty minutes walk up and down as if in contemplation. He could only assume he was getting into a relaxed frame of mind. 'Attilo was a nice man and not a nervous person, or it seemed to me. He surprised me by his approach.'

William Young got on well with Colonel O'Kelly and regarded him as a man's man with a definite air of authority about him. He was impressed by the way he supervised things backstage, ensuring that all was correct on the night. Once, he was singing in *Traviata* and sharing a dressing room with Paddy Ring and Peter McBrien when there was a knock on the door and on opening it, found Colonel O'Kelly standing in the corridor. He sensed immediately that something was wrong. 'Bill looked at me and said, "William, I've made a terrible mistake." I asked him what was the problem and he said straightaway, "I've offered you too much money, I mean I can't pay you what I said I would." After a pause, he added, "I'll give you half the fee and make it up some other time to you. Will you do that for me?"'

Young looked at him and nodded, "Sure, Colonel, I'm an artist, I hope. The show must go on." The Colonel shook his hand warmly and walked down the corridor.

The year ended on a sad note with the death of Dr John F Larchet at the grand age of 83. For twenty-six years he had served the society wholeheartedly as its esteemed president, chairing management committee meetings, joining deputations for talks with the Radio Éireann authorities, and always being on hand to advise Colonel O'Kelly and his colleagues on operatic matters. On DGOS gala nights the Larchets, John and his wife Madeline, were familiar figures in the Gaiety Theatre foyer as they greeted civic dignitaries and diplomats. And for years they welcomed musicians, singers and actors to their home at St. Mary's Road, Ballsbridge, where they enjoyed glowing hospitality and lively conversation and anecdotes.

'My father died a peaceful death,' recalls Gerry Larchet. 'I don't remember him ever being seriously ill and at the end he just grew fatigued and passed away. His life was music, so was my mother's. Involvement with the DGOS meant a great deal to him and I suppose that he, Colonel O'Kelly and Jim Doyle could be described as buddies.'

To Sheila Larchet, her father had been very happy serving the Dublin Grand Opera Society and she knew he derived immense satisfaction from the visits of the Hamburg and Munich companies as well as the principals of Opéra-Comique. And whenever the society presented little known operas of the time such as *Werther, Andrea Chénier* and *Nabucco* he regarded it as further artistic advancement and was very proud of the achievement.

In his appreciation, Dr Anthony Hughes, who had succeeded Dr Larchet as Professor of Music at UCD in 1958, and who would shortly be elected DGOS president, stated that Dr Larchet had served on many committees in the Royal Dublin Society and the Dublin Grand Opera Society and elsewhere to ensure that they in Ireland might be enabled to hear the world's finest musicians. Through more private committees he expressed his concern to relieve the plight of fellow musicians who through illness or old age were in need. There were few who did not benefit from his advice in moments of difficulty and crises.

To Hughes he was a remarkable man who could hold a company that included such brilliant talkers as Walter Starkie and Michael MacLiammoir entranced by his recollections of the Abbey Theatre among which his affection for Lady Gregory was clearly evident. As the years advanced, he preserved his youth. He never succumbed to the closed mind. He maintained a lively interest in new musical developments, and was delighted that his own former students should be so progressive in their style. His own abiding memory would be of Dr Larchet's unfailing courtesy.

This was a sentiment I found echoed by society members like Aileen Walsh and Monica Condron. In their opinion, Dr Larchet presented the society in the very best light and his easy working relationship with Colonel O'Kelly was an important factor in the society's progress. Ms Walsh said that the Colonel greatly respected Dr Larchet's musical judgment. They all had agreed that his death was a grievous blow.

Mary Sheridan

Mary Sheridan had made her debut with the society in 1962 as the Shepherd Boy in *Tannhauser* and in the subsequent six years sang secondary roles in *Tosca, Aida, Macbeth, Carmen and Die Fledermaus;* in between she had performed with the Irish National Opera Company, getting a particularly good notice for her Donna Elvira in *Don Giovanni*.

Sharing the same stage with stars like Margherita Rinaldi, Giuseppe di Stefano, Gian Giacomo Guelfi and Piero Cappuccilli had been on her own admission a thrilling experience and she was eagerly looking forward to more big nights. It was by now early in 1968 and she had heard of the DGOS programme for the spring season and that it included a revival of Puccini's *Turandot*. For a long time she had a secret ambition to sing Liu, the slave girl, in the opera.

One morning Colonel Bill O'Kelly telephoned and said he wanted her to sing Mercedes in *Carmen*, but she told him she was singing as a soprano and not a mezzo and added, 'You're doing *Turandot* and I know I can sing a good Liu.' The Colonel said, 'Leave it with me, Mary, I'll have a word with Annovazzi about it.' Three weeks later he rang again to say the conductor was in agreement.

She knew it was the break she had been waiting for and was determined to make the most of it. At that moment it seemed to her she had waited a long time for growing up in Naas, Co. Kildare she began singing at the age of four. It was not surprising since her family, her mother and grandmother especially, were keen musicians and leisure time in the Sheridan home usually meant making music together. Young Mary was a pretty red-head with green eyes, being quick and intelligent, and went on to study under Dr Oliver O'Brien and after some Feis Ceoil successes auditioned in 1956 for the Radio Éireann Singers.

'I was successful,' she recalls, 'and proud that I'd achieved my ambition of making singing my profession. It was a grand feeling and I remember it imbued me with a new-found confidence. I was joining a bunch of talented young people with splendid voices and the camaraderie was good.'

She took a year off later to avail of a scholarship awarded by the Italian government and went to study in Como with Carmen Melis who had been Tebaldi's teacher. She immersed herself in the Italian vocal tradition and says it was most useful to her when she came to sing operas by Italian composers. 'I wouldn't have missed it for anything. I got new insights into interpretation and phrasing and vocal technique generally.'

Mary Sheridan also found romance through opera. She met her Dutch husband, Rinus de Bruin at the Gaiety Theatre in 1963 when he had a walk-on part. He had come to Ireland in January of that year and his contract as engineer was for seven weeks, but he applied for a permanent transfer from Holland and it was granted. After their marriage in 1966, Mary continued to perform with the Radio Éireann Singers. The young couple settled down in the lovely Vale of Shanganagh where soon the Dutch influence was very evident with prints of Vermeer, Van Gogh and other Dutch masters on display, and the crest of the Royal Dutch Marines hung in place of honour in the hall.

The cast of *Turandot* was cosmopolitan with the title role being sung by the Bulgarian soprano Margarita Radulova, the leading soprano of the Sofia Opera. The Calaf was the talented Italian tenor Lino Martinucci who appeared extraordinarily young to be cast in the role.

Timur, the exiled King of Tartary (Calaf's father) was taken by the Romanian bass Helge Bömches who had sung Mephistopheles in Faust with Maestro Annovazzi conducting at the Bucharest Opera. Italian baritone Enrico Fissore was making his debut with the society as Ping and Irish artists, Patrick Ring and Brendan Cavanagh were Pang and Pong respectively. The opera was being directed by Enrico Frigerio.

To Mary Sheridan the director was being over-worked - he was also directing in that spring season a new production of *Donizetti's La Favorita*, with Piso and Cortez, *Tosca* starring Magda Olivero, *Traviata* with Piso as Alfredo and *Rigoletto*. She could not understand why he was being asked to do so much. At rehearsals she found him inventive and there always appeared to be something 'going on' but after a while she feared he'd lose his reason with so many demands on his time. 'I had sympathy for him and regarded him as an incredibly gifted director. That he found time to do all he was being asked to do was unbelievable.'

There was, she recalls, a good atmosphere at rehearsals and some magnificent voices. Margarita Radulova swept through the role of Turandot, making light of the difficult music, and she came to admire a lot the fresh tenor voice of Lino Martinucci who hit every high note in 'Nessun dorma'. Helge Bömches's towering figure matched his powerfully resonant bass voice. She had to admit it was challenging working with these artists but it was also very stimulating. As opening night approached she remembers she used to cry at rehearsals because the part of Liu was so emotional. 'I couldn't help it,' she said, 'and I began to wonder if I could stop myself doing it on the first night. But the répétiteur on the piano kept saying to me, "Cry away Mary, it doesn't matter, by the first night you'll have it under control."'

The advice turned out to be correct. The soprano sang with a secure voice and wasn't emotionally affected. Mary Sheridan also remembers the performance for another reason. In act three of the opera when she and Timur are brought before Princess Turandot who proceeds to question Timur about the name of the Prince, Liu steps forward saying she is the only one to know the secret of his name. When the soldiers try to force the name from her, her love for Calaf gives her the strength to resist. Liu turns to Princess Turandot and in despair grabs a soldier's dagger and stabs herself to death. Normally her supine body is carried off in a mournful procession, followed by Timur. But on this occasion the director had other ideas.

'I remember that Helge Bömches lifted me up in his arms and carried me off stage, something which is never done,' Ms Sheridan said. 'I'm sure it looked very moving, even dramatic, and I could hear a pin fall in the theatre.'

There are other aspects of that *Turandot* that are still talked about today by DGOS choristers. Paddy Brennan remembers they needed a Super to play the part of the executioner and when Attilio d'Orazi was told of the problem, he said casually, 'What do you want me to do?' Someone mentioned the executioner. The baritone nodded, and said, 'I don't mind doing it.' To Brennan it exemplified the unique spirit that existed in the society.

It was also manifested in Magda Olivero's attitude to Margarita Radulova. Recognising that the Bulgarian soprano had a thrilling voice but was no actress and was even gauche on stage, she became her mentor, as it were, and taught her deportment and how to walk across the stage; and off-stage she advised her how to dress and look smart. As one veteran chorister was to say, 'In no time at all Radoluva was a new woman both on and off stage.'

Choristers also like to recall that Olivero in order to ensure that everything went exactly right for the soprano in the actual performance, became a trainbearer to Princess Turandot, a kind of super Super. Everyone agreed it was a marvellous gesture by the diva. 'I couldn't get over it when I heard that Magda was acting as trainsbearer' said Aileen Walsh. 'I mean, here was a star playing second fiddle to someone not in her class as an actress-singer. Where else but in Dublin could you have that?'

Paddy Ring thought that Lino Martinucci was too young for the role of Calaf, though he did concede the young Italian had a perfectly placed voice, both warm and natural, and singing the role didn't seem a problem to him. Choristers will tell you that when Martinucci hit the optional highC it brought a glowing smile to Annovazzi's face. He wasn't given to smiling as he conducted but on this occasion his gold tooth sparkled.

To Ann Deegan (then Ann Weafer), Martinucci looked baby-faced but liked to be sociable with choristers. 'We used to purchase foodstuffs in Lipton's and cook them upstairs in a room in the Gaiety. Although he hadn't a word of English, he'd sit around and if someone had a few words of Italian he'd join in the conversation. I got the impression that he and his Italian colleagues were enjoying themselves hugely in Dublin and were finding the scene much different from abroad where principals don't mix with the professional choristers. Lino had a grand voice and I sensed that one day he would be a big star. I found Mary Sheridan's Liu spellbinding and Radulova's Princess Turandot just awesome. It was a very spectacular production.'

Turandot was acclaimed by the majority of the critics, with Mary Sheridan emerging as a star performer. She admits she usually read reviews and of course was delighted to with the critics' reaction. 'I felt I had sung well but it's nice to get the critics' imprimatur. I had rehearsed very hard and gave the part everything I'd got. And, of course, the Gaiety audiences were wonderful to me.'

Mary MacGoris noted in the *Irish Independent* that 'Mary Sheridan's gently passionate Liu was beautifully sung with warmth and richness and a great sympathetic quiet tenderness.' Charles Acton in the *Irish Times* was no less enthusiastic. 'Many opera seasons are remembered for some outstanding features,' he observed. 'This one will be the year of Mary Sheridan's Liu.'

Margarita Radulova won praise for her 'splendour of tone and regal presence' while Lino Martinucci was described as 'a personable young tenor of lovely quality and a true, top voice with a ring to it.' But at least one reviewer felt the heroic role strained him vocally. Martinucci had already sung an impressive Cavaradossi in *Tosca* but as expected he was overshadowed by the sheer artistry of Magda Olivero's Floria Tosca, a performance that both Maureen Lemass and Florrie Draper found riveting. There was also a good deal of interest in the production of *La Favorita* and opera-goers were richly rewarded by Viorica Cortez' performance as Leonora di Gusman, the king's mistress, and Jon Piso's Fernando, a novice monk. His singing of 'Spirto Gentil' received about the same volume of applause as Cortez' magnificently sung 'O Mio Fernando'.

Chorus master Giuseppe Giardina remembers that spring season of `67 for its excellent *Turandot, Tosca* and *La Favorita*. He felt the DGOS chorus showed further improvement and it was a source of utmost satisfaction to him. Since it would probably be Magda Olivero's last season in Dublin it was wonderful that Irish opera-goers had heard her Tosca. Barry Hodkinson's first experience of the chorus was singing in *La Favorita* and said that Giardina had prepared them well. Being on stage with people like Cortez, Piso and D'Orazi was a splendid experience for any newcomer and the memory has stayed with him to this day. He was studying accountancy at the time and although rehearsing was time-consuming, he believed the whole exercise was worthwhile. He decided to give it a few years at least.

There had been disappointment, meanwhile, in Cork operatic circles when the proposed visit by the society fell through. Lengthy talks took place between both parties with Colonel O'Kelly, the DGOS chairman making it clear to Opera House manager Bill Twomey and his board directors that unless a firm guarantee against loss was forthcoming from Cork it would be foolhardy for the society to enter into any arrangement. When no such guarantee could be secured all thought of the proposed visit was abandoned.

Looking back, Donnie Potter said they had no other option, though he sympathised with true lovers of opera in Cork. Harold Johnson, an Opera House shareholder, says he was bitterly disappointed by the news. But he was determined to press the Opera House directors to 'make it happen in the future'. He believed the obstacles were far from insurmountable.

There was more disappointment awaiting the society as they planned the winter season. It had been hoped to stage *Eugene Onegin* for the first time but these hopes were shattered when the Russian army occupied Czechoslovakia and protests followed all over the world. The management committee met and it was unanimously felt that to go ahead with the production might place the society and the visiting artists in a very uncomfortable situation should any protest meetings be organised in Dublin. Reluctantly it was decided to defer the production and, instead, stage *The Barber of Seville*.

It was hoped in early January 1969 that the Italian subvention would be available for the spring season and in this respect Colonel O'Kelly and Donnie Potter travelled to Rome to meet the Minister for Spectacolo and present their case. Potter recalls they tried very hard to make a strong case but by the end of that month were informed the subvention could not be granted. The season's programme had to be revised with *I Puritani* and *Simon Boccanegra* omitted from the list. The society once again was struggling financially. Losses of £10,500 and £6,400 were reported on the spring and winter seasons of '68 repectively, however the Arts Council grant of £10,000 backed by a rise in box-office receipts and patrons' subscriptions made the picture look less desperate.

The line-up of artists for the '69 spring season looked more than promising and included Ugo Benelli, Helge Bömches, Attilio D'Orazi, Lino

Martinucci, Margarita Radulova and a newcomer in the Spanish tenor, Pedro Lavirgen. Giuseppe Giardina was returning as chorus master. He was prepared to work with the chorus twenty-four hours a day but they were available at only certain times. In his spare time he bought antiques at auctions and stored them in his bed-sitter in Leeson Street. As usual he bought his fruit and vegetables in Moore Street and often cooked for himself and his friends.

Living in Dublin in the sixties was in his view cheap and he paid only £5 a week for his bed-sitter and eating out, if one wished, was not expensive. The destruction of Georgian Dublin at this time was, he considered, a black mark on the civic authorities, although he was relieved to hear that it ceased before the seventies. Sometimes after chorus rehearsals he joined members in Italian restaurants for fish and chips. 'It was all we could afford at the time,' the ebullient chorus master says with amusement. 'It was fun,' recalls John Brady, 'and made the thought of rehearsals all the more enjoyable. Giuseppe was a great character and he was much enjoyed by us all.'

There were numerous highlights that season with Donizetti's *L'Elisir d'Amore* on top of the list. Ugo Benelli, as the lovelorn Nemorino, used his lovely lyric voice to colour the melodies and his innate comic flair did the rest. Barry Hodkinson says it was marvellous to sing on stage with him and remembers the hilarious scene when Nemorino gets deliciously drunk after taking Dr Dulcamara's supposed love potion. He felt also that Attilio d'Orazi was perfectly cast as the swashbuckling Sergeant Belcore and that Valeria Mariconda sang well as Adina. Both Benelli and d'Orazi, as well as Mariconda figured in a delightful *Don Pasquale* in that same season.

Any baritone singing Nabucco had to contend with the vivid legacy of Gian Giacomo Guelfi in the role, but I do remember that Giuseppe Scalco, who hailed from Padua, was very impressive, displaying a strong musical voice and acting with conviction. Helge Bomches, as the High Priest Zaccaria, was close behind, while Margarita Radulova sang with fire and passion as Abigaille. In conversation in Rome, Giuseppe Giardina told me that the chorus gave its best performance of the season in *Nabucco*. It is one of his favourite Verdi operas and rehearsing the chorus was a joy. He agreed it was by no means easy for the chorus but on this occasion the blend of voices was right and they had worked very hard with him throughout rehearsals. 'I was proud of them and it made my job a little easier. What enthusiasm and dedication those men and women brought to it all!'

Pedro Lavirgen won a lot of admirers as Manrico in *Trovatore* by the ardour of his singing and dramatic power. 'Lavirgen has the makings of a heroic tenor voice,' commented one morning newspaper reviewer, 'though it is at present too constricted on top and he has not yet achieved command of expressive phrasing.'

Barry Hodkinson was one of those who thought that Lavirgen's Manrico showed great promise, so much so that in the Gaiety green room afterwards he introduced the tenor to his father, who blurted out, 'It takes an Italian...' Lavirgan gave no hint of what he thought of the remark.

The *Madama Butterfly* will be remembered for the moving performance of Japanese soprano Atsuko Azuma as Cio-Cio-San. Lino Martinucci looked an extremely young Pinkerton but his voice blended well with Azuma in the great love duet. Ann Deegan and Florrie Draper felt she was a natural Cio-Cio-San and really credible in every scene. William Young, who played Prince Yamadori and the Imperial Commissioner, fully agreed and found both her singing and acting touching in the extreme.

A notable feature of the `69 winter season was the society's first production of Tchaikovsky's *Eugene Onegin* with what looked in the programme a formidable cast. 'Jon Piso was a glorious Lensky,' recalled Paddy Brennan, 'and his singing of the aria before the duel was unforgettable. Once again, he confirmed his mastery of non-Italian roles.'

Dublin-born mezzo Ruth Maher was making her debut with the society, singing Madame Larina, an estate owner. A former member of the RTÉ Singers, she graduated to Sadler's Wells, London in the middle sixties and understudied leading roles and also toured with the company. After 'living out of a suitcase', she decided to return to Dublin and resumed her work with the RTÉ Singers. Some months before, Colonel O'Kelly invited her to sing for the DGOS and offered her Larina.

She recalled it was a compelling production, with Jon Piso a superb Lensky and the Romanian soprano, Aida Abagieff, a worthy Tatyana. Her Letter Scene was beautifully done. Paddy Ring, who sang Monsieur Triquer, a Frenchman, thought that Philippe Perrottet's production was imaginative and he let the music flow. It got mixed reviews from the critics, ranging from 'drab costumes' to 'an uninspired performance by Emil Rotundo in the title role.' However, Charles Acton did state, 'The performance seems to me real value for money and it and the characteristic beauty of Tchaikowsky's music should bring in the crowds. I hope they do.'

Robert Johston in the *Irish Press* commented that it was a brave decision on the society's part to stage *Onegin* for the first time - a Russian opera sung in Russian - and he sincerely wished the society success in the shape of large attendances, which it deserved.

In that season Dublin audiences were to encounter Albert Rosen for the first time when he conducted *Die Fledermaus*. He had been first invited to Ireland by Dr Tom Walsh in 1965 to conduct *Don Quichotte* at the Wexford

Festival and on his own admission, instantly liked Ireland and the Irish people. He was back in 1966 for Donizetti's *Lucrezia Borgia*. This led to engagements with the Radio Éireann Symphony Orchestra and to his appointment as principal conductor in 1968.

Born in Vienna in February 1924, he was to admit that his talents were slow to emerge - he had to be persuaded to audition for the Vienna Academy and was surprised when accepted. His progress was quick as he studied piano and composition under Joseph Marx, and conducting with Hans Swarowsky. He moved to Prague in 1960 as resident conductor at the National Theatre, later becoming director of the Smetana Theatre, now the State Opera. He quickly made his mark with the DGOS, with some people feeling he should have been asked to conduct *Eugene Onegin* instead of *Die Fledermaus*.

'With his background, I think it would have been very interesting,' recalls Brian O'Rourke, who felt that Rosen simply loved conducting whether it was opera or symphonic music, though opera was really his background. He could be difficult with singers and throw a tantrum and he belonged to that school of conducting where the maestro was the absolute boss. He didn't have a great deal of time for operatic directors as he saw opera as a musical experience.

From the outset, Paddy Brennan was impressed by his dynamic approach and his capacity to wring the best out of performers. When he came first to the society his burly figure, gruff voice and no-nonsense air was to prove somewhat off-putting to some choristers. 'Sometimes he put the fear of God into me, but only where music was concerned,' says Monica Condron. His eastern European background was new to us and we didn't know what to expect. Off the podium, though, he could be charming and friendly and was a singers' conductor. He wasn't the one to parade his talents. I know that Bill O'Kelly was very happy to have him as one of his conducting team, regarding him as both versatile and talented. Some people felt their personalities were not dissimilar.'

Sadly, the society continued to lose friends and patrons. Colonel O'Kelly was bereaved by the unexpected death of his wife Margaret, affectionately known as Meg. She rarely missed important first nights, usually being accompanied by a friend as her husband was occupied backstage. Afterwards they would dine out together with friends. She encouraged him to invite singers and conductors back to their house in Terenure where she knew they could relax. She herself was the first to join the society as a patron member in 1946, and was also a member of the first Ladies' Committee which did such splendid fund-raising. Her final night at the opera had been the winter season of 1968, when she joined with the performing members in celebrating the end of the season.

Earlier, the society suffered another severe blow by the death of 'Boodie' Caracciolo. For years she had shared her husband's great love of opera. Things were never to be the same for Prince ('Freddie') Caracciolo thereafter. Her delightful hosting of post-opera parties at the Caracciolo home in Rathfarnham would be greatly missed. To this day singers like Paolo Silveri, Ugo Benelli and Virginia Zeani talk of her generosity; indeed, Zeani was once introduced to Tyrone Power in the house, as well as other celebrities. Despite the shattering blow of his wife's death, 'Freddie' Caracciolo not only kept up his interest in the DGOS but also in the Wexford Opera Festival.

The decade had also seen a changing Dublin with a significantly expanding suburbia and consequent rise in population. Regrettably, subversives had destroyed Nelson's Pillar, that monolithic landmark on O'Connell Street, while the grand old Theatre Royal had given way to a new and unattractive office block; otherwise the cultural institutions like the DGOS, the R&R and the Symphony Orchestra were going strong, though the city still awaited its much needed new concert hall.

Honour for Chairman

The indomitable Bill O'Kelly was by now almost thirty years the society's elected chairman. Since he had been honoured by the Italian government for his services to Italian music his full title read: Lieut.-Colonel, Cav. UFF, William O'Kelly; but to his colleagues and friends he remained simply the Colonel. 'I never called him anything else except Colonel,' recalled Norris Davidson. To Donnie Potter, he was 'Bill' as he was to Prince Caracciolo and Thomas McMahon, the society's vice-presidents. Joint treasurer Aileen Walsh felt that the Colonel was very proud of his honour. 'I think he saw it as the country's official recognition of what he had done for Italian opera and culture in Ireland.'

It was perhaps understandable that many people should believe he was solely pre-occupied with opera matters, and although he did devote a lot of his time to auditioning singers in London, Rome, Bucharest and elsewhere, he was also involved in the Irish film industry in an advisory capacity after he had left the army in 1959. Seán Kelly, his son, recalls that it was Louis Elliman who first invited his father to Ardmore Studios in Bray and considered him very useful for productions that required military knowledge about arms, tactics and positions.

'I think his first movie was *Shake Hands with the Devil,* where he got to know its star James Cagney. There were scores more, including *The Blue Max, The Spy Who Came in from the Cold, The Viking Queen, Darling Lili* and much later, *Ryan's Daughter.* My father enjoyed meeting people whether it was a diva or a film star; he was a man who liked some variety in his life. He had great faith in the emergent film industry and he used to chat about it with John Huston and others. The movie people evidently thought a lot about him for during the making of Ryan's Daughter in Kerry they gave him a house for the duration of the shooting. My father was also very loyal to his ex-army colleagues and when it came to employing extras he gave them priority. He made a comfortable living as an advisor and enjoyed this facet of his life enormously and loved to retail stories about the stars he met, but the DGOS remained his most abiding interest. It was his life more than anything else.'

It was by now 1970 and as early as January there were enough problems to keep Colonel O'Kelly's mind fully focused on the society. A letter was received from RTÉ stating that 'owing to additional costs they could not in future make the same arrangements for the availability of the orchestra as for former seasons.' When the question was discussed at a DGOS management committee meeting, O'Kelly said he thought this was a breach of contract for the coming spring season. It was agreed that he himself head a deputation to RTÉ consisting of Dr Anthony Hughes, Donnie Potter and John Lovatt-Dolan. After discussions, it was pointed out to them by Gerard Victory, head of music at the station, that the extra costs for the National Symphony Orchestra must be paid. Apparently, these amounted to £1,500. It was a severe blow to the society and something it had not expected as up to then RTÉ had charged nothing for the orchestra, being satisfied with the arrangement of broadcasting in lieu the operas from the Gaiety.

There was a further setback for Colonel O'Kelly when Cagliari Opera informed him that it would be unable to visit Dublin. He and Donnie Potter had earlier travelled to Rome and met impresario Signor Ferrari who told them that Cagliari company were interested in visiting Ireland and had applied for a subvention from the Italian government to pay the artists. O'Kelly was still hoping to get a subvention; indeed, he and Maestro Annovazzi had compiled a list of operas that would be staged with the help of the subvention, with one of the guest artists being the renowned tenor Mario del Monaco. At the same time he had drawn up an alternative programme - assuming there was no subvention - and this was now adopted by the management committee.

The society's problems weren't over by any means. It was almost certain that their premises at 11 South Leinster Street would be taken over. 'It came as a big shock to us,' recalls Monica Condron, hon. sec. 'We had resided there for nearly thirty years and held our rehearsals there, so you can imagine our quandary. We had also some props and scenery stored in the premises. We hastily looked around for an alternative place and eventually John Lovatt-Dolan phoned me to say that the Augustinian Fathers in Thomas Street would be happy to oblige us with rehearsal facilities.'

Colonel O'Kelly was undaunted and felt the society could mount an exciting spring season. Dr Anthony Hughes liked to say, 'To our chairman obstacles existed to make life a little more difficult. However, the greater the obstacles, for him the more ingenious his plans became to surmount or circumvent them. 'To Donnie Potter, who began to accompany him abroad more regularly, it was O'Kelly's optimism and dynamic spirit that got him over the difficult moments.' Bill was resilient and knew how to deal with bureaucracy.'

By now everyone in the society knew about the 'Colonel's Throne', as it came to be known. It was a chair by the side of the stage and out of the audience's view. Usually he was ensconced in it during a performance and became as familiar a figure as the tall and kilted Patrick McClellan. O'Kelly supervised the order of entries, the chorus and the principals, and he ensured that the sequence of curtain calls was observed. If anything untoward happened he'd jump up suddenly from the chair and want to know the circumstances. He could on the other hand give a word of encouragement to a soprano and as she came off stage, whisper, 'Well done.' He would berate a tenor, for instance, who went off pitch or forgot his lines. His motto was that the public were paying for their tickets and the performance must be right.

'Bill O'Kelly looked after people,' said Paddy Brennan. 'His was a constant and reassuring presence on the 'Throne'. He encouraged and cajoled and saw that everything was in order. He became a father-figure as he got older and was respected. Yes, I believe the "Colonel's Chair" did serve a positive purpose and is remembered today by choristers and principals alike.'

There are those who hold that the Colonel pushed the amateur chorus almost beyond its limits, but not everyone I found agreed with this claim. 'Bill O'Kelly gave us something to strive for in the chorus,' says Dick Hanrahan, 'and I don't think we let him down. It is the chorus master or chorus mistress who really matters and at this time, we had Jeannie Reddin and John Brady, two of the best.' Both John and Tom Carney agreed, and added that after singing big choral works like *Nabucco, Aida* and *Ernani,* they were confident and welcomed any new challenges. Ann Deegan and Dympna Carney said they had made a commitment to the society and were prepared to make sacrifices to prepare themselves for operas new to them and sung in different languages.

And that spring season of 1970 was undeniably a challenging one with a programme comprising *Andrea Chénier, La Traviata, Rigoletto, La Bohème* and *Tosca;* the latter had been substituted for *La Favorita* when both Jon Piso and Viorica Cortez were unavailable to sing the Donizetti work. Among the returning artists were: Aldo Protti, Pedro Lavirgen, Helge Bomches, Giuseppe Scalco, Angela Rosati and Mario d'Anna. When casting was discussed at a management committee meeting earlier in the year, John Lovatt-Dolan asked about the possibility of engaging the Italian tenor Flaviano Labo. Donnie Potter assured him it was possible except that the fee would be substantial. Lovatt-Dolan, who followed opera abroad and knew of the tenor's worth, suggested they should try to get him for *Bohème.*

Eventually his wish was granted and the news that Labo would sing Rodolfo was greeted enthusiastically by the more knowledgeable opera buffs. Born in Piacenza, Labo had made his operatic debut in his home town and rose quickly to the top rank. By the time he was engaged by the DGOS he had been singing for ten years and earlier in that year, 1970 had sung Manrico at La Scala and Ernani in Turin, and he was a regular guest artist at the New York Met, where he had first sung in 1957. He was once described in America as 'a short man with a beautiful voice and fine style.' One Met veteran said of him, 'He had a thrilling top, with a beautiful legato throughout his wide and entire range. We used to love to yell out "Bravo Labo"'.

The records show that he sang nine seasons at the Met but left under strange circumstances. He was on a weekly contract as opposed to a performance fee. He therefore had tax withheld each week which made his fee smaller than the amount he had been told would be his weekly pay, with the result that the tenor suspected the management was pocketing the difference. Eventually, he stopped going to the Met, which was perhaps one of the reasons why he was available to the DGOS.

The society was stretching its limited resources in engaging him; it was claimed at the time that his fee was between £750 and £1,000 per performance which of course fell somewhat short of the £1,500 paid for each *Tosca* performance to Giuseppe di Stefano. 'We couldn't afford another penny,' says Donnie Potter. 'But we were naturally delighted to get him.'

Colonel O'Kelly was shrewd when it came to casting. He knew that occasionally the society must engage an exceptional voice in order to heighten interest among opera fans who had come to expect something special for the spring season. *Bohème* was a magical evening in the theatre and the memory has stayed with me long after I've long forgotten others. Puccini might have tailored the role of Rodolfo for Labo. The voice was smooth, expressive and notable for its musical sensitivity. There was spontaneous applause as he ended his first big aria, 'Che Gelida Manina' and this was followed by more rapturous applause after he and soprano Maria Angela Rosati had sung the love duet at the end of the act. From there on Labo could do no wrong. His Rodolfo remains the best I have ever heard. At the final curtain he was accorded the kind of reception once reserved for Silveri, Stignani, Mancini, Borso and Cappuccilli.

Irish soprano Ann Moran sang an impressive Musetta, displaying a secure and sweet-toned soprano and natural acting ability, while Mario d'Anna looked a youthful Marcello. Helge Bömches made a totally credible Colline. This is a *Bohème* vividly remembered by choristers like Paddy Brennan - a great admirer of Labo's voice - John Carney and Barry Hodkinson. Neither *Traviata* nor *Tosca* pleased the critics for different reasons. Fanny Feehan in the *Evening Press* blamed the ineffectual performance by Giuseppe Scalco as Scarpia as one of the real reasons, and she felt that *Traviata* was spoiled by applause at the wrong time. She described the audience behaviour as boorish.

It was proving a busy season for Ruth Maher. Besides playing Flora in *Traviata,* she was singing Giovanna in Rigoletto and the roles of Contessa and Madelon in Andrea Chénier. 'I was getting a good run,' she recalls, 'and I was enjoying the experience.

Rehearsing *Andrea Chénier,* she noticed the chorus members were visibly moved by the impassioned singing of tenor Pedro Lavirgen as Chénier. 'I thought he was incredible in the part, singing at times with the utmost intensity, and I'll never forget his final scene. Strangely, though, he did not repeat this performance on the first night; perhaps he was a bit nervous - I can't say. Maria Angela Rosati was an excellent Maddalena and she brought out the anguish in the part very well and at times her singing was thrilling.'

Ruth Maher resents some people's attitude to small parts in opera, particularly those who tend to dismiss singers who play them. She considers this cruel. 'They believe that anybody can sing them which of course is not true; musically they can be extremely difficult.' Interestingly, she was mentioned by most of the critics that season and her blind woman in *Chénier* was praised. And she gained some new insights into the society and concluded that Bill O'Kelly was the real force behind nearly all the activities and she doubted if the society could have existed at all without him. She came to admire Annovazzi's musicianship and his total commitment. He was a singers' conductor and appreciated their feelings. As for the Italian singers, they were self-assured and gave the impression that music was their sole life and that they cared about little else except singing.

Irish singers figured prominently in the winter season, with Mary Sheridan, Ruth Maher and Paddy Ring in the *Tales of Hoffmann.* Soprano Violet Twomey was Micaela in Carmen and both operas were being directed by Philippe Perrottet. Albert Rosen was conducting Beethoven's *Fidelio,* a production that was eagerly awaited. A feature of *Carmen* was that three of the principals, including Pedro Lavirgen, were Spanish, and though the critics generally expressed reservations, apparently the tenor's performance as Don José excited Gaiety audiences.

Lavirgen had one weak leg but he never allowed this to interfere with his acting; if anything it tended to make the final scene in *Carmen* incredibly emotional, as he confronted Carmen, pleading for her love, then suddenly raging at her rejection. 'Watching him was frightening,' recalls Ruth Maher. 'Pedro seemed to throw himself entirely into the part. As he played the scene the house was deadly silent as though no one dared to speak. I pitied any Carmen trying to match his passion and intensity.'

Mary Sheridan received very good notices for her acting and singing as Nicklause in *Hoffmann*, though she told me later that the show really belonged to Jon Piso who sang the title role. 'He was terrific,' she says, 'singing with typical elegance and style. As an artist he was one of the best to sing with the society at this time.' Ann Moran won praise for her singing of the Doll's Song, but Mary MacGoris was far from pleased with Paddy Ring's 'harlequin costume' and stated that 'he stood out like a sore thumb.' Everyone seemed impressed by the chorus.

Albert Rosen, as expected, made his mark by his skilful conducting of Beethoven's compelling *Fidelio score*. 'The opera and the music suited his talents,' recalled Brian O'Rourke, principal clarinettist of RTÉ Symphony Orchestra. 'Actually I preferred him in this kind of work than in bel canto, although he was a versatile conductor as we all know from his Wexford and DGOS days.'

Paddy Ring, who was praised for his performance as the lovelorn Jacquino in the production, remembers that Albert Rosen contributed a considerable amount to its success and showed a wonderful understanding of the music. 'I always believed that Albert was a risk-taker on the podium and adhered to the motto that there were a lot of people out there behind his back and he had to keep them entertained. He created atmosphere and excitement when it was needed and his musicianship was never in question. In my opening scene in *Fidelio*, for instance, he adopted a certain tempo and when I told him it was perhaps too fast, he explained it had to be like that as the whole thing would slow down later on.'

To Ring, Annovazzi was less effusive as a person than Rosen and never went overboard about things. 'I regarded him as a splendid conductor who knew his music inside out; indeed, it was a miracle the way he held some productions together musically. He was a private person, lacking in small talk, but sincere all the same. I had no problem with him, nor for that matter with Albert Rosen. Both were steeped in opera tradition. To everyone, including the visiting artists, Annovazzi was 'Maestro', the boss, and you were not supposed to argue with him. He might not have been a world beater in musical inspiration, nevertheless he was respected for his solid professionalism and you could rely on him totally. If it went wrong it was your fault, not his.'

Ring says he was fortunate that as an RTÉ Singer he was allowed time off to perform both in Wexford and for the DGOS. 'I must say that this added a great variety to my career and getting a chance to sing with established stars was both an education and a challenge. It was also my pocket money.'

It was considered a good year both artistically and commercially, with *Chénier* and *Bohème* proving the highlights of the spring season and

Hoffmann, which sold out for all performances, and *Fidelio*, being the most talked about operas of the winter season. With a guarantee against loss of £15,000 from the Arts Council, and continuing support from patron members and guarantors - not to mention the opera fans themselves. Colonel O'Kelly and his management committee could be forgiven for thinking that the omens were good for at least another decade. O'Kelly was also encouraged that Annovazzi had fitted so well into the Dublin operatic scene and appreciated the meaning of budgets. 'He was able to come up with the kind of package that suited us,' recalls Donnie Potter, 'and we were still getting some first-class singers. It was after all Annovazzi who brought Pedro Lavirgen and other Spanish singers to our 1970 spring season. We felt he was a man we could trust and continue to do business with, and that was of course important to us.'

Year of the Tenors

In a lighter moment, Ugo Benelli described 1971 as the 'Year of the Tenors'. He probably meant the spring season of that year, for the line-up looked impressive, featuring as it did Benelli himself as Nemorino in *L'Elisir d'Amore,* Flaviano Labo alternating with Lino Savoldi as Calaf in Puccini's *Turandot* and a little known name, Giuseppe Giacomini singing Edgardo in *Lucia di Lammermoor* and Pinkerton in *Madama Butterfly* - he was making his first visit to Dublin.

At the pre-season press reception, at which Lino Savoldi sang a ringing 'Nessun dorma', Colonel O'Kelly told the convivial gathering that in his opinion they were able to parade before the public some smashing new voices. 'You've heard what Signor Savoldi can do, but we also have a good one in Giuseppe Giacomini... I'll say no more.' It was the Colonel's way of indicating that he had yet again discovered another outstanding voice in Italy. With his exemplary record to date, no one dared to question his judgment. For diplomacy's sake, he did go on to refer to the 'array of female talent' and mentioned the names of Japanese soprano Atsuku Azumo, the Cio-Cio-San that season, Carol Wyatt, the attractive young American mezzo making her Dublin debut as Amneris in *Aida*, the Spanish soprano Francina Girones, singing the title role in *Lucia,* and the return of popular Maria Angela Rosati as Princess Turandot. In addition, Mary Sheridan was back to take the role again of Liu in the same production while Ruth Maher was Suzuki in *Butterfly.*

'We had auditioned a crop of singers in Italy months before the season began,' recalled Donnie Potter, 'and we heard some very promising young voices. I remember that Bill O'Kelly was more pleased than usual and coming back on the plane he'd say to me, "Wait 'til they hear this fellow Giacomini." Bill always wanted to hear singers before he engaged them for the first time. Annovazzi was agreeable to this, mainly because it saved time. Engaging singers blindly can be risky because if they fail at rehearsal, say, they'd have to be replaced at short notice.'

It was a year in which the Gaiety Theatre was celebrating the centenary of its opening and the society decided to stage *Aida* to mark the occasion - it was first heard in Cairo in December of 1871. And it commissioned artist James Malcolm to execute a framed drawing of the Gaiety's original auditorium and this was presented to Joe Kearns, the manager, by the DGOS president Professor Anthony Hughes. It was a time also when evening newspapers devoted copious space to the coverage of the seasons and Colonel O'Kelly made no secret of his satisfaction. For instance, on Monday, April 19, 1971 the *Evening Press* gave an entire page to a feature on *Aida*, with its star columnist Terry O'Sullivan describing the scene at the final dress rehearsal in his own inimitable style. Among Pat Cashman's photographs was one of the principals and chorus on the Gaiety stage and this extended fully across the eight columns in the page. A truly magnificent photograph.

'I used to think that all opera is vulgar,' commented O'Sullivan. 'Now I think that I only like vulgar opera... and having the head blown off me by a quartet of rare trumpets in the Green Room of the Gaiety last night, I know my limitations. These fanfare trumpets, over two feet long, and loaned to the conductor Napoleone Annovazzi, are rich and rare indeed, and in the Green Room the quartet of RESO brass made a sound like four Gabriels. And, as for the chorus, male and female, they made massive sounds, enough to satisfy the most gluttonous stereo fan. The show looked a bit sexy, too, in that the men were wearing hot pants, and the leading ladies were beautiful even without make-up. But they would not allow themselves to be photographed... and that's Grand Opera, you see. 'So, it's me for the big sound of *Aida*, and the more cultured for the delicacies of *L'Elisir d'Amore*... and the song we have all been waiting for... "Una furtiva Lagrima."

Donnie Potter believes that such extensive pre-season coverage helped in no small way to sell tickets at the box-office and between them, the *Evening Press* and *Evening Herald* were doing opera proud. 'I always said we couldn't have paid for such publicity, so naturally all of us in the society were very grateful.'

It was adjudged an enjoyable *Aida*, with Fanny Feehan in the Evening Press being much taken by Carol Wyatt's 'sumptuously beautiful Amneris, her dramatic singing and her regality.' She found Renato Francesconi a bit wooden as Radames, though he sang with commendable feeling; and in her view, soprano Milkana Nikolova lacked variety of tone as Aida. The sets and costumes came in for general praise, being described as very effective. Undoubtedly, two of the most eagerly awaited productions of that spring season of `71 were *Lucia di Lammermoor* and *Madama Butterfly*, though *Turandot* was not far behind in the brisk box-office booking.

It was during the final rehearsals of *Lucia* that chorus members began to take real notice of tenor Giuseppe Giacomini as he sang Edgardo's melodious music, and their reaction was summed up in the words, star quality. Everyone spoke of his warm vocal timbre and the way he spun long, legato lines. To Tom Carney, the voice was powerful and flexible and lovely to listen to, because of its depth of quality and tonal colour. He felt Donizetti's music suited the tenor to perfection. Barry Hodkinson thought him simply superb and his ringing top notes very exciting. He believed he would be equally effective singing either Verdi's or Puccini's music. To Dympna Carney, the voice projected magnificently and was never forced and he paid much attention to phrasing. She was sure he would make an ideal Edgardo. It was a voice that also deeply impressed both Florrie Draper and Ann Deegan because of its musicality and strength.

As a tenor in the chorus, Paddy Brennan was inclined on his own admission to take more than a passing interest in the latest tenor imports. He wondered what they could expect from Signor Giacomini. He remembers that on his way to morning rehearsals at the Gaiety Theatre his car broke down in Dame Street, opposite the Olympia Theatre, leaving him with no option except to push it to one side of the street. He then proceeded to the Gaiety on foot and as he entered by the stage door, where he had a good view of the bare stage, he picked out an individual with a coat slung over his shoulders who was rehearsing the final scene from *Lucia*. 'It was an unbelievable sound coming back at me,' he recalls, 'and at that moment I forgot about my broken down car and concentrated instead on Signor Giacomini. I realised I was listening to a glorious voice, big and expressive and full of feeling for both words and music.'

Paddy Ring was singing Arturo in the same production and was struck by Giacomini's voice. 'It was well developed and would no doubt develop more. He had good musicianship and no problem with intonation or range. I saw a big future for him. He was self-effacing and of quiet disposition and perhaps even shy.'

It was soon evident, however, that the tenor was troubled by poor sight. 'I think it was a problem with him,' says Barry Hodkinson. 'But he was able to get around the stage alright.' Whether the critics suspected this failing or not is not easy to say. Charles Acton, in the *Irish Times*, found him 'a fine Edgardo, with a commanding, convincing voice.' Mary MacGoris described his voice as 'of heroic quality, though not perfectly produced.' I liked the opening paragraph of her review, 'Lucia went mad in primrose and chiffon on the Gaiety stage last night, and certainly it was better than the usual obviously nylon nightie.' As a critic, she knew how to inform as well as entertain her readers, which couldn't be said of all her colleagues of what was really a golden era in grand opera in Ireland.

Giacomini was a most convincing Pinkerton in that season's *Madama*

Butterfly and his love duet with soprano Atsuko Azuma proved to be a vocal highlight of the highest order. *Butterfly* was one of Colonel O'Kelly's favourite operas and he confided in friends that the combination of Giacomini and Azuma was among the greatest he had heard on any stage. Ruth Maher was cast as Cio-Cio-San's servant Suzuki and regarded Azuma's portrayal of the ill-fated wife of the American naval officer as superb. 'I do recall that people were saying that she was picked for the part because she was Japanese, but that is not true. She came to Dublin with an international reputation and lived up to her billing. It was an exciting *Butterfly* and I agree that Giacomini was brilliantly cast as Pinkerton. I should add that Atsuko Azuma had her own little daughter with her and she was the child in the opera. She was very precocious and used to conduct the orchestra behind the scenes, and one evening she said to Albert Rosen, "Leave your wife and run away with me."'

Ruth Maher admitted she was conscious of her height - she stood at five feet and nine inches, and particularly felt it because Atsuko Aziuma was only five feet and three inches. People could be thoughtless and cruel and tended to comment on disparity in height between singers. 'Coming up to the first night I had taken some stick about my height and one chorister said to me, "Ruth, you're going to look very foolish." However as soon as I got on stage I didn't feel self-conscious at all. It was such a joy singing and acting with Atsuko that I forgot about everything else. And I do think we managed alright in the opera and Atsuko looked taller than she was and at least one critic remarked he hadn't noticed a big difference between us.'

She played Giannetta, a village girl, in *L'Elisir d'Amore* and considered the cast particularly talented, with Angelo Romero outstanding as Sergeant Belcore; she was not surprised to learn that earlier in the year he had made his La Scala debut in *The Barber of Seville*. While she conceded that Ugo Benelli had perfected the characterisation of Nemorino, she couldn't understand why on occasions he wanted, in her view, to upstage his colleagues. 'I thought this was completely out of character. Ugo was a gentleman and a lovely lyric tenor with a grand flair for comedy, and so it was silly of him carrying on stage business behind people's backs as they tried to sing. I didn't expect that from him. He should have known it was distracting.'

I found that some chorus members as well as seasoned opera buffs, were inclined to attribute this to over-exuberance and a tendency sometimes on his part to go over the top. Others, like Barry Hodkinson, felt the tenor was a wonderful team man and was only endeavouring to enliven the show, especially if the stage direction was weak, as it sometimes happened to be in DGOS productions. Nevertheless, he remained hugely popular in Dublin and Wexford and unlike a lot of his Italian colleagues, was a real personality with a remarkable zest for life, exuding charm and bonhomie. In the eyes of the vast majority of the opera-going public he was unflawed, yet Ruth Maher's point had been echoed in some quarters and found some support.

Remembering Enrico Frigerio's imaginative production of *Turandot* in the spring season of '68, Mary Sheridan expressed disappointment to me about the staging of the opera in '71, though she was delighted to be asked again to sing Liu, the slave girl. She felt unhappy about Sanzio Levratti's direction and as rehearsals progressed had reason to complain to Colonel O'Kelly that she required more time to work out the scene after her death when she is supposed to be carried off the stage. She suspected that Levratti lacked experience for such a large scale work and this in her opinion was borne out with the arrival of Flaviano Labo to rehearse the role of Calaf.

'I remember he found fault with some of the chorus groupings and suggested ways of improving them with the director; he was also annoyed with a certain stage flat and asked that it be removed. He knew his stagecraft and in no time was co-directing the production. I could speak to him in Italian and found him very helpful. He was also a witty man and on the opening night of *Turandot,* in the scene where he is trying to find the answer to the riddle, he looked at me and grinned as he whispered, "You have got beautiful eyes."' I can still remember the wonderful way he sang "Nessun Dorma" and despite the fact that he was small, he did have a certain stage presence. Lino Savoldi was also a fine Calaf and though obviously an inexperienced actor possessed a most promising tenor voice.'

While she agreed that Maria Angela Rosati sang and acted well as Princess Turandot her performance did not erase the memory of Margarita Radulova's magnificence in the same role in the '68 production, nor was the Timur of Eftimios Michalopoulos quite up to the same standard as Helge Bomches's who had made so much of her death scene. That scene in her view in '71 lacked impact as it was left to two 'supers' to carry her off the stage. As she began to get better parts she was surprised that principals were expected to do their own make-up, with the result that she went to veteran Irish comic Cecil Nash for some tips. And whenever she asked Colonel O'Kelly for an increase in fee, he invariably replied, "Aren't you getting a decent fee for singing only a few performances?"
Usually she left it at that.

Four years had passed without the society's visit to the Opera House Cork, something that Harold Johnson found completely unacceptable. By now he had been co-opted onto the Opera House board and on the occasion the chairman Commander George Crosbie had said to him, 'You've been at our

AGMs for some years, urging us to invite the DGOS to come to the Opera House, so off you go now to make it happen.' It was the green light that Johnson was waiting for and before long had arranged a meeting with Colonel O'Kelly and Donnie Potter in a Dublin hotel.

'Bill Twomey, manager of the Opera House, came along with me to Dublin and we had an amicable discussion,' recalls Johnson. 'I told them that we wanted the society to re-visit Cork. Donnie Potter turned to me and said, "Harold, you're banging on an open door. Of course we'd love to return if we can work out the mechanics. I could see that Colonel O'Kelly was also enthusiastic. He said the Taoiseach, Jack Lynch, was anxious also that we'd go back.'

Johnson 'did his sums' and before he approached business interests in Cork for sponsorship knew exactly what he wanted, right down to the cost of the RTÉ Symphony Orchestra. In fact, he was able to get a sponsor for each performance of *Aida* and Lucia in that week. He was assured that the Opera House bars would do brisk business and would be a real source of revenue; as events transpired they made a considerable profit. The DGOS visit was to prove a huge success with almost full attendances for every performance. To Johnson and his fellow directors on the Opera House board it was tremendously reassuring. 'We broke even on the week,' he says, 'and that was a big achievement. And it also meant that we could go along to Colonel O'Kelly and invite the society back.'

The week had opened with a special concert at which the Italian, Romanian and Irish artists participated. It turned out to be a big artistic and commercial success. As Harold Johnson said, 'We were introducing the artists who would be singing in the week's operatic performances, so the audience knew what they could expect.'

The chorus members were thrilled to be returning. 'It was a week's holidays for us,' said John and Tom Carney, 'and we were looking forward to the visit.' The same sentiment was echoed by their colleagues in the chorus. Dr Dermot O'Kelly, who by now was a member of the DGOS management committee, and his wife, planned to take a week-end in Cork and have a good time. The local breweries and business firms organised receptions and invited along the company. What made it special, recalls Donnie Potter, was the fact that the society wasn't going to lose money on the venture. Cork was really playing its part to ensure that our visit would be a success in every way. We owed a lot to Harold Johnson. Best of all, we could see the arrangement continue for at least another decade, if not more.'

Harold Johnson was to assert later, 'I believe that the great age of grand opera in Cork commenced at precisely 8.10 on the evening of Monday, May 3, 1971 as Aida heralded the first of the DGOS's regular visits to Cork, and at 8.10 on that evening grand opera really returned to us when Italian tenor Renato Francesconi and the splendid acoustics of the new Opera House combined to give us as fine a rendering of "Celeste Aida" as ever we heard in the pre-1939 era. The week was an unqualified success and had been planned like a military operation. Following the final Gaiety Theatre performance on the previous Saturday, the transport of scenery and instruments, and the mass movement of some two hundred singers, dancers, musicians and others got under way to Cork on Sunday, May 2.

It was Albert Rosen who had suggested to Colonel O'Kelly the revival of Smetana's *The Bartered Bride* for the `71 winter season. The society, it will be remembered, had previously staged this delightful Czech folk opera in 1953 when Vilem Tausky conducted and it was sung in English. On this occasion it would be sung in Czech and the costumes were by courtesy of Prague Opera. Rosen had travelled to Prague to select some of the principals including Gabriela Benackova, Milan Karpisek and Zdenek Svehla. The director was Jaroslav Horacek, who would also play Kecal, a marriage broker, in the production.

The task of teaching the chorus to sing in Czech was given to John Brady, the assistant chorus master. He had joined the chorus in the middle 1960s and was an accountant by profession; he was also an accomplished organist and pianist. He found that all his spare time was being devoted to chorus work and he was never free at Easter as they prepared for the spring season. But he had found it absolutely wonderful to sing with the cream of the international guest artists and wouldn't have missed it for the world.

It was Albert Rosen, as conductor of *The Bartered Bride* who first asked him to take the chorus. 'One day I had a cup of coffee with Albert in his room and he told me the society was thinking of staging the opera and if I would be interested. I didn't know anything about it but assured him I'd learn Czech and take the chorus during the summer months and in my own time. He took out a piece of paper and wrote out for me the phonetics of the Czech language and later on gave me the opera's score and I proceeded to write the whole chorus out by hand. Only those chorus members who came to rehearsals during the summer were allowed to sing in the production. I worked very hard and so did the chorus. As the first rehearsal with Albert Rosen approached I worried for fear of anything going wrong, but to my surprise he got emotionally upset when he heard the Dublin chorus singing in Czech and was almost in tears.'

'John Brady did a remarkable job,' recalls Paddy Brennan. 'I do remember that first rehearsal with Albert Rosen and his words were, "Let's start," and after we ran through the chorus part he suddenly closed the music score and walked out of the room. We all wondered if we had got it wrong. John Brady followed him and came back to tell us that Albert was in tears and told him that not only had we got the language correct but conveyed the spirit of the work as well.'

'I feel this was a tremendous compliment to John Brady,' says Barry Hodkinson. 'I understand he got a Czech member of the RTÉ Symphony Orchestra to teach him how to pronounce the language and at rehearsals, with the use of a blackboard, he was able to write out the words so that we could speak them as well as sing them. It was a novel approach and fascinating in its own way.'

To John Carney, Czech was a difficult language to adapt for singing, particularly when one was accustomed to highly musical sounds as in Italian. 'We learned it phonetically with the aid of a blackboard. It was hard work during those summer months but it was more than re-paid by the surprised reaction of Albert Rosen at the first rehearsal. He was very moved and proud, both musically and linguistically.'

To Ann Deegan, Albert Rosen seemed very excited about *The Bartered Bride* and took over the production and his enthusiasm was infectious. And he was fully supported by Czech director Jaroslav Horacek who shared his vision of the work and together they made a great job of it.'

Gabriela Benackova made quite an impression at rehearsals. Some of the chorus members, especially the more romantic males, who described her to me as 'stunningly beautiful' and one member dared to say 'she was the most beautiful creature he had ever laid eyes on.' She was in her early twenties and the role of Marenka was ideal for her talents. Mary Sheridan, who was singing her mother Ludmilla in the opera, recalls that she sang radiantly and conveyed to perfection the simple characteristics of the village girl in the story.

Carmel McHale was a member of the Ladies' Committee and a close friend of Albert Rosen, told me later that he was absolutely thrilled by the success of the production. 'It was an ambition of his, ever since he had come to Ireland, to conduct this opera for the DGOS and felt the cast and chorus had done justice to the work. I know he had predicted a very bright future for Gabriela Benackova; she was a charming young woman with a delightful personality and her singing impressed everyone in the Gaiety.'

Baritone William Young was cast as Krusina and believed singing the work in Czech underlined the artistic progress being made by the society. It was another important milestone in its history. Paddy Ring, who played the Ringmaster, was to agree and added that the talented Czech singers injected an idiomatic touch necessary for such a work. 'I think that both Czech and Irish singers blended very well.' To Ruth Maher (Hata) it was an excellent thing for the society to contrast the spring and winter programmes as a surfeit of Italian opera would probably not please the purists. 'I enjoyed working in *The Bartered Bride* and got some valuable insights into Smetana's music.'

John Brady would say that RTÉ's Gerard Victory had told him that *The Bartered Bride* was one of the best recordings made of any opera from the Gaiety. For his own part, the production was very satisfying and one that had been brilliantly cast. He felt the mixture of Czech and Irish voices had worked very well. He could not say enough about the performance of the chorus.

Mary MacGoris *(Irish Independent)* summed up: 'An Irish and Czech cast, singing in Czech, brings out all the natural lilt of Smetana's flowing music which has the fresh sweetness of a bowl of ripe cherries, with Albert Rosen flexibly guiding the singers and the RTÉ Symphony Orchestra into sympathetic phrasing, perfect tempi and an easy but unflagging impulsion throughout the whole piece.'

The society presented Wagner's *Lohengrin* for the first time that season and Philippe Perrottet's production was lauded by the critics. Ruggero Orofino fared well in the title role, though his singing lacked the great heroic ring needed for this part, yet, as one veteran critic pointed out, he was never strained vocally and his acting was convincing. The most memorable singing apparently came from Eldemira Calomfirescu, who brought to Ortrud 'a notable feeling of passion and drama.' The chorus won very favourable mention. Tom Carney recalls that it was enjoyable to sing in and was well directed. 'We always looked forward to the society staging Wagner. I suppose you could say his operas were neglected in Dublin, which was a pity for when well produced they can find warm audience response.'

It wasn't all work and no play for DGOS members and opera buffs generally. The social side was in full swing as usual, with Nico's and other city restaurants opening their doors to post-opera diners. 'I remember some fabulous nights at Nico's' says Barry Hodkinson, 'when the place was full of principals, chorus members and maybe a film celebrity or two. Once, Peter O'Toole made his entry accompanied by an entourage and he was in great form and stayed for the sing-song. 'I can still see him going around the tables and shaking hands with the diners.'

At other times principals and chorus members gathered in a top room in the Gaiety Theatre and enjoyed the best of Italian cuisine prepared by Luciano Pecchia. Luciano had begun coming to Dublin in the late fifties and sang small roles as well as being one of the Italian leaders in the chorus. Once, Barry Hodkinson lent him an old electric cooker, a relic of the forties, and Pecchia cooked some delicious pastas and other opulent viands. Sometimes a bottle of wine was produced to enhance the culinary enjoyment. To Hodkinson and others, they were fun times, part of a scenario that would be hard to recapture. Colonel O'Kelly was happy enough to see the Irish and Italians enjoying themselves together as long as it didn't interfere with the 'serious business of opera.'

Rehearsals Abandoned

At around 7.30 on Friday evening, December 1, 1972, DGOS guest principals, chorus members and musicians of the RTÉ Symphony Orchestra assembled at the Metropolitan Hall, Upper Abbey Street (off O'Connell Street) for rehearsals of Tchaikovsky's tragic opera *The Queen of Spades*. It was being staged by the society for the first time and sung in Russian and also featured a children's choir who were in attendance in the hall.

Albert Rosen was among the first to arrive, and with the opening night on December 5, he was anxious to get on with the rehearsals. Among the guest artists present were Oldrich Spisar, cast in the key role of Hermann, the gambler, Marcela Machotkova, singing Lisa, his lover, Andrea Snarski (Prince Yeletsky) and the English mezzo Johanna Peters who was singing the old countess who is said to know the secret of the three cards that always win. Director Jaroslav Horacek was at that moment talking to the principal singers - he was playing two small parts, Tomsky and Plutus.

Irish singers Ruth Maher and Terry Reid were among those waiting to be called. Ms Reid was Donegal-born and after study at the Royal Irish Academy proceeded to the St. Cecilia Conservatory of Music, Rome, graduating with her final diploma in 1970. Her light soprano voice was considered very promising. Seated at the piano, near the stage, was chorus master John Brady with the score in front of him; he had been asked by Albert Rosen to take charge of the chorus and says he was privileged to do so. In a room off the balcony, the 16-strong children's choir was being rehearsed on their own.

According to John Brady, rehearsals had up to that day been proceeding satisfactorily and the chorus members had come to grips with the Russian language, even if some of them found it more difficult than others. It was by now about 7.45 and he was checking some notes before the chorus would be called on to perform. They were lined up on the stage, the women outnumbering the men by at least two to one, while at the same time Albert Rosen, with baton in hand, was explaining a point to the musicians. Suddenly at about 8 o'clock there was a loud bang in the vicinity of the hall, coming from the direction of Liberty Hall on the nearby quays. Such was the impact that some windows were blown inwards in the Metropolitan Hall.

'There was a horrible bang like the powerful crash of a car,' recalls chorus member Seán Kelly. 'When the stained-glass windows at the other end of the hall fell in, I knew instantly it was very serious.' To Barry Hodkinson, it seemed like an explosion but he couldn't be sure. John Carney felt the blast was quite near and remembered the windows crashing to the floor; his thoughts immediately turned to the safety of the children's choir. Tom Carney described it as 'an almighty roar' and he exchanged a quick glance with his wife Dympna who at that moment looked shocked. 'I could see that most of the musicians had hastily left and for a few moments it seemed that Albert Rosen was frozen on the podium. I realised there were kids involved and wondered what was happening to them. All of us were told to get out of the hall as fast as possible.'

'I've a vivid picture in my mind of the windows coming in,' says Paddy Brennan, 'and of seeing cellist Vincenzo Caminiti, with the flowing hair, and he still bowing as he made for the door. I remember also the hurried, nervous glances among chorus members and of looking down at Albert Rosen who still hadn't moved away. Looking back, it was a frightening experience.' To Monica Condron, it had all happened so quickly that it left those present in the hall in some confusion. 'I thought it was a bad car crash or something worse and I can recall someone being asked to go out to try and find out what was happening. I was thinking of the children and their safety, for I knew that if there had been a serious explosion, their parents would be in a terrible state. I helped to organise them into groups and tried to get volunteers to bring them to their homes.'

Brian O'Rourke, who by now had put away his clarinet in its case, remembered Albert Rosen saying to them immediately after what seemed to him 'a weighty thud', 'It's better for all of you to stay here in the hall. If you go into the streets, you're in more danger.' But no one listened to him; instead they picked up their instruments and made for the door. 'I do remember a second explosion at around 8.20 and then the last of us, including Albert, went away as quickly as possible through the lane at the rear, where we were met by the sound of police car sirens and ambulance sirens. It was an eerie experience and I wanted only to get out of the city.'

Civic guards were patrolling the streets and telling people to clear the area near O'Connell Bridge. Chorus members heard rumours about car bomb explosions for the first time. 'It was then that the grim reality of the situation dawned on us,' says Barry Hodkinson. Monica Condron was relieved they had found volunteers to ferry the children's choir to their homes. Aileen Walsh says she failed to make the rehearsals that night because gardaí had stopped her and others entering O'Connell Street. 'I finished up in the

Teachers'Club later.'

Two people had died in the car bomb explosions with 126 injured, some seriously. The first had taken place at Liberty Hall, where many windows were smashed, and the second in Sackville Place. One of the bomb cars had been hired in Belfast. The worst fears of Southerners were being realised - the Northern violence had come to Dublin for the first time. It would undoubtedly cast a cloud over the society's winter season of grand opera; in fact they were already looking for a premises to continue with rehearsals. For a while, says Aileen Walsh, there was a strange atmosphere in the city but we were determined to carry on and not be thwarted by violence.

The Queen of Spades was a success, particularly in the artistic sense. The chorus singing in Russian for only the second time, did surprisingly well and as one critic commented, 'made a spirited attempt to look at ease singing the language.' Charles Acton eulogised about the production : 'With *The Queen of Spades* the DGOS last night rose to marvellous heights and gave me a total operatic experience, virtually never exceeded and very rarely equalled. Albert Rosen welds Tchaikovsky's score into a single unit in which solos, ensembles, chorus, orchestra, all form a part of a whole theatre event. In Dublin alone, the conductor has now given us *Eugene Onegin, The Bartered Bride* and *Fidelio,* and now this great performance. Why not put him in charge of the complete season this time next year?'

It was a point pungently made but despite Colonel O'Kelly's admiration for Rosen, it was doubtful whether he would invest him with any such authority. In theory at least Maestro Annovazzi remained the society's artistic director and he held the key to the 'package'.

It had been a sparkling spring season with Ugo Benelli proving a good judge of Irish operatic taste. He had, he told me later, suggested Rossini's *La Cenerentola* to Colonel Bill O'Kelly, saying he would be free to sing the role of Don Ramiro. 'I had sung it many times in Continental houses and it appeared to me that audiences liked the opera very much. You can imagine my pleasure when Colonel O'Kelly said the society would do it for the first time!'

Besides the popular lyric tenor, the cast also included the talented Angelo Romero, who made a believable character out of Dandini, Ramiro's valet, and sang Rossini's music most stylishly. Aileen Walsh recalls mezzo-soprano Giuseppina Dalle Molle's fine performance as Angelina (known as Cinderella) and how beautifully she sang in the final scene of the opera. Paddy Brennan regarded the cast as excellent with Benelli showing how good a Rossini singer he could be. But Angelo Romero, he said, handled the most difficult music in the opera in commendable fashion. Ruth Maher and

Terry Reid, as the Baron's daughters, fitted easily into Philippe Perrottett's production. 'I enjoyed the whole thing immensely,' Ms Maher told me later. 'And what a cast we had!'

She was giving sterling service to the society and showed her versatility when she sang the important role of Fenena, Nabucco's daughter, in the Verdi opera, which was being revived that season. The Turkish soprano Ozglu Tanyeri was making her debut with the society as Abigaille but despite her impressive CV disappointed vocally. By contrast, the Spanish-born baritone Pedro Farres gave a *tour-de-force* performance as Nabucco, displaying a vibrant and resilient voice and acting ability above the ordinary. Lino Savoldi, who had already sung Calaf successfully with the society, coped impressively with Ismaele's music.

The biggest single success of the season was, however, Puccini's *Manon Lescaut* starring Giuseppe Giacomini and Anna Maria Balboni. Chorus members still love to recall Perrottet's production and the superb singing by Giacomini and Balboni in the passionate love duet in act two. 'It had tremendous impact,' says Paddy Ring, who sang the role of Edmondo, a student. 'I think we heard Giacomini at his very best in this opera.' To Paddy Brennan, it was a fabulous evening in the Gaiety. 'Anyone who listens to a tape of the performance today will agree, I've no doubt, with this.'

I myself have listened to the tape (courtesy of Tom Carney) and thoroughly agree, but something else also struck me forcibly - the exquisite playing by the RTÉ Symphony Orchestra under Maestro Annovazzi who managed to convey the magnificent sweep of the music and its inherent passion. Undeniably it was an inspiration to the cast in which the part of a naval captain was played by young Irish baritone Pádraig O'Rourke. 'There was one great voice in that production,' he recalls, 'and that was Giuseppe Giacomini.'

Ironically, though, it caused him one uncomfortable moment at rehearsal. It occurred when the tenor placed his hand on O'Rourke's shoulder and sang full out into his ear. 'I never felt such discomfort in my life. Giacomini had a wonderful voice but unfortunately he couldn't see beyond my head when he took his glasses off and so didn't realise how close he was to me. He nearly blew my head off. I suspect that Annovazzi was a blur to him and I think he was the only singer that the conductor made a concession to - I mean, he followed the tenor instead of the other way round. My own problem was that I hadn't a big voice and singing in the Giacomini/Balboni company one felt under pressure. It struck me at the time that Gaiety audiences wanted to hear big voices. I learned also that singers like Giacomini and Jon Piso were fearless when it came to singing; they knew their capabilities and had supreme confidence in their own ability. Opera was their life, and it was in their blood. I don't think Irish artists sing as naturally as these people; perhaps it's the language and our particular difficulties with pronunciation. Gian Giacomo Guelfi was, for example, the ultimate singing machine, with a big, powerful voice that shook rafters. I remember an Irish baritone, who sang with him in Tosca, coming to my dressing room afterwards and holding the side of·his head and when I asked what was wrong, he replied, "That Guelfi - he sang straight into my ear."'

It was Verdi's *The Force of Destiny*, however, in the `73 spring season that really hooked Pádraig O'Rourke on opera, and once again it was Giacomini who helped to make it a memorable experience. 'He was in great voice as Alvaro and doing full justice to Verdi's inspired score. Pedro Farres was little behind him as Don Carlo.' But if he had experienced discomfort during the rehearsals of Manon Lescaut, it was a different story in the case of Verdi's opera. 'Looking back, it was quite funny. I remember I was sitting in the parterre with my eyes on the stage when suddenly there was a screech from Maestro Annovazzi. I wondered what had happened, but it appears he was startled by the Gaiety cat as it strode across the stage. I had heard he was supersitious but he could also be a difficult little man and I got the feeling that because one was Irish he wasn't terribly interested in you.'

The *Bohème* that spring was notable for the appearance of Terry Reid as Musetta and she aquitted herself admirably. Colonel O'Kelly liked to remind people at the society's AGMs that the society was giving ample opportunities to Irish singers and few could refute his claim. William Young, Brendan Cavanagh, Paddy Ring, Terry Reid, Ruth Maher and Peter McBrien were only some of the names well worthy of their places in any company. The Colonel, contrary to some people's views, was prepared to listen to guest artists who wanted to sing a particular role in Dublin, so that when the popular baritone Attilio d'Orazi asked him to give him a shot at Falstaff he did agree in 1972, though he had refused him earlier. As anyone in the DGOS will tell you, it was a resounding success, with the baritone's temperament perfectly suited to expose all facets of the Fat Knight's character. As one of the quartet of ladies, Ruth Maher excelled herself, singing and acting delightfully.

Cavalleria Rusticana and *I Pagliacci* was the double bill chosen for the gala occasion and since it was the last appearance at the opera of Eamon de Valera as President of Ireland, the Gaiety management arranged to have printed a special programme on silk to commemorate the event. The society's chorus paid their tribute to the President on his arrival by singing from the stage the National Anthem. Everyone agreed it was a very touching moment.

With the majority of Irish opera-goers by now steeped in Italian opera, with its glorious melody and exciting choruses, the staging of a Janacek work like *Jenufa* would always be a box-office gamble and unfortunately this was the case in that winter season of `73. Paddy Brennan believes the name of the opera put people off, which was a pity because it was a very convincing production. To John Brady, the human drama in the piece was moving and Albert Rosen was naturally keen to see it staged in Dublin and probably suggested it to Colonel Bill O'Kelly. It attracted the lowest attendance ever and proved a severe blow to the society's finances. 'We all agreed that it would take us some time to recover from the blow,' recalls Donnie Potter, 'but in artistic terms we felt we owed it to opera-goers to be adventuresome and do lesser known works. It was disheartening, though, when it turned out like this.'

It was even more discouraging for members of the cast who believed in the work totally and had worked hard at rehearsals with director Jaroslav Horacek. Dublin-born mezzo-soprano Deirdre Grier Delaney was singing Karolka in the opera and felt it was sung with tremendous passion by the Czech principals. She found the music and the drama at times intensely moving. 'I could see that Albert Rosen was proud to be conducting it and it should of course have been better supported.' To Ruth Maher, who played the downtrodden peasant grandmother, it was a gripping piece of drama with the music matching the underlying tensions. She felt it must have been an emotional experience to sing the part of Jenufa. Like Ms Delaney, she had no doubt that it deserved more public support than it received. 'I was disappointed, so was everyone else. *Jenufa* is a fine opera of its kind and it's in the repertory today of many leading opera houses.'

It would be some years more however before conservative Irish opera-goers accepted Janacek. But it showed another aspect of Albert Rosen's total commitment, as well as his understanding of the psychology of performers. The wedding dance being performed in *Jenufa* by the village girls had been causing problems in rehearsals so something had to be done to ease the women's obvious inhibitions. Summoning them to the Gaiety's Green Room during the second interval on opening night the conductor presented them with glasses of brandy, urging them at the same time to 'knock it back' and go out and enjoy their dance. Apparently this magic potion had the desired effect and drew a beaming smile from 'Doctor' Rosen in the pit.

Jenufa wasn't the only box-office loser that winter for it seems neither *Don Carlo* nor *Mignon* packed the Gaiety with the result that the society in a desperate bid to recoup its losses, decided to increase ticket prices for the following spring season. In the annual report for 1973, it was stated, 'We are from time to time reproached for continuing to include pot boilers in our choice of programme. Naturally we ourselves get tired of the tried and trusted operas and would love to have the finance to arrange a season of not one but three or four lesser known works, but the old reliables act as our safety valve and keep our feet on the ground.' It was a frank admission and didn't augur well for the operas of Britten, Janáček, Massenet and Rimsky-Korsakov.

Eighteen years had passed since the society had staged Verdi's noble work *Simon Boccanegra*, which is notable for its superb musical characterisation, so its revival in the spring of `74 was timely and undoubtedly welcomed. Colonel O'Kelly and Donnie Potter had earlier visited Rome to complete the casting. At this time the young Cork-born bass-baritone John O'Flynn was studying there with Paolo Silveri and usually had voice lessons in the famous singer's home.

A year before he had decided to make opera his career and was encouraged in his decision by Silveri who thought his voice had both flexibility and resonance. O'Flynn was surprised one afternoon to be introduced to Bill O'Kelly and Donnie Potter. 'Colonel O'Kelly said they were auditioning singers for the DGOS spring season and Paolo Silveri had told him, it seems, that I was suitable for certain parts. Paolo and myself then sang a duet from *Don Carlo* and afterwards O'Kelly said he would probably get in touch with me later. Subsequently he offered me the roles of Pietro in *Boccanegra*, Monterone *(Rigoletto)*, Bonze *(Butterfly)* and Zuniga in Carmen. 'I liked the idea of starting my operatic career n Dublin, although some years previously I had sung in musical comedy in London's West and enjoyed myself. I had started my career as an actor and worked in the Abbey Theatre for a year.'

Rehearsals of *Boccanegra* went well in Dublin and he was pleased to be working with such an able cast that included the outstanding soprano Anna Maria Balboni as Maria, Boccanegra's daughter and Salvatore Sassu as Boccanegra. Chorus members remember the production as first-rate both vocally and dramatically. To John O'Flynn the music had wonderful nobility and eloquence and he loved being part of it. Paddy Brennan says it is remembered as one of the best Verdi productions staged by the society. Although Salvatore Sassu was small and lacked a commanding stage presence, he won over audiences by his velvety and warm baritone voice that projected excellently. To Tom Carney the voice was ideal in strength and quality for Verdi's music and it was a joy to listen to him sing.

When the opera was presented at the Opera House, Cork, a few weeks later it made a profound impact on everyone, including the local critics.

Singing before his own people brought back a flood of memories to John O'Flynn. As a boy he had accompanied his parents to the old Opera House and seeing Rigoletto there for the first time was to prove a marvellous experience. He was now delighted to find that Cork's operatic tradition was alive and well with the theatre packed almost every night of that week. Harold Johnson had also enjoyed *Boccanegra* and compared its impact to that of *The Force of Destiny* which had been acclaimed in Cork in the previous year. 'Any of us who heard Giacomini sing Alvaro will never forget it.'

The annual visits by the DGOS to the Opera House were, in his view, enhancing local opera-goers' appreciation of grand opera and singers such as Benelli, Giacomini, Lavirgen, Guelfi, Sassu and Balboni had become household names. Corkonians were also pleased to welcome John O'Flynn and already he had shown he could sing beside the best. The society's visit was organised in a most professional manner with everything in readiness for the company on arrival. 'Most of the principals stayed in the Imperial Hotel where we arranged special rates for them,' recalls Harold Johnson, 'and in addition we got business firms to sponsor the different operas, thus ensuring that neither the Opera House nor the DGOS lost money. The Opera House bars were also a great money-spinner for us and there were times when it was almost impossible to get people to go home. They talked endlessly and some of them sang and the whole atmosphere was fantastic. It was after all Cork's biggest music week in the year.'

Aurio Tomicich had made his DGOS debut as Jacopo Fiesco in that season's *Simon Boccanegra,* having been auditioned earlier in Rome by Maestro Annovazzi. It was a big and demanding role for a young bass of twenty-six years - Samuel Ramey had put off singing it until his late thirties. Tomicich, who hailed from Trieste and studied at the Palermo Conservatory, was strongly built with a well-focused bass voice, dark in colour and of rich tonal quality. A bright future was predicted for him by Maestro Annovazzi who liked nothing better than to see his predictions come true. During my visit to Rome in April 1998, I found that Aurio Tomicich hadn't changed from his Dublin days - he last sang with the DGOS in 1990 - and it seemed to afford him pleasure to reminisce about the past.

He speaks good English, is articulate and self-effacing and has a ready sense of humour. When he arrived in Dublin for the first time he says everything was strikingly different compared to Italy: the houses, the bars, the streets. But he liked the place from the beginning and gradually felt at home. He was warmly welcomed by Colonel O'Kelly and the chorus, and although they were an amateur chorus, he could see at the rehearsals of *Boccanegra* that they were well coached and heroic in the way they unselfishly gave of their time to the society. He was, though, surprised to be told that none of them got paid for all their work and dedication.

Looking back, he says that Dublin fulfilled an important purpose as it afforded him an opportunity to take on principal roles and develop them musically and dramatically. In Italy he would, for instance, have to wait for some time before being given a part like Fiesco but singing these roles early in his career gave him confidence and belief in himself. 'I don't think Maestro Annovazzi would have asked me to sing Fiesco if he didn't think I could sing it. He was encouraging to me and I learned a lot from him musically. He knew his operas and the characters in them and how these parts should be sung. Dublin was very good to me in that way and I increased my repertoire in a short time.'

During that `74 spring season, he also sang Raimondo in *Lucia di Lammermoor* and his voice seemed well suited to bel canto roles. He soon learned that the fees paid by the society were small but he wasn't worried. He saw himself as a young singer trying to gain experience and he knew he was singing with some very good artists. And he liked the friendly atmosphere around the place and from his early days regarded the Gaiety Theatre a his spiritual home. He believes Colonel O'Kelly managed the society wisely and as long as you gave of your best he was happy. He was intrigued by the way the Colonel used to sit in the wings and watch everything closely on stage.

'He imposed his own kind of discipline,' Tomicich said, 'and I didn't see anything wrong with that. Every opera company does the same to varying degrees and as long as it is fair you accept it. I was young and eager and didn't take much notice. I came to love the Gaiety audiences and their enthusiasm; a young singer appreciates that kind of thing and applause can get to him. I could see that singers enjoyed coming to Ireland and spoke to their friends in Italy about the country, its people and its opera. I counted myself lucky to be invited back so often.'

He is still singing and his large repertoire embraces a good deal of contemporary opera. I liked his parting words, 'I would like again to go back to my old spiritual home and sing for my Irish friends.'

Tom Hawkes

'I was, you could say, thrown in at the deep end,' declared Tom Hawkes. 'I was asked by Colonel Bill O'Kelly to come to Dublin to direct three operas for the spring season of `75, *Traviata, Un Ballo in Maschera* and *I Puritani* which they were staging for the first time. I had been recommended to O'Kelly by Philippe Perrottet who up to then had directed for about eight years with the society. We had worked together at the London Opera Centre training young singers and I was amused once when Philippe said to me he was going to Dublin to direct five operas in three weeks. What a handful, I thought. But my agent knew a good deal about the Dublin Grand Opera Society and believed it was a good thing for a young director like myself to be thrown in at the deep end.'

Hawkes hailed from Devon in the West Country and set out to be an actor and eventually became a lecturer in drama at the Royal Manchester College. It was music initially that attracted him to opera and the emotional response to music, something that had always appealed to him. He regarded it as a powerful force and as a form of theatre opera could be most spectacular. But first you had to find the musical and dramatic core of the work. He joined the staff of Sadler's Wells Opera and after that became a freelance director of both opera and drama. Later, he directed productions of *Madama Butterfly* and *A Masked Ball* - both in English - at the London Coliseum. Directing the Verdi opera in Italian for the DGOS would be a new experience for him. 'I knew I could not handle three operas inside a few weeks unless I did my homework first in London,' he recalled, 'so I did some serious preparation, especially on *Puritani* which was new to me.'

Although he had been Director of Productions for Northern Ireland Opera for four years, Hawkes did not know Dublin nor anything about the DGOS. He had no written contract with the society or Colonel O'Kelly, just a letter from honorary secretary Monica Condron saying what his fee was going to be - his agent had evidently asked about the size of the fee. His first impressions of Colonel O'Kelly were he admits somewhat extraordinary. 'He exuded enthusiasm and when he looked at you with those sharp eyes of his and spoke in rather gruff tones you never were quite sure whether he approved of you. Before long I heard stories about the discipline he imposed but I seemed to get along well with him. As for the amateur chorus, I had worked with similar choruses in England and that was no problem. It was, however, the volume of work I was expected to get through in two or three weeks that worried me. I hadn't tackled such a heavy volume before and it was a big commitment.'

It was a help that he had worked before with Albert Rosen - he was conducting his *Traviata*. He liked his tremendous enthusiasm and his passion for opera and it was always a joy making music with him. He knew nothing of Annovazzi, though he suspected he was a different personality entirely to Rosen. He got no idea of the size of the budgets he had but from what he could see they were very tight.

With the spring season costing in the region of £30,000, the society feared that there would be resistance among opera-goers to the increased ticket prices but happily, says Monica Condron, this did not happen. 'I do remember that the advanced booking was very good and that was a relief to us all. Patron members' subscriptions went up to £7 in that year and that, too, was a help, though increases in postage and telephone costs would almost certainly cancel out any profit.'

The Arts Council's guarantee of £20,000 against loss was the society's lifeline and, in addition, their sponsors were also making a good contribution as was the Ladies' Committee. Musically, it was to prove a highly enjoyable season with keen interest in Terry Reid's debut in a major role for the society. As Norina in Donizetti's *Don Pasquale* she delighted audiences by her grace and gaiety and agile singing. Fanny Feehan was to comment in the *Evening Press:* 'The DGOS are to be congratulated on having learnt the Wexford lesson that good unknown singers can often be a better buy than the well-known "big" names, and in giving Terry Reid this opportunity they have earned our gratitude.' The season had opened with *Traviata* and as it turned out, Tom Hawkes got off to a promising start with the society. His production showed thought, care and rehearsal, noted Mary MacGoris *(Irish Independent),* 'and it had clearly been worked out as a whole and even the chorus, singing with fine responsiveness and balance, behaved quite naturally as guests at the parties where contretemps occurred.' She was impressed by Gianni Bavaglio's beautifully sung Alfredo and his voice had a kind of soft, golden quality reminiscent of Gigli.

She expressed mixed feelings about that season's *Tosca*, mainly because of what she described as Gian GiacomoGuelfi's 'antics': firstly, in the first-act finale when he turned his back on the ceremony and sang to the audience with hand uplifted like a revivalist preacher; and secondly while Floria Tosca was singing 'Vissi d'arte' he kept walking in and out of the French windows.

She did comment however on his magnificent voice and commanding stage presence as Scarpia, but his restlessness was unforgivable. She was more pleased by Pedro Lavirgen's ringing tenor as Cavaradossi, though 'he should have been shot long before he was for his disgraceful hanging on to the third syllable of 'Vittoria' - semantically and musically outrageous, but it could be forgiven for his exquisite singing of 'O dolci mani'.

Tom Hawkes remembers the tenor's performance that season in *Un Ballo in Maschera* for the sheer passion he brought to the role of Riccardo and considered it a bravura performance. 'He was easy to direct because he was totally involved in the singing and in the drama,' he says, 'and he was the kind of tenor who roused an audience. Very exciting. Salvatore Sassu sang well as Renato and Florida Norelli, as Amelia, made up a first-rate trio of principals.'

Bellini's opera *I Puritani,* written for Paris and premiered there in January 1835, was chosen by the society because in Antonio Bevacqua both Colonel O'Kelly and Maestro Annovazzi believed they had a tenor who could cope with the extremely difficult role of Arturo, and that the experienced Romanian soprano Niculina Mirea Curta was ideal for Elvira, the heroine in the opera. Aurio Tomicich was singing Sir George Walton and Salvatore Sassu was cast as Riccardo, a most rewarding part for a baritone of his talent.

Paddy Brennan recalls that at a concert in Cork in the previous year Bevacqua sang "A te, o cara" from *Puritani* and this more than anything else convinced Bill O'Kelly that he was right for Arturo. Some of them in the chorus had been pushing for years to have the opera staged because of the lyric beauty of its music and one had only to listen to the Callas/diStefano recording for confirmation of this. Tom Hawkes, who was directing, says he loved the opera and that at rehearsals knew he had an excellent cast who would do justice to Bellini. He thought the mad scene most affecting and the final scene touching.

The story is set in the 17th century during the Civil War between the supporters of Cromwell and the Stuarts and is the composer's last opera. There is a happy ending as Elvira's sanity is restored and she and Arturo are blissfully reunited. The DGOS production pleased Mary MacGoris, and she summed up, 'A good deal of credit must be given to Tom Hawkes who saw the possibilities of story, cast and stage, not to mention the admirably grouped and well-dressed chorus which moved gracefully and sang magnificently.' Chorus members such as Anne Deegan, Maura Mooney and Mary Troy told me they found the mad scene both moving and compelling and beautifully sung by Niculina Mirea Curta, while Charlie Dunphy and Barry Hodkinson thought that Antonio Bevacqua was outstanding as

Arturo, singing with ease and real bel canto style.

Aurio Tomicich remembered the opening night's performance for a less musical reason. 'Elvira is supposed to be my daughter in the opera and at one point we were singing a duet together and embraced. She happened to be wearing an embroidered costume and I had a hook in my costume and we got caught and remained hooked together until the end of the act. All we could do was to laugh and hope we didn't look too foolish. It was the same night that Brendan Cavanagh, who was playing Sir Bruno Robertson, came on in heavy armour and suddenly fell flat on the floor. I can still hear the noise of the armour as he hit the floor. That, too, caused us to laugh.'

It had been a good season for Irish artists, for apart from Terry Reid's beguiling performance as Norina in *Pasquale* - Brendan Cavanagh was the Notary - Monica Condron had sung Flora in *Traviata* with Paddy Ring as Gaston and Peter McBrien (Baron Douphol), Pádraig O'Rourke (Marquis d'Obigny) and Seán Mitten (Doctor Gremnvil). McBrien also figured in *Un Ballo in Maschera*, as Silvano, and Sciaronne, Scarpia's aid, in *Tosca* and as he told me, marvelled once more at the sheer volume of Gian Giacomo Guelfi's voice. Soprano Mary O'Sullivan was the Shepherd in that production while Paddy Ring was Spoleto and Seán Mitten, the escaped prisoner Angelotti. The society was fortunate to have such able Irish singers to fill these parts and their fees though small were, according to Paddy Ring, improving.

The week's season at the Opera House, Cork was a sell-out, but the choice of operas - *Tosca, Traviata* and *Ballo* - had a lot to do with this. Some of the chorus members, though, including Paddy Brennan and Tom Carney, believed an opportunity was lost in not bringing *Puritani* so as to give Cork's opera lovers bel canto sung at its best. The operatic concert scheduled for the Sunday night prior to opening night of the opera 'died a death' as the normal 40-minute air journey from Dublin became a virtual nightmare for the artists. Because of the petrol strike, the plane had to fly from Dublin to Cardiff before returning to Cork. The concert, meanwhile, having got off to a late start was kept going by Aurio Tomicich, Paddy Ring and Peter McBrien.

To Harold Johnson, a board member of the Opera House, it was another memorable week of opera and today he likes to recall Guelfi's 'frightening' Scarpia and Pedro Lavirgen's passionately sung Riccardo in *Ballo*. He was thrilled also by the performance of Turkish soprano Gunes Ulker as Violetta. 'I think we would also have liked to have heard Terry Reid sing Norina in *Pasquale* and I suppose Antonio Bevacqua in *Puritani* - he had sung very well at our concert in the previous year. But we couldn't really complain. Hearing three fine operas in the course of one week was tremendous.'

Tom Hawkes had clearly made an excellent impression on Colonel O'Kelly as he was invited back to Dublin to direct *Der Rosenkavalier* and *The Tales of Hoffmann* for the winter season, with both operas to be conducted by Maestro *Annovazzi*. *Rosenkavalier* appealed to him enormously, although in retrospect he felt he hadn't had enough time to do it full justice. 'It requires style and elegance and that takes time to get right. Nevertheless, I enjoyed tackling it for the first time and its music is in parts sublime.'

Patrick Murray was the designer. A native of Cork, he was trained in the local School of Art and also studied music. It was the late 1950s and one morning he got a 'phone call from Joan Denise Moriarty to see her at her ballet studio. She was staging *The Sleeping Beauty* and gave him a list of props she wanted designed. He brought them back to her in record time. She looked at him and said, "I'm going to be your patron. I asked you to do something, you did not delay, and they're beautiful." My mistake was that I designed them too well,' Murray quips today. 'And I kept designing for her for years and years. Joan was a wonderful lady and very inspiring to work with.'

Early in 1975, he had designed *Swan Lake* for her, and Colonel O'Kelly happened to see it and later contacted the young designer. 'We talked for a while, Murray recalls, 'and I said I heard he was tricky to deal with and he laughed. He wanted me to design *Der Rosenkavalier* and when I asked about the budget available, he shrugged and said, "Don't mind the costs." He agreed that the stage sets could be built at the Opera House, Cork. We had struck up a good working relationship and I trusted him.'

He had designed *Faust* and *Trovatore* for Cork's new opera house after it opened in the mid-sixties. When conductor Nicky Braithwaite saw his set for *Trovatore*, he said to him, 'It's very modern and resembles something we're doing at the Bayreuth Festival. Can I have your design?' Murray was taken by surprise but agreed he could take it away with him. 'Next thing that happened was, Nicky sent it off to Friedelind Wagner, one of the family in charge there, and she offered me a travelling scholarship. But how was I going to get there? I hardly knew where the place was in Germany.'

But Cork rallied round their gifted young designer. International concert pianist Charles Lynch gave him a 'crash course' in Wagner's famous Ring and the local School of Art awarded him a scholarship. He was soon on his way to the renowned festival town where he would study design for six months, as well as attending the performances of Wagner's works in the Festspielhaus. As one of eight scholarship students, he was the only one to have designed for both ballet and opera. After some months, he got a telegram from the Wexford Festival. 'Dr Tom Walsh, the festival director, had heard about my work and wanted me to come to Wexford to help out in that year 1966 with the productions of *Lucrezia Borgia* and *Fra Diavolo,* whose sets were being designed by Reginald Woolley. Seemingly, he had fallen off a ladder and was indisposed. Dr Walsh was sufficiently impressed to invite me back there the following year to design Gounod's *Romeo & Juliet.'*

He found the Bayreuth experience invaluable and had to make a decision either to stay in Germany or return to Ireland; he chose the latter course. 'Although I had got offers from Hamburg, I felt in honour bound to work in Ireland.' Tom Hawkes says that Murray did lovely sets for *Rosenkavalier.* 'I found him to be very musical and his sets reflected his musicality. I felt though he was somewhat restricted by the small budget available to him.' Colonel O'Kelly was so pleased that he invited Murray to return the following year to design Faust. Hawkes felt that Annovazzi was engaging talented singers and tenor Franco Bonanome's performance in both *Hoffmann* and *Rosenkavalier* was commendable and for an Italian his French was very good in *Hoffmann.*

For Monica Condron, the hard-working singer-secretary, the season was not without its problems. She recalled that on the day of the dress rehearsal of *Rosenkavalier* Kay Griffel who was to have sung the Marschallin, became ill and was told by her doctor not to sing for at least three days. Since the first performance on the following evening was also gala night something had to be done quickly to find a replacement. Eventually when they had almost given up, the English National Opera agreed to release Lois McDonnall. She proved a true artist. In spite of the fact that she only arrived off the plane at 5 o'clock, she was ready to go on stage at 7.30 leaving her scant time to walk through the production with the other artists whom she was meeting for the first time. In the circumstance, she gave a first-rate performance and soon forgot she was singing her part in English.

To Ms Condron, the rest of the cast also did very well. Helga Anjervo repeated her success as Octavian - she had sung in the 1972 winter season; Niculina Mirea Curta was a newcomer to the part of Sophie but was very impressive while Peter McBrien scored a personal triumph as Sophie's father, Faninal. A problem arose with that season's *Trovatore,* when tenor Renato Francesconi, as Manrico, contracted a bad sore throat and had to be replaced at the second performance by Ciro Pirotta who had previously sung Samson in the Saint-Saens opera in the winter of `74.

The social side, meanwhile, remained an integral part of the DGOS seasons, with the fund-raising events organised by the Ladies' Committee a highlight. Some of the more enjoyable were still being held at "Dalguise", the home of Mrs Margaret McDonnell and her husband Colm. Carmel McHale, a long-serving member of the Ladies' Committee, recalled the recital in the house by the celebrated pianist Jacques Klein and how he had come to be there. Shortly before, he had performed at the RDS and afterwards Professor Anthony Hughes and his wife had entertained him at a party in their home - both men had studied in Vienna - and Carmel McHale got talking to the pianist. 'He asked me about the Dublin Grand Opera Society and I said we were trying to raise funds and to my astonishment he offered to give a free recital to raise some money. Great, I thought to myself, but wondered if he would forget all about it by the next day. But instead he repeated his offer and I immediately got in touch with Margaret McDonnell and suggested the recital be held in her house. Margaret and her husband Colm agreed and it was given to an over-flow attendance of over one hundred friends and music lovers who contributed generously. It turned out to be one of our most memorable fund-raising events.'

There were other events such as the fashionable ball held in a large marquee in the grounds and, according to Carmel McHale, it was a magnificent occasion as friends made up parties and more than two hundred people were treated to a champagne reception. Having the ball under the big top made all the difference and the society benefited handsomely. And on other occasions the McDonnells ran a casino in the house and attracted people from judges to politicians to opera buffs. They played cards and roulette and other games with all the proceeds going to the society. Charlie Haughey was one of a small group who played cards at a table in a first floor room and was happy to hand over the winnings to fund-raisers. For years he was good to the society and as Minister for Finance was always sympathetic to approaches for assistance. 'He nudged the Arts Council to give us grants against loss and in that way took us out of more than one crisis,' said Donnie Potter. In addition, there were tennis tournaments held on the lawns and these according to Máire Hogan, a member of the Ladies' Committee, not only raised money but forged new friendships. 'Margaret and Colm McDonnell were marvellous the way they made their home available to fund-raising and it was something everyone appreciated.'

The sense of camaraderie in the society was tremendous. There was general satisfaction, for instance, when John Lovatt-Dolan received the Order of Merit from the Italian government for his services to the arts. He was the society's advisor as well as an energetic worker on themanagement committee. He was the third member to receive such an honour, the others being Bill O'Kelly and John F MacInerney.

Meanwhile, the post-opera suppers gaily continued with guest singers being among those invited to homes to share in true Irish hospitality and bonhomie. Paddy Fagan and his wife Anne, longtime patrons of the society, kept up the tradition at their home in Park Avenue and enjoyed listening to

Italian artists rendering Neapolitan songs after their refreshments. 'Opera-going wouldn't have been the same without these get-togethers,' Paddy Fagan said. 'We always ensured the conversation was lively and needless to say the wit flowed. Of course visiting singers loved to be part of it all.' To Dermot O'Kelly it was a tradition that had begun during the society's Italian Festival of Opera seasons in the late fifties and had become accepted as a vital part of the social scene.

There were others who frequented Nico's hoping to combine their steaks with songs and arias sung by Italians and Romanian artists. It was generally held that the city's dining places did a brisk business during these seasons. Singers and chorus members, on the other hand, usually had post-opera drinks in pubs near the Gaiety Theatre and by now Neary's was a kind of unofficial opera club where Irish and Italian voices were heard above the clink of glasses. Arthur Guinness reigned supreme and was recognised as the patron saint of opera singers. This was indisputable.

Dario's Mission

'You want to come to Dublin, Dario?' asked Maestro Annovazzi early in 1975.
'Why not, Maestro?' replied the director.
'I can promise you no big money.'
'I don't care about money. I come if you want me. So I will come.'

The two men were sipping their cappuccinos in a small restaurant in Benevento where Dario Micheli had directed a spectacular and highly successful production of Puccini's *Turandot,* starring Emma Renzi and Flaviano Labo. Annovazzi, who had conducted the performances, admired Micheli's flair, work-rate and imaginative approach and told Colonel O'Kelly later he was the sort of director/designer he could use in Dublin. Micheli was by now in his middle forties and in Italy had directed Mario del Monaco in Verdi's *Otello,* Virginia Zeani in *Manon, Lescaut and Tosca,* and Gian Giacomo Guelfi in *Nabucco.* Meeting him in Rome in April 1998 was a special pleasure for me as he is a quintessential Roman who has filmed in its streets, played its theatres, and dined in its restaurants. DGOS chorus members talk about him with a mixture of warmth, admiration and occasionally with awe.

He has a relaxed presence, an easy manner and is identifiable by his wide moustache, penetrating eyes and soft voice. As we dined in an atmospheric little restaurant in the shadow of the ruins of the Colisseum, he reminisced for a while and in no time at all had convinced me he was a *Figlio d'arte* - both his parents had worked at the Teatro Reale del' Opera di Roma and, he says, it was no secret that his mother had to hurry to ensure her son wasn't born in the theatre on that October day in 1930. She worked in the costume department while his father, a master tailor, had served there for forty years.

Young Micheli adapted naturally to the theatre, being child actor, boy singer and on occasions ballet dancer, not to mention his obvious gift for mimicry. Within a few years he had developed his theatrical skills, and in 1953, after military service, became active in film-making, assisting in costume design. Gradually he moved to opera and directed *Madama Butterfly* in the lyric season of Udine and later *Carmen, Faust* and *Aida* in

Rimini, Ancona and Mexico City. And he managed to divide his time between opera and the cinema most successfully, designing for such movies as *Morgan il Pirata* and *Violenza Segreta*.

'My work as director/designer has taken me to four continents,' he told me. 'I like to travel and to direct. It is so exciting.' A prodigious worker with boundless energy, his talents were soon recognised in Ireland and his gregarious personality and good humour endeared him to DGOS members and choristers. According to John Carney, though, Dario Micheli did not suffer fools gladly; he was a man who knew what he wanted in production terms and at times could appear unreasonable, but it was always for the sake of the opera and almost invariably he was proved right. 'In my view, he was to accomplish astonishing feats in opera in Dublin. When you remember that he probably had no more than four or five evenings' rehearsal with the chorus before even the biggest show like *Aida* or *Nabucco*, it's hard to believe the results he would achieve.'

'Dario was soon as popular in his own way as Colonel O'Kelly,' recalls Joan Rooney. 'We all considered him a gifted man capable of turning his hand at anything, whether it was fixing bulbs or painting his own scenery.' To Tom Carney he became a kind of legendary figure as was the case with Giuseppe Giardina and they were both brilliantly talented individuals who were also lacking both pretension and egotism.'

It was by now the spring of 1976 and Micheli had arrived in Dublin to direct *Otello* and Andrea Chénier. His first impressions of the Gaiety stage were disappointing insofar as he realised that it was perhaps small for big and grandiose production ideas so he was prepared to tailor his sets to its size. As he said, 'I would have no problem with the smaller operas but with *Aida* and *Nabucco* I could not be as spectacular as I wished.' He was renewing acquaintance with Gian Giacomo Guelfi and regarded the baritone's voice as 'a hurricane' and his Gerard in *Chénier* as an exceptional characterisation - and he was easy to direct. He recalled that in rehearsal Guelfi would say to him, 'Dario, you ask and I follow. Do not worry.' To Micheli, most of the star singers, with the exception of Mario del Monaco, were easy to direct and he had no problems with them. It was the smaller ones with the pretensions who could be difficult.

Singing the title role in *Otello* was tenor Angelo Marenzi, who hailed from Rome, and worked in public transport before he took up opera as a career. He was married to New Zealand-born soprano Lorraine Jones. Merenzi quickly impressed the chorus members by his vocal powers. To Paddy Brennan, in the tenor line, his voice was special, being naturally produced, even and well-focused. 'I remember he sailed through the most difficult parts of the music in a surprisingly effortless way. Off-stage he had a fetish though about his health - his throat especially.'

Fanny Feehan (*Evening Herald*) thought Marenzi produced some splendid singing, while Charles Acton commented that he had a true tenor voice of considerable flexibility which he used at full power at climactic moments. There were mixed views regarding Joshua Hecht's performance as Iago, but nearly everyone agreed that Hagint Vartanian's Desdemona was beautifully sung and acted. She was a late replacement for Linda Vajna who because of a broken leg sustained in Italy, was unable to come to Dublin.

Otello wasn't altogether a happy experience for tenor Paddy Ring. He was due to sing the role of Cassio but because he regarded it as more important than Roderigo, asked Colonel O'Kelly for a bigger fee. The Colonel, however, took umbrage at the request, so Ring decided to sing Roderigo for his original fee, letting Brendan Cavanagh sing Cassio, 'I would like to have sung the part a few years before if I'd been asked, but it didn't happen that way.' It would be 1980 before he'd be invited to sing another role for the society and that would be *Fidelio*.

Dario Micheli had reason to be pleased with the critics' reaction to his stage designs and direction. Charles Acton *(Irish Times)* in particular was impressed and found his opening act 'gripping and a *tour de force.*' Fanny Feehan found it 'a colourful production' while Judith Segal *(Evening Press)* stated the 'production had celerity, colour in costume, good handling of crowds and altogether showed Micheli as a visionary of musical theatre.'

He also designed the sets and directed that season's *Andrea Chénier* which was strongly cast with Irish singers like Ruth Maher, Brendan Cavanagh, Mary Sheridan and Peter McBrien holding their own in distinguished company. Indeed, McBrien proved a very credible Schaunard in *La Bohème* with Terry Reid excelling as Musetta and Aurio Tomicich confirming his status as a first-rate singing-actor. Franco Bonanome and Hagint Vartanian were thoroughly convincing as Rodolfo and Mimi and according to Robert Johnson *(Irish Press)* sang a magnificent first act.

For Dario Micheli it was both an enjoyable and successful first season in Dublin. He was not altogether surprised when Colonel O'Kelly called him aside one afternoon and said he wanted him to work regularly for the society. Although he was being extremely busy directing opera in Italy, Malta and elsewhere he assured the DGOS chairman that he would like to return. 'I got on well with Bill O'Kelly and he left me alone to do my work. I told him I liked working with the company and that the backstage staff was helpful and the chorus very loyal.'

It was perhaps an understatement. To Pat McClellan and George McFall, the quiet Italian was a tremendous worker who knew his job from A to Z. 'He tried to make our backstage work easy,' McFall says, 'and quickly took the measure of the Gaiety stage.' Chorus members were amused by Micheli's gift for mimicry and by now he was able to take off Colonel O'Kelly, Albert Rosen and others to perfection. 'It was fun working with Dario,' recalls Tom Carney. 'He ensured there wasn't a moment's boredom in rehearsal.' To Barry Hodkinson, he was unique, and to Paddy Brennan, he was simply a wonderful asset to the society, the miracle worker.

Donizetti's *L'Elisir d'Amore* was to prove one of the big successes of that `76 spring season, mainly because it had been well cast and in Paddy Ryan, who was making his debut as director with the society, was imaginatively staged. Ugo Benelli, as Nemorino, was singing one of his most famous roles and could expect a great reception from his adoring Irish public. Terry Reid looked ideal casting as Norina and the same could no doubt be said for Attilio d'Orazi as Sergeant Belcore. Discussing the production in Rome with Aurio Tomicich, the genial bass felt he was miscast as the quack 'Doctor' Dulcamara. 'The truth is I wasn't ready for the part which requires me to sell love potions to a love-lorn tenor. The Dublin critic who said I wouldn't be able to sell ice-cream in a desert was on this occasion right. You see, critics can be right ... sometimes!

Paddy Ryan had directed for Irish National Opera in the sixties and with productions such as *Don Giovanni,* James Wilson's *Twelfth Night* and Archie Potter's *The Wedding* had built up an impressive reputation as a man of the theatre. At the same time he regularly attended DGOS seasons at the Gaiety and admired the work it was doing to bring grand opera to the people. He was a part-time theatrical producer - his day job was in Guinness - and he must have been somewhat surprised to get a call from Colonel O'Kelly. Around this time he had directed the Waterford Grand Opera Company in a new production of *L'Elisir d'Amore* but when he set out to meet O'Kelly this was behind him. 'He was cordial and said he had seen my work and wanted me to direct *L'Elisir d'Amore* for the 1976 spring season,' recalls Ryan. 'I told him I'd be happy to accept the offer. With that, he produced a contract and I signed it. Turning to me, he said, "Take it away with you." He was an extraordinary man and must have had a struggle on his hands to keep all the different elements in the society working smoothly.'

Rehearsals were harmonious and Ryan admitted he had a first-class cast. He found Ugo Benelli a gentle, good-humoured soul and an outstanding professional blessed with a lovely lyric tenor voice. 'Ugo is a Florentine and an elegant man in all sorts of ways and as an artist is very polite. He was born to sing Nemorino. He could be tricky though on stage; I mean, you could rehearse him in scenes and he'd follow you but he always reserved a bit of horse-play for the actual performance. It was almost impossible to stop him doing this.'

One inspired innovation by the director drew spontaneous applause and gave the show an added sparkle. He brought four mettlesome horses onto the stage as part of Sergeant Belcore's Cavalry and they were an immediate hit. Mary MacGoris put it succinctly: 'Once those handsome horses walked two-legged onto the stage one knew exactly where one was - and in general the style was sustained throughout.' Another critic described them as 'human' horses. But they achieved their purpose. They were made by a craftsman in Churchtown, Co. Dublin, and according to Paddy Ryan, were wonderfully managed and 'brought the house down' at each performance.

No one knew however that conductor Albert Rosen hadn't wanted them in the opera. 'He took strong exception to their introduction at rehearsals,' says Ryan, 'and I remember he passed them off to me as silly nonsense. I had other ideas, though. I knew that if I timed their entry correctly it would lift the whole scene. And the fact that each horse had a slightly different caste of face and looked so real enthralled audiences. The critics without exception said my idea had worked.' To Patrick Murray, who designed the sets, Ryan's idea was very inventive. 'It's a fun opera and it's perfectly valid to try something original. The audience loved it.'

Murray himself shared in the triumph. 'The sets were delightful as well as viable,' commented Mary MacGoris *(Independent)* while Fanny Feehan *(Herald)* described the sets as 'a delight to the eye'. Ms MacGoris was fond of pinpointing unusual aspects and found a few gems. Having lauded Ugo Benelli's well-sung Nemorino, she noted, 'He should not, however, make use of such Dickensian shifts as wiping his nose on his sleeve and of course he should not wear grey nylon stockings.' I'm sure that the irrepressible Signor Benelli was never 'corrected' like that in either Milan or New York. It was, of course, justifiable comment.

As he expected, Paddy Ryan found the tenor as incorrigible as ever. In the scene in act two where Adina discovers the lengths Nemorino has gone to win her and she begins to sing of her rekindled love for him, Benelli refuses to remain quiet as in rehearsal; instead, he moves around behind her and goes to the table where he proceeds to cut the wedding cake and place the slices on two plates to the amusement of the audience. To the director this is distracting to the soprano and shouldn\t be done. 'I decided not to say a word about it to Ugo. I would get my own back in the sweetest possible way.'

Together, he and the props man Pat McClellan get a biscuit tin and place inside it what to all appearances is a real wedding cake but in reality is a metal object. At the performance a few nights later he watches from the wings as Nemorino, true to form, moves to the table as Adina is singing and lifts the lid off the tin and proceeds *(as he thinks)* to slice the cake but can't.

'Ugo realises immediately he has been caught,' recalls Paddy Ryan, 'and he knows by whom. He gets the message and moves away from the table. What can I do but chuckle to myself.'

Predictably, the production thrilled audiences at the Opera House, Cork. To board member Harold Johnson it had everything - colourful sets, graceful singing and comedy that never descended into broad farce. 'I remember I complimented Bill O'Kelly on bringing the show to Cork, for up to then we were inclined to get the heavier operas and while we had no complaint about that, comedies were also worth getting and I felt our audiences loved them. Ugo Benelli was of course a great favourite by the Lee, both inside and outside the theatre.'

It was in the Opera House on the final night that Paddy Ryan played his final trick on the tenor. On this occasion, he put a real wedding cake on the table but Benelli avoided it, thinking by now it was a fake. After the final curtain the company gathered on stage to celebrate Ugo's birthday and Ryan asked the tenor to cut the cake. 'I can still see his face as he takes the knife and finds that it's real cake and that he could have after all played his tricks earlier on poor Adina. He's a good sport, though, and was the first to join in the fun and laughter.'

The winter season of `76 was notable for a number of reasons. Franco Bonanome showed how good he could be in French opera when he sang a stylish Faust; while Mary Sheridan maintained her excellent record with the society by singing an impressive Siebel. Irish baritone William Young, who got good notices for his performance of Valentine, says this was the second plum part he would be handed by Colonel O'Kelly, the reason being that some years before he had agreed to the chairman reducing his fee because the society was in financial trouble. 'Bill O'Kelly never forgot it for me,' said Young. 'He was like that - he never forgot loyalty.'

Patrick Murray's sets for *Faust* again caught the eye and Tom Hawkes as usual directed with a keen eye for detail. In his view, Franco Bonanome was an excellent Faust, singing the high music with typical ease. He thought Patrick Murray's sets were visually attractive and also very effective. He had noted that Colonel O'Kelly seldom said much about his own productions. 'He might say to me in the Green Room afterwards, "A good show, Tom," or "Not bad, boy." I preferred it that way.'

When it came to directing *Eugene Onegin* that season he ran into a problem. It arose when both Colonel O'Kelly and Annovazzi wanted to go straight through from the Garden Scene to the Letter Scene in act one, but he pointed out to them that this would not work because the scene could not be changed inside of fifteen minutes at least. 'I remember that the Colonel accused me of being unfair to Mervyn Rowe, but I persisted that the change would be too complicated. I was proven right on the first night. The orchestra stopped playing and the audience sat in semi-darkness waiting for the hammers to stop on stage. I went to the bar and Donnie Potter came round to ask me what was the matter. I said the scene change doesn't work because it's too elaborate and added that I had pointed out this weeks before to Colonel O'Kelly. For the remaining performances we played it with an interval. The Colonel told me later I was right in the first place. I was relieved that he respected my judgment.'

Not surprisingly, the critics gave the production a mixed reception, pointing to the delay in the opening act and blaming Mervyn Rowe's 'over-elaborate sets' as the main reason. Vocally, though, it won praise, especially Hagint Vartanian's Tatyana and Franco Bonanome's Lensky. Ruth Maher was an impressive Madama Larina and Nikola Mitic was described by most critics as superb in the title role.

Undeniably the biggest success of the season was the revival of *The Bartered Bride* and it must have been a source of utmost satisfaction to everyone in the society that the Irish singers in the cast acquitted themselves so well. William Young says much of the inspiration came from director Jaroslav Horacek and conductor Albert Rosen. It was their understanding of Smetana's work that made the difference between a good and an outstanding production. Mary Sheridan, who sang Ludmila, agreed and felt that musically the whole thing went with a sparkle. Brendan Cavanagh added yet another fine comprimario role - that of the ringmaster - to his impressive collection. To Ruth Maher, cast as Hata, Albert Rosen always seemed to bring something extra to his conducting of Slav or Russian operas.

Operas apart, there were other matters that tended to occupy Colonel O'Kelly's mind in that year of `76. Earlier, the society had received a letter from Colm O'Briain, director of the Arts Council, stating it was proposed to set up a special committee on Opera in Ireland and that it was intended to include representatives of the major opera promoting bodies on the committee.

The DGOS chairman, believing that the council wanted to exert some control over the affairs of the society, wondered at the outset whether it was wise for them to be represented on the advisory committee. Donnie Potter felt it was better to be 'in' rather than 'out' of the new body and that others had signalled their intention of being represented.

Dr Tom Walsh, director of the Wexford Festival, would head the committee and the Arts Council was represented by Veronica Dunne, Norris Davidson, Bill Skinner and Gerard Victory, RTÉ's head of music. Colm O'Briain made it known he had 'no big stick to wave' and that in reality he was trying to fill what he saw as a vacuum and that opera in general should have an active lobby to press for what it needed and to act as a pressure group for more money. He was quick to add however that quite irrespective of the OAC, the Arts Council no longer considered itself just an animated cheque book but believed it should take some responsibility with the opera-makers. He did not outline any possible conditions to be imposed on the DGOS in the future, although in this respect Colonel O'Kelly raised the question at a society's management committee meeting later whether the council would in time seek control over the selection of the operas. He hated interference with his 'democratic society', though he was happy to accept money from the council.

It was by now common knowledge in the society that the council felt an artistic director should be appointed as in the case of the Wexford Festival. The society's reply was that in its president, Professor Anthony Hughes and Maestro Annovazzi they had people thoroughly qualified to advise artistically. It was clear however that the council wanted a significant say in the running of opera in the country, which was understandable in view of the funding it was supplying, although the £24,000 being donated to the DGOS against loss was a paltry amount and totally inadequate to the society's growing needs. The council had also made it known that it wanted higher standards with regard to DGOS productions and it was felt that this would not happen until an artistic director was appointed. Colonel O'Kelly was the first to admit that the standard of the society's productions varied, mainly because of the limited budget available. As he liked to say, 'Give us the money and we'll give you the productions you want.'

Monica Condron in her comprehensive report for the year stated, 'In closing my report last year I said the winds of change might be approaching and the future of the society could well be in the balance. Well, I am happy to say that by and large things seem to have settled into calmer waters.'

As though to show that the society could draw on revenue from other sources than the Arts Council, the report stated that more than 40,000 people had seen its eight productions at the Gaiety Theatre, and that in addition their guarantors had been supportive, the Ladies' Committee had donated £2,000 and that it was hoped the number of patron members could be soon raised to the 1,000 mark.

However, wiser heads in the society privately felt that the Arts Council wanted the society's structures changed and the amateur tag replaced in time by a professional one. Few dared to predict the ultimate changes, at least within earshot of Colonel O'Kelly who up to now had been lord of all he surveyed.

The year meanwhile ended on a particularly happy note with the marriage of pretty dark-haired Terry Reid and Franco Bonanome, the tenor with the handsome Mediterranean looks. They had fallen in love in Cork during the run of *La Bohème* in which she sang Musetta and Franco the poet Rodolfo, and inside no time at all he had popped the question and Terry was happy to accept his proposal.

It was perhaps appropriate that Fr Peter Shields, head of the Dundalk Gramophone Circle, should officiate at the wedding ceremony as he had rarely missed their performances at the Gaiety Theatre and, of course, they had sung at his fund-raising concerts in Dundalk Town Hall with other guest artists. It will be remembered that soprano Adéle Leigh and bass James Pease met also in opera in Dublin in the fifties and were wed in London.

Earlier in the sixties, the romance and wedding of tenor Ruggero Bondino and Diana Edge created considerable interest. Diana hailed from a wealthy Dublin family and was exceedingly good-looking and glamorous. Bondino was dark and handsome and had made his name with the DGOS in operas such as *Traviata and La Sonnambula*. They had first met at a post-opera supper and party and later settled in Italy.

And it was not unusual for chorus members to meet and marry; one such couple were John Carney and Brigid Finucane. In addition, there were numerous affairs, some tense, others fleeting, involving choristers and visiting guest artists and inevitably some broken hearts. There were liaisons also between Italian and Romanian artists and Irish people on the fringe of opera or perhaps DGOS patrons.

I once went to the old Royal Hibernian Hotel in Dawson Street to interview a visiting star for the *Sunday Independent* and found a well-known Abbey Theatre actress waiting for him with a bouquet of flowers. His plane had been delayed so I discreetly left a message instead for him. When one tried to contact a star in her dressing room after a performance it was often virtually impossible because of her adoring Irish friends. It was no different to the Wexford Festival where voluptuous sopranos and mezzo-sopranos invariably attracted opera buffs.

Florrie Draper enjoyed watching the romantic scene surrounding the DGOS, and while working in the costume department had sometimes to listen to sopranos complain that their boyfriends or husbands overseas were upset because they hadn't heard from them. Florrie found it all amusing, though understandable, and had sympathy for some of the artists. 'Some of them could be emotional and I used to be afraid it would upset their singing. I'd give a bit of advice for what it was worth and I don't know whether they took it or not.'

It was said that Maestro Annovazzi frowned on female artists staying out late if they had a demanding week of opera. He was known to get cross and rebuke them. Mostly, however, artists were discreet about their affairs and it was sometimes difficult to draw a distinction between friendship and a relationship. Once or twice Annovazzi was called on by Colonel O'Kelly to sort out 'messy affairs' and 'infatuations' and he did not hesitate to remind a tenor or baritone of their marital responsibilities back home in Italy.

For the most part the visitors enjoyed themselves and made the Gaiety their spiritual home, cooking pasta and spaghetti in room No. 7 upstairs (The Wardrobe) and trying at the same time to make themselves understood to their Irish friends.

Colonel in Bronze

As a man of action Colonel O'Kelly could be restless and in the words of his daughter Máire (Hogan) found it hard to sit still. So when she and the family learned that the society had commissioned a bust of him in bronze they naturally wondered how he would adapt to his new role of sitter. To everybody's relief, however, the Colonel settled in comfortably to the task and was even chuffed when told by Prince Caracciolo that he was being immortalised at the bequest of the society.

'I found Bill a most entertaining sitter,' Gary Trimble would say later. As a portrait painter and sculptor, Trimble was widely known and had executed portraits of celebrities, including Eamon de Valera and Micheál MacLiammoir. But he agreed that Colonel O'Kelly was somewhat different for during his six sittings he wanted operatic music played gently in the background, so Trimble played overtures, arias and tuneful duets. O'Kelly at the same time regaled him with stories about Michael Collins and Dick Mulcahy and the film stars he encountered on location such as Robert Mitchum, John Mills and Sarah Miles and lots of others, and although he wasn't a drinking man graciously accepted a drop of Irish whiskey.

To Trimble, the DGOS chairman was an earthy character, good-humoured and knowledgeable about a variety of subjects. 'I enjoyed Bill talking about swimming, rugby, Irish history and war heroes, yet he always seemed to come back to grand opera and was proud to recall the famous singers he had brought to Dublin. He spoke about Verdi as though he knew him and it was easy to see he was by far his favourite composer.'

'Bill wasn't getting any younger,' recalled Donnie Potter, 'so we agreed among ourselves in the management committee that it was time to have a bust done of him and in this respect we had the support of the patrons and the Ladies' Committee. The idea was to have it unveiled during the 1977 spring season in the Gaiety where it would be displayed as a tribute to his thirty-six years as chairman of our society.'

Máire Hogan says her father was very proud of the society's thoughtful gesture and liked the bust very much. 'We all agreed in the family that it bore a true likeness to him and I remember we complimented Gary Trimble. I've now the original bronze bust in my home and the plaster cast one is in the Gaiety.'

Despite his advancing years, Colonel O'Kelly showed no visible signs of slowing down. Donnie Potter still accompanied him to Italy and elsewhere to audition singers, and to Paddy Brennan and other chorus members he was proud to occupy his 'throne' in the Gaiety wings observing every curtain rise or fall, his ears sharply attuned also to singers in case of a wrong note or uncertain entrance. 'He was alert as ever,' said Aileen Walsh, the long-serving joint treasurer. 'Bill hardly ever missed a management committee meeting and was in control as always.'

Earlier, he had asked Dario Micheli to direct a revival of Verdi's *Falstaff* and was delighted as everyone else when it was an unqualified success. Patrick Murray, who designed the set, remembers that Colonel beamed when he saw how good Attilio D'Orazi was in the title role. He felt like everyone else that it was one of the best things the baritone had done for the society. Dario Micheli told me that D'Orazi was as convincing a fat knight as he had seen anywhere. 'We had fun working it out in production. Attilio is a very good singing-actor and he was easy to direct.' The critics thought likewise and described the production as 'delicious'. Dario Micheli's direction was lauded for its 'aptness' while Patrick Murray, who told me he enjoyed working with the director, must have been pleased by the critics' views of his sets. One picked out his 'lovely fantasy for Windsor Forest', describing it as 'visually striking'.

Inevitably every season produced a big talking point and that spring season of `77 was no exception. In fact the 'talk' began in rehearsal as chorus members listened to a new voice - that of baritone Antonio Salvadori - singing the stirring arias from *Nabucco*. He was twenty-six and formerly a glass blower from Venice. Paddy Brennan was instantly impressed, as were Barry Hodkinson, the Carneys, Tom and John, and Seán Kelly. They agreed that it was a big, vibrant and expressive voice that appeared ideally suited to Verdi's music. 'It was a meaty sound,' said Paddy Brennan, 'and Salvadori was in the best traditions of the other outstanding baritones who had sung Verdi roles for us. His voice would further develop, of course, but even then his vocal technique was sound and he coped well with Nabucco's music.' We agreed among ourselves that the Colonel had discovered another prize singer.'

The critics would also agree, although at least one felt that the young baritone, for all his power and impressive range, needed more musical colour and deeper characterisation. The Gaiety audiences found him exciting but he was singing a role that Piero Cappuccilli would not attempt until well into his thirties. One of the joys of that season's *Nabucco* was undoubtedly Aurio

Tomicich's commanding High Priest; his voice had darkened appreciably and coloured and he was in the words of Dario Micheli, showing tremendous promise as an all-round artist.

No one could accuse the society of neglecting any Irish singer worth hearing in opera. Bernadette Greevy was given the role of Charlotte in Werther alongside the experienced tenor Jon Piso, who was then attached to Munich Opera. The critics expressed reservations about the production and suggested the opera needed sharper direction and perhaps more rehearsal time. While Piso dominated proceedings as Werther, singing with style and assurance, it was felt that Ms Greevy's lovely singing did not make up for her lack of emotional depth and this was most apparent during Werther's death scene. Albert Rosen and the RTÉ Symphony Orchestra did, however, emerge from a disappointing first night with honour.

It was a very different story in the case of Wagner's *Tannhauser* in November `77, for it was unanimously voted a brilliant success. Strangely, it hadn't been staged by the DGOS for twenty-five years but now with Ken Neate available to direct the revival there was an air of confidence in the camp. 'I think this is correct,' recalled Tom Carney who always welcomed an opportunity to sing the composer's majestic music. And Patrick Murray was being entrusted with designing both the sets and the costumes, including those for members of Joan Denise Moriarty's Irish Ballet Company, collaborating for the first time with the society. Having tasted the unique Wagnerian atmosphere of Bayreuth Festival, Murray was enthusiastic about his music and regarded *Tannhauser* as a noble work and an obvious challenge for a designer. He decided to use a cyclorama all round the stage and in front of that gold hessian, hand-painted - again the full way round - and he encased it in gold and when lit from behind became like a starry sky. It would enhance the effect of the glorious aria, 'O Star of Eve.'

Except for what he says was 'a stand-up row' on opening night, Murray could look back with pride on the production. The problem arose over the big pilgrims' cross placed downstage (left), which to his dismay had been changed and at the interval he demanded to know who changed its position. As his anger grew, both Colonel O'Kelly and Donnie Potter looked on. The answer he got from a stagehand was that the pantomime was coming in and they wanted a line for a border for *Red Riding Hood*.

'Until hell freezes over I'm not leaving this stage until that cross is put back where it's supposed to be,' Murray declared. O'Kelly said, 'The boy is right.' I explained the cross was lit that way. But this could happen occasionally in the Gaiety, with someone saying, "Jaysus, who cares whether it's moved back or forward." It did matter as in this case the singers were placed around the cross so if you moved it the lighting is out of focus.'

He tended to be amused by a critic's comment that 'one can only hope that the more staid opera-goers will not be shocked at the seductiveness of the choreography by Joan Denise Moriarty or at least the costumes designed for the dancers by Patrick Murray...' He says today he didn't get a single letter one way or the other so assumed that opera-goers were mature enough to appreciate good dancing and appropriate costumes. He was especially pleased for Joan Denise's success and glad to share his own with her. She had always held that a ballet company must be of service to opera as well as ballet, and if need's be, pantomime. She didn't recognise any boundaries in dance and made her views known. 'I admired Joan for that,' says Murray, 'and I fully agreed with her.'

Apart from what was described as 'a moderate production of *The Barber of Seville,* the season was an enjoyable one with the tiny American soprano Sharon Bennett surprising everyone with her stunning mad scene in *Lucia di Lammermoor.* 'She was a classic canary,' quipped one female chorus member, while a male colleague remarked, 'She was a comet who appeared out of nowhere to thrill us all and disappeared again without trace.' Dario Micheli, who directed, told me the soprano had a silvery coloratura and flexible voice and, despite her size, could command the stage. He would remember her Lucia.

Ugo Benelli had by now thrilled Gaiety audiences as Nemorino, Ernesto and Almaviva *(Barber of Seville)* and was looking forward to singing the role of Tonio in Donizetti's *The Daughter of the Regiment* in the spring season of `78. He had already sung it with success at La Scala where, he told me, he brought his parents along to hear him on the opening night. 'Lots of high Cs,' he joked in his typical way, 'but Ugo can manage them.' He loved the part and had sung it also with Mirella Freni in her home town of Modena in Italy. Unfortunately, it was soon evident to him as he rehearsed in Dublin that the opera was being under-directed and the soprano singing Maria was unsure of her lines. He admitted that if he had not known his own part already he would have been confused. 'I felt sad because this had not happened to me before in Dublin. I like rehearsals to be enjoyable.'

Ruth Maher, who was playing the Marchesa, says there were underlying tensions in rehearsals because the soprano playing the daughter of the regiment was either unwell or wasn't familiar enough with her part. At times it could be embarrassing and it didn't seem the production was coming together. 'I'm afraid these tensions were manifested on the opening night, for after Ugo Benelli sang his act one duet with Maria he came off the stage in a rage and banged his clinched fist off a wall and might have injured himself. This, I knew, was out of character for him and I put it down to his frustration. It was such a pity really for as an opera it's truly delightful and very popular abroad. I can say though that Ugo Benelli sang superbly and probably saved the show from being a disaster.'

Paddy Brennan, a chorus member on the occasion, recalls that the production bordered on the disastrous, partly because the company was being over-extended and there was even uncertainty in the chorus. 'I do remember the prompter was kept very busy and although Maria Clausova sang well as the daughter she did not seem to know the role well enough so was dramatically weak. I was left with the impression that Ugo Benelli dragged us through the performance.'

When I discussed the production with the tenor and reminded him that at least one critic suggested he over-acted as Tonio, he replied that he probably had but only because the opera was under-directed, so he tried to supply some extra business of his own. 'I was disappointed as Bill O'Kelly had agreed to put it on for me. For myself, I was satisfied with my singing but I wanted the opera to be a success for everybody else in the cast.'

The critics had a field day and the heading over Mary MacGoris' piece in the *Irish Independent* echoed the general reaction: 'THIS REGIMENT MARCHES INTO TROUBLE.' When the opera was presented during the week's season at the Opera House, Cork, the *Examiner* critic Geraldine Neeson, commented, 'An easy work to stage, I would have thought but the production last night was untidy with many late entrances, clumsy grouping and on one important occasion, the Marquise Birkenfeld had to burrow her way through the members of the chorus to reach her position.'

The Daughter of the Regiment apart, there were some memorable performances during that `78 spring season, among them Antonio Salvadori's Don Carlo in the revival of Verdi's *Ernani* and his singing as the hunchbacked jester in *Rigoletto*. His voice appeared more shaded and coloured than the year before and he invested his singing with telling conviction. He may have lacked the subtlety of a Silveri or Cappuccilli in these parts but he was still only twenty-seven and able to rouse an audience. Terry Reid was busy adding to her growing repertoire and her Gilda was sung with feeling and in fuller voice than before and her "Caro nome" was loudly applauded.

It was turning out to be another remarkable season for Aurio Tomicich, undeniably one of the most popular of the visiting artists. Although he was a towering in *Ernani,* it was not the role that really afforded him the most satisfaction that season; it was in fact Mustafa in Rossini's comedy *The Italian in Algiers* which was now being directed and designed by Dario Micheli. Discussing the production in Rome with Tomicich, he chuckled as he recalled the fun he had in rehearsal. 'Dario was great to work with; he was never pushy. He would always discuss with you your role and let you do what you instinctively felt. If something was wrong he would point it out to you and show you what to do. In that way he was helpful and inventive.'

Like Micheli, he expressed unstinted admiration for the young German mezzo Helga Muller who as the 'Italian Girl' charmed everyone by her acting and singing. 'Helga was a joy to direct,' said Micheli, 'a coming star, a born artist.' Ruth Maher, who sang Zulma, described the opera as a champagne comedy with a fine sparkle, while Peter McBrian thought it was a delicious soufflé.

Around this time the society had been given the temporary use by Guinness Brewery of a large old empty hop store in an adjacent building, and it was here that Micheli set up his workshops. Working long hours, often in splendid isolation, he recycled old scenery and flats and repainted them. Sometimes he had a helper or two with him if he was dealing with perhaps three major productions at a time. Paddy Brennan, as well as others, was intrigued by his ingenuity and methods. 'I had wonderful times watching him at work. The man's ability to take a huge canvas and put perspectives on it was remarkable. Dario was an all rounder and very gifted as designer, director and set builder.'

The Irish interest in the revival of *Don Carlo* centred on Bernadette Greevy's singing of the role of Princess Eboli and Patrick Murray's set designs. As it turned out, both artists emerged successfully from what was described as 'a compelling production.' I can still vividly remember the prolonged applause that greeted Ms Greevy's great aria, 'O don fatale' in act four, and her regal appearance was quite striking. However, it was soprano Lorenza Canepa, as Queen Elizabeth, who scored the biggest personal triumph with her eloquent singing and convincing acting. Patrick Murray counts the production as one of his most rewarding experiences, although one evening newspaper reviewer referred to the 'economy sets' which prompted me to ask the designer later on if he was limited in his designs for the society because of the small budgets at his disposal.

'Money was never a question in my designing for the DGOS,' he said, 'because one knew how much one could spend. Instead of showing a whole sumptuous garden, for instance, you showed the section that was necessary to display. I subscribe to the view that if the set stars, no one stars. You've got to give the singers scope for they are after all singing the opera and you must also be truthful and respectful to the composer.'

Colonel O'Kelly made no secret of his admiration for Murray's designs and at this time regularly engaged him for the society. And the two men remained on friendly terms, with the designer able to say, 'He was a man of his word.' Earlier in the year, the DGOS chairman was the recipient of an honorary degree of Doctor of Law by University College, Dublin and in the course of his address Professor Maurice Kennedy stated, 'His colleagues can think of Colonel O'Kelly in so many ways - on the stage in the chorus of Trovatore; in the foyer of the theatre greeting the high and the low; off-stage through the microphone announcing that an artist was ill but that an alternative one had been flown in from Rome or Munich; at the society's AGM bellicosely defending his views; in the opera houses of Europe negotiating for artists. What baritone - and he is a fine one - could more truthfully sing "Largo al factotum"?'

It was noticeable at the conferring ceremony, though, that the legendary Colonel looked drawn and had lost weight. 'Bill didn't appear well that day,' recalls Aileen Walsh. 'I think we were worried about him. But he was very proud of the honour conferred on him and that helped to cheer him up.'

Nineteen seventy-nine, meanwhile, began badly, not only for the society but for the rest of the country. For the postal strike, which started in February, stretched into the spring season and while it was possible to hand deliver most of the priority information to their patrons and guarantors, the strike and the subsequent bus dispute would it was feared have an effect on the box-office. Four operas were scheduled for the season, including Rossini's *La Cenerentola* which was being directed by Dario Micheli - he was also directing Verdi's *Macbeth*. While both productions were acclaimed by the critics they found apathetic response at the box-office and the industrial disputes were not entirely to blame. Helga Muller-Molinari enchanted audiences as Angelina in *Cenerentola* and got wholehearted support from Aurio Tomicich (the Baron) Ruth Maher and Ernesto Palacio, as the prince, displayed a true lyric tenor voice of lovely quality.

DGOS members, including Donnie Potter, Paddy Brennan and Jack Doyle liked to recall the *Macbeth* of that season as tremendously exciting, mainly because of the performances by Antonio Salvadori and Lorenza Canepa as the key protagonists in the dark and bloody plot.

Both were stated to be in magnificent voice, with Mary MacGoris *(Independent)* adding, 'Miss Canepa's voice could, and did, express venom, urgency, scorn, tension and finally despair, all without losing its beauty of tone and she moved and acted with graceful purpose.' Charles Acton *(Irish Times)* added the names of Maestro Annovazzi and Dario Micheli, saying they shared with the cast in the success of the production. In conversation, Micheli praised the work done by chorus master John Brady. 'I remember they sang extremely well because they were well prepared. This was true also of the women singing the Witches.' Aurio Tomicich (Banquo) agreed, adding that it was one of the best Verdi productions he had sung in and thought that Maestro Annovazzi contributed a huge part.

Jack Doyle had joined the chorus two years before and on his own admission was enjoying himself. A banker by day, he says he learned a great deal from chorus master John Brady. 'It was marvellous to be singing in a big opera like *Macbeth* and in actual fact we all thought we were principals. You gave it all and singing on the same stage as Salvadori - the best singer I'd heard - was both a joy and an honour. I remember his big baritone voice boomed out and you wondered at its power and resonance. I thought his performance the previous year in *Ernani* was every bit as exciting.'

Tosca was a major talking point, not only because of the excellent cast - Canepa as Floria Tosca, Attilio D'Orazi as Scarpia and the impressive Ernesto Veronelli (Cavaradossi) - but because Patrick Murray's vivid sets caught the eye, particularly his real Roman church in act one, San' Andrea della Valle with the alter on stage (right), the grille with the life-size holy statues and all done in black and grey marble. Scarpia's room at the Farnese Palace depicted the more sinister aspect and his idea throughout was to contrast the good with the evil in the opera. When it was staged that season at the Opera House, Cork, board chairman Harold Johnson, as well as the local critics, found the production riveting. 'I've no hesitation in saying,' recalls Johnson, 'that Lorenza Canepa's Tosca was one of the finest seen in Cork and anyone who heard her "Vissi d'arte" will not easily forget it. And she was also a first-class dramatic actress and her act two confrontation with Scarpia (D'Orazi in this case) still lives in my memory.'

As winter approached it was apparent that Colonel O'Kelly's strength was waning and there were occasions when he no longer occupied his 'throne' in the Gaiety stage wings. However, since he had always appeared indestructible the society's members believed he would soon get well again, but his close friends like Donnie Potter, Monica Condron and Aileen Walsh were less optimistic. 'Let's say we hoped and prayed, even up to the last time he went into hospital, that he would pull through,' says Aileen Walsh. 'We knew how resilient he was and of his great heart.'

For three years Colonel O'Kelly had tried to get Luciano Pavarotti to give a concert for the society in Dublin and had at last succeeded and it was scheduled to take place in the following month, December. 'Bill always wanted to have Pavarotti for a concert,' recalls Monica Condron, 'mostly to make money for the society, but Luciano kept putting it off. When Bill was in hospital in autumn of `79, I told him I was going to Covent Garden to see the tenor in *La Bohème* and he suggested I go around and see him.

Eventually I contacted his agent and we finally agreed on a date for the conert. It was sold out in no time at all. But Bill saw an opportunity for a second concert and we wrote to Luciano suggesting that since he was coming to Dublin, and in view of the immense interest his visit was arousing, perhaps he might consider a second concert around the same time. Incredibly, he said "yes". I think he felt he owed the society a debt of gratitude for engaging him in the early sixties when he was beginning his career. Ever since then Bill and he had remained very good friends. It was a wonderful coup for us and we stood to make badly needed revenue.'

Unfortunately, Colonel O'Kelly died on November 7, some weeks before the opening concert. 'It was the last thing we hoped would happen,' Monica Condron said, 'for everybody in the society wanted Bill to be there to greet his friend Luciano with a curtain speech. We were all left shattered.' His death came on the night of the third performance of *The Tales of Hoffmann*. Chorus members told me the atmosphere of the first night was unreal in the Gaiety. Before the rise of curtain, the Prelude to the final act of *Traviata* was played by the RTÉ Symphony Orchestra under Maestro Annovazzi. Donnie Potter said it was one of the most moving moments he had experienced in an opera house. To Paddy Brennan, it was even more touching later at the Requiem Mass in a packed Dublin church. 'We attempted to sing some of Bill's favourite music, like "Va, pensiero" and it wasn't easy at all. All of us were choked with emotion. To John and Tom Carney and other chorus members it evoked a strange feeling, as though they were singing the great chorus in the Gaiety with Bill as the only member of the audience.'

Bill's death was traumatic,' Monica Condron said, 'and left us all a bit dazed and wondering where to turn next.' Donnie Potter had travelled back and forth to the Continent with the DGOS chairman and remembered once in the seventies when he collapsed with a diabetic attack in Vienna and was confined for a few days in a clinic. It had been, he says, recommended by the Intendant of the Vienna State Opera which was an indication of the esteem in which Bill was held. Aileen Walsh, the society's joint treasurer, had been in close touch with Colonel O'Kelly during his illness and recalled that he remained alert and talked about problems affecting the society. 'I felt somehow he might make it for the first night of Pavarotti's concert as he didn't give up easily.'

The O'Kelly family were still very much part of the society. Máire Hogan, Bill's daughter, was an active member of the Ladies' Committee, while Seán and Liam, his sons, were chorus members. To Seán Kelly, his father would always remain 'Mr Opera' and he and the family were very proud of his long involvement with the DGOS. 'My father held the society together in all kinds of weather and, in the final analysis, that was his greatest achievement.'

To Florrie Draper the Colonel's passing was like losing a dear friend, while Dympna Carney, another staunch chorus member, said Bill O'Kelly was part of their big operatic family and would be an incalculable loss. Maureen Lemass had served on the Patrons' Committee as well as the management committee, and found it almost impossible to imagine the DGOS without its father-figure. The first question that came to Paddy Brennan's mind on hearing from Monica Condron of his passing was how the society was going to cope without his guiding hand. 'We had seen Bill's highs and lows and had admired what he had done for opera and the chorus. I had no idea now what the future held for the society.'

Many tributes, both national and international, were paid to him. 'Bill O'Kelly lived to see the society he had founded in difficult days become a thriving force in the cultural life of the community,' commented Professor Anthony Hughes, the society's president. 'Bill O'Kelly was an extraordinary man with a solid military background which was so important for establishing our opera society against massive financial odds and general apathy,' stated Prince Caracciolo. 'But he conquered them all. And in Bill's dictionary the word "impossible" could not be found.' To Gerard Victory, RTÉ's head of music, he was the primary embodiment of opera in Ireland for over thirty years. His enthusiasm and energy were unbounded and his ability to surmount the formidable problems of opera production won universal admiration. 'We will all miss Colonel O'Kelly greatly,' said Joan Denise Moriarty, 'but I feel with his quiet smile he will be watching over us all.' To designer Patrick Murray, he was an unforgettable character, and for the DGOS he always strove for the best. 'I shall always remember the "throne" in the wings from which he watched every performance and equally his regular greeting to me which I now return, "Ah farewell, me ould segotia."'

The tickets meanwhile for Pavarotti's two concerts on December 18 and 20 had been quickly snapped up. It was one of those fabulous nights in the Gaiety Theatre with an unmistakable buzz around the auditorium and the dress circle. What the audience did not know on the occasion however was that the tenor was suffering from a cold, but he was adamant the show must go on. And before he sang, he paid his own tribute to Colonel O'Kelly, describing him as his friend, the man who had opened doors for him in the operatic world and how he would be forever grateful to him. He was delighted, he told the audience, to be able to sing in his memory and for the society he helped to establish.

To Paddy Brennan, the great tenor sang on technique because of his cold. 'It was sheer professionalism and I imagine quite a few people in the packed house hardly noticed the difference. He displayed no temperament except a smile and a white handkerchief and his personality was warmth personified. It was the kind of evening that Bill O'Kelly would have cherished. The Gaiety itself was freezing but Luciano never complained. The management, I remember, promised next day to ensure the theatre was heated for his second concert.'

For the DGOS, the decade had ended with a feeling of both joy and sorrow. Looking back, chorus member Caroline Phelan summed up: 'When Bill O'Kelly died he had achieved all that he could for the society and changes were needed. Notwithstanding, he was quite unique in both his vision and the implementation of that vision. One of his most endearing qualities was that he always gave credit where credit was due, and was fully aware of the importance of the contributions of those around him to the realisation of his own dream. He was far from perfect, but suffice to say that in the context of a biographical analysis it must be pointed out to the citizens of Dublin and the country generally that Bill founded an opera company that has survived to this day. When we remember that it had to cope with the war and the financial constraints this is no mean achievement.

'And despite the seriousness of the job in hand, humour was always present and Bill possessed a great sense of fun. Being the lovable old rogue that he was, he was fond of protesting his passion for anonymity and preference for being with the "troops" backstage but at the same time delighted in bringing his heavily minked prima donnas into the dress circle bar after the performance to meet patrons and public alike. He was unique.'

Chairmanship Contested

Filling the chair vacated by Colonel O'Kelly was not going to be the formality many members of the society had expected in January 1980. It was thought that Donnie Potter, who had been the acting chairman since his death, would be elected unopposed at the spring AGM, but soon however popular Prince (Freddie) Caracciolo let it be known that he was a candidate and at the age of sixty-nine did not consider himself too old. Both men were long and devoted servants of the society and well capable of following in the Colonel's footsteps, even if they lacked his powerful personal drive and expansive personality.

Potter became a patron in 1954 and by 1962 was serving on the management committee and a year later made his first trip to the Continent with Colonel O'Kelly to audition and contract artists for Dublin. Apart from his opera commitments, he was a businessman, vice-chairman of the Mountjoy Prison Visiting Committee, and an keen golfer and swimmer. Since the mid-seventies he and his wife Moyra - she was also prominent in the Ladies' Committee - had been organising special opera trips to European and North American capitals and these had become deservedly popular with DGOS members.

Freddie Caracciolo, as he was known to his friends, was associated with the society since the late forties and helped to swing the Italian government subvention that opened the doors for the appearance in Dublin of singers such as Silveri, Gobbi, Stignani, Zeani, Protti and others. Over the years he served on the patrons' committee as well as the management committee and edited the society's brochure for fifteen years. Behind his charm and amiability though, he was a tough and successful businessman, and a member of the Irish Georgian Society and An Taisce. The election of either candidate ensured continuity insofar as both were totally committed to the ideals of the society and its future well-being. It promised to be a bonny fight.

'We were expecting a close contest,' recalls Aileen Walsh, 'and both men I knew were eager for victory. Donnie Potter had the edge on age and the experience of working more closely with Bill O'Kelly.' In the weeks leading up to the AGM there had been, according to chorus members, friendly banter and some mudslinging between both camps. To some, Caracciolo was the better qualified candidate artistically while the Potter camp believed their man's influence in political circles, especially Fianna Fáil, was an extremely useful asset to the society in times of financial crisis - and had been so in the past. He was also the society's representative on the Arts Council.

The AGM took place in the Central Hotel, Exchequer Street, and attracted an over-flow attendance of the society's patrons and performing members. Aileen Walsh recalls that as their president Tony Hughes took his seat to preside over the meeting, there was a definite air of expectancy. 'I can still remember people saying there would be only a few votes between them. I felt that Donnie Potter would win the contest and so did others.'

Her prediction was proved correct, though the voting was close and exciting. Afterwards, there were cordial exchanges and Potter was applauded as he was declared the society's new chairman and, of course, successor to Colonel Bill O'Kelly. He was very much his own man and determined to do it his way, which meant strenghtening the existing structures and to continue to press the Arts Council for more money. Before long, Mary Sheridan found him easier to deal with than Bill O'Kelly with regard to fees. 'It could be a hassle with Bill,' she said, 'but Donnie gave me what I asked for. I think that Irish singers benefited under his chairmanship and fees rose.'

One of the first things he did was to set up within the management committee a number of small sub-committees to help ease the burden of some and to allow others to find their feet in a particular field. He pledged also to continue with the William O'Kelly Memorial Concerts and in this respect had been fortunate, he said, to engage the outstanding Spanish tenor José Carreras and his recital was scheduled for September 29 at the RDS. It was plain that things would not change radically under Potter's chairmanship and anyway most of the members, including the chorus, wanted it to remain that way.

Musically, the 1980 spring season soon ran into trouble. On the first night of *Trovatore* Ernesto Veronelli (Manrico) lost his voice, having succumbed to an attack of laryngitis. It was too late to find a replacement so the tenor was prevailed upon to continue, which he bravely agreed to do. Monica Condron recalls that this naturally proved a strain on himself and his colleagues. For the remaining performances two replacement tenors, Tom Swift and Derek Blackwell, alternated in the role of Manrico singing in English. Veronelli was back to his best later to sing Enzo in *La Gioconda*; in fact during the company's visit to the Opera House Cork he also sang Manrico to great acclaim.

Bernadette Greevy sang Laura in Dario Micheli's production of *Gioconda* and Patrick Murray did the sets which were described as 'both evocative and spectacular'. According to Mary MacGoris (*Irish Independent*) it was an absorbing first night with the Irish Ballet Company performing beautifully in the 'Dance of the Hours' and the opera principals, notably soprano Lorenza Canepa in the title role and Antonio Salvadori (Barnaba) first-rate. In her view, Bernadette Greevy's voice was 'strong and splendid' as Laura while Ruth Maher, as the blind woman, conveyed the part beautifully.

If there is a role that should suit Ms Greevy to perfection, it is I believe that of *Orfeo in Gluck's Orfeo ed Euridice*. It is written for a contralto voice of depth and rich quality, so her success came as no surprise. Patrick Murray, who designed the costumes, agreed. 'Bernadette loved working with dancers and since she's graceful herself her scenes with them were visually striking. I can still see her being gracefully led around by the company's leading dancer Anna Donovan. I designed a full-length costume in grey and black for Bernadette as a contrast to the white of the blessed spirits. Seán Burke's lighting did the rest.'

Paddy Ryan, meanwhile, was directing a revival of *Madama Butterfly* and told me he saw Puccini's opera as an intensely personal drama. 'I regarded it also as intensely emotional music and we had I believe a very fine cast. As Butterfly, the Japanese soprano Yoko Watanabe was stunning to look at and blessed with a lovely voice. I remember that she worked so hard in rehearsal that she cried if anything went wrong. I counted her right for the part in every way. Ironically, she was in love with the Italian tenor Renato Grimaldi who in this production was the Pinkerton who would leave her for someone else.'

Looking back, he says that this was the best production he staged for the society, for both musically and dramatically everything in his opinion worked. He recalled that in the final moments Colman Pearce and the orchestra held the last chord of the music until Butterfly dies in Pinkerton's arms. 'I feel that her performance was unforgettable and I find that people still come up to me and recall her portrayal. For one thing, she brought out all the heart-breaking longing and final despair as I had not before experienced it. Incidentally, I didn't suspect that Yoko and Renato were off-stage lovers - I thought she was in love with me!'

Inevitably their romance was taken up by the media, first though by journalist Sheila Walsh whose engagement column in the *Irish Press* was widley read. She told me she had got 'a hint of it' from a DGOS chorus member and it turned out to be one of her best stories of the year and in the paper was accompanied by a striking photograph of the young lovers. To Donegal-born Sheila, everyone loved to read about romance and she worked hard to meet the demand. It seemed that Yoko Watanabe and Renato

Grimaldi had met four years before in a singing competition in Tokyo where they shared the top prize. Since he spoke no Japanese and she no Italian, they went their separate ways, only to meet a few years later at La Scala Opera Studio where their love began to blossom. To Sheila Walsh it was the classic showbusiness romance.

By now Ruth Maher had made the part of Suzuki *(Madama Butterfly)* her own and in the outstanding production of that season had gained more kudos for her performance. 'I was in total sympathy with the part and in Yoko Watanabe I realised we had an exceptionally talented Cio-Cio-San.' Fanny Feehan *(Evening Herald)* commented, 'Ruth Maher has played many Suzukis to different and indifferent Butterfly's, but here she excelled; in fact, all the small parts were well cast, Seán Mitten as The Bonze and Prince Yamadori and Brendan Cavanagh as Goro.'

The winter season was notable for an enjoyable *Fidelio* and what was described as a 'moderate *Faust'*. Irish singers figured prominently, with bass-baritone John O'Flynn a sturdy Valentine and Colette McGahon being praised for her Siebel. It was left to Ken Neate's skilful production of Beethoven's *Fidelio* to redeem the season and here again Irish artists such as Paddy Ring (Jaquino), Peter McBrien (Fernando) and Ann Moran (Marzelline) did extremely well. Ring felt that at this point the society was under pressure from the Arts Council to engage more Irish and although the fees still remained small there was an improvement.

With veteran stage manager Pat McClellan 'threatening' to retire, the society reckoned it was time to look around for an assistant to Pat, who had given such herculean service over the years. Josephine Scanlon was their choice and with her operatic background she was well qualified. She was married to well-known Cork-born actor and entertainer Chris Curran and had taken leading roles in grand opera, including Violetta *(Traviata)* and Leonora *(Trovatore)*.

After a few months as assistant to Pat McClellan she had to admit it was demanding work. 'I was mainly in charge of supplying stage properties and I quickly came to know every antique shop in Dublin. I even took materials out of my own house for props as well as cajoling friends to lend me some. I was amused sometimes when visiting artists thought I was the society's treasurer and asked me to get them accommodation or help them to buy jewellery. My job was really to supply the opera director with all the props he required and in this respect I got excellent advice from Pat McClellan. He had a habit of saying, "We must work 'til we drop, Jo." I don't think the critics were aware of the problems that existed backstage, for it was sometimes touch and go whether productions actually went on on time.'

When Monica Condron (hon. sec.) sat down to write her report for that year of 1980, it was not surprising that she should open it with a reference to the late Colonel O'Kelly. She stated that the year in a sense had been a trial period for the society and that during his thirty-eight years as chairman he had built a fortress to withstand almost all onslaughts. Following his death, the society seemed to be, as it were, holding its breath and waiting under its new management. 'Now that waiting is over,' she added, 'and it can breathe again. Very little has changed. There is, of course, a new chairman, who with the co-operation of the members is carrying on the traditions already set. No two people can work or think alike but as long as their aims are the same then the continuation and success of the society is assured and we need have no fears for the future.'

Ms Condron's was an interesting report and clearly hinted that in the years ahead there would perhaps be 'onslaughts' on the society's policies, artistic and otherwise. How long more it could remain a 'fortress' was a moot point. There was, it could be surmised from the report, no immediate need for apprehension.

Meanwhile, the passing of Dr Colm McDonnell, husband of Margaret McDonnell, who remained the driving force behind the Ladies' Committee and its fund-raising efforts, was genuinely mourned by DGOS members. The McDonnells had always been a very united couple and Colm had supported his wife in all of her activities for the DGOS, going so far on numerous occasions to host events in their home and grounds in order to raise money. As Margaret was to tell me once, 'Colm like myself, knew the society badly needed funds and whenever I sought his support it was always forthcoming. Going to the opera gave him a lot of enjoyment and we always made a social night out of it - he had good friends.'

Carmel McHale, Máire Hogan, Moyra Potter and others in the Ladies' Committee felt that Margaret could not have achieved so much for the society without Colm's support and encouragement. 'He was always there in the background helping her,' added Carmel McHale, who remembered some outstanding fund-raising functions at the McDonnell home.

Dario Micheli was back in Dublin in March 1981 to direct Verdi's *Otello* as well as *A Masked Ball*. He was to be found most days at his workshops in Guinness, close to the brewery, recycling scenery, painting it and building sets. Sometimes chorus members dropped in to watch him at work but he told me that he never minded working in isolation. 'I do my best work in quiet surroundings,' he mused. His scenery for *La Bohème*, the first production of that spring season, was highly praised by the critics, and the principals, Maria Clausova as Mimi and Michele Molese (Rodolfo), were regarded as ideal casting. Patrick Murray teamed up with the director for

Otello, with Murray designing the sets. 'Dario never interfered with my designs,' he said. 'Usually I gave them to him in advance and he always seemed to get the best out of them. You had to go to him with your work prepared, otherwise we could not work as a team.'

Pat O'Kelly commented in the *Evening Press*: 'Visually, this *Otello* looks well. Patrick Murray's sets show how economy need not be distasteful, and Dario Micheli's direction moves capably.' To the director, *Otello* was one of Verdi's greatest operas and he welcomed the opportunity of staging it. There were mixed feelings about Gilbert Py's portrayal of the moor, as was the case also with Gian Koral's Iago, leaving Maria Luisa Garbato to emerge as the star as Desdemona.

Micheli's direction of *A Masked Ball* was acclaimed and there was general satisfaction with the cast, notably tenor Ernesto Veronelli who sang convincingly as Riccardo and the Uruguaian baritone Juan Carlos Gebelin made a great impression as Renato. It was proving a good season for Irish artists, including Ann Moran, Peter McBrien and baritone Frank O'Brien, who had first sung with the society in the late seventies and his well-focused voice marked him out as a singer to note. He told me he was intrigued by Italian baritone Attilio D'Orazi and considered him a wonderful make-up artist. 'I remember he used to arrive in the theatre early to begin preparing himself and getting his make-up right. He also paid a lot of attention to the wig he was wearing. I once met him in the corridor before he went on stage as Scarpia and didn't recognise him. And he also spoke good English which was rare enough in case of Italians.'

O'Brien says he was delighted to be learning his operatic craft from artists like D'Orazi, Maestro Annovazzi and Dario Micheli. 'Working with Dario made me feel confident and secure. I thought he was an inventive director and he was an excellent communicator as regards giving directions. And as he told you in what position to stand, he'd sing your lines; he was experienced and knew his operas.'

Paddy Ryan welcomed the opportunity to direct *Lucia di Lammermoor* which he regarded as a very dramatic work with the mad scene as the highpoint. He was fortunate in his Lucia, for not only was Carla Basto a beautiful woman but could sing like an angel. However, she would not rehearse in full voice, with the result that conductor Eugenio Marco was fit to throw his baton at her. 'I can't work with her,' he screamed on one occasion, but she had her way. In Bill O'Kelly's time she would be singing full out at dress rehearsals, something he insisted on. What made it seem worse was the fact that the other principals were singing in full voice. Ryan was greatly impressed by baritone Carlo Desideri, who was singing Enrico. 'Listening to his resonant voice and phrasing, I felt he had an outstanding future, which of course he went on to have.'

On the second night the tenor singing Edgardo, Antonio Savastano, caught a virus and collapsed after the finale of act two and was replaced by Michele Molese who at that moment was actually in the green room having a pint of stout. He sang act three and the remaining performances. It confirmed Paddy Ryan's opinion that directing opera was like living on a knife edge and was definitely a risky business. 'I sometimes felt I was living on a high wire with the danger immediately below me.' Although Frank O'Brien found the Italian and Romanian artists very assured they seemed to be always anxious for fear of catching colds. He remembered one particular Italian tenor who arrived at rehearsals croaking and without a voice and he himself went off and got honey and vinegar for him and after taking it he was miraculouly able to sing. 'I remember Maestro Annovazzi was very thankful for what I had done. They recognised genuine friendship.'

Opera in English? To the purists it was no longer either desirable or fashionable, yet in the winter season of `81 Tom Hawkes' production of Rossini's *The Barber of Seville* (designed by Patrick Murray) was, despite being sung in English, a resounding success; indeed, Hawkes thought that comedies like the *Barber* were often better understood in that language, something he had first noted as a director at the English National Opera. He told me later he still enjoyed coming to Dublin although it had become by now an expensive city. Since the death of Colonel Bill O'Kelly he suspected there was much more internal politics in the society and dealing, for instance, with Donnie Potter was not the same as with the Colonel - he could be tricky. And there was incredible rivalry among the chorus members with all sorts of cliques, but apart from that he found them a splendid bunch of men and women dedicated to the cause of opera and prepared to make endless sacrifices.

Dario Micheli directed *Carmen* at short notice and as expected, staged it with his usual aplomb. He both designed and directed Bellini's *Norma* which had an Italo-American soprano, Lynne Strow Piccolo in the title role. The critics differed about the merits of the production though it was generally agreed that Piccolo was very impressive, singing incisively and in true bel canto style. The year, meanwhile, ended on an auspicious note with a recital by soprano Montserrat Caballe in the National Concert Hall. Billed as the William O'Kelly Memorial Recital, it featured Maestro Annovazzi as the piano accompanist; he was a friend of Caballe's since the 1950s when he was artistic director of the Teatro del Liceo in Barcelona. She admitted she learned her first operatic roles with him and was to say later, 'In a year he showed me how to produce a steady stream of tone with no effort, and taught me never to force my voice.'

Not only had Annovazzi persuaded for her to come to Ireland but broke a personal rule so as to accompany her for since devoting himself to operatic conducting, he rarely accompanied soloists. But the soprano insisted and made it a condition of her coming. The recital drew a large and representative audience who listened enthralled to a mixed programme of Italian, German and Spanish songs as well as some arias. Nonetheless, opera buffs came away feeling disappointed, having hoped to hear her in a succession of great arias; yet her profound musicianship and vocal technique left the more fastidious music lovers well satisfied. Annovazzi, for his part, had shown resilience since the death of his close friend Bill O'Kelly and made no secret of his satisfaction at the success of Caballe's visit. Remembering the Colonel figured high among his priorities and he felt that Monserrat Caballe had paid due homage to his memory.

The year was not without its sadness. Maura Mooney, one of the great stalwarts of the society, was bereaved by the death of her husband Gerard, who had been an active member of the society since its foundation. He served both as chorus member and honorary treasurer and he also found time to play small parts. 'The DGOS was part of Gerry's life,' recalled Monica Condron, 'and his familiar figure would be missed. He played the waiter in *Café Momus,* for example, with great aplomb.'

One of the highlights of the spring season of `82 was unquestionably the appearance in concert of Piero Cappuccilli, accompanied by the RTÉ Symphony Orchestra with Proinnsias O Duinn conducting. The society was presenting the famous baritone at the Gaiety Theatre on Saturday, April 17 in order to raise funds and Toyota Ireland helped to defray the costs. Since he had been in Dublin in the sixties Cappuccilli had become a world name, a recording star and the preferred baritone of Herbert von Karajan at the Salzburg Festival. He had a repertoire of fifty operas but it was as a Verdi exponent that he had won fame and fortune. His Dublin concert, however, was orchestrally dominated with the result that once again avid opera-lovers felt cheated. When he did sing the big Verdi arias for which he was renowned, the voice was as steely as ever with a palette of vocal colours.

'Vocally, Piero was in top form,' said Monica Condron, 'and those of us who remembered him in *Rigoletto and Ernani* marvelled once more at his pure legato line and clear vocal projection. We counted ourselves fortunate to get him for Dublin.'

But he was not the only fine Italian baritone to sing in the capital during that spring. The name of Licinio Montefusco would soon be on everyone's lips. He was engaged to sing two important roles - Alfonso, King of Castile, in Donizzetti's *La Favorita* and the title role in Verdi's *Nabucco*. Paddy Brennan remembers collecting Montefusco at the airport and driving him to his hotel and then to the Gaiety, where the RTÉ Symphony Orchestra, under Maestro Annovazzi, was rehearsing *La Favorita*. To Brennan's surprise the baritone began to sing the act two aria. "Vien, Leonora" while still wearing his overcoat and hat and looking like any businessman. 'I found it a little amusing but Licinio was to prove a great guy, genial and warm-hearted and good company. And he did sing the aria from Favorita magnificently. We were lucky to be getting singers of his calibre and he was also very popular with audiences.'

Bernadette Greevy was to have sung the key role of Leonora, the king's mistress, but had to cancel because of illness. The society was fortunate to be able to call on Kumiko Yoshii and she sang most beautifully. Tom Hawkes, who directed, recalls that it was a formidable and well-balanced cast and he greatly enjoyed directing the opera.

That season's *Tosca* will be remembered not only for Attilio D'Orazi's powerfully sung and acted Scarpia but for the brief appearance in act one of the white-bearded Noel Purcell as the Cardinal, but only after they'd found a gold cape long enough to fit his gangling frame. In 1963, he had played the same role in the *Tosca* starring tenor Giuseppe di Stefano and his return came as a surprise to himself and to the audience. Noel was by now in his eighties. 'It's great to be back on the old Gaiety stage again,' he beamed, 'but they've got me just in time. I wouldn't have lasted another second, the bloody legs were going from under me.'

The production was distinguished by Patrick Murray's 'brilliant sets', as one evening newspaper critic described them, while Lorenza Canepa, a first-rate Floria Tosca, sang 'Vissi d'arte' with exquisite feeling and beauty. Dario Micheli's direction came in for favourable comment and was said to be 'thoughtful'. At this time Italian conductor Giovanni Veneri was proving a real acquisition to the society, especially in operas by Puccini and Verdi.

Nabucco, as usual, packed the Gaiety. Licinio Montefusco made a powerful impact as Nabucco and showed he was the natural successor to Gian Giacomo Guelfi in the role. Mary Sheridan, who was singing Fenena, says their voices were different with Guelfi's the more compelling. 'I remember that Montefusco was smaller in stature and less commanding on stage, but his voice projected exceedingly well and he tackled the big Verdi arias fearlessly.'

To Dario Micheli, Montefusco was a Verdi baritone in the true Italian tradition and he thought he built up the character very well. He was surrounded by a fine cast in Lorenza Canepa, as Abigaile, whose act two aria was stunning, and Aurio Tomicich as the High Priest, one of the bass's favourite parts.

A notable feature of the winter season of `82 was the popularity of Verdi's *Il Trovatore,* directed by Dario Micheli and conducted by Albert Rosen. It was effectively cast with soprano Hagint Vartanian displaying a voice of true Verdian quality and tenor Michele Molese a most convincing Manrico, singing his big arias with panache and ringing tones. Aurio Tomicich made the most of Ferrando's dark music and Kumiko Yoshii's interpretation of the gypsy woman Azucena was, according to Mary McGoris *(Irish Independent)* 'well-conceived and well sung.'

It was puzzling though why the society was unprepared to take risks with Verdi's operas. It still had not staged *Luisa Miller, Attila, I due Foscari, I Lombardi or I vespri siciliani* and, in retrospect, this seemed to me at the time a serious omission especially in view of the outstanding Verdi baritones at the society's disposal. Unfortunately the audiences appeared to be calling the tune with the result that no one was prepared to risk a *Foscari or Miller.* It was I believe a wonderful opportunity lost. But DGOS policy-makers of the time will argue that for the most part they could not afford to be risk-takers however much they revered Verdi and his works and that their hands were tied. It seemed a somewhat lame excuse.

The seasonal *Hansel and Gretel,* meanwhile, was another success in that `82 winter season, thanks to Paddy Ryan's inventive direction and Proinnsias O'Duinn's able conducting of the RTÉ Symphony Orchestra. Mary Sheridan was convincing as the mother while in the title roles Jill Washington and Helga Anjervo caught the mood of the piece beautifully. Frank O'Brien was excellent as the father. Pat O'Kelly, in the *Evening Press,* summed up, 'Anyone seeking an escape from the hustle, bustle and anxiety of everyday life should hasten to the Gaiety for a totally magical experience.'

Suzanne's Violetta

DGOS old-timers who vividly remembered May Devitt's English-sung Violetta were, in the winter of 1983, eagerly awaiting Suzanne Murphy's debut in the role in Dublin which she would sing in Italian. She had already achieved a major success in the part with Welsh National Opera, having first joined the company in 1976, and told me after a performance of *Traviata* in the Welsh resort of Llandudno how she hoped one day to sing it in Dublin.

Those Irish opera fans who had yet to hear the Limerick-born soprano sing leading Verdi, Bellini and Mozart heroines with WNO could be forgiven for asking when the DGOS would engage her. The truth was that the society had to wait until she was available for her schedule was an extremely busy one. When it was eventually announced she would sing Violetta, I do remember the news was greeted with genuine enthusiasm.

'It was very exciting having Suzanne for this Verdi part,' recalled Tom Hawkes. 'I had followed her success with the Welsh and knew that her Violetta with them had won critical acclaim in Cardiff and on tour. It was inevitable that the DGOS would ask her to sing it.'

The opera was not long in rehearsal when he was able to say, 'I found Suzanne lovely to work with as she was both painstaking and intelliegent and had this unmistakable aura about her, a glamour and presence that makes some artists stand out from others. Working with her, I began to learn a lot more about *Traviata*.'

'Suzanne came with a reputation, there's no question about that,' reflected Paddy Brennan. 'I think it was at the dress rehearsal that we realised how good this *Traviata* was going to be. She brought to the part pathos, vulnerability and a vocal dynamic that was most convincing. And she was inventive in the way she kicked off her shoes in act one as if to show the carefree side of the character at that moment. In the garden scene with Attilio D'Orazi, I thought their singing and acting was in the very best traditions of the society.'

To Tom Hawkes, the soprano had the courage to look ghastly in the final scene of the opera. 'She had a wig which she had brought from Cardiff with her and which had a lot of grease in it and this gave the impression that her hair was matted with sweat; for a woman dying of consumption it was credible and to me heightened the drama of the death scene.'

Hawkes felt the buzz around the theatre on the first night. 'It was tangible,' he said, 'and I got it right up to the rise of the curtain.' Chorus member Ann Deegan sensed it also and added that everyone wanted Suzanne to do well in her first Violetta in Dublin. I know that for weeks people had been talking about her appearance in the opera and were excited at the prospect of seeing her as Violetta.'

Although Suzanne herself was comfortable in the role and knew it intimately, she agreed that singing it with the DGOS was a very different thing. 'As I made up in my dressing room, I felt nervous on that first night. I didn't want to let down those people who had supported me and in some cases had come to hear me sing in Britain. When, however, they asked me later how I felt, I had to tell them I was too involved to think of anything except Violetta. I'm told some people gave me a standing ovation on the first night but I don't remember. What I heard was a wall of sound coming from the auditorium. In subsequent performances I was better able to appreciate the enthusiasm of audiences. These are moments I'll always cherish.'

According to Tom Carney, Suzanne Murphy's performance certainly came up to expectations and all the tickets were snapped up. 'I remember she got a terrific reception from the fans.' Josephine Scanlon, the assistant stage director, has mixed memories of the occasion. Apart from the hundred and one chores she was required to do, ranging from setting sixty drinking glasses for the big opening party scene, to fetching flower plants for the garden scene in act two, she was horrified to be told earlier that day that stage director Patrick McClellan had suddenly been laid low by flu, which in effect meant she had 'to carry the can for everything.' She was not helped by the fact that during the building of the *Traviata* set most of it collapsed like a house of cards.

'I can still see the wooden pillars split and collapse, leaving the construction crews to start all over again with the nails and hammers. I think they were still lighting the set with fifteen minutes to go to the opening. Naturally tension was high and anyone who inadvertently walked across the stage was at the receiving end of abuse.'

Fanny Feehan, the *Sunday Tribune* critic, enthused about the production, as did most of her newspaper colleagues. 'Suzanne Murphy has a sweet, dark-toned soprano voice which is very agile and with a wide range of expression and is remarkably consistent,' she noted. 'And she has an assured stage manner as one would expect from an actress who has been carefully nurtured over the years by Welsh National Opera.'

Feehan was also impressed by the Alfredo of the young tenor Berardino di Domencio, as well as by D'Orazi's elder Germont, even though the baritone sang "Di Provenza" with an obvious hoarseness on the first night. Monica Condron was playing Annina, servant to Violetta, for more times than she could remember. For Veronica Dunne it was a very special occasion. She had been Suzanne Murphy's first voice tutor and from the beginning was enthusiastic about the voice. 'When Suzanne came to me her voice was small because she had been using a microphone with the vocal group WE 4, but I managed to get her up a few octaves until she sounded like a fully fledged soprano. The beauty was that at any register her voice never lost its sheen.'

It was a proud occasion also for Tony O'Dálaigh, a founder member in 1965 of the Irish National Opera Company. 'I wasn't surprised by the tremendous success of Suzanne's Violetta in Dublin,' he said. 'Ever since she sang in Rossini's *La Cenerentola* and Cimarosa's *Secret Marriage* for INOC I was confident she would be an international star. I remember she had absolute belief in what she was doing and total identification with the role she was playing. Once she said to me, "Tony, I'm going to make it" and I didn't doubt her words for a moment.'

That winter season of `83 would not only be remembered for *Traviata* but also for the sparkling modern dress production of Mozart's *Cosi fan tutte,* directed by Steven Pimlett and conducted by Albert Rosen. It owed a lot to the brilliant teamwork of the cast, headed by Aurio Tomicich whose portrayal of the cynical bachelor Don Alfonso was a gem, as was Terry Reid's frivolous maid Despina, a delightful performance in every way.

Ferrando and Guglielmo, the officers in love with Dorabella and her sister Fiordiligi, re-appear in this production dressed as Arabs to test the fidelity of the two ladies and it is then of course that the fun really begins. The casting of the young Spanish tenor Eduardo Giménez as Ferrando was inspired, both vocally and dramatically. His warm lyric voice with its lustrous sheen and purity of tone was ideal for Mozart's music. I don't think I've ever heard the aria, "Un aura amorosa" more eloquently sung.

Frank O'Brien was thoroughly convincing as Guglielmo and sang and acted above himself. To my surprise, he told me later that the opera was produced by Steven Pimlott within seven days. 'I remember we started on a Monday and the first night was to take place on the following Monday. I was singing Guglielmo for the first time and it was a great experience. Musically, Albert Rosen was inspiring and Tim Reed's costumes helped us a lot as the show was in modern dress. I must say I enjoyed myself.'

According to Norris Davidson, Mary Burgess's performance as Fiordiligi was one of the best he had seen, being both beautifully sung and acted, and he also remembered Kumiko Yoshii as a first-class Mozartian singer. Davidson loved Mozart's music and expressed disappointment that the DGOS had more or less neglected the composer. Albert Rosen shared this view; indeed up to this he had conducted only two Mozart works for the society, *The Marriage of Figaro* in the spring season of 1973 and *Don Giovanni* in 1974. There is no doubt that his ebullient musicality in the modern-dress Cosi fan tutte helped to make it one of the society's most memorable creations.

Earlier, the spring season had been notable for some highly impressive performances by Licinio Montefusco as the jester in *Rigoletto* and Gerard in *Andrea Chénier*, evoking in the Verdi work fond memories of Silveri, Cappuccilli and Protti who in the past had electrified Gaiety audiences. Interestingly, there was a father and daughter partnership in the *Rigoletto*, Bruno and Suzanna Rigacci, he conducting and she singing the part of Gilda.

Monica Condron felt that on the opening night this family link may have caused some tension but it was happily missing in subsequent performances. The very promising young Dublin-born contralto, Patricia Bardon, was singing Maddalena and displayed I remember a rich voice of power and beauty. She went on in that year to win second place in the Cardiff Singer of the World Competition, while the tall Irish mezzo Therese Feighan, who was doubling the roles of the Countess and Madelon in *Chénier*, proceeded to win the Voice of Ireland.

The country was beginning to produce some excellent voices, although there was an inexplicable scarcity of talented tenors. Anna Caleb, for instance, was to make a big impact as Suzuki in *Madama Butterfly*, confirming the reports from Germany of her success there. Maestro Annovazzi continued to show great faith in the creative talents of Dario Micheli who directed both *Chénier and Manon Lescaut* during that season.

'I was enjoying myself in Dublin and stayed in an apartment,' he told me later in Rome. 'I missed Colonel O'Kelly of course but there were still most of my friends around. When Maestro Annovazzi asked me to come to Ireland I tried to make myself available. I like to think we worked well as a team, Napoleone remained my friend and I returned his loyalty.'

Those firm favourites of Irish audiences, Attilio D'Orazi and Maria Luisa Garbato, excelled in *Manon Lescaut;* the former was in his 25th year with the society and his versatility as a singer was a decided asset. He sang Sharpless in *Madama Butterfly* with Micié Akisada in the name part. Paddy Ryan's direction was lauded by the majority of the critics. Irish artists Mary Sheridan, Peter McBrien, Brendan Cavanagh, Frank O'Brien and Seán

Mitten again played prominent parts in that season and by now had become almost indispensible to the society. Strangely, the week in Cork proved disappointing financially with bookings well down on previous years. Monica Condron was to state later, 'It was quite clear that *Rigoletto* could have been staged for the whole six nights of the week.'

As if the society wasn't burdened with enough problems, financial and otherwise, the state of the Gaiety Theatre was at this time giving rise for serious concern. The true position was highlighted for the public when journalist Deirdre Purcell reported in the *Sunday Tribune* what she found backstage in a special feature on *La Traviata* in the winter of `83. 'There is a drip, drip of water down through the flies, from the leaky roof,' she wrote. 'Now the DGOS is worried about the theatre. After forty-two years, they won't have a venue for their next spring season, as the planned refurbishment will close the Gaiety. In the quiet sad passages of act two I can still hear the steady drip, drip marking its own tempo.'

To the selfless chorus members it was becoming an intolerable situation. 'There were a lot of problems with the Gaiety,' recalled Tom Carney. 'Backstage for example did not bear thinking about. With the roof leaking, buckets had to be placed on the floor of our dressing-rooms to take the water. I think the Supers were as annoyed as ourselves.'

Genial manager Joe Kearns was naturally embarrassed, particularly on gala nights when he had to escort President Patrick Hillery and his wife Maeve to the presidential box in the dress circle. They were obliged to step on threadbare carpets that no doubt would have horrified the theatre's former owner Louis Elliman who had always striven to maintain the theatre in splendid fashion. Unfortunately Éamonn Andrews and his co-directors didn't seem to have the same commitment, despite the fact that manager Joe Kearns repeatedly prevailed on them 'to do something about the place.' When Andrews and his partners invested in the *MV Arran* and converted it into a floating restaurant on the Liffey, the *Evening Herald* was prompted to remark, 'It's time the Gaiety was refurbished. May we also suggest that a few paint brushes from the Liffey restaurant are needed urgently to brighten the theatre.'

Later, when the Andrews' Irish £1 million business empire collapsed with the loss of jobs, Monica Condron was to write in her DGOS annual report, 'Mention must be made of the Gaiety Theatre which has now closed for an indefinite period. The owners appear willing and anxious to refurbish the theatre at a cost of £350,000 but cannot take possession of the lease. Does this mean that the Gaiety must remain in the dark? Surely the influential people in our city can do something quickly to ensure that the theatre is restored to its former glory and thus preserve one of the famous landmarks. Whatever the outcome, to its former manager Joe Kearns and to the staff, the DGOS say thank you for the happy memories associated with the Gaiety.'

It was agreed that the society's spring season in 1984 would be held in the Olympia Theatre in Dame Street; happily, the Gaiety was being restored, especially the backstage amenities. To its credit, the management of the Olympia set about improving facilities and decorating front of house. 'We had no other option except to move there,' recalls Donnie Potter. 'It was a case of the only port in a storm.'

That season, too, he had another pressing problem on his mind - Maestro Annovazzi was ill and would shortly undergo a bladder operation. He was by now seventy-seven and not nearly as energetic as he was even a year before. Potter flew to Rome to discuss with him details of the `84 spring season and on his return was able to say, 'I'm convinced that Napoleone will be well enough to come to Dublin during some stage of the season. It means a great deal to him as he hasn't missed a season with us for more than twenty years. He said to me before I left his apartment, "I will do my utmost to be with you all in Dublin, that I can promise."'

Apparently, he had asked his doctor for a postponement of the operation so as he could come to Dublin but he was refused. Earlier that year his former intrepid friend Lt. Colonel Bill O'Kelly was remembered when the society held a memorial recital in his memory at the National Concert Hall. It featured the distinguished tenor Nicolai Gedda and in the words of *Irish Independent* critic Mary MacGoris, 'Gedda cast a moonlit lustre over the Scandinavian and Russian songs he chose.'

But in March the operatic world mourned the passing at the age of sixty-eight of the legendary baritone Tito Gobbi. It was an occasion for old-timers to recall his masterly Scarpia for the society in the early 1950s, when even Paolo Silveri's avid fans agreed that there was little between the singers in their subtle and powerful interpretations of the great Puccini role.

Meanwhile, the `84 spring season at the Olympia Theatre would open on April 24th with a performance of *Aida* directed by Dario Micheli and conducted by Giacomo Zani, the replacement for Maestro Annovazzi who was not now expected to arrive in Dublin until well into the season. Since the Olympia was mostly used for variety shows, pantomime, light musicals and drama, it was going to be difficult to create a true grand opera atmosphere, not to mention the necessary touch of glitter and glamour associated with DGOS gala nights at the Gaiety. I must admit I found this to be the case on that opening night, when even the RTÉ Symphony Orchestra looked somewhat cramped for space.

Ostensibly, the cast for *Aida* looked formidable with Aurio Tomicich singing Ramfis, Licinio Montefusco as Amonasro , and Angelo Marenzi as Radames. The theatre was well filled on opening night though not to its capacity but there seemed to be a lack of atmosphere and expectancy. Later, Tom Carney would say, 'As far as we were concerned in the chorus there wasn't the same feeling of excitement as we'd have in the Gaiety, although the actual acoustic was probably better. And we found the backstage and wings cramped and uncomfortable.

Aida got mixed newspaper reviews with some critics disappointed by Marenzi's Radames. I do remember though that his forceful 'Celeste Aida' pleased the audience, as did his controlled singing in the thrilling final duet with Aida, sung here by Hagint Vartanian. Critic Fanny Feehan commented in her *Sunday Tribune* review that Vartanian's costumes were atrocious, altogether too tight and revealing every curve of her body. But she conceded that vocally the soprano was a splendid contrast to the Amneris, sung by the Chilean mezzo soprano Claudia Parada.

If *Aida* had got off the society's first ever season outside the Gaiety off to a tame start, the following night's performance of Donizetti's *Lucia di Lammermoor* caused the first semblance of a real buzz in the 'house'. Dympna Carney, cast as Alisa, thought that the Brazilian soprano Maria Angela Peters was an exciting Lucia and made the most of her mad scene. She herself, however, got a strange impression that they were playing to a different audience to that at the Gaiety. 'It's hard to explain really. Maybe it was the Olympia itself which didn't seem as homely as the Gaiety. I'm sure that most of the operagoers were the same as those who normally supported us at the Gaiety but this "different" feeling persisted. And the backstage became easily crowded with choristers, Supers and principals and this made it uncomfortable for everybody.'

Puccini's *La Bohème* opened on May 1 under somewhat trying circumstances. The conductor Giacomo Zani was returning to the podium after the death of his son in an accident in Italy and understandably showed some emotional strain but at no time, said the opera's director Paddy Ryan, did he let his feelings get in the way of the music. Furthermore, the young Berardino di Domencio, who was singing Rodolfo, had brought along his pretty wife to rehearsals and this in Paddy Ryan's view was a mistake. 'I think the chap became a little embarrassed as he rehearsed the love scene in act one with Mimi. He would have been happier I feel left to himself.'

It was no help either when the Mimi, Maria Luisa Garbato, was stricken by a flu bug but she bravely agreed to sing the performance. In the circumstances, she performed convincingly with few people I imagine in the audience suspecting she was on anti-biotics. Charles Acton in the *Irish Times* did comment on her courage and felt she created a telling portrait of Mimi, the little seamstress. It was one of the best performances of the opera he had attended.

At the third performance on the evening of May 7, it fell to Donnie Potter, the society's chairman, to go before the curtain at the outset to tell the packed audience of the unexpected death in Rome that day of their friend and musical director Maestro Annovazzi. The cast and chorus, he said, wished to dedicate that night's performance of *Bohème* in the maestro's honour. He asked those present to stand in silence as a tribute to his memory. Afterwards, the RTÉ Symphony Orchestra played the Prelude from the last act of *Traviata*.

Since he spoke the language, Paddy Ryan sympathised in turn with each of the Italians in the cast. 'I remember I spoke to them as a brother. They are an emotional people and do relate to one another and in the case of Annovazzi he was as it were like a father or elder brother to them and they really respected him as conductor and musician. I think I held more weeping Italians in my arms than I ever could have imagined. They had lost someone they came to admire and it was also true he had given many of them their first opportunity to sing major roles. I could understand their grief.'

Paddy Brennan recalls that his death came as a shock to both himself and his fellow chorus members. 'Although we had known he was ill for some time none of us was prepared for his unexpected passing. When the news first broke, I remember nobody wanted to sing. The next best course was to make the *Bohème* our tribute to him.

To Paddy Ryan that May 7 performance of *Bohème* was not only a worthy tribute to Maestro Annovazzi but vocally and dramatically outstanding. 'To me, it caught the poignancy of the occasion and it also revealed how much the cast was affected by his death. I can vividly recall seeing Aurio Tomicich in tears as he sang Colline's farewell to his coat.'

When I talked this year in Rome with Tomicich and Dario Micheli - he was the designer for *Bohème* - they both remembered the occasion. Tomicich felt indebted to the maestro for inviting him to sing in Dublin where he got the opportunity to tackle plum operatic parts. 'I don't forget these things. Napoleone was a great man and a great musician.' Dario Micheli described him as 'fantastic,' which was his way of saying that he liked him as an individual and admired his artistry.

Donnie Potter travelled to Rome for the funeral. His friendship with Annovazzi went back a long way and since the death of Bill O'Kelly they had worked more closely together in planning the society's seasons. To Potter, the maestro had been a devoted servant who also understood the unique operatic climate in Ireland. 'We weren't in a position to pay him large sums for his dedicated work with us, but we provided the friendly conditions that made that work enjoyable for him. He simply loved coming to Dublin and meeting his friends, as did also his charming wife Nanny. His death was a terrible blow to the society.'

'He was a perfectionist,' said Monica Condron, 'and a gentleman. I used to visit Italy a lot in those years and could never go there without telling him. As for work, sometimes sparks flew between Napoleone and Bill O'Kelly and since I knew Italian he would call on me to explain a point to Bill. It was all part of the scenario and afterwards they'd be the best of friends.'

I found that most society members, from choristers to minor principals, could express an opinion about the maestro. To Brian O'Rourke, chief clarinettist with the RTÉ Symphony Orchestra, Annovazzi continued to be under-rated in Ireland and perhaps was taken for granted. Generally he was liked by musicians. In Caroline Phelan's view, great credit was due to him for managing to juggle the financial budget so that the luminaries still came to sing some memorable performances. To Tom Hawkes, Annovazzi was an accomplished musician and as he got to know one he tended to relax more. 'He was always sympathetic to the chorus,' said Joan Rooney. 'Yet he could be a stern taskmaster with principals and his face was a study if any of them made mistakes.' To Ruth Maher, the conductor could be very helpful to a singer when he offered technical advice. 'He was a natural voice coach and one respected his knowledge.'

Maureen Lemass was a good friend of Napoleone and his wife Anne Maria, affectionately known as 'Nanny' and used to visit them occasionally at their apartment near Rome's Appian Way. There, she remembered, the conductor had an extensive stamp collection as well as many valuable operatic scores. Although he projected a studious, if serious, disposition and was to an extent a disciplinarian, he was at the same time a sensitive man and musician.

He was convalescing in hospital after the operation when he died unexpectedly. Maureen Lemass had been told that his wife had gone out to a nearby shop to fetch him something and on her return found he was dead. It was very unexpected. 'Napoleone, like Nanny, loved Ireland and greatly enjoyed going with the society to Cork where sometimes after a performance he would be visited by broadcaster Tommy O'Brien. In Dublin, he was friendly with Freddy Caracciolo and Ruggero Nico, the owner of Nico's restaurant in Dame Street, where he and Nanny sometimes dined.'

To Ms Lemass, he was a superb teacher and years before in Barcelona counted among his pupils Victoria de Los Angeles and Montserrat Caballe. 'I know that he coached soprano Terry Reid for leading parts with the DGOS and he also took a personal interest in the career of her husband-to-be, tenor Franco Bonenome. I think he regarded Franco as the son he never had.'

Around this time she was honorary secretary of the Patrons' Committee whose city and country membership numbered more than 1,200. They were by now contributing nearly £25,000 annually in subscriptions to the society. Like others, Maureen Lemass felt that Annovazzi was almost irreplaceable and his death left a huge void. John Carney was to agree and recalled the remarkable contribution he had made to opera in Ireland. Another great friend of the society's, John F. MacInerney, had retired from the civil service and had gone to Italy to live. He, too, would be missed.

The Cork operatic scene, meanwhile, had undergone a significant change with the establishment of Cork City Opera, but the DGOS had gone ahead nevertheless with plans to visit the southern capital in that spring of `84 where they would present *Aida, Lucia di Lammermoor and La Gioconda.* The latter, as it turned out, was regarded as the most successful production of the week, partly due to Patrick Murray's visually striking sets as well as the impassioned singing by Lorenza Canepa as Gioconda and Licinio Montefusco as the spy Barnaba.

Harold Johnson, chairman of the Opera House Board of Directors, compared the performance with among the best given by the DGOS in Cork but like his co-directors worried whether Cork had sufficient opera fans to support two spring seasons. It was inevitable that comparisons would be made; indeed this was being done already, for after the opening night of *Aida,* for instance, *Cork Examiner* critic Tomas O'Cannainn noted that the first act set was uninspiring and fell below the standard by the Cork City Opera in a recent staging of *Carmen.* However, matters improved apparently for *Lucia* and especially in the cast of *Gioconda* and both musically and dramatically there was, according to O'Cannainn, 'a sparkle about the productions' with Maria Angela Peters showing star quality as Lucia.

In Dublin the operatic scene was also changing, mainly due to the Arts Council's pressure on the DGOS to adopt a more professional approach. The first steps in this direction were taken with the appointment of English-born Philip Gilbert as full-time chorus master - he had worked with Welsh National Opera and in Wexford. In November 1985 David Collopy was appointed the first DGOS administrator; he was Wexford-born and had filled a similar post with Wexford Festival Opera. It now appeared only a matter of time until an artistic director was appointed, although the fact remained that there was still stern resistance by some members who argued that there was simply no need for one.

In a special report commissioned by the Arts Council as far back as the mid-seventies the society was urged to appoint an artistic director but at the time the council was told that Maestro Annovazzi was acting in this capacity and that the society's president, Professor Anthony Hughes, was also musical advisor. In fact, chairman Bill O'Kelly told one daily newspaper journalist that they were a democratic society and would never renounce their democracy in favour of any sort of 'director'. It could be said however that since the death of Annovazzi the musical climate had changed and there was an urgent need for an artistic director.

Nonetheless, the 1985 spring season, reduced by now to three productions, went ahead without an artistic director. The choice of operas, *Tosca, Don Carlo* and *Macbeth* seemed to lack contrast and one missed a Rossini or Donizetti comedy. Not that the casting lacked enterprise; indeed Frank O'Brien sang two performance of *Don Carlo* and acquitted himself admirably. 'Frank's voice sounded very good on the night,' said Barry Hodkinson, a chorus member. 'He did himself proud.'

Macbeth was voted by the critics as the most rewarding production of the season. Under the heading 'MAGNIFICENT MACBETH', Mary MacGoris in the *Irish Independent* stated that the drama and excitement of the music was brilliantly conveyed in the singing of the principals. Giovanni di Angelis made a stalwart Macbeth, his strong baritone coping exceptionally with Verdi's music, while as his goadingly ruthless Lady, Radmilla Bakocevic was magnificent. The conductor Giovanni Veneri and the RTÉ Symphony Orchestra treated the score with sensitivity as well as colour. In her view, the chorus unfortunately continued its sub-form of the season.

Irish artists could hardly complain of lack of opportunities. Ben Barnes was engaged to direct *Tosca* and Wendy Shea was the set designer.

The winter season of that year was notable for a number of reasons: soprano Virginia Kerr's debut as Micaela in *Carmen* and Patricia Bardon's first Olga *(Eugene Onegin)* for the society. Trained in London, Ms Kerr had first come to the notice of Irish audiences when she sang Donna Anna in Irish National Opera's production of *Don Giovanni* and the critics predicted a bright future for her. She was to confirm this as Micaela. Likewise, Patricia Bardon showed further vocal and dramatic promise as Olga and I remember she told me at the time of the overwhelming feeling singing the part gave her. She looked forward to singing it again when she was more mature.

The year closed on a high note for Frank O'Brien when he sang Figaro in Paddy Ryan's lively production of Rossini's *The Barber of Seville* in English. It was a strong cast that included Della Jones - a natural Rosina - Patrick Power, a sweet-toned Almaviva, and Aurio Tomicich, a marvellous Don Basilio and like the rest of the cast singing in English. Although Rossini's delightful comedy has never been Paddy Ryan's favourite opera to direct ('too much business') he thought that Frank O'Brien matched up well to the international cast.

As the year drew to a close the society still seemed a ship without a captain and lacking real direction. How long more could it put off appointing an artistic director of strength and vision who would point the way forward? It was a question that still divided the society.

Epilogue

Prospects for the following decade (1986 -'96) did not appear particularly bright and predictably it was to be marked by mixed fortunes both on and off stage. The professionalism of the society proceeded gradually, ultimately resulting in the shedding of the various committees and advisory committees as well as the big amateur chorus. For many it was a painful experience, others were more philosophical and accepted the inevitable.

Yet, to this day, there are chorus members who complain that the attitude from the top was insensitive and not enough recognition was given to the contribution they had made. The Arts Council, however, did not view the issue in such sentimental terms. When in 1986 the Council felt the DGOS was 'dragging its feet' it stepped in and reduced its grant to a mere £45,000, landing the society in an unexpected financial crisis. This action was seen as a warning to the management to put its foot on the accelerator. With the appointment prior to the '86 winter season of Michael McCaffery as its first artistic director, the grant was not only restored but raised from the '85 figure of £85,000 to £120,000.

While progress could be expected in the administrative and artistic levels the society's weak infrastructure remained a problem with perhaps too many committees, and although these consisted of intelligent, well-meaning and hard-working volunteers, their roles would have to be examined in any future professional set-up. To David Collopy, the society was at a cross-roads - either it was going to continue as an amateur organisation and hopefully flourish, or it was going to become professional. The idea of mingling the two was in his opinion just not going to work.

More than once in the eighties it struck him that if the society had its way it would not espouse professionalisation nor did most members see the need for it. In their view the society was proceeding nicely but this was to ignore the fact that people were doing jobs like marketing and selling that were normally carried out in other companies by professionals. Furthermore, the Arts Council was by now funding the society to the extent of over £100,000 annually and it was one of the reasons why the council was concerned about the question of accountablility.

He acknowledged that as an amateur society it was well developed and the various committees knew exactly what they were doing, nevertheless it eventually became clear that not enough thought had been put into the grafting of the professional onto the amateur and this created a problem that would take time to iron out. As a newcomer, though, he was aware of the society's long and proud tradition especially in the vocal sense, so was terribly keen to play his part in steering it successfully into the nineties and beyond.

As for the opera fans, I felt myself at the time that either they did not know what was going on behind the scenes or did they greatly care as long as they continued to get value for money in the spring and winter seasons. The more discerning however must have guessed that the halcyon days were over and that in future they would have to be satisfied with singers not quite in the sublime class of Cappuccilli, Protti, Guelfi, Rinaldi, Zeani and Pavarotti. They also knew it was a question of money, that the DGOS could no longer pay the fees demanded. Nonetheless, this did not deter the fans in that spring season of 1986 with the result that booking at the Gaiety box-office was very brisk for the performances of *Nabucco*.

The opera was being directed by Dario Micheli and designed by Patrick Murray, who travelled to Rome for meetings with Micheli. With Licinio Montefusco singing the title role and Radmila Bakocevic the Abigaille, vocal fireworks were promised; the first-night audience certainly wasn't disappointed and the dramatic intensity of their big duet was breath-taking. There were fireworks of another kind following the exploding fall of the statue of Baal, though Montefusco remained singing while at the same time endeavouring to extinguish the fire with his cloak. Eventually it took the quick action of a backstage manager George McFall to restore normality. From my seat in the dress circle it didn't appear that anyone on stage was at risk, but talking to Aurio Tomicich later - he was singing the High Priest - he assured me it was a scary experience and he couldn't understand why some people were chuckling. 'I sensed danger almost immediately the statue caught fire and seeing Licinio use his cloak was very unnerving. I did not experience such a thing on stage before.'

Radmila Bakocevic was back for the winter season to sing the title role in Puccini's *Turandot* and her penetrating dramatic soprano was heard to excellent effect, although at least one critic found the tone rasping when she forced her voice. Virginia Kerr scored a personal triumph as Liu, revealing her quality both as actress and singer. 'I loved the role,' she told me later. 'I was fully in sympathy with the character and playing it could be quite touching.'

The staging by Dario Micheli - he also designed the production - was spectacular and showed once more how skilful and imaginative he could be with big operatic works. *Turandot* was one of his favourite operas and it was undeniably a fitting way to say farewell to Dublin. Strangely, he wasn't invited back in spite of the tremendous service he had given the society since the seventies. I suspect this both surprised and disappointed him. He does however visit Dublin occasionally to renew friendships and he is always delighted to greet members of the society on holidays in Italy.

Gluck's *Orfeo ed Euridice* was that season the ideal musical contrast, and since it was immortalised by Kathleen Ferrier years before - her recording of the famous aria 'Che faro' proved a bestseller - there was unsurprisingly a good deal of interest shown in the DGOS revival. Patrick Murray was both director and designer and his great friend Joan Denise Moriarty was choreographer. I do recall looking forward to hearing Patricia Bardon sing Orpheus and reckoned it would reveal the richness and expressive qualities of her voice. Patrick Murray suggested to DGOS chairman Donnie Potter that it might be a practical thing for the principals to rehearse in Cork. 'Since I was doing the set the cast would be able to rehearse with it on stage, and of course with Joan, Denise and the Irish National Ballet Company based in the city everything soon fell into place. Later, we rehearsed for a few days in Dublin with the chorus and the RTÉ Symphony Orchestra under Albert Rosen.'

He regards the production as one of his most memorable experiences in opera. As he said, 'To be asked to direct and design a work of this grandeur and nobility is an honour really. The rehearsals went well and I considered Patricia Bardon perfect for the part of Orpheus.'

I remember she told me that she didn't consider herself too young to tackle the role.

Off-stage, meanwhile, the struggle by the society to make ends meet meant that more sponsors - foundation, corporate and individual - were constantly being sought and according to David Collopy, the response was encouraging. 'It was a vital source of income for us and we were also helped by the fact that under Section 32 of the 1984 Finance Act, nett contributions between £100 and £10,000 qualified for tax relief.'

At this point the twenty foundation sponsors were contributing a minimum of £1,500 each per annum, the corporates giving £500, and about sixty-five individuals happy to donate a minimum of £125 p.a. In addition, the Arts Council's grant had risen but it was not sufficient; indeed a lottery with modest prizes had to be run to boost income.

Chartered accountant Barry Hodkinson - he was also a DGOS chorus member - was by 1987 one of the finance committee and admitted that the society was always short of money and in fact were still paying off an old bank loan so could not be expected to show a profit on their seasons. It was a tough situation and one not easy to manage. Dr Dermot O'Kelly, chairman of the Patrons' Committee tried to be optimistic and got good support from his colleagues, Vivian Kenny, Dermot Kinlen, Maureen Lemass, Tim Mahony and Bill Phelan. 'The patrons' subscriptions brought in a substantial amount to the society,' said Dr O'Kelly, 'and we tried as best we could to recruit new members, which wasn't always the easiest of tasks.'

Likewise, the Ladies' Committee, spearheaded by chairwoman Mary Egan, hon. secretary Moyra Potter and Máire Hogan (hon. treas.) - not to mention the indefatigable Margaret McDonnell - continued to hand over thousands of pounds annually from fund-raising activities, ranging from a midsummer ball to post-opera suppers; the ball alone raised £6,500 towards the society's general fund. And the pre-opera buffet on gala nights in the Gaiety was proving an unqualified success, indicating that the convivial social side was vibrant with members regarding opera as more than merely a musical occasion. In such an atmosphere it was difficult for anyone to imagine the society shedding its amateur elements. It still belonged to the members who were as eager as ever to maintain the glamour and excitement associated with what I like to call the golden years.

Meanwhile, new artistic director Michael McCaffery arrived to take up his appointment. He was English-born, aged thirty, and had worked closely with Peter Hall in various productions at Glyndebourne and at the Bayreuth Festival. Irish operagoers first came to hear about him at the Wexford Festival where in 1986 he directed Engelbert Humperdinck's *Konigskinder* and I remember the production was well received by both the critics and the festival-goers. Albert Rosen conducted and the greatly talented Russian baritone Sergei Leiferkus sang the role of the Fiddler. McCaffery fitted easily into the Wexford scene and was already looking forward to working in Dublin.

Being young and enthusiastic, he was keen, if possible, to expand DGOS's repertory that had a preponderance of Verdi and Puccini to the neglect it seemed of Mozart, Britten and Janacek. Furthermore, he encountered an elderly artistic culture that was enshrined in a forty-five year old operatic tradition and as he was determined to reflect a young approach, he foresaw some problems ahead. But at least the Arts Council had a policy which it wanted implemented and this gave him confidence, though he felt affecting changes would not be easy.

At times during that first year he came up against some indecision which was to prove frustrating for him. When he thought for example he had worked out a programme the management committee might suggest alterations, which of course raised the question of artistic freedom. However, he tried to get on with the job and for his first spring season of 1987 chose *La Bohème and L'Elisir d'Amore* because they were first-rate operas, the society could successfully stage them, and people would want to see them. He engaged Mike Ashman to direct *Bohème* and Patrick Young for the Donizetti work. Although working on a modest budget, he still believed he had talented casts, with Virginia Kerr singing Musetta and the promising French tenor Jean Luc Viala as Rodolfo. He cast the well-known German baritone Hartmut Singer as Marcello. *L'Elisir d'Amore* remained one of his own favourite comedies and the cast was headed by Italian soprano Antonella Muscente as Adina and as her lover Nemorino, Justin Lavender. While the attendances for both productions were good the reviews unfortunately were mixed and this did not augur well for the society's revived spring visit to the Opera House, Cork.

'I think the rather poor reviews affected our attendances,' recalled Harold Johnson, a board director. 'This was a pity really for we were making a last big effort in the Opera House to make the visit by the DGOS an annual one. The society had made their annual week's visit for nearly twenty years and it was particularly memorable for the big chorus of men and women. It was a holiday for them and their friends and lively parties were organised and of course the Opera House bars did great business. I was sad when it all ended for those opera occasions were a large chunk of both my own and my wife Chloe's life.'

Michael McCaffery decided to direct his first opera for the society in the `87 winter season, Donizetti's comic masterpiece *Don Pasquale* and travelled to Milan to audition singers for the principal roles. He counted himself fortunate to be able to engage the brilliant young lyric soprano Nuccia Focile for Norina, a poor widow in love with Ernesto, who would be sung by her fellow Italian Giuseppe Costanzo. And he signed up the experienced Enrico Fissore, a buffo singer of note, for the title role with Russell Smythe singing Doctor Malatesta. As far as I can recall, there was a sparkle about the production and some wonderfully comic moments.

There could be no complaints that Irish artists were being ignored, for there were ten of them alone in *Rigoletto*, including Peter McBrien who made a brave shot at the taxing role of the jester. The third production that season, Bizet's tuneful *Les Pêcheurs de Perles,* was to prove a lively talking point because of director Mike Ashman's odd demands on soprano Virginia Kerr, who was singing Leila, the priestess. In the first act, for instance, she was raised some ten feet above the stage in an iron swing and remained swaying there until the curtain fell. Later, she was obliged to skip over a stage-full of prone bodies in a full-length strait-jacket that curtailed her use of arms and balance. I remember asking myself how relevant it all was and could only conclude that the director was trying to be unconventional. Mary MacGoris in her review for the *Irish Independent* also questioned its relevance. Virginia Kerr told me later she thought Mike Ashman was being daring and she had no complaints. 'I'll try anything as long as it doesn't affect my voice.'

By now the problem of inconsistency was puzzling even the most loyal of the DGOS's followers. And it was sadly noticeable during the spring season of 1988 with *Il Trovatore* being gloomily lit and Tosca proving in the words of one newspaper critic, 'dark and dull' saved only by some ardent singing by the principals. Mozart's *Don Giovanni* was an altogether different matter and showed how on occasions the society could rise remarkably above the mediocre. Michael McCaffery had asked Patrick Mason, the brilliant theatrical director, to produce the opera, his first for the society, and he proved an inspired choice as indeed was designer Joe Vanik. Mason set the work in the Rome of 1960, reflecting an atmosphere evoking Fellini's *La Dolce Vita* - stills from the film were exhibited later in the programme book.

He had two years previously begun directing opera at the Wexford Festival with considerable success and as a Mozartian always wanted to direct *Giovanni* which he saw as a sophisticated, playful opera with an ironic view of life. Setting it in 1960 was a way, he felt, of getting a fresh look at it and he was determined to bring out its humour. As he said, 'Whatever about its tragic undertones, if you can't get a laugh out of *Giovanni* there's something wrong with the production, for it's one of the most witty librettos in all opera.'

He saw advantages in updating it to the sixties; it was a period of moral change and society itself was changing, so in a way it was traditional morality versus a new kind of liberalism. Audiences in the eighties could readily identify with the references and see for themselves how modern an opera it was. As for the Don, he was suave and lecherous as he moved around in his tie and dinner jacket and he had echoes of Marcello Mastroianni and even James Bond. He was pleased by Michael McCaffery's casting and they had a great double act in Maarten Flipse's Don and Tom Haenen's Leporello and a striking Commendatore by Jean-Jacques Cubaynes. It owed its musical strengths, Mason said, to Janos Furst's superb conducting of the RTÉ Symphony Orchestra. He also paid tribute to the chorus, a mixture of imported professional choristers and singing alongside the DGOS members.

To Virginia Kerr, who was singing Donna Elvira, the production was a milestone in the society's development and updating the piece was a master stroke. 'It worked brilliantly,' she said, 'and I don't think this is always true when one takes operas out of their time.'

Michael McCaffery's choice of Bellini's masterpiece *Norma* for the spring season of 1989 gave the society another resounding success. Because the Gaiety Theatre was unavailable it was decided to stage the opera in the National Concert Hall and alternate it with a Viennese concert programme. The fact that Suzanne Murphy was to sing Norma aroused considerable interest and tickets were snapped up. The society was creating a precedent in paying the soprano the highest fee in its history. Up to then the £1,500 a performance paid to Giuseppe di Stefano in the sixties was a record. 'We wanted Suzanne for the role and we were prepared to pay the fee asked by her agent,' said Donnie Potter. 'We knew also our patrons and friends wanted to hear her in a part that she had sung so successfully with Welsh National Opera.'

She told me later she had asked the DGOS if Angela Feeney could sing the role of Adalgisa in the opera and this was agreed. 'Angela and I wanted to make the production our tribute to Ronnie Dunne for all she had done for our voices in the past. She had followed our careers and attended performances in Cardiff, London and elsewhere.' Suzanne says she enjoyed the *Norma* rehearsals and she had no worries about singing in the National Concert Hall. Italian designer Ulderico Manani's visual flair resolved the problems of dressing the hall with an appropriate set; it rose sharply over the choir seats giving the stage a marvellous three-dimensional appearance.

The first night reminded me of those exciting DGOS evenings in the sixties with the Gaiety audiences full of expectancy at the prospect of hearing Rinaldo, Zeani or Cappuccilli. Suzanne Murphy rose to the occasion, as did Angela Feeney and the rest of the cast. No one was more delighted by her success than Michael McCaffery as they had worked well in rehearsal. 'She was in radiant voice,' he said later, 'and the good hall acoustic did the rest. Looking back, I think we could have charged more for the best seats. In view of the demand for tickets we would have got £40 instead of £30.'

Despite his success with *Norma*, McCaffery was on his own admission finding it increasingly difficult to do his job as artistic director the way he wanted. 'Every day was a battle,' he admitted later. 'There was a lot of interference by committee members and times when I had fixed on a repertoire it was chopped and changed for some peculiar reason. It was frustrating and I began to ask myself how long more I can go on.' I believed I was on the right track but some individuals seemed to feel threatened.'

Like others, I was surprised some time later when he submitted his resignation and it was accepted. He had still some months to go to the expiry date of his three-year contract. It was decided as a temporary measure to invite Elaine Padmore to take control of the society's artistic side and she agreed. Her work as artistic head of the Wexford Festival was greatly admired and she could count on some good friends in the DGOS who always regarded her as the ideal choice as artistic director and regretted the fact she could not accept the role on a long-term basis. However, problems remained and the Arts Council's professionalisation plans still had to be fully implemented. And could Ms Padmore combine successfully the DGOS and Wexford jobs?

The 1990s saw the battle within the organisation between the conservatives and the progressives intensify with the forces on either side making strong cases. Because the Arts Council held the purse strings it was not difficult to predict the final outcome, but there were some years still to go. Meanwhile, an interesting artistic experiment took place when the society re-staged in the Gaiety Theatre two of Opera Northern Ireland's productions, *Tosca and The Magic Flute* with mostly different casts. The Puccini work fared better musically. Around this time Elaine Padmore, due to pressing commitments could not continue her good work with the society. 'We were sorry to lose Elaine,' said David Collopy, 'but during her period with us her advice was very helpful.'

Shortly afterwards the appointment of Kenneth Richardson, from Covent Garden Opera House, was announced and he had the responsibility of choosing the operas for the spring season of 1991, the society's golden jubilee year and another landmark in its history. His choice of Puccini's *Manon Lescaut* and *Rossini's Il Barbiere di Siviglia* did not please everyone; old-timers indeed felt that *Nabucco and Aida* would have been more appropriate for the historic celebratory occasion.

After more than ten years as chairman, Donnie Potter bowed out gracefully, having given sterling service since the late fifties to the organisation. Undeniably he had played a key role in ensuring that it had survived the uncertain years. Finance ministers in successive governments usually responded positively in times of crisis to his appeals for assistance. 'The trouble was, we seemed to be in crisis a lot of the time,' he once remarked to me. 'But Bill O'Kelly and myself were far too involved to let the DGOS go under. I suppose you could say our fierce optimism never waned.'

He was replaced by recently retired banking executive Frank O'Rourke, an opera lover from his youth. He usually took his bank holidays in May and December to coincide with DGOS seasons. He now saw the urgent need for re-organisation and felt the society couldn't survive in the way that it had been going on. As he said, 'The issues of what went with being a *society,* a predominantly amateur organisation, had to be faced up to in terms of artistic standards as well as in terms of organisation itself. For example, the financial constraints on the company were so great that we were really prevented from taking too many risks.'

He was disappointed by some sections of the Irish business and industrial world. They tended to regard opera as elitist and it was extremely difficult to try to persuade them otherwise. 'I found that most of them wanted to sponsor things of benefit to themselves and populist in nature. While I didn't at all subscribe to the this claim of elitism it didn't make our task of getting sponsorship any easier'

Happenings on stage in the spring of 1991 were also a sore disappointment to both Frank O' Rourke and David Collopy as well as the amateur chorus. The critics also vented their displeasure and soon artistic director Kenneth Richardson was obliged to answer questions as to why *Manon Lescaut and Il Barbiere di Siviglia* had failed to satisfy Gaiety audiences.

'The DGOS anniversary season proved to be a rather sorry affair,' Ian Fox stated in the *Sunday Tribune.* 'Both operas should have been surefire hits but unfortunately neither work produced the kind of buzz normally associated with it and the overall standard of the singing was little short of dismal.'

Opera lovers were critical of the direction of the productions, i.e. Stephen Daldry's updating of *Manon Lescaut* to the second World War period, and Robert Chevara's hyper-active *Barber.* 'This production is totally devoid of style or wit,' commented Mary MacGoris *(Irish Independent),* 'and Rossini's joyous ensembles were lost in strange novelties and various vulgarities, culminating in behaviour from the Count to Rosina which would be accounted crude if offered to a prostitute.'

Despite general condemnation, Kenneth Richardson seemed to be unperturbed. He told Michael Dervan *(Irish Times)* that he had considered *Manon Lescaut* a 'great production' and had learned a lot about the opera and thought it had made a positive statement. At the same time, he stoutly defended the Rossini staging, stressing that 'opera has to be relevant to the people and can't exist in a vacuum.'

For those people who had shared the joys of former DGOS presentations the Richardson era did not at this stage seem to offer a great deal. Had no one in the organisation told him that the traditional view of opera was strongly represented in Dublin and fans were concerned by directors who did not take this into account. Later on Richardson's contract was not renewed and once again Elaine Padmore was asked back on a consultancy basis until a new artistic director was appointed.

Padmore's second period in artistic control was to prove controversial. In line with the Arts Council's desire to complete the professionalisation of the society, it was decided to re-audition the chorus and this resulted in the shedding of fifty per cent of them. Understandably, it was a traumatic experience for those men and women with lengthy service. 'More people failed to come up to standard than I certainly expected,' recalled Frank O' Rourke. 'I thought this was going to happen more slowly, but it had to be faced. It was a part of what had to be done to face the future, because the sound that comes from the chorus cannot be put in a compartment with a note saying, "By the way, this will be different".

Tears were shed, particularly by the women choristers whose commitment had long become an integral part of their social lives. Their reaction was a mixture of dismay and anger. The attitude of male members was the same. 'I went along to an audition by the chorus master,' recalls Seán Kelly, 'and like others I felt I was unfairly discarded. I was hoping to sing in the chorus for another two years. It struck me at the time that the auditions were being held to suit another agenda? Jack Doyle represented the chorus committee and in his own words 'fought like mad' to save the amateur chorus from extinction. When he wrote to the chorus master Jonathan Webb to find out what was going on, he was advised 'to audition again in the following year.' His reply was, 'Do you really think I'll get better as I get older?' I knew the same thing would happen again anyway. Jonathan Webb was a first-rate chorus master and I presumed he was only carrying out artistic instructions. I was I remember gutted, as were my colleagues who had failed the audition. Singing with them had become part of my social and artistic life.'

Inevitably, a sense of disillusionment set in. Seán Kelly, whose father Bill O' Kelly had helped to establish the society, felt that its ethos had altered from the mid-eighties onwards. 'I think we all felt this and it was hard to accept.' There were others who felt that the society's shouldn't have been renamed DGOS Opera Ireland. But the disappearance of half the chorus remained the biggest bone of contention. Some members believed it should have been a gradual process, others actually argued against the need at all of 'stripping the chorus' of excellent voices and pointed to the position of Opera Northern Ireland where an amateur chorus still operated. Both John and Tom Carney, who were retained after the auditions, still felt there was an element of insensitivity shown in the way their colleagues were treated. 'I think it was done the wrong way,' Tom Carney said, 'and this rankled among those who lost out.'

Professional choristers from Britain were engaged for the spring and winter seasons and sang beside the remaining amateur members. This arrangement did of course prove costly but no one complained, least of all the Arts Council. By 1992 the council grant amounted to £265,000 and Frank O' Rourke acknowledged this support, saying, 'If they'd had money to give us this year, on their view of our merits, I think they would have given it to us. They're doing all that they can.' Like his colleagues he had been most disappointed by the lack of public support for the society's production in the spring season in 1990 of Britten's *Peter Grimes*. 'I thought it was tremendous and deserving of everyone's support. I'm still baffled as to why so few people wanted to see such a compelling opera.'

There were some other worthy performances. The *Un ballo in Maschera* of '92 afforded me considerable pleasure, mainly because of Dublin soprano Frances Lucey's captivating portrayal of Oscar, the Page. Combining agility and musicianship, she tended to 'steal' the scenes in which she sang. 'Ms Lucey uses her voice with poise and precision,' commented Michael Dervan in the *Irish Times*.

Furthermore, there was a delightful *Martha* in that same year with Irish soprano Marie-Claire O' Reirdan singing the lovely aria, "The Last Rose of Summer" with both feeling and style. She displayed an engaging new confidence as both actress and singer and obviously was benefiting from her work in Germany. Meanwhile, a production of Puccini's *Turandot* had to be cancelled due to financial problems, another indication that it had become a hit-and-miss era for the society.

Musically, the year 1993 was I can recall satisfying and indeed quite memorable. For the spring season the revival of John Lloyd Davis's 1990 production of *Madama Butterfly* with its stunning set, was revived successfully with mezzo Lynda Lee proving a splendid Suzuki and the diminutive Russian suprano Katerina Kudriavchenko singing a passionate "Un Bel Di". The Cosi fan tutte got a mixed reception, particularly due to its vocal inadequacies.

Highlight of the winter season was *Lakmé* by the French composer Delibes and premiered at the Opéra-Comique in April 1883. It owed much of its success to the famous Bell Song and the equally melodious duet, but had not been seen in Ireland since the unforgettable Christiane Eda-Pierre performance at Wexford Festival in 1970. Now with the American coloratura soprano Elizabeth Futral in the title role producing a thrilling vocal sound, the packed Gaiety audience responded enthusiastically. It was one of those elegant evenings that made one forget some mediocre DGOS productions in the eighties. Irish mezzo-soprano Kate McCarney proved an outstanding partner for Futral in the Flower Duet. In that same winter season, Regina Nathan sang a moving Mimi opposite the fine American tenor Stuart Neill while Cork soprano Majella Cullagh made the most of her appearance as Musetta in the Café scene.

By now the professionalisation of the company was almost complete, although a few familiar names remained. Professor Anthony (Tony) Hughes was still a popular president while his vice presidents were Margaret McDonnell, J F McInerney, Donnie Potter and Aileen Walsh. President Mary Robinson was patron and Frank O' Rourke presided over a board of five: Paddy Brennan, Barry Hodkinson, Adrian Burke, Denis Magee and Paul Smith. Gone were the ten different voluntary and advisory committees, which had been considered 'unwieldy' by the Arts Council, so the company had now a professional and spare look about it. Fortunately the numerical strength of the Friends and Patrons was growing and the income from them was vitally important. Yet not everybody was happy about the 'break up' of the various committees who had contributed wholeheartedly in keeping the DGOS a vibrant force.

'For some time,' said John Carney, 'all the many tasks which were in the past performed voluntarily were now carried out by paid personnel and paid choristers began to be used much more frequently. I could see that the old society spirit was being gradually lost. I still believed that this was a mistake for a city like Dublin with no opera house and a relatively small local population for opera would find it extremely difficult to sustain a professional company for two short seasons each year.'

As the year drew to a close both John and Tom Carney had decided to leave the chorus. Tom Carney wrote to Frank O' Rourke explaining his reasons and received a reply thanking him for his long and loyal service. In his case, he had become annoyed during rehearsals of *Bohème* when it seemed the amateur members of the chorus were obliged to 'hang round' and repeat the Café scene unnecessarily so as to await the bus to convey the professional choristers to their city hotel. To Carney it was frustrating and the kind of thing that would never have been allowed to happen in Colonel O 'Kelly's days. 'Bill would have directed the chorus master to get on with it as chorus members had homes to go to.' It confirmed his own view that the society wanted a fully professional chorus who could rehearse during the day, which the amateurs could not always do.

As the nineties proceeded it was noticeable that none of the big works such as *Nabucco, Don Carlo, Ernani and The Force of Destiny* were any longer in the society's repertory and this, I remember, was a real source of regret to the composers' admirers. DGOS old-timers found it hard to accept seasons without two or more of these operas. When Elaine Padmore was eventually appointed artistic director of the Danish Royal Opera and left for Copenhagen, she was replaced by the mature Dorothea Glatt who was attached to the Bayreuth Festival. A woman of quiet disposition and considerable operatic experience, she obviously faced a difficult path ahead of her in Dublin because of the society's lack of money, so I'm afraid I could not see her enjoying notable success, although in due course she did invite Michael McCaffery to direct for the society again and his production of *The Magic Flute* was particularly enchanting.

For the most part Ms Glatt kept a surprisingly low public profile and during her stay in Dublin scarcely became known to the rank and file operagoer. Eventually, as in the case of Kenneth Richardson, her contract was not renewed, although in musical circles she had won much respect. The newspapers barely noticed her departure from Dublin. Had the post of artistic director lost its status?

DGOS Opera Ireland, meanwhile, carried on experiencing more artistic highs and lows. Occasionally critics expressed puzzlement at its failure to keep its artistic directors. Came 1996, and the society said it was pleased to announce the appointment of the celebrated Swiss director Dieter Kaegi as its new head of artistic affairs. Again hopes rose. Could this be the man to set the Liffey on fire? Both Frank O' Rourke and David Collopy were confident that Kaegi had the energy and experience to do the job.

At the same time it was further announced that Ireland had a new professional national opera company, Opera Ireland and as part of its commitment to nurturing Irish talent it had offered the National Chamber Choir a twice yearly contract that would see the choir become the nucleus of the company's professional chorus. And the announcement ended, 'This is an exciting phase of activity in the new company and we are looking forward to building good relationships with our audiences, the Arts Council and the broader arts building committees.'

Kaegi, an outgoing personality, quickly made his mark and advocated that the Gaiety Theatre be made the permanent home of Opera Ireland, that this grand old theatre in South King Street be taken over by either Dublin Corporation, the Arts Council or some other responsible body to secure the future of opera in the capital. It was a grand proposal and certainly deserved the support it got. Artistically, he got off to a good start and productions such as *Macbeth, Eugene Onegin* and *The Tales of Hoffmann* seemed to please operagoers and most of the critics. Like Elaine Padmore, he showed an appreciation of Dublin's opera needs. But he requires time to bring the company around fully to his way of thinking; above all the Arts Council must be aware that he needs more money if the society is to revive *Don Carlo, Norma or The Force of Destiny*.

One can only hope that the new generation of operagoers will get behind him and give him their full support. Anything less will not ensure sucess in a musical and entertainment scene that is becoming intensely competitive.

DUBLIN GRAND OPERA SOCIETY

DGOS OPERA IRELAND • OPERA IRELAND

(Chronology of Opera Performances with casts 1941 - 1998)

Compiled by PADDY BRENNAN

The 50th Anniversary Exhibition of DGOS memorabilia displayed in the National Concert Hall, Dublin through the first Quarter of 1991 proved the catalyst for the establishment of a permanent archive for the organisation. At that time there were neither central records nor a full set of programmes available. What follows has been gleaned from programmes, newspapers, surviving minute/cash books, scrap books [especially those of the late Larry Dowd] and personal memories.

The objective of this chronology has been to record all opera performances with principal cast lists and any changes that occurred during the run of performances. Inevitably errors of omission or commission have occurred in assembling these facts and I would be grateful if anybody were to bring them to my attention either through Opera Ireland or by e-mail to <nozzari@tinet..ie>.

The innumerable concerts and recitals organised and promoted during and outside the seasons of opera lie beyond the scope of this study. Suffice it to say that apart from the pleasure afforded the audiences, many charities throughout the country benefited from the generosity of both artists and DGOS.

Opera in the vernacular was the norm for the1940's. Mixed language performances were common in the early 1950's with chorus and local singers usually performing in English and guests singing either in the original or their native language. By 1955 all Spring Season operas were uniformly sung in Italian while for the Winter it was either English or original language for all performers. Since 1966, all operas have been performed in their original language with the small number of exceptions sung in English as noted in the chronology.

My grateful thanks are due in particular to Andrew Percival, Seamus Kearns and Gerard Moriarty for their invaluable help and advice. Following the chronology is a roll of honour of DGOS performing members taken from roll books, programmes and brochures. They are listed here as a small tribute to that disparate group of dedicated amateurs who by their unique contribution enabled Irish audiences to enjoy the best of opera at affordable prices.

Paddy Brennan
October 1998
Dublin Grand Opera Society

SPRING 1941: GAIETY THEATRE DUBLIN; SAVOY THEATRE LIMERICK

LA TRAVIATA - VERDI Dublin May 19, 23; Limerick Jun 2, 6
May DevittVioletta James JohnstonAlfredo Robert IrwinGiorgio Marjorie BarryFlora C
ByromGastone N J LewisBaron Ben EnnisMarchese Sam Mooney/Thomas Peacock[Jun 2,
6]Dr Grenvil Carmel McAseyAnnina Capt J M DoyleConductor John LynskeyProducer
IL TROVATORE - VERDI Dublin May 20, 24; Limerick Jun 3, 7
John TorneyManrico Moira GriffithLeonora John LynskeyDi Luna Patricia BlackAzucena
Sam Mooney/N J Lewis[Jun 3, 7]Ferrando Capt J M DoyleConductor John
LynskeyProducer
LA BOH_ME - PUCCINI Dublin May 21, 24m; Limerick Jun 4, 7m
May DevittMimi John TorneyRodolfo Eily MurnaghanMusetta John LynskeyMarcello N J
LewisColline Sam Mooney/Robert Irwin[Jun 4, 7m]Schaunard Stephen BlackBenoit Capt J
M DoyleConductor John LynskeyProducer
FAUST - GOUNOD Dublin May 22, 25; Limerick Jun 5
James JohnstonFaust Helen PaxtonMarguerite John LynskeyMéphistophélès Robert
IrwinValentin Patricia BlackSiébel Cathleen O'ByrneMartha Thomas PeacockWagner Capt J
M DoyleConductor John LynskeyProducer

WINTER 1941: GAIETY THEATRE DUBLIN

CARMEN - BIZET Nov 3, 8m, 15
Patricia BlackCarmen John TorneyDon José May DevittMicaëla John LynskeyEscamillo
Josephine O'HaganFrasquita Carmel McAseyMercédès W PorterDancaïre William
MillarRemendado N J LewisZuniga S BlackMoralès Capt. J M DoyleConductor Eily
MurnaghanProducer
LA TRAVIATA - VERDI Nov 4, 15m
Renée FlynnVioletta James JohnstonAlfredo N J LewisGiorgio Marjorie BarryFlora C
ByromGastone G JonesBaron W BrennanMarchese J G CuthbertDr Grenvil Ruby
HuntAnnina Capt J M DoyleConductor Eily MurnaghanProducer
TOSCA - PUCCINI Nov 5, 12
May DevittTosca John TorneyCavaradossi John LynskeyScarpia Sam MooneyAngelotti
Stephen BlackSacristan C ByromSpoletta E HartneySciarrone Charles LynchConductor Eily
MurnaghanProducer
CAVALLERIA RUSTICANA - MASCAGNI Nov 6, 10, 13
Patricia BlackSantuzza James JohnstonTuriddu Sam MooneyAlfio Kitty VaughanLucia Kay
LynchLola Charles LynchConductor Eily MurnaghanProducer
PAGLIACCI - LEONCAVALLO Nov 6, 10, 13
John TorneyCanio Renée FlynnNedda John LynskeyTonio T E AtwoolSilvio
William MillarBeppe Capt J M DoyleConductor Eily MurnaghanProducer
RIGOLETTO - VERDI Nov 7, 11
John LynskeyRigoletto Moira GriffithGilda John Torney/James Johnston[Nov 11]Duke F
ClarkeSparafucile Cathleen O'ByrneMaddalena Sam MooneyMonterone Charles
LynchConductor Eily MurnaghanProducer
FAUST - GOUNOD Nov 8, 14
James JohnstonFaust May DevittMarguerite J C BrownerMéphistophélés T E AtwoolValentin
Patricia BlackSiébel Anne FrayneMartha Jack CarrollWagner Capt J M DoyleConductor Eily
MurnaghanProducer

SPRING 1942: GAIETY THEATRE DUBLIN; OPERA HOUSE CORK

MESSIAH - HANDEL Dublin Apr 13, 19m [Bicentenary performances]

Rita LynchSoprano Patricia BlackContralto James JohnstonTenor Hooton MitchellBass Capt
J M Doyle/J Turner Huggard[Apr 19m]Conductor
TOSCA - PUCCINI Dublin Apr 14, 18m
May DevittTosca John TorneyCavaradossi John LynskeyScarpia Sam MooneyAngelotti
N J LewisSacristan C ByromSpoletta W BrennanSciarrone Charles LynchConductor Sydney
RussellProducer
IL TROVATORE - VERDI Dublin Apr 15, 21; Cork May 5, 10
James Johnston/John Torney[May 5,10]Manrico Moira GriffithLeonora John LynskeyDi
Luna Patricia BlackAzucena Sam MooneyFerrando Charles LynchConductor Sydney
RussellProducer
SAMSON ET DALILA - SAINT-SA_NS Dublin Apr 16, 22, 25
John TorneySamson Patricia BlackDalila Sam MooneyAbimélech Michael O'HigginsHigh
Priest J C BrownerOld Hebrew Capt J M DoyleConductor Sydney RussellProducer
LE NOZZE DI FIGARO - MOZART Dublin Apr 17, 25m; Cork May 10m
Michael O'HigginsFigaro Rita LynchSusanna Renée FlynnCountess Sam MooneyCount
Josephine O'HaganCherubino J C BrownerBartolo Moira GriffithMarcellina William
MillarBasilio William HogartyAntonio Jean TongeBarbarina L W KennedyCurzio Capt J M
DoyleConductor Sydney RussellProducer
CAVALLERIA RUSTICANA - MASCAGNI Dublin Apr 18, 23; Cork May 6, 9m
Moira GriffithSantuzza James JohnstonTuriddu Sam MooneyAlfio Kitty VaughanLucia
Cynthia Flynn/Cait Pleimann[May 6, 9m]Lola Charles LynchConductor Sydney
RussellProducer
PAGLIACCI - LEONCAVALLO Dublin Apr 18, 23; Cork May 6, 9m
John TorneyCanio Renée FlynnNedda John LynskeyTonio N J LewisSilvio William
MillarBeppe Charles LynchConductor Sydney RussellProducer
MADAMA BUTTERFLY - PUCCINI Dublin Apr 20, 24; Cork May 8
May DevittCio-Cio San John TorneyPinkerton Patricia BlackSuzuki Michael O'Higgins/John
Lynskey[May 8]Sharpless Joseph FloodGoro N J LewisBonze Ben EnnisYamadori Maire
DoyleKate Capt J M DoyleConductor Sydney RussellProducer
LA TRAVIATA - VERDI Cork May 4, 9
Renée FlynnVioletta James JohnstonAlfredo N J LewisGiorgio Marjorie BarryFlora C
ByromGastone G JonesBaron W BrennanMarchese J G CuthbertDr Grenvil Capt J. M.
DoyleConductor Sydney RussellProducer
FAUST - GOUNOD Cork May 7
James JohnstonFaust May DevittMarguerite J C BrownerMéphistophélès N J LewisValentin
Patricia BlackSiébel Kitty VaughanMartha Capt J M DoyleConductor Sydney RussellProducer

WINTER 1942: GAIETY THEATRE DUBLIN

IL BARBIERE DI SIVIGLIA - ROSSINI Nov 30, Dec 12m
John LynskeyFigaro Moira GriffithRosina John TorneyAlmaviva Sam MooneyBartolo John
NolanBasilio William BrennanFiorello Marie SloweyBerta T J StewartOfficer Charles
LynchConductor Sydney RussellProducer
LE NOZZE DI FIGARO - MOZART Dec 1, 5m, 10
Michael O'HigginsFigaro Rita LynchSusanna Renée FlynnCountess Sam MooneyCount
Josephine O'HaganCherubino Richard MasonBartolo Moira GriffithMarcellina Joseph
FloodBasilio William HogartyAntonio Jean Tonge/Maire DoyleBarbarina Luke
KennedyCurzio Capt J M DoyleConductor Sydney RussellProducer
LA TRAVIATA - VERDI Dec 2, 12
Renée FlynnVioletta James JohnstonAlfredo N J LewisGiorgio C O'ByrneFlora C
ByromGastone G JonesBaron W BrennanMarchese J G CuthbertDr Grenvil Ruby
HuntAnnina Charles LynchConductor Sydney RussellProducer
LA BOH_ME - PUCCINI Dec 3, 7
May DevittMimi John TorneyRodolfo Josephine O'HaganMusetta John LynskeyMarcello N J
LewisColline Sam MooneySchaunard Peter MorganBenoit William HogartyAlcindoro Capt J
M DoyleConductor Sydney RussellProducer
AIDA - VERDI Dec 4, 8, 11

May DevittAida John TorneyRadames Patricia BlackAmneris John LynskeyAmonasro Richard MasonRamfis Sam MooneyKing Marjorie BarryPriestess Harry SheridanMessenger Capt J M DoyleConductor Sydney RussellProducer

LA FAVORITA - DONIZETTI Dec 5, 9
Patricia BlackLeonora Herman SimbergFernando Michael O'HigginsAlfonso John NolanBaldassarre Rita LynchInes Pearse SheridanGasparo Capt J M DoyleConductor Sydney RussellProducer

MESSIAH - HANDEL Dec 20
Mabel ThriftSoprano Patricia BlackContralto James JohnstonTenor Richard MasonBass J Turner HuggardConductor

---

SPRING 1943: GAIETY THEATRE DUBLIN; SAVOY THEATRE LIMERICK

LA BOH_ME - PUCCINI Dublin May 3, 8m; Limerick May 17
Joan HammondMimi John TorneyRodolfo Josephine O'HaganMusetta John LynskeyMarcello J C BrownerColline Sam MooneySchaunard Peter Morgan/William Hogarty[May 17]Benoit William HogartyAlcindoro Charles Lynch/Commdt J M Doyle[May 17]Conductor Sydney RussellProducer

CARMEN - BIZET Dublin May 4, 15; Limerick May 20
Patricia BlackCarmen John TorneyDon José Rita LynchMicaëla John Nolan/John Lynskey[May 20]Escamillo Josephine O'HaganFrasquita Carmel McAseyMercédès Ignatius PorterDancaïre Joseph FloodRemendado Richard Mason/Sam Mooney[May 20]Zuniga Thomas J StewartMoralès Commdt J M DoyleConductor Sydney RussellProducer

FAUST - GOUNOD Dublin May 5, 10; Limerick May 18, 21
James JohnstonFaust May Devitt/Renée Flynn[May 18]Marguerite J C BrownerMéphistophélès Seán Mooney/John Lynskey[May 18, 21]Valentin Patricia BlackSiébel Kitty Vaughan/Anne FrayneMartha Jack CarrollWagner Charles LynchConductor Sydney RussellProducer

TANNHÄUSER - WAGNER Dublin May 6, 11, 14
John TorneyTannhäuser Joan HammondElisabeth John LynskeyWolfram J C BrownerHerrmann Renée FlynnVenus Joseph FloodWalther Sam MooneyBiterolf Pearse SheridanHeinrich Richard MasonReinmar Ruby HuntShepherd Commdt J M DoyleConductor Sydney RussellProducer

MADAMA BUTTERFLY - PUCCINI Dublin May 7, 13; Limerick May 19, 22
May DevittCio-Cio San John TorneyPinkerton Patricia BlackSuzuki Michael O'HigginsSharpless Joseph FloodGoro Richard MasonBonze William HogartyYamadori Maire DoyleKate Commdt J M DoyleConductor Sydney RussellProducer

DON GIOVANNI - MOZART Dublin May 8, 12, 15m
Michael O'HigginsGiovanni Renée FlynnAnna Sam MooneyLeporello Marie SloweyElvira James JohnstonOttavio Rita LynchZerlina John NolanCommendatore Richard MasonMasetto Commdt J M DoyleConductor Sydney RussellProducer

---

WINTER 1943: GAIETY THEATRE DUBLIN

MADAMA BUTTERFLY - PUCCINI Nov 15, 16
May DevittCio-Cio San Walter WiddopPinkerton Patricia BlackSuzuki Michael O'HigginsSharpless Joseph FloodGoro Richard MasonBonze Ben EnnisYamadori Maire DoyleKate Charles LynchConductor Sydney RussellProducer

IL TROVATORE - VERDI Nov 17, 25
James JohnstonManrico Moira Griffith/Joan Hammond[Nov 25] Leonora Sam MooneyDi Luna Patricia BlackAzucena Richard MasonFerrando Commdt J M DoyleConductor Sydney RussellProducer

HÄNSEL UND GRETEL - HUMPERDINCK Nov 18, 27m
Rita LynchGretel May DevittHänsel Michael O'HigginsFather Kitty Vaughan Mother Marie SloweyWitch Cathleen O'ByrneSandman Carmel McAseyDew Fairy Commdt J M DoyleConductor Sydney RussellProducer

AIDA - VERDI Nov 19, 22

Joan HammondAida Walter WiddopRadames Patricia BlackAmneris Michael
O'HigginsAmonasro Richard MasonRamfis J C BrownerKing Marjorie BarryPriestess James
BrittainMessenger Commdt J M DoyleConductor Sydney RussellProducer
LE NOZZE DI FIGARO - MOZART Nov 20m, 26
Michael O'HigginsFigaro Rita LynchSusanna Renée FlynnCountess Sam MooneyCount
Josephine O'HaganCherubino J C BrownerBartolo Marie SloweyMarcellina Joseph
FloodBasilio Seamus FitzpatrickAntonio Margaret Folan/Maire DoyleBarbarina Luke
KennedyCurzio Commdt J M DoyleConductor Sydney RussellProducer
TOSCA - PUCCINI Nov 20, 24
May DevittTosca Frank WalshCavaradossi Sam MooneyScarpia Richard MasonAngelotti
Joseph FloodSacristan Commdt J M DoyleConductor Sydney Russell
THE BOHEMIAN GIRL - BALFE Nov 23, 27[Centenary Performance]
Rita LynchArline James JohnstonThaddeus Patricia BlackGypsy Queen J C
BrownerDevilshoof Seán MooneyArnheim Joseph FloodFlorestein Una BodieBuda Commdt J
M DoyleConductor Sydney RussellProducer

Spring 1944: Gaiety Theatre Dublin; Opera House Cork

LA TRAVIATA - VERDI Dublin Apr 17, 22, 26; Cork May 1, 6
Renée FlynnVioletta James JohnstonAlfredo John LynskeyGiorgio Marjorie BarryFlora C
ByromGastone Ben EnnisBaron Gwylim JonesMarchese Sam MooneyDr Grenvil Ruby
HuntAnnina Charles LynchConductor Sydney RussellProducer
IL TROVATORE - VERDI Dublin Apr 18, 28; Cork May 4
James JohnstonManrico Moira GriffithLeonora John LynskeyDi Luna Patricia BlackAzucena
Richard MasonFerrando Commdt J M DoyleConductor Sydney RussellProducer
MADAMA BUTTERFLY - PUCCINI Dublin Apr 19, 25; Cork May 2, 7m
May DevittCio-Cio San Joseph McLaughlinPinkerton Patricia BlackSuzuki Michael
O'HigginsSharpless Joseph FloodGoro Richard MasonBonze Ben EnnisYamadori Alice
FrayneKate Commdt J M DoyleConductor Sydney RussellProducer
FAUST - GOUNOD Dublin Apr 20, 24, 29; Cork May 3, 7
James JohnstonFaust Renée Flynn/May Devitt[May 3]Marguerite J C
BrownerMéphistophélès Richard MasonValentin Patricia BlackSiébel Kitty VaughanMartha P J
TobinWagner Charles LynchConductor Sydney RussellProducer
SAMSON ET DALILA - SAINT-SA_NS Dublin Apr 21, 27; Cork May 5
Frank WalshSamson Particia BlackDalila Sam MooneyAbimélech Michael O'HigginsHigh
Priest J C BrownerOld Hebrew Commdt J M DoyleConductor Sydney RussellProducer
HÄNSEL UND GRETEL - HUMPERDINCK Dublin Apr 22m, 29m
Rita LynchGretel May DevittHänsel Michael O'HigginsFather Moira GriffithMother Marie
SloweyWitch Kitty VaughanSandman Carmel McAseyDew Fairy Commdt J M
DoyleConductor Sydney RussellProducer

Winter 1944: Gaiety Theatre Dublin

RIGOLETTO - VERDI Nov 20, 25m, 30
John LynskeyRigoletto Marion DaviesGilda James JohnstonDuke Dermot BrownerSparafucile
Commdt J M DoyleConductor Sydney RussellProducer
LA GIOCONDA - PONCHIELLI Nov 21, 25; Dec 1
May DevittGioconda Joseph McLaughlinEnzo Patricia BlackLaura Michael O'HigginsBarnaba
Nora FinnCieca Richard MasonAlvise Commdt J M DoyleConductor Sydney RussellProducer
CARMEN - BIZET Nov 22, 27, Dec 2
Patricia BlackCarmen James JohnstonDon José Rita LynchMicaëla John LynskeyEscamillo
Josephine O'HaganFrasquita Marie SloweyMercédès Sam MooneyDancaïre Joseph
FloodRemendado Richard MasonZuniga Ben EnnisMoralès Commdt J M DoyleConductor
Sydney RussellProducer
DON GIOVANNI - MOZART Nov 23, 29
Michael O'HigginsGiovanni Marion DaviesAnna Sam MooneyLeporello Marie SloweyElvira
James JohnstonOttavio Rita LynchZerlina Richard MasonCommendatore/Masetto Commdt

J M DoyleConductor Sydney RussellProducer
LA BOH_ME - PUCCINI Nov 24, 28, Dec 2m
May DevittMimi Joseph McLaughlinRodolfo Josephine O'HaganMusetta John
LynskeyMarcello Richard MasonColline Sam MooneySchaunard Hubert O'ConnorBenoit
Joseph FloodAlcindoro Commdt J M DoyleConductor Sydney RussellProducer

SPRING 1945: GAIETY THEATRE DUBLIN; OPERA HOUSE CORK

ROMÉO ET JULIETTE - GOUNOD Dublin May 7, 15, 19; Cork May 31
May DevittJuliette Joseph McLaughlin/Francis Russell[May 31]Roméo Richard
MasonLaurent Leslie JonesMercutio Josephine O'HaganStéphano Dermot BrownerCapulét
Joseph FloodTybalt Commdt J M DoyleConductor Sydney RussellProducer
AIDA - VERDI Dublin May 8, 10, 16
Eva TurnerAida Parry JonesRadames Patricia BlackAmneris John LynskeyAmonasro Richard
MasonRamfis Dermot BrownerKing Marjorie BarryPriestess Thomas SynnottMessenger
Commdt J M DoyleConductor Sydney RussellProducer
MADAMA BUTTERFLY - PUCCINI Dublin May 9, 12, 19m; Cork May 29
May DevittCio-Cio San Joseph McLaughlinPinkerton Patricia Black/Cathleen
O'Byrne[May9]Suzuki Leslie JonesSharpless Joseph FloodGoro Dermot BrownerBonze
William HogartyYamadori Marie DoyleKate Arnold PerryConductor Sydney RussellProducer
LA GIOCONDA - PONCHIELLI Dublin May 11, 17
May DevittGioconda Joseph McLaughlinEnzo Patricia BlackLaura John LynskeyBarnaba
Cathleen O'ByrneCieca Richard MasonAlvise Edgar W BouchierConductor Sydney
RussellProducer
**LES CONTES D'HOFFMANN - OFFENBACH Dublin May 12m, 14, 18; Cork
May 28, Jun 2**
Parry Jones/Francis Russell[May 28, Jun 2]Hoffmann Josephine O'HaganOlympia Patricia
BlackGiulietta John Lynskey Coppélius/Miracle/Dapertutto Molly MurphyNicklausse
Maureen Harold/Maureen Keane[May 14]Antonia Joseph FloodSpalanzani/Frantz Richard
MasonCrespel/Schlemil Robert J CareyCochenille/Pitichinaccio Arnold PerryConductor
Sydney RussellProducer
LA BOH_ME - PUCCINI Cork May 27, Jun 1
May DevittMimi Joseph McLaughlinRodolfo Josephine O'HaganMusetta John
LynskeyMarcello Richard MasonColline Leslie JonesSchaunard Commdt J M
DoyleConductor Sydney RussellProducer
CARMEN - BIZET Cork May 30, Jun 3
Patricia BlackCarmen Francis RussellDon José May DevittMicaëla John LynskeyEscamillo
Josephine O'HaganFrasquita Marie SloweyMercédès Leslie JonesDancaïre Joseph
FloodRemendado Richard MasonZuniga Ben EnnisMoralès Commdt J M DoyleConductor
Sydney RussellProducer

WINTER 1945: GAIETY THEATRE DUBLIN

FAUST - GOUNOD Nov 26, Dec 1, 5
James Johnston/Frank Sale[Dec 1]/Tudor Davies[Dec 5]Faust Victoria SladenMarguerite
Vere LaurieMéphistophélès Richard Mason/Roderick Jones[Nov 26]Valentin Patricia
BlackSiébel Kitty VaughanMartha P J TobinWagner Commdt J M DoyleConductor Sydney
RussellProducer
IL TROVATORE - VERDI Nov 27, 29, Dec 1m
James JohnstonManrico Ruth PackerLeonora John LynskeyDi Luna Patricia BlackAzucena
Richard MasonFerrando Arthur HammondConductor Sydney RussellProducer
MADAMA BUTTERFLY - PUCCINI Nov 28, Dec 7
Victoria SladenCio-Cio San Ivan Dixon/James Johnston[Dec 7]Pinkerton Patricia
BlackSuzuki Roderick JonesSharpless Joseph FloodGoro Richard MasonBonze Brendan
RobertsYamadori Mary de Riva O'PhelanKate Arthur HammondConductor Sydney
RussellProducer
LA BOH_ME - PUCCINI Nov 30, Dec 3, 8m

Victoria SladenMimi Tudor Davies/Ivan Dixon[Nov 30]Rodolfo Josephine O'HaganMusetta John Lynskey/Roderick Jones[Nov 30]Marcello Owen BranniganColline Richard MasonSchaunard Joseph FloodBenoit/Alcindoro Commdt J M DoyleConductor Sydney RussellProducer

RIGOLETTO - VERDI Dec 4, 6, 8
Roderick JonesRigoletto Gwen CatleyGilda James JohnstonDuke Owen BranniganSparafucile Patricia BlackMaddalena Richard MasonMonterone William O'KellyMarullo Arthur Hammond/Commdt J M Doyle[Dec 4]Conductor Sydney RussellProducer

Spring 1946: Gaiety Theatre Dublin

TOSCA - PUCCINI May 13, 16, 18m
Victoria SladenTosca Ivan DixonCavaradossi John LynskeyScarpia Sam MooneyAngelotti Joseph FloodSacristan R J CareySpoletta Luke KennedySciarrone Arthur HammondConductor Sydney RussellProducer

OTELLO - VERDI May 14, 17, 20
Parry JonesOtello Ruth PackerDesdemona Edmond DunlevyIago Joseph FloodCassio Joseph G BlackRoderigo Dermot BrownerLodovico P J TobinMontano Patricia BlackEmilia Luke KennedyHerald Commdt J M DoyleConductor Sydney RussellProducer

LA TRAVIATA - VERDI May 15, 24, 25m
Ruth PackerVioletta Ivan DixonAlfredo John LynskeyGiorgio Mary de Riva O'PhelanFlora R J CareyGastone Ben EnnisBaron Brendan RobertsMarchese Sam MooneyDr Grenvil Kathleen AdamsAnnina Commdt J M DoyleConductor Sydney RussellProducer

IL TROVATORE - VERDI May 18, 22
Parry JonesManrico Ruth PackerLeonora Bernard RossDi Luna Patricia BlackAzucena Sam MooneyFerrando Commdt J M Doyle/Arthur Hammond[May 22]Conductor Sydney RussellProducer

DER FLIEGENDE HOLLÄNDER - WAGNER May 21, 23, 25
Robert ParkerDutchman Mary CherrySenta Dermot BrownerDaland George ChittyErik Patricia BlackMary Joseph FloodSteersman Arthur HammondConductor Sydney RussellProducer

Autumn 1946: Royal Hippodrome Belfast

LA TRAVIATA - VERDI Sep 16, 19[11.30pm]
Ruth PackerVioletta Ivan DixonAlfredo John LynskeyGiorgio Marjorie BarryFlora Thomas J. SynnottGastone P J TobinBaron Brendan RobertsMarchese Dermot BrownerDr Grenvil Kathleen AdamsAnnina Arthur HammondConductor Sydney RussellProducer

FAUST - GOUNOD Sep 17, 19, 21m
James JohnstonFaust Victoria SladenMarguerite Vere LaurieMéphistophélès Roderick JonesValentin Patricia BlackSiébel Kitty VaughanMartha P J TobinWagner Commdt J M DoyleConductor Sydney RussellProducer

IL TROVATORE - VERDI Sep 18m, 21
Frank SaleManrico Ruth PackerLeonora John LynskeyDi Luna Patricia BlackAzucena Dermot BrownerFerrando Commdt J M DoyleConductor Sydney RussellProducer

RIGOLETTO - VERDI Sep 18, 20
Roderick JonesRigoletto Gwen CatleyGilda Ivan DixonDuke Dermot BrownerSparafucile/Monterone Patricia BlackMaddalena William O'KellyMarullo Arthur HammondConductor Sydney RussellProducer

Winter 1946: Gaiety Theatre Dublin

FAUST - GOUNOD Dec 2, 6, 7m
Ivan DixonFaust Ruth Packer/May Devitt[Dec 6]Marguerite Howell GlynneMéphistophélès John LynskeyValentin Josephine O'HaganSiébel Kitty VaughanMartha P J TobinWagner Commdt J M DoyleConductor Vere LaurieProducer

CARMEN - BIZET Dec 3, 5, 7

Patricia BlackCarmen Henry WendonDon José May DevittMicaëla George HancockEscamillo
Josephine O'HaganFrasquita Molly MurphyMercédès Dermot BrownerDancaïre Joseph
FloodRemendado Vere LaurieZuniga P J TobinMoralès Arthur HammondConductor Sydney
RussellProducer

OTELLO - VERDI Dec 4, 13
Frank SaleOtello Ruth PackerDesdemona George HancockIago Joseph FloodCassio Joseph G
BlackRoderigo Dermot BrownerLodovico P J TobinMontano Patricia BlackEmilia Gerard
DugganHerald Commdt J M DoyleConductor Sydney RussellProducer

MADAMA BUTTERFLY - PUCCINI Dec 9, 11, 14m
May DevittCio-Cio San Frank SalePinkerton Patricia BlackSuzuki John LynskeySharpless
Joseph FloodGoro Dermot BrownerBonze/Yamadori Nuala PerryKate Commdt J M
DoyleConductor Vere LaurieProducer

LA TRAVIATA - VERDI Dec 10, 12, 14
Ruth PackerVioletta Ivan DixonAlfredo George HancockGiorgio Marjorie BarryFlora Thomas
J. SynnottGastone P J TobinBaron William O'KellyMarchese Dermot BrownerDr Grenvil
Kathleen AdamsAnnina Arthur HammondConductor Sydney RussellProducer

SPRING 1947: GAIETY THEATRE DUBLIN

AIDA - VERDI Apr 28, 30, May 9
Ruth PackerAida Frank SaleRadames Patricia BlackAmneris George HancockAmonasro
Richard MasonRamfis Vere LaurieKing Marjorie Barry/Maura Mooney[Apr 30]Priestess
Thomas SynnottMessenger Commdt J M DoyleConductor Sydney RussellProducer

RIGOLETTO - VERDI Apr 29, May 10
Leyland WhiteRigoletto Gwen CatleyGilda James Johnston/John Myrridan[May 10]Duke
Owen BranniganSparafucile Patricia BlackMaddalena Richard MasonMonterone William
O'KellyMarullo Arthur HammondConductor Vere LaurieProducer

CARMEN - BIZET May 1, 3, 6
Patricia BlackCarmen James Johnston/Ivan Dixon[May 3]Don José Blanche TurnerMicaëla
George HancockEscamillo Josephine O'HaganFrasquita Molly MurphyMercédès Richard
MasonDancaïre Joseph FloodRemendado Vere LaurieZuniga Ailfrid MacGabhannMoralès
Arthur HammondConductor Sydney RussellProducer

LA BOH_ME - PUCCINI May 2, 3m, 8
Blanche TurnerMimi Walter MidgleyRodolfo Josephine O'HaganMusetta Leyland
White/George Hancock[May 2]Marcello Owen BranniganColline Vere LaurieSchaunard
Joseph FloodBenoit/Alcindoro Commdt J M DoyleConductor Sydney RussellProducer

DON GIOVANNI - MOZART May 5, 7, 10m
Leyland WhiteGiovanni Ruth PackerAnna Owen BranniganLeporello Mary CherryElvira
Walter MidgleyOttavio Winifred RadfordZerlina George HancockCommendatore Richard
MasonMasetto Arthur HammondConductor Vere LaurieProducer

AUTUMN 1947: ROYAL HIPPODROME BELFAST

CARMEN - BIZET Oct 27, 29
Patricia BlackCarmen Henry WendonDon José Victoria SladenMicaëla Redvers
LlewellynEscamillo Arthur HammondConductor Sydney RussellProducer

LA TRAVIATA - VERDI Oct 28, 29m
Ruth PackerVioletta James JohnstonAlfredo Leyland WhiteGiorgio Commdt J M
DoyleConductor Sydney RussellProducer

AIDA - VERDI Oct 30, Nov 1
Ruth PackerAida Henry WendonRadames Patricia BlackAmneris Henry GillAmonasro Howell
GlynneRamfis Dermot BrownerKing Marjorie BarryPriestess Thomas SynnottMessenger
Commdt J M DoyleConductor Sydney RussellProducer

MADAMA BUTTERFLY - PUCCINI Oct 31, Nov 1m
Victoria SladenCio-Cio San James Johnston/Ivan Dixon[Nov 1m]Pinkerton Patricia
BlackSuzuki Arnold MattersSharpless Joseph FloodGoro Howell GlynneBonze Jack
O'ConnorYamadori Molly MurphyKate Arthur HammondConductor Sydney RussellProducer

WINTER 1947: GAIETY THEATRE DUBLIN

TOSCA - PUCCINI Dec 8, 10, 13m
Victoria SladenTosca Ivan Dixon/James Johnston[Dec 8]Cavaradossi Roderick JonesScarpia
Dermot BrownerAngelotti Joseph FloodSacristan Lt-Col J M DoyleConductor Vere
LaurieProducer

IL TROVATORE - VERDI Dec 9, 11, 12
Walter MidgleyManrico Ruth PackerLeonora Leyland WhiteDi Luna Patricia BlackAzucena
Dermot BrownerFerrando Arthur HammondConductor Sydney RussellProducer

MADAMA BUTTERFLY - PUCCINI Dec 13, 17, 20m
Ruth Packer/Joyce Gartside[Dec 13]Cio-Cio San Ivan Dixon/Henry Wendon[Dec
13]Pinkerton Patricia BlackSuzuki Roderick Jones/Arthur Copley[Dec 20m]Sharpless Joseph
FloodGoro Dermot BrownerBonze/Yamadori Molly MurphyKate Arthur
HammondConductor Sydney RussellProducer

SAMSON ET DALILA - SAINT-SA_NS Dec 15, 19
Henry WendonSamson Particia BlackDalila Dermot BrownerAbimélech Arthur CopleyHigh
Priest Vere LaurieOld Hebrew Arthur HammondConductor Vere LaurieProducer

LA TRAVIATA - VERDI Dec 16, 18, 20
Margery FieldVioletta Walter MidgleyAlfredo Leyland White/Arthur Copley[Dec 16]Giorgio
Molly MurphyFlora Joseph FloodGastone Jack O'ConnorBaron Brendan RobertsMarchese
Vere LaurieDr Grenvil Carmel McAseyAnnina Lt-Col J M DoyleConductor Vere
LaurieProducer

SPRING 1948: GAIETY THEATRE DUBLIN

AIDA - VERDI Apr 26, 28, 30
Ruth PackerAida Frank Sale/Henry Wendon[Apr 28]Radames Patricia BlackAmneris Henry
GillAmonasro Dermot BrownerRamfis Sam MooneyKing Marjorie Barry/Maura
Mooney/Monica CondronPriestess Gerald V MooneyMessenger Lt-Col J M DoyleConductor
Sydney RussellProducer

LA BOH_ME - PUCCINI Apr 27 May 3, 7
Margery Field/Barabara Lane[May 7]Mimi Tom Culbert/James Johnston[May 3]/Charles
Danson[May 7]Rodolfo Barbara Lane/Margery Field[May 7]Musetta John LynskeyMarcello
Dermot BrownerColline Vere LaurieSchaunard Joseph FloodBenoit/Alcindoro Lt-Col J M
DoyleConductor Vere LaurieProducer

RIGOLETTO - VERDI Apr 29, May 1m
John LynskeyRigoletto Joan ButlerGilda Ivan Dixon/Ken Neate[May 1]Duke Dermot
BrownerSparafucile Patricia Black/Kay O'Byrne[May 1]Maddalena Sam MooneyMonterone
Jack O'ConnorMarullo Lt-Col J M DoyleConductor Sydney RussellProducer

FAUST - GOUNOD May 1, 5, 8
James Johnston/Ivan Dixon[May 8]Faust Margery FieldMarguerite Henry
GillMéphistophélès Bruce DargavalValentin Joyce NelsonSiébel Kitty VaughanMartha P J
TobinWagner Lt-Col J M DoyleConductor Sydney RussellProducer

PELLÉAS ET MÉLISANDE - DEBUSSY May 4, 6, 8m [Opéra Comique, Paris]
Jacques JansenPelléas Irene JoachimMélisande Henri EtcheverryGolaud M ClavencyArkel
Marguerite MyrtalGenevéve Jacqueline CellierYniold Vere LaurieMédecin Roger
DesormièreConductor Vere LaurieProducer

SUMMER 1948: BUTLIN'S HOLIDAY VILLAGE THEATRE, MOSNEY, CO. MEATH

FAUST - GOUNOD Jul 12, 14
James JohnstonFaust Margery FieldMarguerite Hervey AlanMéphistophélès Bruce
DargavalValentin Patricia BlackSiébel Kitty VaughanMartha P J TobinWagner Lt-Col J M
DoyleConductor Sydney RussellProducer

RIGOLETTO - VERDI Jul 13, 15
John LynskeyRigoletto Joan ButlerGilda Ivan DixonDuke Dermot BrownerSparafucile

Page 328

Patricia BlackMaddalena Bruce DargavalMonterone Jack O'ConnorMarullo Lt-Col J M
DoyleConductor Sydney RussellProducer

RIGOLETTO - VERDI Dec 6, 8, 11m
Edmond DonlevyRigoletto Audrey BowmanGilda Ken NeateDuke Jack HarteSparafucile
Betty SagonMaddalena Sam MooneyMonterone Jack O'ConnorMarullo Lt-Col J M
DoyleConductor Sydney RussellProducer
CARMEN - BIZET Dec 7, 10, 14, 18
Patricia BlackCarmen Frans VroonsDon José Margery FieldMicaëla Bruce DargavalEscamillo
Josephine O'HaganFrasquita Betty SagonMercédès Sam MooneyDancaïre Joseph
FloodRemendado Jack O'ConnorZuniga John PearceMoralès Vilem Tausky/Lt-Col J M
Doyle[Dec 10]Conductor H A Powell-LloydProducer
TOSCA - PUCCINI Dec 9, 11
Joan HammondTosca Frans VroonsCavaradossi Stanley PopeScarpia Jack HarteAngelotti
Joseph FloodSacristan Sam MooneySciarrone Lt-Col J M DoyleConductor H A Powell-
LloydProducer
IL TROVATORE - VERDI Dec 13, 15, 17
John MyrrdinManrico Audrey BowmanLeonora Bruce DargavalDi Luna Patricia
BlackAzucena Jack HarteFerrando Vilem TauskyConductor Sydney RussellProducer
LE NOZZE DI FIGARO - MOZART Dec 16, 18m
Edmond DonlevyFigaro Joan WalkerSusanna Barbara LaneCountess Denis DowlingCount
Josephine O'HaganCherubino Jack HarteBartolo Betty SagonMarcellina Joseph
FloodBasilio/Curzio Sam MooneyAntonio Monica CondronBarbarina Lt-Col J M
DoyleConductor H A Powell-LloydProducer

LA TRAVIATA - VERDI Apr 25, 27, 30m
Audrey BowmanVioletta Ken NeateAlfredo Melvin Bartell/Roderick Jones[Apr 30m]Giorgio
Nuala PerryFlora Joseph FloodGastone Jack O'ConnorBaron Frank GormleyMarchese Vere
LaurieDr Grenvil Monica CondronAnnina Vilem TauskyConductor Sydney RussellProducer
DIE ENTFÜHRUNG AUS DEM SERAIL - MOZART Apr 26, 28, 30
Margaret RitchieKonstanze Richard LewisBelmonte Ingrid HagemanBlonde Owen
BranniganOsmin John KentishPedrillo Joseph O'DeaSelim Lt-Col J M DoyleConductor Vere
LaurieProducer
FAUST - GOUNOD Apr 29, May 2, 4
James JohnstonFaust Joyce GartsideMarguerite Owen BranniganMéphistophélès Roderick
JonesValentin Patricia BlackSiébel Anne BishopMartha P J TobinWagner Lt-Col J M
DoyleConductor Sydney RussellProducer
UN BALLO IN MASCHERA - VERDI May 3, 5, 7
Ken NeateRiccardo Audrey BowmanAmelia Melvin BartellRenato Patricia BlackUlrica Barbara
LaneOscar Martin DempseySamuel Jack HarteTom Joseph FloodSilvano Vilem
TauskyConductor Vere LaurieProducer
MADAMA BUTTERFLY - PUCCINI May 6, 7m
Korina HellasCio-Cio San James JohnstonPinkerton Patricia BlackSuzuki Melvin
BartellSharpless Joseph FloodGoro Jack HarteBonze Anthony NolanYamadori Maureen
RyanKate Vilem TauskyConductor Joseph FloodProducer

RIGOLETTO - VERDI Dec 5, 7, 10
Edmond Donlevy/Otakar Kraus[Dec 10]Rigoletto Marjorie ShiresGilda Ken NeateDuke Jack
HarteSparafucile Patricia BlackMaddalena Martin DempseyMonterone Lt-Col J M
Doyle/Vilem Tausky[Dec 10]Conductor Sydney RussellProducer
IL TROVATORE - VERDI Dec 6, 8, 12, 14

James JohnstonManrico Doris DoréeLeonora Bruce DargavalDi Luna Patricia
Black/Catherine Lawson[Dec 14]Azucena Jack HarteFerrando Vilem Tausky/Lt-Col J M
Doyle[Dec 12]Conductor Sydney RussellProducer
TOSCA - PUCCINI Dec 9, 10m, 17
Doris DoréeTosca Frans Vroons/James Johnston[Dec 9]Cavaradossi Otakar KrausScarpia
Jack HarteAngelotti Joseph FloodSacristan/Spoletta Martin DempseySciarrone Lt-Col J M
DoyleConductor Joseph FloodProducer
LES CONTES D'HOFFMANN - OFFENBACH Dec 13, 15, 16
Frans VroonsHoffmann Jean MountfordOlympia Blanche TurnerGiulietta/Antonia Otakar
KrausCoppélius/Miracle/Dapertutto/Lindorf Catherine LawsonNicklausse Joseph
FloodSpalanzani/Frantz Martin DempseyCrespel/Schlemil Robert J
CareyCochenille/Pitichinaccio Cathryn CorcoranMother Lt-Col J M DoyleConductor Powell
LloydProducer
HÄNSEL UND GRETEL - HUMPERDINCK Dec 17m, 19, 20
Jean MountfordGretel Josephine ProustHänsel Edmond DunlevyFather Maureen
KeaneMother Cathryn CorcoranWitch Ada GeogheganSandman Monica CondronDew Fairy
Vilem TauskyConductor Powell LloydProducer

AIDA - VERDI Apr 24, 26, 28
Doris Dorée/Elfriede Wasserthal[Apr 28]Aida Emilio MarinescoRadames Patricia
BlackAmneris Bruce DargavalAmonasro Stanley ClarksonRamfis Vere LaurieKing Marjorie
BarryPriestess Gerald V MooneyMessenger Lt-Col J M DoyleConductor Vere LaurieProducer
DON GIOVANNI - MOZART Apr 25, 27, 29 [Hamburg State Opera]
Matthieu AhlersmeyerGiovanni Clara EbersAnna Theo HermannLeporello Elfriede
WasserthalElvira Walter GeislerOttavio Lore HoffmanZerlina Sigmund RothCommendatore
Gustav NeidlingerMasetto Arthur GrüberConductor Günther Rennert Producer
CARMEN - BIZET Apr 29m, May 1, 3
Patricia BlackCarmen Frans Vroons/Ken Neate[May 3]Don José Veronica DunneMicaëla
Bruce DargavalEscamillo Josephine O'HaganFrasquita Barbara LaneMercédès Sam
MooneyDancaïre Joseph FloodRemendado Vere LaurieZuniga John DuffyMoralès Vilem
TauskyConductor Sydney RussellProducer
COSI FAN TUTTE - MOZART May 2, 4, 6 [Hamburg State Opera]
Lore HoffmanFiordiligi Walter GeislerFerrando Martha MödlDorabella Georg
MundGuglielmo Theo HermannAlfonso Annaliese RothenbergerDespina Arthur
GrüberConductor Günther Rennert Producer
LA TRAVIATA - VERDI May 5, 6m, 10
Irma BeilkeVioletta Ken NeateAlfredo Otakar KrausGiorgio Pauline NolanFlora Joseph
FloodGastone Martin DempseyBaron Sam MooneyMarchese Vere LaurieDr Grenvil Monica
CondronAnnina Vilem Tausky/Lt-Col J M Doyle[May 5]Conductor Joseph FloodProducer
LA BOH_ME - PUCCINI May 8, 12, 13m
Irma BeilkeMimi Horst TaubmannRodolfo Josephine O'HaganMusetta Otakar KrausMarcello
Stanley ClarksonColline Vere LaurieSchaunard Joseph FloodBenoit/Alcindoro Lt-Col J M
DoyleConductor Vere LaurieProducer
UN BALLO IN MASCHERA - VERDI May 9, 11, 13
Ken NeateRiccardo Doris DoréeAmelia Bruce DargavalRenato Patricia BlackUlrica Barbara
LaneOscar Martin DempseySamuel Sam MooneyTom Joseph FloodSilvano Vilem
TauskyConductor Vere LaurieProducer

IL TROVATORE - VERDI Dec 4, 7, 19
Rowland Jones/Frank Sale[Dec 19]Manrico Serafina di Leo/Gré Brouwenstijn[Dec
7]Leonora Bruce Dargaval/Frederick Sharp[Dec 7]Di Luna Constance Shacklock/Edith
Coates[Dec 4]Azucena Harold BlackburnFerrando Vilem TauskyConductor Sydney
RussellProducer

CAVALLERIA RUSTICANA - MASCAGNI Dec 5, 14, 16m
Serafina di LeoSantuzza James McKennaTuriddu Arthur CopleyAlfio Rita CullenLucia
Josephine O'HaganLola Lt-Col J M DoyleConductor Joseph FloodProducer
PAGLIACCI - LEONCAVALLO Dec 5, 14, 16m
Arthur Servant/James Johnston[Dec 5]Canio Minnia BowerNedda Roderick JonesTonio
Arthur CopleySilvio Brendan CavanaghBeppe Lt-Col J M DoyleConductor Joseph
FloodProducer
FAUST - GOUNOD Dec 6, 9m, 16, 18
Robert Thomas/James Johnston[Dec 9m]/Rowland Jones[Dec 18]Faust Margery
Field/Amy Shuard[Dec 16, 18]Marguerite Howell Glynne/Hervey Alan[Dec
6]Méphistophélès Otakar Kraus/Roderick Jones[Dec 6]Valentin Josephine O'HaganSiébel
Anne BishopMartha Gus MaddenWagner Vilem TauskyConductor Sydney RussellProducer
DON CARLO - VERDI Dec 8, 9, 11
John DavidCarlo Serafina di LeoElisabetta Bruce DargavalFilippo Roderick JonesRodrigo
Patricia BlackEboli Harold BlackburnInquisitore Sheila McPhillipsTebaldo Martin
DempseyFrate Vilem TauskyConductor Powell LloydProducer
TOSCA - PUCCINI Dec 12, 13, 15, 20
Gré BrouwenstijnTosca Frans VroonsCavaradossi Otakar Kraus/Roderick Jones[Dec
20]Scarpia Martin DempseyAngelotti Joseph FloodSacristan Brendan CavanaghSpoletta
Gerard MooneySciarrone Lt-Col J M DoyleConductor Powell LloydProducer

SPRING 1951: GAIETY THEATRE DUBLIN

RIGOLETTO - VERDI May 7, 9, 11
Tom WilliamsRigoletto Joan Butler/Vera Terry[May 9]Gilda Walter MidgleyDuke Stanislav
PieczoraSparafucile/Monterone Betty SagonMaddalena Vilem TauskyConductor Sydney
RussellProducer
TOSCA - PUCCINI May 8, 10, 12
Gré Brouwenstijn/Doris Dorée[May 8]Tosca Christopher ReumerCavaradossi Scipio
ColomboScarpia Martin DempseyAngelotti Joseph FloodSacristan Brendan CavanaghSpoletta
Gerard MooneySciarrone Lt-Col J M DoyleConductor Powell LloydProducer
LA TRAVIATA - VERDI May 12m, 17, 19
Rosanna GiancolaVioletta Christopher ReumerAlfredo Tom WilliamsGiorgio Jean HealyFlora
Brendan CavanaghGastone Joseph FloodBaron Thomas BradyMarchese Martin DempseyDr
Grenvil Monica CondronAnnina Lt-Col J M DoyleConductor Powell LloydProducer
**IL BARBIERE DI SIVIGLIA - ROSSINI May 14, 15, 16, 18, 19m, 21 [Hamburg
State Opera]**
Horst GüntherFigaro Annaliese RothenbergerRosina Fritz LehnertAlmaviva Adolf Meyer-
BremenBartolo Sigmund RothBasilio Guido DiemerFiorello Hedy GuraBerta Arthur
GrüberConductor Günther RennertProducer
**DIE ENTFÜHRUNG AUS DEM SERAIL - MOZART May 22, 23, 25, 26m
[Hamburg State Opera]**
Clara EbersKonstanze Walter GeislerBelmonte Annaliese RothenbergerBlonde Theo
HermannOsmin Kurt MarschnerPedrillo Guido DiemerSelim Arthur GrüberConductor
Günther RennertProducer
LA BOH_ME - PUCCINI May 24, 26
Victoria ElliottMimi James JohnstonRodolfo Arda MandikianMusetta Jess WaltersMarcello
Stanislav PieczoraColline Martin DempseySchaunard Joseph FloodBenoit/Alcindoro Lt-Col J
M DoyleConductor Sydney RussellProducer

WINTER 1951: GAIETY THEATRE DUBLIN

CARMEN - BIZET Dec 3, 8m, 12, 19
Patricia BlackCarmen Frans Vroons/James Johnston[Dec 19]Don José Veronica
DunneMicaëla Alfred Orda/Roderick Jones[Dec 8m,19]Escamillo Josephine
O'HaganFrasquita Jean HealyMercédès Sam MooneyDancaïre Joseph FloodRemendado
Martin DempseyZuniga Brendan CavanaghMoralès Lt-Col J M DoyleConductor Powell

LloydProducer
FAUST - GOUNOD Dec 4, 6, 8
James Johnston/Rowland Jones[Dec 8]Faust Veronica DunneMarguerite Howell
GlynneMéphistophélès Bruce DargavalValentin Patricia LawlorSiébel Anne BishopMartha
Ralph MorrisWagner Lt-Col J M DoyleConductor Sydney RussellProducer
MADAMA BUTTERFLY - PUCCINI Dec 5, 7, 10, 15m
Amy Shuard/Victoria Elliott[Dec 15m]Cio-Cio San Frans VroonsPinkerton Betty
SagonSuzuki Alfred OrdaSharpless Joseph FloodGoro Sam MooneyBonze Martin
DempseyYamadori Maureen RyanKate Vilem TauskyConductor Sydney RussellProducer
LA FORZA DEL DESTINO - VERDI Dec 11, 14, 17
Kyra VayneLeonora Corrado d'OttaviAlvaro Roderick JonesCarlo Bruce DragavalGuardiano
Powell Lloyd/Ernest Davies[Dec 11]Melitone Betty SagonPreziosilla Martin
DempseyMarquis Vilem TauskyConductor Powell LloydProducer
IL TROVATORE - VERDI Dec 13, 15, 18, 20
Corrado d'Ottavi/James Johnston[Dec 13]Manrico Franziska PetriLeonora Bruce DargavalDi
Luna Patricia BlackAzucena Sam Mooney/Ernest Davies[Dec 13 Act1]Ferrando Lt-Col J M
Doyle/Vilem Tausky[Dec 18,20]Conductor Sydney RussellProducer

SPRING 1952: GAIETY THEATRE DUBLIN

LA FORZA DEL DESTINO - VERDI Apr 28, 30, May 3m
Luisa MalagridaLeonora Rinaldo PelizzoniAlvaro Gwyn GriffithCarlo Bruce
DragavalGuardiano Ernest DaviesMelitone Betty SagonPreziosilla Martin DempseyMarquis
Vilem TauskyConductor Powell LloydProducer
LA BOH_ME - PUCCINI Apr 29, May 1, 3, 7, 10m
Veronica DunneMimi Giuseppe ZampieriRodolfo Sandra BaruffiMusetta Giulio
FioravantiMarcello Gino BelloniColline Arturo La PortaSchaunard Brendan CavanaghBenoit
Joseph FloodAlcindoro Karl RanklConductor Sydney RussellProducer
LA TRAVIATA - VERDI May 2, 5, 8, 10
Luisa MalagridaVioletta Rinaldo PelizzoniAlfredo Giulio Fioravanti/Otello Bersellini[May
8,10]Giorgio Jean HealyFlora Brendan CavanaghGastone Arturo La PortaBaron Martin
DempseyMarchese Gino BelloniDr Grenvil Monica CondronAnnina Lt-Col J M
DoyleConductor Powell LloydProducer
MANON - MASSENET May 6, 9, 12, 14
Barbara BrittonManon Richard Lewisdes Grieux Otakar KrausLescaut Joseph FloodGuillot
Jess WaltersCount Ernest DaviesBrétigny Clothilde JohnstonPousette Monica
CondronJavotte Betty SagonRosette Reginald GoodallConductor PowellLloydProducer
MADAMA BUTTERFLY - PUCCINI May 13, 16, 20, 22
Joan HammondCio-Cio San Ivan CecchiniPinkerton Betty SagonSuzuki Bruce
DargavalSharpless Joseph FloodGoro Sam MooneyBonze Martin DempseyYamadori Maureen
RyanKate Vilem Tausky/Lt-Col J M Doyle[May 16]Conductor Powell LloydProducer
RIGOLETTO - VERDI May 15, 17, 21, 24m
Otello Bersellini/Giulio Fioravanti[May 21, 24m]Rigoletto Sandra BaruffiGilda Giuseppe
ZampieriDuke Gino BelloniSparafucile Arturo La PortaMonterone Betty SagonMaddalena
Vilem Tausky/Lt-Col J M Doyle[May 15, 24m]Conductor Powell LloydProducer
DON PASQUALE - DONIZETTI May 17m, 19, 23, 24
Ronald StearPasquale Veronica DunneNorina Ivan CecchiniErnesto Bruce DargavalMalatesta
Barry O'SullivanNotary Vilem TauskyConductor Powell LloydProducer

AUTUMN 1952: OPERA HOUSE CORK

IL TROVATORE - VERDI Sep 1, 3
James Johnston/Ivan Dixon[Sep 3]Manrico Victoria ElliottLeonora Bruce DargavalDi Luna
Edith CoatesAzucena Richard MasonFerrando James GibsonConductor Powell
LloydProducer
FAUST - GOUNOD Sep 2, 4, 6m
James JohnstonFaust Veronica DunneMarguerite Howell GlynneMéphistophélès William

EdwardsValentin Betty SagonSiébel Lt-Col J M DoyleConductor Powell LloydProducer
LA TRAVIATA - VERDI Sep 5, 6
Ruth PackerVioletta Ivan DixonAlfredo Bruce DargavalGiorgio James GibsonConductor
Powell LloydProducer

WINTER 1952: GAIETY THEATRE DUBLIN

FAUST - GOUNOD Dec 1, 5, 6
James Johnston/Rowland Jones[Dec 5]Faust Joyce GartsideMarguerite Howell
GlynneMéphistophélès William EdwardsValentin Betty SagonSiébel Anne BishopMartha
Ralph MorrisWagner Lt-Col J M DoyleConductor Powell LloydProducer
IL BARBIERE DI SIVIGLIA - ROSSINI Dec 2, 4, 6m, 13
Paolo SilveriFigaro Maria EratoRosina Rodolfo MoraroAlmaviva Arturo La PortaBartolo
Plinio ClabassiBasilio Sam MooneyFiorello Giannella BorelliBerta Giuseppe MorelliConductor
Bruno Nofri Producer
L'AMICO FRITZ - MASCAGNI Dec 3, 8, 10, 12
Alvinio MiscianoFrtiz Veronica DunneSuzel Arturo La PortaDavid Brendan
CavanaghFrederico Noel ReidHanezò Maura MooneyCaterina Giuseppe MorelliConductor
Bruno NofriProducer
CARMEN - BIZET Dec 9, 11, 13m
Constance ShacklockCarmen Frans VroonsDon José Dolores BurkeMicaëla Bruce
DargavalEscamillo Patricia O'KeefeFrasquita Betty SagonMercédès Sam MooneyDancaïre
Joseph FloodRemendado Harold BlackburnZuniga Brendan CavanaghMoralès Vilem
TauskyConductor Powell LloydProducer
IL TROVATORE - VERDI Dec 15, 17, 19, 20
Giorgio BardiManrico Licia RossiniLeonora Rodolfo AzzoliniDi Luna Maria SalvoAzucena
Plinio ClabassiFerrando Lt-Col J M DoyleConductor Sydney RussellProducer
TOSCA - PUCCINI Dec 16, 18, 20m
Maria KinasiewiczTosca Frans VroonsCavaradossi Bruce DargavalScarpia Harold
BlackburnAngelotti Joseph FloodSacristan Brendan CavanaghSpoletta Gerard
MooneySciarrone Vilem TauskyConductor Powell LloydProducer

SPRING 1953: GAIETY THEATRE DUBLIN

**TRISTAN UND ISOLDE - WAGNER Apr 20, 22[Act 3], 24, 29 May 3 [Munich
State Opera]**
Paula Baumann/Erna Schluter[Apr 20]Isolde August SeiderTristan Hans Hermann-
NissenMarke Ira MalaniukBrangäene Rudolf GrossmannKurwenal Albrecht PeterMelot
Rudolf WunzerSteersman Paul KuenSailor/Shepherd Robert Heger/Hans Gierster[Apr
29]Conductor Ulrich ReinhardtProducer
MADAMA BUTTERFLY - PUCCINI Apr 21, 25, 28 May 2m
Elena RizzieriCio-Cio San Alvinio MiscianoPinkerton Gianella BorelliSuzuki Giuseppe
ForgioneSharpless Joseph FloodGoro Umberto FrisaldiBonze/Yamadori Maureen RyanKate
Giuseppe MorelliConductor Bruno NofriProducer
IL BARBIERE DI SIVIGLIA - ROSSINI Apr 23, 30, May 5, 7
Giuseppe ForgioneFigaro Erina ValliRosina Rodolfo MoraroAlmaviva Umberto
FrisaldiBartolo Plinio ClabassiBasilio Sam MooneyFiorello Giannella BorelliBerta Giuseppe
MorelliConductor Bruno Nofri Producer
LA BOH_ME - PUCCINI Apr 25m, 27 May 1, 4 [Munich State Opera]
Gerda SommerschuhMimi Hans Hopf/Josef Traxel[Apr 25m]Rodolfo Kathe
NentwigMusetta Albrecht PeterMarcello Rudolf WunzerColline Benno KuscheSchaunard
Adolf KielBenoit/Alcindoro Karl TutineConductor Oscar Arnold-PaurProducer
LE NOZZE DI FIGARO - MOZART May 2, 6, 8, 11 [Munich State Opera]
Benno KuscheFigaro Kathe NentwigSusanna Cäcilie ReichCountess Karl Schmitt-
WalterCount Herta TopperCherubino Ruolf WunzerBartolo Ian GerheinMarcellina Paul
KuenBasilio Adolf KeilAntonio Hildegard LimmerBarbarina Emile GrafCurzio Rudolf
Kempe/Hans Gierster[May 2]Conductor Heinz ArnoldProducer

LA TRAVIATA - VERDI May 9m, 13, 15, 16 [Munich State Opera]
Sari BarabasVioletta Richard HolmAlfredo Karl Schmitt-WalterGiorgio Antonie FahbergFlora
Emile GrafGastone Josef KnappBaron Robert HagerMarchese Rudolf WunzerDr Grenvil Ian
GerheinAnnina Hans GiersterConductor Heinz ArnoldProducer
RIGOLETTO - VERDI May 9, 12, 14, 16m
Paolo SilveriRigoletto Erina ValliGilda Alvinio MiscianoDuke Plinio ClabassiSparafucile
Umberto FrisaldiMonterone Giannella BorelliMaddalena Lt-Col J M DoyleConductor Powell
LloydProducer

THE BARTERED BRIDE - SMETANA Nov 30 Dec 2, 4, 5
Dolores BurkeMarenka Rowland Jones/Thomas Round[Dec 4, 5]Jeník Bruce DargavalKecal
Powell LloydVasek Leslie PearsonKrusina Jean HealyLudmilla Patricia LawlorHáta Sam
MooneyMícha Josephine O'HaganEsmeralda Joseph FloodCircus Master Lt-Col J M
DoyleConductor Powell LloydProducer
DON GIOVANNI - MOZART Dec 1, 3, 5m, 7, 9, 11 [Hamburg State Opera]
James PeaseGiovanni Clara EbersAnna Toni BlankenheimLeporello Elfriede WasserthalElvira
Walter GeislerOttavio Lore HoffmanZerlina Sigmund RothCommendatore Horst
GüntherMasetto Leopold LudwigConductor Günther RennertProducer
CARMEN - BIZET Dec 8, 10, 12m
Constance Shacklock/Gita Denise[Dec 12]Carmen Frans VroonsDon José Dolores
BurkeMicaëla Bruce DargavalEscamillo Josephine O'HaganFrasquita Patricia LawlorMercédès
Sam MooneyDancaïre Joseph FloodRemendado Leslie PearsonZuniga Brendan
CavanaghMoralès Lt-Col J M DoyleConductor Powell LloydProducer
DIE ENTFÜHRUNG AUS DEM SERAIL - MOZART Dec 12, 14, 16, 18 [Hamburg
State Opera]
Valerie BakKonstanze Fritz LehnertBelmonte Annaliese RothenbergerBlonde Theo
HermannOsmin Kurt MarschnerPedrillo Guido DiemerSelim Heinz Günther-
Wallberg/Reinhard Linz [Dec 16, 18]Conductor Günther RennertProducer
LA BOH_ME - PUCCINI Dec 15, 17, 19
Victoria ElliottMimi Oreste KirkopRodolfo Dolores BurkeMusetta Bruce DargavalMarcello
Harold BlackburnColline Leslie PearsonSchaunard Brendan CavanaghBenoit Joseph
FloodAlcindoro Vilem TauskyConductor Ande AndersonProducer

CECILIA - REFICE May 3, 5, 7, 10
Iselle FavatiCecilia Tommaso FrascatiValeriano GiuseppeForgioneTiburzio Palmira Vitali
MariniBlind Woman Plinio ClabassiUrbano Arturo La PortaAmachio Monsignor Licinio
ReficeConductor Bruno NofriProducer
MADAMA BUTTERFLY - PUCCINI May 4, 6, 8
Rina GigliCio-Cio San James JohnstonPinkerton Betty SagonSuzuki Bruce DargavalSharpless
Joseph FloodGoro Sam MooneyBonze Brendan CavanaghYamadori Maureen RyanKate
Vilem TauskyConductor Powell LloydProducer
IL TROVATORE - VERDI May 11, 13, 15, 27
James Johnston/Brychan Powell[May 13]/Giorgio Bardi[May 27]Manrico Victoria
Elliott/Caterina Mancini[May 27]Leonora Bruce Dargaval/Paolo Silveri[May 27]Di Luna
Jean Watson/Gita Denise[May 11]/Palmira Vitali Marini[May 27]Azucena Sam
Mooney/Plinio Clabassi[May 27]Ferrando Lt-Col J M Doyle/Giuseppe Morelli[May
27]Conductor Powell LloydProducer
TOSCA - PUCCINI May 12, 14, 17, 19
Maria BoiTosca Alvinio MiscianoCavaradossi Tito Gobbi/Paolo Silveri[May 19]Scarpia Plinio
ClabassiAngelotti Arturo La PortaSacristan Brendan CavanaghSpoletta Clem MorrisSciarrone
Giuseppe MorelliConductor Bruno NofriProducer
LA FORZA DEL DESTINO - VERDI May 18, 21, 25, 29
Caterina ManciniLeonora Giorgio BardiAlvaro Giuseppe Forgione/Antonio Manca Serra[May

18]Carlo Plinio ClabassiGuardiano Arturo La PortaMelitone Palmira Vitali MariniPreziosilla Sam MooneyMarquis Giuseppe MorelliConductor Bruno NofriProducer

LA TRAVIATA - VERDI May 20, 22, 24, 26, 28
Rina GigliVioletta Alvinio MiscianoAlfredo Paolo SilveriGiorgio Bernadette DalyFlora Brendan CavanaghGastone Arturo La PortaBaron Joseph FloodMarchese Plinio ClabassiDr Grenvil Monica CondronAnnina Lt-Col J M DoyleConductor Bruno NofriProducer

LA BOH_ME - PUCCINI Nov 29, Dec 1, 3, 8
Veronica DunneMimi Walter MidgleyRodolfo Elizabeth FretwellMusetta Jess Walters/Roderick Jones[Nov 29]/William Dickie[Dec 8]Marcello Kenneth StephensonColline Bernard HootonSchaunard Brendan CavanaghBenoit Joseph FloodAlcindoro Lt-Col J M DoyleConductor Powell LloydProducer

FIDELIO - BEETHOVEN Nov 30, Dec 2, 4, 7, 9 [Munich State Opera]
Esther Mühlbauer Leonora August SeiderFlorestan Hans Hermann-NissenPizzaro Helmut FehnRocco Antonia Fahberg/Uta Graf[Dec7]Marzelline John KuhnJaquino Heinz Maria LinsFernando Hans GiersterConductor Bruno von NiessenProducer

AIDA - VERDI Dec 6, 10, 17
Elizabeth FretwellAida Paul Asciak/Walter Midgley[Dec 10]Radames Jean WatsonAmneris William DickieAmonasro Kenneth StephensonRamfis Bernard HootonKing Sheila RyanPriestess Brendan CavanaghMessenger Lt-Col J M DoyleConductor Powell LloydProducer

HÄNSEL UND GRETEL - HUMPERDINCK Dec 11, 13, 15, 20 [Munich State Opera]
Uta GrafGretel Doris PillingHänsel Hans Hermann-NissenFather Hanna MünchMother Esther Mühlbauer Witch Alma McIntyre/Joan RooneySandman Monica Condron/Mary HealyDew Fairy Hans GiersterConductor Bruno von NiessenProducer

CARMEN - BIZET Dec 14, 16, 18, 21
Marianna RadevCarmen Brychan PowellDon José Veronica DunneMicaëla Jess Walters/William Dickie[Dec 14]Escamillo Josephine O'HaganFrasquita Betty SagonMercédès Bernard HootonDancaïre Joseph FloodRemendado Kenneth StephensonZuniga Brendan CavanaghMoralès Milan HorvatConductor Ande AndersonProducer

UN BALLO IN MASCHERA - VERDI Apr 25, 27, 29, May 19
Antonio GaliéRiccardo Caterina ManciniAmelia Paolo SilveriRenato Giannella BorelliUlrica Maria Luisa GiorgettiOscar Marco StefanoniSamuel Tito DolciottiTom Giorgio OnestiSilvano Giuseppe MorelliConductor Elisabeth WoehrProducer

TOSCA - PUCCINI Apr 26, 30, May 4, 7
Maria Curtis Verna/Maria Caniglia[Apr 26]Tosca Giovanni Millo/Antonio Galié[May 4, 7]Cavaradossi Antonio Manca SerraScarpia Tito DolciottiAngelotti Giorgio OnestiSacristan/Sciarrone Brendan CavanaghSpoletta Francesco ManderConductor Elisabeth WoehrProducer

LA TRAVIATA - VERDI Apr 28, May 2, 12, 17
Virginia ZeaniVioletta Gianni Raimondi/Alvinio Misciano[May 2, 17]Alfredo Antonio Manca Serra Giorgio Maria Luisa GiorgettiFlora/Annina Brendan CavanaghGastone Giorgio OnestiBaron Joseph FloodMarchese Tito DolciottiDr Grenvil Lt-Col J M DoyleConductor Elisabeth WoehrProducer

NORMA - BELLINI May 3, 6, 10, 14
Caterina ManciniNorma Ebe StignaniAdalgisa Primo ZambrunoPollione Marco StefanoniOroveso Joseph FloodFlavio Maria Luisa GiorgettiClothilde Alberto Erede/Giuseppe Morelli[May14]Conductor Elisabeth WoehrProducer

RIGOLETTO - VERDI May 5, 9, 16, 21
Paolo SilveriRigoletto Gianna d'AngeloGilda Gianni RaimondiDuke Marco StefanoniSparafucile Tito DolciottiMonterone Giannella BorelliMaddalena Giuseppe

MorelliConductor Elisabeth WoehrProducer
LUCIA DI LAMMERMOOR - DONIZETTI May 11, 13, 18, 20
Gianna d'AngeloLucia Alvinio MiscianoEdgardo Antonio Manca SerraEnrico Tito
DolciottiRaimondo Brendan CavanaghArturo/Normanno Maria Luisa GiorgettiAlisa
Giuseppe MorelliConductor Elisabeth WoehrProducer

Winter 1955: Gaiety Theatre Dublin

CAVALLERIA RUSTICANA - MASCAGNI Nov 26, Dec 2, 5, 8, 14, 16
Arda Mandikian/Amy Shuard[Nov 26]Santuzza Paul Asciak/Brychan Powell[Dec
5,8]Turiddu William DickieAlfio Olwen Price/Patricia Johnson[Dec 2]Lucia Celine
MurphyLola Stanford Robinson/Lt-Col J M Doyle[Dec 14, 16]Conductor Powell
LloydProducer
PAGLIACCI - LEONCAVALLO Nov 26, Dec 2, 5, 8, 14, 16
Antonio AnnaloroCanio Veronica DunneNedda William DickieTonio William EdwardsSilvio
Brendan CavanaghBeppe Stanford Robinson/Lt-Col J M Doyle[Dec 14, 16]Conductor
Powell LloydProducer
FAUST - GOUNOD Nov 28, 30, Dec 3, 7, 10
Brychan PowellFaust Veronica DunneMarguerite Michael Langdon/David Ward[Dec
10]Méphistophélès William EdwardsValentin Celine MurphySiébel Anne BishopMartha Leo
O'BrienWagner Lt-Col J M DoyleConductor Powell LloydProducer
MADAMA BUTTERFLY - PUCCINI Nov 29, Dec 1, 6, 9, 13
Leonora Lafayette/Amy Shuard[Nov 29, Dec 1]Cio-Cio San Paul AsciakPinkerton Olwen
Price/Patricia Johnston[Nov 29, Dec 1]Suzuki William DickieSharpless Joseph FloodGoro
William EdwardsBonze Leo O'BrienYamadori Monica CondronKate Milan HorvatConductor
Ande AndersonProducer
LA BOH_ME - PUCCINI Dec 12, 15, 17
Joan Stuart/Veronica Dunne[Dec 12]Mimi Charles CraigRodolfo Arda MandikianMusetta
Frederick Sharp/Ronald Lewis[Dec 12]Marcello Harold BlackburnColline Peter
Glossop/John Probyn[Dec 15]Schaunard Brendan CavanaghBenoit Joseph FloodAlcindoro
Bryan BalkwillConductor Powell LloydProducer

Spring 1956: Gaiety Theatre Dublin:2nd Festival of Italian Opera

IL TROVATORE - VERDI Apr 30, May 3, 7, 10
Antonio AnnaloroManrico Caterina ManciniLeonora Paolo SilveriDi Luna Ebe
StignaniAzucena Tito DolciottiFerrando Giuseppe MorelliConductor Elisabeth
WoehrProducer
LUCIA DI LAMMERMOOR - DONIZETTI May 1, 4, 24, 26, 29 Jun 1
Antoinetta Pastori/Gianna d'Angelo[May 24, 26]/Virginia Zeani[May 29]/Franca
Ottaviani[Jun 1]Lucia Antonio Galié/Alvinio Misciano[May 1, 4]Edgardo Giuseppe
ForgioneEnrico Ferruccio Mazzoli/Tito Dolciotti[Jun 1]Raimondo Brendan
CavanaghArturo/Normanno Dodi ProteroAlisa Giuseppe Morelli/Alberto Leone[Jun
1]Conductor Elisabeth WoehrProducer
LA BOH_ME - PUCCINI May 2, 5, 9, 14
Virginia ZeaniMimi Antonio GaliéRodolfo Celine MurphyMusetta Giuseppe Forgione/Paolo
Silveri[May 2]Marcello Ferruccio MazzoliColline Osvaldo PetricciuoloSchaunard Giorgio
OnestiBenoit/Alcindoro Nino VerchiConductor Elisabeth WoehrProducer
MANON - MASSENET May 8, 11, 16, 18
Virginia ZeaniManon Alvinio Miscianodes Grieux Giuseppe ForgioneLescaut Joseph
FloodGuillot Ferruccio MazzoliCount Osvaldo PetricciuoloBrétigny Lt-Col J M
DoyleConductor Elisabeth WoehrProducer
UN BALLO IN MASCHERA - VERDI May 12, 15, 19, 22
Antonio GaliéRiccardo Caterina ManciniAmelia Paolo SilveriRenato Giannella BorelliUlrica
Dodi ProteroOscar Ferruccio MazzoliSamuel Tito DolciottiTom Giorgio OnestiSilvano Nino
VerchiConductor Elisabeth WoehrProducer
IL SEGRETO DI SUSANNA - WOLF-FERRARI May 17, 21, 23, 25

Osvaldo PetricciuoloGil Dodi ProteroSusanna Giorgio OnestiSante Giuseppe
MorelliConductor Elisabeth WoehrProducer
PAGLIACCI - LEONCAVALLO May 17, 21, 23, 25
Antonio AnnaloroCanio Marisa PintusNedda Paolo Silveri/Giuseppe Forgione[May 23,
25]Tonio Osvaldo PetricciuoloSilvio Brendan CavanaghBeppe Giuseppe MorelliConductor
Elisabeth WoehrProducer
RIGOLETTO - VERDI May 28, 30
Paolo SilveriRigoletto Gianna d'Angelo/Franca Ottaviani[May 30]Gilda Antonio
AnnaloroDuke Ferruccio MazzoliSparafucile Tito DolciottiMonterone Giannella
BorelliMaddalena Giuseppe MorelliConductor Elisabeth WoehrProducer
LA TRAVIATA - VERDI May 31, Jun 2
Virginia ZeaniVioletta Antonio Annaloro/Antonio Galié[Jun 2]Alfredo Giuseppe
ForgioneGiorgio Dodi ProteroFlora Brendan CavanaghGastone Brendan RobertsBaron
Joseph FloodMarchese Tito DolciottiDr Grenvil Monica CondronAnnina Giuseppe
MorelliConductor Elisabeth WoehrProducer

WINTER 1956: GAIETY THEATRE DUBLIN

TOSCA - PUCCINI Nov 26, 28, Dec 1
Joan HammondTosca James JohnstonCavaradossi Ronald LewisScarpia Peter Forbes-
RobertsonAngelotti Howell Glynne/Joseph Flood[Nov 28]Sacristan Brendan
CavanaghSpoletta Walter KaneSciarrone Emmanuel YoungConductor Alfred SierckeProducer
DIE WALKÜRE - WAGNER Nov 27, 30 Dec 3, 14 [Essen Municipal Opera]
Tilla BriemBrünnhilde Gunther Treptow/Rudolf Lustig[Nov 30]Siegmund Herbert
FlietherWotan Elfriede Wasserthal/Paula Brivkalne[Nov 27]Sieglinde Xavier WaibelHunding
Trude RoeslerFricka/Waltraute Gustav König/Paul Belker[Nov 30, Dec 3]Conductor Hans
HartlebProducer
IDOMENEO - MOZART Nov 29, Dec 4, 13, 15 [Essen Municipal Opera]
Willi FriedrichIdomeneo Paula BrivkalneElettra Annie StudentIlia Louis de VosIdamante
Julius JüllichArbace Xavier WaibelHigh Priest Herbert FlietherOracle Gustav König/Paul
Belker[Dec 4]Conductor Hans HartlebProducer
SIMON BOCCANEGRA - VERDI Dec 5, 7, 10, 12
Roderick JonesSimon Victoria ElliottAmelia James JohnstonGabriele Howell GlynneFiesco
Frederick SharpPaolo Ronald LewisPietro Charles MackerrasConductor Werner
WiekenbergProducer
CARMEN - BIZET Dec 6, 8, 11
Margareta ElkinsCarmen William AikenDon José Celine MurphyMicaëla Ronald
LewisEscamillo Nancy CreightonFrasquita Anne EdwardsMercédès Brendan
CavanaghDancaïre/Moralès Joseph FloodRemendado Donald CampbellZuniga Lt-Col J M
DoyleConductor Werner WiekenbergProducer

Spring 1957: Gaiety Theatre Dublin:3rd Festival of Italian Opera

LA TRAVIATA - VERDI Apr 22, 24, May 3, 8, 11
Gabriella TucciVioletta Ferrando FerrariAlfredo Carlo TagliabueGiorgio Silvia BertonaFlora
Brendan CavanaghGastone Arturo La PortaBaron Girogio OnestiMarchese Renzo
GonzalesDr Grenvil Monica CondronAnnina Giuseppe MorelliConductor Bruno
NofriProducer
ANDREA CHÉNIER - GIORDANO Apr 23, 26, May 1, 4
Antonio GaliéChénier Caterina ManciniMaddalena Giulio MastrangeloGérard Ferruccio
MazzoliRoucher Silvia BertonaBersi Arturo La PortaMathieu Giannella
BorelliMadelon/Countess Franco TainoIncroyable Renzo GonzalesFléville/Dumas Giorgio
OnestiFouquier-Tinville/Schmidt Brendan CavanaghAbbé Giuseppe MorelliConductor Bruno
NofriProducer
DON PASQUALE - DONIZETTI Apr 25, 27, 30
Giorgio OnestiPasquale Maria dalla SpeziaNorina Fernando BanderaErnesto Giuseppe
ForgioneMalatesta Brendan CavanaghNotary Nino VerchiConductor Bruno NofriProducer

TOSCA - PUCCINI Apr 29, May 2, 6, 9
Simona dall'ArgineTosca Umberto BorsòCavaradossi Carlo TagliabueScarpia Renzo
GonzalesAngelotti Arturo La PortaSacristan Brendan CavanaghSpoletta Giorgio
OnestiSciarrone Nino VerchiConductor Bruno NofriProducer
MADAMA BUTTERFLY - PUCCINI May 7, 10, 14, 17, 23
Miki KoiwaiCio-Cio San Antonio GaliéPinkerton Giannella BorelliSuzuki Giuseppe
ForgioneSharpless Brendan CavanaghGoro Renzo GonzalesBonze Arturo La PortaYamadori
Vera Power-FardyKate Franco PatanèConductor Bruno NofriProducer
AIDA - VERDI May 13, 16, 20, 22, 25
Caterina ManciniAida Umberto BorsòRadames Lari ScipioneAmneris Giuseppe
ForgioneAmonasro Ferruccio MazzoliRamfis Renzo GonzalesKing Rhona WoodcockPriestess
Brendan CavanaghMessenger Franco PatanèConductor Bruno NofriProducer
IL BARBIERE DI SIVIGLIA - ROSSINI May 15, 18, 21, 24
Giulio MastrangeloFigaro Maria dalla SpeziaRosina Fernando BanderaAlmaviva Arturo La
PortaBartolo Ferruccio MazzoliBasilio Giorgio OnestiFiorello Giannella BorelliBerta
Giuseppe MorelliConductor Bruno Nofri Producer

WINTER 1957: GAIETY THEATRE DUBLIN

LES CONTES D'HOFFMANN - OFFENBACH Nov 25, 30, Dec 9, 14
James Johnston/Edgar Evans[Nov 25]/Brychan Powell[Nov 30]Hoffmann Margaret
NisbettOlympia Joyce BarkerGiulietta Bruce
DargavalCoppélius/Miracle/Dapertutto/Lindorf Barbara HowittNicklausse Veronica
DunneAntonia Niven MillerSpalanzani Othmar Rémy ArthurCrespel/Schlemil Kevin
MillerCochenille/Pitichinaccio/Frantz Monica SinclairMother Peter GellhornConductor
Ande AndersonProducer
TURANDOT - PUCCINI Nov 26, 28, Dec 2, 12
Sylvia Fisher/Maria Kinces[Dec 2, 12]Turandot Walter MidgleyCalaf Eizabeth RustLiù
Marian NowakowskiTimur Niven MillerPing Kevin MillerPang Brychan PowellPong Brendan
CavanaghAltoum Ronald EvansMandarin Peter GellhornConductor Ande AndersonProducer
FAUST - GOUNOD Nov 27, 29, Dec 4, 13
Walter MidgleyFaust Patricia Bartlett/Anne Bollinger[Dec 13]Marguerite Marian
NowakowskiMéphistophélès Ronald EvansValentin Margaret NisbettSiébel Vera Power-
FardyMartha P J TobinWagner Lt-Col J M DoyleConductor John CopleyProducer
LA BOH_ME - PUCCINI Dec 3, 6, 11
Adèle LeighMimi William McAlpineRodolfo Elizabeth RustMusetta John HauxvellMarcello
James PeaseColline Niven MillerSchaunard Brendan CavanaghBenoit/Alcindoro Warwick
BraithwaiteConductor Christopher WestProducer
LE NOZZE DI FIGARO - MOZART Dec 5, 7, 10
James PeaseFigaro Adèle LeighSusanna Anne BollingerCountess Geraint Evans/Bruce
Boyce[Dec 10]Count Patricia KernCherubino Howell GlynneBartolo Barbara
HowittMarcellina Kevin MillerBasilio Martin DempseyAntonio Margaret NisbettBarbarina
Niven MillerCurzio Bryan BalkwillConductor Christopher WestProducer

SPRING 1958: GAIETY THEATRE DUBLIN:4TH FESTIVAL OF ITALIAN OPERA

UN BALLO IN MASCHERA - VERDI Apr 7, 9, 11, 14
Antonio GaliéRiccardo Caterina Mancini/Elisabetta Barbato[Apr 14]Amelia Carlo
MelicianiRenato Maria TassiUlrica Gioi GiovannettiOscar Ferruccio MazzoliSamuel Renato
SpagliTom Arturo La PortaSilvano Alberto EredeConductor Bruno NofriProducer
RIGOLETTO - VERDI Apr 8, 10, 16, 18
Aldo ProttiRigoletto Renata OngaroGilda Ermanno LorenziDuke Ferruccio
MazzoliSparafucile Renato SpagliMonterone Valeria EscalarMaddalena Giuseppe
MorelliConductor Bruno NofriProducer
AIDA - VERDI Apr 12, 15, 19, 23
Gloria DavyAida Umberto BorsòRadames Ebe StignaniAmneris Giuseppe ForgioneAmonasro
Ferruccio MazzoliRamfis Renato SpagliKing Diana RobertiPriestess Gabriele de

JulisMessenger Alberto EredeConductor Bruno NofriProducer

MANON LESCAUT - PUCCINI Apr 17, 21, 25 May 1

Elisabetta BarbatoManon Umberto Borsòdes Grieux Giuseppe ForgioneLescaut Arturo La
PortaGeronte Gabriele de JulisEdmondo, Dancing Master/Lamplighter Valeria EscalarSinger
Ledo FreschiSergeant Renato SpagliCaptain Alberto EredeConductor Bruno NofriProducer
LUCIA DI LAMMERMOOR - DONIZETTI Apr 22, 24, 29, May 3
Virginia ZeaniLucia Antonio GaliéEdgardo Carlo MelicianiEnrico Ferruccio
MazzoliRaimondo Gabriele de JulisArturo Diana RobertiAlisa Brendan CavanaghNormanno
Giuseppe MorelliConductor Bruno NofriProducer
L'ELISIR D'AMORE - DONIZETTI Apr 26, 28, 30, May 2
Renata OngaroAdina Alvinio MiscianoNemorino Franco MiolliBelcore Arturo La
PortaDulcamara Diana RobertiGiannetta Giuseppe MorelliConductor Bruno NofriProducer

WINTER 1958: GAIETY THEATRE DUBLIN

DON GIOVANNI - MOZART Nov 24, 26, 28, Dec 1
Geraint EvansGiovanni Joan SutherlandAnna Martin LawrenceLeporello Patricia BartlettElvira
Dermot TroyOttavio Patricia ClarkZerlina Bruce DargavalCommendatore Harold
BlackburnMasetto Bryan BalkwillConductor Anthony BeschProducer
TOSCA - PUCCINI Nov 25, 27, 29, Dec 2
Joan HammondTosca James JohnstonCavaradossi Otakar KrausScarpia Martin
LawrenceAngelotti Harold BlackburnSacristan/Sciarrone Joseph SomersSpoletta Bryan
BalkwillConductor Anthony BeschProducer
LA BOH_ME - PUCCINI Dec 3, 5, 8
Ofelia di MarcoMimi Luigi RumboRodolfo Santa ChissariMusetta Marco StecchiMarcello
Loris GambelliColline Ernesto VezzosiSchaunard Giorgio OnestiBenoit/Alcindoro Franco
PatanèConductor Bruno NofriProducer
LA TRAVIATA - VERDI Dec 4, 6, 10, 12
Dora Carral/Ofelia di Marco[Dec 10, 12]Violetta Renato Cioni/Luigi Rumbo[Dec 10,
12]Alfredo Atilio d'Orazi/Renzo Scorsoni[Dec 10, 12]Giorgio Santa ChissariFlora Joseph
SomersGastone Giorgio OnestiBaron Ernesto VezzosiMarchese Camillo RighiniDr Grenvil
Licia MaragnoAnnina Lt-Col J M DoyleConductor Bruno NofriProducer
MADAMA BUTTERFLY - PUCCINI Dec 9, 11, 13
Joan Hammond/Dora Carral[Dec 9: Act 1]/Ofelia di Marco[Dec 9: Acts 2 & 3]Cio-Cio San
Renato CioniPinkerton Licia MaragnoSuzuki Atilio d'OraziSharpless Ernesto VezzosiGoro
Camillo RighiniBonze Giorgio OnestiYamadori Vera Power-FardyKate Franco
PatanèConductor Bruno NofriProducer

SPRING 1959: GAIETY THEATRE DUBLIN:5TH FESTIVAL OF ITALIAN OPERA

AVE MARIA - ALLEGRA March 30, Apr 1, 3, 6
Ines BardiniMadre Regolo RomaniBista Silvano BazzoniLena Renzo ScorsoniSagro Salvatore
AllegraConductor Bruno NofriProducer
CAVALLERIA RUSTICANA - MASCAGNI March 30, Apr 1, 3, 6
Ines BardiniSantuzza Umberto BorsòTuriddu Renzo ScorsoniAlfio Luciana PalombiLucia
Licia MarangoLola Giuseppe Patanè-CaravagliosConductor Bruno NofriProducer
DON PASQUALE - DONIZETTI Mar 31, Apr 2, 4, 10
Leo PudisPasquale Anna MoffoNorina Salvatore GioiaErnesto Atilio d'OraziMalatesta Sergio
FelicianiNotary Ottavio ZiinoConductor Bruno NofriProducer
RIGOLETTO - VERDI Apr 7, 9, 11, 14
Carlo MelicianiRigoletto Ornella GiacchettiGilda Antonio GaliéDuke Umberto
GiacoboniSparafucile Camillo RighiniMonterone Maria Teresa MandalariMaddalena Ottavio
ZiinoConductor Bruno NofriProducer
ANDREA CHÉNIER - GIORDANO Apr 8, 20, 22, 24

Umberto BorsòChénier Ines BardiniMaddalena Renzo ScorsoniGérard Loris
GambelliRoucher Silvana BazzoniBersi Ernesto VezzosiMathieu/Fléville Maria Teresa
MandalariMadelon Licia MaragnoCountess Sergio FelicianiIncroyable/Abbé Umberto
GiacoboniDumas Camillo RighiniFouquier-Tinville/Schmidt Franco PatanèConductor Bruno
NofriProducer

IL BARBIERE DI SIVIGLIA - ROSSINI Apr 13, 15, 17, 23
Atilio d'OraziFigaro Margherita RinaldiRosina Salvatore GioiaAlmaviva Giorgio OnestiBartolo
Umberto Giacoboni/Loris Gambelli[Apr 23]Basilio Ernesto VezzosiFiorello Licia
MaragnoBerta Franco Patanè/Giuseppe Patanè-Caravaglios[Apr 23]Conductor Bruno
NofriProducer

OTELLO - VERDI Apr 16, 18, 21, 25
Paolo SilveriOtello Ofelia di MarcoDesdemona Afro PoliIago Sergio FelicianiCassio Brendan
CavanaghRoderigo Loris GambelliLodovico Ernesto VezzosiMontano Maria Teresa
MandalariEmilia Camillo ReghiniHerald Franco PatanèConductor Bruno NofriProducer

WINTER 1959: GAIETY THEATRE DUBLIN

CARMEN - BIZET Nov 24, 26, 28, Dec 2
Mafalda MasiniCarmen Umberto Borsò/Paul Asciak[Nov 28, Dec 2]Don José Anne
Edwards/Jeanette Sinclair[Nov 24]Micaëla James PeaseEscamillo Elizabeth RustFrasquita
Johanna PetersMercédès Evan ThomasDancaïre/Moralès Gerald DaviesRemendado Gerald
DuffyZuniga Giuseppe Patanè-CaravagliosConductor Christopher WestProducer

LE NOZZE DI FIGARO - MOZART Nov 25, 27, Dec 1, 4
James PeaseFigaro Adèle LeighSusanna Patricia BartlettCountess Jess WaltersCount Celine
MurphyCherubino David KellyBartolo Johanna PetersMarcellina Gerald DaviesBasilio/Curzio
Gerald DuffyAntonio Elizabeth RustBarbarina Charles MackerrasConductor Christopher
WestProducer

FAUST - GOUNOD Dec 3, 5, 8, 10
Ken NeateFaust Denise MonteilMarguerite Georges VaillantMéphistophélès Julian
HaasValentin Lena PastorSiébel Tina RutaMartha Evan ThomasWagner Jean
FournetConductor Bruno NofriProducer

IL TROVATORE - VERDI Dec 9, 11, 16, 18
Primo ZambrunoManrico Claudia ParadaLeonora Antonio CampoDi Luna Mafalda
MasiniAzucena Federico DaviáFerrando Franco PatanèConductor Bruno NofriProducer

FEDORA - GIORDANO Dec 12, 15, 17, 19
Nora de RosaFedora Giuseppe Savio/Augusto Ferrauto[Dec 12]Loris Antonio CampoDe
Siriex Celia Alvarez BlancoOlga Vittorina MagnaghiDimitri/Voice Valiano
NataliDesiré/Baron Federico DaviáCirillo Ernesto VezzosiBoroff/Lorek Camillo
RighiniGretch Brendan O'RiordanNicola/Sergio Charles DunphyMichele Franco
PatanèConductor Bruno NofriProducer

SPRING 1960: GAIETY THEATRE DUBLIN:6TH FESTIVAL OF ITALIAN OPERA

FALSTAFF - VERDI Apr 18, 20, 22, 27
Piero GuelfiFalstaff Nora de RosaAlice Enzo SordelloFord Nicoletta VerzieriNanetta Angelo
MarchiandiFenton Myriam PirazziniQuickly Ezio BoschiBardolph Ferruccio MazzoliPistol
Rina CorsiMeg Valiano NataliCaius Ottavio ZiinoConductor Bruno NofriProducer

LUCIA DI LAMMERMOOR - DONIZETTI Apr 19, 21, 23, 25
Margherita RinaldiLucia Ruggero BondinoEdgardo Felice SchiaviEnrico Loris
GambelliRaimondo Valiano NataliArturo Rina CorsiAlisa Ezio BoschiNormanno Ottavio
ZiinoConductor Bruno NofriProducer

TURANDOT - PUCCINI Apr 26, 28, 30, May 2
Lucille UdovickTurandot Umberto BorsòCalaf Aureliana BeltramiLiù Ferruccio
MazzoliTimur Ernesto VezzosiPing Valiano NataliPang Ezio BoschiPong Evaristo
OrlandiniAltoum Loris GambelliMandarin Franco PatanèConductor Bruno NofriProducer

LA SONNAMBULA - BELLINI Apr 29 May 4, 9, 12

Page 340

Virginia Zeani/Margherita Rinaldi[May 9, 12]Amina Ruggero BondinoElvino Ferruccio
MazzoliRodolfo Nicoletta VerzieriLisa Rina CorsiTeresa Ernesto VezzosiAlessio Franco
PatanèConductor Bruno NofriProducer

LA TRAVIATA - VERDI May 3, 6, 10, 14
Virginia Zeani/Aureliana Beltrami[May 10, 14]Violetta Ruggero Bondino/Enzo Tei[May 10,
14]Alfredo Enzo SordelloGiorgio Nicoletta VerzieriFlora Valiano NataliGastone Ernesto
VezzosiBaron Ezio BoschiMarchese Loris GambelliDr Grenvil Giovanna RalliAnnina Franco
PatanèConductor Bruno NofriProducer

TOSCA - PUCCINI May 5, 7, 11, 13
Nora de RosaTosca Umberto BorsòCavaradossi Piero GuelfiScarpia Loris GambelliAngelotti
Ernesto VezzosiSacristan/Sciarrone Ezio BoschiSpoletta Franco PatanèConductor Bruno
NofriProducer

WINTER 1960: GAIETY THEATRE DUBLIN

ORFEO ED EURIDICE - GLUCK Nov 22, 24, 26, 30
Hanna LudwigOrfeo Marlies BehrensEuridice Enja GabrieleAmor Arthur GrüberConductor
Alfred SierckeProducer

DIE ENTFÜHRUNG AUS DEM SERAIL - MOZART Nov 23, 25, 29, Dec 1
Gertie CharlentKonstanze Peter FlottauBelmonte Doris Lorenz/Enja Gabriele[Dec 1]Blonde
Elfego EsparzaOsmin Martin HæuslerPedrillo Guido DiemerSelim Arthur GrüberConductor
Alfred SierckeProducer

LA BOH_ME - PUCCINI Dec 3, 6, 9, 12
Ofelia di MarcoMimi Antonio Galié/Enzo Tei[Dec 9, 12]Rodolfo Santa ChissariMusetta
Marco StecchiMarcello Giovanni AmodeoColline Arturo La PortaSchaunard Ernesto
VezzosiBenoit/Alcindoro Giuseppe RuisiConductor Bruno NofriProducer

IL BARBIERE DI SIVIGLIA - ROSSINI Dec 7, 10, 14, 16
Atilio d'OraziFigaro Santa ChissariRosina Ismildo TedeschiAlmaviva Arturo La PortaBartolo
Giovanni AmodeoBasilio Ernesto VezzosiFiorello Rina CorsiBerta Giuseppe RuisiConductor
Bruno NofriProducer

CAVALLERIA RUSTICANA - MASCAGNI Dec 8, 13, 15, 17
Teresa ApoleiSantuzza Umberto Borsò/Achille Braschi[Dec 8]Turiddu Marco StecchiAlfio
Eleanor KirwinLucia Rina CorsiLola Mario CordoneConductor Bruno NofriProducer

PAGLIACCI - LEONCAVALLO Dec 8, 13, 15, 17
Umberto Borsò/Achille Braschi[Dec 8]Canio Mafalda MicheluzziNedda Atilio d'OraziTonio
Marco StecchiSilvio Ismildo TedeschiBeppe Mario CordoneConductor Bruno NofriProducer

SPRING 1961: GAIETY THEATRE DUBLIN:7TH FESTIVAL OF ITALIAN OPERA

AIDA - VERDI Apr 3, 5, 7, 11
Claudia ParadaAida Angelo Bartoli/Umberto Borsò[Apr 11: Acts 3 & 4]Radames Myriam
PirazziniAmneris Piero CappuccilliAmonasro Lorenzo GaetaniRamfis Giovanni AmodeoKing
Luciana PalombiPriestess Brendan CavanaghMessenger Napoleone AnnovazziConductor
Carlo Acly AzzoliniProducer

MANON LESCAUT - PUCCINI Apr 4, 6, 8, 12
Elena TodeschiManon Umberto Borsòdes Grieux Attilio d'OraziLescaut Leo PudisGeronte
Edwin FitzgibbonEdmondo Brendan CavanaghDancing Master/Lamplighter Jole di
MariaSinger Ernesto VezzosiSergeant Loris GambelliCaptain Napoleone AnnovazziConductor
Carlo Acly AzzoliniProducer

IL MATRIMONIO SEGRETO - CIMAROSA Apr 13, 15, 18, 24
Margerita RinaldiCarolina Salvatore GioiaPaolino Ledo FreschiGeronimo Mafalda
MicheluzziElisetta Leo PudisRobinson Jole di MariaFidalma Napoleone AnnovazziConductor
Carlo Acly AzzoliniProducer

NORMA - BELLINI Apr 14, 17, 19, 22
Lucille UdovichNorma Myriam PirazziniAdalgisa Umberto Borsò Pollione Lorenzo
GaetaniOroveso Edwin FitzgibbonFlavio Luciana PalombiClothilde Ottavio ZiinoConductor
Carlo Acly AzzoliniProducer

RIGOLETTO - VERDI Apr 20, 23, 26, 28
Piero CappuccilliRigoletto Margherita RinaldiGilda Antonio GaliéDuke Giovanni
AmodeoSparafucile Loris GambelliMonterone Bernadette GreevyMaddalena Ottavio
ZiinoConductor Carlo Acly AzzoliniProducer
DON PASQUALE - DONIZETTI Apr 21, 25, 27, 29
Leo PudisPasquale Mariella AdaniNorina Salvatore GioiaErnesto Atilio d'OraziMalatesta
Ernesto VezzosiNotary Ottavio ZiinoConductor Carlo Acly AzzoliniProducer

WINTER 1961: GAIETY THEATRE DUBLIN

CARMEN - BIZET Nov 28, 30, Dec 2, 11
Josephine VeasyCarmen Raymond ChiarellaDon José Jeanette SinclairMicaëla Raimund
HerincxEscamillo Elizabeth RustFrasquita Bernadette GreevyMercédès Peter
McBrienDancaïre David TreeRemendado Elfego EsparzaZuniga John Rhys EvansMoralès
Charles MackerrasConductor Anthony BeschProducer
MADAMA BUTTERFLY - PUCCINI Nov 29, Dec 1, 6, 9
Leonora Lafayette/Marie Collier[Dec 9]Cio-Cio San John DobsonPinkerton Anna
PollakSuzuki John HauxvellSharpless David TreeGoro Elfego EsparzaBonze John Rhys
EvansYamadori Elisabeth RustKate Charles MackerrasConductor Anthony BeschProducer
FAUST - GOUNOD Dec 5, 7, 13, 15
Ronald DowdFaust Ana-Raquel SatreMarguerite Elfego EsparzaMéphistophélès John
CameronValentin Bernadette GreevySiébel Maureen McDonnellMartha Peter McBrienWagner
Charles MackerrasConductor Michael GeliotProducer
COSI FAN TUTTE - MOZART Dec 8, 12, 14, 16
Patricia BartlettFiordiligi Edward BylesFerrando Margareta ElkinsDorabella Geoffrey
ChardGuglielmo Neil EastonAlfonso Elizabeth RobinsonDespina John MathesonConductor
Michael GeliotProducer

SPRING 1962: GAIETY THEATRE DUBLIN;8TH FESTIVAL OF ITALIAN OPERA

IL TROVATORE - VERDI Apr 23, 25, 27, 30
Umberto Borsò Manrico Luisa MaraglianoLeonora Piero CappuccilliDi Luna Lucia
DanieliAzucena Loris GambelliFerrando Luciana Palombi/Margherita Rinaldi[Apr23]Ines
Ottavio ZiinoConductor Enrico FrigerioProducer
LA BOH_ME - PUCCINI Apr 24, 26, 28, May 2
Edy AmedeoMimi Umberto GrilliRodolfoValeria MaricondaMusetta Enzo SordelloMarcello
Plinio ClabassiColline Giorgio GiorgettiSchaunard Ernesto VezzosiBenoit Giorgio
OnestiAlcindoro Ottavio ZiinoConductor Enrico FrigerioProducer
GIANNI SCHICCHI - PUCCINI May 1, 4, 11, 14
Scipio ColomboSchicchi Valeria MaricondaLauretta Angelo MarchiandiRinuccio Anna di
StasioZita Luciana PalombiNella Loris GambelliSimone Ernesto VezzosiMarco Giorgio
GiorgettiGherardo Napoleone AnnovazziConductor Enrico FrigerioProducer
SUOR ANGELICA - PUCCINI May 1, 4, 11, 14
Edy AmedeoSuorAngelica Paola MantovaniLa Zia Principessa Anna di StasioLa Badessa
Valeria MaricondaSuorGenoveva Luciana PalombiLaSuoraZelatrice Noreen RyanSuorDolcina
Dympna CarneySuorOsima Kitty Vaughan Maestra delle Novizie Monica Condron/Joan
RooneyCercatrici Mary TroyUnaNovizia Napoleone AnnovazziConductor Enrico
FrigerioProducer
IL MEDICO SUO MALGRADO - ALLEGRA May 1 ,4, 11, 14
Scipio ColomboSganarello Anna di StasioMartina Angelo MarchiandiLeandro Margherita
RinaldiLucinda Giorgio OnestiGeronte Loris GambelliValeria Edwin FitzgibbonLuca
Napoleone AnnovazziConductor Enrico FrigerioProducer
LUCIA DI LAMMERMOOR - DONIZETTI May 3, 5, 9, 12
Margherita RinaldiLucia UmbertoBorsò Edgardo Enzo SordelloEnrico Plinio
ClabassiRaimondo Edwin FitzgibbonArturo Luciana PalombiAlisa Brendan
O'RiordanNormanno Ottavio ZiinoConductor Enrico FrigerioProducer
LA TRAVIATA - VERDI May 8, 13, 16, 18

Elena TodeschiVioletta Umberto GrilliAlfredo Piero Cappuccilli/Enzo
Sordello[May18]Giorgio Luciana PalombiFlora/AnninaJames BrittainGastone Giorgio
OnestiBaron Ernesto VezzosiMarchese Loris GambelliDr Grenvil Napoleone
AnnovazziConductor Enrico FrigerioProducer
NABUCCO - VERDI May 10, 14, 17, 19
Gian Giacomo GuelfiNabucco Luisa MaraglianoAbigaille Ferruccio MazzoliZaccaria Angelo
MarchiandiIsmaele Paola MantovaniFenena Loris GambelliHigh Priest Edwin
FitzgibbonAbdallo Luciana PalombiAnna Napoleone AnnovazziConductor Enrico
FrigerioProducer

TANNHÄUSER - WAGNER Nov 27, 29, Dec 1, 4
Wilhelm ErnstTannhäuser Nelde ClavelElisabeth Alexander LorenzWolfram Gerd
NienstedtHerrmann Herta WilfertVenus Edwin FitzgibbonWalther Gerald DuffyBiterolf
James BrittainHeinrich Joseph DaltonReinmar Mary SheridanShepherd Tibor PaulConductor
André DiehlProducer
MANON - MASSENET Nov 28, 30, Dec 3, 7
Veronica DunneManon Edward Bylesdes Grieux Russell CooperLescaut Edwin
FitzgibbonGuillot Noel ManginCount Bryan DrakeBrétigny Hazel WilliamsPousette Beryl
BrierJavotte Christine PalmerRosette Charles MackerrasConductor Rowland Holt
WilsonProducer
DON GIOVANNI - MOZART Dec 6, 8, 11, 13
Carlos AlexanderGiovanni Herta WilfertAnna Benno KüscheLeporello Elizabeth
SchwarzenbergElvira Glade PetersonOttavioEdith MathisZerlina Zvi BorodoCommendatore
Georg PappasMasetto Tibor PaulConductor André DiehlProducer
DIE FLEDERMAUS - STRAUSS Dec 10, 12, 14, 15
Adèle LeighRosalinda Peter GrantEisenstein June BartonAdele Geoffrey ChardFalke Patricia
Kern/Marion Davies[Dec14, 15]Orlofsky Joseph PowellAlfred Evan ThomasFrank Noel
Mangin Frosch Hazel WilliamsIda Edwin FitzgibbonBlind Charles Mackerras/William
Reid[Dec14, 15]Conductor Anthony BeschProducer

UN BALLO IN MASCHERA - VERDI May 20, 22, 24, 30
Umberto Borsò Riccardo Luisa MaraglianoAmelia Piero Cappuccilli/Gianni Maffeo[May
30]Renato Lucia DanieliUlrica Leila BersianiOscar Loris GambelliSamuel Guido PasellaTom
Ernesto VezzosiSilvano Napoleone AnnovazziConductor Carlo Acly AzzoliniProducer
LA SONNAMBULA - BELLINI May 21, 23, 25, 28
Margherita RinaldiAmina Ugo BenelliElvino Plinio Clabassi/Ferruccio Mazzoli[May
28]Rodolfo Leila BersianiLisa Anna di StasioTeresa Ernesto VezzosiAlessio Guido
PasellaNotary Ottavio ZiinoConductor Carlo Acly AzzoliniProducer
RIGOLETTO - VERDI May 27, 29, 31, Jun 3, 7
Piero CappuccilliRigoletto Margherita RinaldiGilda Luciano PavarottiDuke Plinio
Clabassi/Ferruccio Mazzoli[Jun 7]Sparafucile Loris GambelliMonterone Anna di
StasioMaddalena Ottavio ZiinoConductor Carlo Acly AzzoliniProducer
MACBETH - VERDI Jun 1, 4, 6
Dino DondiMacbeth Sofia BandinLady Macbeth Carlo MenippoMacduff Ferruccio
Mazzoli/Plinio Clabassi[Jun 1]Banquo Edwin FitzgibbonMalcolm Anna di StasioLady in
waiting Loris GambelliDoctor Napoleone AnnovazziConductor Carlo Acly AzzoliniProducer
TOSCA - PUCCINI Jun 8, 11, 14, 17
Luciana Serafina/Marina Cucchio[Jun 8]Tosca Giuseppe di StefanoCavaradossi Gian
Giacomo GuelfiScarpia Loris GambelliAngelotti Guido PasellaSacristan
ErnestoVezzosiSciarrone Edwin FitzgibbonSpoletta Napoleone AnnovazziConductor Carlo
Acly AzzoliniProducer
AIDA - VERDI Jun 10, 12, 15, 18

Simona dell Argina/Luisa Maragliano[Jun 10]Aida Umberto BorsòRadames Lucia DanieliAmneris Gianni MaffeoAmonasro Ferruccio MazzoliRamfis Loris GambelliKing Mary SheridanPriestess Edwin FitzgibbonMessenger Napoleone Annovazzi/Tristano Illesberg[Jun 10]Conductor Carlo Acly AzzoliniProducer

WINTER 1963: GAIETY THEATRE DUBLIN

CARMEN - BIZET Nov 26, 28, 30, Dec 4
Joyce BlackhamCarmen Robert ThomasDon José Elaine BlightonMicaëla John Hauxvell/Michael Maurel[Nov 26, Dec 4]Escamillo Mary SheridanFrasquita Laura SartiMercédès Evan ThomasDancaïre/Moralès Edwin FitzgibbonRemendado Derek DaviesZuniga Warwick BraithwaiteConductor Douglas CraigProducer
TRISTAN UND ISOLDE - WAGNER Nov 27, 29, Dec 3, 7
Liane SynekIsolde Rudolf LustigTristan Gerd Nienstedt/Edouard Wollitz[Nov 29, Dec 7]Marke Erika Wien/Ruth Hesse[Nov 27]Brangäene Alfons HerwigKurwenal Edwin FitzgibbonMelot /Sailor Joseph DaltonSteersman Patrick RingShepherd Tibor PaulConductor Manfred HubrichtProducer
LE NOZZE DI FIGARO - MOZART Dec 2, 5, 10, 12
Dieter Behlendorf/Derek Davies[Dec 5]Figaro Ingrid PallerSusanna Veronica DunneCountess Hans Otto Kloose/Rudolf Jedlicka[Dec 12]Count Cora Canne-Meier/Frances Bible[Dec 10, 12]Cherubino Edouard WollitzBartolo Mary SheridanMarcellina John Kentish/Hans Blessin[Dec 2]Basilio Edwin FitzgibbonCurzio Gerald DuffyAntonio Eithne TroyBarbarina Tibor PaulConductor Manfred HubrichtProducer
DIE FLEDERMAUS - STRAUSS Dec 9, 11, 13, 14
Adèle LeighRosalinda Kevin MillerEisenstein June BartonAdele Geoffrey ChardFalke Iona JonesOrlofsky Rowland Jones/Brychan Powell[Dec13, 14]Alfred Evan ThomasFrank Derek DaviesFrosch Mary SheridanIda Edwin FitzgibbonBlind William ReidConductor Douglas CraigProducer

SPRING 1964: GAIETY THEATRE DUBLIN:10TH FESTIVAL OF ITALIAN OPERA

TURANDOT - PUCCINI May 18, 20, 22, 28
Carla FerrarioTurandot Angelo Lo ForeseCalaf Ileana SinnoneLiù Giannicola PigliucciTimur Alberto OroPing Edwin FitzgibbonPang Brendan CavanaghPong James BrittainAltoum Ernesto VezzosiMandarin Napoleone AnnovazziConductor Enrico FrigerioProducer
LA BOH_ME - PUCCINI May 19, 21, 27, Jun 1
Ivana TosiniMimi Luciano PavarottiRodolfo Ileana SinnoneMusetta Attilio d'OraziMarcello Ferruccio MazzoliColline Alberto OroSchaunard Ernesto VezzosiBenoit/Alcindoro Napoleone AnnovazziConductor Enrico FrigerioProducer
LA TRAVIATA - VERDI May 23, 25, 29, Jun 8
Margherita RinaldiVioletta Luciano PavarottiAlfredo Giuseppe Taddei/Cesare Bardelli[Jun 8]Giorgio Mary SheridanFlora Brendan CavanaghGastone Alberto OroBaron Ernesto VezzosiMarchese Loris GambelliDr Grenvil Monica CondronAnnina Ferdinando GuarnieriConductor Enrico FrigerioProducer
NABUCCO - VERDI May 26, 30, Jun 3, 5
Gian Giacomo GuelfiNabucco Luisa MaraglianoAbigaille Ferruccio MazzoliZaccaria Enzo TeiIsmaele Anna di StasioFenena Loris GambelliHigh Priest Edwin FitzgibbonAbdallo Mary SheridanAnna Napoleone AnnovazziConductor Enrico FrigerioProducer
OTELLO - VERDI Jun 4, 6, 10, 12
Pier Miranda FerraroOtello Virginia ZeaniDesdemona Cesare BardelliIago Brendan CavanaghCassio Patrick RingRoderigo Loris GambelliLodovico Ernesto VezzosiMontano Anna di StasioEmilia Alberto OroHerald Tibor PaulConductor Enrico FrigerioProducer
ANDREA CHÉNIER - GIORDANO Jun 7, 9, 11, 13
Angelo Lo ForeseChénier Luisa MaraglianoMaddalena Gian Giacomo GuelfiGérard Loris GambelliRoucher Anna di StasioBersi/Madelon Ernesto VezzosiMathieu Mary SheridanCountess Napoleone AnnovazziConductor Enrico FrigerioProducer

DER FLIEGENDE HOLLÄNDER - WAGNER Nov 23, 25, 27 [Wiesbaden State Opera]
Tomislav NeralicDutchman Liane SynekSenta Almar HeggenDaland Hermin EsserErik Natalie Hinsch-GrondahlMary Richard GsellSteersman Ludwig KaufmannConductor Peter KertzProducer

DIE ENTFÜHRUNG AUS DEM SERAIL - MOZART Nov 24, 26, 28[Wiesbaden State Opera]
Elisabeth VerlooyKonstanze Reinhold BartelBelmonte Claire RainerBlonde Helmut IblerOsmin Wolfgang FreyPedrillo Heinz PetersSelim Ludwig KaufmannConductor Wolfgang BlumProducer

DER ROSENKAVALIER - STRAUSS Dec 1 ,3, 5, 7
Elisabeth ThomaFeldmarschallin Margarethe SjostedtOctavian Erich WinkelmannOchs Veronica DunneSophie Rudolf KnollFaninal Ann MoranMarianne Erich KlausValzacchi Glenys BirchAnnina EdwinFitzgibbonSinger Joseph DaltonNotary Napoleone AnnovazziConductor Ernst August SchneiderProducer

DER ZIGEUNERBARON - STRAUSS Dec 2, 4, 9, 11
Rhonda BruceSaffi Peter GrantBarinkay Geoffrey ChardZsupan Gita DeniseCzipra June BartonArsena Raymond MyersHomonay Glenys BirchMirabella John Rhys EvansCarnero John StoddartOttokar William ReidConductor Douglas CraigProducer

LES P_CHEURS DE PERLES - BIZET Dec 8, 10, 12
Veronica DunneLeila Rowland JonesNadir Raimund HerincxZurga James PeaseNourabad Napoleone AnnovazziConductor Douglas CraigProducer

ERNANI - VERDI May 10, 12, 15
Pier Miranda FerraroErnani Marcella de OsmaElvira Piero CappuccilliCarlo Plinio ClabassiSilva Mario FerraraRiccardo Loris GambelliJago Napoleone AnnovazziConductor Augusto CardiProducer

IL BARBIERE DI SIVIGLIA - ROSSINI May 11, 13, 19, 25
Aldo Protti/Atilio d'Orazi[May 25]Figaro Lucia CappellinoRosina Luigi PontiggiaAlmaviva Leo PudisBartolo Franco VentrigliaBasilio Ernesto VezzosiFiorello Lina RossiBerta Napoleone AnnovazziConductor Augusto CardiProducer

LUCIA DI LAMMERMOOR - DONIZETTI May 14, 20, 30, Jun 1, 4
Gianna d'Angelo/Margherita Guglielmi[May 14, 20]Lucia Enzo TeiEdgardo Attilio d'OraziEnrico Plinio Clabassi/Loris Gambelli[Jun1]Raimondo Mario FerraraArturo/Normanno Lina RossiAlisa Giuseppe MorelliConductor Augusto CardiProducer

DON CARLO - VERDI May 18, 21, 24
Ruggero OrofinoCarlo Maria Pia FabrettiElisabetta Raffaele AriéFilippo Giulio FioravantiRodrigo Dora MinarchiEboli Franco VentrigliaInquisitore Lina RossiTebaldo Loris GambelliFrate Napoleone AnnovazziConductor Augusto CardiProducer

MADAMA BUTTERFLY - PUCCINI May 22, 27, 29, Jun 3
Luisa Maragliano/Jeanette Pilou[May 29, Jun 3]Cio-Cio San Michele MolesePinkerton Licia GalvanoSuzuki Attilio d'OraziSharpless Mario FerraraGoro Loris GambelliBonze Ernesto VezzosiYamadori Lina RossiKate Giuseppe MorelliConductor Augusto CardiProducer

RIGOLETTO - VERDI May 26, 28, 31, Jun 2, 5
Giulio Fioravanti/Piero Cappuccilli[Jun2, 5]Rigoletto Margherita GuglielmiGilda Luciano SaldariDuke Franco VentrigliaSparafucile Loris GambelliMonterone Rosemarie de RivaMaddalena Napoleone AnnovazziConductor Augusto CardiProducer

CARMEN - BIZET Nov 30, Dec 2, 4, 6, 8
Edith EvansCarmen Robert ThomasDon José Ann MoranMicaëla Raymond MyersEscamillo

Beverly BohanFrasquita Margaret NordenMercédès Peter McBrienDancaïre Patrick
RingRemendado Joseph DaltonZuniga Paschal AllenMoralès Warwick BraithwaiteConductor
Powell LloydProducer
LA BOH_ME - PUCCINI Dec 1, 3, 11, 13
Veronica DunneMimi Charles CraigRodolfo June BartonMusetta John HauxvellMarcello
James PeaseColline John Rhys EvansSchaunard Raymond FarrellBenoit Terence
ConoleyAlcindoro Harold GrayConductor Ann MakowerProducer
FAUST - GOUNOD Dec 7, 9, 15, 17
Donald PilleyFaust Sylvia StahlmanMarguerite William McCueMéphistophélès John
HauxvellValentin Beverly BohanSiébel Margaret NordenMartha Paschal AllenWagner John
MathesonConductor Rowland Holt WilsonProducer
DON GIOVANNI - MOZART Dec 10, 14, 16, 18
Forbes RobinsonGiovanni Elizabeth RustAnna James PeaseLeporello Veronica DunneElvira
Edmond BohanOttavioAnnMoranZerlina James PeaseCommendatore Joseph DaltonMasetto
Myer FredmanConductor Powell LloydProducer

SPRING 1966: GAIETY THEATRE DUBLIN:12TH FESTIVAL OF ITALIAN OPERA

DON PASQUALE - DONIZETTI May 18, 20, 23
Paolo WashingtonPasquale Valeria MaricondaNorina Ugo BenelliErnesto Atilio
d'OraziMalatesta Augusto PedroniNotary Giuseppe MorelliConductor Augusto
CardiProducer
TOSCA - PUCCINI May 19, 21, 25
Luisa MaraglianoTosca Enzo TeiCavaradossi Giulio FioravantiScarpia Loris GambelliAngelotti
ErnestoVezzosiSacristan/Sciarrone Augusto PedroniSpoletta Giuseppe MorelliConductor
Augusto CardiProducer
LA TRAVIATA - VERDI May 24, 26, 28, 31, Jun 2
Margherita RinaldiVioletta Veriano LuchettiAlfredo Attilio d'OraziGiorgio Carmel
O'ByrneFlora Augusto PedroniGastone Ernesto VezzosiBaron Luciano PecchiaMarchese Loris
GambelliDr Grenvil Monica Condron Annina Napoleone AnnovazziConductor Augusto
CardiProducer
IL TROVATORE - VERDI Jun 3, 6, 8, 10
Ruggero OrofinoManrico Marisa BaldazziLeonora Renato BrusonDi Luna Anna Maria
RotaAzucena Loris GambelliFerrando Giuseppe MorelliConductor Augusto CardiProducer
RIGOLETTO - VERDI Jun 4, 7, 9, 11
Piero CappuccilliRigoletto Anna MacciantiGilda Enzo TeiDuke Loris Gambelli
Sparafucile/Monterone Valeria EscalarMaddalena Napoleone AnnovazziConductor Augusto
CardiProducer

Winter 1966: Gaiety Theatre Dublin:Principals of Bucharest Opera

SAMSON ET DALILA - SAINT-SA_NS Dec 6, 8, 10, 15
Ion BuzeaSamson Zenaida PallyDalila Joseph DaltonAbimélech David OhanesianHigh Priest
Nicolae FloreiOld Hebrew Napoleone AnnovazziConductor Augusto CardiProducer
UN BALLO IN MASCHERA - VERDI Dec 7, 9, 13, 16
Jon PisoRiccardo Elena DimaAmelia David OhanesianRenato Elizabeth BergmanUlrica
Niculina Mirea CurtaOscar Nicolae FloreiSamuel Joseph DaltonTom Mugur BogdanSilvano
Napoleone AnnovazziConductor Augusto CardiProducer
MIGNON - THOMAS Dec 12, 14, 17
Viorica CortezMignon Jon PisoWilhelm Niculina Mirea CurtaPhiline Nicolae FloreiLothario
Ann Moran Frédéric Joseph DaltonJarno Mugur BogdanLaërte Napoleone
AnnovazziConductor Augusto CardiProducer

SPRING 1967: GAIETY THEATRE DUBLIN; OPERA HOUSE CORK
:13TH FESTIVAL OF ITALIAN OPERA

ADRIANA LECOUVREUR - CILEA Dublin May 22, 24, 29

Magda OliveroAdriana Jon PisoMaurizio Alberto RinaldiMichonnet Maria Luisa NavePrincess
Loris GambelliPrince Ernesto VezzosiQuinault/Poisson Vittorina MagnaghiJouvenot Clara
BetnerDangeville Gabriele deJulisAbbé Napoleone AnnovazziConductor Maria Sofia
MarascaProducer
LA BOH_ME - PUCCINI Dublin May 23, 25, 30, Jun 3; Cork Jun 19, 22
Rita Talarico/Irma Capece Minutolo[May 30, Jun 3]/Maria Angela Rosati[Jun 19, 22]Mimi
Ettore BabiniRodolfo Limbania Leoni/Vittorina Magnaghi[Jun 19, 22]Musetta Silvano
Carroli/Franco Pagliazzi[Jun 19, 22]Marcello Alfonso Marchica/Loris Gambelli[Jun 19,
22]Colline Alberto OroSchaunard Ernesto VezzosiBenoit/Alcindoro Adolfo
Camozzo/Napoleone Annovazzi[Jun 19, 22]Conductor Maria Sofia MarascaProducer
AIDA - VERDI Dublin May 27, Jun 1, 5, 11
Linda Vajna/Alba Bertoli[Jun 11]Aida Giovanni Gibin/Bruno Rufo[Jun 11]Radames Viorica
CortezAmneris Silvano Carroli/Silvano Verlinghieri[Jun 5, 11]Amonasro Nicolae
FloreiRamfis Loris GambelliKing Vittorina MagnaghiPriestess Gabriele deJulisMessenger
Napoleone Annovazzi Conductor Maria Sofia MarascaProducer
**LUCIA DI LAMMERMOOR - DONIZETTI Dublin May 31, Jun 2, 7, 13; Cork
Jun 21, 24**
Jolanda Meneguzzer Lucia Ettore Babini/Jon Piso[Jun 13, 21, 24]Edgardo Franco
PagliazziEnrico Loris GambelliRaimondo Gabriele di JulisArturo Patrick RingNormanno
Vittorina MagnaghiAlisa Adolfo Camozzo/Napoleone Annovazzi[Jun 21, 24]Conductor
Maria Sofia MarascaProducer
DON CARLO - VERDI Dublin Jun 6, 12, 15, 17
Jon PisoCarlo Maria Angela RosatiElisabetta Nicolae FloreiFilippo Franco PagliazziRodrigo
Viorica CortezEboli Alfonso MarchicaInquisitore Vittorina MagnaghiTebaldo Loris
GambelliFrate Napoleone AnnovazziConductor Maria Sofia MarascaProducer
MADAMA BUTTERFLY - PUCCINI Dublin Jun 8, 10, 14, 16; Cork Jun 20, 23
Edy AmedeoCio-Cio San Bruno Rufo/Ettore Babini[Jun 10]Pinkerton Clara BetnerSuzuki
Alberto OroSharpless Gabriele deJulisGoro Loris GambelliBonze Ernesto VezzosiYamadori
Vittorina MagnaghiKate Adolfo Camozzo/Napoleone Annovazzi[Jun 20, 23]Conductor
Maria Sofia MarascaProducer

WINTER 1967: GAIETY THEATRE DUBLIN:PRINCIPALS OF BUCHAREST OPERA

MIGNON - THOMAS Dec 4, 6, 8, 12
Viorica CortezMignon Jon PisoWilhelm Niculina Mirea CurtaPhiline Nicolae FloreiLothario
Ann Moran Frédéric Joseph DaltonJarno Mugur BogdanLaërte Napoleone
AnnovazziConductor Mladen SabljicProducer
CARMEN - BIZET Dec 5, 7, 9, 13, 15
Zenaida PallyCarmen Constantin IliescuDon José Renée CorenneMicaëla
DanJordachescuEscamillo Olive DuncanFrasquita Patricia DolanMercédès Peter McBrien
Dancaïre Patrick RingRemendado Joseph DaltonZuniga Mugur BogdanMoralès Vladimir
BenicConductor Mladen SabljicProducer
WERTHER - MASSENET Dec 11, 14, 16
Jon PisoWerther Viorica CortezCharlotte Mugur BogdanAlbert Ann MoranSophie Joseph
DaltonBailli Patrick RingSchmidt William YoungJohann Napoleone AnnovazziConductor
Mladen SabljicProducer

SPRING 1968: GAIETY THEATRE DUBLIN

LA FAVORITA - DONIZETTI Jun 3, 5, 8
Viorica CortezLeonora Jon PisoFernando Attilio d'OraziAlfonso Helge BömchesBaldassarre
Ann MoranInes Raimondo BotteghelliGasparo Napoleone AnnovazziConductor Enrico
FrigerioProducer
RIGOLETTO - VERDI Jun 4, 6, 12, 14
Nicolae HerleaRigoletto Daniela Mazzucato MeneghiniGilda Franco GhittiDuke Helge
BömchesSparafucile Enrico FissoreMonterone Sandra delGrandeMaddalena Assen
NaydenovConductor Enrico FrigerioProducer

TOSCA - PUCCINI Jun 7, 11, 13, 19

Magda OliveroTosca Lino MartinucciCavaradossi Cesare BardelliScarpia Helge BömchesAngelotti Enrico FissoreSacristan Raimondo BotteghelliSpoletta William YoungSciarrone Ann MurrayShepherd Napoleone AnnovazziConductor Enrico FrigerioProducer

LA TRAVIATA - VERDI Jun 10, 15, 18, 21

Aida AbagieffVioletta Jon PisoAlfredo Attilio d'OraziGiorgio Evelyn DowlingFlora Raimondo BotteghelliGastone Enzo FranciBaron William YoungMarchese Joseph DaltonDr Grenvil Monica Condron Annina Assen NaydenovConductor Enrico FrigerioProducer

TURANDOT - PUCCINI Jun 17, 20, 22

Margarita RadulovaTurandot Lino MartinucciCalaf Mary SheridanLiù Helge BömchesTimur Enrico FissorePing Patrick RingPang Brendan CavanaghPong Raimondo BotteghelliAltoum William YoungMandarin Napoleone AnnovazziConductor Enrico FrigerioProducer

WINTER 1968: GAIETY THEATRE DUBLIN

DON GIOVANNI - MOZART Dec 2, 4, 6, 11

Walter AlbertiGiovanni Irma LanducciAnna Enrico FissoreLeporello Aida AbagieffElvira Corneliu FenateanuOttavio AnnMoranZerlina Helge BömchesCommendatore Joseph DaltonMasetto Napoleone AnnovazziConductor Maria Sofia MarascaProducer

MUSIC HATH MISCHIEF - VICTORY Dec 3, 5, 9, 13

Patricia McCarryKate William YoungJohn Patrick RingPostman Napoleone AnnovazziConductor Gene MartinProducer

PAGLIACCI - LEONCAVALLO Dec 3, 5, 9, 13

Redento ComacchioCanio Lucia StanescuNedda Octav EnigarescuTonio Angelo RomeroSilvio Patrick RingBeppe Vladimir BenicConductor Maria Sofia MarascaProducer

IL BARBIERE DI SIVIGLIA - ROSSINI Dec 7, 10, 12, 14

Angelo Romero Figaro Niculina Mirea CurtaRosina Corneliu FenateanuAlmaviva Enrico FissoreBartolo Helge BömchesBasilio William YoungFiorello Gillian HullBerta Napoleone AnnovazziConductor Maria Sofia MarascaProducer

SPRING 1969: GAIETY THEATRE DUBLIN

IL TROVATORE - VERDI Apr 7, 9, 11, 14

Pedro LavirgenManrico Marina StoicaLeonora Attilio d'OraziDi Luna Bianca BeriniAzucena Helge BömchesFerrando Napoleone AnnovazziConductor Enrico FrigerioProducer

NABUCCO - VERDI Apr 8, 10, 16, 19

Giuseppe ScalcoNabucco Margarita RadulovaAbigaille Helge BömchesZaccaria Marco VilleggianteIsmaele Giovanna CanettiFenena Joseph DaltonHigh Priest Raimondo BotteghelliAbdallo Anna AssandriAnna Giuseppe MorelliConductor Enrico FrigerioProducer

MADAMA BUTTERFLY - PUCCINI Apr 12, 17, 22, 25

Atsuko AzumaCio-Cio San Lino MartinucciPinkerton Giovanna CanettiSuzuki Angelo RomeroSharpless Raimondo BotteghelliGoro Helge BömchesBonze William YoungYamadori Anna AssandriKate Napoleone AnnovazziConductor Enrico FrigerioProducer

DON PASQUALE - DONIZETTI Apr 15, 18, 24

Alfredo MariottiPasquale Valeria MaricondaNorina Ugo BenelliErnesto Atilio d'OraziMalatesta Raimondo BotteghelliNotary Giuseppe MorelliConductor Enrico FrigerioProducer

L'ELISIR D'AMORE - DONIZETTI Apr 21, 23, 26

Valeria MaricondaAdina Ugo BenelliNemorino Attilio d'OraziBelcore Alfredo MariottiDulcamara Anna AssandriGiannetta Napoleone AnnovazziConductor Enrico FrigerioProducer

WINTER 1969: GAIETY THEATRE DUBLIN

EUGENE ONEGIN - TCHAIKOVSKY Dec 1, 3, 5, 8

Emil RotundoOnegin Aida AbagieffTatyana Jon PisoLensky Helge BömchesGremin

Margareta TomazianOlga Ruth MaherLarina Ana ManciuleaFilippyevna Patrick RingTriquet
Joseph DaltonZaretsky Napoleone AnnovazziConductor Philippe PerrottetProducer
DIE FLEDERMAUS - STRAUSS Dec 2, 4, 6, 10   [Sung in English]
Jennifer CaronRosalinda Malcolm RiversEisenstein Ann MoranAdele Brian KempFalke
Marjory McMichael Orlofsky Stefano CurrisAlfred Eric ShillingFrank Evan ThomasFrosch
Monica CondronIda Terry JenkinsBlind Albert Rosen Conductor Philippe PerrottetProducer
MANON - MASSENET Dec 9, 11, 13
Mila CovaManon Jon Pisodes Grieux Elizeu SimulescuLescaut Patrick RingGuillot Helge
BömchesCount Evan ThomasBrétigny Ann MoranPousette Marjory McMichaelJavotte Ruth
MaherRosette Napoleone AnnovazziConductor Philippe PerrottetProducer

LA BOH_ME - PUCCINI Mar 30, Apr 1, 3
Maria Angela RosatiMimi Flaviano LabòRodolfo Ann Moran Musetta Mario d'AnnaMarcello
Helge BömchesColline Maurizio PiacentiSchaunard Alberto CarusiBenoit/Alcindoro
Napoleone AnnovazziConductor Sanzio LevrattiProducer
RIGOLETTO - VERDI Mar 31, Apr 4, 7, 10
Aldo ProttiRigoletto Niculina Mirea CurtaGilda Pedro LavirgenDuke Helge
BömchesSparafucile Alberto CarusiMonterone Margarita TomazianMaddalena Giuseppe
MorelliConductor Sanzio LevrattiProducer
TOSCA - PUCCINI Apr 2, 6, 9, 13
Lucia StanescuTosca Daniele BarioniCavaradossi Giuseppe ScalcoScarpia Alberto
CarusiAngelotti Maurizio PiacentiSacristan Raimondo BotteghelliSpoletta Gino de
RossiSciarrone Napoleone AnnovazziConductor Sanzio LevrattiProducer
LA TRAVIATA - VERDI Apr 8, 11, 15, 17
Agneta KrizaVioletta Giancarlo PastineAlfredo Mario d'AnnaGiorgio Ruth MaherFlora
Raimondo BotteghelliGastone Maurizio PiacentiBaron Alberto CarusiMarchese Joseph
DaltonDr Grenvil Monica Condron Annina Giuseppe MorelliConductor Sanzio
LevrattiProducer
ANDREA CHÉNIER - GIORDANO Apr 14, 16, 18
Pedro LavirgenChénier Maria Angela RosatiMaddalena Giuseppe ScalcoGérard Helge
BömchesRoucher Margarita TomazianBersi Ruth MaherMadelon/Countess Raimondo
BotteghelliIncroyable/Abbé Napoleone AnnovazziConductor Enrico FrigerioProducer

CARMEN - BIZET Nov 30, Dec 2, 4, 8
Rosario GomezCarmen Pedro LavirgenDon José Violet TwomeyMicaëla Pedro
FarresEscamillo Olive DuncanFrasquita Ruth MaherMercédès Brian Donlan Dancaïre Patrick
RingRemendado Helge BömchesZuniga Brendan CavanaghMoralès Napoleone
AnnovazziConductor Philippe PerrottetProducer
FIDELIO - BEETHOVEN Dec 1, 3, 5, 11
Alena MikovaLeonora Oldrich SpisarFlorestan Jaroslav HoracekPizzaro Elfego EsparzaRocco
Ann MoranMarzelline Patrick RingJaquino Brendan KeyesFernando Albert RosenConductor
Philippe PerrottetProducer
LES CONTES D'HOFFMANN - OFFENBACH Dec 7, 9, 10, 12
Jon PisoHoffmann Ann MoranOlympia Aida AbagieffGiulietta/Antonia Helge
BömchesCoppélius/Miracle/ Lindorf Pedro FarresDapertutto/Crespel Mary
SheridanNicklausse Patrick RingSpalanzani/Pitichinaccio Patrick O'RourkeSchlemil Brendan
CavanaghCochenille/Frantz Ruth MaherMother Napoleone AnnovazziConductor Philippe
PerrottetProducer

TURANDOT - PUCCINI Dublin Apr 12, 14, 16, 22
Maria Angela RosatiTurandot Flaviano Labò/Lino Savoldi[Apr 16, 22]Calaf Mary

SheridanLiù Eftimios MichalopoulosTimur Franco PivaPing Patrick RingPang Brendan CavanaghPong Michele BuenzaAltoum William YoungMandarin Napoleone AnnovazziConductor Sanzio LevrattiProducer

LUCIA DI LAMMERMOOR - DONIZETTI Dublin Apr 13, 15, 17, 20; Cork May 4, 6, 8
Francina Girones Lucia Giuseppe GiacominiEdgardo Renato BorgatoEnrico Carlo Micalucci Raimondo Patrick Ring Arturo Michele BuenzaNormanno Olive DuncanAlisa Albert Rosen/Napoleone Annovazzi[May 4, 6, 8]Conductor Sanzio LevrattiProducer

AIDA - VERDI Dublin Apr 19, 21, 23, 26; Cork May 3, 5, 7
Milkana Nikolova Aida Renato Francesconi Radames Carol WyattAmneris Pedro Farres Amonasro Carlo MicalucciRamfis Eftimios MichalopoulosKing Monica CondronPriestess Patrick RingMessenger Napoleone Annovazzi Conductor Sanzio LevrattiProducer

L'ELISIR D'AMORE - DONIZETTI Dublin Apr 24, 28, 30
Fiorella PediconiAdina Ugo BenelliNemorino Angelo RomeroBelcore Gianni SocciDulcamara Ruth MaherGiannetta Napoleone AnnovazziConductor Sanzio LevrattiProducer

MADAMA BUTTERFLY - PUCCINI Dublin Apr 27, 29, May 1
Atsuko AzumaCio-Cio San Giuseppe GiacominiPinkerton Ruth MaherSuzuki Renato BorgatoSharpless Brendan CavanaghGoro Eftimios MichalopoulosBonze William YoungYamadori Monica CondronKate Albert RosenConductor Sanzio LevrattiProducer

WINTER 1971: GAIETY THEATRE DUBLIN

LOHENGRIN - WAGNER Nov 29, Dec 1, 3, 7
Ruggero OrofinoLohengrin Anna Maria BalboniElsa Pedro FarresTelramund Eldemira CalomfirescuOrtrud Helge BömchesHenry Brian DonlanHerald Napoleone AnnovazziConductor Philippe PerrottetProducer

IL BARBIERE DI SIVIGLIA - ROSSINI Nov 30, Dec 2, 4, 9
Attilio d'Orazi Figaro Niculina Mirea CurtaRosina Angelo degl'InnocentiAlmaviva Sergio PezzettiBartolo Helge BömchesBasilio Brian DonlanFiorello Ruth MaherBerta Napoleone AnnovazziConductor Philippe PerrottetProducer

THE BARTERED BRIDE - SMETANA Dec 6, 8, 10, 11 - [Principals of Czech National Theatre Prague]
Gabriela BenackovaMarenka Zdenek SvehlaJeník Jaroslav HoracekKecal Milan KarpisekVasek William YoungKrusina Mary SheridanLudmilla Ruth MaherHáta Brendan KeyesMícha Marta BohacovaEsmeralda Patrick RingCircus Master Albert RosenConductor Jaroslav HoracekProducer

SPRING 1972: GAIETY THEATRE DUBLIN; OPERA HOUSE CORK

LA CENERENTOLA - ROSSINI Dublin Apr 3, 5, 7
Giuseppina Dalle MolleAngelina Ugo BenelliRamiro Angelo RomeroDandini Sergio PezzettiMagnifico Terry ReidClorinda Ruth MaherTisbe Alberto CarusiAlidoro Napoleone AnnovazziConductor Philippe PerrottetProducer

NABUCCO - VERDI Dublin Apr 4, 6, 8, 12
Pedro FarresNabucco OzglüTanyeriAbigaille Gianfranco CasariniZaccaria Lino SavoldiIsmaele Ruth MaherFenena Alberto CarusiHigh Priest Brendan CavanaghAbdallo Olive DuncanAnna Mario BraggioConductor Charles JannsensProducer

IL TROVATORE - VERDI Dublin Apr 10, 13, 15, 19; Cork Apr 25, 27, 29
Lino SavoldiManrico Maria Angela RosatiLeonora Pedro FarresDi Luna Adriana StamenovaAzucena Gianfranco CasariniFerrando Mario Braggio/Napoleone Annovazzi[Apr 25, 27, 29]Conductor Philippe PerrottetProducer

LA TRAVIATA - VERDI Dublin Apr 11, 14, 18, 21; Cork Apr 24, 26, 28
Susanna GhioneVioletta Bernardino TrottaAlfredo Gabriele Floresta/Renato Borgato[Apr 26, 28]Giorgio Olive DuncanFlora Patrick RingGastone Alberto CarusiBaron Brendan KeyesMarchese William YoungDr Grenvil Monica CondronAnnina Napoleone AnnovazziConductor Charles JannsensProducer

MANON LESCAUT - PUCCINI Dublin Apr 17, 20, 22

Anna Maria BalboniManon Giuseppe Giacominides Grieux Renato BorgatoLescaut Sergio PezzettiGeronte Patrick RingEdmondo Brendan CavanaghDancing Master/Lamplighter Monica CondronSinger Alberto CarusiSergeant Patrick O'RourkeCaptain Napoleone AnnovazziConductor Philippe PerrottetProducer

WINTER 1972: GAIETY THEATRE DUBLIN

FAUST - GOUNOD Dec 4, 6, 8, 14
Gennaro de SicaFaust Wilma VernocchiMarguerite Robert el HageMéphistophélès Gabriele FlorestaValentin Terry ReidSiébel Ruth MaherMartha Brian DonlanWagner Napoleone AnnovazziConductor Philippe PerrottetProducer
THE QUEEN OF SPADES - TCHAIKOVSKY Dec 5, 7, 9, 12
Marcela MachotkovaLisa Oldrich SpisarHermann Jaroslav HoracekTomsky Andrea SnarskiYeletsky Johanna PetersCountess Ruth MaherPauline Joan DaviesGoverness Terry ReidChloë Albert RosenConductor Jaroslav Horacek
DER ROSENKAVALIER - STRAUSS Dec 11, 13, 15, 16
Kay GriffelFeldmarschallin Helga AnjervoOctavian Rolf PolkeOchs Margaret GaleSophie Armand MacLaneFaninal Terry ReidMarianne Brendan CavanaghValzacchi Joan DaviesAnnina Gennaro de SicaSinger Brian DonlanNotary Napoleone AnnovazziConductor Philippe PerrottetProducer

SPRING 1973: GAIETY THEATRE DUBLIN; OPERA HOUSE CORK

CAVALLERIA RUSTICANA - MASCAGNI Dublin Apr 23, 25, 27, May 3; Cork May 17, 19
Maria Angela RosatiSantuzza Nunzio TodiscoTuriddu Pedro Farres/Salvatore Sassu[May 17, 19]Alfio Olive DuncanLucia Ruth Maher/Deirdre Grier[May 3, 17, 19]Lola Albert RosenConductor Sanzio LevrattiProducer
PAGLIACCI - LEONCAVALLO Dublin Apr 23, 25, 27, May 3; Cork May 17, 19
Renato FrancesconiCanio Rita LantieriNedda Salvatore SassuTonio Giorgio GattiSilvio Patrick RingBeppe Albert RosenConductor Sanzio LevrattiProducer
LA BOH_ME - PUCCINI Dublin Apr 24, 26, 28, May 1, 4; Cork May 15, 18
Anna Maria BalboniMimi Antonio BevacquaRodolfo Terry ReidMusetta Attilio d'OraziMarcello Giovanni Gusmeroli/Aldo Frattini[Apr 28, May 1, 4]Colline Alberto Carusi Schaunard Patrick RingBenoit/Alcindoro Napoleone AnnovazziConductor Philippe PerrottetProducer
LA FORZA DEL DESTINO - VERDI Dublin Apr 30, May 2, 5; Cork May 14, 16
Maria Angela RosatiLeonora Giuseppe GiacominiAlvaro Pedro Farres/Nikola Mitic[May 14, 16]Carlo Giovanni GusmeroliGuardiano Alberto CarusiMelitone Deirdre GrierPreziosilla Brendan KeyesMarquis Napoleone AnnovazziConductor Philippe PerrottetProducer
FALSTAFF - VERDI Dublin May 7, 9, 11
Attilio d'OraziFalstaff Anna Maria BalboniAlice Giorgio GattiFord Niculina Mirea CurtaNanetta Antonio BevacquaFenton Silvana MazzieriQuickly Angelo MercurialiBardolph Giovanni GusmeroliPistol Ruth MaherMeg Brendan CavanaghCaius Napoleone AnnovazziConductor Philippe PerrottetProducer
LE NOZZE DI FIGARO - MOZART Dublin May 8, 10, 12
Renato CesariFigaro Terry ReidSusanna Ileana SinnoneCountess Aldo FrattiniCount Silvana MazzieriCherubino Sergio PezzettiBartolo Ruth MaherMarcellina Patrick RingBasilio Brendan CavanaghCurzio Brendan KeyesAntonio Monica CondronBarbarina Albert RosenConductor Sanzio LevrattiProducer

WINTER 1973: GAIETY THEATRE DUBLIN

DON CARLO - VERDI Dec 3, 5, 7, 13
Renato FrancesconiCarlo Anna Maria BalboniElisabetta Helge BömchesFilippo Walter MonachesiRodrigo Katia Kolceva AngeloniEboli Giovanni GusmeroliInquisitore Deirdre

Grier Tebaldo Napoleone AnnovazziConductor Philippe PerrottetProducer
JENUFA - JANACEK Dec 4, 6, 8, 11 - [Principals of Czech National Theatre Prague]
Mlada SubrtovaJenufa Alena MikovaKostelnicka Oldrich SpisarLaca Milan KarpisekSteva Ruth MaherGrandmother Jaroslav HoracekStarec Albert RosenConductor Jaroslav HoracekProducer
MIGNON - THOMAS Dec 10, 12, 14, 15
Carmen GonzalesMignon Antonio BevacquaWilhelm Niculina Mirea CurtaPhiline Giovanni GusmeroliLothario Deirdre Grier Frédéric Patrick O'RourkeJarno Mugur BogdanLaërte Napoleone AnnovazziConductor Philippe PerrottetProducer

SPRING 1974: GAIETY THEATRE DUBLIN; OPERA HOUSE CORK

RIGOLETTO - VERDI Dublin Apr 15, 17, 19, 25; Cork May 7, 10
Gabriele FlorestaRigoletto Niculina Mirea CurtaGilda Antonio BevacquaDuke Giovanni GusmeroliSparafucile John O'FlynnMonterone Ruth MaherMaddalena Albert RosenConductor Philippe PerrottetProducer
SIMON BOCCANEGRA - VERDI Dublin Apr 16, 18, 20, 22; Cork May 9, 11
Salvatore SassuSimon Anna Maria BalboniAmelia Gianni BavaglioGabriele Aurio TomicichFiesco Mugur BogdanPaolo John O'FlynnPietro Napoleone AnnovazziConductor Jaroslav HoracekProducer
LUCIA DI LAMMERMOOR - DONIZETTI Dublin Apr 23, 27, May 1
Gunes UlkerLucia Franco BonanomeEdgardo Mugur BogdanEnrico Aurio Tomicich/Giovanni Gusmeroli[Apr 27]Raimondo Patrick Ring Arturo Brendan CavanaghNormanno Olive DuncanAlisa Albert RosenConductor Jaroslav HoracekProducer
MADAMA BUTTERFLY - PUCCINI Dublin Apr 24, 26, 29, May 3; Cork May 6, 8
Atsuko AzumaCio-Cio San Franco BonanomePinkerton Ruth MaherSuzuki Giorgio Gatti/Gabriele Floresta[May 8]Sharpless Patrick RingGoro John O'FlynnBonze Mugur BogdanYamadori Gemma KavanaghKate Napoleone AnnovazziConductor Philippe PerrottetProducer
LA FAVORITA - DONIZETTI Dublin Apr 30, May 2, 4
Silvana MazzieriLeonora Antonio BevacquaFernando Gabriele FlorestaAlfonso Giovanni GusmeroliBaldassarre Terry ReidInes Brendan CavanaghGasparo Napoleone AnnovazziConductor Philippe PerrottetProducer

WINTER 1974: GAIETY THEATRE DUBLIN

CARMEN - BIZET Dec 2, 4, 6, 10, 12
Carmen GonzalesCarmen Franco BonanomeDon José Deirdre Grier Delaney/Aida Abagieff[Dec 10]Micaëla Louis ManikasEscamillo Olive DuncanFrasquita Suzanne MurphyMercédès Peter McBrienDancaïre Brendan CavanaghRemendado John O'FlynnZuniga Brian DonlanMoralès Napoleone AnnovazziConductor Philippe PerrottetProducer
DON GIOVANNI - MOZART Dec 3, 5, 7
Peter GlossopGiovanni Silvana GherraAnna Aurio TomicichLeporello Aida AbagieffElvira Antonio BevacquaOttavio Terry ReidZerlina John O'FlynnCommendatore Brian DonlanMasetto Albert RosenConduct Philippe PerrottetProducer
SAMSON ET DALILA - SAINT-SA_NS Dec 9, 11, 13, 14
Ciro PirottaSamson Katia Kolceva AngeloniDalila John O'FlynnAbimélech Octav EnigarescuHigh Priest Aurio TomicichOld Hebrew Napoleone AnnovazziConductor Philippe PerrottetProducer

SPRING 1975: GAIETY THEATRE DUBLIN; OPERA HOUSE CORK

LA TRAVIATA - VERDI Dublin Mar 31, Apr 2, 4, 10; Cork Apr 21, 23
Gunes UlkerVioletta Gianni BavaglioAlfredo Giorgio GattiGiorgio Monica CondronFlora Patrick RingGastone Peter McBrienBaron Patrick O'RourkeMarchese Seán MittenDr Grenvil Olive DuncanAnnina Albert RosenConductor Tom Hawkes Producer

UN BALLO IN MASCHERA - VERDI Dublin Apr 1, 3, 5; Cork Apr 24, 26
Pedro LavirgenRiccardo Florida NorelliAmelia Salvatore SassuRenato Wally SallioUlrica
Niculina Mirea CurtaOscar Aurio TomicichSamuel Seán MittenTom Peter McBrienSilvano
Napoleone AnnovazziConductor Tom Hawkes Producer
I PURITANI - BELLINI Dublin Apr 7, 9, 11, 16
Niculina Mirea CurtaElvira Antonio BevacquaArturo Salvatore SassuRiccardo Aurio
TomicichGiorgio Suzanne MurphyEnrichetta Brendan CavanaghBruno Seán MittenGualtiero
Napoleone AnnovazziConductor Tom Hawkes Producer
TOSCA - PUCCINI Dublin Apr 8, 12, 15, 18; Cork Apr 22, 25
Mirna LacambraTosca Pedro Lavirgen/ Gianni Bavaglio[Apr 12, 15]Cavaradossi Gian
Giacomo GuelfiScarpia Seán MittenAngelotti James O'NeillSacristan Patrick RingSpoletta
Peter McBrienSciarrone Napoleone AnnovazziConductor Rocco SpataroProducer
DON PASQUALE - DONIZETTI Dublin Apr 14, 17, 19
Sergio PezzettiPasquale Terry ReidNorina Antonio BevacquaErnesto Giorgio GattiMalatesta
Brendan CavanaghNotary Albert RosenConductor Rocco SpataroProducer

WINTER 1975: GAIETY THEATRE DUBLIN

DER ROSENKAVALIER - STRAUSS Dec 1, 3, 5, 9
Lois McDonall/Kay Griffel[Dec 5, 9]Feldmarschallin Helga AnjervoOctavian Rolf PolkeOchs
Niculina Mirea CurtaSophie Peter McBrienFaninal Terry ReidMarianne Brendan
CavanaghValzacchi Joan DaviesAnnina Franco BonanomeSinger James O'NeillNotary
Napoleone AnnovazziConductor Tom Hawkes Producer
IL TROVATORE - VERDI Dec 2, 4, 6, 11
Ciro Pirotta/Renato Francesconi[Dec 2]Manrico Milla AndrewLeonora Salvatore SassuDi
Luna Wally SalioAzucena Seán MittenFerrando Albert RosenConductor Rocco
SpataroProducer
LES CONTES D'HOFFMANN - OFFENBACH Dec 8, 10, 12, 13
Franco BonanomeHoffmann Niculina Mirea CurtaOlympia Nicole LorangeGiulietta/Antonia
Joshua HechtCoppélius/Miracle/ Lindorf/Dapertutto Mary SheridanNicklausse Patrick
RingSpalanzani/Pitichinaccio Seán MittenCrespel /Schlemil Brendan
CavanaghCochenille/Frantz Ruth MaherMother Napoleone AnnovazziConductor Tom
Hawkes Producer

SPRING 1976: GAIETY THEATRE DUBLIN; OPERA HOUSE CORK

ANDREA CHÉNIER - GIORDANO Dublin Apr 19, 21, 23
Piero ViscontiChénier Maria Angela RosatiMaddalena Gian Giacomo GuelfiGérard Alessandro
SabbatiniRoucher Mary SheridanBersi Ruth MaherMadelon/Countess Brendan
CavanaghIncroyable/Abbé Napoleone AnnovazziConductor Dario MicheliProducer
LA BOH_ME - PUCCINI Dublin Apr 20, 22, 24, 28; Cork May 11, 14
Hagint VartanianMimi Franco BonanomeRodolfo Terry Reid Musetta Salvatore
SassuMarcello Aurio TomicichColline Peter McBrienSchaunard Patrick RingBenoit/Alcindoro
Albert RosenConductor Rocco SpataroProducer
AIDA - VERDI Dublin Apr 26, 29, May 1, 7; Cork May 10, 13
Maria Angela RosatiAida Piero ViscontiRadames Wally SalioAmneris Salvatore SassuAmonasro
Franco PuglieseRamfis Alessandro SabbatiniKing Monica CondronPriestess Patrick
RingMessenger Napoleone Annovazzi Conductor Rocco SpataroProducer
OTELLO - VERDI Dublin Apr 27, 30, May 3, 5
Angelo MarenziOtello Hagint VartanianDesdemona Joshua HechtIago Brendan
CavanaghCassio Patrick RingRoderigo Seán MittenLodovico Peter McBrienMontano/Herald
Ruth MaherEmilia Napoleone AnnovazziConductor Dario MicheliProducer
L'ELISIR D'AMORE - DONIZETTI Dublin May 4, 6, 8; Cork May 12, 15
Terry ReidAdina Ugo BenelliNemorino Attilio d'OraziBelcore Aurio TomicichDulcamara
Sheila MoloneyGiannetta Albert RosenConductor Paddy RyanProducer

THE BARTERED BRIDE - SMETANA Nov 29, Dec 1, 3, 9 -[Principals of Czech National Theatre Prague]
Daniela SounovaMarenka Bohumil CernyJeník Jaroslav HoracekKecal Alfred HampelVasek William YoungKrusina Mary SheridanLudmilla Ruth MaherHáta Brendan KeyesMícha Terry ReidEsmeralda Patrick RingCircus Master Albert RosenConductor Jaroslav HoracekProducer

EUGENE ONEGIN - TCHAIKOVSKY Nov 30, Dec 2, 4, 7
Nikola MiticOnegin Hagint VartanianTatyana Franco BonanomeLensky Zivan SaramandicGremin Breda KalefOlga Ruth MaherLarina Elvira Kohenoff d'Alboni Filippyevna Brendan CavanaghTriquet Brendan KeyesZaretsky Napoleone AnnovazziConductor Tom HawkesProducer

FAUST - GOUNOD Dec 6, 8, 10, 11
Franco BonanomeFaust Lorraine Nawa JonesMarguerite Zivan SaramandicMéphistophélès William YoungValentin Mary SheridanSiébel Ruth MaherMartha Brendan KeyesWagner Napoleone AnnovazziConductor Tom HawkesProducer

MADAMA BUTTERFLY - PUCCINI Dublin Apr 11, 13, 15, 19, 21
Atsuko AzumaCio-Cio San Carlo TuandPinkerton Joan Clarkson/Ruth Maher[Apr 11, 13]Suzuki Roberto Ferrari AcciaioliSharpless Brendan CavanaghGoro Seán MittenBonze Brendan KeyesYamadori Mary O'SullivanKate Giuseppe MorelliConductor Dario MicheliProducer

FALSTAFF - VERDI Dublin Apr 12, 14, 16
Attilio d'OraziFalstaff Gabriella NovielliAlice Roberto Ferrari AcciaioliFord Elena BaggioreNanetta Claudio RazziFenton Corinna VozzaQuickly Angelo MercurialiBardolph Vito BrunettiPistol Ruth MaherMeg Brendan CavanaghCaius Napoleone AnnovazziConductor Dario MicheliProducer

MANON LESCAUT - PUCCINI Dublin Apr 18, 20, 23, 27; Cork May 2, 6
Maria ClausovaManon Franco Bonanomedes Grieux John vanZeltzLescaut Giovanni SavoiardoGeronte Brendan Cavanagh Edmond /Dancing Master Robert Hammond Lamplighter Monica CondronSinger Brendan KeyesSergeant Seán MittenCaptain Napoleone AnnovazziConductor Rocco SpataroProducer

IL BARBIERE DI SIVIGLIA - ROSSINI Dublin Apr 22, 25, 29; Cork May 3, 5
John vanZeltzFigaro Terry ReidRosina Ugo BenelliAlmaviva Giovanni SavoiardoBartolo Aurio TomicichBasilio Brendan KeyesFiorello Joan ClarksonBerta Giuseppe MorelliConductor Paddy RyanProducer

NABUCCO - VERDI Dublin Apr 26, 28, 30; Cork May 4, 7
Antonio SalvadoriNabucco Carla FerrarioAbigaille Aurio TomicichZaccaria Franco BonanomeIsmaele Joan ClarksonFenena Seán MittenHigh Priest Brendan CavanaghAbdallo Dympna CarneyAnna Napoleone AnnovazziConductor Rocco SpataroProducer

LUCIA DI LAMMERMOOR - DONIZETTI Nov 28, 30, Dec 2, 6
Sharon BennettLucia Franco BonanomeEdgardo Salvatore SassuEnrico Aurio TomicichRaimondo Brendan CavanaghArturo Frank DunneNormanno Dympna CarneyAlisa Napoleone Annovazzi/Colman Pearce[Dec 2, 6]Conductor Dario MicheliProducer

WERTHER - MASSENET Nov 29, Dec 1, 3, 8
Jon PisoWerther Bernadette GreevyCharlotte William YoungAlbert Terry ReidSophie Seán MittenBailli Brendan CavanaghSchmidt Peter McBrienJohann Albert RosenConductor Dario MicheliProducer

TANNHÄUSER - WAGNER Dec 5, 7, 9, 10
Connell ByrneTannhäuser Maria ClausovaElisabeth Peter BinderWolfram Aurio TomicichHerrmann Irene SandfordVenus Frank DunneWalther Peter McBrienBiterolf Brendan CavanaghHeinrich Seán MittenReinmar Terry ReidShepherd Napoleone

AnnovazziConductor Ken NeateProducer

SPRING 1978: GAIETY THEATRE DUBLIN; OPERA HOUSE CORK

RIGOLETTO - VERDI Dublin Mar 27, 29, 31, Apr 8
Antonio SalvadoriRigoletto Terry ReidGilda Franco BonanomeDuke Aurio
TomicichSparafucile Seán MittenMonterone Angela FeeneyMaddalena Colman
PearceConductor Ann MakowerProducer
TURANDOT - PUCCINI Dublin Mar 28, 30, Apr 1, 4; Cork Apr 17, 20
Kazue ShimadaTurandot Angelo MarenziCalaf Maria Clausova/Lorraine Marenzi Jones[Apr
4, 17, 20]Liù Franco PuglieseTimur Salvatore SassuPing Michele BuenzaPang Brendan
CavanaghPong Frank O'BrienAltoum Peter McBrienMandarin Napoleone
AnnovazziConductor Dario MicheliProducer
ERNANI - VERDI Dublin Apr 3, 6, 11, 15; Cork Apr 19, 22
Angelo MarenziErnani Nadia SavovaElvira Antonio SalvadoriCarlo Aurio TomicichSilva
Brendan CavanaghRiccardo Peter McBrienJago Napoleone AnnovazziConductor Dario
MicheliProducer
L'ITALIANA IN ALGERI - ROSSINI Dublin Apr 5, 7, 13
Helga MüllerIsabella Franco BonanomeLindoro Aurio TomicichMustafà Lorraine Marenzi
JonesElvira Salvatore SassuTaddeo Ruth MaherZulma Peter McBrienHaly Napoleone
AnnovazziConductor Dario MicheliProducer
**LA FIGLIA DEL REGGIMENTO - DONIZETTI Dublin Apr 10, 12, 14; Cork Apr
18, 21**
Maria ClausovaMaria Ugo BenelliTonio Salvatore SassuSulpizio Ruth MaherMarchesa Peter
McBrienHortensio Joan RooneyDuchessa Albert RosenConductor Rocco SpataroProducer

WINTER 1978: GAIETY THEATRE DUBLIN

LA BOH_ME - PUCCINI Dec 4, 6, 8, 12, 14
Gabriella NovielliMimi Franco BonanomeRodolfo Elena Baggiore Musetta Giorgio
GattiMarcello Franco PuglieseColline Peter McBrienSchaunard Brian DonlanBenoit Frank
O'BrienAlcindoro Albert RosenConductor Dario MicheliProducer
DON GIOVANNI - MOZART Dec 5, 7, 9
Helge BömchesGiovanni Anastasia DimitrovaAnna Aurio TomicichLeporello Licia
FalconeElvira Gianni SergeOttavio Elizabeth JarosewichZerlina Seán MittenCommendatore
Brian DonlanMasetto Napoleone AnnovazziConductor Dario MicheliProducer
DON CARLO - VERDI Dec 11, 13, 15, 16
Antonio SavastanoCarlo Lorenza CanepaElisabetta Aurio TomicichFilippo Gianni
deAngelisRodrigo Bernadette GreevyEboli Franco PuglieseInquisitore Elizabeth
JarosewichTebaldo Napoleone AnnovazziConductor Ken NeateProducer

SPRING 1979: GAIETY THEATRE DUBLIN; OPERA HOUSE CORK

LA TRAVIATA - VERDI Dublin Apr 16, 18, 20, 23, 28; Cork May 7, 10
Mariana Niculescu/Maria Luisa Garbato[May 7, 10]Violetta Aldo FilistadAlfredo Attilio
d'OraziGiorgio Ruth MaherFlora Brendan CavanaghGastone Peter McBrienBaron Frank
O'BrienMarchese Brendan KeyesDr Grenvil Monica CondronAnnina Napoleone
AnnovazziConductor Dario MicheliProducer
TOSCA - PUCCINI Dublin Apr 17, 19, 21, 25, 27; Cork May 9, 12
Elena Duma/Lorenza Canepa[May 9, 12]Tosca Ernesto VeronelliCavaradossi Walter
Alberti/Attilio d'Orazi[May 9, 12]Scarpia Brendan KeyesAngelotti Peter McBrienSacristan
Brendan CavanaghSpoletta Frank O'BrienSciarrone Albert RosenConductor Ken
NeateProducer
LA CENERENTOLA - ROSSINI Dublin Apr 24, 26, May 1, 3; Cork May 8, 11
Helga MüllerAngelina Ernesto PalacioRamiro Franco BoscoloDandini Aurio
TomicichMagnifico Elizabeth JarosewichClorinda Ruth MaherTisbe Brendan KeyesAlidoro
Napoleone AnnovazziConductor Dario MicheliProducer

MACBETH - VERDI Dublin Apr 30, May 2, 4, 5
Antonio SalvadoriMacbeth Lorenza CanepaLady Macbeth Ernesto VeronelliMacduff Aurio TomicichBanquo Brendan CavanaghMalcolm Ruth MaherLady in waiting Brendan KeyesDoctor Napoleone AnnovazziConductor Dario MicheliProducer

LES CONTES D'HOFFMANN - OFFENBACH Dec 3, 5, 7, 11, 13
Renato CazzanigaHoffmann Niculina Mirea CurtaOlympia Elena BaggioreGiulietta/Antonia Gian KoralCoppélius/Miracle/ Lindorf/Dapertutto Gloria FoglizzoNicklausse Frank DunneSpalanzani/Pitichinaccio Seán MittenCrespel /Schlemil Brendan CavanaghCochenille/Frantz Christine CadolMother Luigi MartelliConductor Giampaolo ZennaroProducer

LOUISE - CHARPENTIER Dec 4, 6, 8
Carolina DumasLouise Georges LiccioniJulien Solange MichelMother Frederic VassarFather Guy GabelNoctambulist/King of the Fools Colette McGahonRag Picker/Suzanne Aideen LaneCoal Gatherer/Errand Girl Mary TroyPaper Girl/Marguerite Joan RooneyMilkwoman/Madeleine John CarneyJunkman Seán Mitten The Ragman Brendan Keyes1st Policeman/Barrel Vendor Derek Carroll2nd Policeman Christine Cadol StreerSweeper/Gertrude Sheila MoloneyStreet Arab/Elise Frank DunnePainter/Artichoke Vendor Frank O'BrienSculptor/Old Clothes Man Brendan CavanaghSongwriter/Ragman/Green Peas Vendor Raymond HayesStudent Peter McBrien1st Philosopher Tom Carney2nd Philosopher Jack HughesPoet Tony ByrneApprentice Adrienne DoyleChairmender Paddy BrennanCarrot Vendor Catherine FitzgeraldBirdfood Girl Hila GharakhanianBlanche Gloria FoglizzoIrma Deirdre GrierCamille Adrienne CarrollForewoman Napoleone AnnovazziConductor Marcel FeruProducer

SAMSON ET DALILA - SAINT-SA_NS Dec 10, 12, 14, 15
Gilbert PySamson Bernadette GreevyDalila Peter McBrienAbimélech Gian KoralHigh Priest Frederic VassarOld Hebrew Napoleone AnnovazziConductor Ken NeateProducer

MANON - MASSENET Dublin Apr 7, 9, 11, 17
Maria Luisa GarbatoManon Gines Sirerades Grieux Pierre van FroshemLescaut Brendan CavanaghGuillot Marzio LauricellaCount Peter McBrienBrétigny Hila GharakhanianPousette Colette McGahonJavotte Deirdre GrierRosette Napoleone AnnovazziConductor Gabriel CouretProducer

MADAMA BUTTERFLY - PUCCINI Dublin Apr 8, 10, 12, 21, 25; Cork Apr 29, May 2
Yoko WatanabeCio-Cio San Renato GrimaldiPinkerton Ruth MaherSuzuki Peter McBrien/Attilio d'Orazi[Apr 8, 10, 21]Sharpless Brendan Cavanagh/Frank Dunne[Apr 29]Goro Seán MittenBonze/Yamadori Joan RooneyKate Colman PearceConductor Paddy RyanProducer

IL TROVATORE - VERDI Dublin Apr 14, 16, 18; Cork May 1, 3
Ernesto Veronelli/Tom Swift[Apr 16]/Derek Blackwell[Apr 18]Manrico Lorenza CanepaLeonora Antonio SalvadoriDi Luna Stella SilvaAzucena Aurio TomicichFerrando Albert RosenConductor Marcel FeruProducer

ADRIANA LECOUVREUR - CILEA Dublin Apr 15, 19, 23
Maria Luisa GarbatoAdriana Renato GrimaldiMaurizio Attilio d'OraziMichonnet Stella SilvaPrincess Marzio LauricellaPrince Seán MittenQuinault Frank DunnePoisson Hila GharakhanianJouvenot Colette McGahonDangeville Brendan CavanaghAbbé Napoleone AnnovazziConductor Dario MicheliProducer

LA GIOCONDA - PONCHIELLI Dublin Apr 22, 24, 26; Cork Apr 28, 30
Lorenza CanepaGioconda Ernesto VeronelliEnzo Bernadette GreevyLaura Antonio SalvadoriBarnaba Ruth MaherCieca Aurio TomicichAlvise Frank Dunne Isepo/Singer Seán MittenZuane Frank O'BrienPilot/Monk Napoleone AnnovazziConductor Dario MicheliProducer

FAUST - GOUNOD Dec 1, 3, 5, 11
Fernando BanoFaust Caroline DumasMarguerite Louis Hagen WilliamsMéphistophélès John O'FlynnValentin Colette McGahonSiébel Mary O'SullivanMartha Frank O'BrienWagner Luis BertholonConductor Denise & Marcel FeruProducers

FIDELIO - BEETHOVEN Dec 2, 4, 6, 9
Nelli SkolnikLeonora Maurice MaievskiFlorestan Gian KoralPizzaro Frederic VassarRocco Ann MoranMarzelline Patrick RingJaquino Peter McBrienFernando Albert RosenConductor KenNeateProducer

ORFEO ED EURIDICE - GLUCK Dec 8, 10, 12, 13
Bernadette GreevyOrfeo Lorraine Marenzi JonesEuridice Hila GharakhanianAmor Napoleone AnnovazziConductor Dario MicheliProducer

LA BOH_ME - PUCCINI Dublin Apr 20, 22, 24, 27, 30; Cork May 11, 14
Maria ClausovaMimi Michele MoleseRodolfo Mary BurgessMusetta Carlo DesideriMarcello Frederic VassarColline Peter McBrienSchaunard Michael CarlyleBenoit Frank O'BrienAlcindoro Napoleone AnnovazziConductor Flavio TrevisanProducer

UN BALLO IN MASCHERA - VERDI Dublin Apr 21, 23, 25, 29, May 2
Ernesto VeronelliRiccardo Lorenza CanepaAmelia Juan Carlos GebelinRenato Katia Kolceva AngeloniUlrica Ann MoranOscar Seán MittenSamuel Brendan KeyesTom Frank O'BrienSilvano Giovanni VeneriConductor Dario MicheliProducer

OTELLO - VERDI Dublin Apr 28, May 1, 5, 7; Cork May 13, 16
Gilbert PyOtello Maria Luisa GarbatoDesdemona Gian KoralIago Silvio EupaniCassio Brendan CavanaghRoderigo Frank O'BrienLodovico Peter McBrien/John Morgan[May 7, 13, 16]Montano John MorganHerald Mary O'SullivanEmilia Napoleone AnnovazziConductor Dario MicheliProducer

LUCIA DI LAMMERMOOR - DONIZETTI Dublin May 4, 6, 8, 9; Cork May 12, 15
Carla BastoLucia Michele Molese/Antonio Savastano[May 4, 6 (Acts 1 & 2)]Edgardo Carlo DesideriEnrico Frederic VassarRaimondo Silvio EupaniArturo Brendan CavanaghNormanno Dympna CarneyAlisa Eugenio MarcoConductor Paddy RyanProducer

IL BARBIERE DI SIVIGLIA - ROSSINI Nov 30, Dec 2, 4, 8 [Sung in English]
Alan OpieFigaro Cynthia BuchanRosina Anthony RodenAlmaviva Peter McBrienBartolo Paul HudsonBasilio Frank O'BrienFiorello Rosalind HorsingtonBerta Colman PearceConductor TomHawkesProducer

CARMEN - BIZET Dec 1, 3, 5, 10
Cleopatra CiurcaCarmen Michele MoleseDon José Maria Luisa GarbatoMicaëla Platon ShvetsEscamillo Rita HarpurFrasquita Mary O'SullivanMercédès Peter McBrienDancaïre Brendan CavanaghRemendado Seán MittenZuniga Frank O'BrienMoralès Albert RosenConductor Dario MicheliProducer

NORMA - BELLINI Dec 7, 9, 11, 12
Lynne Strow PiccoloNorma Kumiko YoshiiAdalgisa Maurice MaievskiPollione Franco PuglieseOroveso Brendan CavanaghFlavio Rita HarpurClothilde Napoleone AnnovazziConductor Dario MicheliProducer

LA FAVORITA - DONIZETTI Dublin Apr 12, 14, 16, 20, 22
Kumiko YoshiiLeonora Antonio BevacquaFernando Licinio MontefuscoAlfonso Aurio TomicichBaldassarre Marie Claire O'ReirdanInes Brendan CavanaghGasparo Napoleone

AnnovazziConductor Tom HawkesProducer
TOSCA - PUCCINI Dublin Apr 13, 15, 21, 24; Cork May 3, 6
Lorenza CanepaTosca Michele MoleseCavaradossi Attilio d'OraziScarpia Seán
MittenAngelotti Peter McBrien/Frank O'Brien[May 3, 6]Sacristan Brendan
CavanaghSpoletta Frank O'BrienSciarrone Giovanni VeneriConductor Dario MicheliProducer
NABUCCO - VERDI Dublin Apr 19, 23, 26, 30; Cork May 5, 8
Licino MontefuscoNabucco Lorenza CanepaAbigaille Aurio TomicichZaccaria Antonio
BevacquaIsmaele Mary SheridanFenena Seán MittenHigh Priest Brendan CavanaghAbdallo
Dympna CarneyAnna Napoleone AnnovazziConductor Dario MicheliProducer
L'ELISIR D'AMORE - DONIZETTI Dublin Apr 27, 29, May 1; Cork May 4, 7
Marta TaddeiAdina Ugo BenelliNemorino Giorgio GattiBelcore Maurizio PicconiDulcamara
MarieClaire O'ReirdanGiannetta Proinnsías _'DuinnConductor Paddy RyanProducer

IL TROVATORE - VERDI Nov 29, Dec 1, 3, 7, 9
Michele MoleseManrico Hagint Vartanian/Lynne Strow Piccolo[Dec 7, 9]Leonora
Alessandro CassisDi Luna Kumiko YoshiiAzucena Aurio TomicichFerrando Albert
RosenConductor Dario MicheliProducer
**HÄNSEL UND GRETEL - HUMPERDINCK Nov 30, Dec 2, 4   [Sung in
English]**
Jill WashingtonGretel Helga AnjervoHänsel Frank O'BrienFather Mary SheridanMother
Rosalind HorsingtonWitch Marie Claire O'ReirdanSandman/Dew Fairy Proinnsías
_'DuinnConductor Paddy RyanProducer
MARTHA - FLOTOW Dec 6, 8, 10, 11
Mary BurgessMartha Eduardo GiménezLionel Marla VolovnaNancy André OrlowitzPlunkett
Aurio TomicichTristram Peter McBrienSheriff Napoleone AnnovazziConductor Tom
HawkesProducer

MANON LESCAUT - PUCCINI Dublin Apr 4, 6, 8, 13, 16; Cork Apr 26, 29
Maria Luisa GarbatoManon Doro Antoniolides Grieux Attilio d'OraziLescaut Miguel
ChimientiGeronte Peter RichfieldEdmond/Lamplighter Brendan CavanaghDancing Master
Patricia BardonSinger John CarneySergeant Peter McBrienCaptain Napoleone
AnnovazziConductor Dario MicheliProducer
RIGOLETTO - VERDI Dublin Apr 5, 7, 9, 12, 15; Cork Apr 25, 28
Licinio MontefuscoRigoletto Susanna RigacciGilda Andrea ElenaDuke Franco
PuglieseSparafucile Peter McBrienMonterone Patricia BardonMaddalena Bruno
RigacciConductor Loris SolenghiProducer
MADAMA BUTTERFLY - PUCCINI Dublin Apr 11, 14, 18, 20, 22
Micié AkisadaCio-Cio San Doro AntonioliPinkerton Anna CalebSuzuki Attilio
d'OraziSharpless Brendan CavanaghGoro Seán MittenBonze Frank O'BrienYamadori Maura
DevineKate Takuo YuasaConductor Paddy RyanProducer
ANDREA CHÉNIER - GIORDANO Dublin Apr 19, 21, 23; Cork Apr 27, 30
Doro Antonioli/Herman Malamood[Apr 19]Chénier Martha ColalilloMaddalena Licino
Montefusco/Attilio d'Orazi[Apr 27]Gérard Franco PuglieseRoucher Mary SheridanBersi
Thérèse FeighanMadelon/Countess Brendan CavanaghIncroyable/Abbé Napoleone
AnnovazziConductor Dario MicheliProducer

LA TRAVIATA - VERDI Nov 28, 30, Dec 2, 6, 8
Suzanne MurphyVioletta Berardino di DomenicoAlfredo Attilio d'OraziGiorgio Thérèse
FeighanFlora Brendan CavanaghGastone Peter McBrienBaron Frank O'BrienMarchese Seán
MittenDr Grenvil Monica CondronAnnina Ernesto GordiniConductor Tom HawkesProducer

COSI FAN TUTTE - MOZART Nov 29, Dec 1, 3
Mary BurgessFiordiligi Eduardo GiménezFerrando Kumiko YoshiiDorabella Frank
O'BrienGuglielmo Aurio TomicichAlfonso Terry ReidDespina Albert RosenConductor Steven
PimlottProducer
LOHENGRIN - WAGNER Dec 5, 7, 9, 10
Ruggero OrofinoLohengrin Tiziana SojatElsa Antonin SvorcTelramund Pauline
TinsleyOrtrud Aurio TomicichHenry Brian DonlanHerald Napoleone AnnovazziConductor
Mladen SablicProducer

SPRING 1984: OLYMPIA THEATRE DUBLIN; OPERA HOUSE CORK

AIDA - VERDI Dublin Apr 24, 26, 28, May 2; Cork May 14, 17
Hagint VartanianAida Angelo MarenziRadames Claudia ParadaAmneris Bruno dal
Monte/Licinio Montefusco[May 14, 17]Amonasro Aurio TomicichRamfis Armando
CaforioKing Thérèse FeighanPriestess Brendan CavanaghMessenger Giacomo ZaniConductor
Dario MicheliProducer
**LUCIA DI LAMMERMOOR - DONIZETTI Dublin Apr 25, 27, 30, May 3, 5; Cork
May 15, 18**
Maria Angela PetersLucia Gianni BavaglioEdgardo Bruno dal MonteEnrico Armando
CaforioRaimondo Patrick McCarthyArturo Brendan CavanaghNormanno Dympna
CarneyAlisa Stephen BarlowConductor Loris SolenghiProducer
LA BOH_ME - PUCCINI Dublin May 1, 4, 7, 9, 11
Maria Luisa GarbatoMimi Berardino di DomenicoRodolfo Gabriella NovielliMusetta Attilio
d'OraziMarcello Aurio TomicichColline Peter McBrienSchaunard Brian
DonlanBenoit/Alcindoro Giacomo ZaniConductor Paddy RyanProducer
LA GIOCONDA - PONCHIELLI Dublin May 8, 10, 12; Cork May 16, 19
Anna Maria Pizzoli/Lorenza Canepa[May 16, 19]Gioconda Gianni BavaglioEnzo Claudia
ParadaLaura Licinio MontefuscoBarnaba Deirdre Cooling-NolanCieca Aurio TomicichAlvise
Brendan CavanaghIsepo Frank O'Brien Zuane/Singer/Monk John CarneyPilot Janos
AcsConductor Dario MicheliProducer

WINTER 1984: GAIETY THEATRE DUBLIN

COSI FAN TUTTE - MOZART Dec 4, 6, 8
Monica TeodorescuFiordiligi Eduardo GiménezFerrando Kumiko YoshiiDorabella Frank
O'BrienGuglielmo Aurio TomicichAlfonso Terry ReidDespina Albert RosenConductor Steven
PimlottProducer
DER ROSENKAVALIER - STRAUSS Dec 5, 7, 11, 13
Celestina CasapietraFeldmarschallin Helga Müller-Molinari Octavian Heinz FeldhoffOchs
Nicola SharkeySophie Peter McBrienFaninal Thérèse FeighanMarianne Brendan
CavanaghValzacchi Deirdre Cooling-NolanAnnina Anthony RodenSinger Brian
DonlanNotary Stephen BarlowConductor Tom HawkesProducer
DIE FLEDERMAUS - STRAUSS Dec 10, 12, 14, 15   [Sung in English]
Catherine WilsonRosalinda Geoffrey PogsonEisenstein Marilyn Hill SmithAdele Martin
McEvoyFalke Lynn BarberOrlofsky Anthony RodenAlfred John AyldonFrank Frank
KellyFrosch Frances LuceyIda Brendan CavanaghBlind Robin StapeltonConductor Tom
HawkesProducer

SPRING 1985: GAIETY THEATRE DUBLIN

DON CARLO - VERDI Apr 10, 12, 16, 23
Walter DonatiCarlo Lorenza CanepaElisabetta Carlo CavaFilippo Licinio Montefusco/Frank
O'Brien[Apr 16, 23]Rodrigo Jadranka JovanovicEboli Armando Caforio/David Gwynne[Apr
23]Inquisitore Kathleen TynanTebaldo Gianfranco RivoliConductor Giampaolo
ZennaroProducer
TOSCA - PUCCINI Apr 11, 13, 19, 26, 27
Radmila BakocevicTosca Giorgio TieppoCavaradossi Attilio d'OraziScarpia Armando

Caforio/Carlo Cava[Apr 26, 27]Angelotti Peter McBrienSacristan Brendan CavanaghSpoletta Frank O'BrienSciarrone Stephen BarlowConductor Ben BarnesProducer
MACBETH - VERDI Apr 17, 20, 22, 24
Giovanni de AngelisMacbeth Radmila BakocevicLady Macbeth Walter DonatiMacduff Carlo CavaBanquo Ted RyanMalcolm Thérèse FeighanLady in waiting Frank O'BrienDoctor Giovanni VeneriConductor Dario MicheliProducer

IL BARBIERE DI SIVIGLIA - ROSSINI Dec 3, 5, 9, 13 [Sung in English]
Frank O'BrienFigaro Della JonesRosina Patrick PowerAlmaviva Peter McBrienBartolo Aurio TomicichBasilio Roland PurcellFiorello Deirdre Cooling-NolanBerta Albert Rosen/Bryden Thomson[Dec 9, 13]Conductor Paddy RyanProducer
CARMEN - BIZET Dec 4, 6, 7, 11
Rodica Mitrica BadirceaCarmen Constantin EneDon José Virginia KerrMicaëla Dan ZancuEscamillo Anne-Maria SmithFrasquita Carolann LoweMercédès Peter McBrienDancaïre Brendan CavanaghRemendado Pompei HarasteanuZuniga Frank O'BrienMoralès Vladimir ContaConductor A E ArboreProducer
EUGENE ONEGIN - TCHAIKOVSKY Dec 10, 12, 14
Emil IurascuOnegin Monica TeodorescuTatyana Ionel VoineagLensky Pompei HarasteanuGremin Patricia BardonOlga Ruth MaherLarina Deirdre Cooling-NolanFilippyevna Brendan CavanaghTriquet Nigel WilliamsZaretsky Ervin AcelConductor A E ArboreProducer

LA TRAVIATA - VERDI Apr 1, 3, 5, 7
Maria Luisa GarbatoVioletta Ionel VoineagAlfredo Peter McBrienGiorgio Carolann LoweFlora Brendan CavanaghGastone Brian DonlanBaron Andrew MurphyMarchese Nigel WilliamsDr Grenvil Joan O'FarrellAnnina Ervin AcelConductor Tom HawkesProducer
MADAMA BUTTERFLY - PUCCINI Apr 2, 4, 9, 11
Yasuko SatoCio-Cio San Walter DonatiPinkerton Deirdre Cooling-NolanSuzuki Frank O'BrienSharpless Brendan CavanaghGoro Brian DonlanBonze Nigel WilliamsYamadori Patricia RyanKate David ParryConductor Wilfred JuddProducer
NABUCCO - VERDI Dublin Apr 8, 10, 12
Licino MontefuscoNabucco Radmila BakocevicAbigaille Aurio TomicichZaccaria Walter DonatiIsmaele Thérèse FeighanFenena Brian DonlanHigh Priest Ted RyanAbdallo Dympna CarneyAnna Giovanni VeneriConductor Dario MicheliProducer

ORFEO ED EURIDICE - GLUCK Dec 4, 8, 10, 12
Patricia BardonOrfeo Angela FeeneyEuridice Kathleen TynanAmor Mary ClarkeHappy Shade Albert RosenConductor Patrick MurrayProducer
TURANDOT - PUCCINI Dec 5, 9, 11, 13
Radmila BakocevicTurandot Walter DonatiCalaf Virginia KerrLiù Liu YueTimur Peter McBrienPing Frank DunnePang Brendan CavanaghPong Ted RyanAltoum Nigel WilliamsMandarin Giovanni VeneriConductor Dario MicheliProducer

LA BOH_ME - PUCCINI Dublin Apr 22, 24, 27, 30, May 2; Cork May 5, 7, 9
Anna Maria FerranteMimi Jean-Luc VialaRodolfo Virginia KerrMusetta Hartmut SingerMarcello Curtis WatsonColline Bruno CaproniSchaunard Brian DonlanBenoit Nigel WilliamsAlcindoro Albert RosenConductor Mike AshmanProducer
L'ELISIR D'AMORE - DONIZETTI Dublin Apr 23, 25, 29, May 1; Cork May 4, 6,

8

Antonella MuscenteAdina Justin LavenderNemorino Alan WattBelcore Maurizio
PicconiDulcamara Kathleen TynanGiannetta James BlairConductor Patrick YoungProducer

WINTER 1987: GAIETY THEATRE DUBLIN

RIGOLETTO - VERDI Dec 3, 5, 8, 11
Peter McBrienRigoletto Ilena VinkGilda Ingus PetersonDuke Curtis WatsonSparafucile Frank
O'BrienMonterone Deirdre Cooling-NolanMaddalena Albert RosenConductor Jan
BouwsProducer
DON PASQUALE - DONIZETTI Dec 4, 6, 10
Enrico FissorePasquale Nuccia FocileNorina Giuseppe CostanzoErnesto Russell
SmytheMalatesta Ciaran Rocks/Duncan McKenzie[Dec 6]Notary David ParryConductor
Michael McCafferyProducer
LES P_CHEURS DE PERLES - BIZET Dec 7, 9, 12
Virginia KerrLeila Gines SireraNadir Peter Coleman WrightZurga Jack O'KellyNourabad
Valentin ReymondConductor Mike AshmanProducer

SPRING 1988: GAIETY THEATRE DUBLIN

TOSCA - PUCCINI Apr 6, 8, 11, 14
Margareta HavarinenTosca Giorgio TieppoCavaradossi Anthony BaldwinScarpia Jean-Jacques
CubaynesAngelotti Peter McBrienSacristan Marc ThomsonSpoletta Nigel WilliamsSciarrone
Albert RosenConductor Susan ToddProducer
IL TROVATORE - VERDI Apr 7, 9, 13, 16
Fabio ArmiliatoManrico Francesca ArnoneLeonora Luis Giron MayDi Luna Evghenia
DundekhovaAzucena Alistair MilesFerrando David ParryConductor Michael
McCafferyProducer
DON GIOVANNI - MOZART Apr 10, 12, 15
Maarten FlipseGiovanni Tiziana DucatiAnna Tom HaenenLeporello Virginia KerrElvira
Christian PapisOttavio Kathleen TynanZerlina Jean-Jacques CubaynesCommendatore Jack
O'KellyMasetto Janos FurstConductor Patrick MasonProducer

SPRING 1989: NATIONAL CONCERT HALL, DUBLIN

NORMA - BELLINI Mar 28, 31, Apr 3
Suzanne MurphyNorma Angela FeeneyAdalgisa Osvaldo di PianduniPollione Giancarlo
BoldriniOroveso Paul McCannFlavio Marie WalsheClothilde Roderick BrydonConductor
Michael McCafferyProducer

WINTER 1989: GAIETY THEATRE DUBLIN : ELAINE PADMORE ARTISTIC DIRECTOR

LA TRAVIATA - VERDI Dec 2, 4, 6, 8
Karen Huffstodt/Bronwen Mills[Dec 8]Violetta Patrick PowerAlfredo Dimitri
KharitonovGiorgio Susan DanielFlora Francis EgertonGastone Peter LoehleBaron Frank
O'BrienMarchese Nigel WilliamsDr Grenvil Sylvia O'ReganAnnina David ParryConductor
Michael HuntProducer
CARMEN - BIZET Dec 3, 5, 7, 9
Luretta BybeeCarmen Stefano AlgieriDon José Mariette KemmerMicaëla Balazs
PokaEscamillo Regina NathanFrasquita Susan DanielMercédès Brendan CavanaghDancaïre
Francis EgertonRemendado Peter LoehleZuniga Frank O'BrienMoralès Albert
RosenConductor Jean-Claude AuvrayProducer

SPRING 1990: GAIETY THEATRE DUBLIN

PETER GRIMES - BRITTEN Apr 25, 28, May 1, 4
William NeillGrimes Pamela MyersEllen Keith LathamBalstrode Elizabeth BainbridgeAuntie

William MackieSwallow John DanieckiBoles Peter SavidgeKeene Angela HickeyMrs Sedley
Yvonne Brennan/Kathleen TynanNieces Brendan CavanaghAdams Thomas LawlorHobson
Simon JolyConductor Tim HopkinsProducer
MADAMA BUTTERFLY - PUCCINI Apr 26, 29, May 2, 5
Nikki Li HartliepCio-Cio San Hans Gregory AshbakerPinkerton Thérèse FeighanSuzuki
Victor LedbetterSharpless Philip DoghanGoro John TranterBonze Frank O'BrienYamadori
Carolann LoweKate Marco GuidariniConductor John Lloyd DaviesProducer
DON GIOVANNI - MOZART Apr 27, 30, May 3
Russell SmytheGiovanni Lauren FlaniganAnna Joseph McKeeLeporello Phyllis TreigleElvira
Paul Austin KellyOttavio Regina NathanZerlina John TranterCommendatore Mark
HollandMasetto Alan HackerConductor Patrick MasonProducer [Revival restaged by Paul
Maloney]

DIE ZAUBERFLÖTE - MOZART Dec 2, 4, 6, 8   [Sung in English]
Mark NicholsonTamino Linda KitchenPamina Russell SmythePapageno Jennifer Rhys-
DaviesQueen Jonathan BestSarastro Lynne Davies/Thora Ker/Hyacinth NichollsLadies
Owen Edward Brady/Alan Carroll/David Cregan/Anthony Doyle/Kevin Kelly/Paul
ReaBoys Michael NeillSpeaker Howard HaskinMonostatos Sally-Ann ShepherdsonPapagena
Brendan McBride/Paul ParfittPriests/ArmedMen
David ParryConductor John RamsterProducer
TOSCA - PUCCINI Dec 3, 5, 7, 9
Susan McCullochTosca Maurizio SaltarinCavaradossi Sigmund CowanScarpia Michael
NeillAngelotti Paul ParfittSacristan Brendan McBrideSpoletta Proinnsias
O'RaghallaighSciarrone Christopher BellConductor Mike AshmanProducer

IL BARBIERE DI SIVIGLIA - ROSSINI Apr 6, 8, 10, 12, 14
Adrian ClarkeFigaro Tamara MitchellRosina Luigi PetroniAlmaviva Terence SharpeBartolo
William MackieBasilio Paul ParfittFiorello Frances McCaffertyBerta Nicholas KokConductor
Robert ChevaraProducer
MANON LESCAUT - PUCCINI Apr 7, 9, 11, 13
Alison PearceManon Stefano Algieri/Richard Burke[Apr 11]des Grieux Paul ParfittLescaut
Tom HaenenGeronte Paul HarrhyEdmond Robert CroweDancing Master Frances
McCaffertySinger James NelsonLamplighter Paul McNamaraSergeant Graham WebberCaptain
Marco GuidariniConductor Stephen DaldryProducer
DGOS OPERA IRELAND

LUCIA DI LAMMERMOOR - DONIZETTI Dec 1, 3, 5, 7
Alexandrina PendatchanskaLucia John FowlerEdgardo Albert DolinEnrico Jan
GallaRaimondo Adrian MartinArturo David OwenNormanno Regina HanleyAlisa Maurizio di
RobbioConductor Francesca ZambelloProducer
LE NOZZE DI FIGARO - MOZART Dec 2, 4, 6, 8   [Sung in English]
Kurt LinkFigaro Regina NathanSusanna Valerie MastersonCountess Victor LedbetterCount
Pamela Helen StephenCherubino Richard CristBartolo Colette McGahonMarcellina John
FryattBasilio James NelsonCurzio Thomas LawlorAntonio Majella CullaghBarbarina Jonathan
WebbConductor John Lloyd DaviesProducer

UN BALLO IN MASCHERA - VERDI Apr 26, 28, 30, May 2
Maurizio SaltarinRiccardo Carol NeblettAmelia Vladimir RedkinRenato Jacalyn BowerUlrica
Frances LuceyOscar Frank O'BrienSamuel Mark GlanvilleTom Tim MorganSilvano Guido

Ajmone-MarsanConductor Ceri SherlockProducer
MARTHA - FLOTOW Apr 27, 29, May 1, 3
Marie Claire O'ReirdanMartha Kip WilbornLionel Ulrika PrechtNancy James WoodPlunkett
Peter-Christoph RungeTristram Peter McBrienSheriff James LockhartConductor Dieter
KaegiProducer

WINTER 1992: GAIETY THEATRE DUBLIN

L'ITALIANA IN ALGERI - ROSSINI Dec 2, 4, 6, 8
Luretta BybeeIsabella Mark CalkinsLindoro Valentin PeytchinovMustafà Virginia KerrElvira
Patryk WroblewskiTaddeo Pauline TinsleyZulma Eric RobertsHaly Guido Ajmone-
MarsanConductor Tim ColemanProducer
DIE FLEDERMAUS - STRAUSS Dec 3, 5, 7, 9 [Sung in English]
Valerie MastersonRosalinda Stephen O'MaraEisenstein Mary HegartyAdele Karl Morgan
DaymondFalkeThérèse FeighanOrlofsky Adrian MartinAlfred Eric RobertsFrank Thomas
LawlorFrosch Anna JenningsIda James Drummond NelsonBlind Albert RosenConductor Paul
BaillieProducer

SPRING 1993: GAIETY THEATRE DUBLIN

MADAMA BUTTERFLY - PUCCINI Apr 17, 19, 21, 23
Katerina KudriavchenkoCio-Cio San Joseph WolvertonPinkerton Lynda LeeSuzuki Victor
LedbetterSharpless Philip DoghanGoro Gerard O'ConnorBonze Frank O'BrienYamadori
Niamh MurrayKate Stephen BarlowConductor John Lloyd DaviesProducer
COSI FAN TUTTE - MOZART Apr 18, 20, 22, 24
Mariette KemmerFiordiligi Kip WilbornFerrando Yvona SkvarovaDorabella Paul
WhelanGuglielmo Eric RobertsAlfonso Mary Callan ClarkeDespina Simon JolyConductor
Dieter KaegiProducer

WINTER 1993: GAIETY THEATRE DUBLIN

LA BOH_ME - PUCCINI Nov 29, Dec 1, 3, 5, 7
Regina NathanMimi Stuart NeillRodolfo Majella CullaghMusetta Patryk WroblewskiMarcello
Egils SilinsColline Martin HigginsSchaunard Peter McBrienBenoit Frank O'BrienAlcindoro
Roderick BrydonConductor Jean-Claude AuvrayProducer
LAKMÉ - DELIBES Dec 2, 4, 6
Elizabeth FutralLakmé Donald GeorgeGérald Kate McCarneyMallika Georgi
SelesnevNilakantha Mark PedrottiFrédéric Mary Callan ClarkeEllen Roisin McGibbonRose
Meriel DickinsonMistress Bentson Emmanuel JoelConductor Nicolette MolnárProducer

SPRING 1994: GAIETY THEATRE DUBLIN : DOROTHEA GLATT ARTISTIC DIRECTOR

RIGOLETTO - VERDI Apr 9, 11, 13, 15, 17
Robert McFarlandRigoletto Nicola SharkeyGilda Kip WilbornDuke Michael
MilanovSparafucile Peter McBrienMonterone Deirdre Cooling-NolanMaddalena David
ShawConductor Eric VigiéProducer
FIDELIO - BEETHOVEN Apr 10, 12, 14, 16
Anna LindenLeonora Patrick RafteryFlorestan Louis ManikasPizzaro Klaus DammRocco
Marie-Claire O'ReirdanMarzelline Peter MausJaquino Max WittgesFernando Karl
SollakConductor Albert-André Lheureux Producer

WINTER 1994: GAIETY THEATRE DUBLIN

LA TRAVIATA - VERDI Nov 29, Dec 1, 3, 5, 7, 9
Marie-Claire O'ReirdanVioletta John FowlerAlfredo Evgenij DemerdjevGiorgio Sarah
FryerFlora Leonardo di LisiGastone Detlef RothBaron Richard WhitehouseMarchese Anthony
SmithDr Grenvil Margaret MaguireAnnina David Lloyd-JonesConductor Vivian

CoatesProducer
HÄNSEL UND GRETEL - HUMPERDINCK   Dec 2, 4, 6, 8
Eva KirchnerGretel Jane TurnerHänsel Klaus DammFather Ruthild EngertMother Cynthia
BuchanWitch Deirdre MastersonSandman/Dew Fairy David HeuselConductor Michael
McCafferyProducer

SPRING 1995: GAIETY THEATRE DUBLIN

IL TROVATORE - VERDI   Apr 22, 24, 26, 28, 30
Scott FlahertyManrico Tatiana ZakhartchoukLeonora Mark RuckerDi Luna Anne
WilkensAzucena Alan EwingFerrando Dejan SavicConductor Inga LevantProducer
DON GIOVANNI - MOZART   Apr 23, 25, 27, 29
James Michael McGuireGiovanni Madeleine KristoffersonAnna Sami LuttinenLeporello
Deanne MeekElvira Eric AshcraftOttavio Marit SauramoZerlina Scott WildeCommendatore
Giles DaviesMasetto Ira LevinConductor Michael McCafferyProducer

WINTER 1995: GAIETY THEATRE DUBLIN

FAUST - GOUNOD   Dec 1, 3, 5, 7, 9
Patrick RafteryFaust Jane Leslie MacKenzieMarguerite Victor BraunMéphistophélès Matthew
ThomasValentin Jane TurnerSiébel Anne WilkensMartha Richard WhitehouseWagner Paul
EthuinConductor Neville Carlyle-StyleProducer
LA CENERENTOLA - ROSSINI   Dec 2, 4, 6, 8
Alison BrownerAngelina Jing-Ma FanRamiro Christopher GoldsackDandini Gerolf
SchederMagnifico Katerina BeranovaClorinda Imelda DrummTisbe David
StephensonAlidoro David HeuselConductor Klaus FroboeseProducer

SPRING 1996: GAIETY THEATRE DUBLIN

TOSCA - PUCCINI   Apr 11, 13, 15, 17, 19, 21
Jane ThornerTosca Paul LyonCavaradossi Max WittgesScarpia David StephensonAngelotti
Peter McBrienSacristan Peter ButterfieldSpoletta Desmond CaplissSciarrone Martin
MerryConductor Eric VigiéProducer
DIE ZAUBERFLÖTE - Mozart   Apr 14, 16, 18, 20   [Sung in English]
Philip SalmonTamino Marina LevittPamina Steven PagePapageno Cara O'SullivanQueen
Greg RyersonSarastro Claire Daniels/Marie Walshe/Cynthia BuchanLadies Claire
Wallace/Roisín Toal/Clíona McDonoughBoys David StephensonSpeaker Alexander
OliverMonostatos Deirdre MastersonPapagena Tom Cregan/Charles Munro/Nyle P
WolfePriests Alan Beck/Nyle P Wolfe ArmedMen David HeuselConductor Michael
McCafferyProducer
OPERA IRELAND

WINTER 1996: GAIETY THEATRE DUBLIN : ELAINE PADMORE ARTISTIC ADVISOR

LA BOH_ME - PUCCINI   Nov 27, 29, Dec 1, 3, 5, 7
Maria SpacagnaMimi Maurizio Comencini/Gianni Mongiardino[Dec 5, 7]Rodolfo Kathryn
SmithMusetta Andrea ZeseMarcello Gerard O'ConnorColline Andrea PicciniSchaunard Philip
O'ReillyBenoit/Alcindoro Rico SaccaniConductor Daniel SlaterProducer
L'ELISIR D'AMORE - DONIZETTI   Dec 2, 4, 6, 8
Majella CullaghAdina David NewmanNemorino Steven PageBelcore Roderick
EarleDulcamara Roisín ToalGiannetta Mark Shanahan/Fergus Sheil[Dec 8]Conductor Mike
AshmanProducer

SPRING 1997: GAIETY THEATRE DUBLIN

LE NOZZE DI FIGARO - MOZART   Apr 5, 7, 9, 11, 13
Desmond ByrneFigaro Mary HegartySusanna Mariette KemmerCountess Karl

DaymondCount Kristina HammarströmCherubino Jonathan VeiraBartolo Pauline
TinsleyMarcellina Ugo BenelliBasilio James NelsonCurzio Gerard O'ConnorAntonio Deirdre
MastersonBarbarina Simon JolyConductor Michael McCafferyProducer
MACBETH - VERDI Apr 6, 8, 10, 12
Anatoly LochakMacbeth Karen NotareLady Macbeth Raul MeloMacduff Stanislav
SchwetsBanquo Niall MorrisMalcolm Regina HanleyLady in waiting Gerard O'ConnorDoctor
Alexander AnissimovConductor Dieter KaegiProducer

WINTER 1997: GAIETY THEATRE DUBLIN : DIETER KAEGI ARTISTIC DIRECTOR

THE MERRY WIDOW - LEH_R Nov 27, 29, Dec 1, 3, 5, 7 [Sung in English]
Alwyn MellorHanna Patrick RafteryDanilo Susanne ElmarkValencienne Peter
Gr¢nlundCamille Gerard O'ConnorBaron Stephen BrennanNjegus Anthony NortonCascada
Niall MorrisRaoul Kieran AhernBogdanowitsch Dearbhla WalshSylviane Nicholas
GrennellKromow Niamh O'BrienOlga Joe ConlanPritschitsch Anne DeeganPraskowia
Philippe JordanConductor Alan StanfordProducer
EUGENE ONEGIN - TCHAIKOVSKY Nov 30, Dec 2, 4, 6
John HancockOnegin Tatyana PoluektovaTatyana Ivan ChoupenitchLensky Michael
DruiettGremin Mary Ann McCormickOlga Yvonne LeaLarina Sheila NadlerFilippyevna
Neville AckermannTriquet Frank O'BrienZaretsky Vadim MunsterConductor James
RobinsonProducer

SPRING 1998: GAIETY THEATRE DUBLIN

LES CONTES D'HOFFMANN - OFFENBACH Apr 18, 20, 22, 24, 26
Jean Pierre FurlanHoffmann Ana Camelia StefanescuOlympia Mary Ann McCormickGiulietta
Regina NathanAntonia Laurence AlbertCoppélius/Miracle/ Lindorf/Dapertutto Marianne
R¢rholmNicklausse Neville AckermannNathaniel/Spalanzani Jean-Jacques
CubaynesLuther/Crespel Camille RenoHermann/Schlemil André
GrégoireAndreas/Cochenille/Frantz/Pitichinaccio Deirdre Cooling-NolanMother Claude
SchnitzlerConductor Joël Lauwers Producer
FALSTAFF - VERDI Dublin Apr 19, 21, 23, 25
Roy StevensFalstaff Anne Margarethe DahlAlice Richard ByrneFord Daniella LojarroNanetta
Jean-Luc VialaFenton Hanna SchaerQuickly Marc AcitoBardolph Gerard O'ConnorPistol Kari
Hamn¢yMeg William SaetreCaius Antonello AllemandiConductor Dieter KaegiProducer

Chorus Members: 1944 - '98

Abell Rita
Carroll Ursula
Geoghegan Ada
Adams Kathleen
Carwood Geraldine
Gibney Evelyn
Adams May
Cashman Aileen
Gleeson Myra
Ahern Kay
Caverly Miriam
Gleeson Patricia
Allen Dorothy
Chammartin Katherine
Goff Barbara
Andrews Gertrude
Clancy Ita
Gordon Joan
Assouad Jacqueline
Clyne Nancy
Grecen Charlotte
Bambrick Helena
Coen Noreen
Grey Patricia
Barry Ann
Coers Ellen
Griffin Aileen
Barry Marjorie
Condron Monica
Guilfoyle Maeve
Bartley Breda
Colgan Ann
Guilfoyle Sylvia
Bassett Marjorie
Doyle Adrienne
Gunning Eileen
Bedford Erinn
Dwyer Roisin
Hamill Carmel
Bird Miriam
Edwards Aileen
Hamill Phil
Bishop Anne
Edwards Marie
Handy Olive
Blake Sheila
Egan Geraldine
Hanley Patricia
Bligh Noreen
Ellison June Conaghan
Hanrahan Aisling

Bodie Una
Ely-O'Carroll Aideen
Harrington L
Boylan Philomena
Ely-O'Carroll Triona
Harrington P
Bracken Deirdre
Eustace Gertie
Hawkins Anne
Branagan Kathleen
Fagan Aureen
Hayden Pauline
Brasè Mona
Fanning Angela
Healy Jean
Breene Joan
Fanning Marie
Healy Mary
Brennan Aoife
Farrar Barbara
Heffernan Evelyn
Brennan Claire
Farrell Sheila
Henry H
Brennan Marie
Feeley Claire
Hickey Ann
Brennan Pauline
Fenning Eileen
Hickey Sadie
Breslin Clare
Fields Florence
Hillery Margaret Flynn
Brophy Peggy
Finlay Linda
Hodgins Deirdre
Broughal J
Finn Joan
Hogan Mary
Bruce Eva
Finnegan Patricia
Holley Kathleen
Buckley Nancy
Finucane Brida Carney
Hough Fionnuala
Bugler Dympna- Carney
Finucane Nuala
Hughes Maureen
Burke Catherine
Fish Myrtle
Humphries Dorothea

Burke Mary
Fitzgerald Kathryn
Hunt Ruby
Butler Anne
Fitzgerald Kay
James Patricia
Byrne Carmel
Folan Margaret
Jeacle Mona
Byrne Eileen
Foley Evelyn
Jennings Carmel
Byrne Joan
Foran Mona
Jennings Eva
Byrne Joy
Foran Sylvia
Johnston Colette
Byrne M
Forde Emer
Kavanagh Eithne
Byrne Nuala
Fortune Deirdre
Kavanagh Gemma
Byrne Stella
Foster Hilda
Kavanagh Marion Saunders
Byrom Joan
Fowler Ursula
Kavanagh Maura
Callaghan Louise
Franklin Margaret
Kavanagh Nellie
Cameron-O'Hagan Louie
Frayne Anne
Kavanagh Patricia
Campbell May
Furlong Kathleen
Keane Fiona
Cantwell Attracta
Gahan Patricia
Keating Mary
Cantwell Patricia
Galloway Patricia
Kelly Chris
Carroll Adrienne Duffy
Garb J
Kelly Eithne
Carroll Edina
Gaughan Catherine
Kelly Fidelma

Kelly June
McDermott Pauline
Newman Edith
Kelly Marie
McDonald Kay
Newport Nuala
Kelly Mary
McDonald Minnie
Nolan Bella
Kelly Mary B
McDonnell Maureen
Nolan Ena
Kelly Rita
McDonough Cliona
Nolan Pauline
Kennedy Adrienne
McGauran Alice
Nolan Teresa
Kennedy Anne
McGovern Sheila
O'Brennan Deirdre
Kenny Dorothy
McGovern Teresa
O'Brien Dorothy
Kenworthy Patricia
McGrath Mary
O'Brien Kathleen
Kemp Anne
McGuane Ann
O'Brien Maeve
Keogh Maire M
McGuinness Helena
O'Byrne Cathleen
Keogh Margaret
McHugh Pauline
O'Callaghan Byna
Keogh Maura
McIntyre Alma
O'Callaghan Dympna
Kiely Eilis
McIntyre Margaret
O'Callaghan Peg
Kinirons Una
McKeown Anne
O'Connell Anne
Kirwan Eileen
McKeown K
O'Connor Bridget
Kirwan Nellie
McLoughlin Brid
O'Connor Maura Devine
Krotschin Alice
McMahon Charlotte
O'Connor Miriam
Laheen Maureen
McMahon Clare
O'Connor Nell

Laheen Rosaleen
McPhillips Sheila
O'Doherty Maureen
Lancen R
McShane Noreen
O'Donoghue Breda
Larkin May
McSweeney Teresa
O'Donoghue Mary
Larkin Pauline
McSwiney Marie
O'Donovan Juliette
Larkin Una Faughnan
McVey M
O'Farrell Aoife
Lawless Assumpta
Mee Eileen
O'Flaherty Emer
Leach Angela
Mee Kathleen
O'Gorman Joan
Ledwidge Bonnie
Mee Peggy
O'Grady Clare
Lemass Flora
Meers Brenda
O'Hagan J
Lollar Elizabeth
Metcalfe Clare
O'Hara Patricia
Long May
Millea Anne
O'Keeffe Doreen
Lynch Deirdre
Mitchell Stella
O'Keeffe Florence
Lynch K
Moffat Alice
O'Kennedy Peggie
Macaura Beatrice
Moloney Sheila
O'Leary M
Mackey Marie
Monaghan Margaret
O'Loughlin Moira
Mackey May
Mooney Maura
O'Malley Molly
Madden Josephine
Morgan Marie
O'Neill Aine
Maddison Irene
Moriarty Mary Hanratty
O'Neill Barbara
Maguane Ann
Morris Marie
O'Neill Bernadette

Maguire Helen
Morrison Cecily Lynch
O'Neill Patricia
Maher Maeve
Morrissey Betty
O'Phelan May de Riva
Maher Sheila
Mullen Kathleen
O'Reilly Carmel
Maher Sue
Mulvey Phyllis
O'Reilly Caroline
Malone Nuala
Murnane Denise
O'Reilly R
Manders Mary
Murphy Catherine
O'Reilly Tara
Mangan Terry
Murphy Kathleen
O'Shaughnessy Orma
Manning Eileen
Murphy Margaret
O'Shea Elizabeth
Mannion C
Murphy Mary
O'Shea Fidelma
Markey Fay McGowen
Murphy May
O'Siochain Aisling
Markey Maureen
Murphy Molly
O'Siochain Orla
Martin Vera
Murphy Roma
O'Sullivan Assumpta
Mason Muriel
Murray Catherine
O'Sullivan Finnula
McAsey Carmel
Murray Eithne
O'Sullivan Karen
McCall Nora
Murray Maureen
O'Sullivan Mary
McCallum Eileen
Musgrave Pat
O'Sullivan Noreen
McCarthy Catherine
Nangle Fiona
O'Toole Barbara
McCarthy Mary
Naughton Maude
O'Toole Patricia
McConnell Hester
Nelson Joyce
Oireachtaig Maebh Nic

McCourt Magda
Nestor Kathleen
Oireachtaig Sinead Nic
McCrone Angela
Neville Mary
Oman Sandra
Owens Ita
Scott Irene
Weir Nicola
Palmer Joy
Sharkey Clare
Whelan Sylvia
Perry Nuala
Sheehan Joan
Whelan U
Peters Eithne
Sheehan Una
Whelan Veronica
Phillips Maureen
Sheridan Christine
White Blaithin
Phelan Caroline Millar
Sheridan Mary
White Dorothy
Pleimann Cait
Shiels Nora
Williamson Marie
Powell Charlotte
Slowey Marie
Willis Maureen
Powell Gypsy
Smith Doris
Wilson Jennifer
Power Josephine
Smith Maura
Woodcock Rhona
Power-Fardy Vera
Smith Sheila
Woods Bernie
Prendergast Eithne
Soffe Eileen
Woolaghan Elizabeth
Prendergast Maeve
Solan Lorrie
Young Patricia
Purcell Eileen
Souhey Mary
Quigley Joan
Stack Deirdre
Quinn Deirdre
Stanley Noreen
Reddy Doreen
Stone Pat
Reeves Maureen
Sugrue Maura
Reid Maura
Sweeney Shirley

Reilly R
Taylor Patricia
Robinson P
Thompson Sheila
Roche Hilda
Thomson Dorothy
Rock Vera
Thornton Peggy
Roddy Alison
Tiernan Patricia
Roden Ann
Tonge Jean
Rooney Joan O'Farrell
Troy Mary
Rowe Carol
Tuite Lilian
Ruane Mary
Vaughan Kitty
Rumbold M
Wakely Vivienne
Russell Margaret
Waldron Eileen
Russell Yvonne
Walsh Aileen
Ryan Evelyn
Walsh Betty
Ryan Margaret
Walsh Dearbhla
Ryan Mary
Walsh Stella
Ryan Maureen
Walsh Veronica
Ryan Noreen Hanratty
Ward Carol
Ryan Sheila
Ward Catherine
Ryan Therese
Waters Ann
Sands Bree
Weafer Ann Deegan

GENTLEMEN

Agnew Seamus
Cuthbert James G
Grace Noel
Allen John
Daly Michael
Grehan Austin
Armstrong Frank
D'Arcy Patrick
Griffin Eugene
Barriscale William
Davidson John
Griffith J
Barry David
Dawson Owen

Hackett A J
Bermingham James
Deegan Dermot
Hall Harry
Biggs Conor
Delaney Patrick
Hammond Robert
Bishop Joseph
Dempsey Robert
Hanrahan Richard
Black Joseph G
Diffney Patrick
Hargadone Michael
Black Stephen
Dignam Alec
Harper Aidan
Blanche Gerry
Dillon Jim
Hartney Edward J
Bloomfield Jack
Dillon John
Haugh Peter
Brady John
Dineen Liam
Hayes Brendan
Brady John P
Dinnigan Michael
Hayes Larry
Brady Patrick
Doherty A
Hayes Raymond
Brady Thomas
Doherty S
Hayes Richard
Brawn Oliver
Donnelly Leo
Henshaw David
Brennan Paddy
Douglas Christopher
Hickey Paul
Brennan William
Doyle Andrew
Higgins Martin
Brittain Harry
Doyle Conan
Higginson J
Brittain James
Doyle George
Hodkinson Barry
Brophy Colm
Doyle Jack
Hogan Patrick
Browne Marcus
Doyle Michael
Hogarty William C
Buckley Sean
Doyle Sean

Hourigan Eamon
Byrne Tony
Duffy John
Hughes Jack
Byrne James M
Duggan Gerald
Hughes Michael
Byrne Philip
DugganEdward
Hurley Brian
Byrom Chris J
Dunn Peter
Hutchins Walter
Caplis Des
Dunne John
Hywell John
Carey Michael
Dunphy Charles
Jackson John
Carey Robert J
Dwyer Dermot
Jackson Richard J
Carney John
Edwards P J
Jennings Redmond
Carney Tom
Ennis Ben
Jones Gerrard
Carroll Derek
Fagan J
Jones Gwilym
Carroll Jack
Fahy Michael
Kane Walter
Casey Jack
Farrell Benjamin
Kavanagh Brendan
Cassidy Hugh
Farrell Henry
Kavanagh Paul
Cassidy Sean
Fetherstone Leslie
Keane Desmond
Claffey Tom
Fitzgerald Denis
Keane Frank
Clarke T
Fitzpatrick Seamus
Kearney Phil
Claxton Denis
Fitzsimons Paul
Kearns Brendan
Clery Dermot
Flanagan Con
Keenan Noel
Coates Gerry
Flanagan Sean

Keoghan Donald
Coates Vivian
Fletcher Ken
Kerrigan Edward
Coleman George F
Flynn Maurice
Kiely Noel
Collins Tom
Foley W J
Kiernan Tom
Condon P
Forde H
Kinsella Brendan
Conn Noel
Foster William
Kelly Jim
Connolly Maurice
Fowler W
Kelly Patrick
Coulter Gordon
Frazer Edward
Kelly Paul
Courtney Randal
Gaffney Martin
Kenna Thomas A
Cowley William
Glynn Gerard
Kennedy Luke W
Cross Vincent
Goodwin Anthony
Kenny Michael
Cullen Brendan
Gormley Frank
Laheen Chris
Culleton Tom
Grace Edward
Larkin James
Lavelle J
Morgan Sean
O'Toole James
Leggette John A
Moriarty Ken
Ormonde Noel
Lenihan John
Morris Clem
Packenham Cecil
Lewis N
Morris Ralph
Peacocke Tom
Linehan John
Morrissey Martin
Pearce John
Lynskey W
Morrissey Vincent
Pelessier Robert W
MacDonald Charles
Mowlds Desmond

Porter Ignatius W
MacGabhann Ailfrid
Munnelly Austin
Power Martin
Madden Aubrey
Murphy Andrew
Price Jim
Madden Gus
Murphy Gerard
Quigley Michael
Madden Peter A
Murphy John
Quilligan Pat
Madden Tony
Murphy Patrick
Raymond Con
Madeley George
Murphy Robert
Redmond P
Maguire William
Murphy Sean
Reid John
Malone Matt
Murphy William
Reid Noel
Mangan Henry
Murray Denis
Reilly Brendan
Mannix Edward J
Murray Fergus
Roberts Brendan
Martin Patrick
Murray Jack
Rooney Eamon
Martin W
Nagle Michael
Rocks Ciaran
McArdle Eamon
Nolan Anthony
Rothwell A I
McAuliffe Michael
Nolan Denis
Ruffli Annesley Collins
McCarthy Patrick
Nolan William G
Ryan Brendan
McCarthy Tom
Noonan John
Ryan John
McCormack Derek
Noonan Richard
Salmon Arthur
McCormack Thomas
O'Brien Conor
Shannon T
McDonald Vincent
O'Brien Pat

Sheridan Dermot
McGahon Niall
O'Brien Stephen
Sheridan Harry
McGowan Dermot
O'Callaghan Noel
Sheridan Pearse
McGuiggan M
O'Carroll Proinnsias
Shields Tom
McGuinn Dermot
O'Cleirigh Tiernan
Sinnott Thomas
McGuinness Peter
O'Connell Dermot
Slattery David
McGuinness Sean
O'Connell John
Somerville Patrick
McGuirk G
O'Connell Louis
Stanbridge William
McKeown John
O'Connor Dan
Staunton Patrick
McKevitt Robert
O'Connor Hubert
Stewart Thomas
McMahon Dick
O'Connor Liam
Sweeney Frank
McManus Peter
O'Connor Thomas
Sweeney John
McQuillan Fred
O'Donnell Graham
Tallon Chris
McSharry Michael
O'Donoghue Patrick
Thornley David
Merriman Frank
O'Donovan Michael
Timlin A E
Millar George
O'Farrell Michael
Timoney Eamon
Millar William
O'Flanagan Sean
Tobin Patrick J
Milne David
O'Hanrahan Brian
Tobin William
Milne Thomas
O'Hara Michael
Traynor Frank
Milner Harold
O'Kane Fergus

Tucker Noel
Mooney Desmond
O'Kelly Jack
Tuke Joe
Mooney Eamonn
O'Kelly Liam
Twomey Michael
Mooney George
O'Kelly Seamus
Veale Peter
Mooney Gerard V
O'Kelly Sean
Wallace Eric H
Mooney John
O'Kelly William
Wallace Ken A
Mooney Matthew
O'Neill Donal
Walsh Basil
Mooney Patrick
O'Neill Harry
Walsh Declan
Mooney Phil
O'Neill Terry
Walsh Derek
Moore Louis
O'Reilly C
Walsh Kevin
Moore Paul
O'Reilly Colm
Walsh Thomas
Moran Chris
O'Riordan Billy
Warren Frank
Moran William
O'Riordan Brendan
Waters Terence
Moreland Chris
O'Sullivan Austin
Westby Alan
Morgan P J
O'Sullivan Barry
Whelan Andrew D
Whelan Thomas
Wilson Thomas
Withers Ronnie
Young Desmond
Chorus Masters
d'Angelo Alfredo
Barbieri Vittorio
Benaglio Roberto
Bodley Seoirse
Bottino Riccardo
Brady John
Broome Oliver
Büchler Claudio
Cleveland Kenneth

Contardo Olinto
Coussell David
Dillon Maureen
Egea Giorgio
Evans David
Fanfani Adolfo
Feist Robert
Friend Lionel
Gabard Ann Marie
Giacconi Tullio
Giannini Vincenzo
Giardina Giuseppe
Gilbert Philip
Gray Julia
Griffith Moira
Hutchinson Stuart
Lambert Edward
Leone Alberto
McSwiney Veronica
O'Callaghan Lt. Fred
O'Reilly Peadar
Olbrich Volkmar
Owens Teresa
Pecchai Angelo
Pelosi Luciano
Prestia Francesco
Reddin Jeannie
Richards William
Rigolin Amelio
Robinson Peter
Rosen Hans Waldemar
Sheil Fergus
Smedley Michael
Somerville Patrick
Webb Jonathan
White Philip